D0847975

BLOOD, SWEAT, AND TOIL

HD
8391
F54
2011
WEB

Blood, Sweat, and Toil

*Remaking the British Working
Class, 1939–1945*

GEOFFREY G. FIELD

OXFORD
UNIVERSITY PRESS

OXFORD
UNIVERSITY PRESS

Great Clarendon Street, Oxford OX2 6DP

Oxford University Press is a department of the University of Oxford.
It furthers the University's objective of excellence in research, scholarship,
and education by publishing worldwide in

Oxford New York

Auckland Cape Town Dar es Salaam Hong Kong Karachi
Kuala Lumpur Madrid Melbourne Mexico City Nairobi
New Delhi Shanghai Taipei Toronto

With offices in

Argentina Austria Brazil Chile Czech Republic France Greece
Guatemala Hungary Italy Japan Poland Portugal Singapore
South Korea Switzerland Thailand Turkey Ukraine Vietnam

Oxford is a registered trade mark of Oxford University Press
in the UK and in certain other countries

Published in the United States
by Oxford University Press Inc., New York

© Geoffrey G. Field 2011

The moral rights of the author have been asserted
Database right Oxford University Press (maker)

First published 2011

All rights reserved. No part of this publication may be reproduced,
stored in a retrieval system, or transmitted, in any form or by any means,
without the prior permission in writing of Oxford University Press,
or as expressly permitted by law, or under terms agreed with the appropriate
reprographics rights organization. Enquiries concerning reproduction
outside the scope of the above should be sent to the Rights Department,
Oxford University Press, at the address above

You must not circulate this book in any other binding or cover
and you must impose the same condition on any acquirer

British Library Cataloguing in Publication Data
Data available

Library of Congress Cataloging in Publication Data
Data available

Typeset by SPI Publisher Services, Pondicherry, India
Printed in Great Britain
on acid-free paper by
MPG Books Group, Bodmin and King's Lynn

ISBN 978–0–19–960411–1

1 3 5 7 9 10 8 6 4 2

Acknowledgements

It's a depressing thought but this book has taken me a lot longer to write than the war lasted. On the bright side, along the way, I have received a great deal of help and encouragement from individuals and institutions for which I am very thankful.

Purchase College, where I have taught for many years, has supported my work with Sabbatical leave. In addition I am most grateful to Patrick Fridenson for inviting me to be a visiting scholar at the École des Hautes Études in Paris, a wonderful place to think and write. I also want to thank François Poirier for inviting me to spend a semester and give a course at the Centre de Recherches Interculturelles sur les Domaines Anglophones et Francophones [C.R.I.D.A.F.], Paris 13. Portions of my research were presented to seminars at Columbia University, the European Studies Center at Harvard, Princeton University, the École des Hautes Études en Sciences Sociales, Paris, and the Paris colloques organized by the journals *International Labor and Working-Class History* and *Le Mouvement Social*.

I am indebted to the many librarians and archivists who have helped me over the years, including those at Purchase College, the New York Public Library, the British Library, Columbia University, Britain's National Archives, the Modern Records Centre at Warwick, the Imperial War Museum, the National Museum of Labour History at Manchester, the Fawcett Library at the London Guildhall University, and other institutions too numerous to mention by name. I especially want to thank Dorothy Sheridan who helped me in my early efforts at Mass-Observation, before I even knew my topic and also Fr David Lannon for his kind hospitality and help at the Salford Diocesan Archives.

In writing such a broad study I am, of course, indebted to many scholars who have written on different aspects of Britain during the Second World War. I have mentioned many in my footnotes. In particular, I wish to thank friends who have read and criticized earlier drafts of chapters and offered suggestions. Louise Yelin, with whom I have taught interdisciplinary courses on twentieth-century British history and literature, has been the perfect colleague, critic, and friend throughout. Helmut Gruber offered encouragement and criticism over the years; so have our other colleagues on the editorial board of *ILWCH*. I owe a special debt to Eric Foner who not only read and commented on early drafts, but read through the whole of the originally much longer manuscript and offered suggestions about where it might be slimmed down. Other friends who have given me support and practical advice include: David Cannadine, Jane Caplan, Marianne Debouzy, Maurizio Gribaudi, Jean Herskovits, James Hinton, Jim Jaffe, Peter Linebaugh, Andy Rabinbach, Carl Resek, Judith Stein, and my colleagues at Purchase, past and present, especially Ren Yu and Wayne Te Brake. A summer stipend from the American Council of Learned Societies enabled me to begin research on evacuation. I am also grateful to the Greenwood-Labadorf funds of Purchase College for a grant that aided my research and I wish to express my appreciation to the Warner

Fund at the University Seminars at Columbia University for help in preparing the book for publication. Material in this work was presented at the University Seminars on Labor History and Twentieth-Century Politics and Society.

My thanks to the editorial collective at *ILWCH*, to Cambridge University Press for permission to use material I have published in *ILWCH*, and to the UK Data Archive, Colchester, Essex for permission to cite the British Institute of Public Opinion (Gallup Polls) 1939–46, the data from which were converted to computer searchable form by J. Hinton, P. Thompson, and I. Liddell. I am also most grateful to the Trustees of the Mass-Observation Archive, University of Sussex, for allowing me to use the archive and for permission to quote from its collections.

My thanks to the anonymous readers for Oxford University Press for their acute observations and suggestions. I am also grateful to my copy-editor, Jeremy Lang-worthy, and the production staff at Oxford. Most especially, I should like to thank my editors Stephanie Ireland and Christopher Wheeler who were undaunted by a much longer original manuscript and encouraged me to believe that it could be reduced to a more manageable size.

Finally, I want to thank my brothers, Les and Brian, their wives, and families for their hospitality and support on my many research trips to Britain. Above all, my thanks to my wife Linda, who makes life worth living and has for too long lived with this project. It is dedicated to her with much love.

Contents

List of Illustrations

List of Abbreviations

ABCA	Army Bureau of Current Affairs
AEU	Amalgamated Engineering Union
ATS	Auxiliary Territorial Service
BIPO	British Institute of Public Opinion (Gallup Polls)
BIPO (Gallup Polls) UK Data Archive Essex	J. Hinton, P. Thompson, I. Liddell, British Institute of Public Opinion (Gallup) Polls 1938–46 (computer file), British Institute of Public Opinion (original data producer(s)). Colchester, Essex. UK Data Archive (distributor) April 1996, SN 3331
CEMA	Council for the Encouragement of Music and Art
CP/CPGB	Communist Party of Great Britain
CW	Common Wealth Party
ENSA	Entertainments National Service Association
EWO	Essential Works Order
Gallup International Polls	The Gallup International Public Opinion Polls of Great Britain 1937–75 (New York, 1976)
IWM	Imperial War Museum
JBDA	Jewish Board of Deputies Archive
JPC	Joint Production Council
LCC	London County Council
M-OA DR	Mass-Observation Archive Directory Reports
M-OA FR	Mass-Observation Archive File Reports
M-OA TC	Mass-Observation Archive Topic Collection
MoH	Ministry of Health
MoL	Ministry of Labour
MRC	Modern Records Centre, Warwick University
NA	National Archives, Kew, Richmond, Surrey
NEC	National Executive Committee (Labour Party)
NSCN	National Society of Children's Nurseries
NUGM	National Union of General and Municipal Workers
PD	Parliamentary Debates (Commons) (Lords)
RIRO	Regional Industrial Relations Officer
ROF	Royal Ordnance Factory
TGWU	Transport and General Workers' Union
TUC	Trades Union Congress
WAAF	Women's Auxiliary Air Force
WGPW	Women's Group for Public Welfare
WVS	Women's Voluntary Service
WWA	War Widows Archive. The Iris Strange Collection, Staffordshire University Library, Stoke-on-Trent

Journal Abbreviations:

AHR	*American Historical Review*
EHR	*English Historical Review*
HJ	*Historical Journal*
HWJ	*History Workshop Journal*
ILWCH	*International Labor and Working-Class History*
JBS	*Journal of British Studies*
TCBH	*Twentieth Century British History*

Introduction

Now that the twentieth century has ended, the Second World War seems more than ever to have been its pivotal event—if, indeed, such a vast conflict can be called 'an event'—or the 'hinge' on which it turned. Precipitated by the multiple crises of the century's first four decades, the war revolutionized the global balance of power for the next fifty years. In popular memory and academic histories alike, it constitutes a great divide. The devastation it caused was unprecedented. So was the level of violence which engulfed the lives of both soldiers and civilians on a global scale and at Auschwitz and Hiroshima redefined the moral landscape and the limits of man's destructive capacity. For most Europeans the war brought occupation, genocide, the collapse of political structures, and massive casualties. After 1945 most were eager to draw a veil over their recent past; the tasks of re-establishing 'normality' demanded carefully constructed myths and selective silences, although repressed truths, whether in French trials or Swiss bank accounts, constantly resurfaced, igniting controversy and social division.

By comparison, Britain had a good war. Never a battleground for massive armies, its casualties were lighter than many countries and far fewer than in 1914–18, and it never experienced the persecutions, deportations, guilt, and division of occupied states. Popular perceptions of Britain's war have reflected this good fortune, being mostly positive and consensual and largely unaltered by the passage of time. A never-ending stream of films, novels, anniversary celebrations, and popular memoirs attests to continuing public fascination with the war as a heroic, defining moment of British national character, when the nation was tested as never before and emerged stronger, revitalized, more united. This was the gist of Churchill's patriotic oratory at the time and, with few modifications, it has been the theme of hugely successful TV serials like *A Family at War* and *Foyle's War*. It was difficult for historians to break free of popular mythology and most older accounts echoed the theme of national rebirth—even a normally sceptical A. J. P. Taylor concluded that this was the time when the British people 'came of age'. Beginning with Angus Calder's *The People's War* (1969), however, academic studies have branched out in new and more critical directions: questioning claims of consensus within the wartime Coalition, examining racial attitudes and ethnocentrism, debating whether 1945 constituted a radical break in politics, even whether the conflict produced a new sense of national unity bridging pre-war class divisions. New research on the language of patriotism and nationalism has centred on the war; so have oral histories and the burgeoning study of collective memory. Above all, the war years have become a focus of gender studies, examining masculine and feminine roles and, in particular, the war's impact on the lives and self-consciousness of women.

The result of this varied body of research has been to resuscitate the war as a subject of controversy and a period whose conceptualization is vital to our understanding of the major themes of British history in the twentieth century. One area of comparative neglect, however, has been the history of the working class and of class relations; there is no comprehensive account of the British working class (or for that matter the middle classes) in the war years. Studies of specific topics like trade unionism or the Communist Party exist but, with very few exceptions, broader analyses of working-class experience either end in 1939 or 1940 or take 1945 as their point of departure.[1] This is particularly surprising since a dominant trope of the 1940s was the rise of labour—politically in Labour's 1945 victory over Churchill, institutionally in the prestige of trade unionism, and materially in workers' higher wages and the shift to a full employment economy.

Two possible reasons for the gap come to mind. First, there is what we might call the 'People's War' effect, by which I mean that numerous books have taken the 'people' as their focus, where the phrase becomes virtually indistinguishable from 'the civilians' war'. In many of the more popular accounts this reflects—directly stated or implicitly—a view that the war blurred or eroded social distinctions; it also stems from the tendency to personalize or domesticate the war's social history, so that it emphasizes the shared dangers and hardships of family life, with less attention devoted to work, business, trade unions, class, and the structures of inequality. More importantly, perhaps, the lacuna reflects a broader shift away from labour history and class-centred history in the last two decades. Once the major organizing principle of the period since industrialization, class analysis has been rocked by simultaneous critiques from different quarters and found wanting, disavowed, dethroned. The sources of this historiographical shift have been widely dissected in books and journals and the debate itself requires only a brief comment here. The collapse of the Soviet Union and the general retreat of socialism and trade unionism in Britain and elsewhere in the 1990s have played an important part, so have feminist critiques of the significance of class compared to gender and growing sensitivity to the complexity and instability of identity. As historians of women correctly point out, most labour history and the assumptions underlying it privileged male workers and excluded much of women's experience. But arguably the most powerful and fundamental challenge was presented by the growing influence of the 'linguistic turn' and postmodernism with its emphasis on deconstructing meta-narratives, including those anchored to class, and grounding history in the analysis of discourse.[2] Together these critiques amounted to a thoroughgoing

---

[1] The exceptions include: J. E. Cronin, *Labour and Society in Britain, 1918–1979* (London, 1984); R. Price, *Labour in British Society* (London, 1986).

[2] G. Stedman Jones, *Languages of Class. Studies in English Working-Class History 1832–1982* (Cambridge, 1983); *idem*, 'Anglo-Marxism, Neo-Marxism and the discursive approach to history' in Al Lüdtke (ed.), *Was bleibt von marxistischen Perspecktiven in der Geschichtsforschung?* (Göttingen, 1997). P. Joyce, *Visions of the People: Industrial England and the question of class, 1840–1914* (Cambridge, 1991); *idem* (ed.), *Class: A reader* (Oxford, 1995).

redefinition of historical practice in which the study of culture, discourse, and webs of representation displaced the 'social' as the leading-edge of new research. By the late 1990s social and, in particular, working-class history were widely seen as being 'in crisis' and suffering from a loss of purpose and direction.

The central focus of many critiques was a rejection of Marxist models of class with their implicit teleology and the view of class as primarily production- and work-determined. There was a good deal of exaggerated rhetoric on all sides as some called for recentring history upon discourse analysis, while others sprang to the defence of traditional practices. In truth *Marxisant* studies were a good deal more nuanced, eclectic, and open-ended than many critics allowed and in Britain focused less on modes of production than on the constitutive role of culture in the formation of class consciousness.[3] Also attractive to many historians were Weberian-influenced models, which conceived of class as rooted in unequal market relationships rather than the labour process. For Weber classes were not by definition cohesive social collectivities; they merely represented possible bases for collective consciousness and can either constrain or enable political action. Another appealing feature of Weber was his belief that classes would become more diffuse and fragmentary over time. Growing scholarship on gender, ethnicity, craft divisions, and regionalism underscored diversity and internal differentiation within classes—so much so that some historians prefer to speak of 'working classes' as a way of distinguishing themselves from bolder advocates of homogeneity.[4] Over time the heat and passion in these debates subsided and there were more and more calls for eclecticism—in Ira Katznelson's words, for 'a playful multi-dimensionality'[5] in which different approaches are kept 'in useful tension'. Geoff Eley and Keith Nield have also been in the forefront of those calling for a conceptual pluralism that engages constructively with the postmodernist challenge while retaining much of social history's insights into socio-economic structures of industrial society.[6]

Blood, Sweat, and Toil has been written against the backdrop of these controversies and among the few advantages in working so slowly is that the most extreme rejections of class have faded and one can spot a definite movement 'to bring class back in'.[7] The proclivity of people to categorize themselves in class terms

[3] D. Dworkin, *Cultural Marxism in Postwar Britain* (Durham and London, 1997); Harvey Kaye, *The British Marxist Historians* (Oxford, 1984).

[4] Trevor Griffiths, *The Lancashire Working Classes c.1880–1930* (Oxford, 2001). The problem for labour and socialist movements was how to forge collective solidarities out of this diversity. What is perhaps most striking in retrospect is how successful they were in the brief period between the 1880s and the 1920s in building national movements—with the spread of mass trade unionism and the rapid growth of alternative working-class political parties, culminating in the period of heightened class militancy which began prior to the First World War and continued into the early 1920s.

[5] I. Katznelson, 'The "bourgeois" dimension: A provocation about institutions, politics and the future of labor history', *ILWCH*, 46 (1994).

[6] Geoff Eley, *A Crooked Line: From cultural history to the history of society* (Ann Arbor, 2005); Geoff Eley and Keith Nield, *The Future of Class in History: What's left of the social?* (Ann Arbor, 2007).

[7] S. G. McNall, R. F. Levine, and R. Fantasia (eds.), *Bringing Class Back In: Contemporary and historical perspectives* (Boulder, 1991); J. R. Hall (ed.), *Reworking Class* (Ithaca, 1997); F. Devine *et al.*, *Rethinking Class. Culture, Identities and Lifestyles* (Basingstoke and New York, 2005). L. Heerma van Voss and M. van der Linden (eds.), *Class and Other Identities: Gender, religion and ethnicity in the*

is so pervasive in modern British society that, even if definitions of class are vague and its agency hard to pin down, historians have discovered that they cannot do without it as a way of theorizing social and economic inequality and (to use David Cannadine's shorthand[8]) what culture does to them. The main question now is how best to write about it. Simply put, I have tried to examine the impact of the Second World War on workers in the varied contexts of the family, military service, the workplace, local communities, the nation, and politics. Class is understood as structured inequality which is produced and reproduced in economic, social, cultural, and political relations. The workplace and work relations are seen as one highly important arena in which class consciousness is shaped and experienced, but others including family, community, culture, and politics are also formative. My approach to class is also necessarily dualistic, exploring not only the outlook of workers in the war years, but (as much as possible) how they were represented in public debate and the media and how class assumptions were encoded in state policies, administrative practices, and wartime symbolism or iconography.

Class is only one element of self-understanding, albeit an important one. As a growing corpus of work on identity-formation illustrates, people have multiple identities of varying prominence at different times and an ongoing difficulty for historians is to show how class interacts with gender, ethnicity, confession, region, and generational difference. In addition, recent work on political language and parties has increasingly conceived of the political sphere as more autonomous than before, uncoupling the social and the political, questioning interpretations that see politics as simply a reflection of social reality, and emphasizing the creative agency of parties in forging their constituencies, including class constituencies. David Cannadine, for example, has identified three dominant tropes or models which Britons have used since the eighteenth century to represent their unequal social order—as a finely graded 'great chain' of hierarchy; a triad of upper, middle, and lower class layers; and a dichotomous, polarized model that contrasts people and privileged in adversarial blocs. Cannadine's formulation underscores the significance of politics in shaping and manipulating social identities. The work of Jon Lawrence and others on political parties' impact on popular perceptions has also helped historians get away from preconceived notions about the relationship of class consciousness and political action; not least it replaces older preoccupations with explaining the lack of working-class militancy in Britain with more open-ended narratives of working-class politics, including recent studies of popular liberalism and renewed attention to moderate Labour Party politics as a conscious and reasonable choice. It is important, however, not to exaggerate the role of politics and thereby downplay other social processes. At different periods class identity may be stronger or weaker, more or less cohesive, and to understand this we need to recognize the shifting mix of contributory factors operative at any given

---

writing of labour history (New York and Oxford, 2002). J. Belchem and N. Kirk, *Languages of Labour* (Aldershot, 1997). Also, D. Kalb, *Expanding Class: Power and everyday politics in industrial communities, the Netherlands 1850–1950* (Durham and London, 1997), especially the Introduction.

[8] D. Cannadine, *Class in Britain* (London, 2000).

time—the role of specific events, cultural patterns, and a variety of processes in which institutions, politics, ideologies, and language play a vital part. Finally, because of the diversity of the working class, it is important to distinguish between situations where status differences between workers are of chief importance and those circumstances where the divide between workers and non-workers is paramount. Too intense a focus upon divisions can obscure important unities, shared visions, and purposes that link workers together; tendencies to fragmentation are in constant contention with processes that draw a class together.

Viewed from today's perspective, it is easy to forget how deeply segregated the British nation was by class between the wars. If anything, growing middle-class movement away from city centres to commutable suburbs between the wars increased the social separation. Over 75 per cent of the working population was engaged in manual labour, with huge numbers employed in basic industries like textiles, coal, steel, shipbuilding, and engineering or in transport; they mostly lived in cities and in many cases in conurbations that sprawled across the industrial regions of Scotland and England. Workers' neighbourhoods were largely insular and self-enclosed; those middle-class figures who were encountered were employers, teachers, the local doctor, the magistrate if you broke the law, and the local vicar or priest when a marriage, baptism, or funeral took place. These interlopers were a race apart: different by way of education, security, accent, pastimes, social networks, and family life. Workers' associational life was well developed, if largely male-centred, and a fairly standardized national pattern of life existed, readily identifiable as working-class; regional differences existed, to be sure, but when we examine photographs of the period—the street life of women and children, rows of terraced houses, workplace football teams, the Co-op and street-corner shops, tallymen and bookies, pubs, and markets—we recognize an urban culture that, superficially at least, endured until the early 1950s.

Savage and Miles have argued that the interwar decades produced a more homogeneous working class: that the proliferation of semi-skilled work narrowed skill barriers and eroded wage differentials, while lower levels of social mobility into the ranks of the middle class meant that intra-class mobility and intermarriage increased.[9] Others have pointed out that the religious sectarianism and ethnic conflicts that were so deeply ingrained in cities like Liverpool and Manchester seemed less significant and divisive than before 1914. Some historians have suggested that the economic insecurity of these years, when underemployment and unemployment transcended the usual craft and skill divisions, may also have promoted a common sense of class identity.[10] However, the salient fact of those decades was the sharp disparities in the social experience of workers produced by markedly different regional economies and the geographical concentration of mass unemployment. The collapse of the old Victorian staple industries had a devastating, pauperizing impact on working-class communities in the north, Scotland, and South Wales. Unemployment never dropped below 10 per cent of insured workers

[9] M. Savage and A. Miles, *The Remaking of the British Working Class, 1840–1940* (London, 1994).
[10] R. McKibbin, *Classes and Cultures: England 1918–1951* (Oxford, 1998), pp. 161ff.

Blood, Sweat, and Toil

nationally. This was bad enough, but in towns like Oldham, Merthyr Tydfil, Jarrow, Motherwell, and Dundee it was double or triple that figure in the early 1930s and many were jobless for years. Large numbers of young workers migrated from what Hugh Kearney identifies as 'outer Britain'[11] to the South and Midlands; others made do with life on the dole. By contrast, on the London periphery and in towns like Oxford, Coventry, and Luton new industries and new manufacturing plants mushroomed; the work was hard and labour discipline often harsh, but here workers began to get a first hint of what in the 1950s was called an 'affluent lifestyle'. Class disunity was also evident in the retreat of trade unionism, its shrinkage in the old industrial strongholds and slow, fitful growth in the new areas. The wave of labour militancy that extended from 1916 to the early 1920s had passed, superseded by an environment more favourable to business interests. Workers were also divided in political allegiance; fewer than half voted for the Labour Party and Conservative political dominance in the period relied on both a solid coalition of middle-class voters and substantial working-class support. Labour made some real gains in specific areas, but could never claim to be *the* working-class party. Arguably, one of the key forces that helped to build a measure of working-class solidarity was exogenous: Conservative use of the twin threats of socialism and the organized working class as a means of rallying a broad anti-labour alliance. None of this prevented people from having a deep sense of class difference from those higher up the social scale or from freely categorizing themselves into social classes, but in terms of organization and political solidarity the context reinforced working-class fragmentation.

The Second World War transformed this situation. Far from bridging or blurring the gulf between social classes, as many contemporaries and later accounts have suggested, the war deepened a sense of class identity and reshaped class relations in important ways—ways that could not have been predicted in, say, 1925 or 1931. Not only did the conflict enhance the power and prestige of organized labour and create a new framework of industrial relations, full employment lifted the older industrial communities out of depression and revitalized their political cultures. The war experience nationalized workers, both in a patriotic sense and in forging closer class unity and the sense of a common political agenda. Distinctive regional class identities remained and continued to be important, but the war had increased the sense of belonging to a national class, superimposed upon more parochial loyalties. *Blood, Sweat, and Toil* examines the combination of factors that contributed to this transformation and process of social integration.

Organized thematically, but to some degree chronologically so as to underscore the differences between the context of the first three war years and the period from 1943, the book begins with two chapters on the evacuation of women and children in the first months of the war and German air raids against British cities in 1940–1.

---

[11] H. Kearney, *The British Isles: A history of four nations* (Cambridge, 1995). Kearney uses the term 'outer Britain' for Scotland, Wales, Ireland, the North, and South-west. Economic depression also gave impetus to Scottish and Welsh nationalist movements and reinforced a popular sense of cultural distinctiveness.

The first government-organized evacuation, involving 1.4 million people, many from the poorest districts of the nation, resulted in sudden and often acrimonious confrontations; it touched the nation's raw nerves, disclosing deep class, confessional, and regional divisions and making society transparent to itself in new and unsettling ways. While today in memoirs and oral histories, evacuation is often personalized or portrayed in terms of the contrasts between urban and rural, for historians it provides graphic illustration of the extent of childhood poverty and of class attitudes at the outbreak of war. The second chapter on the Blitz examines the responses of working-class communities to the raids on London and provincial cities. The dangers and hardships and the disruption of communities, as many contemporaries noted, produced a shift in public discourse about workers and poor neighbourhoods and also a surge of popular nationalism and defiance—but it was a patriotism that was more assertive, less deferential than before, forged in the context of growing criticism of the pre-war social and political order.

Three chapters analyse the impact of full-scale mobilization on people's lives. Chapter 3 examines the conversion to a war economy and its effect upon industrial relations, the spread of trade unionism, and the changing balance of power between employers and organized labour. The workplace is not the only context in which class consciousness develops—indeed factories can also be sites for investigating gender, ethnic, and confessional relationships—but in wartime they were particularly important if only because of the amount of time that workers spent in them and the vast numbers of new recruits drawn into various sectors of war work. While women are integral to every chapter of the book, chapter 4 examines the experiences of working-class women in war factories and the uniformed services and tries to gauge the broader impact of wartime participation on their social and political outlook. Several excellent studies by Penny Summerfield and others have shown that contemporary claims that the war was transforming conventional gender relations were vastly exaggerated, but they also reveal how these years were seen by many women as a powerful formative period in their lives and self-awareness.[12] Chapter 4 focuses upon the ways that working-class women were addressed in wartime as part of the national community and suggests ways in which war work shaped their material aspirations and their unprecedented support for Labour in 1945. Finally, surprising though it may seem, most accounts of the home front largely ignore men in the armed forces even though much of the army spent most of the war on British soil. Chapter 7 takes as its focus the transformation of Britain's small professional army into a mass conscript army for the second time in the space of a quarter century. Armies reflect the values, attitudes, and priorities of the nation they represent, and the British army was no exception: this chapter shows how military hierarchy replicated and reinforced class divisions and analyses the continuing tensions between the democratic propaganda of a 'People's

---

[12] P. Summerfield, 'Approaches to women and social change in the Second World War' in B. Brivati and H. Jones (eds.), *What Difference Did the War Make?* (Leicester, 1993); *idem, Reconstructing Women's Wartime Lives: Discourse and subjectivity in oral histories of the Second World War* (Manchester, 1998).

War' and a military code that was deeply ambivalent about the rights of 'civilians' in uniform.

The portrayal of working-class men and women by films, radio, advertising, and official publicity changed quite dramatically during the course of the war. More than ever before workers and 'ordinary' people came to symbolize the nation; workers' social identification inevitably involves the interplay of self- and external definition—an individual's outlook is constantly tested and compared to representation in public discourse. It would take a book in itself to adequately trace this feature of war culture. Instead I have focused on two very different aspects. Chapter 5, 'Family in Crisis', is really a counterpoint to the cosy, unifying, populistic messages of so much national propaganda. It shows how growing public and official alarm about the dissolution of families, juvenile delinquency, and the putative decline in sexual morality was centred upon the working-class family. As with the furore over the first evacuation which focused upon feckless parents and incompetent slum mothers, so a few years later public debate about irresponsible, promiscuous 'good time girls' was also class-freighted. Chapter 6, on the other hand, examines the growing wartime involvement of the state and private organizations in the provision of recreation for workers. Here again the focus was on changing and improving workers—but the tone was idealistic, not negative, rooted in pre-war critiques of mass entertainment and notions about positive leisure and the forging of a unified national culture.

The last two chapters of the book examine wartime politics and 'the road to 1945'. Few topics in twentieth-century British history have attracted more attention—and yet scholars remain deeply divided about whether the war produced a cross-party consensus for reform, if the vote in 1945 was really a mandate for sweeping change, or if public opinion was radicalized by the war or could be described as disaffected and disengaged at its end. In these chapters my chief focus is not the elite or 'high politics' of the period, but the development of popular opinion. The sources for such a study are patchy and their meaning sometimes ambiguous, but opinion polls, Mass-Observation, Home Intelligence, trade union documents, and personal letters and diaries make it possible to piece together a clear picture of early radicalization, while in the final war years popular attitudes became more volatile, conflicted, and contradictory. Interpretations of Labour's 1945 victory have stressed many things: tracing it, for example, to the 1940 political crisis which discredited pre-war Conservatism, or viewing it as a victory for 'middle opinion' or for Labour's superior political organization. But most importantly, it reflected the multiple processes which had strengthened working-class collective power and confidence and the momentum produced by wartime mobilization for a social democratic reform agenda. This agenda, informed by ideals of democratic citizenship and greater equality, was radical by the standards of the 1930s. Workers emerged from the war conscious of their role in saving the nation and convinced that they were owed a better life and opportunities post-war. Central to this rhetoric and to the 1945 political campaign was a narrative of interwar failure, poverty, and social division—a narrative which the furore over the first evacuation in 1939 powerfully reinforced.

1

Evacuation

In autumn 1933, the novelist J. B. Priestley set off on a journey around England. Published in the following year *English Journey* became one of the key texts of the decade, shaping the views of contemporaries and later generations. Famously, Priestley's journey, which started at Southampton and moved through the Midlands and Lancashire to the depressed shipbuilding and mining communities of the Tyne and east Durham, led him to define three very different 'Englands'. There was the historic, tourist England of cathedrals, colleges, manor houses, and quaint byways. Then there was nineteenth-century industrial England with its decaying slump-ridden industries and much of its workforce reduced to poverty and life on the dole. And, finally, there was the newly emergent 'Americanized' one, located chiefly in Greater London and parts of the Midlands, with its highways, giant cinemas, filling stations, and modern, electrified, mass-production factories. Though seemingly the result of random choices with little forethought, in reality Priestley's odyssey was carefully planned; his chatty style camouflaged a serious and well-crafted rumination on the state of English society and the deep gulf between the prosperous regions and the blighted areas where workers, 'flung on the scrap heap', were living in 'worktowns' that had no work for them. He was an angry patriot, eager to get readers to face society's failures, betrayals, and injustices.

Priestley's was also a post-war book. Almost every chapter referred to his service in the Great War: his embarkation for France, recovery from injuries, the death of all but one of his childhood friends on the Somme, and a reunion of his battalion in Bradford that jobless comrades were too ashamed to attend because they lacked decent clothes. 'If Germans had been threatening these towns instead of Want, Disease, Hopelessness, Misery,' he wrote, 'something would have been done quickly enough.'[1] Over the next years many other writers, photographers, and documentary film-makers took to the road to examine the 'condition of England' (or, more rarely, of Wales and Scotland). In these later journeys, written after the worst of the depression was over, the theme of war was equally pervasive; but now with the growing threat from Nazi Germany the underlying question was whether so unequal and deeply fragmented a British nation could withstand the test of another war. Would the nation's morale hold firm or snap when tested by poison gas or the aerial bombardment of cities? Rapid advances in aircraft technology

---

[1] J. B. Priestley, *English Journey* (Jubilee edition, London, 1984), p. 307.

produced a flood of speculation about the horrors that civilians might face. Already in 1934 in a speech to the Commons Winston Churchill warned:

> We must expect that, under the pressure of continuous air attack upon London, at least 3 million or 4 million people would be driven out into the open country around the metropolis. This vast mass of human beings . . . without shelter and without food, without sanitation and without special provision for the maintenance of order, would confront the Government of the day with an administrative problem of the first magnitude . . .

'London', Cambridge philosopher Bertrand Russell prophesied, 'will be one vast raving bedlam, the hospitals will be stormed, traffic will cease, the homeless will shriek for help, the city will be a pandemonium.' Government planners, pessimistic about mounting an effective defence against high-speed bombers, were equally apocalyptic in their forecasts.[2]

In the previous war, battlefronts and home front had remained largely distinct. Soldiers on leave could travel in a few hours from Flanders to London where, if things were far from normal, a semblance of peace remained. But now air power had nullified the protection that geography and the Channel had afforded. Recognizing this, Britain devoted more attention than other nations to devising a plan for the mass evacuation of cities.[3] The threat of air war was regularly discussed by the Committee of Imperial Defence in the late 1920s although a subcommittee to consider the feasibility of evacuation was not established until 1931 and it took three years to complete its report. However, the accelerating pace of Nazi expansionism injected much greater urgency into official preparations and by late 1938 a detailed plan had been worked out, which gave priority to four 'non-essential' groups of civilians in the likely target areas: schoolchildren, mothers with pre-school infants, expectant mothers, the blind and handicapped. Schoolchildren, who constituted the largest of the categories, were to be evacuated in school units accompanied by their teachers, while infants would travel to safety with their mothers. Believing that public opinion would oppose compulsion, the scheme relied on voluntary participation, but few people were expected to reject the chance of escaping heavy air attacks. Evacuees were to be accommodated in private homes rather than camps or special facilities; transportation costs were to be paid by the government, as were the billeting allowances awarded to householders who boarded evacuees.[4]

---

[2] Churchill in *PD* (Commons) 28 November 1934; B. Russell, *Which Way to Peace?* (London, 1936). Also, U. Bialer, *The Shadow of the Bomber: The fear of air attack and British politics, 1932–1939* (London, 1980); I. F. Clarke, *Voices Prophesying War* (Oxford, 1966).

[3] In Germany there was no mass evacuation of children at the start of the war since Goering was confident that his air force could protect German cities and Hitler was concerned not to alarm the population. France evacuated children in 1939 and early 1940, mostly from the Paris region and Alsace-Lorraine but the planning seems to have occurred very late in the midst of mobilization for war. Gerhard Kock, *'Der Führer sorgt für unsere Kinder . . . 'Die Kinderlandverschickung im Zweiten Weltkrieg* (Paderborn, 1997); Laura Lee Downs, *Childhood in the Promised Land: Working-class movements in the colonies de vacances in France 1880–1960* (North Carolina, 2002).

[4] Richard Titmuss, *Problems of Social Policy* (London, 1950). Many middle-class rate-payers viewed compulsory billeting as a real injustice and mobilized petitions against it; R. A. Skelton, *Anderson's Castle: An Englishman's house is his (Sir John Anderson's) castle* (London, 1939).

But in September 1938 when the Sudetenland crisis pushed Europe to the brink of war, planning was still incomplete; administrators breathed a sigh of relief at the Munich settlement, which granted them another year of peace and a much-needed reprieve in which to revise a scheme that was still seriously deficient. By February 1939 the whole of Britain had been classified as either evacuation, reception, or neutral regions (where no population change was contemplated), and local authorities had conducted surveys of habitable rooms in the reception areas. It was estimated that around 4 million people would be evacuated in the first weeks of a war (1.4 million from the Greater London area alone); in addition, the general public had to be informed and persuaded to participate, social welfare and educational facilities were needed, and numerous official and voluntary agencies required careful coordination. No government would have dreamed of implementing a scheme of this magnitude but for the terrifying vision of aerial bombardment prevalent in official circles. In 1937 it was estimated that the first two months of a conflict might result in as many as 600,000 dead and 1.2 million injured, while in 1939 Liddell Hart anticipated nearly 250,000 casualties in the first week. The London region, covering 750 square miles with over 9 million people, was the worst defensive nightmare, but other conurbations appeared almost as vulnerable. Critics of the scheme later claimed that transportation timetables had been emphasized to the exclusion of 'competent psychological and social planning'. But, convinced that 'the bomber will always get through' and believing that a major bombing offensive would be launched at the very beginning of a war, officials focused on the logistics of moving unprecedented numbers of people without panic or a disorderly flight with thousands clogging road and rail routes out of urban areas. Probably, too, the logistical problems seemed more tractable and solvable than the likely human repercussions from so vast a migration.[5]

On 31 August, shortly after German troops entered Poland, the code-name for evacuation, 'Pied Piper', was passed to local and educational authorities throughout Britain. The next morning and for days thereafter thousands of mothers and children could be seen assembling in playgrounds, filing into railway stations behind school placards, and crowding onto waiting trains and buses. Some 4,000 special trains had been laid on—over 1,500 for London alone, and over 300 each for major centres such as Manchester, Merseyside, and the Clyde area. The plan seemed to operate almost flawlessly. There was outward calm and order; school parties seemed to have profited from summer rehearsals; and in many places the speed of dispatch was remarkable. At one London station 8,000 people an hour were sent off; Leeds entrained 40,000 in seven hours; and other cities boasted equal efficiency—all without a single casualty.[6] Early reports, made before accurate information was available, were universally congratulatory. There were glowing

---

[5] For London planning: LCC: EO/WAR/1, 3, 4, 5, 6, 11, 13; for Yorkshire's West Riding, Leeds Educ. Papers, Boxes 370–4 (Evacuation, 1938–9). Also, G. A. N. Lowndes, *The Silent Social Revolution* (Oxford, 1969), ch. 12.

[6] R. Padley and M. Cole (eds.), *Evacuation Survey: A report to the Fabian Society* (London, 1940); also O. S. Nock, *Britain's Railways at War, 1939–45* (London, 1971).

commentaries on the BBC; press photographs and newsreels captured tearful mothers and excited schoolchildren, symbols of the nation's unity of purpose.[7] Fewer, rather 'staged', pictures showed evacuees being welcomed by beaming foster mothers in the reception areas. In fact, as participating teachers and volunteers recognized, appearances were misleading. Many parents who had registered their children simply changed their minds at the eleventh hour; others had made their own private arrangements during the summer months; and some were still away on holiday when the war began. Official secrecy about the destination of evacuees also troubled many families, while young wives with infants balked at leaving husbands and elderly parents to fend for themselves. Places now within easy reach by car also seemed both distant and alien to a working class that in 1939 travelled infrequently, rarely telephoned, wrote few letters, and generally worked close to home. But in Newcastle and Liverpool, at least, the evidence suggests that many of the poorest families opted out of the scheme because they could not meet the costs of outfitting a child or the fares for visits; rumours about expected parental contributions for a child's upkeep and the fact that evacuation meant the loss of child assistance payments also played a role.[8]

'Pied Piper' evacuated a total of 1,473,000 people, far fewer than originally predicted. The vast majority travelled in the first four days, but efforts were made to supplement the numbers over the following two weeks. Regional participation rates also varied considerably, reflecting in part the energy and efficiency of local government structures. In Manchester, Salford, Liverpool, and Newcastle around 70 per cent of eligible schoolchildren (for whom statistics are more accurate) took part in the scheme; roughly 24 per cent participated from the Midlands; the figure for London was 42 per cent, while other towns sent off a much smaller proportion, only 25 per cent in Bradford and a paltry 15 per cent in Sheffield. The average participation was 47 per cent for England and 38 per cent for Scotland. Throughout the country the turn-out of mothers and infants was significantly lower than this.[9] Because there were fewer evacuees than anticipated, last-minute changes were made to evacuation timetables designed to telescope the process into fewer days. This played havoc with a scheme that was already seriously compromised by the fact that some 2 million people, who could afford to do so, had self-evacuated over the summer months as the Polish crisis deepened.[10] As a result earlier reports of available billets lost their utility. The eagerness of dispatchers to send off parties as quickly as possible also produced confusion in the reception areas. Many evacuees ended up in the wrong places. Large urban secondary schools found themselves mistakenly deposited in small villages without adequate facilities or were spread over wide areas so that teachers took days reassembling them; brothers

[7] BBC Archives: 'Home News Bulletins' for September 1939; H. Marshall, 'How the children went', *The Listener*, 7 September 1939.

[8] A. M. Preston, 'The evacuation of schoolchildren from Newcastle upon Tyne, 1939–1942', *History of Education*, 18(3) (September 1989), 232–3.

[9] Titmuss, *Problems of Social Policy*, Appendix 4; Padley and Cole (eds.), *Evacuation Survey*, ch. 3.

[10] Titmuss, *Problems of Social Policy*, Appendix 2; H. C. Dent, *Education in Transition* (London, 1944).

and sisters were split up despite previous assurances to parents; and reception committees often found themselves with evacuees of quite different numbers, sex, and age than anticipated.

The distances travelled—in many cases 40 miles or so—were small by today's standards, but some of the journeys were particularly arduous. A Glasgow teacher sent to Aberdeenshire described his school's experience as 'the most depressing, deplorable and disgusting journey I have ever had the misfortune to make', adding that his party were 'so exhausted and depressed that the term refugees applied to them by some of the householders seemed more appropriate than offensive'. Dagenham and East London children who went by sea to Yarmouth and Lowestoft found there was no transport to convey them to nearby villages and had to be housed in schools and sheds. The small north Wales village of Aberdaron was thrown into turmoil by the unexpected arrival of 424 mothers and young children from the Edge Hill district of central Liverpool. The women thought they were going to Wrexham with the schools of their district, but had instead been sent 120 miles in a non-corridor train to the remote Lleyn peninsula. 'Lancashire children and mothers were overjoyed to finish their journey on the legendary coasts of Wales and Cumberland', ran the Panglossian commentary of *The Times*.[11] It took about two weeks for the true facts to percolate into radio and press commentary; but these logistical mistakes were quickly overshadowed by the human and class implications of the scheme, either ignored or minimized by bureaucratic minds up to this point.

Several conclusions can be drawn about the administrative preparations for 'Pied Piper'. So preoccupied were government planners with pessimistic casualty estimates and doubts about civilian morale that they focused almost exclusively on the swift dispersal of evacuees. Amazingly little attention was devoted to the myriad social problems of integrating so many people, many of them from the poorest areas of the nation, into very different communities.[12] Inner-city working-class neighbourhoods, clustered around factories and docks, accounted for a high proportion of areas slated for evacuation under the government scheme. But too often prior links between evacuation and reception areas were minimal, many receiving authorities felt overwhelmed, and understandably few were ready to incur costs for additional community services without clear Treasury guarantees that they would be reimbursed. In its preconceptions the scheme was also, as Margaret Cole put it, 'military, male and middle class'.[13] It was framed by officials who had mostly spent their youth in boarding schools and had no grasp of how working-class families might respond to extended separations. It took little account of the precariousness of household economies among the poor or of the role of close

---

[11] Scottish Women's Group for Public Welfare, *Our Scottish Towns: Evacuation and the social future* (Edinburgh, 1944), p. 8. Padley and Cole, *Evacuation Survey*; *PD* (Commons), 14 September 1939; *The Times*, 4 September 1939, p. 5.

[12] The Board of Education and the Ministry of Health were the principal agencies responsible for administering the scheme. Scotland organized its own evacuation, mainly from Edinburgh, Glasgow, Clydebank, Dundee, Rosyth; it was much smaller, accounting for about 175,000 evacuees at the outbreak of war.

[13] Padley and Cole (eds.), *Evacuation Survey*, p. 4.

kinship ties in these communities. And it assumed the willingness of vast numbers of women to take over the childcare of others without pay for an unspecified period of time. Once the evacuees arrived in their billets, what had begun as an aspect of military planning was suddenly transformed into a vast social experiment.

'TWO NATIONS' OR 'TOWN CHILDREN THROUGH COUNTRY EYES'

In retrospect, what is surprising about the 'spasm of horror'[14] that convulsed reception areas in early September 1939, is that so few people predicted it. Evacuation brought together in sudden and unprecedented fashion town and country, different classes, confessional, and ethnic groups. Evacuees included large numbers of impoverished families and the policy of preserving school units helped to concentrate the poorest children in specific localities. Liverpool Catholics arrived in the strongholds of Welsh vernacular culture and Nonconformism, East End Jewish mothers were sent to Norfolk, and children from industrial towns where long-term unemployment had become a way of life found themselves in suburbia or scattered across rural counties. In such circumstances acrimonious confrontations were almost inevitable.

In this war the first 'atrocity' stories were spread by Britons about each other on the home front. Members of Parliament were inundated by complaints from their constituents and repeated them as truth in the Commons, while the press avidly publicized the ill-feeling that swept the nation.[15] Very quickly caricatures hardened into folkloric truth. There were tales of ragged, lice-ridden evacuees who had never seen cows and slept under their beds or soiled them; of evacuated mothers who were dirty, ungrateful, simply having a holiday, incapable of boiling an egg, or drunken and abusive. On the other side, hosts were frequently decried as cold and exploitative. Phrases like 'slave auction', 'treated like bits of dirt', and 'treated like cattle in a market' became common parlance to describe billet selection. Strapping boys, it was said, were chosen for farm work, while teenage girls were expected to be skivvies.[16] Summarizing her view of Luton, one London mother said: 'I hate the place and I hate the people . . . I never met such a snobbish, selfish, unfriendly, rude lot in all my life.'[17] There were, of course, hosts and evacuees who adjusted successfully and many evacuees were welcomed with sympathy and kindness.

---

[14] H. C. Dent's phrase in *Education in Transition*, p. 8.

[15] M-OA: TC, Evacuation, Box 1; M-OA: FR 11 (1939); NA: HLG 7/73–83 (Evacuation: Regional Officers' Reports). Newspaper and magazine correspondence columns were full of the debate over evacuation in September and October 1939. The Commons debate of 14 September 1939 was particularly heated with MPs trading stories and accusations; by 2 November the tone in the Commons was a good deal more constructive.

[16] M-O, *War Begins at Home* (London, 1940); letters in Leeds Educ. Papers, Box 372. Apparently in one Lincolnshire town and in Rugby cattle markets were used for selection purposes.

[17] The Luton News, *Luton at War* (Luton, 1947), pp. 21–2 (Luton, it should be remembered, was barely 30 miles from her home). By 21 September some 50% of the mothers with young children had left Luton.

Thousands of volunteers also spent exhausting hours trying to make people comfortable. But positive experiences were less newsworthy; it was the mismatches that dominated public debate. The scheme had misfired badly, but its failings were compounded by exaggeration and distortion.

At the centre of the controversy was the simple fact that many reception committees were completely unprepared for the condition and behaviour of the poorest evacuees. There were widespread reports of evacuees arriving in rags, with newspapers stuffed into their clothes for additional warmth, and without proper footwear, raincoats, overcoats, or changes of clothing. William Boyd's survey of Glasgow and Clydebank evacuees judged the clothing of almost 40 per cent to be 'bad or deplorable'; the same was true for groups from central Liverpool, Manchester, Grimsby, and London's East End.[18] Local authorities circulated lists of necessary items, but they proved too expensive for some parents. Thus, at evacuation rehearsals in Manchester some 20 per cent of children had only plimsolls, while the Newcastle corporation acknowledged that of its 31,000 children registered for evacuation, 13 per cent lacked adequate footwear and 21 per cent sufficient clothing. In October 1939 half of the parents included in a Liverpool survey had 'serious difficulty in providing the necessary clothes', especially if they had two or more children.[19] Public appeals were made and teachers were instructed to collect cast-off garments and old boots for emergency distribution. But very little public money was made available and even that was deliberately under-publicized for fear that it might weaken parental responsibility. As the novelist Alan Sillitoe, then an eleven-year-old from Nottingham, recalled: 'The four of us went up the street to school with a carrier bag each. We'd been given a list of what to take with us, which included pyjamas and underwear, but I for one had none of these things. I had what I stood up in with an extra shirt in the bag.' His father had been on the dole for several years.[20]

Some billetors claimed children had been sent off in their oldest clothes 'relying on the generosity of the hostess to supply them with new things'. And when evacuees were asked if they had brought all their clothes, they sometimes replied untruthfully that they had left their Sunday things at home. To those brought up in neighbourhoods where parents would keep them indoors on Sunday rather than publicly admit poverty by sending them out without 'best' clothes, anything would seem better than to admit to total strangers that they had nothing for 'best'. In fact, many parents had pawned and gone into debt, and their children had gone away with more clothes than they had ever had before. A teacher from a poor district of Tynemouth and South Shields was surprised to find her pupils had new pyjamas, toothbrushes, shirts, and underwear, but also learned that some mothers would be

[18] WGPW, *Our Towns. A Close-up: A study made during 1939–42* (London, 1943), pp. 54–62; National Federation of Women's Institutes, *Town Children through Country Eyes* (Dorking, 1940); William Boyd (ed.), *Evacuation in Scotland* (London, 1944), pp. 57–8.

[19] Titmuss, *Problems of Social Policy*, p. 115; Liverpool University School of Social Sciences and Administration, *Preliminary Report on the Problems of Evacuation* (London, 1939). Also, LCC: EO/WAR/1/60 (Clothing, 1939).

[20] Alan Sillitoe in B. S. Johnson (ed.), *The Evacuees* (London, 1968), p. 238.

paying for them until Christmas.[21] Often evacuee parents could not understand why billetors requested more clothing or wrote that what a child had was inappropriate for country living; they could not afford new things and were often embarrassed to send second-hand clothes from market stalls and jumble sales. Hosts with children argued that it was impossible to have two very different standards of dress in one household, and many were annoyed when parents sent little treats like comics and sweets or visited, spending money on fares, instead of sending socks and underwear. Government funds were made available for the neediest cases, but procedures were slow and cumbersome. Clothing and footwear problems intensified once winter arrived. A Leeds headmaster whose school was evacuated to Louth, Lincolnshire, wrote angrily in February 1940: 'Since December 1st, we have received only two pairs of footwear here from the U.A.B. and P.A.C. [Unemployment Assistance Board and Public Assistance Committee] in Leeds, and there are nearly two hundred children from the poorest schools of Leeds passing through weeks of the severest weather. No clothing from Leeds has ever come to my aid. Lists have been sent periodically, but no tangible result seems to accrue.' Shortages persisted and though evacuating authorities eventually established their own clothing schemes, the LCC scheme, for example, did not begin until early 1941.[22]

Many of the children looked pale and undernourished, while their bad language, rough manners, and food habits occasioned widespread comment. 'Some', wrote a Chepstow schoolteacher, 'will not sit at the table but want to sit on the floor and have the food handed to them . . . Some do not know how to use a knife and fork . . . Others have never been used to sanitation and foul the paths and gardens.'[23] Even more shocking to many billetors was the high incidence of verminous heads and skin diseases like scabies and impetigo. 'Some of the heads were in a terrible condition', reported a School Medical Officer in Suffolk, 'and an experienced school nurse told me that she had never seen such heads in this area since 1920.' 'The children were nearly all verminous', claimed a Yorkshire doctor. 'Tooth combs and Derbac soap were sold out in Northallerton by the end of the week; the only subject of conversation on market day was the best methods of delousing.' In places like Wigtown in Cumbria, the hair of evacuees was shaved off by local doctors and nurses; elsewhere their clothes were burnt and their heads painted with gentian violet which became a mark of Cain. Public cleansing stations were hastily set up and later special hostels were established for the worst cases.[24]

Soon a veritable war of statistics erupted between evacuation and reception authorities. Anywhere from 22 per cent to 50 per cent among the groups of

[21] Liverpool University School of Social Sciences, *Our Wartime Guests: Opportunity or menace?* (London, 1940), p. 28. M-OA: FR 11, p. 7; M-O, *War Begins at Home*.
[22] Leeds Educ. Papers, Box 375S: O. Walmsley to G. Guest (Leeds Director of Education), 7 February 1940 and 20 March 1941. Also, Box 385 (Provision of Clothing); LCC: EO/WAR/1/63, 109, 202.
[23] M-OA: FR 11.
[24] WGPW, *Our Towns*, p. 66; E. S. Turner, *Phoney War* (New York, 1961), pp. 82–3; PRO: CAB 102/761; PRO: HLG 7/74; IWM, diary of D. M. Hoyles, headmistress of a south London junior school evacuated to Weymouth.

Merseyside evacuees were said to be verminous, while for London children the figures ranged from 8 per cent to 35 per cent. The average for Scotland was put at 30 per cent, with figures as high as 50 per cent and even 90 per cent for some parties. In fact, all estimates were unreliable since many householders simply combed and washed evacuees without reporting cases, while others treated any scratching as lousiness and protested loudly. Reception authorities argued that stringent inspections should have been made prior to departure and there was a lot of grumbling about wasteful expenditure and incompetence in big city social programmes. Councils in the evacuation zones blamed overcrowded travel conditions and the fact that during the summer vacation the children had been beyond the reach of school medical services. Clearly, however, the figures routinely collected as a result of perfunctory visits by school doctors were seriously flawed (almost 98 per cent of inspected children had been declared free from vermin in 1938).

In the wake of the uproar Dr Kenneth Mellanby, Research Fellow of the Royal Medical Society, was engaged by MoH and the Board of Education to study the population of ten industrial cities and four rural areas. He found a low percentage of head infestation in country areas, but a huge reservoir of undetected cases in cities, especially among girls under fourteen years of whom he estimated, around 50 per cent were infested or lousy, while among boys the figures were lower, around 20 per cent among those aged fourteen. Mellanby's report was an embarrassment for the School Medical Service and some officials advised against its publication, although it did appear eventually and was widely covered in the press. Public anger also led to a change in procedures: medical inspections were conducted before evacuating children and the parents of those rejected as having vermin, scabies, or other skin diseases were told to follow a course of treatment and reapply for a further inspection.[25]

Bed-wetting was another widespread and much-publicized problem that officials had failed to anticipate, although it was commonplace in orphanages and middle-class boarding schools. Highly exaggerated at the time, enuresis was usually temporary, a testimony to the psychological stress experienced by children often away from home for the first time. But it was often blamed on 'low social standards' and 'defective training' rather than the emotional strains of separation. Cases of faecal incontinence were far fewer, although one psychiatrist spoke of 'a sort of sphincter holiday. The child goes "native" as it were.'[26] The national government was slow to provide assistance or guidance to householders and it was often months before hostels were established to accommodate the most chronic cases. Outraged at the ruin of bedding and the burden of washing sheets, a few billetors resorted to harsh

---

[25] LCC: EO/WAR/1/185, 186 and PH/WAR/1/21; 'Problems of evacuation', *Manchester Guardian*, 14 September 1939, p. 12; *PD* (Commons) 2 November 1939; *The Health of the School Child: Report of the Chief Medical Officer of the Ministry of Education, 1939–45* (HMSO, 1947); School Medical Officer, 'Verminous children', *The Spectator*, 6 October 1939. Routine school medical inspections were brief (in large schools less than one minute was devoted to each child) and since they were announced beforehand, some children were kept away and others were combed and cleaned more carefully than usual by their parents.

[26] E. Miller, 'The bedwetting problem', *Mental Health*, 1 (January 1940), 4.

discipline. In one case a child psychiatrist visited a boy of nine boarded with 'a well-meaning but feeble foster mother and a foster father of the worst sergeant-major type': the child was 'wet and dirty; cowed; bewildered and . . . shut in the scullery, his shoes and stockings taken off so that he should not run away . . . covered with weals from a severe thrashing'. Fortunately, such methods were not common.[27]

Questionnaires filled out by the members of some 1,700 Women's Institutes in England and Wales recorded the shock of rural and suburban hosts. Many purchased clothes and boots for their evacuees and reacted sympathetically to their adjustment difficulties. But complaints and recrimination abounded, directed particularly at working-class parents, especially mothers. Some of the harshest critics were doctors and Medical Officers who repeatedly pointed to a 'lack of early training', and deplored 'the parents' gross neglect or lack of interest in their children, either because their mother is at work all day, or because of the desire for drink or amusement on the part of both parents'.[28] The dichotomy of town and country, another long-established trope of social analysis, was also repeatedly invoked. Poverty and primitive living conditions were common enough in the countryside—and came as a shock to some evacuees—but they took more acceptable, even picturesque forms, and many voluntary organizations involved in evacuation, like the Women's Institutes, were disposed to think of rural life as more wholesome. 'The London woman', concluded a government committee of 1941, 'is not over-burdened by domesticity. She has a partiality for tinned foods and readily resorts to fish and chip shops . . . The life of her sister in the country parish or provincial town is more often centred in her home. She is more house proud and a better cook.'[29]

But it was not only the condition of evacuee children that provoked criticism of poor mothers; even stronger hostility focused on those women who had evacuated with their babies and infants. Lily Boys, a vicar's wife and WVS organizer in Lincolnshire complained that 'the low, slum type form the majority of mothers, some out for what they can get, most of them dirty, many of them idle and unwilling to work or pull their weight'. She added that the most appropriate solution would be to put them in camps or hostels where they could 'live dirtily (and happily) together and be a nuisance

---

[27] H. St Loe Strachey, *Borrowed Children* (London, 1940), p. 27; H. V. Nicholson, *Prisoner of War. True Stories of Evacuees: Their lost childhood* (London, 2000). Nicholson, a journalist, spent five years as an evacuee in Northumberland and was badly mistreated. She estimates that perhaps as many as 75,000 children were abused (p. 3) but gives no hard evidence for her figure. In 1999 a BBC series on evacuation asked 500 former evacuees whether they thought they had suffered physical or sexual abuse; some 12% answered affirmatively, although it is hard to gauge if this group should be viewed as 'typical' and the figure may also reflect changes in public attitudes towards physical punishment in homes and schools since the 1940s.

[28] NFWI, *Town Children through Country Eyes*; Dr S. E. Gill, 'Nocturnal enuresis: Experiences with evacuated children', *British Medical Journal*, 10 (August 1940), 200. One concern of Medical Officers of Health was that, in mixing populations from very different epidemiological environments, evacuation would increase the spread of certain diseases common in inner-city areas. M. Smallman-Raynor, C. Nettleton, and A. D. Cliff, 'Wartime evacuation and the spread of infectious diseases: Epidemiological consequences of the dispersal of children from London during World War II', *Journal of Historical Geography*, 29(3) (2003).

[29] *Report on Conditions in Reception Areas* (HMSO, 1941), pp. 3–4.

to no-one but themselves'.[30] Similar comments abounded: 'The young mothers were the worst'; 'a great many lacked the will or the knowledge to train their children in good habits'; 'the mothers had not the most elementary ideas of decency and home-training'; and their 'appalling apathy . . . was terrible to see'. In the Wantage area of Berkshire, locals declared 'that the mothers left at a moment's notice' and that it was the 'hysterical type' that had gone away; they added, 'a decent woman would not leave her husband'.[31] The neglectful and irresponsible 'slum mother' became the chief culprit for the scheme's failure: the accusations were wildly exaggerated, but they masked the profound short-comings of official preparations. This was arguably the most deficient and poorly conceived aspect of the whole scheme. The women were expected to cook for themselves in the billetor's kitchen; few nurseries, social clubs, or canteens existed for them, and many found themselves roaming the villages, pushing prams, and standing in shop doorways: 'I feel such an intruder', one said, 'I know they don't really like me in the house, but what can I do? I can't be out all day.' Not surprisingly, feeling unwelcome and uprooted, many mothers returned home within a matter of days.[32]

Conceived as a way of saving lives and reducing panic, evacuation rapidly turned into a national debate about the causes of poverty and the culture and standards of the urban working classes. It raised serious doubts about the validity of school medical inspections, which were now viewed as far too complacent; it also rekindled pre-war controversy about the extent of child malnutrition. In the 1930s the debate had become highly politicized with widely different sets of statistics being bandied about concerning the adequacy of wage rates and relief payments to sustain family health. Groups like the Children's Minimum Council, who advocated free milk and meals programmes, had long accused official reports of downplaying the physical condition of a substantial minority of children. These critics regarded evacuation as a complete vindication. There had been no shortage of surveys of poverty in the 1930s, but the human consequences made a far deeper impression when they came through the front door in the form of an undernourished schoolchild or 'slum' mother. As was true when German raids began, government agencies at first looked to local authorities and voluntary effort to plug gaps in social provision, but over time clothing collections became more organized and school meals and milk programmes expanded dramatically. But in early 1940 the most pressing issue was how to deal with the uproar in the reception areas, some of which were described as 'not far removed from open revolt'[33] and how to dissuade large numbers of evacuees from quitting the scheme altogether.

---

[30] Lily Boys, 'Preliminary report on evacuation of children and others to Lindsey (Lincolnshire)', 11 September 1939 NA: HLG 7/74 (also WRVS archive, London, R3/5 Lincolnshire/Lindsey).

[31] NA: HLG 7/74 (Report on evacuation to Lindsey, Lincs., 11 September 1939); NFWI, *Town Children through Country Eyes*, pp. 20–1. On Wantage: Association of Architects, Surveyors, and Technical Assistants, *Evacuation in Practice: Study of a rural reception area* (London, 1940), p. 14.

[32] Titmuss, *Problems of Social Policy*, pp. 168ff.; M-O, *War Begins at Home*, p. 314; *The New Era* (September–October 1939), 241–2. The scheme made no distinction between married and unwed mothers, but in practice the latter were almost impossible to billet: see LCC: PH/GEN/3/20.

[33] MoH regional officer quoted by Titmuss, *Problems of Social Policy*, p. 163.

RELIGIOUS DIFFERENCES: CATHOLICS AND JEWS

Not all of the cultural differences exposed by evacuation were class-based or rooted in the separation of town and country; in some instances they were compounded by religious and ethnic factors. Catholics from Glasgow, Clydebank, and Liverpool went to overwhelmingly Protestant rural communities in southern Scotland and northern Wales, while evacuees from the Jewish neighbourhoods of London, Manchester, and Leeds were dispersed to small towns and villages, posing enormous problems in terms of religious observance. Evacuation planners had given little attention to religious confession, which was not even specified on the registration forms. Not only did the Anglican Church play a minor role in the planning process, but concerns voiced by the Catholic hierarchy and the Jewish Board of Deputies elicited few firm assurances from officials who were so preoccupied with the physical movement of evacuees.[34]

Problems surfaced quickly, especially in the isolated valleys of north Wales, which received large groups of Catholic evacuees from Liverpool.[35] Even where a Catholic church existed in the vicinity, billetors often resented rearranging domestic timetables to suit evacuees' hours of worship, while in many small villages observant householders, not wishing to leave young evacuees at home alone, had to choose between missing services themselves or taking the children with them, which brought accusations of proselytizing.[36] At Launceston in Cornwall, London children were dispersed over a large area with little access to religious services and billetors accused teachers of sabotaging their efforts by instructing pupils to demand that their parents recall them. A head teacher wrote: 'They see and hear things in non-Catholic houses that to my mind are far more detrimental . . . than any danger from bombing.'[37] Evacuees, teachers, and some of the priests who accompanied them complained of anti-Catholic bigotry in some areas. By October 1939 the Archbishop of Westminster, Cardinal Hinsley, was demanding the transfer of Catholic children from unsuitable areas; several schools were relocated, but such moves were largely undercut by a rapid return to the cities, significantly higher

---

[34] On evacuation and religious upbringing: T. Tatlow, 'The results of an enquiry on evacuation', *Religion in Education* 7(3) (July 1940); M. L. Jacks, 'Teaching religion in war-time', *Religion in Education* 7(2) (April 1940); Commission of the Churches for International Friendship and Social Responsibility, *Evacuation and the Churches* (London, 1941); for a criticism of evacuation planning and its lack of consultation with the churches, see S. M. Gibbard, 'The Church and evacuation', *Theology* 43 (July 1941), 253.

[35] Archbishop Downey of Liverpool complained: 'It is notorious that Liverpool children have been sent to the most non-Catholic part of the kingdom where facilities for the practice of their religion are practically non-existent': *Universe*, 25 July 1941. See also *Catholic Times*, 25 July 1941. While many Welsh householders welcomed evacuee children, the Welsh Nationalist Party was deeply opposed to the scheme. Its leader, Saunders Lewis, feared that the 'monoglot English school populations' would 'destroy the continuity of Welsh education, of Welsh religious life, of Welsh rural and social conditions': Letter of 26 January 1939 in NA: ED/136/117.

[36] C. Jackson, *Who Will Take our Children?* (London, 1985), pp. 47–51. Also, Leeds Educ. Papers, Box 372 (G. Paling to G. Guest, 17 November 1939).

[37] LCC: EO/WAR1/188; Catholic Diocesan Archives, Southwark, Box File 'Education 1940–41' and 'Evacuation of Schools 1940–42', which includes quote: Mrs Ramage to Canon Thompson, 7 July 1940; *Catholic Times*, 26 March and 12 April 1940.

among Catholics than other groups—no less than 92 per cent of Clydebank Catholic children went home within four months.[38] After Christmas 1939, with declining numbers still evacuated, the pressure to merge school groups increased and the Catholic authorities grew increasingly troubled by this intermingling of faiths in billets and school units. Bishops urged parents to write 'Catholic' in large letters at the top of registration forms. Bishop Marshall of the Salford diocese, for example, prepared detailed instructions for his clergy requiring that he be contacted immediately if there were any difficulties in provision for 'spiritual care'. By November 1941 he had concluded, though he was unwilling to say so publicly, that further evacuation of Catholic children was inadvisable. 'I repeat', he wrote to the deans of his diocese, 'that I would rather see children killed than that they should lose their precious gift of faith, purity, and piety.'[39]

Ingrained anti-Irish prejudice also played a role in the reception of Catholic evacuees; it comes as no surprise that in Evelyn Waugh's evacuation novel, *Put Out More Flags*, the unbilletable family is named Connolly. Irish Catholics came from some of the poorest and most overcrowded urban areas and mothers with infants, always very difficult to billet, constituted a high proportion in many of these groups. A volunteer escorting Islington Catholic schoolchildren was overwhelmed by their poverty; most of them carrying their few belongings in pillow cases, cushion covers, or paper bags.[40] A Mass-Observer in Cheshire reported: 'Six Irish slum women with 15 children arrived. They were given one room in a big house, which was not properly panelled, but which could be properly locked up from the rest of the house. All the women were to sleep in this room . . . After two days evacuation, they wanted to go back.'[41] The legacy of the first evacuation was also evident when preparations got underway for a second exodus in spring 1940. In one Scottish county, for example, among 5,000 householders contacted, only 97 expressed real willingness to take evacuees and these specified that only Protestants should be sent. Similarly, the local education officer at Truro warned the LCC that 'the presence of more than 300 Catholic children in any Cornish town is going to create considerable difficulty'. He was assured by the London authorities that efforts were being made 'to get as many as possible allocated to other detraining stations'.[42]

[38] NA: ED138/50 (copy of letter from Hinsley to MoH, 9 October 1939). Clydebank children: Boyd (ed.), *Evacuation in Scotland*, pp. 93, 96, 114–16.

[39] Marshall Papers (Salford Diocesan Archive, Bolton) 200/16, 2 November 1941. Also, J. Davies, 'Evacuation during World War II: The response of the Catholic Church', *North West Catholic History*, 25 (1998), 49. Archbishop Williams of Birmingham (in a letter to his clergy, 8 June 1940) also urged that if Catholic children could not be billeted close to a Catholic community, then evacuation should be resisted. S. Parker, *Faith on the Home Front: Aspects of church life and popular religion in Birmingham, 1939–45* (Oxford, 2006), p. 134.

[40] N. Longmate, *How We Lived Then* (London, 1971), p. 55.

[41] M-OA: TC, Evacuation Box 1/b (letter signed G.W. and dated 6 September 1939). See also the comments of WVS organizer Vera Dart about the verminous Liverpool Irish: 'The only sensible thing to do with people who are a lower type of civilization altogether is to put them into huts': J. Hinton, *Women, Social Leadership and the Second World War* (Oxford, 2002), p. 151.

[42] NA: CAB 102/761, p. 98; LCC: EO/WAR1/188 includes the Truro case (T. E. Jervis to C. L. Hart, 5 April 1940 and subsequent correspondence). Also, NA: HLG 7/73 (22 June 1940). The issues were also discussed in the *Catholic Times*.

Jewish evacuation also produced special difficulties both in terms of religious needs and the responses of billeting communities. Very few synagogues existed in reception areas, kosher food was unavailable for the most part, and in many places there were few Jewish families to act as foster parents even if officials had wanted to allocate billets on a confessional basis. The London Board of Deputies quickly became very active in the reception areas, setting up kosher and communal eating facilities, appointing local liaison officers who worked with local officials and clergy, and raising money for regular religious instruction where it was lacking. Remarkably, by July 1941 regular Jewish instruction was provided at 250 centres in reception areas for over 7,000 children.[43] Some 14,000 Jewish evacuees from London and smaller groups from other towns participated in the government scheme in September 1939. Most were sent to communities in Bedfordshire, Buckinghamshire, Oxfordshire, Cambridgeshire, and East Anglia. It is impossible to generalize about their reception, since individual and group experiences varied from place to place. There was the usual clash of town and country and friction produced by class differences when, for example, poor mothers and children from the East End arrived in affluent suburbs. Among hosts, knowledge of Judaism was rare and many billetors who had expected evacuees to fit easily into their families felt thwarted by children whose ways seemed so 'foreign', especially when they were orthodox, refusing to eat foods prepared for them or to participate in activities on the Sabbath.[44] 'No one in the village', wrote Ruth Fainlight, nine years old when she was evacuated with her mother and brother to South Wales, 'seemed to have met or had any personal contact with a Jewish person before. We were told that we could not possibly be Jews as if it were a delusion we were all suffering from and of which, in natural kindness and humanity, we should be cured.'[45] There was fear that children evacuated for a long time might simply conform to the routines of Christian households and lose contact with their roots, although allegations that foster parents were attempting to convert children were very few. Misunderstandings were often quickly overcome, especially where communal feeding facilities and the efforts of Jewish organizers eased the burdens of householders.[46] However,

---

[43] The Jewish Board of Deputies Archives (JBDA), C9/1–C9/5 contain detailed records of the special problems of organizing Jewish evacuation. Also, LCC: EO/WAR/2/46 ('Jewish school children: Special problems', June 1939–June 1940). On the provision of instruction see *Joint Emergency Committee for Jewish Religious Education in Great Britain: Second report, August 1941–December 1942* (Woburn House, 1942); B. Steinberg, 'Jewish education in Britain in World War II', *Jewish Social Studies*, 29 (1967).

[44] Tony Kushner, 'Horns and dilemmas: Jewish evacuees in Britain during the Second World War', *Immigrants and Minorities*, 17(3) (November 1988); JBDA, C9/1e: letter from Rabbi J. Ferber, 4 January 1942.

[45] Johnson (ed.), *The Evacuees*, p. 90. Also, Bernard Kops, *The World is a Wedding* (New York, 1963).

[46] For a Jewish secondary school very successfully relocated from Stoke Newington, London to Bedfordshire: J. Grunfeld, *Shefford: The story of a Jewish school community in evacuation, 1939–45* (Essex, 1980). A Cambridge rabbi complained to the Board of Deputies in September 1941 that the Billeting Officer in St Ives was 'making every effort to convert our Jewish children to Christianity . . . not even the Ministry of Health has been able to turn her from her path': JBDA, C9/1e. See also *Cambridge Daily News*, 12 September 1941 and the correspondence in C9/1e on Ely and Cambridge.

in rural areas of East Anglia, according to Titmuss, there was less tolerance of cultural and religious differences.[47]

Anti-Semitism was a persistent concern, especially in small towns and country regions that had little previous experience of Jews and where even strangers from a neighbouring county were often regarded as 'foreigners'. As a Mass-Observation survey of its panel of observers in spring 1939 showed, negative stereotypes of Jews were widespread. Respondents invariably asserted that there was no 'Jewish question' in their area and many expressed their horror at Nazi persecution of Jews; but self-examination also revealed distaste for Jews and strong inclination to believe accusations about their sharp business practices, lack of public spirit, and clannishness; images of Shylock or of rich, pushy Jews sprang quickly to mind. Typical comments explained: 'I have an antipathy to Jews, and while realizing it is unreasonable, I am unable to overcome it', and 'I believe in a policy of live and let live . . . In fact I don't object to Jews at all. There's something about them which is alien and slightly repellent, and I avoid coming into too close personal contact with it, that's all.'[48] Some Jewish evacuees undoubtedly encountered prejudice, either inadvertently in jokes and daily conversation or in the taunts that village children sometimes directed at them; but more virulent forms of anti-Semitism were rare, at least until the summer and autumn of 1940. At that time several factors seem to have contributed to the increase: the string of military failures, invasion fears, fifth-column hysteria, and the government's internment of aliens together probably intensified customary inclinations towards scapegoating, while the Blitz produced a crop of accusations that Jews were prone to panic, overcrowding communal shelters, and flocking to safe billets.[49] It is difficult to gauge the prevalence of such prejudice. Many negative reports came from sympathetic observers, including Jews who were anxious that co-religionists might be causing offence, and they were addressed to a Board of Deputies that was particularly sensitive to signs of anti-Semitism. The Board's staff responded with a campaign to encourage higher standards of behaviour, warning Jews against gambling and card-playing on trains between London and nearby reception areas, and suggesting that 'word should be put in the Jewish press asking Jewish people . . . to be very careful of their conduct and not to give any cause for complaint to fellow travellers'.[50] To combat prejudice

---

[47] Titmuss, *Problems of Social Policy*, p. 179.

[48] M-OA: DR, Anti-Semitism and Racial Research Survey February–March 1939; M-OA: TC, Anti-Semitism survey (3 boxes). G. G. Field, 'Antisemitism with the boots off', *Wiener Library Bulletin*, Special Issue 1983: 50 Years of the Wiener Library, pp. 25–46. For a comprehensive study of anti-Semitism in the war years, see Tony Kushner, *The Persistence of Prejudice: Antisemitism in British society during the Second World War* (Manchester, 1989).

[49] M-OA: TC, Evacuation, Box 2/i: 'In Leicester, after the air raid, the rumour spread that the Londoners, having run from one town, were running away again. There were no good words to be said for them at all. The words "evacuees" and "Jews" are used interchangeably; all those who have run away are thought to be Jews' (report of 27 November 1940). Also, M-OA: FR 482.

[50] Quote comes from S. London to A. Petrie, 16 March 1942, JBDA C9/1e. For other complaints to the Board of Deputies: M. Morris and S. G. Pick in June 1942, JBDA, C9/1e; A. Petrie, 'Notes on Hyde park', 12 August 1941, C9/4/2. Also, A. Petrie to W. Rubinstein, 5 February 1942; S. L. Bensusan, 20 January 1942; letter to Mrs J. B. Priestley, 5 February 1942, JBDA, C9/5; Mr Israel to Rev. M. Katz, 3 October 1941 which includes 'Criticisms against Jews in the Berkhamstead

the Board promoted lecture series on Jewish history, religion, and Anglo-Jewry's contributions to Britain at adult education programmes, church societies, the Women's Co-operative Guild, and rotary clubs.

The major stimulus to anti-Jewish feeling, however, was the spontaneous departure of London raid victims to surrounding areas so that villages and provincial cities rapidly became overcrowded and supplies, accommodation, and services were strained to breaking-point. Towns like Luton, Leicester, Beaconsfield, Windsor, Stevenage, High Wycombe, Horsham, Reading, and Oxford were thrown into considerable chaos by refugees arriving daily. In Reading, for example, the pre-war population of about 100,000 had grown by 50 per cent in October 1940, much of it in the previous two months. Its Jewish community of roughly thirty families rose to over 1,500 people, many poor and some recent refugees from the Continent. Reports to the London Board of Deputies described mounting resentment, some of it directed at Jews, while the local congregation was said to have offered little assistance and 'if anything, give the impression that they are anxious not to be associated with the Londoners'.[51] Whatever their actual numbers, 'East End Jews' provided a convenient scapegoat for residents' accumulated frustrations. Faced with impossible demands for billets, the mayor of Windsor was said to have blurted out: 'You're a lot of Jews anyway, and you ought to go back to Whitechapel. We don't want Jews here.' In some places local anger was directed towards poor Jews from Poplar and the East End, many of them left destitute by the raids and forced to crowd into makeshift accommodation in rest centres and local institutions. Elsewhere discontent fixed upon 'rich Jew' stereotypes. In Oxford, for example, affluent Jews were criticized as pushy and inconsiderate, promenading in large groups, buying up scarce supplies, and spending their time in cinemas while offering no help to local voluntary services. One volunteer at a communal rest centre told Mass-Observation: 'We get rather a lot of Jews. I don't say anything against them myself, but they're so different from us—trousers and lipstick and head in a scarf—we aren't used to that sort of thing... Then we get some rich Jews—come down in cars and expect to find a room waiting for them.'[52]

VOTING WITH THEIR FEET: THE GREAT RETURN AND RE-EVACUATIONS

By January 1940 the failure of 'Pied Piper' was widely acknowledged. Government press releases about the improving health and happiness of evacuees could not

---

area', C9/1a; 'Report on investigation of conditions in reception areas', 28 August 1944, C9/1d. For complaints about Jews playing cards on trains, see C9/4 especially February and March 1942.

[51] Report of 29 October 1940, JBDA, C9/1e.

[52] M-OA: TC, Evacuation, Box 2 (2/m Windsor and Reading; 2/j Beaconsfield and Witney; 2/k Windsor and Reading and 2/r Stevenage); M-OA: FR 451, 482, 565A. On Reading: JBDA, C9/5/3, N. Walmsley–A. Petrie correspondence, April 1941; JBDA, C9/1e, 'Position of evacuees at Windsor', 23 October 1940 and letter from Rev. J. S. Choate, 10 December 1940; JBDA C9/1d, 'Brief notes on reception areas', 26 November 1941.

disguise the plain facts: many who were eligible for evacuation had never participated in the scheme and a large percentage of those who did had gone home
almost immediately. As the government feared, many children who went home
for Christmas 1939 did not return. Official statistics, released in the spring of 1940,
confirmed months of rumour. Of a total of 1,473,000 persons evacuated in
September, some 900,000 had returned within four months, including 88 per
cent of evacuated mothers, 86 per cent of pre-school children, and 43 per cent of
the schoolchildren. Those still in reception areas (some 570,000) represented only 14
per cent of pre-war government estimates for evacuation. The absence of raids
in the early months of the war was a major factor, leading many evacuees and
many of their hosts to conclude that the disruption of their lives far outweighed
the dangers.[53]

As these statistics indicate, the most glaring failure was the evacuation of mothers
with young infants and pregnant women. Both groups proved exceptionally
difficult to billet and politicians' comments about the inability of two women to
share the same kitchen or water tap demonstrated masculine incapacity to grasp the
problems of such doubling up, especially in homes that were already crowded.[54]
Similarly, press reports that women were returning to their husbands because of
jealous concerns about 'the woman round the corner' made light of the fact that
many had left aged parents, as well as husbands, to fend for themselves or had
given up part-time earnings and now could not meet their additional expenses.
A prevalent comment that many had simply jumped at the chance for a brief
holiday was a sad travesty of these women's experiences.[55]

Among school parties the scheme was more successful, although surveys indicated that the rate of return was highest among the poorest children. This reflected
both the resistance of foster parents to having them and the difficulties of their
families in meeting additional expenses for travel, clothes, and other items, especially if their unemployment benefit had been reduced or if the conscription of
fathers and older brothers had caused family income to drop. In the first three
months of the war over 20 per cent of the parents of Liverpool evacuees were on
some form of public relief. A government announcement in October 1939 that it
would means-test billeting allowances also increased the rate of return, even though
the poorest families were not required to contribute. Older and better-off schoolchildren were more likely to remain evacuated than those in elementary schools;
parents did not want to disrupt their education and since schools were closed in the
big cities they worried that returning evacuees would 'run wild' and get into serious

---

[53] Titmuss, *Problems of Social Policy*, p. 172. These statistics do not include those who made private
arrangements whose movement cannot be calculated with any accuracy. The rate of return of
government evacuees was higher in Scotland (by January 1940 28% of Scottish evacuees remained
in reception areas, compared to 40% in England).

[54] *PD* (Commons) 14 September 1939 (Ede) and *PD* (Commons) 2 November 1939 (Wilkinson).

[55] A survey by The Standing Joint Committee of Working Women's Organizations in September
1939 strongly criticized the scheme for mothers. Memorandum October 1939 SJCWWO Papers
(Labour History Archive and Study Centre, Manchester).

trouble. Later, with the expansion of the labour market, poor families were more likely to bring home teenagers so they could find jobs or look after siblings while mothers worked.

Aside from obvious 'misfits' where hosts and evacuees disliked each other from the first, or where children were undisciplined or enuretic, most children were taken home simply because they were homesick or lonely.[56] Few people had telephones and writing letters was a difficult and unfamiliar task for many. In general, parents were troubled by the idea that their children's characters were being moulded by strangers and this was especially where they sensed that hosts viewed their own standards critically. Explaining why she had fetched her eight-year-old daughter home, one woman told a BBC interviewer: 'You see, at present some children are having so much luxury that they will never be satisfied with their own simple homes again.' Another mother with children billeted in a middle-class home complained that they 'were being brought up "narky"' and that she wasn't going to have it.[57] Sometimes, of course, a foster parent's circumstances changed or the task became too burdensome. But parents also rationalized their own needs claiming that 'the child felt unwanted, or that the hostess seemed . . . anxious to get rid of the child'. In a Liverpool survey of returning children, hosts attributed 67 per cent of the cases to parents and 10 per cent to the wishes of the child, while parents blamed the host in 40 per cent of the cases (41 per cent were ascribed to homesickness and 19 per cent to their own wishes). Studies suggested that children settled down better where the distances were greater and parental visits fewer. It was also widely argued that they were more contented (and relations between parents and hosts were more agreeable) in billets that resembled the social level of their own homes. This was probably true, although it also served as a rationalization for an unfair distribution of billets.[58]

Only a third of those who had participated in the first evacuation remained in the reception areas in June 1940 when France capitulated, sharply increasing the threat of German air raids against British cities. Plans for a second evacuation met with stubborn resistance, despite an intensive campaign of personal visitation to get children registered.[59] The new scheme was scheduled to get underway only when serious air bombardment began, but many parents nursed bitter memories from the previous exodus and refused to commit in writing that they would not bring children home. Reception areas were equally resistant; the phrase 'once bitten, twice shy' was repeatedly used to describe their mood, despite higher billeting allowances and the fact that the government originally decided to

---

[56] Leeds Educ. Papers, Box 380 (Return of Evacuees, 1939–40); M-OA: FR 87, 299. It was regarded as unfair that billeting should be compulsory and its duration unspecified, although parents could suddenly remove their evacuee children without notice. The absence of raids in the first months of the war also led hosts to feel that their lives had been precipitously thrown into confusion.

[57] BBC Archives: 'Talking it over', 18 April 1941; M-O, *War Begins at Home*, p. 330.

[58] Liverpool University, *Our Wartime Guests*, pp. 29–34; S. Isaacs, *Cambridge Evacuation Survey* (London, 1941), pp. 140, 132–3. Also, G. M. Lindsay, 'The physical, social, and educational effects of evacuation upon West Hartlepool evacuated schoolchildren', MA Diss., West Hartlepool, 1942; J. F. Dow, *A Survey of Evacuation in Westmorland* (Kendal, 1943).

[59] LCC: EO/WAR/1/46.

exclude mothers and infants from the new plan.[60] Opinion polls revealed a strong preference for the construction of special evacuee camps, although this was unrealistic given the numbers required and the urgent demands now being made on all the nation's raw material resources.[61] Once heavy air raids started, a second mass movement got underway. Between September 1940 and the end of 1941 about 1,250,000 children and mothers with infants (who were once again included) travelled to reception areas. This time the movement was spread over many months, rising and falling with the intensity of enemy attacks. As in the first case, some evacuees returned quickly and there were indignant press stories about those who went back and forth several times. But, in general, billeting mismatches were far fewer than in the previous year. In most places arrivals were staggered and destinations known beforehand; evacuating authorities medically screened children before departure;[62] and many mothers took advantage of a new 'assisted scheme' which provided travel and billeting vouchers and allowed them to arrange their own accommodation.

Without doubt the evacuation scheme functioned far better in this second mass evacuation and during the next two years than it had at the outbreak of war. Some historians have attributed this to the greater sympathy of receiving communities once the bombs started falling and to the more inclusive and generous ethos of the 'People's War' that developed in late 1940.[63] There is truth in this, but the value of later evacuations as a yardstick of public attitudes is limited. They were scarcely comparable to September 1939; no later migration could have the same shock effect as the first, none was so concentrated in time, or included so many parties of poor women and children; indeed, there is some evidence that many of the poorest families never participated in later schemes. Government spending increased, making it easier for reception areas to provide a range of services; more social workers and psychologists were appointed; special hostels were established for so-called 'unbilletables' along with residencies for mothers with babies; billeting allowances were raised; and the numbers of communal canteens, clothing schemes, and social clubs grew. In addition, as the war continued, full employment, higher wages, and a huge expansion of school meals and milk programmes helped to

[60] The weekly allowance paid for billeting at the outbreak of war was 10s 6d for one child and 8s 6d for additional children. Hosts complained about its inadequacy and the rate was raised at intervals. By June 1940 it was 10s 6d for each child of 10–14 years, 12s 6d for those 14–16, and 15s for those over 16. For mothers with pre-school infants (who were responsible for their own meals) the rate was originally 5s for the mother and 3s for each child. A major problem was sharp regional disparities in living costs.

[61] A BIPO poll in the *News Chronicle*, 26 March 1940 showed 72% of the sample in favour of camps, 25% in favour of billeting, and 3% don't knows. One aspect of evacuation for which enthusiasm grew was the Children's Overseas Reception Board (CORB), which began sending children overseas to the United States and the Dominions in June 1940. But few of the 200,000 applications received and even fewer of the 3,500 children sent abroad before sinkings in the Atlantic ended the scheme, came from the working class. Home Intelligence reported that the scheme provoked sharp recrimination against the rich, whose children were enabled to sail.

[62] After May 1940 children were examined and details were entered onto cards in a coded form; these were then copied onto the labels worn by children so that those requiring special attention could be quickly identified upon reaching a reception area.

[63] A. Marwick, *Class, Image, and Reality in Britain, France and the USA since 1930* (Oxford, 1980), p. 218.

1. London schoolchildren being evacuated, 13 June 1940.

improve the general health of working-class children, even if they were pale and tired from spending their nights in air-raid shelters.[64] Finally, official statistics for evacuees reflect simply the number of billeting allowances paid; they do not take into account changes in the rules for eligibility. Those who had privately evacuated before the outbreak of war—including better-off working-class and lower-middle-class families—and were therefore originally ineligible for billeting allowances, were now brought into the government scheme.[65]

One, often neglected, reason for improvement in the scheme's functioning was the hard work of teachers, 'the invisible evacuees', whose lives were dramatically disrupted

---

[64] Ministry of Education, *The Health of the School Child, 1939–45* (HMSO, 1947). Official documents and surveys stressed evacuation's beneficial impact in improving the health and appearance of urban children. Country air, more nourishing meals, and a more structured existence, it was claimed, produced rapid gains in weight, height, and general alertness. The claims were impressionistic and those based on anthropometric examinations were seriously flawed. When the statistics in some camp schools actually showed retarded growth, officials were perplexed. It appeared healthier, wrote one puzzled official in August 1942, for 'a child to stay in East London sleeping irregular hours in ill-ventilated shelters and eating fish and chips than to have fresh air conditions in one of our Camps with regular hours of sleep and plenty of well-prepared wholesome food'. See, J. Macnicol, 'The evacuation of schoolchildren' in H. L. Smith (ed.), *War and Social Change: British society in the Second World War* (Manchester, 1986), p. 20.

[65] On eligibility for allowances, see Leeds Educ. Papers, Boxes 383–4.

by being transplanted to reception areas for several years. Often short of classroom space and using school buildings in shifts with little in the way of equipment, they adapted and experimented, anticipating the more child-centred pedagogies of the post-war era. Evacuation greatly enlarged their responsibilities, at times blurring the boundaries between education and social services, although many later recalled that it made for closer, less formal contact with pupils and their families. If some felt conscripted by the extra duties or worried that parents were 'throwing off more and more responsibility to teachers', many had a real sense that education was at the centre of plans for construction of a better, more inclusive society.[66] Among other things, they took a large role in finding suitable billets for evacuees, which as school logbooks and official documents show, was a never-ending battle.

By the middle of the war, not surprisingly, many hosts were weary and somewhat resentful, believing themselves the victims of a government-sponsored regional division of labour that allowed urban mothers to take lucrative war jobs while they assumed the responsibilities of childcare for little payment or recognition. Even where householders were ready to take in boarders, they preferred military personnel (especially Americans), factory workers, and evacuated civil servants who paid more and were less trouble. Above all, foster parents resented the fact that many people evaded the responsibility. A Lancashire 'farmer's wife with three children and two men in the house' complained about the wealthier landowners in her area: 'They all have big houses, and when you ask why they have none, they just say can't be bothered with them. I do not think it is fair, when such as we and people with little houses has to have them.'[67] Such complaints surfaced from the very beginning and never let up. The popular media's attention might focus on cases of slum children lodged with gentry farmers, duchesses, or affluent retirees who previously had 'only a dog or a parrot or a temperamental liver to worry about'.[68] But as weeks went by and re-billeting took place, most districts saw a trend; as a Mass-Observer in rural Yorkshire put it, 'The billeting officers were rather successful in transferring evacuees from the houses of the well-to-do to those of the lower-middle and working classes.'[69] The 'real hard core of resistance is the upper middle classes', reported one Medical Officer in 1941; fines were sometimes levied but officials were generally reluctant to use compulsory powers where children were clearly unwelcome. Social matching, it was widely claimed, was the key to success, but this did not assuage local anger and cries of favouritism.[70]

[66] M. Lawn, 'What is the teachers' job? Work and welfare in elementary teaching, 1940–1945' in M. Lawn and G. Grace, *Teachers: The culture and politics of work* (London, 1987). Also, National Union of Teachers (NUT) Archive (London), Box 1992 Folders 1–4 on difficulties for evacuated teachers.
[67] Lancs. County Council (Preston), RDG 17/13, letter dated 12 February 1941; also MBF 23/6. Also, for billeting difficulties: the NUT archives (London), e.g. NUT: Box 1992 (A); 1992 (B).
[68] *The Listener*, 5 October 1939, p. 662. Two films that fostered the mythic view are *Those Kids from Town* (1942) and *Gert and Daisy's Weekend* (1942).
[69] M-OA: FR 592; also, F. Le Gros and R. W. Thoms, 'Evacuation: Failure or reform', Fabian Society Tracts, no. 249 (1940), p. 6.
[70] Titmuss, *Problems of Social Policy*, pp. 392–3. Also, NA: HLG 7/75. INF 1/292, 15–25 June 1941. The turnover of billeting officers was rapid and over time the job fell more and more to women. In one town Titmuss found that 37 prominent citizens (including the town clerk, the vicar, the

By September 1942 the frequency of enemy raids had greatly diminished and evacuation slowed to a trickle. Indeed, after the so-called Baedeker raids that singled out poorly defended provincial cities, Churchill himself admitted that 'children were in no more danger in London than in the country'. A growing number of urban schools also reopened, further stimulating the drift back to the cities. All classes of evacuees for the whole country numbered around 350,000 in the period from the summer of 1943 until that of 1944. As Titmuss argued, the function of evacuation had been transformed; it was now less a means of saving the population from bombs than a 'safety-valve for social distress in the cities', a possible solution for the multiple problems faced by families in wartime: finding homes for children when their mothers were sick or giving birth and there was nobody to care for them; relieving the pressures on working wives whose husbands were in the services or had been directed into war jobs away from home.[71] Social workers developed networks of contacts with billeting officers and evacuated children for therapeutic reasons— placing them in hostels or private billets or farm-training colonies for young people. A typical example involved a young serviceman's wife, with four small sons, living in 'very bad conditions', demoralized by their disobedience and unable to cope. 'We arranged', wrote the caseworker, 'for the two older boys to be evacuated to billets with a party from their school and they settled down and stayed away 12 months.' In other cases the children's removal was more punitive: 'She was not allowed to forget them and was fully conscious of the purpose of their temporary absence.'[72]

A final wave of evacuation began in July 1944 when the sudden and enormously destructive 'buzz bomb' and V2 rocket attacks convinced many citizens to leave target areas in the south. With victory seemingly so close at hand, the government was at first reluctant to resort to another mass scheme. But, to an exhausted population, this new danger seemed particularly intolerable and terrifying. By early September over 700,000 people left London and the south-east, many making their own arrangements and going to formerly 'neutral' areas that had not taken evacuees before. The mood this time was different, since nobody expected the conflict to last much longer. Most returned within a few months and by the summer under 20,000 schoolchildren remained in the reception areas. This final exodus had none of the social fall-out of earlier phases.

THE IMPACT OF EVACUATION: SOCIAL AND PSYCHOLOGICAL VERDICTS

While later evacuations in 1940 and 1944 went more smoothly, it was the first mass exodus, 'Pied Piper', that set the pattern for future discussions. Scores of

billeting officer, the chairman of the billeting committee, and the bank manager) had not taken a single evacuee as late as April 1942.

[71] P. H. J. H Gosden, *Education in the Second World War* (London, 1976), p. 59; Titmuss, *Problems of Social Policy*, p. 423. Also, Leeds Educ. Papers, Box 377 (Mrs O. Calder to G. Guest, 18 August 1942).

[72] P. Starkey, *Families and Social Workers: The work of the Family Service Units 1940–85* (Liverpool, 2000), pp. 22–3.

postmortems of 'Pied Piper' appeared in addition to extensive coverage in newspapers and magazines. Many had an immediate and practical purpose: suggesting various administrative ways to ease the pains of separation; calling for more hostels, nurseries, and childcare professionals; or giving advice on how to cope with pediculosis and other infestations. Other analyses took a broader approach, continuing interwar debate about public health, the causes of poverty, and child psychology.

The most influential investigation of the causes of poverty and the urban environment from which the poorest evacuees came was *Our Towns* produced by the Women's Group on Public Welfare (WGPW). It developed from a national conference on the problems of evacuation organized by the National Council of Social Service at the urging of the Women's Institutes and the Townswomen's Guilds. Non-partisan, with representatives from groups active in child welfare and social work, it was chaired by Margaret Bondfield, the first woman of Cabinet rank in the Labour government of 1929.[73] The WGPW established several subcommittees which spent over two years gathering evidence about unsanitary housing, health, hygiene, the needs of children under five, and credit structures in working-class areas. They interviewed health visitors, teachers, housing managers, billeting officers, and voluntary workers. The views and preoccupations of committee members differed in emphasis and the final report reflected this in its uncertainty about the relative weight to be ascribed to environmental causes of poverty and those rooted in moral failings and individual incapacity. What emerged, then, was a synthesis of the dominant strands of progressive thinking about the poorest stratum of working-class families—one that looked forward to a more beneficent social service state but also contained strong echoes of interwar ideas about the 'undeserving' poor with severe mental and character defects. Its dominant premise was strongly environmentalist. *Our Towns* viewed low income as the root cause of poverty and gave detailed attention to substandard housing, pitifully inadequate budgets, and deficient education. Rehabilitation was achievable through education, higher wages, better housing, nursery schools and child welfare centres, and the expert interventions of social-work professionals. At the same time the report called for stiffer punishment of parents whose children were verminous and outlined a syndrome of attitudes and customs—including apathy, ignorance, and wasteful spending habits—that were nurtured by life 'below standard'.

Ironically, though the original investigation—in the spirit of public responses to the first evacuation—focused on the scale of urban poverty that still existed in England, its long-term influence was in refurbishing and popularizing the concept of 'problem families'. This was really a recasting of what in the interwar decades was called 'the social problem group' and a forerunner of 'the underclass' concept of the 1980s.[74]

---

[73] J. Welshman, 'Evacuation, hygiene, and social policy: The *Our Towns* report of 1943', *HJ*, 42(3) (1999). The WGPW Papers are in the Fawcett Library, London; see, WF/D3, 5, 7, 8, 9, 12, 13, 14, 15. Unsuccessful efforts were made to have the report issued as a Penguin Special and a documentary film.

[74] J. Macnicol, 'From "problem family" to "underclass", 1945–1995' in R. Lowe and H. Fawcett (eds.), *Welfare Policy in Britain: The Road from 1945* (London, 1999); *idem*, 'In pursuit of the underclass', *Journal of Social Policy*, 16 (July, 1987); J. Welshman, *Underclass: A history of the excluded 1880–2000* (London, 2006).

Evacuation, the WGPW argued, had reaffirmed 'that the "submerged tenth"' described by Charles Booth in the 1890s 'still exists in our towns like a hidden sore . . . always on the edge of pauperism and crime, riddled with mental and physical defects, in and out of the Courts for child neglect, a menace to the community of which the gravity is out of all proportion to their numbers'.[75]

These 'problem families' were not occasional exceptions, but constituted a distinctive stratum of the working class (the bottom 10–13 per cent): a whole subculture in which poverty determined character, producing an unending cycle of squalor, child neglect, ill health, and criminality. In fact, the WGPW made no attempt to define the group precisely or substantiate estimates of its size. 'Problem family' served as a catch-all sociological category for a socially maladjusted minority that had wrecked evacuation; they were the 'unbilletable families' whom decent householders would not take. Beginning in 1940 Pacifist Service Units, composed of conscientious objectors, worked with such families offering 'friendship', practical advice, and monitoring their family budgets, standards of childcare, and housekeeping. After the war, with a new framework of social legislation in place, what were now called Family Service Units greatly expanded this kind of social casework and the 'problem family' concept became a fixture in the vocabulary of social workers, public-health officials, and housing managers. The concept aggregated multiple causes under one label so that 'problem family' became a convenient shorthand for those who stubbornly resisted rehabilitation—'a sore thumb held downwards in the cheery face of the welfare state'.[76]

The initial public outcry over evacuation, as we have seen, ascribed much of the blame for its failure to the low standards of working-class mothers. *Our Towns* echoed this, despite the committee's sympathy with the plight of poor women and the difficulties they faced. The rhetoric is significant: mothers were labelled as 'degenerate', 'degraded', and 'low grade', while the nursery school was championed as 'the only agency capable of cutting the slum mind off at the root'.[77] And while the WGPW reminded readers that 'problem families' were a minority in no way representative of the working class as a whole, the distinction at times gets blurred. Describing the 'poorer type of factory worker' who had little prospect of becoming an efficient home-maker, the report went on:

> Education has left her where it found her, the ignorant offspring of ignorant parents, with a child's mind in a woman's body, fit neither to be wife nor mother . . . [A] girl of this type goes rapidly downhill in the first year of marriage. The smartness which she enjoyed when care-free and earning is often no longer called for because with the first pregnancy her husband ceases to take her out. From thence onwards she sinks into sluttishness and brings her children into it.[78]

[75] WGPW, *Our Towns*, p. xiii.
[76] On Pacifist Service Units, T. Stephens, *Problem Families: An experiment in social rehabilitation* (Liverpool, 1947). Also, Starkey, *Families and Social Workers*. Quote from P. Seed, *The Expansion of Social Work in Britain* (London, 1973), p. 60.
[77] WGPW, *Our Towns*, pp. 3, 40.
[78] *Ibid.*, pp. 108–9.

The tone here is all too reminiscent of Victorian efforts to reform the manners and morals of the working class or the prescriptions of Lady Bell's analysis of the family in Middlesbrough. As Pat Starkey has argued, 'problem family' was virtually a synonym for 'problem mother'.[79]

While the WGPW's report was finished by 1941 paper scarcity and other difficulties delayed its publication until March 1943. By then, with full employment and higher wartime wages, poverty as a general issue had receded, although the poverty of children, those in large families especially, continued to be a central issue for social reformers and family-welfare groups. By then the actual number of evacuees had declined with the lower incidence of enemy raids, but the report's appearance coincided with the sudden intensification of debate about post-war reconstruction, Beveridge's proposals for comprehensive social insurance, and renewed legislative efforts to enact child allowances as a partial solution to poverty in large families. Asserting that 'great and radical reforms are needed to give humanity its chance', the report was designed to influence policy-makers ('no whit of the impetus resulting from the shock to the public conscience should pass unused').[80] Public response was huge and immediate: the first edition of 5,000 copies sold out in days. It was cited in parliamentary debates and was widely reviewed in the national media as well as specialized journals. In fact, it contained little that was new in the way of social analysis but, by accommodating a plurality of approaches to the problem of poverty, it could be used and referenced by a wide variety of groups—its combination of 'radical' and 'reactionary' tones, its 'Janus-faced character' as John Welshman puts it, was crucial to its success.[81] *Our Towns* was the most significant social analysis to originate with evacuation, but its focus on the environment of poverty also meant that it had nothing to say about the role of policy miscalculations and administrative failures in undermining the first evacuation nor did it mention those evacuees who adapted well to conditions in the reception areas.[82]

If one result of evacuation was increased public debate about poor families, another was growing recognition of the family's role as a psychological unit. This vast dislocation of family life was a golden opportunity for psychologists and child-guidance experts to test their theories and demonstrate their professional utility. In the early planning stages, psychologists were barely consulted.[83] Official attitudes

---

[79] F. Bell, *At the Works: A study of a manufacturing town* (London, 1985; orig. 1907); Anna Davin, 'Imperialism and motherhood', *History Workshop Journal*, 5 (1978); Jane Lewis, *The Politics of Motherhood: Child and maternal welfare in England 1900–39* (London, 1980); P. Starkey, 'The feckless mother: Women, poverty and social workers in wartime and post-war England', *Women's History Review*, 9(3) (2000).

[80] WGPW, *Our Towns*: quote is from p. 101; also Scottish WGPW, *Our Scottish Towns: Evacuation and the social future* (Edinburgh, 1944).

[81] Welshman, 'Evacuation, hygiene, and social policy', p. 807.

[82] For a more positive view: Barnett House Study Group, *London Children in Wartime Oxford: A survey of social and educational results of evacuation* (Oxford, 1947). Research for the study was mostly carried out in 1942 and 1943.

[83] In the first days of the war, psychiatrist and educationalist Susan Isaacs recommended the establishment of an advisory committee on emotional stress among evacuees; she was fobbed off and

changed with the outcry over 'Pied Piper'. Within a few months large numbers of psychiatrists and childcare specialists were recruited to work with 'unbilletable' children, while the Child Guidance Council quickly expanded its activities and founded numerous clinics, aided financially by the American Commonwealth Fund.[84] D. W. Winnicott worked with delinquent and disturbed children sent to special hostels in Oxfordshire; Anna Freud and her co-worker Dorothy Burlingham ran a residential nursery; Susan Isaacs, Cyril Burt, and others led teams of researchers, studying specific groups of evacuees. Most of those who later became well known in British child psychology became involved in some fashion with evacuees.[85]

Briefly put, for their findings cannot be analysed in detail here, we can summarize the general consequences of this corpus of work as both professional and theoretical. First, evacuation represents an important stage in the expansion and authority of psychiatric social workers and child-welfare specialists. Their influence over social policy grew steadily throughout the war years and working with large numbers of children in families, foster care, nurseries, and special hostels was important in the development of new therapies. Secondly, evacuation marks a dramatic breakthrough in official perceptions of the family as a psychological entity; the distinction between normality and maladjustment became more blurred as the dislocations of war produced growing awareness of the emotional fragility of 'normal' children. Most importantly, the splitting up of so many families underscored earlier assumptions about the causal connection between maladjustment and maternal deprivation. As the war continued, the quality of mothering and especially early rupture of the mother–child bond played an increasingly central role in theorizing neurosis formation and the psychodynamics of childhood. Already before the war John Bowlby of the Tavistock Clinic had linked juvenile criminality and prolonged separations in early childhood.[86] And already in December 1939, together with Winnicott and Emanuel Miller, he published a letter in *The British Medical Journal* warning that evacuating children under five without their mothers might result in 'very serious and widespread psychological disorder' and create delinquent children in the next decades.[87] German raids did not alter this view; indeed, the main thrust of psychiatric work was that evacuation was potentially

a marginal note to her letter by some official commented that she was merely trying to find herself a job. NA: ED 138/5, S. Weitzman draft of a 'History of education in wartime' (p. 143).

[84] By 1944 there were over 70 clinics (17 in London alone) affiliated to the Child Guidance Council. The archives of the Commonwealth Fund (Rockefeller Archives, Pocantico, New York) contain detailed reports on its role in the evacuation scheme.

[85] S. Isaacs, *The Cambridge Evacuation Survey: A wartime study in social welfare and education* (London, 1941); D. W. Winnicott, *Deprivation and Delinquency*, ed. C. Winnicott, R. Shepherd, and M. Davis (London, 1984); Cyril Burt, 'The incidence of neurotic symptoms among evacuated school children', *British Journal of Educational Psychology (BJEP)* 10(1) (1940); idem, 'The billeting of evacuated children', *BJEP*, 11(2) (1941). For a bibliography of psychological studies of evacuation: K. M. Wolf, 'Evacuation of children in wartime: A survey of the literature', *The Psychoanalytic Study of the Child*, 1 (1945).

[86] Bowlby's book *Forty-Four Thieves* was not published until 1946, but its findings were anticipated in widely known essays and lectures. J. Bowlby, 'Forty-four juvenile thieves: Their characters and home lives', *International Journal of Psychoanalysis*, 25 (1944).

[87] Letter in *The British Medical Journal*, 16 December 1939, pp. 1202–3.

more damaging emotionally than bombing. 'Love for parents is so great', Anna Freud wrote, 'that it is a far greater shock for a child to be suddenly separated from its mother than to have a house collapse on top of him.' 'It would be tragic', Bowlby argued, 'if more damage were to be caused by our precautions than by the weapons they were designed to protect us against.' The American psychiatrist Dr J. Louise Despert concluded in 1942 that 'if the British had to do it over again there might not be any evacuation'.[88]

What, in conclusion, was the significance of evacuation for this study of the working class—aside that is from the immediate experiences of millions of people, both those evacuated and those who took them in? One result is that evacuation was one of several aspects of the early war that forced the state to take a more active role. It loosened Treasury purse strings and helped to introduce reforms—from improvements in the school medical programme to school meal and milk programmes. It was also a catalyst for the rapid growth of family professionals in the war and early post-war years, whose views—shaped by their wartime experience—influenced the design of social policy and its practical implementation. Belief that wartime had left family life in disarray, requiring urgent restoration, was one factor in a complex web of causation that for the first time gave Britain a unified set of family policies in the late 1940s. And while many of these ideas were framed in the class-neutral explanatory concepts of psychology, in fact working-class families were perceived as the prime object of social welfare reform, just as working-class youth was at the centre of debate about juvenile delinquency. A broadly shared orientation towards child-rearing evolved during the war years—one that combined the insights of social workers and psychiatrists. Indeed, the war saw the triumph of an intensely familialist view of child welfare centred upon the nuclear family and especially the mother as the key to successful socialization. The distinctiveness of this amalgam of ideas is easily forgotten except when compared to a more collectivist, less family-focused tradition like the French. As Laura Lee Downs writes: 'What no one worried about ever throughout the entire French evacuation of 1939, nor during the subsequent evacuations of 1940–45, was the impact that separation of children from their biological mothers might have on children's psychological development . . . the major question that haunted the British [experts] *never even came up* in the many discussions of French evacuation.'[89]

But beyond these consequences, there was also what we might call the sociopolitical impact of evacuation. Richard Titmuss, in his volume in the official series of war histories, argued that evacuation and then German raids against British cities

---

[88] A. Freud and D. Burlingham, *Infants Without Families* (New York, 1944); *idem, Young Children in Wartime* (London, 1942); Padley and Cole (eds.), *Evacuation Survey*, ch. 16 (J. Bowlby, 'Psychological aspects'); Bowlby, 'The problem of the young child' in *The New Era*, 21 (March 1940); J. L. Despert, *Preliminary Report on Children's Reactions to the War* (New York, 1942), p. 85. Also, J. C. Kenna, 'Evacuation? Educational and psychological problems of evacuation: An analysis of the experience of England', Australian Council for Educational Research (Melbourne, 1942).

[89] Laura Lee Downs, 'Milieu social or milieu familial? Theories and practices of childrearing among the popular classes in 20th century France and Britain: The case of evacuation (1939–45)', *Family and Community History*, 8(1) (May 2005), 60.

produced a fundamental change in public attitudes; that the revelations of poverty which evacuation disclosed, combined with the shared danger of the moment, helped to create a new social climate conducive to social reform. Certainly there were many in 1940 who hoped that might be true. Hilde Marchant of the *Daily Express*, called it a 'silent social revolution, the significance of which will be seen long after the devastation of this war', and as late as 1943 the *Economist* described it as 'the most important subject in the social history of the war'.[90] But, as John Macnicol has argued, the dominant reaction of Whitehall officials and much of the middle class to 'Pied Piper' was to cling to their preconceptions about poverty and the irresponsibility of the poor—indeed, in the short run it may even have boosted moral and eugenic explanations.[91] Dr Gertrud Wagner who studied Liverpool evacuees wrote: 'Many of the upper classes have come into contact with the workers for the first time and have been horrified. The minority, mainly represented in the women's organizations, have turned their horror into pity, and have determined that the appalling conditions . . . shall be swept away and very soon; the majority have turned their horror into fear and even hatred, seeing in this level of humanity an animal threat . . .'[92]

The outcry over evacuation touched the nation's raw nerves, disclosing deep class and confessional divisions and making society transparent to itself in new ways. It answered the question Priestley and others had posed about national solidarity. The Kingdom, it seemed, was far from United; it looked more like Benjamin Disraeli's 'Two Nations'. But while Titmuss may have ascribed too much to the singular impact of evacuation, he was right about its symbolic significance and its longer-term contribution to a new ethos of democratic collectivism. In the early war years evacuation, German bombing, the threat of invasion, and repeated battlefield defeats together went far to weaken the legitimacy of the pre-war social and political order. In the summer of 1940 Priestley broadcast his famous 'Postscripts' after the nine o'clock news. In them he outlined the concept of a 'People's War' and sketched a powerful narrative of the interwar decades—as an era of broken promises, dole queues, and political failure. A populist counterpoint to the ornate style of Church-ill's radio addresses, he proclaimed the war as a new beginning, but one umbilically linked to the past. As the nation fully mobilized over the next two years, evacuation became integral to this imagery: a *crise révélatrice* as Runciman has called it,[93] which graphically recalled the bad old days. In this political mythology where children so often represented a better future, the ragged evacuees conjured up an unequal and divided past—but also hinted at the possibility of a New Britain that might emerge from the hardships of war.

---

[90] H. Marchant, *Women and Children Last* (London, 1941), p. 151; *Economist*, 1943, quoted in Lowndes, *The Silent Social Revolution*, p. 203. Also, M. Cosens, 'Evacuation: A social revolution', *Social Work* (January 1940).

[91] Macnicol, 'The evacuation of schoolchildren'. For views closer to Titmuss, see Bob Holman, *The Evacuation* (Oxford, 1995); J. Welshman, 'Evacuation and social policy during the Second World War: Myth and reality', *Twentieth Century British History*, 9(1) (1998).

[92] M-O, *War Begins at Home* (London, 1940), p. 336.

[93] W. R. Runciman, *A Treatise on Social Theory*, III: *Applied Social Theory* (Cambridge, 1997), p. 270. Even today memories of evacuation—unlike so many nostalgic references to national solidarity—are much more likely to contradict myths of national unity and cosy community.

2
Class and Community in the Blitz, 1940–1

The first evacuation took place before the nation had time to adjust to war; the public at large had little idea of what to expect or how quickly and completely their lives would change. A year later Poland was subdued, Denmark and Norway invaded, the British army driven from the Continent, and France defeated and occupied, bringing British cities within striking distance of Hitler's air force and the strong possibility of a full-scale invasion of southern England. At home Conservative political hegemony was undermined and Neville Chamberlain's government had collapsed, replaced by Churchill's Conservative–Labour coalition whose strength and cohesion appeared anything but certain at the time. Not surprisingly, with everything seeming to disintegrate around them, fear and shocked uncertainty were among the general public's strongest reactions and, deeply concerned that defeatism would spread, the government took extraordinary steps to monitor morale on a daily basis. Writer and diplomat Harold Nicolson, now working for the Ministry of Information, had the feeling that 'an old-toothed civilization is breaking now'. Britain, he wrote, 'must put forward a positive and revolutionary aim admitting that the old order has collapsed and asking people to fight for a new order'.[1]

Nicolson's view reflected a radical shift in the nation's mood. It seemed clear that, if Britain was to survive, sweeping changes must be introduced which committed all the nation's energies to the war. Not everyone imagined it was possible: military expert and historian Captain Basil Liddell Hart was convinced that Britain should negotiate a truce with Hitler and warned against both Churchill's 'grandiloquent nonsense' and 'idealists out of touch with military factors'. His friend, the novelist Irene Rathbone, nourished one glimmer of hope in mid-November 1940: that 'new men will take hold, new methods will be used ... It will be a leap into the blue, an unimaginable blue, but there is the chance it will be taken and for that chance I hang on.'[2] But as German bombing reduced London and other cities to rubble, the nation's morale did not break, the atmosphere of desperation subsided; indeed, people, albeit with frayed nerves and sleep-deprived, seemed to grow acclimatized to new routines. Official publicity and the media recast the conflict as a 'People's War' in which the Blitz was soon mythicized as a

[1] H. Nicolson, *Diary and Letters*, II: *1939–45* (New York, 1967), p. 99 (entry for 3 July 1940).
[2] Liddell Hart to I. Rathbone, 18 November 1940; Liddell Hart to Kingsley Martin, 2 November 1940; I. Rathbone to Liddell Hart, 16 November 1940: Basil Liddell Hart Papers, Liddell Hart Centre for Military Archives, King's College, London University.

regenerative force, a purgatorial trial by fire and high explosives, from which a more united and better Britain would emerge. That the events of 1940–1 transformed political and social attitudes is largely accepted by historians. Far less agreement exists about the degree of change, whether it was lasting or ephemeral, and the extent to which the nation was truly unified or remained fractured by class, gender, and other internal divisions. My answer to these questions will emerge in the course of several chapters; this one focuses primarily upon a dramatic shift in public discourse about the nation and the working classes during the months of the 'Blitz'—a term that is often loosely used to cover the whole air war, but strictly speaking refers to the sustained period of aerial bombardment from September 1940 until the following May.

GOVERNMENT, PEOPLE, AND AIR-RAID PRECAUTIONS

Although German Zeppelin and aircraft raids against Britain in the First World War had produced only minor casualties and relatively little structural damage, the nightmare of heavy aerial bombardment was a constant preoccupation in official circles over the next two decades. Yet, in contrast to most European countries, planning for civil defence was largely carried on in secret until the Abyssinian crisis and the Spanish Civil War graphically publicized the dangers. Casualty and damage estimates were revised upwards as technology improved and fuller data became available, but government policy seemed stalled by a mixture of budgetary concerns and policy assumptions.

Several factors were mutually reinforcing. First, few funds were allocated to Air Raid Precautions (ARP) research and the projected costs of providing adequate shelters (i.e. capable of sustaining a direct hit) were deemed prohibitive, especially at a time when rearmament already threatened to put a growing strain on the national budget. Instead, in a 1935 circular the government urged local councils to adopt measures voluntarily and counselled house owners on elementary ways of protecting against blast from near misses.[3] Behind official thinking there still lurked a belief that the government's foreign policy could avoid a European war and, if that were not the case, there remained the hope that Britain's heavy investment in bombers would act as a deterrent. If, indeed, the bomber could always get through, as Stanley Baldwin had suggested, then the threat of mutual devastation might compel some restraint. In addition, government civil defence policy anticipated that most air raids would be of short duration, intense, and during daylight hours. Few, if any, predicted the nightly assaults that would force Londoners to sleep and spend long hours sheltering from early September 1940. And, finally, a great deal of attention and disproportionate funding was devoted to anti-gas measures. Poison gas had been used by Mussolini in Abyssinia and there were fears that it might be used on a wide scale although, as one government scientific adviser later suggested,

---

[3] T. H. O'Brien, *Civil Defence* (London, 1955).

the distribution of some 38 million gas masks was also politically shrewd, enabling everybody to be issued with a protective device at a very cheap cost and diverting attention, perhaps, from the paucity of shelters.[4]

By 1938, amid heightened international tensions over Hitler's absorption of Austria and the Czech crisis, public debate over civil defence intensified. Central government plans continued to devolve much of the responsibility for air-raid precautions, in addition to evacuation planning, on local authorities while at the same time refusing to guarantee their expenditures. Some were overwhelmed by the growing array of new tasks; others put forward proposals for the construction of deep shelters and the reinforcement of existing underground tunnels. The Labour-controlled borough of Finsbury in London proposed several deep, bomb-proof shelters, each capable of holding 7,600 to 12,000 people. Accessible by broad, spiral ramps, they were designed for easy peacetime conversion to underground parking garages. Along with several other local proposals, this scheme was rejected in early 1939. A government report, ostensibly examining the case for deep shelters, but in reality bolstering its case against them, expressed fears that they might incubate a defeatist 'shelter mentality'.[5] The Labour Party grew more vocal in its criticism of government inaction and called for larger expenditures on underground communal shelters. A spate of books and pamphlets also appeared, including a widely read Penguin Special and a Left Book Club selection by geneticist J. B. S. Haldane, who had made a close study of aerial warfare in Spain. Haldane became a tireless campaigner for deep, mass shelters, forming an ARP Coordinating Committee of architects, engineers, and scientists, and lecturing and writing regularly in the press; his columns for the *Daily Worker* gave lustre to the Communist Party's increasingly successful efforts to mobilize opinion around ARP at a time when the Nazi–Soviet pact had left it otherwise in serious disarray. And when the Women's Voluntary Service (WVS) was formed in June 1938, initially to assist local authorities in recruiting volunteers for ARP work, some women's groups, especially Labour ones, refused to participate. Some of their concerns sprang from organizational rivalry and there was considerable criticism of the undemocratic structure and perceived Tory, upper-class ethos of Lady Reading's WVS. But there was also a feeling among left groups that giving assistance would remove pressure on the government to construct credible air-raid defences. As a woman officer of the radical Civil Service Clerical Association wrote to the TUC, her union believed 'that the only way to drive the Government into making ARP more adequate by the expenditure of considerable sums of money upon bomb-proof shelters, is for this dearth of volunteers to continue'.[6]

---

[4] J. F. Baker, *Enterprise versus Bureaucracy: The development of structural air-raid precautions during the Second World War* (Oxford, 1978).

[5] J. S. Meisel, 'Air raid shelter policy and its critics', *TCBH*, 5(3) (1994), 311–14.

[6] Replies of organizations to Lady Reading's appeal can be found in the WVS Archive, London (V/38 series of folders, nos. 34, 36, 40, 51, 95, 107, 121, etc.); L. M. Sweet of the Civil Service Clerical Assoc. to Walter Citrine, 20 June 1938, TUC Papers in MRC (Warwick University) MSS 292/883.212/8.

Opinion polls showed that the vast majority of people wanted deep shelters and, by May 1939, 53 per cent of those surveyed by Gallup actively criticized the government's refusal to build deep underground bunkers. But by early 1939 official policy was set. It did not aim at providing the maximum possible safety from aerial bombardment, but was shaped by several goals: protection from blast and splinters but not direct hits; cost containment; the conservation of scarce supplies of steel, cement, and labour; and anxieties about the possible impact of mass shelters on morale. This translated into a preference for dispersed, family shelters (named after the Home Secretary Sir John Anderson) that could be constructed in backyards. Once the shelter space was dug out, it was covered by a sheet of corrugated steel and about eighteen inches of earth; simple, trench shelters were also built in parks, sometimes lined with wooden duckboards and covered by corrugated steel roofs. With both these types, damp and flooding were serious problems. Family shelters and the accompanying publicity that made each household unit largely responsible for its own defensive preparations, suited best the circumstances of suburban living. In areas of flats and tenements where people were less likely to have gardens, small brick and concrete surface shelters were built. Few of them had any amenities and many were badly built and unsafe; however, a steel shortage in 1940 resulted in increasing reliance on surface shelters which came to represent a high proportion of the available spaces in some inner-city areas. Factories often had basements or they reinforced specific areas for their workforce while schools that remained open usually adapted basements or dug slit trenches in the playgrounds.[7] But when war came the supply of shelters was seriously deficient in towns like Birmingham and Coventry, while in April 1941 Belfast still had spaces for only a quarter of its population.

Official predictions about the likely consequences of aerial attack were particularly grim, forecasting widespread panic, floods of terrified refugees, and hospitals full of psychological as well as horrific physical casualties.[8] A 1938 report presented to MoH by a group of leading psychiatrists anticipated that there would be a three to one ratio of psychiatric to physical casualties in the first six months, with about 3–4 million people suffering from various degrees of neurosis and panic. They urged the creation of mobile teams of psychiatrists and a complex structure of outpatient clinics and hospital provision.[9] As it happened, the destructiveness of enemy bombing was far less than predicted, but when set alongside the catastrophic estimates prevalent at the time, government preparations were little short of scandalous.[10] They also reflected the

[7] In 1938 the country was divided into twelve civil defence regions, each with a Regional Commissioner responsible for coordinating the different government departments and organizations. Where real progress had been made prior to September 1939 was in the recruitment of air-raid wardens, auxiliary firemen, ambulance drivers, etc., the vast majority of them volunteers. By the end of 1938 (influenced by the Munich crisis) 1.4 million adults had volunteered.

[8] J. Rugg, 'Managing "civilian deaths due to war operations": Yorkshire experiences during World War II', *TCBH*, 15(2) (2004). There were plans for 17,000 troops and 20,000 reserve constables to be drafted in London to cope with the predicted mass exodus and prevent panic.

[9] Tom Harrisson, *Living Through the Blitz* (New York, 1976), p. 39; R. M. Titmuss, *Problems of Social Policy* (London, 1950), pp. 20–1.

[10] A 1937 report by the Committee of Imperial Defence had calculated that a 60-day offensive might result in as many as 600,000 deaths and 1.2 million injured.

social assumptions of policy-makers; in particular, resistance to large, communal shelters was predicated not only on worries about potential loss of life in the event of a direct hit, but fears that they might become incubators of defeatism or political disaffection, especially in working-class districts. Civil defence discussions between the wars worried that the poorest social groups were 'likely to form the most unstable element—an element very susceptible to panic. The worst of all will, doubtless, be found in the East End, and those who had experience in the last war will recall the appalling scenes which occurred in this area.'[11] Ironically, it was in the East End and similarly poor and densely populated areas that shortages of shelter accommodation were most acute.

'CIVILIANS IN THE FRONT LINE': THE LONDON BLITZ

It was always assumed that the first and the chief target would be London—indeed, nervous anticipation led to a false alarm immediately after Neville Chamberlain finished his radio broadcast announcing that the nation was at war. Altogether the sirens sounded 1,124 times—an average of once every thirty-six hours for five years. There were 101 daylight and 253 night raids and over 40 per cent of the V1s and V2s fell on London. Its population sustained half the deaths from air attacks, while about 30 per cent of the City, 20 per cent of the East End, and large sections of many other areas were reduced to ruins. Eighty thousand dwellings were estimated to have been destroyed altogether and 700,000 were damaged to some degree. No other city was targeted so continuously.[12]

The number of alerts climbed steadily during the summer of 1940 as German bombers struck several cities and air bases around London, but the first major raid on London took place in daylight on 7 September when some 375 German bombers began raining down bombs on the densely packed streets, docks, warehouses, and factories of West Ham, Bermondsey, Poplar, Stepney, Shoreditch, and Bethnal Green. Night brought a second assault. In twenty-four hours some 430 people had been killed, over 1,600 seriously wounded, and thousands made homeless.[13] Thereafter the city was attacked continuously, mainly at night, for a period of over two months. The main period of the Blitz, however, extended until 10 May 1941, with particularly destructive raids on 29 December (the so-called 'Fire of London') and on 16 and 19 April when over 1,000 people were killed each

[11] T. L. Crosby, *The Impact of Civilian Evacuation in the Second World War* (London, 1986), p. 15. See also NA: CAB 46/22–23 (Evacuation Sub-Committee, especially 13 and 21 March 1931); M. C. McKenna, 'The development of air raid precautions in World War I' in T. Travers and C. Archer (eds.), *Men at War: Technology and innovation in the twentieth century* (Chicago, 1982).
[12] P. Ziegler, *London at War* (New York, 1995), p. 337; J. Mack and S. Humphries, *The Making of Modern London: London at war, 1939–45* (London, 1985); A. Price, *Blitz on Britain: The bomber attacks on the United Kingdom* (London, 1977); C. Whiting, *Britain under Fire: The bombing of Britain's cities, 1940–45* (London, 1986).
[13] L. Miller and H. Bloch, *The First Day of the Blitz: East London memories of September 7th 1940* (London, 1984); M-OA: FR 392 (20 September 1940); FR 403 (12 September 1940); Peter Stansky, *The First Day of the Blitz* (New Haven, 2007).

night and on 10 May itself when more than 1,400 were killed. Later attacks on London were concentrated in early 1943 and the first three months of 1944 (the so-called 'little Blitz') and then in the war's final year came the flying bombs and V2 rockets, which together destroyed over 30,000 dwellings in the London area.[14]

From the beginning the pattern of German bombing contradicted earlier assumptions. Instead of brief, daylight attacks, Londoners soon found themselves enduring long nightly raids that forced them to sleep in cramped shelters and to completely reorder their daily routines. The inadequacy of shelter facilities quickly became evident, particularly in central London which bore the brunt of the early raids. Trench shelters were overcrowded, poorly lit, cold, often muddy with dripping walls and leaking roofs. Families with Anderson shelters fared better, although often they were liable to flooding. Some brick surface shelters were badly constructed and caved in from bomb blast or the roofs became detached from the walls; doubts about them spread quickly and many people abandoned them for non-official places of refuge. While the number of casualties was much smaller than pre-war estimates, physical damage to houses from incendiaries as well as high explosives was extensive, leaving unexpectedly large numbers of people homeless. Unexploded bombs also wreaked havoc putting many on the streets temporarily until their bomb could be inspected, defused, and disposed of—and this might take several days. Rest centres, set up mostly in former schools or church halls, had been envisioned as places where raid victims might rest for a few hours before returning home or being rehoused; in fact, they soon accommodated people for weeks on end. They were badly understaffed and short of blankets, bedding, soap, towels, first-aid supplies, chairs, and crockery; washing facilities were often primitive and many lacked kitchens for hot meals. At one centre in Stepney, 2–300 people slept on the floor with ten buckets and coal scuttles to serve as lavatories. A social worker recalled: 'Dim figures in dejected heaps on unwashed floors in total darkness: harassed, bustling, but determinedly cheerful helpers distributing eternal corned beef sandwiches and tea—the London County Council's panacea for hunger, shock, loss, misery, and illness.'[15] So rapidly did the crisis of homelessness outpace the ability of local authorities to deal with it that within three weeks over 25,000 were lodged in rest centres and in the first six weeks ten times that number needed rehousing, although only about 1 in 7 passed through a rest centre. The majority simply sought help from friends and relatives, camped out in the shelters, found some other accommodation, or went back home once it was safe to do so.[16]

The intensity and regularity of the raids on London strained emergency services to breaking point and shattered normal routines. Women especially faced heavy burdens. Over half a million children were still in the town when the raids began; schools were closed and the supervision of children was both more imperative and

---

[14] For the V1s and V2 rockets, see N. Longmate, *The Doodlebugs* (London, 1981).
[15] Titmuss, *Problems of Social Policy*, p. 261. See also: M-OA: FR 465 (24 October 1940); NA: CAB 102/731, 733; Randall Swingler, 'Blitz nights and days', *Our Time*, 1(1) (February 1941).
[16] Titmuss, *Problems of Social Policy*, ch. 14. Also, M-OA: FR 406 (September 1940). It was estimated that in all 1.4 million people in the London civil defence region (i.e. one-sixth of the Greater London population) were homeless at some point between September 1940 and May 1941.

time-consuming. Shopping was a constant battle since many shops were closed or bombed and distribution systems were disrupted, resulting in long queues and shortages. When raids cut off gas, electric, and water services, cooking had to be done on coal-burning ranges or over outdoor fires and drinking water might require boiling. After an attack, whole districts were blanketed with dust and soot and even dwellings that were not hit often had windows blown out, ceilings collapsed, and slates stripped from their roofs. Shelter surveys regularly reported that married women got the least sleep and showed the most strain and fatigue as the months passed.[17] For the elderly, especially if they were physically impaired, queuing for shelter spaces, sleeping on hard benches, and negotiating blacked-out streets carpeted with rubble and downed power lines was extremely difficult.

Before the war psychiatrists had made dire predictions about the likely numbers of psychiatric casualties. These proved mistaken in the extreme. The London Emergency Region recorded an average of slightly more than two 'bomb neuroses' cases per week in the first three months of the Blitz. At Guys Hospital, which was close to areas that were severely bombed, the attacks accounted for only a handful of psychiatric cases treated by the outpatient department; at another London hospital only 5 of 200 psychiatric cases admitted in a six-month period were attributable to the raids. Children also adapted far better than anticipated; the pains of family dissolution caused by evacuation, psychologists began to assert, were more trau-matizing than bombs. But, while chronic and incapacitating neurosis was rare, there was no way of knowing how many less serious cases went untreated since physical injury to raid victims preoccupied rescue squads.[18]

However, the strain of the raids manifested itself in a variety of less acute signs of emotional stress: anxiety attacks, extreme fatigue, eating disorders, apathy, feelings of helplessness, trembling, tics, and weeping spells. In children minor symptoms like lack of concentration, excitability, and restlessness were widely detected. A rising incidence of peptic ulcers, coronary symptoms, angina attacks, cerebral haemorrhages, miscarriages, and various menstrual disorders can also be linked to the tension under which people were living.[19] So can higher levels of disorientation and senility among the elderly. Various minor behavioural quirks were also wide-spread. Superstition and fatalism were rife: people carried gas masks, sprigs of

---

[17] Harrisson, *Living Through the Blitz*, pp. 100–9. See also, M-OA: FR 408 (18 September 1940).

[18] R. D. Gillespie, *Psychological Effects of War on Citizen and Soldier* (New York, 1942); Edward Glover, 'Notes on the psychological effects of war conditions on the civilian population', 2 parts in *International Journal of Psychoanalysis*, 22, 23 (1941–2); M. Schmideberg, 'Some observations on individual reactions to air raids', *International Journal of Psychoanalysis*, 23 (1942); Aubrey Lewis, 'Incidence of neurosis in England under war conditions', *Lancet* (July–September 1942); R. H. Thouless, 'Psychological effects of air raids', *Nature*, 148 (1941); P. E. Vernon, 'Psychological effects of air raids', *Journal of Abnormal and Social Psychology*, 36 (1941); W. M. Burbury, 'Effects of evacuation and air raids on city children', *British Medical Journal*, 2 (1941); A. McClure, 'Effects of air raids on schoolchildren', *British Journal of Educational Psychology*, 13 (1943). Also NA: CAB 102/719; INF 1/292 (12–19 February 1941). Also L. Stonebridge, 'Anxiety in a time of crisis', *HWJ*, 45 (Spring 1998).

[19] I. L. Janis, *Air War and Emotional Stress* (London, 1951). Also M. Dyson 'Psychiatric social work during London's wartime bombing', Association of Psychiatric Social Workers Archive Folder 11/1, Birmingham, now relocated to the MRC (Warwick University).

heather, lucky charms, and other talismans; some refused to wear green; others avoided sheltering with those they thought unlucky. 'I have become superstitious about cleaning my rubber boots' a fireman admitted. 'After cleaning my boots we generally suffer a blitz, and I am out all night fighting fires. The same thing occurs if I am short of cigarettes while on duty.'[20] Many claimed that, 'like lightning', bombs never strike twice in the same place or argued fatalistically: 'If your name's on a bomb it will get you.' On weekends large sightseeing crowds, drawn compulsively to bomb sites, hampered civil-defence work. The public cheerfulness, so often referred to in the press, was not just a fiction but there was a manic quality to the merriment, a silly giddiness that reflected the supercharged nature of life and the need for cathartic release. Everyone, it seemed, had a 'bomb story' and a pressing need to tell it.

Stepney and London's dockside communities soon lost much of their population. Some families now registered their children for evacuation or sought refuge with relatives in quieter districts of London. After big raids there was a great deal of short-term flight with crowds boarding trains for nearby towns like Windsor, Stevenage, Reading, Leicester, and Oxford, which were already overfull. Hilde Marchant of the *Daily Express* described scenes comparable to those she had witnessed in war-torn Spain: a 'ragged, sleepless army' carrying suitcases, pushing prams overflowing with their belongings, old people in makeshift wheelchairs, others with carts or piling into old cars and lorries formed a convoy of refugees, a steady stream heading out towards the rural hinterland. The town of 'Reading is like Bordeaux,' commented a resident, recently back from France, 'queues of women and children with their possessions done up in pillow-cases; nowhere to go—storming the YMCA and the buses—it's very bad.' Friction spiralled between local populations, town officials, and the shifting tide of newcomers.[21] Deficient shelter provision in their own areas also led families to 'trek' to open spaces like Hampstead Heath, Epping Forest, or the Kent countryside while others sought out commercial basements in the West End that had been reinforced as shelters.

In many neighbourhoods, people soon selected their own communal places of refuge. Shelters sprang up spontaneously in church crypts, beneath factories and under railway arches; some had even been sanctuaries from raids in the previous war. In the worst of them coughs, colds, and 'shelter throat' spread freely, as did lice and skin diseases like impetigo and scabies. The numbers of TB cases also rose, but luckily the incidence of diseases like influenza, diphtheria, meningitis, and scarlet fever remained lower than medical opinion feared.[22] These massively overcrowded public shelters—extensively covered by journalists like Ritchie Calder and Hilde Marchant—finally brought the long-festering shelter debate to crisis point. Among the most publicized was the Tilbury, a huge underground warehouse and goods

[20] M-OA: FR 975 (21 November 1941); also, FR 739 (April 1941); FR 521 (6 December 1940).
[21] H. Marchant, *Women and Children Last* (London, 1941), p. 55; M-OA: FR 482 (4 November 1940); also, FR 451 (11 October 1940).
[22] CMD 6340, *Summary Report by the Ministry of Health, April 1, 1939 to March 31, 1941* (London, 1942).

depot between the Commercial Road and Cable Street in Stepney. At times as many as 14,000 people squeezed into its vaults and loading bays, surrounded by crates and rubbish, with only a few earth buckets for lavatories. 'I felt sick', wrote Nina Masel of Mass-Observation: 'You just couldn't see anything, you could just smell the fug, the overwhelming stench... thousands and thousands of people, lying head to toe, all along the bays and with no facilities.'[23] A safer and even larger refuge on London's outskirts were the caves around Chislehurst in Kent. Though privately owned, they were quickly occupied and by mid-October gave shelter to as many as 15,000 people.

But the most important communal shelters were those in the stations of the London Tube or Underground. Although thousands had gone down there during the First World War, the government rejected their use as shelters, arguing both that unhindered movement of commuters and troops must be guaranteed and that occupants might easily acquire a 'deep shelter' mentality and refuse to leave. The regularity of the raids, however, made it easy for increasing numbers of people to enter the Tube and remain there. Minor confrontations occurred (orchestrated in some cases by Communist Party activists) between crowds waiting to go below and Underground officials whose instructions were to lock the entrances once a raid began.[24] By the second week of heavy bombing, however, the authorities had yielded to popular pressure and orderly queues outside the stations became a familiar sight, waiting for 4.00 p.m. when they were allowed onto the platforms. As captured by Bill Brandt's magnificent photographs, people sat or slept huddled together on platforms, between the lines themselves once the power was shut off, and propped against escalator stairs. The unfinished Aldwych–Holborn spur and the Liverpool Street extension were turned into the vast tubular dormitories of sleeping figures depicted in Henry Moore's drawings. Especially in the deepest stations the detonation of bombs and anti-aircraft barrages was muffled and rest came easier than above ground. But the subterranean peace recorded by Brandt and Moore was far from secure: several stations were hit by bombs (Marble Arch, Balham, Bank, Liverpool Street, etc.), some with heavy casualties.

By mid-September about 150,000 people a night were sleeping in the Tube, although by the winter and spring months the number had declined to 100,000 or even less on raid-free nights. Official estimates are, however, somewhat misleading for in many of the poorest working-class areas where the number of people in communal shelters was significantly higher, the percentage of families that at some point took refuge in the Tube, even if they were not 'regulars', was far higher than contemporary estimates suggested.[25] Only a minority of Londoners went to the

---

[23] Mack and Humphries, *London at War*, p. 59.

[24] A. Hern and J. Chen, 'The people of the tubes', *Tribune*, 27 September 1940.

[25] A rough census (November 1940) placed about 4% of Londoners in the Tube and equivalent large communal shelters, 9% in public surface shelters, and 27% in domestic Anderson shelters. This left over half the population unaccounted for—presumably spending the night in basements or cupboards under the stairs or, more often, simply staying in bed or downstairs in their living rooms. Harrisson, *Living Through the Blitz*, p. 112. Also, M-OA: FR 436 (3 October 1940); for public criticism of tube-shelterers: M-OA: FR 425 (28 September 1940); FR 421 (27 September 1940).

mass shelters, but they soon captured the nation's imagination, becoming the focal point of debate over civil defence and by extension a yardstick of governmental failure. They illustrated dramatically the tragedy of modern war and the resilience of ordinary people and, like evacuation, underscored the glaring inequities of pre-war society. The large public shelters were also easily accessible. Many churchmen, journalists, and social workers visited them, followed by celebrities and a stream of socially curious sightseers and 'slummers' on a new version of a pub-crawl. Anyone travelling by Underground in the evening could not avoid encountering rows of reclining figures on the platforms, families camped out, and private life being lived in public. The trains continued to run until half-past ten at night and painted white lines reserved a walkway for passengers, juxtaposing everyday normality and startling, surreal images of wartime dislocation. 'The train had its windows covered with opaque or black-out material,' wrote the architect Sidney Troy 'and when it stopped at a station and the doors were opened from the centre the effect was remarkably like that of a stage.'[26] Early on, some Tube riders were critical of these troglodytes who got in their way, abusing them as dirty, cowardly, diseased, work-shy, or simply foreign. Even those more sympathetic could slip into language that underscored social distance. Thus, novelist Naomi Mitchison, who spent much of the war in a Scottish fishing village, commented: 'All so like the Russian stations in 1932, with the families camped in them. I think the *indigènes* are a slightly different race, a shade darker and smaller . . . They hardly gaze back but go on reading the papers, drinking tea from mugs, knitting . . . We don't exist for one another.'[27]

Very quickly certain basic forms of organization began to develop in large shelters, sometimes spontaneously among those seeking refuge, sometimes organized by local clergymen and air-raid wardens. 'Each shelter', wrote Tom Harrisson, 'became more and more a self-sufficient community, with its own leaders, traditions, laws.' Collections were taken up to buy disinfectants and brushes or to tip porters and cleaners at Tube stations. In the largest shelters, spaces were allocated for smoking, recreation, nurseries, children's play, and sleeping; rules developed about keeping gangways clear, making noise, and respecting other people's space. While in some locations individuals took the lead and acted as shelter marshals, in many places committees were organized to run things, settle disputes, assign chores, arrange entertainments, and put pressure on local authorities to make improvements. As so often with such ad hoc structures, however, not much was committed to paper and our information about their operation is fragmentary and impressionistic. In the Tube more than thirty stations established committees and by December they had joined forces holding a Tube shelterers' conference to share ideas and discuss a common strategy for obtaining more bunks, canteens, and better lighting and sanitary facilities.[28] Where local government was

[26] Troy, quoted in C. FitzGibbon, *The Winter of the Bombs: The story of the Blitz of London* (New York, 1957), p. 151.

[27] D. Sheridan (ed.), *Among You Taking Notes: The wartime diary of Naomi Mitchison, 1939–45* (London, 1965), p. 115.

[28] Harrisson, *Living Through the Blitz*, pp. 118–21. 'Have you a shelter committee?', *Daily Worker*, 13 September 1940; also 17 September (Tufnell Park Tube committee), 20 September (Belsize Park);

2. Elephant and Castle Tube station, November 1940.

passive and slow to respond, as in West Ham and Stepney, there were angry exchanges between local officials and shelter delegations. The police intervened in a meeting held in early October at a large shelter under the Spitalfields Fruit Exchange in Stepney and, shortly afterwards, a deputation from the Tilbury demanding, among other things, a ticketing system to reserve places and public access to shelters under private firms in the area ended in a mêlée with the police and several arrests. Elsewhere borough councils established welfare committees on which diverse groups were represented. Shelter inspection was at first deficient but things improved rapidly once Labour's Herbert Morrison took over as Home

28 November and 14 December (on the Tube shelterers' conference). See also, E. Trory, *Imperialist War: Further reflections of a communist organizer* (Brighton, 1977), pp. 134ff.; M-OA London Survey, 1940, Box 4, 65/3/H 'East Ham', 28 August 1940.

Secretary in October 1940 and put pressure on local authorities to take more decisive action.[29]

Some of this grass-roots organizational activity aroused official concern. Ritchie Calder of the *Daily Herald* wrote that most shelter committees developed spontaneously concluding that the role of militants was often exaggerated. But Whitehall was quick to blame political agitators for any unrest. Local activists took the lead in demonstrations to open the London Underground, picketed commercial buildings where basements were locked at night, and demanded that empty flats and houses in more affluent neighbourhoods be requisitioned for homeless raid victims. Home Intelligence warned that 'people sleeping in shelters are more and more tending to form committees among themselves, often communist in character, to look after their own interests and to arrange dances and entertainments'. Certainly, in Stepney, where the Communist Party already had a solid base in local tenants' groups, it did play a prominent role; moreover, the Nazi–Soviet pact and the dispersal of people with evacuation had weakened the party in some areas and the push to organize shelters was an effort to reconstitute local party structures. The party's most widely publicized venture was a sit-in, organized by Phil Piratin, Stepney's Communist councilman, at the luxuriously appointed shelter in the Savoy Hotel. In general, however, the main cause of public anger was the paucity of emergency services and glaring evidence of class differences during the crisis.[30]

It was voluntary organizations that reacted first to the crisis, helping to plug gaps in services until state structures responded to new needs. Public shelters soon became sites for social activism and experiments in community formation. The Red Cross and St John Ambulance set up first-aid posts; the Charity Organization Society distributed blankets, food, and clothing; and heroic work was done to improve shelters and rest centres by the WVS, the YMCA, Salvation Army, settlement houses, and church groups. Local doctors donated their time and a number of devoted clergymen, like John Groser, the socialist vicar of Christ Church, Stepney, toured the shelters assisting the sick and aged, distributing food, making arrangements for the homeless to be evacuated, and trying to deal with a growing youth problem. A survey of 150 London shelters by a committee of the Church of England Temperance Society found few of them suitable for young people and urged the government and youth organizations to provide more

---

[29] *Daily Worker*, 2 and 21 October 1940; H. R. Srebrnik, *London Jews and British Communism, 1935–45* (Ilford, 1995), p. 45. On West Ham, see E. D. Idle, *War over West Ham: A story of community and adjustment* (London, 1942); also on the East End: R. Bell, *The Bull's Eye: A tale of the London target* (London, 1943).

[30] NA: INF1/292 (28 October–4 November; 4–11 December; 11–18 December; 18–24 December 1940). M-OA: FR 431 (27 September 1940); *Daily Worker*, 18 September 1940. For Piratin's raid on the Savoy: P. Piratin, *Our Flag Stays Red* (London, 1948). When socialist reporter Hilde Marchant guided Ralph Ingersoll, the editor of the New York magazine *PM*, around the mass shelters, they went first to Liverpool Street Tube and the Tilbury warehouse and then—for contrast—to the de luxe shelter at the Dorchester Hotel with its waiters, curtained spaces, and fluffy eiderdowns. Writing a 'London Letter' for the leftist New York periodical *Common Sense*, the poet Louis MacNeice also counselled possible visitors: 'If you want a Hogarthian contrast, go down . . . into one of the Tube stations and follow it up by a visit to the Ritz bar.' R. Ingersoll, *Report on England: November 1940* (New York, 1940), pp. 81–103; Alan Heuser (ed.), *Selected Prose of Louis MacNeice* (Oxford, 1990), p. 101.

recreation centres. The Warden of the Jewish Settlement, Basil Henriques, reinforced the building and turned it into a public shelter. Concerned about delinquency, drunkenness, and promiscuity in the large shelters, he expanded the youth club, admitted non-members, and set up a system of patrols to accompany young women in the blackout. This settlement, like others, also distributed clothing and each night carried soup and sandwiches to shelterers and firemen.[31] Old people were found to have taken up permanent residence in some public shelters and rest centres and official efforts to get the elderly to leave their neighbourhoods met with only limited success: 'The blind, the crippled, and the very old would say, "Yes Miss; thank you Miss; I'll go, Miss",' wrote London air-raid warden, Barbara Nixon, 'but they never went.'[32] There were few places for them in hostels and, despite public appeals, few private billetors were willing to take them.

It has been argued that London's shelter crisis was becoming more extreme until German bombers allowed some respite by focusing on provincial targets. What the consequences would have been for neighbourhood solidarity or public order had London not gained some relief after January 1941 is hard to say. But by the end of 1940 significant improvements had been made in the Underground and in many of the more notorious mass shelters. Local authorities distributed heating stoves, washing and sanitary facilities were upgraded, and food services were greatly improved by, for example, regular canteen trains on the Tube. In time, thousands of tiered bunks were installed in the larger shelters and tickets were issued to regulate the numbers of people and reduce the amount of time spent queuing. In November 1940, at Herbert Morrison's prodding, the Cabinet also reversed its policy, authorizing the construction in the London Underground of deep bomb-proof tunnels capable of accommodating about 80,000 people. Completed after the period of heavy raids, they were, in fact, never used. By December 1940 Home Intelligence was reporting that recent improvements had brought a general decline in Communist representation on shelter committees.[33]

Efforts were also made to combat boredom and raise morale by introducing a range of shelter entertainments like darts matches, dances, amateur singing nights, discussion groups, and sewing circles, while at Christmas parties were held for the children and the shelter walls were festooned with paper chains and decorations.

---

[31] Titmuss, *Problems of Social Policy*, ch. 14. Oral history recordings and transcripts describing the Blitz experiences of members of St John Ambulance (many of them working-class in background) are kept at the St John Ambulance Museum and Library, St John's Gate, London. On the WVS Housewives Service see the Women's Royal Voluntary Service Archive (London), files for the Housewives Service and the London region narrative reports for 1940. K. Brill (ed.), *John Groser: East London priest* (London, 1971); Rev. John Groser Papers, MSS 3428–35, Lambeth Palace Archive, London. L. L. Loewe, *Basil Henriques* (London, 1976). On local community initiatives see also M-OA: FR 592 (27 February 1941); on London adolescents: NA: INF 1/292 (4–11 November 1940).

[32] B. Nixon, *Raiders Overhead: The record of a London warden* (London, 1943), p. 62. Also, NA: HO 199/442 rest centre report on Manchester, 6 January 1941.

[33] NA: INF 1/292 (18–24 December 1940). The files of the MoH (e.g. NA: M-O 76 series) and the Home Office (e.g. NA: HO 207 series) contain detailed information on shelter improvements. Also, Violet Markham Papers (BLPES, London School of Economics) 5/18–19 detail improvements to London shelters 1940–3.

Other activities were introduced from outside, some inspired by the goal of improving popular cultural tastes. The Entertainments National Service Association (ENSA) began holding concerts in shelters and the WVS set up play centres and story-corners for young children. There were also religious services, film shows, and dramatic performances by several troupes, including the Unity Theatre which adapted its pre-war experience with co-operatives, trade unions, and civic clubs and began performing in the Tilbury and the Tube. Representatives of the newly formed Council for the Encouragement of Music and the Arts (CEMA) braved the mass shelters armed with their instruments or with gramophones and classical music recordings,[34] while several local councils developed library schemes. The borough of St Pancras soon had up to 2,000 books circulating and Bermondsey about 600, which were left weekly with shelter marshals. The London County Council in February 1941 announced that some 464 evening classes were meeting in the shelters.[35]

Impressive though the record of voluntarism is, however, it is important not to overstate the level of communal activity. Most people, as has been said, did not use public shelters or went to the Tube infrequently. And a great many of those who slept in the large shelters took little or no part in collective activities or organization but simply bedded down with their own kin and got as much rest as possible before returning home or to work in the early morning. 'It would be a mistake', Tom Harrisson wrote, 'to make too much of these temporary associations' among strangers.[36] Similarly, despite the frequent claim that Blitz life broke down class barriers and that people were now more willing to talk to strangers ('You can't be standoffish and toffee-nosed with the person who sleeps in the bunk above yours'[37]), the social profile of most shelters was fairly clearly defined. Those who claimed there was greater social cohesion than before were invariably middle class and the contacts cited were fleeting and far less intrusive or unsettling than those associated with the evacuation scheme; billeting central-city raid victims in suburban areas, for example, remained extremely difficult.

Against the standard images of altruism and solidarity must also be set contrary evidence of division and selfishness. There were plenty of rows, fights, petty thefts, and arguments about noise and space in public shelters. Vandalism by gangs of youths became a serious problem in many districts, as did theft and looting facilitated by the blackout and the general confusion during raids. Blasted shops and commercial premises could easily be entered and stripped of their stocks, while with so many homes left empty burglaries and thefts from gas and electricity meters became rife. Stealing from the debris of bombed homes also became prevalent, arousing exaggerated public and official anger; in fact, under Defence Regulation

[34] For ENSA and CEMA see the discussion in ch. 6 below.
[35] R. Calder, *Carry on London* (London 1940); J. S. Lawrie, 'The impact of the Second World War on English cultural life', PhD Diss., Sydney University, 1988; B. Sokoloff, *Edith and Stepney: The life of Edith Ramsay* (London, 1987), ch. 7; H. Creaton, *Sources for the History of London, 1939–45: A guide and bibliography*, British Records Association (London, 1998), p. 30.
[36] Harrisson, *Living through the Blitz*, p. 314.
[37] M-OA Diary, N.5163 (23 December 1940).

38A it could even be a capital crime, although nobody was executed for it. In 1940 the Commissioner of the Metropolitan Police cited almost 4,600 cases of looting, 45 per cent by youths under eighteen years, some of them receiving prison sentences of three to twelve months. Firemen, wardens, and rescue squads were also widely suspected. As a south London clergyman and ARP volunteer recalled:

> The usual practice of those who took shelter was to put all their cash, savings certificates, items of personal jewellery, and personal papers such as birth and marriage certificates in their handbags, which they left under the chair on which they were sitting, or by their side if they were in bed. As soon as it was light, I used to take two of my wardens and tunnel through mountains of rubble to find these handbags. We dared not leave them, even for a few hours, or they would be gone.[38]

Most looting was opportunistic rather than organized; culprits simply helped themselves or scavenged household goods usually of little value: 'Everybody is doing it'; 'it was a pity that the goods should be lying about unused'; 'I didn't know I was doing any harm, as I was told the lady was dead.' These were typical excuses, but to survivors returning to the ruins of their homes, this ransacking of what little they had left was the last straw: 'Their fingers should have dropped off, but they done it to most houses, not only mine.' Neighbours engaged in mutual defence of possessions against pilferers from further afield.[39]

Many contemporaries watched anxiously for any signs of the ethnic and confessional conflicts that had troubled pre-war London, especially the East End where relations between Jews and Gentiles had often been stormy and Mosley's fascists had built a base of support. Official reports, Mass-Observation records, and press stories were laced with fears that the strains of shelter life might inflame long-standing prejudices. Talk of the dangers of spies and fifth columnists had been rife in the summer of 1940, sanctioned in part by the badly implemented government policy of interning enemy aliens. Of East Enders' anti-Semitism in the Blitz, Ritchie Calder wrote: 'it was real, it was dangerous; it was fairly widespread'. 'But', he added, 'the pogrom and anti-Jewish riots which so many dreaded never materialized even in the worst situation the East End has ever had to face.' To be sure there were accusations: that Jews grabbed the best places in public shelters, that they were the first to panic and flee, that they controlled the black market, or that as shopkeepers they inflated prices. The *Catholic Herald*, a popular weekly, described the Tilbury as a 'brothel' where 'the ubiquitous Jew and his family' spread disease and accused Jewish communists of 'eagerly fanning' the 'red fire'. In the same shelter, however, Nina Masel found: 'Race feeling was very marked—not so much between Cockney and Jews, as between White and Black. In fact, the presence of considerable coloured elements was responsible for drawing Cockney and Jew together, against the Indian.' There were also charges from Stepney's black

---

[38] Roy Ingleton, *The Gentlemen at War: Policing Britain 1939–45* (Maidstone, 1994), pp. 266, 270.
[39] H. Mannheim, 'Some reflections on crime in wartime', *The Fortnightly*, 157 (January 1942), 44; Ingleton, *The Gentlemen at War*, p. 268. Some looting appears to have been more organized and professional: see D. Thomas, *An Underworld at War* (London, 2003), ch. 4.

population that they were discriminated against in shelters especially by Jews and Jewish police auxiliaries. The picture is, however, mixed; a Nigerian air-raid warden in another part of London recalled the close bonds he formed with residents in his area and a good deal of other evidence suggests that the Blitz promoted greater harmony. Jews and Gentiles cooperated on shelter committees and in civil defence activities. Jewish entertainers were very popular in the public shelters and in some joint religious services were held. In general, popular anger over shelter conditions did not get deflected into racism[40] Mass-Observation's reports also seem to indicate that anti-Semitic prejudice was a good deal more virulent in the suburbs and small towns around the periphery of London to which large numbers of refugees, both Jewish and Gentile, had fled.[41] Similarly, when 173 people were suffocated to death in a freak accident at Bethnal Green Tube station in March 1943 and rumours circulated about panicking Jews they had less currency in the immediate area, where the truth was known, than further afield.[42]

With the German invasion of the Soviet Union in the summer of 1941 the frequency of raids decreased. By then conditions in communal shelters had greatly improved, although homelessness remained an acute problem in many areas. Visiting a Tube station in May, George Orwell found the scene almost too respectable: 'What is most striking is the cleanly, normal domesticated air that everything now has. Especially the young married couples, the sort of homely, cautious type that would probably be buying their houses from a building society, tucked up together under pink counterpanes.' At roughly the same time, Tom Harrisson observed: 'it was difficult to remember the violence of early prejudice against tube crowds . . . when they had been abused *en masse*, as dirty, smelly, lousy, diseased, cowardly, foreign and (especially) work-shy'.[43] Even two years later, a residual few thousand shelterers still resolutely occupied the Tube. Their presence, Mass-Observers argued, had little to do with fear or safety: they had grown used to the extended family atmosphere and found it hard to abandon the communal routine. Some were frightened, some lonely, others were homeless, while for the elderly and frail the

---

[40] R. Calder, *The Lesson of London* (London, 1941), pp. 71–5. NA:INF1/292 includes reports on anti-Semitism (e.g. 30 September–9 October 1940; 16–23 July 1941); *Catholic Herald*, 25 October 1940; Nina Masel quoted in T. Harrisson, 'War adjustment', *New Statesman and Nation*, 28 September 1940; M. Banton, *The Coloured Quarter* (London, 1955), pp. 76–9; D. Watson, 'Research note: Black workers in London in the 1940s', *Historical Studies in Industrial Relations*, 1 (March 1996); E. I. Ekpenyon, *Some Experiences of an African Air-Raid Warden* (London, 1943); Sokoloff, *Edith and Stepney: The life of Edith Ramsay*, p. 100.

[41] Tony Kushner, *The Persistence of Prejudice* (Manchester, 1989), pp. 51–8; NA: INF 1/293 (special report on anti-Semitism, 15 January 1942) illustrates a widespread tendency to blame Jews for black-market trading, overcrowding provincial centres, avoiding war work etc.; INF 1/292 (7–14, 14–21 October 1940).

[42] Kushner, *The Persistence of Prejudice*, pp. 60–4, 125–6.

[43] George Orwell's diary entry for 6 May 6 1941 in S. Orwell and I. Angus (eds.), *The Collected Essays, Journalism and Letters of George Orwell* (1940–43), II (New York, 1968), p. 399; Harrisson, *Living through the Blitz*, p. 130. Occasionally the introduction of improvements led to disturbances; resistance to ticketing and bunks was sometimes connected to fears that they would be used to exclude people and reduce the numbers admitted. Idle, *War Over West Ham*, p. 110.

shelters, especially in areas where many neighbours had moved away, were places where they could find food and company and access welfare services.[44]

LONDON AND THE NATION

London was the first and most consistent German target in the Blitz of 1940–1. It received the lion's share of media coverage at the time, far more than provincial towns, and has continued to dominate later accounts. Today the word 'Blitz' almost always conjures up pictures of the capital city, drawn from newsreels, photographs, and, to a lesser extent, paintings and drawings: of St Paul's miraculously preserved and silhouetted by the fires that consumed everything around it; of Westminster ablaze with searchlights jerkily raking the sky; and, above all, of Londoners crammed head to toe in the Underground or being dug out of their ruined homes. So firmly are these images tied to our notions of the nation at war that it is easy to overlook the novelty of this situation.

Between the wars the landscape that was most closely associated with Britain and Britishness was that of the English countryside, usually located vaguely in the south, quiet, tended, domesticated—a 'Constable country of the mind', as one writer has called it, replete with scenic villages, church spires, hedgerows, and rural craftsmen.[45] This imagery, commercially exploited in Shell's travel guides and billboard ads for insurance companies, was predominantly conservative and inherently anti-urban, achieving its fullest political evocation in the speeches and radio broadcasts of Stanley Baldwin, although one can also find radical populist variants.[46] The second iconic landscape of these decades, popular with 1930s writers and film-makers on the left, was the urban north, a terrain of factories and mills, unemployed miners and cotton operatives which had once symbolized the manufacturing might of the nation, the sinews of its imperial power, but after 1920 came increasingly to connote a national economy in trouble and multiple social problems. Now, even more than in the nineteenth century, these two geographies remained separate and at odds, neither capable of incorporating the other.

London did not figure much in either of them; indeed, the city was often depicted as somehow divorced from the true nation. In Victorian national imagery, of course, London was prominent as the home of Parliament and the monarchy, the 'heart' of the empire. But after the slaughter of the First World War, the language of national identity became quieter, less heroic, less bombastic. The inclination to turn inward and to cultivate an insular Englishness was strong,

---

[44] Mass-Observation, 'The Tube-Dwellers' in L. Russell (ed.), *The Saturday Book* (London, 1943). A January 1942 WVS report to the Ministry of Home Security referred to these residual shelterers as 'Tube limpets'. WVS Archive, London: Misc. Memoranda Box: Wartime, London Region.

[45] A. Potts, 'Constable country between the wars' in R. Samuel (ed.), *Patriotism: The making and unmaking of British national identity* (London, 1989), III.

[46] Bill Schwarz, 'The language of constitutionalism: Baldwinite Conservatism' in *Formations of Nation and People* (London, 1984); P. B. Rich, 'British imperial decline and the forging of English patriotic memory, *c.*1918–1968', *History of European Ideas*, 9(6) (1988).

evoking the rolling countryside and the seasonal rhythms of nature more than an imperial world city. The other side of this association of national values and rural traditions was a critique of the urban, which came to focus especially on Greater London. Aspects of this were already apparent in the Edwardian era, especially during the agitation over the 1905 Aliens Act and Jewish immigration when many viewed the capital as in danger of being swamped by foreign influences. Between the wars London not only doubled in size, pushing suburban sprawl ever outwards, but seemed to have altered its character, becoming more modern, cosmopolitan, and Americanized with its giant cinemas, dance halls, cocktail bars, and arterial and by-pass roads. Distaste for what London had become abounds in contemporary comment. From the urban planners who abhorred its 'formlessness' and championed 'garden cities' to Orwell's and Priestley's indictments of its fast food and cheap commercial products to John Betjeman's 'Come friendly bombs, fall on Slough, it isn't fit for humans now' and the reactionary ruralism of Dean Inge of St Paul's, London's Englishness seemed in doubt.

Ironically, the bombs brought a great reversal. Suddenly, unquestionably, in 1940 the city stood for the nation. 'London bombed, burned and battered', wrote Vera Brittain, 'became the suffering symbol of England's anguish, as well as an indictment of mankind's "spiritual failure".'[47] The *Daily Express* reporter and shelter campaigner, Hilde Marchant, born and bred in the north, had originally felt deeply alienated by the capital; her conversion came with the raids when, she argued, the city rediscovered 'that fine, robust, active spirit of Elizabeth's time, that had been deadened and choked by a hypocrisy of wealth'.[48] Wartime patriotic imagery, as Angus Calder has shown, continued to tap a rich and varied repertoire.[49] Certainly, rural England remained central to expressions of national spiritual values and character—one need only look at recruiting posters for the Women's Land Army or Powell and Pressburger's 1944 paean to the Kent countryside in their film *A Canterbury Tale*. But now it shared or contested the terrain with cities, mining regions, and seaports. And when in October 1940 *Life* magazine did a feature on the village of Churchill in Somerset, J. B. Priestley whose own radio 'Postscripts' had dished out a good helping of ruralism, carped: 'This isn't the England that is fighting the war. The Christmas card caricature of England couldn't fight this war for a couple of days.'[50] Indeed, London had become the object of a kind of urban pastoralism as artists and photographers, many of them hired by the War Artists' Scheme, set about capturing the city under fire: the surreal, luminous beauty of St Paul's, the ruins of the Guildhall, the wreckage of smaller Wren churches, and in the East End, in Graham Sutherland's words, 'the shells of long

[47] V. Brittain, *England's Hour* (New York, 1941), p. 214.
[48] Marchant, *Women and Children Last*, p. 184. See also J. B. Priestley's novel *Wonder Hero* (1933), which depicts London as corrupt and draining the rest of the nation—in many ways the antithesis of the nation's true spirit.
[49] A. Calder, *The Myth of the Blitz* (London, 1991).
[50] Priestley quoted by N. J. Cull, *Selling War: The British propaganda campaign against American neutrality in World War II* (Oxford, 1995), p. 111.

terraces of houses . . . perspectives of destruction [receding] into infinity, the windowless blocks . . . like sightless eyes'.[51]

Above all, however, London was a human story, a landscape peopled with ordinary, anonymous citizens: firefighters, heavy rescue workers, good neighbours, and those who carried on with their jobs. As Priestley told his radio audience: 'We're not really civilians any longer but a mixed lot of soldiers—machine-minding soldiers, milkmen and postmen soldiers, housewife and mother soldiers.'[52] Compared to earlier forms of national iconography, this one was more urban, civilian, popular, and featured workers and women far more prominently and in active roles. At first, especially in the Conservative press, many accounts dusted off and refurbished archaic, stereotypical images of the cheerful cockney: courageous, determined to make the best of things, knowing his social place and therefore not threatening: 'The East End loved it', 'I wouldn't miss it for all the tea in China.' Indeed, the 1937 hit show, *Me and My Girl*, with its quaint cockney stereotypes, played in the West End throughout the Blitz. Ironically, before the war the cockney was less likely to be depicted as a national symbol than as an invasive town-dweller, descending on 'deep' England in charabancs with litter and loud music. As one official noted, much coverage of the Blitz in the press merely underscored social difference: 'The working masses are almost a race apart, the primitively simple and heroic poor, admired from a distance. They, the people, are admired by we, the leaders and those above.'[53] But left-leaning newspapers like the *Daily Mirror* and the *Daily Herald* gave a more complex picture and were quicker to deplore deficiencies in shelter provision and post-raid services, though they too could slip into clichés or a language of 'us' and 'them' which belied the claim of a unitary nation.

This rediscovery of London as a national landscape was part of a broader reorientation in rhetoric as the nation moved to full-scale mobilization and sought to harness all its energies for a struggle that had so far produced little more than failure and military retreats. 'A People's War' was the portmanteau phrase used to capture the new mood. Implicit in it and in the dominant images of London's Blitz was a more prominent role for labour and the working class. Recent historical debate has focused heavily on whether or not the political culture was genuinely radicalized in 1940–1; if opinion moved to the left; or if the talk about social change and collectivism was mostly anodyne and vacuous rhetoric, a short-lived product of national danger, largely engineered by the Ministry of Information (MoI) or quickly taken over and contained by resilient British institutions. These issues are examined fully in later chapters;[54] here our focus is wartime representations or public imagery, which certainly changed, becoming noticeably more inclusive and democratic in spirit. And yet, while patriotic rhetoric became more

[51] M. and S. Harries, *The War Artists* (London, 1983), p. 188.

[52] J. B. Priestley, *Postscripts* (London, 1940). Postscript for 8 September 1940, the day after the first major raid on the East End.

[53] G. Stedman Jones, 'The "cockney" and the nation, 1780–1988' in D. Feldman and G. Stedman Jones, *Metropolis: London. Histories and representations since 1800* (London, 1989), p. 314.

[54] Especially ch. 8.

inclusive, stressing how the war had drawn all civilians together and lowered conventional class barriers, in the early months of the Blitz it was the sharp differences and inequalities between classes that were at the forefront of public discussion. And even later, not only did 'the People's War' mean different things to different people, but in the act of describing how shared dangers forged closer social unity, commentators invariably introduced a contradictory note that underscored the 'Otherness' of workers and the poor.

The new centrality of London and the themes of 'the People's War' are exemplified in Humphrey Jennings' film, *Fires Were Started*, made in 1942 and released the following year. Briefly, this film, his only feature-length production, depicts a day and night in the life of an Auxiliary Fire Service (AFS) crew in West Ham. A new man, a middle-class advertising copywriter, has joined the dockland unit and the story traces his integration into this little working-class community of firefighters and the courage and teamwork that enables them to subdue a dangerous warehouse blaze and save a munitions ship moored nearby. Using real firemen rather than actors, Jennings tried to get beyond the usual lower-class stereotypes. The firemen illustrate both national heroism and cooperation across class barriers; they are also distinctive individuals, placed in a specifically working-class culture with its own humour, pastimes, dialogue, and songs, and their teamwork suggests that a new social order could emerge from the local, democratic, voluntary, achievements of civil defence. While filming in Stepney and Wapping an exhilar-ated Jennings wrote to his wife, that for the first time he was 'really beginning to understand people...and not just looking at them and lecturing or pitying them'.[55] The AFS, as the film indicates, offered new possibilities for class mixing and social exploration. Most firemen were working class, but there were numerous middle-class recruits among its 60,000 volunteers. There was little hierarchy at fire stations and raw recruits came in at the bottom, ate, washed dishes, and often slept at the firehouse with the rest of the crew. The poet Stephen Spender who joined a Cricklewood fire crew in 1942 was fascinated by his co-workers: their nicknames, humour, and their 'amorphous, tuneless, grating and sawing songs'; he viewed the station's Christmas party decorations as 'a classic example of something the writers of the left had spent so much time discussing during the 1930s: proletarian art'. 'It could', he added, 'have been moved piece by piece and erected in a museum, as a perfect specimen of the people's taste in 1942.'[56] Spender's vision is

[55] For Jennings' letter to his wife: A. Aldgate and J. Richards, *Britain Can Take It* (Oxford, 1986), p. 234. P. Stansky and W. Abrahams, *London's Burning: Life, death and art in the Second World War* (Stanford, 1994), ch. 2; R. Colls and P. Dodd, 'Representing the nation: British documentary film, 1930–45', *Screen*, 26 (January–February 1985); D. Millar, 'Fires were started', *Sight and Sound*, 38 (Spring 1989). See also the biography by Kevin Jackson, *Humphrey Jennings* (London, 2004).
[56] S. Spender, *World within World* (London, 1951), pp. 262ff. (quotes on pp. 277–8); *idem*, *The Thirties and After* (New York, 1979); V. Bailey (ed.), *Forged in Fire* (London, 1992); M. Richardson, *London's Burning* (London, 1940); R. Greenwood, *The Squad Goes Out* (London, 1943); W. Sansom, *Westminster at War* (London, 1947). Service in the AFS also produced Henry Green's complex novel, *Caught* (1943), in which much of the action revolves around the tangled, difficult relationship between the main character, Richard Roe, a wealthy upper-class volunteer, and his sub-station's supervisor, a regular fireman. Roe adjusts to the socially foreign environment, consciously adopting working-class

ethnographic—an outsider in a foreign culture, rather like his friend Christopher Isherwood's documentary voice in *Berlin Stories* which begins: 'I am a camera.'

By the time Jennings' film appeared it fit into and helped reinforce a certain image of the Blitz firmly rooted in the social democratic patriotism of the war years. Almost exclusively the narrative of the Blitz had become one of unity and social levelling, a purgatorial trial from which a new and better Britain would arise. In a visual sense, of course, the film is now for many people identical with the raids, since its reconstructed scenes have been repeatedly shown as the real thing (actual newsreel coverage of the fires and bombardment is fairly rare). However, in the autumn of 1940 the dominant narrative of the Blitz had just begun to take shape and, as the next section shows, much of the attention focused on the mass shelters.

UNDERGROUND IN 'DARKEST LONDON'

Of the many *lieux de mémoire* of Britain's Second World War, to use Pierre Nora's term, the mass shelters of 1940 are among the most important. Today they evoke images of wartime patriotism, community, and shared danger and present a picture of national endurance and courage. Even at the time, when compared to the percentage of the population who took refuge there, they received disproportionate attention in contemporary accounts of the Blitz. But before examining how the mass shelters were represented, three general points about the broader context should be mentioned briefly.

First, how the shelters were represented must be set against pre-war concerns in official circles that air raids might well produce widespread panic, disaffection, and defeatism, much of this anxiety being focused on working-class districts. Secondly, the images of the poor generated by the Blitz must be recognized as following hard on the heels of a whole array of negative stereotypes provoked by the government's evacuation scheme. As we have seen, evacuation had placed poor working-class families in the spotlight and while for some the condition of inner-city evacuees was testimony to decades of neglect, a legacy of pre-war failure, for others the blame rested squarely with feckless, 'low grade' mothers and parental irresponsibility. In general, as befitted the theme of 'a People's War', not only was Blitz imagery far more positive and sympathetic, but it offered an implicit rejoinder to the earlier furore—focusing especially on brave, caring mothers who made efforts to retain some semblance of family under the most difficult circumstances and fathers who turned up for work no matter how heavy the bombing had been the night before. The kind of public rhetoric that erupted in the autumn of 1939 had become unacceptable a year later: now the emphasis was on a better Britain that

speech patterns. Some firemen accept him, others find him distant and aloof. Human relations are always complicated by intrigues, fantasies, secrecies, and the psychic isolation of individuals; but class creates further barriers. Green's novel is darker than most accounts, disputing claims that the conflict mitigated class differences or produced a cosy togetherness.

would emerge from the ruins of the old—as the novelist Margaret Kennedy put it: 'England after the war is going to belong to the shelterers.'[57]

Finally, contemporary representations of the shelters formed part of a broader tide of criticism that enveloped the nation in 1940. Its initial targets were Neville Chamberlain and individual Appeasers, but it quickly escalated into a general critique of the pre-war social and political order. As chapter 8 shows, a large, diverse group of liberal and left-wing 'war commentators' advocated radical measures as a requirement of national survival. They included novelists, academics, clerics, journalists, and broadcasters; most were London-based, experienced the Blitz, and visited the shelters. They demanded changes that would revitalize the nation and 'bring the real England to the surface': new blood, new ideas, collective goals over individual or group interest. As Richard Weight has argued, the crisis also brought a rediscovery of patriotism, a 'return to Albion', on the part of British intellectuals—catalyzed in some cases by disillusionment with communism as a result of Stalin's purges and the Nazi–Soviet pact.[58] 'Patriotism,' wrote Orwell, 'against which the socialists fought so long, has become a tremendous lever in their hands.'[59] There was also renewed enthusiasm for what we might call the failed socialist project of the 1930s, when despite the conjuncture of political and economic crisis, British workers had conspicuously failed to display the militancy anticipated by many on the left or to pose much of a challenge to the capitalist order. Though the Labour Party had absorbed much of the blame for this with Ramsay MacDonald cast as chief miscreant, many writers had also suspected that British workers might be just too passive, malleable, or conservative to produce a radical politics. In 1940, however, the combination of German bombs and governmental failure seemed to have shifted opinion to the left and created an opportunity for a radical agenda. This mixture of patriotism and renewed faith in working-class agency pervaded many early accounts of the mass shelters, which were often embraced as experiments in community formation, popular democracy in action. And yet the language used to describe them was often curiously literary and distancing—at times romantic, exotic, or patronizing.

When investigative reporters such as Ritchie Calder descended underground, followed by officials, novelists, correspondents from overseas, artists, and photographers, how did they depict what they saw; on what traditions did they draw? Much has been written about the apocalyptic imagery of Blitz writing and the aesthetic response of many observers to the scary, surreal beauty.[60] But little attention has been paid to the stylistic techniques and conventions of shelter narratives. One influence was the documentary movement of the 1930s and Mass-Observation, and, of course, Mass-Observers were present in London's shelters. Another related influence was the genre of social travel-writing, popular

[57] M. Kennedy, *Where Stands a Winged Sentry* (New Haven, 1941), p. 232.

[58] R. A. J. Weight, 'Pale stood Albion: The formulation of English national identity 1939–56', PhD Diss., London University, 1995; *idem*, 'State, intelligentsia and the promotion of national culture in Britain, 1939–45', *Historical Research*, 69(168) (February 1996).

[59] Orwell, 'The Lion and the Unicorn' in *The Collected Essays, Journalism and Letters*, II, p. 94.

[60] Adam Piette, *Imagination at War* (London, 1995).

between the wars. A best-selling example was H. V. Morton's *In Search of England* (1927) and he followed this in 1940 with *I Saw Two Englands*. Even more influential was J. B. Priestley's *English Journey* (1934), a modern tour of Britain's social and cultural landscape, showing the divisive consequences of the depression and especially its corrosive impact on masculine work cultures. Early in the war Vera Brittain had hoped to write a sequel to it, but petrol shortages and restrictions on travel limited her to London and the Home Counties.[61]

Most of all, however, shelter investigators drew on a long tradition of urban exploration that included Henry Mayhew, Andrew Mearns, James Greenwood, Arthur Morrison, W. T. Stead, Charles Booth, and many others. These middle-class 'urban spectators' traversed the labyrinthine modern city, transgressing normal class boundaries, and mapping for their readers the alien and unfamiliar territory of 'the abyss' or 'outcast London'.[62] Their narratives of social discovery combined social concern and voyeuristic elements; demands for reform and fascination with spectacle; motifs from imperial travel-writing and, sometimes, a good dose of moralizing; and rhetorics of class and poverty that were simultaneously sympathetic and distancing. Sometimes explorers adopted disguises to pass more easily; such subterfuges were, however, unnecessary in war which opened new sites, like shelters, for investigation and allowed writers, under cover of the blackout, to navigate normally closed environments without raising suspicion. London examples can be found between the wars—journalist Hugh Massingham's incognito efforts at ethnographic observation in the East End and Orwell's forays among the down-and-outs in London and Paris come immediately to mind[63]—but by the 1930s, with the industrial depression and mass unemployment, the favoured locales for such journeying had moved north. Orwell braved the Brookers' tripe shop in Wigan, Mass-Observation focused its energies on Bolton, other explorers took on Wales, and John Grierson, the father of British documentary film, sought to escape the West End and 'travel dangerously into the jungles of Middlesbrough and the Clyde'.[64] Yet the original and classic terrain for urban spectatorship was London's East End—which suddenly found itself in 1940 at the centre of the shelter crisis.

Of the many shelter narratives published by contemporaries, two will suffice to illustrate their major themes and stylistic conventions. First, the widely debated exposés of Ritchie Calder, written for the *Daily Herald* and *New Statesman*, which soon appeared in two books that are still often cited by historians. Calder, a lifelong

[61] H. V. Morton, *In Search of England* (London, 1927); *idem, I Saw Two Englands* (London, 1942); J. B. Priestley, *English Journey* (London, 1934; 1984); Vera Brittain, *England's Hour* (London, 1941).

[62] On urban explorers: S. Koven, *Slumming: Sexual and social politics in Victorian London* (Princeton, 2004); J. R. Walkowitz, *City of Dreadful Delight* (Chicago, 1992), ch. 1. For earlier women social travellers: Ellen Ross, *Slum Travelers: Ladies and poverty, 1860–1920* (California, 2007).

[63] Hugh Massingham, *I Took Off My Tie* (London, 1936); George Orwell, *Down and Out in Paris and London* (London, 1933).

[64] George Orwell, *Road to Wigan Pier* (1937); much of M-O's Bolton work remains unpublished, but see D. Sheridan and A. Calder, *Speak for Yourself: A Mass-Observation anthology* (London, 1984); Grierson quote in A. Higson, *Waving the Flag: Constructing a national cinema in Britain* (Oxford, 1995), p. 185.

socialist long interested in the problem of poverty, was in the vanguard of reporters pressing for government action to clean up the mass shelters. In his columns he appears as an active informant, experiencing the city for himself and ferreting out the truth about the shelter crisis; his style is colourful, literary, if sometimes a little overdone. 'The typewriter', he begins in one book, 'is treading flakes of soot into the paper as this chapter is being written . . . I have wandered through the blazing city, down into the back courts and up the side streets, tripping over hoses, cowering as buildings lurched and toppled.'[65] To explore the shelters, like so many urban spectators before him, he relies on 'sponsors' or intermediaries: local clergymen like the Reverends John Groser and W. W. Paton, but even more the Dickensian figure of Mickey Davies, a hunchbacked former optician, not much over 3ft 6 inches tall, who was the chief organizer of a large crypt shelter in Stepney and subsequently became its official marshal.

'Mickey, the midget,' he writes: 'led me out of the shelter into the street. "Come on", he said. "You haven't seen anything yet."' They enter the crypt, descending to a 'dimly lit interior'. It 'was Grand Guignol!' we are told. An old man slept on one stone coffin, another was in use as a card table, while a navvy had levered off the lid of a third large sarcophagus and 'was snoring blissfully, his deep breathing stirring up wafts of white dust . . . bone dust!' People lay packed together in the aisles or sat on narrow benches, hugging hot water bottles. This and similar places, Calder writes, 'made the conditions described by Dickens seem like a mannered novel by Thackeray. The Fleet Prison and the Marshalsea were polite hostelries compared with conditions which existed when the "blitzkrieg" first hit London and drove people underground.' 'The foetid atmosphere of most of them was like the germ-incubation rooms of a bacteriological laboratory, only the germs were not in sealed flasks, but hit you in the face in a mixed barrage.' Most notorious, however, was the Tilbury (described but not named), where 'One had to pick one's way along the roads between the recumbent bodies' and people slept in the warehouse bays beside cartons of rotting foodstuffs. 'To begin with there was practically no sanitary provision, and the filth seeped into the blankets or was spread by trampling feet. Cartons filled with margarine were sometimes stacked up to form latrines.' For Calder, and for many who came after him, such squalor was best communicated through allusions to 'Eastern bazaars', 'Cairo bazaars', 'unequalled by anything west of Suez'; the scene could only be captured by comparison with orientalized 'others'. The strangeness of this urban spectacle required the conventions of imperial travel-writing which always moved in two directions, 'a dialectic of the familiar and unfamiliar'; explorers both explained foreign parts by reference to home-grown rookeries and slums, and re-imported the analogies to capture Britain's urban poverty.[66]

---

[65] Calder, *Carry on London*, p. 17.
[66] *Ibid.*, pp. 36–9; *idem*, *The Lesson of London* (London, 1941), pp. 85–6. Also, R. Calder, 'The danger of disease', *New Statesman and Nation*, 19 October 1940. Compare Kingsley Martin on the Tilbury: 'Whites, Jews and Gentiles, Chinese, Indians, and negroes lie there miscellaneously . . . at nights, [it] looks, as one resident said to me, exactly like a bazaar in Cairo . . .'; K. Martin, 'Report on East London', *New Statesman and Nation*, 5 October 1940; M. Valdeverde, 'The dialectic of the familiar and the unfamiliar: The "jungle" in early slum travel-writing', *Sociology* (August 1996).

3. Asleep in a sarcophagus in Christ Church, Spitalfields.

Like earlier East End explorers, visitors to shelters were particularly struck by the profusion of ethnic and racial types living there. Traditionally the entrepôt for successive waves of immigrants and the abode of foreign seamen, the East End had often been represented as a microcosm of Britain's empire or an alien arena in the heart of the metropolis. Again Calder's language is suggestive of earlier descents into 'darkest London' and the imagery of imperial exploration. Led by Mickey up a ladder in the crypt shelter 'to family tombs high up in the wall', he confronts 'a brown baby face with startled black eyes, under a turban, staring at me for a moment in the flickering candlelight before it disappeared under the bedclothes beside its Indian mother. Stretched on the floor was the tall figure of an ex-Bengal Lancer, his magnificent shovel beard draped over a blanket, his head turbaned and looking, in sleep, like a breathing monument of an ancient Crusader.' Or, still more vividly described, the Tilbury with its residents 'piled in miscellaneous confusion':

Nothing like it, I am sure, could exist in the Western World. I have seen some of the worst haunts on the water front at Marseilles which are a byword, but they were mild compared with the cesspool of humanity which welled into that shelter in those early days. People of every type and condition, every colour and creed found their way there—black and white, brown and yellow; men from the Levant and Slavs from Eastern Europe; Jew, Gentile, Moslem and Hindu. When ships docked, seamen would come in to royster for a few hours. Scotland Yard knew where to look for criminals bombed out of Hell's Kitchen. Prostitutes paraded there. Hawkers peddled greasy, cold, fried fish which cloyed the already foul atmosphere. Free fights had to be broken up by the police. Couples courted. Children slept. Soldiers and sailors and airmen spent part of their leaves there.[67]

Edwardian spectators had reacted both negatively and positively to such diversity, using it to support or contradict prejudicial stereotypes. In 1940, however, such descriptions, besides spicing up a narrative, were deployed to show how shared danger could nullify division and produce cooperation among the most dissimilar groups. Calder's dominant theme is the construction of community. 'As long as I live,' he wrote 'I shall never forget the stampede when the gates were flung open and the swarming multitude careened down the slope, tripping, tumbling, being trodden on, being crushed, and fighting and scrambling for the choice of sleeping berths.' But, miraculously, these people soon established rules, elected delegates, set up committees, and arranged entertainments; here was grass-roots democracy in action with 'natural' leaders like Mickey Davies emerging and helping to produce order among 'people who had been herded across Europe, first by the knout and then by the rubber truncheon, and with them the rough cockneys'.[68] My aim here is not to question the authenticity of Calder's shelter articles, but to suggest that what they offer is not transparent observation, but an interpretation shaped by the well-tried conventions of urban exploration, whose travel and literary references codify the social distance between observer, presumed reader, and those observed even as they express sympathy and admiration.

For Calder, above all, the shelters held the promise of more active forms of citizenship and democratic community. He stressed spontaneity and organization from below. Official confusion and neglect had triggered the natural skills and teamwork of ordinary self-appointed or elected shelter organizers. The element of middle-class surprise in such accounts is also notable, given abundant evidence of community-based systems of mutual support in working-class neighbourhoods and the East End's interwar record of 'Poplarism', rent strikes, and anti-fascist mobilization. Sometimes, of course, the organizational efforts got a well-meaning push from outside. The American psychiatric social worker Noel Hunnybun spent four months in an office-building shelter with 180 people, mostly East Enders. The owner had provided various amenities and staff from the Friends Ambulance Unit worked there. 'The organizers', Hunnybun reported, 'were anxious to develop initiative and community sense within the group, and their preliminary planning was all to this end.' Thus, while the leader of the Friends unit appointed an interim committee, it was replaced by a democratically elected one 'as soon as the shelterers got to know something of each other's worth'. Several 'showed real gifts of leadership' including a cleaning woman, a mother of six who took over the canteen, and a railway worker in charge of entertainment: 'he had an extraordinary knack of controlling a crowd and could produce order without giving offense'.[69]

---

[67] Calder, *Carry on London*, pp. 38–9.
[68] *Ibid.*, pp. 40, 43, 53.
[69] N. K. Hunnybun, 'Work in a shelter', 1940 (no exact date given), in Association of Psychiatric Social Workers Archive, folder 11/1, MRC (Warwick University).

Another account of life in a shelter also deserves mention, *Living Tapestry*, this time a curious piece of fiction completed at the war's end. Its author was 'Peter Conway', a pseudonym for a Russian émigré surgeon and prolific writer, G. A. M. Milkomane. Though he claims to have spent a lot of time in the large shelters and purports to be documenting fact, by adopting a fictional form he has licence to indulge his fantasies and, as a result, rehearses some of the more voyeuristic and erotic elements found in the work of earlier urban explorers. Again we learn of the shelters through interme- diaries. The book begins with the author, a doctor, being given a tour of a mass shelter by a medical friend; there he meets a man in his early thirties, Keith Munro, who seems unlike the other residents. A lower-middle-class bookkeeper with literary pretensions, Munro becomes the informant through whom the author's experience in the shelter is filtered; the bulk of the text is represented as Munro's notes about living for weeks in a vast warehouse shelter modelled on the Tilbury. There he is transformed by cooperation with the residents, losing his natural reserve and becom- ing an organizer and leader. He even gets scabies, conventionally presented as the scourge of the poor, but here seen as a mark of unity. Munro too is shocked by the rich assortment of races and nationalities and finds himself sharing space with a Jewish orthodox family and a tough casual labourer. 'I would talk to a man and find myself in perfect agreement with him, and only later, perhaps when he had turned away, realize that he was a Negro or a Swede.' He adds: 'I became conscious for the first time, I believe, of the underlying sameness of humanity.'[70]

As in Calder's account, 'Conway's' dominant theme is the emergence of 'com- munal life on a scale and intimacy no one could have dreamed of in times of peace'. Democracy and leadership seem to evolve naturally with officialdom 'always one step behind the spontaneous organization of the shelterers themselves'. Improve- ments are secured, tickets issued, canteens opened, entertainments arranged, and abuses controlled by the residents themselves. When a spate of thefts occur, signifi- cantly the culprits are outsiders masquerading as wardens. 'We learnt that the will of the people could be law, that it needed no panoply of police and regulation to give it force and power.' As his social and racial prejudices drop away, so does Munro's initial shock at the forced intimacy of the shelter and at the way in which private life was lived out in public. Here his gaze could light on women breastfeeding, people disrobing, dishevelled frocks, naked thighs unconsciously uncovered in sleep, and the 'rough, sexual horseplay' of the younger people. Going to the shelter entrance one night, he is accosted by a young prostitute and later manages a brief fling with a 'dark, foreign looking' married woman, an Italian, who is terrified by the bombs. Like 'darkest London' in the 1880s, the mass shelter (and the blackout) is a terrain

[70] 'Peter Conway', *Living Tapestry* (London, 1946), p. 61. George Alexis Milkomanovich Milkomane was the son of a tsarist military officer who, after studying medicine in various cities in Western Europe, settled in England in 1932 and became a naturalized citizen in 1938. During the Second World War he was associated with the Emergency Medical Service and subsequently carried on a private practice as a plastic surgeon. His numerous books (novels, histories, and works on medicine) were published under at least five pseudonyms (suitable perhaps for a man whose profession was to change or disguise people's appearance). He even used the pseudonym 'George Sava' for his memoir, *A Surgeon Remembers* (London, 1951) and his 1993 entry in *Who's Who*.

for fantasy, an opportunity for chance sexual encounters. London as 'sin' city gained a new dimension in the war years (and soon gave rise to growing public concern about young girls 'running wild'). Mild guilt follows a fling: 'That was my last adventure of this kind in the shelter . . . during those nights we became different people, our entire scale of values shifted and distorted by the nightmare condition of our lives . . . it is all the more strange in that these lapses go side by side with a growing community consciousness . . .' Having killed off Munro with a bomb fragment, the final parts of the book examine life in the Tube and a shelter shared by a group of middle-class flat dwellers. The new 'informant' is an air-raid warden, but his account is anaemic to say the least, designed merely to indicate for comparative purposes that though these cliquish suburbanites lack the natural gregariousness of the poor, they do draw together and cooperate in response to German bombs. No sex here, just a chaste addendum to the first and more lively part.[71]

The mass shelters found a place in much of the writing of the period. Published collections of letters usually included at least one trip to them. A letter by the novelist and playwright Fry Tennyson Jesse, for example, described a night in a basement shelter with its working-class denizens; she had first tried the Aldwych Tube 'which I had heard was a good one to see', but couldn't get in. She admired the occupants' calmness and ability to sleep: they were 'the real heroes of this war . . . who bear all this so as to go on with their ordinary work'. Novels, many of them by women, also used the shelters to explore class difference with aristocratic women characters who navigate the blitzed inner-city or work at mobile canteens and relief services.[72] Shared grief and danger produce empathy, but the novels make no pretence that social mixing has somehow made their worlds less separate.

But while novels, letters, and press accounts had an impact at the time, the most vivid and enduring images of the mass shelters are visual: the record produced by photojournalists such as Bill Brandt, Bert Hardy, and George Rodger and the pictures of a number of contemporary artists, most famously the remarkable series of shelter drawings by Henry Moore. It was photography especially that captured the London shelters for the rest of the nation: 'All new experiences today seem spoiled by *Picture Post*', wrote one young Mass-Observer on reaching London in October 1940, the Tube being 'exactly like what he had imagined and seen pictures of'. But the photographs also echoed the prose descriptions, capturing similar scenes and portraying the social contrasts between the crowded Tube and the smart patrons of the West End's Hungaria restaurant (photographed by Rodger) comfortable on campbeds. Intertextuality is everywhere: when the poet Louis MacNeice described Tube couples with 'their coloured blankets and patchwork quilts' he was directly quoting Brandt.[73]

---

[71] *Living Tapestry*, quotations from pp. 46, 45, 48, 45, 45, 84, 91 respectively.
[72] F. Tennyson Jesse and H. M. Harwood, *While London Burns* (London, 1941), pp. 117–32. Novels include Susan Ertz, *Anger in the Sky* (London, 1943); Noel Streatfeild, *I Ordered a Table for Six* (London, 1942); J. Nicholson [pseud. M. Steen], *Shelter* (London, 1941).
[73] B. Hardy, *My Life* (London, 1985); Hardy's work appeared in *Picture Post*. George Rodger worked for *Life* and *Picture Post*, see *The Blitz Photography of George Rodger* (London, 1990). Mass-Observer quote: Calder, *The Myth of the Blitz*, p. 143; Heuser (ed.), *Selected Prose of Louis MacNeice*, p. 101.

Bill Brandt came from a prosperous German mercantile family and prior to settling in England in 1934 he had lived mostly in Hamburg, Vienna, and Paris. One of several Central European immigrants who revolutionized the photographic culture of Britain, he rapidly emerged as a leading documentarian of English social life in the thirties. His London scenes soon revealed him as one of the city's most accomplished 'urban spectators'. His first book, *The English at Home* (1936) juxtaposed images of wealth and poverty, moving between the upper-class homes of his German banking relatives, the slums of Whitechapel and Bethnal Green, and the miners' dwellings of South Wales. Influenced by Priestley's *English Journey* and the Jarrow marchers, he also took his camera to the industrial north. Orwell seems to have known Brandt's images, though their influence on *Road to Wigan Pier* is a matter of conjecture. But by 1939, this Continental 'outsider', trained in Man Ray's Paris studio, with an eye for the surreal and fascinated by the rituals and visual language of class in Britain, was regularly contributing to the leading photojournals *Lilliput* and *Picture Post*—photographs that soon became synonymous with 'The Thirties' in the British imagination.[74]

Soon after the Blitz began Brandt was commissioned by MoI to photograph London's shelters; he went to Tube stations, railway arches, church crypts, and private cellars in early November 1940 but the project was cut short when he got sick. There is no record that Brandt and Calder toured together the crypt at Christ Church, Spitalfields, and whether photography emulated prose in this case or the other way round is unclear, but the likeness of their images is extraordinary, for example Brandt's celebrated shots of a navvy asleep in a sarcophagus and a Sikh family in an alcove Brandt recorded the squalor as well as the social aspects of life underground—the slop buckets, primitive toilets, and dripping walls, along with shelterers playing cards, reading, chatting, and sleeping tightly packed together on Underground platforms at the Elephant and Castle and Liverpool Street. He was fascinated by the darkness, the strange spaces, the nativity scenes of mothers and babies. His Tube photographs are mesmerizing and jarring: dim-lit stations, with strong contrasts of light and dark, enhanced by Brandt's flashbulbs and long time exposures; quiet, peaceful images of shelterers asleep or doing very ordinary things (like undoing their boots or snuggling under a quilt); and yet their surreal station milieu and the chaotically intermingled bodies of these Londoners proclaim the larger reality of noise, danger, and terror.[75]

[74] On Brandt: P. Delany, *Bill Brandt: A life* (London, 2004); I. Jeffrey, *Bill Brandt: Photographs 1928–83* (London, 1993); N. Warburton, *Bill Brandt: Selected texts and photography* (Oxford, 1993); J. Buggins, 'An appreciation of the shelter photographs taken by Bill Brandt in November 1940', *Imperial War Museum Review*, 4 (1989); *Bill Brandt behind the Camera: Photographs 1928–1983*, text by M. Haworth-Booth and D. Mellor (New York, 1985).

[75] Recent scholarship on Brandt's work has focused more on its surreal juxtapositions and what David Mellor has called the 'phantasms' that separated him from most social documentary; indeed, this element made his shelter photographs all the more compelling, capturing the fantastic character of the scenes underground (e.g. the *Navvy in a Sarcophagus*). But his style varied; e.g. the work he did on housing conditions for the Bournville Village Trust between 1939 and 1943 falls more squarely in the documentary tradition. P. James and R. Sadler, *Homes Fit for Heroes: Photographs by Bill Brandt 1939–43* (Birmingham, 2004).

4. Sikh family in Christ Church, Spitalfields, November 1940.

If Brandt's shelter compositions have become indelibly inscribed in the history of the Blitz, the same can be said of Henry Moore's drawings. Despite some similarities in their depiction of the mass shelters—the stillness and dark spaces, the crowds of sleepers who seem lifeless or transformed into sculpture—they were very different, of course. Moore, unlike Brandt, seems strangely impervious to the shelter literature and press reportage of the time. But larger forces from the beginning linked the two: selections from their work were published together in the magazine *Lilliput* in December 1941 and both were featured in the exhibit *Britain at War 1941* at the Museum of Modern Art in New York.

Moore's chance encounter with the mass shelters has been described innumerable times. Despite the urging of his friend, Kenneth Clark, chairman of the War Artists' Advisory Committee, Moore who had fought and been wounded in the First World War had little desire to become an official war artist. Travelling into central London in early September to eat with friends, he returned home by Tube and found himself riveted by the crowds of people at every station and by their connection to his own work. As he recalled later:

When we got out at Belsize Park we were not allowed to leave the station because of the fierceness of the barrage. We stayed there for an hour and I was fascinated by the sight of the people camping out deep under the ground. I had never seen so many rows of reclining figures and even the holes out of which the trains were coming seemed to me to be like the holes in my sculpture. And there were intimate little touches. Children fast asleep, with trains roaring past only a couple of yards away. People who were obviously strangers to one another forming tight little intimate groups. They were cut off from what was happening above, but they were aware of it. There was tension in the air. They were a bit like the chorus in a Greek drama telling us about the violence we don't actually witness.[76]

He returned regularly to the shelters, spending nights unobtrusively making the rapid sketches and brief notes from which he recreated the scenes in the daytime. 'The only thing at all like these shelters that I could think of', he later commented, 'was the hold of a slave ship on its way from Africa to America, full of hundreds and hundreds of people who were having things done to them which they were quite powerless to resist.' The claustrophobic spaces of Moore's private nightmares had turned into everyone's reality. His favourite locations included the cavernous Tilbury, but most of all he was fascinated by the unfinished Liverpool Street Tube extension, whose entire length was at night a spiral vortex of sleeping bodies: 'dramatic, dismal lit masses of reclining figures fading to perspective point . . . no lines, just a hole, no platform, and the tremendous perspective'. Through Clark, Moore soon gained official status, working intensely for two months until shelter conditions were improved. By then they seemed almost routine; their regulated, more fixed-up state held less interest for him. The drama had passed and he shifted his attention briefly to coal miners, but was dissatisfied with his drawings of coal hewers. The son of a miner (who had later become a mine engineer), the world of the Father was less compelling to him than that of the Mother and soon he left the War Artists' scheme altogether. But the experience left a permanent mark on his artistic development, softening the abstract aestheticism of his pre-war sculpture and reaffirming his humanist side. 'Without the war,' Moore later commented 'which directed one's attention to life itself, I think I would have been a far less sensitive and responsible person.'[77]

The shelter drawings were done from memory while the scenes were still fresh in Moore's mind. 'You couldn't sit in the shelters and draw people undressing their children', he commented. 'It was too private.' 'I had to behave as though I wasn't trying to look; they were undressing, after all . . . I would have been chased out if I'd been caught sketching.'[78] As always with our 'explorers' there is an element of voyeurism; Moore caught the intimacy of these bodies, arms linked, joined together

[76] Stansky and Abrahams, *London's Burning*, p. 34 and ch. 1 as a whole; H. Moore, *A Shelter Sketchbook* (London, 1988). The date was probably 11 September.

[77] D. Hall, *Henry Moore* (New York, 1966), p. 104; J. Russell, *Henry Moore* (New York, 1968), pp. 81–4; M. and S. Harries, *The War Artists*, p. 192; A.G. Wilkinson, *The Drawings of Henry Moore* (London, 1977), ch. 5; 'Shelter pictures by Brandt and Henry Moore', *Lilliput*, December 1942. Most recently, Julian Andrews, *London at War: The shelter drawings of Henry Moore* (London, 2002).

[78] Stansky and Abrahams, *London's Burning*, p. 36; M. and S. Harries, *The War Artists*, p. 192.

5. The Liverpool Street Tube extension, 1941 by Henry Moore.

under wave-like sheets and blankets. His preoccupation with mothers and maternity well pre-dated the war, but in these dim caverns his productivity exploded. His nurturing mothers, heads of sleeping shelterers, and groups of figures sitting awkwardly or reclining are stripped of circumstantial details; they are not Londoners so much as suffering humanity: passive, austere, ghostlike, and monumental. Unlike Brandt's photographs or the texts of Calder and 'Conway', or indeed the more anecdotal style of other shelter artists, Moore's drawings make no special reference to class, community, or nation, nor do they capture the cluttered, interactive gregariousness of shelter life. They universalize London's raid victims who could, it seems, be anywhere in Europe and whose densely packed bodies seem equally to anticipate the horrors of Bergen-Belsen and Buchenwald. Moore's intensely personal vision had raised life in the mass shelters to epic status; the haunted, static quality of his art must have seemed unreal and far removed from the average shelterer's experience. By contrast, most depictions of the Blitz revolved around the themes of nation, class, and above all community.[79] While the raids, it

[79] Other shelter artists like Edward Ardizzone and Feliks Topolski included more specific references to dress, individual physical features, and gestures and depicted more the socializing that went with

6. Liverpool Street Underground station, November 1940.

was argued, had confirmed the nation's strengths, they had also underscored its class divisions and awakened the need for human as well as physical reconstruction.

Yet, for all their differences one of the powerful motifs that connects the abstractions of Moore, the more literal work of other artists, and the photographers is the imagery of protective, nurturing mothers and young infants. Women and children were represented as those for whom the war was being fought; they were the epitome of defenceless civilians, victims of modern war; and the children pointed to an uncertain future. Some images were explicitly religious—for example, a mother and child on a Tube platform, a nativity scene with 'Angel' the station name prominently displayed. These maternal pictures offer a striking contrast to those two years later which portray women engaged in new non-feminine roles, in uniform or producing munitions. In 1940 few women had been mobilized. Moreover, they should be set against the stereotypes produced by evacuation. To contemporary eyes the class dimension of these scenes was implicit and never far from the surface. Mass shelters might epitomize shared danger and wartime community but it was poor, working-class families who were at the centre of the

shelter life. The Hungarian-born artist Joseph Bato also published a Blitz sketchbook: *Defiant City* (London, 1942). B. Foss, *War Paint: Art, war, state and identity in Britain 1939–45* (New Haven, 2007).

shelter crisis and who largely inhabited the Tubes and the Tilbury. And contemporaries all knew that. A year before, poor mothers were accused of lacking 'the most elementary ideas of decency and home-training'. Their ignorance and apathy was widely condemned while the historian, R. C. K. Ensor, acting as a evacuation volunteer, lambasted slum mothers as 'slatternly malodorous tatterdemailions with children to match'.[80] Now suddenly, like London itself, they stood for the nation. Brandt captures some of this in his wonderfully ironic picture of a sheltering woman with a child huddled next to her. She sits, tight-lipped, her gaze hard to read but with a hint of defiance, next to a makeshift lavatory; the sign 'Ladies' with all its *double entente* leaps out at the viewer.

7. South-east London air-raid shelter, November 1940.

[80] R. C. K. Ensor, 'The Great Evacuation', *The Spectator*, 8 September 1939, p. 349. Ensor's word choice seems to have been strongly influenced by C. Williams-Ellis, *England and the Octopus* (London, 1928), p. 128, suggesting that he viewed these working-class evacuees through the prism of interwar anti-urban literature which depicted the vulgar masses as a threat to England's countryside.

THE PROVINCIAL BLITZ

On the night of 14–15 November 1940, after more than two months of continuous raiding, the skies over London remained strangely quiet. But 90 miles to the north-west, Coventry suffered an intense eleven-hour assault that destroyed its medieval core and shopping area, gutted the cathedral, and left a third of the city's homes uninhabitable, especially in the working-class districts near to the town centre. A combination of high explosives and incendiaries had turned a hundred acres of the city into piles of rubble in one night, killing 568 people—almost half of them unidentifiable—and seriously injuring over 860. Hospitals were hit, sewers breached, transport, gas, water, and electricity services were disrupted, and local Medical Officers soon lived in fear of a serious typhoid outbreak. Thousands were given inoculations and for six weeks after the raid the population was instructed to boil all drinking water. On entering the city the morning after, Hilde Marchant found crowds of people 'trekking out—not sure where they were going, what they would do, but just moving to try and get away from the sounds of the night'. Some simply 'leaned against the railings at the roadside, too exhausted to move, their luggage in heaps around them…bewilderment and frustration in their faces'.[81]

The Coventry Blitz signalled a new stage in the Luftwaffe's campaign. While the incidence of raids on provincial cities had risen steadily since September, attacks now became much more severe and in the next months ports and manufacturing centres like Merseyside, Manchester, Birmingham, Southampton, Portsmouth, and Bristol suffered serious damage. London continued to be a major target of the German offensive, but it no longer experienced nightly raids and gained some respite. Especially ferocious were the attacks of March and April 1941 when Plymouth, Hull, Manchester, Merseyside, Clydeside, Belfast, and once again Birmingham and Coventry sustained massive destruction and heavy casualties. In some cases several heavy raids were clustered followed by intervals of inactivity, while other towns experienced single intense assaults followed by a lull—Coventry, for example, was not hit hard again for five months. Whereas the repetition and predictability of the London raids had quickly induced new blitz routines, these sudden, erratic onslaughts were impossible to prepare for and completely fractured older rhythms of life. The capital's expanse made it an easy target for bomber pilots, but its huge area and vast resources were also an advantage: no single raid could simultaneously disrupt the whole of London or affect directly all its inhabitants. Like living organisms, the larger conurbations could compensate for injury: if transport links were cut or food stocks and processing plant destroyed in some districts, others less damaged were able to fill the gap, and wholesalers and retailers could rush in alternate supplies. By contrast, compact small or medium-sized towns like Southampton (180,000) or Plymouth (200,000) not only underwent more

---

[81] Marchant, *Women and Children Last*, pp. 130–1. N. Longmate, *Air Raid: The bombing of Coventry* (London, 1976); Tony Mason, 'Looking back on the Blitz' in T. Mason and Bill Lancaster (eds.), *Life and Labour in a Twentieth Century City: The experience of Coventry* (Warwick, 1986).

concentrated destruction but their rural hinterlands could not quickly render assistance and supplies; only the irregularity of German attacks gave them breathing space to recover from the blows.

The scale of physical devastation, much of it the result of incendiaries, came as a shock, even though casualties were lower than pre-war estimates. After the March and April 1941 raids on Plymouth, a quarter of the town's dwellings were either destroyed or rendered uninhabitable for at least two years and there were more than 50,000 homeless; in all the city endured fifty-nine raids. In the nearby working-class dockyard area of Devonport almost half the houses were damaged or destroyed. In Southampton, beginning with a ferocious daylight raid at the end of November 1940, the city eventually experienced over 1,600 alerts and 57 attacks which gutted the central shopping area and reduced working-class districts to the east of the city to ruins. Eight raids on successive nights in May 1941 turned much of Merseyside into ruins and killed 1,500 people (and possibly many more) in Liverpool alone. In neighbouring Bootle the raids left 40 per cent of the houses completely ruined or seriously damaged; destroyed a third of the shops; damaged eleven out of twelve rest centres and rendered a quarter of the population homeless. In Hull, in the same month, two raids left only 6,000 out of 93,000 homes undamaged. Worst of all, in terms of physical destruction, was the fate of Clydebank, a working-class town of 47,000 with pitifully inadequate shelters. Here two nights of raids in March 1941 only left an estimated 7 out of 12,000 dwellings unscathed: 33 per cent were totally destroyed and fully 43 per cent were uninhabitable. The death toll was 528, but 35,000 found themselves homeless.[82] Often it was working-class neighbourhoods, clustered around docks and inner-city factories, that were the first to suffer heavy damage, giving rise to feelings that the middle classes—seen heading out in the evenings to suburban safety in their cars—were getting off lightly.

Local governments were unprepared for the scale and intensity of these raids. This was in part a consequence of Treasury parsimony, shifting a disproportionate burden onto the localities. While some towns had few resources, others were often reluctant to commit ratepayers' money for no clear, tangible return or to be prodded into sizeable expenditures by London without firm promises of reimbursement. They especially fell behind targets in the construction of shelters. Less than half Birmingham's population could be sheltered in October 1939 and of these over 80 per cent relied on Andersons that had been distributed by Whitehall. Working-class

---

[82] In addition to Harrison, *Living through the Blitz*, see G. Wasley, *Blitz: An account of Hitler's aerial war over Plymouth in March 1941 and the events that followed* (Exeter, 1991); H. P. Twyford, *It Came to our Door: Plymouth in the World War* (Plymouth, 1945); B. Knowles, *Southampton: The English gateway* (London, 1951); T. M. McKendrick, *Clydebank Blitz* (1986); C. M. MacInnes, *Bristol at War* (London, 1962); S. P. Shipley, *Bristol Siren Nights* (Bristol, 1943); T. H. J. Underdown, *Bristol under Blitz* (1942); NA: INF 1/292, 30 April–7 May 1941: Plymouth; 9–16 July 1941: Merseyside; P. Ayers, *Women at War: Liverpool women, 1939–45* (Birkenhead, 1988); R. Garnett, *Liverpool in the 1930s and the Blitz* (Preston, 1991). On the north-east: Craig Armstrong, 'A northern community at war, 1939–1945: "Tyneside can take it!"', *Northern History*, 44(1) (March 2007); idem, *Tyneside in the Second World War* (Chichester, 2007). On Clydeside: Titmuss, *Problems of Social Policy*, p. 313 (figures from a Home Intelligence report of March 1941); J. MacLeod, *River of Fire: The Clydebank Blitz* (Edinburgh, 2010).

districts in the inner-city mostly had to make do with cheap trench shelters or strengthened basements and even in late 1940 the construction of brick surface shelters lagged way behind schedule. When Coventry was battered in November 1940 it had only seventy-nine public shelters; half were trenches and the rest basements. Only six surface shelters existed for those caught in the streets. Most Lancashire towns also relied heavily on covered trenches; government distribution of Anderson shelters was slow and, in any case, there was little room for them in many working-class districts. In the seaport and industrial town of Barrow, to take one example, there were public shelters for only 3,500 out of a total population of 70,000. Even more unprepared was Belfast which, despite its shipyards and engineering plants, thought itself beyond the range of German bombers: in the summer of 1940 it had only 200 public shelters and 4,000 domestic Andersons for a population of 400,000. The cathedral city of York, which suffered ten raids including a heavy attack in April 1942, was almost undefended; its allotment of Andersons had been halved and most people simply took cover in their homes or basements.[83]

Coverage of the raids in the provincial press during the war was largely intent on bolstering local pride and the spate of civic-sponsored publications in the decade after 1945 were mostly self-congratulatory. Few indicated just how overwhelmed many local authorities had been. In some towns the numbers of air-raid wardens and civil-defence workers were still deficient and serious equipment shortages continued throughout the Blitz. Some local elites guarded their powers jealously and were slow to coordinate with neighbouring authorities for civil defence and evacuation purposes. Conducting a survey of shelter facilities, Violet Markham blasted the Sheffield local authority as 'a self-sufficient, self-satisfied body, dominated by a certain type of Labour politics and very unreceptive to ideas from outside'. A government report on Merseyside in July 1941 criticized local councils as 'too easily satisfied with the provisions made', 'inclined to ignore public opinion', and 'on the defensive and unwilling to discuss difficulties'.[84] Among the chief criticisms was the failure to supply raid victims promptly with basic information about where to obtain new ration books, registration papers, and compensation forms or how to get rehoused. After the Coventry Blitz, according to Mass-Observation, 'Ordinary people had no idea what they should do, and this helplessness and impotence only accelerated depression.' Similarly, the secretary of the Birmingham Labour Party protested that hundreds of people were left to wander the streets after a raid 'without any knowledge or information as to where they

---

[83] A. Sutcliffe and R. Smith, *Birmingham, 1939–1970* (Oxford, 1974), p. 23; G. Hodgkinson, *Sent to Coventry* (Coventry 1970); P. Taylor 'The role of local government in wartime, with emphasis on Lancashire', PhD Diss., University of Lancashire, 1993; E. Little, 'Manchester City Council and the development of air raid precautions, 1935–1939', *Manchester Regional History Review*, 2(1) (Spring/ Summer 1988); Nella Last, *Nella Last's War* (London, 1981), p. 150; R. Fisk, *In Time of War: Ireland, Ulster, and the price of neutrality* (London, 1983), p. 479; B. Barton, *The Blitz: Belfast in the war years* (Belfast, 1989); C. Price, 'The political genesis of air raid precautions and the York raid of 1942', *Northern History*, 36(2) (September 2000).

[84] Violet Markham Papers 8/36–38 (BLPES, LSE); I. McLaine, *Ministry of Morale* (London, 1979), p. 122.

could present themselves for relief'.[85] Certainly, inertia and lack of drive was a problem in many places: in June 1941, for example, the Special Commissioner for London noted that *not one* local authority in England, Scotland, or Ireland had approached his office for information about the way the capital was addressing the problem of homelessness.[86]

Opinion surveys after major raids generally praised wardens, firemen, and rescue squads, but revealed sharp criticism of town bureaucracies for delays and gaps in emergency services and complaints that officials treated raid victims like poor-relief recipients. On the morning after, as numerous government reports pointed out, local government rather than the Germans seemed to be the chief enemy. Perhaps this was inevitable, but, while understaffed local departments were often overwhelmed by heavy raids, the difficulties they faced were also staggering. Usually parts of the civil-defence system operated effectively, while others broke down under the strain. Fire and rescue services were taxed to the limit and there were never enough men and equipment on standby to cope with the cycle of concentrated, spasmodic attacks. Some fire brigades were poorly trained and badly administered and non-matching equipment often hampered regional cooperation; moreover, the long hours they put in reduced efficiency and when water supplies failed there was little they could do.[87] The disruption of transport services, closure of shops, and cut-off of basic utilities made shopping, cooking, and getting to work a nightmare; food distribution and the provision of mobile canteens, water-carts, and blankets, though vital to public morale, were often inadequate in early raids. As was the case in London, much of the burden of providing immediate relief fell on rest centres, often hastily organized in schools and churches and staffed by volunteers. And, as in the capital, people took refuge in church crypts, warehouses, mine shafts, and tunnels, often opposed initially by local officials. In them, conditions were squalid with vast crowds sleeping on floors with only primitive sanitary facilities and food services.[88] Meetings, concerts, and something of a nightlife began to develop in some mass shelters, but the erratic nature of German raids in many towns resulted in less regular routines of sheltering than in London, while

[85] M-OA, FR 495 (Coventry) and Harrisson, *Living through the Blitz*, p. 135; D. Thoms, *War, Industry, and Society: The Midlands, 1939–45* (London, 1989), p. 153. On the Anglican Church in the Birmingham Blitz: S. Parker, *Faith on the Home Front: Aspects of church life and popular religion in Birmingham 1939–45* (Oxford, 2006).

[86] Titmuss, *Problems of Social Policy*, p. 306.

[87] C. Demarne, *The London Blitz: A fireman's tale* (Oxford, 1980); Shane Ewen, 'Preparing the British fire service for war: Local government, nationalisation and evolutionary reform, 1935–41', *Contemporary British History*, 20(2) (June 2006).

[88] It has been suggested that morale levels closely reflected the extent to which enemy attacks destroyed city centres, pubs, cinemas, shops, public utilities, and transportation networks, making everyday life far more difficult. Compared to Manchester and Hull, higher public morale in Liverpool is thus explained in terms of less damage to the central city area. Public attitudes fluctuated rapidly and morale reports for any given area were highly subjective and impressionistic. B. Beaven and D. Thoms, 'The Blitz and civilian morale in three northern cities, 1940–1942', *Northern History*, 32 (1996); B. Beaven and J. Griffiths, 'The Blitz, civilian morale and the city: Mass-observation and working-class culture in Britain, 1940–41', *Urban History*, 26(1) (1999); E. Jones *et al.*, 'Civilian morale during the Second World War: Responses to air raids re-examined', *Social History of Medicine*, 17(3) (2004).

large nightly migrations into surrounding areas also inhibited the growth of tight-knit shelter communities.[89]

In the provinces, as in London, the inadequacy of shelter provision sparked heated controversy and growing public activism around ARP issues. In some districts local communists were the catalyst. Instructed by the party to join civil-defence units, they quickly became embroiled with local ARP leaders, many of whom were local police chiefs, and vocal criticism quickly led to their dismissal in Glasgow, parts of Yorkshire, and other regions. Elsewhere the lead was taken by trades councils, union committees, the Women's Co-operative Guild, and dissident factions within local councils who lobbied hard for better protection. Tenants' groups also organized petition drives and sometimes rent strikes. In South Wales the executive of the miners' federation called a conference on public shelters in September, while in Neath, Port Talbot, and several communities of the Rhondda valley, committees of women worked for shelter improvements.[90] In Birmingham, where the local Labour Party and the trades council spearheaded the opposition, Tory civic leaders were strongly criticized for the lack of deep shelters and the malfunctions of its warning system; sirens were inaudible in some parts of the city and there were times when the all-clear sounded in the middle of raids. 'Each night tells the same tale', went a report from the Vickers' Castle Bromwich plant in August 1940, 'hostile aircraft fly over the factory and bombs are heard dropping in the vicinity before the official warning is received.' After the BSA plant in Birmingham sustained heavy casualties in November 1940, employees' concerns about the inaccessibility of shelters culminated in several thousand workers joining demonstrations and taking control of the factory gates; the crowd disbanded when a raid alert sounded, but many men refused for several days to re-enter the plant.[91] By early 1941 improvements had been made in many areas—including bunk-beds, lavatories, and food and medical provision; better coordination between private firms and local governments; and the use of roof spotters to better evaluate the danger and to minimize production stoppages and allow work to continue after the siren had sounded.[92]

The most dramatic response to the attacks on provincial cities was 'trekking' or spontaneous mass migration into neighbouring areas. This had also occurred after severe London raids, but became much more conspicuous in the provinces. Estimates of the numbers involved vary greatly, but during the 1941 raids on Plymouth between 30,000 and 50,000 people daily trekked out of the town. They began leaving around 4.00 p.m., clogging the major roads, mostly on foot but hoping to catch a bus or thumb a lift from passing vehicles. At night they slept out

[89] NA: INF 1/292 (1–8 January, 9–16 July 1941 on Merseyside shelters; 9–16 July, reports on anti-Semitism in the towns of Merseyside and elsewhere). INF 1/292 (19–24 May 1941, reports on problems of vandalism, truancy, and theft in Portsmouth shelters).

[90] *Daily Worker*, 1 July, 9 July, 12 July, 31 August, 5 September, 1 October. Also, *ibid.*, 14 September (Manchester); 16 September (Liverpool).

[91] D. Thoms, *War, Industry, and Society: The Midlands, 1939–45* (London, 1989), pp. 148, 118–19. *Daily Worker*, 22 August, 7 September 1940.

[92] H. Jones, *British Civilians in the Front Line, 1939–45* (Manchester, 2006).

or crowded into schools, churches, and women's institutes that were hastily converted into rest centres. Some families remained, but many more returned to their jobs and homes in the early mornings. There were similar outflows from Portsmouth, Southampton, Bristol, Merseyside, Manchester, Belfast, and other stricken areas. After an especially severe raid 90,000 were said to have taken shelter in the hinterland of Portsmouth and even after an extended lull in enemy action, 30,000 continued to leave regularly: 'They crowd into houses and halls in the villages, into shelters and holes in the hills, into stables and hop-pickers huts. Some sleep under hedges and some in the vehicles that drove them out... we saw people lying on open banks and a colony of 120 in some disused stables without water or sanitation.'[93] The scale of these movements, which resembled too vividly the retreats of broken armies, aroused official fears that public morale was collapsing and at first many local governments refused to schedule extra buses or dispense with fares. One consequence was that far fewer people were left for fire-watching and civil defence in the inner-city neighbourhoods. Yet, while 'trekking' was a form of flight, it also constituted a fairly orderly, rational response to a specific set of circumstances. Had more deep shelters been available the size of these movements would have been smaller and had provincial cities (like London) possessed large suburban belts that could absorb people from the central danger zone, the migrations would have been less conspicuous. With the destruction of city centres, trekkers were in search of basic amenities: a decent night's sleep, food, cigarettes, and a quiet beer in a pub. And where billeting services had broken down and emergency services were poor, the hinterland could offer a temporary solution to homelessness. Many of those involved returned daily to their homes and jobs. There was considerable chaos initially in areas adjacent to these cities and in some instances trekking produced social confrontations similar to the evacuation scheme, but by the summer of 1941 many authorities had constructed hostels to accommodate these migrants.

***

Far less was written about the blitzing of provincial cities than London which was the centre of the national and foreign media and the chief focus of political life. Many of the social problems were the same while the metropole's experiences in a way prepared provincial populations for the worst and provided a template for patriotic behaviour—for 'taking it' and 'carrying on', as well as for how to report the epic struggle in the press. London symbolized the nation's heart in 1940, but heavy raids on other ports and industrial towns further reinforced the place of urban working-class communities in the national imagery. In London the Blitz both provoked anger at civic authorities' lack of advance preparation and criticisms that working-class communities were left to suffer disproportionately, but *at the same time* it enhanced pride in one's city and a sense of local identification. The same was true for other towns whose inhabitants were quick to criticize the BBC's reports of their raids and local stoicism as inadequate. Life in the Blitz was highly

[93] NA: INF 1/292 (19–24 May 1941); HO 199/543.

localized; knowledge of the larger picture came from carefully edited representations in newsreels, the press, and the BBC. London was different from Coventry or Liverpool, while those who lived in Bolton, Mass-Observation's 'Worktown', heard raiders overhead as they flew towards Manchester but never endured a raid. But everywhere raids and the threat of raids promoted mutual assistance and greater reliance on street, kinship, and neighbourhood networks. As Paul Addison has written, 'egalitarianism, and community feeling became, to a great extent, the pervasive ideals of social life: whether or not people lived up to them, they knew they *ought* to'.[94]

Finally, what significance did the Blitz have for class relations? First, and most important, the endurance of the population, and recognition that the nation's survival required the participation of everyone, did much to transform not only the status and consciousness of workers but public discourse *about* the working class. Historians (and retrospective accounts) of the Blitz have often argued that class mattered less or was driven underground during the Blitz. But when we examine contemporary accounts—in novels, private letters, official documents, press stories—class attitudes and the language of class are omnipresent; but their tone and texture had changed in the course of a year. In her study of the creation of a system of factory lookouts or roof spotters, Helen Jones rightly describes workers as assuming greater risks as they conceived of themselves as 'civilians in the front line'. She criticizes overemphasis upon Henry Moore's imagery of civilians as passive, entombed shelterers simply 'taking it'.[95] Yet, contemporary shelter narratives (correctly or exaggeratedly, it doesn't matter) described not passivity but grass-roots participation and activity. Even as the raids continued, London and other cities began commissioning redevelopment plans. Idealistic and radical, most were scaled back later, but their common theme was fostering closer community through urban design. And class was again central to the discussion, for planners envisioned mixed or 'balanced' neighbourhoods where different social strata would live together and mix freely—a response to the class-segregation which, as one put it, produced 'astonishment at other people's lives' and 'created something like social panic during the 1939 evacuation'.[96]

As for the response of workers themselves, it was always mixed. Home Intelligence and other sources record increased prevalence of class feeling (sometimes deflected onto Jews or other outsiders): about inadequate post-raid services and insanitary shelters, the ineptitude of local government elites, claims that sacrifices were unequal (the impact of food shortages, for example), cynicism about suburban commuters departing in the evenings by car or train to comparative safety. Such examples are not hard to find; the Blitz occurred amid a spreading critique of the pre-war social and political order and a radicalization of large sections of the population and this informed popular experience of it. But the raids also fostered

[94] Addison quoted in N. Hayes and J. Hill (eds.), *'Millions Like Us'? British culture in the Second World War* (Liverpool, 1999), p. 21.
[95] Jones, *British Civilians in the Front Line, 1939–45*.
[96] T. Sharp, *Town Planning* (London, 1940), p. 87.

community across classes—gratitude to local doctors, clergy, and WVS who worked in the shelters or manned Citizens' Advice Bureaux; department stores and firms that opened their basements as refuges. In addition, because so much of the response to aerial attack was left to local authorities, citizens were inevitably drawn into more formal voluntary action on an unprecedented scale—as Home Guard, fire-watchers, wardens, shelter marshals, rescue units, first-aid volunteers, helpers at rest centres, or as boy messengers on bicycles. It was this kind of community or active citizenship that Priestley and Ritchie Calder felt was dissipated after 1945 or that Rose, a young unmarried fellow tenant in Doris Lessing's *In Pursuit of the English* remembered as 'warmth, comradeship, as feeling of belonging and being wanted, a feeling she had never been given before or since'.[97] All of this local activity—and it was soon complemented in myriad ways by an increasing expansion of the central state into every aspect of people's lives—both helped redraw the boundaries of private and public life, changed ideas about the legitimate sphere of state action, and gradually helped to foster a sense of the nation as an authentic democratic community rather than a remote set of structures. But the Blitz experience was not alone in reshaping workers' relationship to the nation. Faced with a growing production crisis and labour famine, Britain moved rapidly towards the construction of a war economy in 1941—which over time had even more profound consequences for labour's power and for redefining class relationships.

---

[97] S. Fielding, P. Thompson, and N. Tiratsoo, *England Arise! The Labour Party and popular politics in 1940s Britain* (Manchester, 1995), p. 121; D. Lessing, *In Pursuit of the English* (London, 1960), p. 123.

3

The Industrial Front and Trade Unionism

As belligerent nations discovered in the First World War, warfare was a struggle of rival economic systems as much as of armies in the field. It placed labour and productivity at a premium, highlighted the deficiencies of a nation's industrial base, and put its structure of industrial relations to the test. This was even truer in 1939 when, according to a Treasury estimate, every soldier required three times as much economic support as his counterpart in the previous conflict. Britain's economy was ill-prepared for the outbreak of war and lagged far behind Germany in such vital sectors as steel and machine tools. By 1942, however, the change was remarkable. A centrally managed war economy had been constructed. Women were mobilized on an unprecedented scale. Expenditure on war-related activities rose from 7 per cent of national income in 1938 to 53 per cent in 1942. Business and labour accepted severe limits on their freedom as the necessary price of military survival. And though domestic consumption was drastically reduced, government policies spread the pain more evenly among the population than in the First World War.[1] Admittedly, popular myth exaggerated the success of British industrial performance. But, in part, this was because the nation had surprised itself; few in the pre-war decade would have confidently predicted its capacity to meet the challenge.

The war revolutionized the role of the state in the economy. Not only did government become the key customer for industrial production, but, as David Edgerton has argued, beginning with large-scale rearmament in the late 1930s, the scale of public ownership in the arms industries ballooned. Edgerton has estimated that some 1.6 million workers were employed in state-owned plant at the peak of the war effort, some of it managed directly (like the forty or so government ordnance factories) and others run by private companies.[2] The role of state enterprises in wartime production was prodigious, but equally important was the rapid extension of state regulation over private business after the formation of the Churchill coalition in May 1940. These changes, which were recognized as a requirement of national survival, established a

---

[1] W. K. Hancock and M. M. Gowing, *The British War Economy* (London, 1949); H. M. D. Parker, *Manpower: A study of wartime policy and administration* (London, 1957); M. M. Postan, *British War Production* (London, 1952). R. J. Overy, 'Great Britain: Cyclops' in D. Reynolds, W. F. Kimball, and A. O. Chubarian (eds.), *Allies at War: The Soviet, American and British experience, 1939–45* (London, 1994). Also, M. Harrison, 'Resource mobilization for World War II: The U.S.A., U.K., U.S.S.R., and Germany, 1938–45', *Economic History Review*, 61(2) (1988); S. Broadberry and P. Howlett, 'The United Kingdom: "Victory at all cost"' in M. Harrison (ed.), *The Economics of World War II: Six Great Powers in international comparison* (Cambridge, 1998).
[2] D. Edgerton, *Warfare State: Britain, 1920–1970* (Cambridge, 2006), ch. 4.

new context for labour relations in Britain, imposing constraints on both labour and business and creating new opportunities for the growth of trade unionism, the spread of industrial welfare, and more enlightened and participatory managerial styles.

The creation of a total war economy also transformed the lives of workers: their wages, working conditions, and the time spent at their jobs. In these years long shifts and constant overtime meant that workers' lives revolved far more around their workplaces which also became social centres and a focus of leisure activities, especially if they lived in hostels or billets away from home. Vast numbers of new workers, many of them women, were recruited into war production; they had little or no experience of industrial work regimes and their presence both feminized many workplaces and necessitated new labour-management practices. Above all, however, the war ushered in an era of full employment. In the south—the Greater London area and the Midlands—this further extended the rapid economic expansion already underway in the late 1930s with towns like Coventry or Oxford bursting at the seams with the influx of new workers. But the war's impact was even more dramatic on the old staple industries of the north, Scotland, and South Wales which had experienced the worst of the interwar depression. There, unemployment and dole payments which had blighted the lives of so many disappeared, although memory of them continued to fester. The huge disparities in the experience of workers that had characterized the interwar decades—between geographical regions and the gulf between employed and unemployed—narrowed rapidly, helping to create a stronger sense of belonging to a national working class. Distinctive regional class identities continued to be important, so did sectional and skill divisions, but a wider consciousness of class emerged superimposed upon older loyalties.

Within the confines of a single chapter, it is impossible to examine all aspects of industrial production. The main focus here is on engineering and its allied trades and coal mining, two of the largest and most vital sectors for the war effort. The most conspicuous change of these years, the mobilization of women and their experiences in war work, is addressed in the next chapter.

THE NEW FRAMEWORK OF WAR PRODUCTION

In the early months of the war little changed: the pace of mobilization was sluggish and central economic direction of the war remained indecisive and uncoordinated. This was especially true of labour mobilization where Neville Chamberlain's government relied heavily on market forces and feared anything resembling industrial conscription—mindful of the unrest this had caused in the First World War. The government did little to control the cost of living which rose sharply and failed to formulate plans to control wage demands or to introduce compulsory arbitration of disputes. National negotiations to allow 'dilution'[3] and the transfer of skilled labour also proceeded at a snail's pace, in part because of official reluctance to make

---

[3] The upgrading of semi-skilled labour onto jobs normally reserved for skilled workers and the breaking down of skilled jobs into separate parts which were then performed by non-skilled workers.

necessary concessions to the trade unions. Ironically, this had the effect of enhancing local union power, especially in the aircraft and armaments sectors, where employers were under great pressure to produce and could do so only by securing plant-level cooperation.

Mutual distrust between Chamberlain's government and the leadership of the trade union movement prevented vigorous action to organize labour supply. As early as October 1939, Walter Citrine, leader of the TUC, made it clear that full cooperation with the war effort must entail close consultation, recognition of the trade unions' right to represent workers' interests, and parity of status with employers. Ernest Bevin was an equally vocal critic of Chamberlain; he deplored the 'middle-class mentality in office' and the insistence that 'private interests must not be touched'. The chief architect of the Transport and General Workers' Union (TGWU), Bevin had become one of the most powerful figures in union and Labour Party circles by the 1930s. Looking back to the First World War, he believed that labour's cooperation had been delivered without adequate safeguards for workers' interests or commensurate sacrifices from employers. And in Chamberlain's policies he saw not simply drift or procrastination, but a determination to preserve pre-war class priorities. 'The whole tendency [of the government and bankers]', he told his union members in February 1940, 'is to create a situation which will enable the ruling class to use this war as a means of thrusting us back into a form of serfdom.' 'No employer', he wrote, 'will make sacrifices unless he is compelled to . . . and in this farcical state of Society for one class to be trying to measure another upon a fodder basis is intolerable.' Now almost sixty years of age, he was determined that this war would both enhance the power of trade unionism and reform the structure of industrial relations.[4]

Hitler's lightning victories in the spring of 1940 and the collapse of Chamberlain's government transformed the situation, making it possible to recast labour policy and the economic direction of the war. The Labour Party joined Churchill's coalition and Bevin was appointed Minister of Labour and National Service. A man who loved power, wielded it despotically, and regarded himself as the voice of the working class, Bevin became, after Churchill, the most important figure in the war Cabinet. He moved quickly to establish control over manpower resources, beating out rivals, including Lord Beaverbrook, who also had ambitions of becoming the tsar of war production. The administrative framework that developed over the next two years reflected a consistent and coherent philosophy which, though rightly attributed to Bevin, was shared by other trade unionists, and especially by Citrine. The two men had little in common. Precise, cautious, a practical committee-man, Citrine cut a very different figure from the pugnacious, imaginative, and openly domineering Bevin who 'personalized almost everything'.[5] Theirs was a

[4] A. Bullock, *The Life and Times of Ernest Bevin*, II: *Minister of Labour 1940–1945* (London, 1967). Quotes in order: *Daily Herald*, 1 April 1940, p. 8; P. Weiler, *Ernest Bevin* (Manchester, 1993), p. 101; Bevin to Seebohm Rowntree, quoted in P. Addison, *The Road to 1945* (London, 1977), pp. 58–9. Citrine lacks a biography, but for his earlier career see N. Riddell, 'Walter Citrine and the British Labour movement, 1925–35', *History*, 85(278) (April 2000).
[5] Lord Citrine, *Men and Work: An autobiography* (London, 1964), I, pp. 238–40.

partnership of ideas and objectives with little warmth or friendship between them and on the one occasion when they locked horns (over Bevin's demands that more skilled workers be drafted into the forces), it was Citrine who prevented the quarrel from becoming a destructive breach.

Bevin and Citrine insisted that labour's full cooperation in the war effort required parity with employers. The key, they believed, was joint consultation of labour, business, and the state at all levels from national economic planning to individual firms. If labour were subjected to constraints and controls, then business must submit equally to regulations and higher taxes. Wage restraint must be balanced with price controls, fair distribution of goods, and a limitation on profits. Concessions by trade unions over dilution and the surrender of long-standing work practices had to be negotiated and provisions made for restoration post-war. Employers must make working conditions and workplace welfare a priority and recognize more readily the right of unions to organize. Wherever possible Bevin preferred to rely on voluntary consent rather than compulsion and he was frequently criticized for the incremental way that he introduced manpower controls. He was also determined to preserve competitive wage bargaining, viewing it as essential if union leaders were to retain authority over their memberships and quite workable so long as rationing and price controls were effective.[6] To those who advocated statutory wage controls and comprehensive labour regulation, Bevin replied that this would only be palatable if industry were nationalized on a wide scale.

The chief instruments of wartime manpower policy can be briefly summarized. Under the Emergency Powers (Defence) Act of 22 May 1940 the Minister of Labour gained sweeping legal authority to impose industrial conscription, by which anyone over sixteen years of age could be instructed to perform any war work in any place; regulation 58A, for example, allowed Bevin to direct workers into priority areas of production, regulate the conditions under which firms operated, and force employers to raise wages and improve working conditions. Collective wage bargaining was retained, as we have indicated, but the ultimate weapon of the strike was removed: under Order 1305 (July 1940), strikes and lockouts were banned. If a dispute occurred that proved impossible to resolve through normal procedures, the two parties involved were to report it to the government's Regional Industrial Relations Officer (RIRO) who then had up to twenty-one days to bring about agreement before referring the matter to the National Arbitration Tribunal (NAT). In practice, the RIROs were often consulted in the earliest stages of potential disputes, well before official notification—not least to allow more time for conciliation since the twenty-one days often proved too tight a constraint. Under this regulation, even if a union was not formally recognized, it could lodge a complaint where a firm was not complying with the agreed wages, terms, and conditions for the industry.

---

[6] At a meeting with the Chancellor of the Exchequer and the TUC General Council, 2 July 1941, Bevin argued forcefully against wage freeze proposals: Citrine Papers (LSE) File Folder 5/20 ('Wages in Wartime').

The shortage of skilled labour created competition among employers and the 'poaching' of workers from one firm to another became a serious problem. Steps were taken to prevent hiring except through a trade union or an employment exchange and specific occupational categories (in engineering and later in such industries as shipbuilding and coal mining) were required to register; this was later extended to all workers. The only long-term remedy for the shortage of skilled labour, however, was dilution as it had been practised in the previous war. Bevin bargained hard to arrive at dilution agreements in most sectors of war production; he was helped both by the atmosphere of crisis and the threat of a German invasion and also by his own standing in the labour movement. He also secured statutory guarantees that traditional trade practices would be restored after the war. Even so, patient coaxing was required and success was uneven; opposition and foot-dragging came from both employers and unions and national accords ran into difficulty when it came to applying them locally. Certain regions—Northern Ireland, for example—and certain unions—the boilermakers and electricians, for example—remained intractable throughout the war.[7] In the shipyards, for example, despite all Bevin's efforts, the proportion of women 'dilutees' never rose above 6 per cent. Yet, in general, the fragmentation of skilled jobs and the use of semi-skilled labour provoked far less unrest than in the First World War.

In addition, to hold skilled workers in priority jobs and check unauthorized movement, Bevin gained the power under the Essential Works Order 302 (EWO) of March 1941 to designate firms as engaged on 'national work'. Workers in these enterprises were virtually exempt from military service and could not leave or be dismissed without permission from locally based National Service Officers who could also discipline workers for absenteeism and other infractions. In this way the government was not only able to reserve particular skills, but could dictate where they were employed, reduce turnover, and prevent 'poaching' by rival firms. EWO employers got priority for scarce labour and fuller control over work processes (since workers had to be flexible about work customs) but lost their power of dismissal and, in order to qualify as scheduled enterprises, they had also to meet prescribed standards of working conditions *and* wages. Workers, for their part, surrendered freedom of movement in return for job security, higher pay, and better conditions. The EWO system, which gave ministry officials unprecedented powers to intervene in the internal affairs of private businesses, covered some 30,000 firms and 5.8 million workers by the end of 1941 and eventually the numbers rose to 67,500 establishments and 8.5 million workers.[8]

A special case of government-sponsored change in the labour market was dock labour. Bevin and the TGWU had long advocated reform of the port labour system, where casual employment (on a daily or half-daily basis) prevailed and unemployment had averaged 25 per cent over the period 1923–39. With the Battle of the Atlantic

[7] The success of dilution varied widely. Some regions, e.g. Belfast, were particularly resistant: B. Black, 'A triumph of voluntarism? Industrial relations and strikes in Northern Ireland in World War II', *Labour History Review*, 70(1) (April 2005).

[8] Bullock, *Ernest Bevin* II, ch. 2; Parker, *Manpower*, p. 499.

underway and enormous congestion, especially in west-coast ports like Liverpool and Glasgow, it was clear that the casual system could not handle the volume of shipping quickly enough or maintain the supply of war *matériel* and food necessary to sustain the nation. Beginning in June 1940 Bevin set up a National Dock Labour Corpora- tion with equal representation of employers and labour to administer the scheme and local joint boards to regulate labour supply. Under this framework, dockers had to register, show up for work daily, and were subject to transfer to other ports where labour was needed. Dockers on the Clyde, Mersey, and ports in the north-west became employees of the Ministry of War Transport and by mid-1941 dockers were subject to the same controls as workers in factories engaged on essential national work. While the scheme raised productivity and brought real gains for the TGWU and dockers, work discipline was harsh, working conditions and welfare amenities remained poor, and the relations of employers and workers continued to be deeply adversarial—something that produced even more disruptive effects when the post-war Labour government put the scheme on a permanent basis.[9]

At first, the Ministry of Labour (MoL) lacked the administrative capacity to fully centralize labour allocation and its powers were used sparingly. Large numbers of men and women were 'combed out' from non-essential sectors and transferred into war work. But at the end of 1940 the Manpower Requirements Committee, chaired by Sir William Beveridge, predicted a labour shortfall of over a million in the coming year. It argued that more comprehensive controls and compulsion, including the conscription of women, was the only way to meet the labour shortage. Bevin wanted to move more slowly, convinced that this was the best way to win acceptance for his policies. As a first step in March 1941 the government instructed women in the twenty–thirty-one age group to register at local labour exchanges. But Bevin was forced to ratchet up the level of compulsion when voluntary recruitment campaigns proved inadequate and female conscription was introduced in December 1941.[10] Under the National Service (No. 2) Act single women and childless widows aged twenty–thirty years were designated as 'mobile' and could be 'directed' into war work; they could also be sent to jobs far from their homes, wherever they were needed.

Women's call-up began in January 1942 with the twenty–twenty-one age group; in theory they could choose between war production, civil defence, and the military auxiliaries, but shortages meant that some intakes were simply assigned to muni- tions or the ATS (Auxiliary Territorial Service, the army auxiliary). The extension of compulsion to married women was more contested.[11] In the end, as Margaret Allen has shown, the guidelines adopted were fairly conservative, seeking where

[9] J. Phillips, 'British dock workers and the Second World War: The limits of social change', *Scottish Labour History Society Journal*, 30 (1995); *idem*, 'Class and industrial relations in Britain: The "long" mid-century and the case of port transport, *c*.1920–60', *TCBH*, 16(1) (2005).

[10] P. Summerfield, *Women Workers in the Second World War: Production and patriarchy in conflict* (London, 1984), ch. 3; S. L. Carruthers, '"Manning the factories": Propaganda and policy on the employment of women, 1939–1947', *History*, 75(244) (June 1990).

[11] Surveys revealed that most women agreed with conscription, but many were equally convinced that they were already fully occupied and would therefore be exempted. NA: RG 23/13 Wartime Social Survey: Women's Registration and Call-Up (19 March–25 April 1942).

possible to preserve 'homes' and respect conventional priorities about women's domestic roles.[12] Mothers with children under fourteen years were exempt from war work and were not required to undergo interviews before local employment committees. Childless wives were classified as 'immobile' but might be forced to take up approved local employment. However, women who could show that they kept house for a husband, father, or brother were given a 'Household R' exemption; looking after an elderly widowed mother was not grounds for this exemption. Churchill and the military chiefs also firmly opposed treating childless servicemen's wives as 'mobile', arguing that it would seriously damage morale. Regional labour markets varied a great deal and these guidelines were implemented differently according to local conditions. In the early war years, National Service Officers were reluctant to coerce married women but by 1943 at the peak of war production older women and mothers came under closer official scrutiny and many took up part-time work. All together an additional 1.5 million women (from 6.2 to 7.7 million) entered the labour force; in the vital sector of engineering and metals they eventually accounted for one-third of the workforce.

It took time to centralize labour control and to introduce what amounted to civilian conscription in all but name, but by 1942 the Manpower Budget, drawn up by the MoL not the Treasury, was a key mechanism determining every facet of the war effort. Aware of trade unionist fears, Bevin was convinced that better results could be achieved through consent than compulsion. Overall the system did secure needed supplies of labour for key areas of production, but the production front remained a continuous source of conflict and Bevin's critics were legion. Radicals demanded more drastic controls over industry and a national takeover of key economic sectors[13] and many workers complained that employers were not subject to the same compulsion. Employers, for their part, were troubled by their reduced powers to discipline workers and the threat to managerial prerogatives inherent in the spreading structures of joint consultation, especially the Regional Boards which coordinated production at the local level.[14] Bevin had succeeded in turning the MoL into a first-rate ministry and he always assumed that labour's wartime gains would become part of a new structure of industrial relations. As he announced to the TUC in May 1940: 'If our movement and class rise with all their energy now and save the people of this country from disaster, the country will always turn with confidence to the people who saved them.' 'There is nothing I am doing', he declared, 'without I am keeping an eye on its possible value when this war is over.'[15]

---

[12] M. Allen, 'The domestic ideal and the mobilization of womanpower in World War II', *Women's Studies International Forum*, 8(4) (1983). Also NA: Lab 8/380, 584, 716.

[13] In December 1941 Labour MP Jim Griffiths called for a national takeover of the armaments industry, coal, and transport during the debate on the National Service Bill. *PD* (Commons) 2 December 1941 (cols. 1039–47). In the same debate Sidney Silverman put up an amendment for immediate nationalization of all industries vital to the war effort; this was rejected, but 40 MPs voted in favour.

[14] N. Tiratsoo and J. Tomlinson, *Industrial Efficiency and State Intervention: Labour 1939–51* (London, 1993); P. Howlett, 'British business and the state during the Second World War' in J. Sakudo and T. Shiba (eds.), *World War II and the Transformation of Business Systems* (Tokyo, 1994).

[15] Bullock, *Ernest Bevin*, II, p. 20; Weiler, *Ernest Bevin*, p. 136.

THE SPREAD OF WORKPLACE ORGANIZATION
IN ENGINEERING

After the failure of the 1926 General Strike the prevailing mood in the trade union movement was largely defensive and disillusioned. Unions lost membership, shop-floor networks established during the First World War came under attack, and within a few years economic depression and mass unemployment made efforts at recovery even more difficult. By 1933 less than one worker in four belonged to a union and membership was reduced to about 4.4 million, almost 4 million below its 1920 peak. After 1934, however, the economy began to revive and trade unionism benefited from a more favourable environment, aided by accelerating rearmament in response to the threat from Nazi Germany. Thus, by the outbreak of war total union membership had reached almost 6.3 million, although it was not until 1943 that the 1920 highpoint was equalled. Almost all economic sectors saw a recovery of organized labour in these years, including staple industries like mining, textiles, shipbuilding, and steel, but the most important expansion occurred in engineering, especially in the new manufacturing regions of the south and Midlands, where unionism had previously been weak.[16] Two industries, aircraft and cars, were the backbone of this revitalization. In the 1930s Britain emerged as the leading car producer in Europe, while at the end of the decade the rearmament drive completely transformed the aircraft industry whose workforce grew roughly ten times from under 34,000 to 355,000 in the five years prior to the war.[17]

In both sectors communist organizers often played a leading role in recruiting new union members, although union leaderships typically regarded them with some suspicion as a potential threat to their own power and their ability to guarantee compliance with union-negotiated agreements. In aircraft firms like Handley Page, De Havilland, A. V. Roe, Napier's, and Hawker, the workforce was made up of highly skilled and unionized craftsmen who had managed to maintain a good deal of workplace control and job security during the depression years, bolstered by a steady supply of government contracts. With aircraft production completely transformed in the late 1930s by rapid expansion and huge profits, they moved to take advantage of the intense shortage of skilled labour, mounting a series of effective strikes over wages, dilution, and craft privileges; they also developed a vigorous shop-steward movement which formed a multi-union national committee in 1935, published its own highly successful paper, *New Propeller*, and campaigned for a national pay agreement for aircraft workers, separate from other sections of the engineering trades. The Amalgamated Engineering Union (AEU) protested this last move as a serious threat to established bargaining procedures and nothing came of it, but the activism of aircraft workers continued

---

[16] R. Price, *Labour in British Society* (London 1986); H. A. Clegg, *A History of British Trade Unions*, III: *1934–51* (Oxford, 1985; 1994); C. Wrigley (ed.), *A History of British Industrial Relations 1914–39* (Brighton, 1987).

[17] T. J. Claydon, 'The development of trade unionism among British Automobile and aircraft workers 1914–46', PhD Diss., University of Kent, 1981, p. 177; R. Whiting, *The View from Cowley: The impact of industrialization upon Oxford, 1918–39* (Oxford, 1983).

to grow in the final years of peace, finding new organizing terrain in the so-called 'shadow' factories that the government began financing in 1937 as the only way of meeting the scale of production required.[18]

Organization was much weaker in car firms, many of whose founders like Herbert Austin and Lord Nuffield were notoriously anti-union. Wages in these firms were good, the pace of work was intense, and work discipline was strict. A rash of disputes at Ford, Morris, and other car firms in the mid-1930s indicated growing militancy among a minority of workers, but overall trade union growth was modest. Immediately before the war, however, the rapid increase in government contracts began to reshape the relationship of unions and managements. The leasing of shadow factories for aero-engines, airframes, and other components to these firms which had experience with the latest mass-production methods meant that they expanded rapidly, taking on large numbers of new, semi-skilled workers who quickly became a target for union organizers. The need to satisfy rapidly changing output targets and design specifications also became a catalyst of organization, forcing managers to work more closely with unions and to cede a good deal of control to their shop-floor representatives—a trend that escalated under Bevin's new regulatory framework in the war years.

Another result of engineering's rapid growth in the late 1930s—again anticipating developments in the war years—was renewed militancy among sections of the engineering apprentices. Poorly paid and unrepresented by the unions, their relative position deteriorated as the value of their work increased. As the gulf between their wages and those of skilled workers widened and facing growing competition from semi-skilled workers, they formed their own militant guilds, some of which operated continuously into the war years, and ignited a wave of strikes which began in the Clydeside shipyards and spread to car and aircraft firms in Manchester, Coventry, and other engineering centres.[19]

Thus, the trade union movement as a whole and particularly the engineering trades entered the Second World War on an upswing. In engineering the number of unionized workers had doubled since 1933 and the rearmament-fuelled recovery had allowed unions to rebuild their local branch structures and make significant gains over national wage rates, hours, paid holidays, and—after 1937—the right to negotiate for apprentices. The context created by the war was even more favourable and, encouraged by the government's growing willingness to consult them, unions pressed for more recognition by private firms and for more influence over all factors shaping production in the workshops. The mood among engineering workers in the first two years of the war was a complicated mixture of patriotic support for government goals and growing unrest. There were very few strikes and in some sectors, especially in the critical period after Dunkirk, workers stayed almost

---

[18] R. Croucher, *Engineers at War, 1939–45* (London, 1982); N. Fishman, *The British Communist Party and the Trade Unions, 1933–45* (London, 1995).

[19] A. McKinlay, 'From industrial serf to wage-labourer: The 1937 apprentice revolt in Britain', *International Review of Social History*, 31(1) (1986); *idem*, 'The 1937 apprentices strike: Challenge "from an unexpected quarter"', *Scottish Labour History Journal*, 20 (1985).

continuously in factories to boost production and make up for the war *matériel* lost during the retreat from France. Nonetheless discontent was widespread. Conversion to war production involved numerous changes in the pricing and grading of jobs and rate-fixers were in short supply, overworked, and in some cases inexperienced. Skilled men on time-work often found themselves losing ground to piece-workers. Sometimes trouble flared up over the upgrading of trainees and semi-skilled workers onto skilled jobs without consultation; sometimes there were clashes over inadequate air-raid protection or over the payment of workers for the time they spent inactive in the shelters. Anger also erupted over unexplained production lulls and bottlenecks which were widely attributed to managerial incompetence: 'There is still no work in the Spitfire shop', an aircraft shop steward's wife wrote in her diary. 'When the enemy is at our gates the workers will be blamed for low output. The whole system is rotten ... Someone is profiteering, and one day that someone will have to pay.'[20] But, whatever the complaint, the general context of dissatisfaction was the nation's poor battlefield performance and growing concern about the direction of the war. Much has been written about the attacks on Chamberlain and the 'Guilty Men' in the press and intellectual circles; less well documented but no less important was the politicization that went on across workbenches and in factory canteens.

While union leaders strongly endorsed Bevin's moves to regulate labour and strikes were rare, especially in the period when the nation anticipated a German invasion, some workers insisted that hard-won trade union rights were being surrendered without sufficient guarantees or equal sacrifices from employers. This was especially true of areas and firms with a long tradition of labour conflict like the shipbuilding and engineering industries of Tyneside and West Scotland. 'One looked and listened in vain', Mass-Observation commented on a group of northern factories, 'for any sign of a unity binding all parties in the fight against Germany. From the men, one got the fight against management. From the management, one experienced hours of vituperation against the men ... the real war which is being fought here today is still pre-war, private and economic.'[21] 'Clydeside workers are *also* having a war of their own', noted another Mass-Observation survey: 'they cannot forget the numerous battles of the last thirty years, and cannot overcome the bitter memory of industrial insecurity in the past ten years and their distrust of the motives of managers and employers.' To J. B. Galbraith, the RIRO for the area, Scottish shipyard employers seemed equally pugnacious; some of them, he wrote, 'seem to imagine that all demarcation is obliterated as a result of the war and that they can do very much as they please'.[22]

Several of the strikes that did occur involved alleged victimization of communist shop stewards, who at this stage led the fight against what they described as employers' attempts to place the burden of the war onto the backs of workers. At Standard's Aero factory in Coventry, for example, the firing of a convenor[23] in

---

[20] Mass-Observation, diary of shop steward's wife, quoted by Croucher, *Engineers at War*, p. 147.
[21] M-O, *People in Production* (London, 1942), p. 15.
[22] M-OA: FR 600 (March 1941). Galbraith: NA: LAB 10/362, 22 March 1941. Also, NA: INF 1/292, 24 April 1941 ('Industrial Areas Campaign for Scotland').
[23] Usually the principal steward in a firm who convenes meetings of the shop stewards.

September 1940 resulted in workers taking a three-week 'holiday' (a euphemism to avoid prosecution) until he was reinstated. Still more serious was a conflict which began the same month at British Auxiliaries in Glasgow over the firing of an AEU convenor for sexually harassing a female employee. The strike lasted several weeks and there was a real danger of it igniting wider discontents and spreading to nearby firms like Beardmore's Parkhead Forge and Rolls-Royce at Hillington. Eventually the convenor was reinstated and then by agreement left voluntarily. In neither of these cases did Bevin take punitive action under Order 1305, wishing to avoid making martyrs or creating situations in which disciplined workers felt obliged to take part in sympathetic job actions. The one time, early in the war, that the no-strike order was invoked was at Swift Scales, a London engineering firm with a long history of labour troubles where a convenor had been dismissed for bad time-keeping. What forced Bevin to take action in this case, as Nina Fishman made clear, was the deliberately confrontational style of the young shop steward leader, Reg Birch, and his outright rejection of official negotiating procedures. However, by the time the case came to court in July 1941, Germany had invaded the Soviet Union, the British Communist Party (CP) had swung behind the war effort, and the offending shop stewards were treated very leniently.[24]

The Nazi–Soviet pact of August 1939 and the ousting of their popular leader, Harry Pollitt, had created havoc in the ranks of CP activists who had established a strong base in many engineering centres. Some quit the party altogether. Those who remained initially adopted the position that democracy must be defended against fascism, but that the Chamberlain government was incapable of defeating Hitler. Support for war was linked to a rejection of Britain's ruling class. This was quickly superseded by the Comintern's characterization of the conflict as an imperialist struggle and the resuscitation of Lenin's doctrine of 'revolutionary defeatism'. Motions passed by some AEU branches, trades councils, and miners' lodges endorsed this, but it was not a popular position and much of the party's 'softer' support began to erode, especially in those areas where its earlier 'popular front' orientation had boosted recruitment. Party organizers found themselves deeply torn between country and party, especially after Dunkirk and the onset of German raids against Britain's cities. They soon toned down the anti-war line and shifted to a position which called for a 'war on two fronts'. In practical terms this allowed them to focus on campaigns for better air-raid shelters, protection of working-class living standards, and the defence of trade union rights and craft practices.[25]

---

[24] Fishman, *The British Communist Party and the Trade Unions*, pp. 290–3. On the British Auxiliaries dispute, see the Circular Letters of the North West Engineering Trades Association, TD 1059/17, 23 December 1940, Mitchell Library, Glasgow. The convenor's side of the story is covered more fully in the Glasgow Trades Council minutes, 15–16 October 1940, Mitchell Library, Glasgow. On Swift Scales: MRC, TUC Papers: MSS 292/251/43 (Swift Scales Dispute, April–June 1941); NA: LAB 10/357 (London Region), 7 December 1940, 26 April 1941.
[25] K. Morgan, *Against Fascism and War: Ruptures and continuities in British communist politics 1935–41* (Manchester 1989); also, N. Branson, *History of the Communist Party of Great Britain 1927–41* (London, 1985).

The union movement as a whole did not use the CP's official anti-war position to instigate a general purge of party activists. This was particularly true of the AEU whose president, Jack Tanner, was sympathetic to left-wing militants. Communist shop stewards acted cautiously and party members continued to be influential on district committees and in local union branches, while the AEU Executive pursued a middle path, reassuring the union's right wing but continuing to value communists as shop-floor recruiters.[26] The party's major organizing work during 1940 was the People's Convention Movement which was an attempt to reinvent a popular front of anti-war critics and a range of groups dissatisfied with the government's organization of the home front. The Convention idea grew out of communist-inspired Vigilance Committees founded in London and various provincial cities to safeguard living standards and trade union rights. Labour's entry into Churchill's government, it was argued, meant that there was no longer a parliamentary outlet for dissent, making some forum for criticism all the more necessary. The Convention's original 'Six Point' platform demanded a 'people's peace' but also a 'people's government' to stiffen national resistance by pushing for higher living standards, shelter improvements, and the defence of workers' rights. It also advocated emergency powers to nationalize banks and industries, demanded friendship with the Soviet Union, and Indian independence. How a 'people's government' might be established without first disrupting the war effort was unclear; similarly, the claim that its achievement would motivate German workers to overthrow Hitler reflected little grasp of conditions or the mood in Nazi Germany. Celia Fremlin, who reported on it for Mass-Observation, concluded that the Convention expressed people's vague 'hope that somehow a way would be found out of the present mess'.[27]

In the autumn of 1940, as the Blitz intensified, Convention supporters campaigned with some success in factories, community groups, and local Labour Party branches. J. T. Murphy wrote that the Convention generated 'Much discussion both in the workshop and trade union branches' and calculated that it had 300 supporters in his London factory alone.[28] Though originally scheduled to take place at the Manchester Free Trade Hall, like its Chartist predecessor a century before, it was moved to London after German raids damaged the hall. Some 2,234 delegates turned up, more than the organizers ever dreamed. Over 45 per cent came from the London area; most were young, male, and working class; most were trade unionists, but there were contingents from tenants' groups, cooperatives, youth organizations, teachers, shelter committees, and various left-wing political groups, including members of the Peace Pledge Union. Among the Convention's supporters were the prominent churchmen Mervyn Stockwood and Hewlett Johnson, novelist Walter Greenwood, the popular band leader Lew Stone, and actor Michael

---

[26] Fishman, *The British Communist Party and the Trade Unions*, p. 266.

[27] A. Calder and D. Sheridan (eds.), *Speak for Yourself: A Mass-Observation anthology, 1937–49* (London 1984), pp. 199–202.

[28] J. T. Murphy, *Victory Production* (London, 1942), pp. 39–43. Murphy, one of the founders of the CP but now a critic, spent 17 months as a turner and then as an inspector in aircraft factories in the London area.

Redgrave. Claims that it represented more than a million workers were vastly inflated, but the gathering was no mean feat at a time of constant raids.

The government's shocked reaction was swift. Police surveillance of communists increased and the party's newspaper, the *Daily Worker*, was banned and remained so until September 1942, long after the Soviet Union became an ally. Most of the general public were hostile to 'the People's Reichstag', as the *Daily Herald* called it, viewing it as a defeatist manoeuvre designed to erode support for the war. The *Daily Mirror* dismissed it as anti-British, but also noted that people had 'expected the Labour ministers in the government to be their champions. They are disappointed in them.'[29] As for the trade union movement, Citrine took steps to discipline trades councils that had participated. Vic Feather, who played a large role in the TUC's efforts to police the trades councils, derided it as a communist swindle 'along the same lines of the Popular Front organizations, established to catch the politically unwary'.[30] The BBC also responded, trying to implement a ban against artists, writers, and musicians who participated, but it quickly ran into a firestorm of protests from other broadcasters whose services it valued. With few exceptions the press also sided with the banned artists, as did Actors' Equity, and the BBC was forced to retreat and rescind the ban.[31] As it happened, the Convention was an end not a beginning. The movement was soon discontinued, in part because delegates 'did not know what to do next' or how to achieve their programme and also because the CP was fearful of being suppressed altogether.[32] Most importantly, within six months Hitler's invasion of Russia had totally transformed the CP's relationship to the war leading some local Convention groups to reconstitute as Anglo-Soviet Friendship committees.

1942 was a crucial year in every respect. On the battlefield Britain suffered some of her worst defeats at Singapore and Tobruk. Confidence in Churchill's leadership declined sharply and even within his own circle of aides there were doubts that he could continue in power much longer without a battlefield success. A March 1942 BIPO poll revealed that half of people questioned were dissatisfied and only 35 per cent satisfied with the government's conduct of the war. On the production front

---

[29] *Daily Herald*, 14 January 1941; *Daily Mirror*, 16 January 1941.
[30] V. Feather, 'Report on the People's Convention', MSS 292/778.29/1, 'People's Vigilance Committees and People's Convention 1940–41', TUC Papers MRC (Warwick). For the TUC's disciplining of trades councils: TUC Papers, MRC (Warwick University): MSS 292/778.29/1 (People's Vigilance Committees and People's Convention 1940–41); MSS 292/778.29/2 (Women's Parliaments); MSS 292/79B/36 (Birmingham Trades Council 1927–44); MSS 292/777/3 (Communism and Trades Councils 1939–41); MSS 292/777/4 (Communism and Trades Councils 1941–42); MSS 292/777/5 (Communism and Trades Councils 1942–49); MSS 292/79B/27 (Bethnal Green and Stepney Trades Council); MSS 292/777/14 (Manchester and Salford Trades Council 1940–41); MSS 292/79M/2 (Manchester and Salford Trades Council 1940).
[31] R. Mackay, '"An abominable precedent": The BBC's ban on pacifists in the Second World War', *Contemporary British History*, 20(4) (December 2006).
[32] J. T. Murphy, *Victory Production* (London, 1942), pp. 43–4; Morgan, *Against Fascism and War*, pp. 205–6; J. Hinton, 'Killing the People's Convention: A letter from Palme Dutt to Harry Pollitt', *Bulletin of the Society for Labour History*, 39 (Autumn 1979). For a breakdown of the groups participating in the Convention: CP/ORG/MISC/1/8 CPGB Archive, The Labour History Archive and Study Centre, Manchester.

too, it was a decisive year. Bevin's policies for an integrated war economy began to take full effect and hundreds of thousands of new, inexperienced workers entered war production, bringing dramatic changes to those industries. But at the same time, complaints in Parliament and the press about inefficiency in the war industries reached new highs, fuelling a bitter climate of accusation and counter-accusation about slack workers and selfish or incompetent employers. Some critics gave priority to the need for more central planning and coordination at the top, a unified Ministry of Production to direct and link the various supply ministries; others prioritized decentralization and the need to devolve more power on the trade associations of business groups or regional production boards of employers and trade unionists—the latter option was especially favoured by trade unionists as a way of augmenting their influence throughout the war economy.

Bevin operated skilfully in the midst of all this to frustrate Lord Beaverbrook's ambition to make himself the tsar of war production and to prevent excessive incorporation of the unions into the state apparatus; he also used the growing unrest about inefficiency and accusations of managerial incompetence as a wedge to carry out an ambitious programme to extend joint consultation down to the level of individual firms. The notion of creating formal plant-level structures to consult workers over ways to improve productivity was a radical, unprecedented step. When Bevin first floated the idea in October 1940, it encountered opposition from most employers, protective of managerial prerogatives, and trade union officials, who were fearful that such committees might usurp normal union activities; the CP also rejected it as another effort to co-opt workers and erode their basic rights. But the public's growing concern about production shortfalls created a more favourable context for the experiment. By the autumn of 1941 some employers had begun to endorse production committees, while a few trade unionists also began to rally around the idea, especially Jack Tanner, the outspoken president of the AEU, who at his union's annual conference in June 1941 bitterly attacked managerial failures and called for the direct involvement of workers in production decisions. Soon after, criticized by the Engineering Employers' Association, he instructed AEU officials to collect substantiating evidence from their local branches and some 3,000 replies flowed in from AEU shop stewards. A few months later in October, the communist-led Engineering and Allied Trades Shop Stewards National Council, galvanized into action by the Soviet entry into the war, organized a production conference at London's Stoll theatre. Attended by over 1,200 delegates, it captured the headlines and won sympathetic coverage in the popular press. Speaker after speaker detailed their experiences of production bottlenecks and other problems, demanding factory-level committees to address the problems. It was the largest gathering of shop stewards in the war and illustrated their growing power within the union movement.

It was this grass-roots pressure, James Hinton convincingly argues, that allowed Bevin to wear down resistance both among employers and the TUC and to draft a compromise.[33] The unilateral decision to create committees in the government's

---

[33] J. Hinton, *Shop Floor Citizens: Engineering democracy in 1940s Britain* (Aldershot, 1994). Also, Croucher, *Engineers at War*, pp. 149–74; Clegg, *A History of British Trade Unions*, III, pp. 227–39.

Royal Ordnance Factories also helped to force the hands of private engineering companies. Finally, in March 1942 an agreement was signed between the AEU and the Engineering Employers' Federation establishing Joint Production Committees (JPCs) in firms with over 150 workers; very quickly many smaller companies also introduced them. By the end of the year over 2,000 committees existed and in 1943 the number reached 4,500 according to one estimate.[34] Composed of an equal number of management representatives and elected workers, their function was an advisory one: to help maximize production and to promote cooperation in resolving technical, organizational, and other kinds of problems that impeded output. Hinton has calculated that roughly 20,000 trade unionists served on them, many of them young activists who became influential figures in the post-war trade union movement.[35]

How much impact JPCs had on production is difficult to gauge. For one thing, the numbers in operation varied greatly from one region to another. By July 1943, according to one estimate, they existed in 65–70 per cent of all firms in engineering and allied industries; but the statistics ranged from 92 per cent of firms in London and the south-east to 35 per cent in Scotland. In general, participation was far greater in the south and the Midlands than the old industrial centres of Scotland and the north.[36] A great many committees seem to have met a few times and then petered out altogether. Their involvement in technical production issues also varied, depending on the readiness of employers to share information and listen to suggestions as well as the experience and effectiveness of the workers' delegates. Officially JPCs were barred from taking up collective bargaining issues, but in practice it was very difficult to separate them from productivity discussions, especially if the workers' representatives were shop stewards. This was the case at Albion Motors outside Glasgow, which built heavy trucks and a variety of munitions; here bonus earnings and company limitation of them were repeatedly debated until in June 1943 all the workers' delegates resigned when the company chairman ruled that a bonus issue be excluded from the JPC's agenda.[37] Some JPCs addressed relatively minor changes that could have been dealt with previously by shop stewards; others played a larger and more constructive role. David Thoms points to two contrasting examples: the JPC at the Humber-Hillman works in Coventry had a major effect on labour flexibility through a system of mobile gangs

---

[34] Yard Committees and Pit Production Committees were also established in shipbuilding and coal mining.

[35] Hinton, *Shop Floor Citizens*, p. 88.

[36] *Ibid.* pp. 80–3. J. Tomlinson, 'Productivity, joint consultation and human relations in post-war Britain: The Attlee government and the workplace' in J. Melling and A. McKinlay (eds.), *Management, Labour, and Industrial Politics in Modern Europe: The quest for productivity growth in Britain, Germany, and Sweden during the twentieth century* (Aldershot, 1996), p. 28. On the efforts, blocked by employers, to include draughtsmen, clerical and administrative workers in JPCs, see TUC Papers, MRC (Warwick) MSS 292/106.44/2 (Joint Works Production Committees 1941–42).There was also some pressure in 1943 for JPCs among local government workers, e.g. in Lambeth, London. This was firmly resisted, in this case by the local Labour Party: TUC Papers MS 292/106.44/3 (Joint Production Works Committees 1942–43).

[37] P. Bain and T. Gorman, 'Keeping the home fires burning: The Albion shop stewards in the Second World War', *Socialist History*, 7 (1995), 55–9.

which could be dispatched wherever they were most needed, while the committee at the huge Castle Bromwich aircraft plant in Birmingham had almost nothing to show for its efforts by the end of 1943.[38] On balance, the committees probably did help to promote understanding and a more co-operative climate between managers and workers in many firms; but where there was little trust to begin with, they quickly replicated old divisions and provided an additional forum in which to vent them.

A large proportion of the time of JPCs was devoted to welfare and absenteeism, but the paucity of women delegates often made the committees insufficiently responsive to the problems of wives and mothers trying to cope with the multiple burdens of work, domestic chores, and child-raising. Many committees also became increasingly involved in discipline—which put stress upon their relations with fellow workers and provoked accusations that they had become management stooges. Hugh Scanlon, the Engineers leader of the 1970s and then a communist steward at Metro-Vickers in Manchester, admitted: 'We broke more strikes than we made ... We had a committee that sat in judgment on the workers—if they were late, absent without good knowledge, we could send them to the National Service Officer—who in extreme cases could send them to prison. That's the extent the trade union movement became involved in the war effort ... I'm not saying the workers gained. I'm saying production increased.'[39] Not surprisingly, after an initial surge of enthusiasm, workers' interest in them declined: participation in elections dropped off and they risked being seen as remote or as too cosy with management.

Once Bevin's regulatory framework for manpower took shape, conditions in the war industries began to change rapidly. With labour a scarce commodity and official propaganda emphasizing 'fair shares' and 'equal sacrifice', a loosening of industrial discipline was inevitable. In any case the huge influx of new workers, many of them women and reluctant conscripts with little factory experience, could not be handled in the same old ways. Bevin's policies placed real restraints on workers: they were tied to their jobs, could be directed anywhere by the MoL and, officially at least, they no longer had the strike weapon to achieve their ends. But, if anything, wartime arrangements placed even more restraints and obligations on employers. Their power to hire and fire was seriously eroded and, if operating an EWO, they came under strong official pressure to meet certain standards in working conditions and welfare facilities. Such firms had to observe union-negotiated pay rates and to register instances of dilution and departures from traditional work practices. Order 1305, which banned strikes, also gave unions de facto recognition—even where firms had refused to grant it before—by providing for compulsory arbitration of disputes. In these cases union officials could appeal to

---

[38] D. Thoms, *War, Industry, and Society: The Midlands, 1939–45* (London, 1989), p. 75.

[39] M. Crowley, 'Communist engineers and the Second World War in Manchester', *North West Labour History*, 22 (1997–8), 65. At another Vickers-Armstrong plant management largely ignored the nine JPCs that were set up: NA: BT 28/377 ('Report on waste etc at Vickers-Armstrong (Aircraft) Ltd, Weybridge', March–May 1943).

Regional Industrial Relations Officers to intervene, in effect forcing managements to recognize them and extracting concessions without strikes. By the war's end all but 2 million out of the nation's 17.5 million workers were covered by voluntary or statutory collective bargaining agreements.

The pace of production also tilted the workplace balance of power to labour's advantage. Employers and managers were under heavy pressure to meet output targets and keep up with frequent changes in product designs; to do so they needed co-operative relationships with unions and workers. Also government cost-plus contracts reduced employer concerns about rising wages, the emphasis being more on production than cost containment. Shop stewards were increasingly consulted to facilitate dilution, the introduction of new technologies, and reorganization of work practices. As Arthur Exell, a steward at Morris Radiators in Oxford, wrote: 'everyone felt confident...we could feel our feet a bit'.[40] The aid of workers' committees was increasingly sought to help with absenteeism. At Morris, for example, Exell was given a green light to unionize women workers in return for help in reducing absentee rates. Government-appointed National Service Officers were available to punish serious offenders and could even send them to jail, but in most instances employers found it easier to invite the cooperation of workers' representatives—making labour discipline an area of joint regulation rather than an employer prerogative. Joint control over canteens became a frequent issue, not simply because of the preoccupation with food in these rationed years, but because they became an important centre of factory social life and a place where meetings (including political meetings in some cases[41]) took place. Having a say over these spaces became an important reflection of workers' position within a firm.

The shop-floor atmosphere grew more relaxed: workers sang, whistled, and talked back to the foreman without fear of arbitrary dismissal. 'We had women in there, and that was the start of us getting our tea-breaks and smoking, which we never had before.'[42] To bolster morale and ease the strain of long shifts, compulsory overtime, and boring repetitive jobs, BBC programmes such as 'Music While You Work' were broadcast to workshops over Tannoy loudspeakers, while employers greatly expanded welfare facilities, lunchtime entertainments, and film shows. Many workers, especially those housed in lodgings or hostels, had little social life outside their factory and so welfare officers and workers' committees became closely involved in recreational activities. At Morris, Arthur Exell recalled, there were social evenings and dances every week, big dances at the Town Hall three or four times a year, mealtime variety shows, and boat trips on the Thames.[43] All of these changes helped to bolster morale and facilitated the integration of new workers into factories

---

[40] A. Exell, 'Morris Motors in the 1940s', *HWJ*, 9 (Spring 1980), 67–8.

[41] NA: LAB 10/170 ('Question of forbidding political meetings in factories, 1941–1944'). Separate dining rooms and even shelter arrangements for managers, clerical staff, and shop-floor workers remained in some firms. On one aircraft factory in 1941: M. Benney, *Almost a Gentleman* (London, 1966), p. 142.

[42] L. Holden, 'Think of me simply as the Skipper: Industrial relations at Vauxhalls, 1920–1950', *Oral History*, 9(2) (Autumn 1981), 29.

[43] Exell, 'Morris Motors in the 1940s'. On 'Music While You Work' see M-OA: FR 348 (August 1940).

previously dominated by skilled craftsmen. In general, dilution caused fewer problems than in the First World War, but the ethos of community should not be exaggerated. In the case of Irish and West Indian workers, for example, it is clear that the wartime context did little to shake old prejudices and divisions.

Some 200,000 crossed the Irish Sea to work in Britain (notwithstanding Eire's neutrality), two-thirds of them male. The vast majority of women went into munitions, while men worked mostly in agriculture or construction at least until the peak of war production in 1943. They made a large and seldom acknowledged contribution to Britain's war effort, but encountered a good deal of prejudice.[44] Very few Irish males were employed in the shipyards and those mostly on the Clyde; they could not work on the south coast for security reasons and employers in the north-east did not want them. They had the least difficulties in cities like Cardiff or London with a sizeable Irish population, but faced more resistance in the Midlands where no significant Irish community existed. Some of this prejudice stemmed from Eire's neutrality and the IRA bombing campaign at the beginning of the war,[45] but mostly it reflected ingrained stereotypes about their being dirty, heavy drinkers, and prone to violence. A far smaller group of workers from the Caribbean[46] also encountered considerable hostility in munitions factories. A plan to employ fifty-nine Jamaicans at Napiers aero-engine factory on Merseyside was blocked by the firm 'partly on grounds of colour and partly on the ground of their alleged unsuitability', while in February 1943 official pressure was required to get De Havillands to take twenty-eight black trainees; the firm argued that white workers had insisted that the West Indians should not be employed on skilled work and had threatened to walk out. There were also problems at the Kirkby and Fazakerley Royal Ordnance factories (ROFs), where West Indian technicians protested poor conditions, prejudice from fellow workers, and their difficulty in securing promotions. MoL officials admitted that the superintendents of these ordnance factories were worried that the promotion of Jamaicans, even if well-qualified, to positions of foremen would fuel the resentments of white workers. Ford's at Dagenham was said to exclude workers of colour, so was Vickers, while a memorandum from headquarters to local managers of Government Training Centres admitted to operating a tacit colour bar: 'We have been in the habit of

---

[44] E. Delaney, *Demography and Society: Irish migration to Britain, 1921–1971* (Liverpool, 2000), ch. 3; B. Girvan and G. Roberts (eds.), *Ireland and the Second World War* (Dublin, 2000). On Tyneside where there was an established Irish community and community relations were good, see Craig Armstrong, 'Aliens in wartime: A case study of Tyneside 1939–1945', *Immigrants and Minorities*, 25(2) (July 2007).

[45] One IRA bombing in Coventry in late August 1939 left five dead and many others seriously injured. 'About two thousand men employed at the Armstrong-Whitworth aircraft factory', reported the local Labour Conciliation Officer, 'considered a resolution urging refusal to work with Irishmen but this was rejected in favour of a public demonstration.' Trade union district committees were urged to 'assist the police in the interrogation of suspects', while Coventry's Irish community met 'to consider steps to identify and organize loyalists and to eliminate IRA sympathizers' (LAB 10/348, 2 September 1939).

[46] Aside from those in the armed forces, there were about 2,000 men evenly divided between forestry and munitions.

accepting only those men whose colour is not too pronounced, on the assumption that less prejudice is likely to be aroused in their case.'[47]

In both cases billeting in private homes was very difficult. The minutes of a Home Office meeting in September 1943 acknowledged that 'the question of billeting was a difficulty everywhere for coloured people'.[48] Tacit complicity with the segregationist practices of the American military also led to exclusions from restaurants and dance halls; even the star cricketer Learie Constantine, employed by the MoL to supervise West Indian volunteers, was denied a room in the Imperial Hotel at Russell Square—ostensibly because American guests might object.[49] The authorities mostly preferred to concentrate Caribbean workers where separate hostels and welfare services could be established. Lodgings were also a constant problem for Irish workers. The Ministry of Health, it was said, 'had an unwritten but rigid rule that compulsory billeting was never to be used, even as a threat, where Irish workers were concerned, as feelings ran so high'.[50] 'There was no social life', one man wrote. 'Since the locals were so distant towards us, we could not go into their houses and talk to them as people do in Ireland, so when I returned from work I either sat on my bed in silence, wrote letters to my friends, or tried to kill time in some simple way.'[51] Employers complained that, once workers took leave in Ireland, many failed to return.

The new wartime environment of production favoured the growth of trade unionism and the extension of shop-floor networks. Bevin's own TGWU was especially active in recruiting semi-skilled war-workers, many of them women, while the AEU's rapid growth followed from its decision to admit women in January 1943. Employers found themselves increasingly on the defensive, forced to make concessions because of what they regarded as the partnership between state agencies and the unions. The number of shop stewards grew rapidly, more than doubling in the engineering and metals sector—and this figure omits many who acted unofficially without union accreditation. Some firms preferred informal recognition of an individual rather than the office, believing that this would make it easier to reverse concessions at a later date. Shop stewards were the vital NCOs of the union movement to whom unions turned to monitor changing pay rates and working conditions, facilitate dilution, and check that union dues were

[47] M. Sherwood, *Many Struggles: West Indian workers and service personnel in Britain, 1939–45* (London, 1985), pp. 66–74; D. Watson, 'Research note: Black workers in London in the 1940s', *Historical Studies in Industrial Relations*, 1 (March 1996), 154–5. As for the trade unions, the Boilermakers' Society was resistant to West Indian engineers in the shipyards, but other unions were more accommodating. West Indian craftsmen and trainees do seem to have joined unions, including the AEU, and in some cases e.g. the electricians served on committees.

[48] NA: HO 45/24748 Minutes, 17 September 1943.

[49] J. Flint, 'Scandal at the Bristol Hotel: Some thoughts on racial discrimination in Britain and West Africa and its relationship to the planning of decolonisation, 1939–47', *Journal of Imperial and Commonwealth History*, 12 (May 1983).

[50] A. V. Judges, 'Irish labour in Great Britain 1939–45', p. 43, NA: LAB 8/1528. Also, K. Lunn, '"Good for a few hundreds at least": Irish labour recruitment in Great Britain during the Second World War' in P. Buckland and J. Belchem (eds.), *The Irish in British Labour History*, Conference Proceedings in Irish History, no. 1 (University of Liverpool, 1993).

[51] C. Holmes, *John Bull's Island* (London, 1988), p. 178.

paid. In engineering especially, national pay agreements had to be interpreted at
the plant level, while constant bargaining was needed over changes in product
design, the introduction of new technologies, and the reorganization of work
practices and layouts. Beyond this, they got involved in a range of welfare issues:
offering advice over military deferments and government allowances, counselling
workers over job transfers and appearances before Appeals Boards, and interven-
ing in matters of hostel accommodation and transport. Many stewards were
themselves young and inexperienced. Some did not know how to respond to
managerial initiatives, and some found it difficult to control workers who had
recently joined a union and were quickly frustrated by the slowness of standard
bargaining procedures. In Coventry Jack Jones, then the TGWU's District
Organizer, developed 'teach-ins, mock negotiating sessions, and educational
courses' for the training of new stewards but recruits mostly gained experience
on the job.[52] These activities were very time-consuming and often lowered their
earnings significantly. Some firms, it is true, compensated stewards for time spent
in meetings and sometimes fellow workers found ways to help out, although
trouble could result from this. At Austin Aero in Birmingham, for example, three
workers, including a shop steward, were dismissed for irregular recording of work
in November 1942. Two of the men had booked some of their work to the
steward, knowing that his heavy time commitment had hurt him financially.
Some 7,000 workers walked off the job, and the dispute was resolved by a local
Appeals Board which reinstated the men.[53]

In many aircraft and engineering firms, CP activists, like Exell, played a leading role
in building these networks. Hitler's invasion of the Soviet Union had turned them
into enthusiastic champions of the war effort; the drive to maximize production
replaced their earlier focus on defending trade practices and customary rights. The
middle years of the war saw the party's most rapid growth ever: membership went
from around 18,000 in September 1939 to 46,000 by March 1942 and by June
reached an all-time high of 60,000. During 1942 membership in the Midlands region,
which included Coventry, Birmingham, and the Black Country, is estimated to have
quintupled. Factory cells multiplied very rapidly—in Coventry, for example, the
number went from eighteen in December 1941 to forty the following September.[54]
Organizers, who already worked long hours, found themselves both exhilarated and
exhausted by the continual round of activities: Russia Weeks, Anglo-Soviet Friendship
rallies, factory-gate meetings, shop-steward work, sessions at the party's industrial

[52] Jack Jones, *Union Man* (London, 1986), p. 93.
[53] NA: LAB 10/352 (Midland Region), 21 November 1942.
[54] J. Hinton, 'Coventry communism: A study of factory politics in the Second World War', *HWJ*,
10(1) (Autumn 1980), 95. In 1942 the party had 6 delegates on the AEU's National Committee. In
Birmingham it boasted 20 members of AEU district committees, 35 convenors, and some 200 shop
stewards and branch officials. Etheridge Papers, MRC (Warwick), quoted in S. Jefferys, 'The changing
face of conflict: Shopfloor organization at Longbridge, 1930–1980' in M. Terry and P. K. Edwards
(eds.), *Shopfloor Politics and Job Controls: The post-war engineering industry* (Oxford, 1988), p. 60. In
Manchester there were 5 CP delegates on an AEU District Committee of 31 members and 4 additional
sympathizers whose votes could be relied upon: Crowley, 'Communist engineers and the Second
World War in Manchester', p. 66; Fishman, *The British Communist Party and the Trade Unions*, ch. 11.

bureaux, Second Front demonstrations, and much more. There were dues to collect, bookkeeping and reporting tasks, large numbers of pamphlets, fliers, and posters to be distributed, and sales of the *Daily Worker* once the publication ban was lifted. Many factories also had regular political discussion groups and lunchtime lectures. At Morris Radiators in Oxford, for example, the party ran Thursday-night education classes on Marxism and organized a bookshop and a factory library for about 200–300 borrowers. At Fairey Aviation in Manchester, a party member recalled: 'There was a personal feeling you had. I felt in many respects that the party owned the factory. They were only too anxious to come to some kind of arrangement with us. They agreed to have the Red Army choir in the canteen. It was almost unheard of.'[55] While most workers were sympathetic to the production drive, there were pockets of resistance among older craftsmen with vivid memories of past battles. 'A considerable body of the rank and file in the workshops', the Glasgow industrial relations officer, Galbraith, reported, 'seem to resent the invocation to do more from the very men who, not so long ago, were advocating a policy of indifference as increased production was dangerous to the workers.'[56] As war strain and the number of disputes increased, shop stewards found themselves more and more in the uncomfortable position of trying to mediate and prise concessions from employers while doing everything possible to avoid strikes and work stoppages.

The specific impetus for the growth of shop-floor networks varied. Sometimes—in many Clydeside firms, for example—it was a matter of rebuilding workplace organization that had existed before, but had been decimated during the depression. Elsewhere—for example, the car and machine tool firms of Coventry, Luton, and Oxford where unions had been weak pre-war—the emergence of a small group of shop stewards often preceded the recruitment of significant numbers of new union members. Sometimes activity spread to car firms from the shadow aircraft factories that they operated. At Vauxhall's in Luton it was militants in the Tank Shop who were a catalyst for organizing other parts of the firm, while communist stewards at Napier's worked hard to penetrate the small engineering firms in London's Great West Road area. At times, non-union firms were deliberately sent activists by pro-union staffs in local labour exchange offices; this was how the tool-room at Ford's Trafford Park aero-engine factory became full of militants. With skilled labour in such short supply, many employers found they had little choice but to take known activists whom they would have refused in peacetime. Regional labour transfers could also provide the spark when new workers came from highly organized areas with higher rates of pay. Tinplate workers brought from South Wales were the catalyst at the Morris Engines Foundry in Coventry, while the transfer of well-paid sheet-metal workers from Wolverton had the same effect at Morris Radiators in Oxford. Efforts were also made by militant stewards

---

[55] Exell, 'Morris Motors in the 1940s'. Crowley, 'Communist engineers and the Second World War in Manchester', p. 68.

[56] NA: LAB 10/362, 25 October 1941; also Croucher, *Engineers at War, 1939–45*, pp. 171–2. In August 1942 Galbraith was still reporting a 'considerable body of opinion' among older workers 'who thought it the duty of the Trade Unions to extract as much as possible from the employers, and they take the view that even in wartime this should be the policy of the organizations': NA: LAB 10/363, 1 August 1942.

to move beyond their own solid factory base to build links with neighbouring plants via area committees and to develop combine committees that included representation from the different plants run by large firms like English Electric, Vickers, and Fairey Aviation.[57]

In his autobiography Jack Jones described the war as 'a long series of victories'.[58] Between 1940 and the peak of war production in 1943 total union membership grew by 1.5 million, notwithstanding the absence of many men in the armed forces. The fastest growth was in the engineering and metals sector with the TGWU expanding from 700,000 to over 1 million members and the AEU more than doubling its size from 334,000 at the start of the war to a high of 825,000. Unions emerged from the war confident about their future role and while membership declined slightly at the war's end, it soon recovered, reaching new highs in the late 1940s. But organized labour's gains were uneven, even within some industries. There were also considerable differences in the density of union membership in different firms: in the car industry, for example, some firms like Standard Motors were overwhelmingly unionized, while at Morris and Austin the figure was closer to 30 and 50 per cent respectively, and at the American-owned Ford and Vauxhall less than 25 per cent. But, despite efforts to dislodge them, the shop-floor organizations that grew so rapidly in the war years largely survived; they were too entrenched to be easily dismantled, especially in a labour market that remained buoyant in the post-war years.[59]

As for the most ambitious experiment to extend joint consultation in the war years, the JPCs, most historians have viewed their accomplishments as fairly meagre. Bevin hoped they would become part of a permanent structure of joint consultation, but most employers saw them only as temporary advisory bodies—a way of defusing tensions and improving industrial relations,[60] not as rungs on the ladder of power-sharing—while union leaders, though in favour of extending the experiment after the war, were also ambivalent suspecting that they could fall under

---

[57] Bill Knox and Alan McKinlay, '"Pests to management": Engineering shop stewards on Clydeside, 1939–45', *Journal of Scottish Labour History*, 30 (1995). S. Tolliday, 'Government, employers and shopfloor organization in the British motor industry' in S. Tolliday and J. Zeitlin (eds.), *Shop Floor Bargaining and the State: Historical and comparative perspectives* (Cambridge, 1985), pp. 112–14. Claydon, 'The development of trade unionism among British automobile and aircraft workers', pp. 125ff.; Fishman, *The British Communist Party and the Trade Unions*, p. 305; Exell, 'Morris Motors in the 1940s', p. 91. On combine committees, see E. and R. Frow, *Engineering Struggles* (Manchester, 1982), ch. 5. On the migration of communists from the depressed north to the south and Midlands in the 1930s and later, see K. Morgan, G. Cohen, and A. Flinn, *Communists and British Society 1920–1991* (London, 2007), esp. pp. 31–48.

[58] Jones, *Union Man*, p. 113.

[59] Thus, in 1950 70% of the 20,000 workers at Austin's Longbridge plant were unionized in 1950 and 220 shop stewards represented them: Jefferys, 'The changing face of conflict: Shopfloor organization at Longbridge', p. 66. Also, N. Tiratsoo, 'The motor car industry' in H. Mercer, N. Rollings, and J. D. Tomlinson (eds.), *Labour Governments and Private Industry: The experience of 1945–51* (Edinburgh, 1992). For Clydeside and employer anti-unionism: A. McKinlay, 'Management and workplace trade unionism: Clydeside engineering, 1945–57' in J. Melling and A. McKinlay (eds.), *Management, Labour, and Industrial Politics in Modern Europe: The quest for productivity growth in Britain, Germany, and Sweden during the twentieth century* (Aldershot, 1996).

[60] North West Engineering Trades Employers' Association, Circular Letters TD 1059/7/30 (Mitchell Library, Glasgow) e.g. 8 July, 20 July, 3 October 1942.

the sway of activists who were difficult to control. The CP, though strongly supportive of the committees during the war, also did little to flesh out ideas about industrial democracy or indicate how it should work in a private enterprise system. And when the party reorganized in 1944, it abruptly dismantled much of the factory organization it had patiently built up. Above all, it had proven difficult to sustain workers' interest in the committees; most workers did not want a partnership with management, viewing their functions and interests as distinct and separate. The JPCs reflected the special circumstances of wartime and Labour's effort to revive them in the late 1940s was largely a failure, with employers and labour, in Hinton's phrase, 'going through the motions'.[61] For some post-war union leaders like Jack Jones and Hugh Scanlon they continued to symbolize the potential for a different kind of industrial relations structure, but the hope that they would lead to some form of industrial democracy proved illusory.

STRIKES AND INDUSTRIAL CONFLICT

For several decades after the Second World War, popular memory and most scholars depicted the early 1940s as a period of industrial harmony, when capital and labour put aside their differences and focused on rescuing the nation from defeat. The number of days lost to strikes, it was pointed out, was about half that of the shorter First World War and there was nothing comparable to the syndicalist unrest that swept the country, no equivalent to Red Clydeside in 1916. However, while most industrial disputes in the Second World War were small scale and of short duration, the period was far from peaceful and the total number of strikes was significantly higher than in the previous war. This simple fact does not contradict claims of national unity in fighting the war, nor does it detract from the mostly favourable verdicts on Bevin's handling of labour—indeed, in many ways it illustrates his successful combination of statutory controls and their flexible implementation. For, although all disputes were subject to arbitration and strikes and lockouts were prohibited under Order 1305, in practice the government preferred to settle illegal labour actions by persuasion rather than by prosecution. Such forbearance may well have produced a higher incidence of strikes, but it acted as an important safety-valve and undoubtedly helped avert more serious unrest.[62]

If we take all industries for the period 1940–4, certain general trends are apparent. The incidence of strikes rose with each year of the war and was markedly

[61] Hinton, *Shop Floor Citizens*, ch. 10; Tiratsoo and Tomlinson, *Industrial Efficiency and State Intervention: Labour 1939–51*; Tomlinson, 'Productivity, joint consultation and human relations in post-war Britain: The Attlee government and the workplace'; also TUC Papers, MRC (Warwick) MS 292/106.44/4 ('Joint production Works Committees 1943–46').

[62] NA: LAB 10/153, Bevin to Hodges, 29 October 1941 described most strikes as an acceptable 'safety-valve and a reaction to wartime conditions accelerated by strain and fatigue'. Between 1915 and 1918 there were 3,099 recorded strikes, involving over 2 million workers, for a total of almost 17 million lost workdays. Between 1940 and 1944 there were 7,455 recorded strikes, involving nearly 2.5 million workers, for a little over 9 million workdays lost: Clegg, *A History of British Trade Unions*, III, p. 240.

higher in 1944, although 90 per cent lasted under a week. Clearly, disputes cannot always be pigeon-holed under a single cause; they often result from multiple grievances which a specific cause triggers into action. But official statistics classified 56 per cent of all stoppages as wage disputes, compared to under 39 per cent in 1938; another 23 per cent were attributed to discipline and work rules. Very few arose over compulsory overtime or the greatly extended hours that workers were called upon to put in, while the sharpest drop from pre-war statistics was in strikes over trade union rights, demarcation, and job classification. This does not mean that dilution was accomplished easily or produced little conflict, but only rarely did it ignite strike action—even in the case of the boilermakers who staunchly and successfully blocked government efforts. During the war years workers could and did draw upon a whole repertoire of job actions short of strikes, including work-to-rule, overtime bans, absenteeism, and brief walkouts lasting only a few hours. But the figures do indicate the extent to which unions and workers cooperated and accepted Bevin's promises of post-war restoration of trade practices. Similarly, aggregate data on the ways in which strikes were settled underscore the success of Bevin's combination of voluntarism and controls. Fifty-one per cent were settled on the basis of direct negotiations between workers and employers or their representatives, a figure not that much different from pre-war.[63]

The upward curve of strike activity has, broadly speaking, been interpreted in two different ways. P. Inman, the official historian of the munitions industries, viewed it chiefly as a reflection of changing war circumstances. The fall of France, an anticipated German invasion, and the bombing of British cities produced, she argued, a patriotic response in 1940 and 1941, labour's 'Dunkirk effect'. Any cessation of work in this period of extreme danger seemed a betrayal of the nation, even though public criticism of employers and political leaders was often intense. As a result fewer days were lost to strikes in 1940 than in any other year since the century began. Higher strike activity in later years, Inman suggested, reflected increasing war fatigue and impatience at the continued sacrifices labour was called upon to make. With an improving situation on the battlefield, the social cohesion of the Blitz period became frayed and workers were less inclined to put patriotism before sectional interests. By contrast, Richard Croucher, the historian of the engineering trades, has interpreted rising strike statistics as a sign of increasing working-class radicalization and militancy. Challenging older mythology about industrial peace, he describes the situation as one of growing conflict. As the war continued, Croucher argues, engineers shifted from mostly defensive actions to larger 'offensive' strikes, covering more firms and sometimes extending over several regions, that sought to redefine the balance between workers and management and to make permanent the gains that workers had achieved.[64]

[63] C. Wrigley, 'The Second World War and state intervention in industrial relations, 1939–45' in *idem, A History of British Industrial Relations, 1939–79* (Cheltenham, 1996), pp. 27–8; P. Inman, *Labour in the Munitions Industries* (London, 1957), p. 398.

[64] Inman, *Labour in the Munitions Industries*, ch. 12. R. Croucher, *Engineers at War 1939–1945* (London, 1982). Also, K. G. J. C. Knowles, *Strikes: A study in industrial conflict* (Oxford, 1952); E. Wigham, *Strikes and the Government, 1893–1974* (London, 1976).

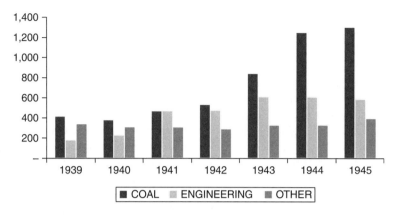

NUMBER OF STRIKES

	1939	1940	1941	1942	1943	1944	1945
COAL	417	381	470	536	843	1,253	1,306
ENGINEERING	181	229	472	476	612	610	591
OTHER	342	312	309	291	330	331	396
TOTAL	940	922	1,251	1,303	1,785	2,194	2,293

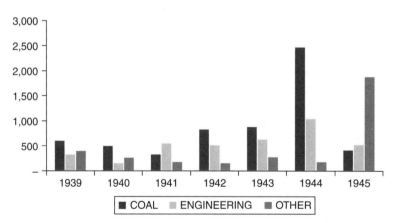

WORKDAYS LOST BY SECTORS (IN THOUSANDS)

	1939	1940	1941	1942	1943	1944	1945
COAL	612	505	335	840	890	2,480	422
ENGINEERING	336	163	556	526	635	1,048	528
OTHER	408	272	188	161	283	186	1,885
TOTAL	1,356	940	1,079	1,527	1,808	3,714	2,835

There is truth in both of these views. A distinct war-weariness and fatigue permeated civilian life by 1944. Years of air raids, overwork, limited leisure, family dislocation, and scarce rations had created a large reserve of easily ignited discontent that could intensify labour disputes. Similarly, as government officials found, clashes between workers and employers became increasingly difficult to defuse or contain in certain industries and regions where enmities were nourished by generations of conflict and resentment. But neither Inman's emphasis on the decreasing power of patriotism to inhibit strikes nor Croucher's picture of rising militancy fully captures the diverse patterns of labour relations between and even within industries. Even within the portmanteau category of 'engineering and allied trades', aggregate figures mask dramatically different configurations of strike activity. Above all, what national strike totals for all industries conceal is the overwhelming concentration of disputes in coal and engineering; together they accounted for almost three-quarters of the workdays lost in the period 1940–4 and coal alone was responsible for over half. Because of their central role in the war economy and in the organized labour movement, the following account focuses on engineering and coal, but it must be remembered that in other economic sectors—say, chemicals, textiles, or transport—industrial relations were much more peaceful and ran a different course.[65]

Engineering and Allied Trades

No economic sector underwent more change during the war years than the many metal industries that in official statistics are categorized as 'engineering and allied trades'. Though grouped together for the sake of convenience, these industries were often markedly different in size, structure, and modernity. Distinctive local political and work cultures created sharp contrasts in their labour relations; so did the outlook and strategies of employers and the past experience of communities, most immediately the interwar decades that brought expansion and relative prosperity to some, while others were overwhelmed by mass unemployment and poverty. In the war some firms had converted from making household goods and consumer durables to munitions, while retaining much of their original workforce; others in shipbuilding, aircraft, and vehicles basically engaged in the same kind of work as before, although new technologies, mass-production methods, and labour dilution transformed many of them. One huge change was the feminization of workplaces. By 1943, at the peak of mobilization, one engineering worker in three was female compared to about one in seven in a much smaller workforce before the war. But some sectors—and, more often, specific parts of large factories—also remained bastions of craft conservatism, firmly resistant to waiving trade practices or de-skilling. Working conditions and welfare amenities varied widely from one factory to another, as did average wages, although pay was generally much lower in Scotland and the north than in the newer car and aircraft firms of the Midlands and London region.

Throughout the war the typical dispute in engineering was a short, sharp tactical skirmish over wage rates and bonus payments, highly localized and usually limited to a single factory or one workshop in a firm. This was true of all parts of the country. Sympathetic strikes were exceptional, as were larger and more protracted conflicts, although some did occur, especially in the shipbuilding and heavy engineering centres of the north and Scotland. Towards the end of the war, the frustrations of workers

---

[65] On the chemical industry: W. J. Reader, *Imperial Chemical Industries*, II: *1926–52* (Oxford, 1975), pp. 298ff.

increased and also their readiness to down tools. These were largely disputes over wages or specific working arrangements; they were not politically motivated or underpinned by any larger goals of securing more power for trade unionism. Indeed, JPCs and shop stewards were sometimes hard pressed to maintain discipline over workers, many of them new and inexperienced, who quickly grew impatient at the delays inherent in the wage-bargaining process. Even towards the end of the war when strike statistics rose sharply, many towns experienced few disputes of real consequence. During 1943 and 1944 there were 182 strikes in the aircraft industry that involved over 10,000 lost man *hours*, but only one occurred in Coventry and this was at the Rootes-Humber factory, the scene of numerous labour problems.[66] Not that there was any dearth of discontent in Coventry or London, of course; quite the reverse. One report from the Midlands Industrial Relations Officer deplored 'the readiness of some classes of workpeople to cease work under the slightest provocation'.[67] But unrest was more apparent in other ways than full-blown strikes: for example, high rates of absenteeism, go-slows, overtime bans, and the speed with which minor altercations with foremen and managers could escalate, requiring mediation.

In the older industrial centres of Scotland, northern England, and Northern Ireland the patterns of strike action were somewhat different. Craft consciousness was strong; scepticism about joint consultation and cooperation between unions and management was widespread; and the legacy of past conflicts and pre-war unemployment weighed heavily. Here, while most disputes were quick, tightly controlled clashes over pay and work rules, there were also larger, protracted struggles which caused more serious production losses and in some cases spread to numerous firms. At Albion Motors in Glasgow, for example, 2,000 workers went on strike for two months in the autumn of 1944. The dispute began with management's refusal to consult with the AEU's convener on the employment of a worker who could not produce evidence of having served an apprenticeship. But it was also the culmination of a whole series of clashes over wages, bonuses, and overtime requirements.[68] In November 1943 a month-long strike over women's pay at the Rolls-Royce aero-engine factory at Hillington near Glasgow involved as many as 16,000 workers and threatened to spread to other firms in the area.[69] This was the largest strike of the war over women's wages; it reflected the growing readiness of a significant minority of female engineers to take action in many areas, but it was also strongly influenced by the radical political culture of the Clyde and rising dissatisfaction among Glasgow militants with the anti-strike position of the CP.[70]

---

[66] T. Donnelly and D. Thoms, 'Trade unions, management, and the search for production in the Coventry motor car industry, 1939–75', *Business History*, 31(2) (April 1989), 102.

[67] NA: LAB 10/352, 7 February 1942. There were also very few strikes in government-run Royal Ordnance Factories, which employed large numbers of new workers, many of them women. By mid-1943 they employed some 270,000 workers and from then until mid-1945 they experienced only 16 mostly short stoppages involving few workers: Inman, *Labour in the Munitions Industries*, p. 406.

[68] Bain and Gorman, 'Keeping the home fires burning', pp. 48–52. Also Glasgow Trades Council Minutes (Mitchell Library, Glasgow), 13 September, 25 October 1944.

[69] For further analysis of the Hillington strike, see pp. 153–4 below.

[70] P. Bain, ' "Is you is or is you ain't my baby": Women's pay and the Clydeside strikes of 1943', *Scottish Labour History Journal*, 30 (1995).

Aside from a few exceptions like the Hillington strike, however, the largest and most serious engineering disputes were all concentrated in marine engineering and shipbuilding. Though shipbuilding and ship repair constituted only about 1.5 per cent of the nation's total workforce, they accounted for well over 9 per cent of all strikes and days lost. As recently as in the years preceding the First World War, British shipyards had produced almost 60 per cent of the world's annual tonnage, but in the following decades the industry had collapsed. In the 1930s output was never more than a third of capacity and unemployment became a way of life affecting in some periods 60 per cent or more of the insured workforce. Shipbuilding firms were mostly small and their managements deeply inbred, conservative, and autocratic. Very little capital investment was made in the interwar decades, so that firms largely relied on antiquated technologies and labour-intensive production techniques that lowered overheads and placed the burden of economic fluctuations onto workers who could simply be laid off when orders declined. Production was in the hands of seventeen major crafts, access to which depended on completing a five-year apprenticeship, and demarcation rivalries were fierce, with each trade struggling hard to maintain control over specific jobs and processes.[71]

The war totally transformed the circumstances of the industry, but not its basic character. Conflict at sea and growing losses of tonnage to U-boats resulted in abundant orders for new merchant and naval vessels, a huge backlog of ships awaiting repairs, and in the final stages of the war a continuous and accelerating demand for landing barges in preparation for the Allied invasion of the Continent. Production soared, as did the pressure on workers and managements to meet targets. Skilled labour was scarce, since many workers had left and few entered the industry in the worst years of the depression; there was also a severe shortage of apprentices. Many men laboured over seventy-two hours a week for long periods. The work was hard and physically exhausting—most of it done outdoors in all weathers—and pay scales were generally well below those in the car and aircraft firms of the Midlands. Mutual antagonism between workers and employers was deeply ingrained and severely impaired government attempts to introduce unskilled workers and subdivide jobs. 'Whenever dilution is raised', commented an MoL official, 'we seem to be brought up short against this ghostly squad of unemployed boilermakers.'[72] Women made up only 6 per cent of shipyard labour, and the ratio

---

[71] L. Jones, *Shipbuilding in Britain* (Cardiff, 1957); J. McGoldrick, 'Crisis and division of labour: Clydeside shipbuilding in the inter-war period' in A. Dickson (ed.), *Capital and Class in Scotland* (Edinburgh, 1982); I. P. Roberts, 'A question of construction: Capital and labour in Wearside shipbuilding since the 1930s', PhD Diss., Durham University, 1988; J. E. Mortimer, *The History of the Boilermakers' Society* (London 1994), III. For a polemic against the industry, see C. Barnett, *The Audit of War* (London, 1986), ch. 6. The labour force in shipbuilding declined by 25% in the period 1924–37.

[72] Inman, *Labour in the Munitions Industries*, p. 130. The Admiralty in 1941 was urging prosecutions of striking boilermakers in Scotland; the MoL resisted this pressure. Dilution went further in the smaller shipyards and in the Royal Dockyards. Women in dockyards were mostly employed as cleaners, labourers, unskilled assistants and also welders. It was in the latter area that their wartime numbers grew rapidly: by 1943–4 about 35% of welders were female. H. Murphy, '"From the crinoline to the boilersuit": Women workers in British shipbuilding during the Second World War', *Contemporary British History*, 13(4) (Winter 1999).

of skilled to unskilled workers changed little from pre-war. Even agreements on the interchangeability of labour between narrowly differentiated trades made little headway. And though the government invested heavily after 1942 in an effort to re-equip and modernize the industry, the growth of prefabrication and the spread of electro-welding and pneumatic riveting also multiplied demarcation conflicts between the Boilermakers, the Shipwrights, and the Constructional Engineering Unions.

The first engineering strike to affect several areas of the country took place in March 1941. It began among the radical Clydeside apprentices, spread rapidly through the towns of western Scotland, then to the shipyard areas of Belfast and Barrow, and eventually to textile apprentices in Manchester and Rochdale. Over 25,000 came out on strike in all, some 6,000 from the Clyde alone. At issue were low wages, poor training, and lack of union representation. As described earlier, dissatisfaction among apprentices had erupted in two large waves of strikes in 1937, after which their situation had improved somewhat. But the war again brought their discontents to boiling point. Firms were treating them as cheap labour, forcing the boys to work adult hours at only a fraction of adult pay rates, while recently hired dilutees were, after a few months, out-earning fourth- and fifth-year apprentices who often had the task of setting up their machines for them. Though the AEU promised to negotiate with employers on their behalf, it did little and months of inaction finally drove the boys, led by the Young Communist League, to form a strike committee and dispatch delegates to other areas to widen the dispute. The speed with which the walkout spread prompted immediate action from Bevin who instituted a Court of Inquiry that rendered a judgment in favour of significant pay raises within twenty-four hours, although at the same time threatening boys who did not return to work with military call-up. When apprentices in the Lancashire textile industry remained out, Bevin's response was tougher: 1,100 of them were ordered to report for military medical examinations and six of the ringleaders were fined and bound over for twelve months under Regulation 1305. Spread over a little more than a month, the strikes could probably have been avoided altogether if employers and the AEU had worked harder and more swiftly to reach a settlement.[73]

Disillusioned with the AEU, the Clyde apprentices had demanded that they be allowed to speak for themselves. By 1942 the union was facing growing discontent from within its own ranks. Now the dissidents were engineers who disliked the union leadership's enthusiasm for JPCs and resisted the unqualified backing given to the production drive by communist shop stewards and union organizers after the invasion of the Soviet Union. In the Glasgow area especially this unrest was encouraged by non-communist radicals from the Independent Labour Party and various small anarchist and Trotskyite groups who remained staunchly opposed to what they called productionist class collaboration. After several strikes in the final months of 1942 Galbraith, the local Industrial Relations Officer, reported that new

---

[73] Croucher, *Engineers at War*, pp. 123–32.

groups of shop-floor dissidents were challenging the authority of union officials and engaging in a 'vendetta' against the communist-led AEU district committee.[74]

Another case where workers clashed with their AEU district committee was the so-called Total Time strike of shipyard workers on Tyneside. Remarkably, what touched off the smouldering unrest here in October 1942 was a reasonable request by employers, designed to ease the burden on clerical staffs, for a change in the day on which workers' pay was calculated. The change involved workers receiving an initial short-week, although firms were willing to make up the money and spread repayment first over five and then over twelve weeks. The AEU district secretary accepted the proposal without fully consulting union members and found himself deluged with protests, followed by a mass walkout that soon spread across the area and involved 20,000 men and the loss of some 135,000 workdays. The immediate issue was relatively minor, but behind it lay grievances about long hours and poor pay and simmering resentment over management breaches of established customs and practices. The chief scapegoats, however, were the men's union officials, among them communist shop stewards who were told by their party to remain at work. Malcolm MacEwen, the party's chief organizer in the north-east, recalled that they were 'isolated and instantly deprived of their positions' although he believed that the men 'would have been willing to listen to them had they not blacklegged'. Few of the communist stewards were reinstated after the dispute and, he added, 'the party never regained the influence it had previously exercised on the Tyne'.[75]

However, the most publicized challenge to the AEU's authority took place in September 1943 at the huge Vickers-Armstrong shipyards and engineering complex at Barrow-in-Furness. The dispute was the most serious of a rash of strikes that grew out of dissatisfaction with a pay award made by the government's National Arbitration Tribunal in March 1943 after negotiations between the AEU and the Engineering Employers Federation became deadlocked. The implementation of national wage settlements was always difficult because they had to be adjusted to suit a complex variety of local rates and work practices that had grown up. Without going into detail in this case, suffice it to say that workers in many regions who had been anticipating a raise found themselves no better off. At Barrow, in fact, Vickers' interpretation of the award would actually have reduced the relatively low earnings of many of its employees. The heart of the dispute was how the new award would affect bonus pay—long a source of grievance since the firm had for many years operated a system that limited bonus earnings.[76] Negotiations with Vickers reached an impasse and the AEU's district committee for Barrow called for a strike. The

[74] T. Milligan, 'Trotskyist politics and industrial work in Scotland 1939–45', *Scottish Labour History Journal* 30 (1995); S. Bornstein and A. Richardson, *War and the International: A history of the Trotskyist movement in Britain, 1937–1949* (London, 1986). Galbraith: NA: LAB 10/363, 7 November 1942, also 24 October 1942; NA: LB 10/146 (includes a Report on the Clyde Shipyards July–August 1941 and October 1941).

[75] Croucher, *Engineers at War*, pp. 181–7; M. MacEwen, *The Greening of a Red* (London 1991), pp. 93–4. Also Craig Armstrong, 'Wartime industrial action on the Tyne 1939–1945', *North East Labour History*, bulletin of the North East Group for the Study of Labour History, 36 (2005).

[76] Bonus earnings were often as much as 40% of a man's weekly pay.

union's national executive opposed this action and suspended the district committee, but the strike proceeded anyway, lasting six weeks and involving almost all Barrow's engineers. To bring it to an end, the AEU leadership eventually sent George Crane, a communist national organizer for the AEU, to reconstitute the district committee and arrange a settlement. Vickers did agree to modify its bonus system and workers made some gains, but the highly publicized dispute left bitter and lasting divisions within the AEU at Barrow.[77]

Finally, in 1944, a spate of strikes swept the shipyard areas of Belfast and Tyneside, coinciding—as we shall see—with the highpoint of unrest in the nation's coalfields. Northern Ireland experienced the same wartime trends as other centres of shipbuilding and engineering with the disappearance of unemployment, a rapid increase of trade union membership, the growth of an assertive shop-steward movement, and by 1942 widespread rank-and-file discontent with management. As Boyd Black has argued, the situation was also complicated by the region's political and religious context; a substantial section of its population was far less committed to the war than other parts of the British Isles.[78] Particularly prone to strikes, Northern Ireland accounted for 2.5 per cent of the insured workforce of the United Kingdom, but was responsible for 10 per cent of the total working days lost, including several of the largest disputes.[79] In 1941 Belfast had been one of the centres of the apprentices' strikes. The following year an engineers' strike forced the reinstatement of two sacked shop stewards at Short Bros. & Harland aircraft factory at a cost of over 120,000 working days lost. But the most costly action of all came in February 1944 from a demand that fitters' rates at the Harland and Wolff shipyards be raised to the level of other smaller yards in the area and to parity with shipwrights and boilermakers. Workers at the Short Bros. & Harland aircraft factory decided upon sympathetic action and as a result their convener and four shop stewards were sentenced to imprisonment and hard labour. This infuriated trade unionists across the region and a general strike was only narrowly avoided when pay increases were conceded and the stewards released. Lasting six weeks, involving some 36,000 munitions workers, and costing over 400,000 lost working days, this was the largest stoppage of the war outside coal. Boyd suggests that the very combustive Northern Ireland situation may have triggered Bevin's decision to push through regulation 1AA designed to crack down harder on subversive elements and those inciting strikes.[80] Just as the trouble at

---

[77] Croucher, *Engineers at War*, pp. 218–18; Clegg, *A History of British Trade Unions*, III, pp. 244–6. For a critical account of the AEU's role, see 'A Special Correspondent', 'The Barrow Strike', *Engineering*, 15 and 22 October 1943.

[78] B. Black, 'A triumph of voluntarism? Industrial relations and strikes in Northern Ireland in World War II', *Labour History Review*, 70(1) (April 2005); G. Cradden, 'Trade unionism and socialism in Northern Ireland, 1939–53', PhD Diss., Queen's University, Belfast, 1988. Also, P. Ollerenshaw, 'War, industrial mobilisation and society in Northern Ireland, 1939–45', *Contemporary European History*, 16(2) (2007).

[79] Boyd Black estimates that the Clyde lost 849,000 working days in principal disputes outside coal mining; Northern Ireland lost 757,000 days; Tyne/Tees lost 146,000 days; and Leeds/Yorkshire 146,000 (p. 12).

[80] Black, 'A triumph of voluntarism?', pp. 14–15. The CP strongly opposed the Harland and Wolff strike but clearly in Belfast the party's ability to prevent or restrain militant unofficial action by shop stewards was very limited.

Harland and Wolff was being resolved, strike action also began to spread in March 1944 among thousands of apprentices on Tyneside and the Clyde, protesting the government's decision to include them in the 'Bevin boy'[81] coal-mine ballot. The walkout soon began to collapse, especially after boys of call-up age were ordered to report for medical examinations. The unions opposed the walkout and refused to recognize the militant apprentices' guild throughout the negotiations.

The growing incidence and scale of strikes in 1943 and even more in 1944 was alarming to MoL officials. The mass actions taken by apprentices and the strikes at Barrow,[82] Hillington, and Belfast, especially when coupled with the unrest in the coalfields, made them believe that industrial strife had entered a dangerous new phase in which national union structures seemed to have decreasing control over the workforce or local union branches. The MoL's regional officer for the north-east warned of 'a spirit of determination on the part of workers . . . not so much to get on with the war as to assert their power, their principles and prerogatives and to ventilate their grievances, not only against their employers but against the whole structure of society'.[83] Investigations of militants and of small Trotskyite groups were stepped up, but Bevin resisted pressures from government departments to prosecute strikers, being convinced that such action would only reveal the inherent weakness of his powers under Order 1305. All this would appear to support Croucher's claim of a rising tide of militancy. But while this was the picture in some of the old centres of heavy industry, it hardly corresponds to the fairly peaceful situation in many other economic sectors. The protracted battles of Belfast, Barrow, and the Clyde had no real counterparts in the car and aircraft factories in the south and the Midlands. In London and the south-east in 1944 in *all* industries there were only eighty-nine strikes. They involved 31,500 workers, but only four lasted a week, fifty-two ended in less than a day, and most were over so fast that only forty-two were actually reported as strikes under Order 1305.[84]

Once the peak of production passed, workers became increasingly concerned about likely plant closures and redundancies. The wartime circumstances that had worked in labour's favour, began to change and employers, who felt that they had been on the defensive for too long, made moves to reassert their authority and settle old scores. Overtime and bonus earnings came under pressure and firms grew more resistant to making concessions that they might have difficulty in reversing later.[85] The largest strike of the war years at Austin Longbridge took place in September 1944, precipitated mostly by fears of layoffs and suspicion that the company intended to roll back prices as soon as possible. Another in October 1944 came

---

[81] Some 36,000 men had left mining for the forces or for less-exhausting and better-paid employment by mid-1943. Because of the extreme shortage of labour for the mines, Bevin began in December 1943 to direct young men eligible for the draft and chosen by ballot into the coal industry.

[82] While the Barrow strike was the most important, J. E. Mortimer (*History of the Boilermakers*, III, p. 25) indicates that in the first half of 1943 there were also 43 strikes in the shipbuilding and repair yards on the Clyde, 10 on the Tyne, and 6 on the east coast of Scotland.

[83] NA: LAB 10/394, 5 November 1943.

[84] NA: LAB 10/443 (29 December 1944) for the London area statistics.

[85] e.g. NA: LAB 10/443, 10 November, 4 August 1944.

after cuts in bonuses.[86] This was echoed elsewhere in Midlands car firms as workers strove to prevent the return of old-style labour relations.[87] Where strikes occurred in this period they were mostly defensive, aimed at upholding previous agreements and preventing the downgrading of jobs, rather than establishing new gains.

Coal Mining

If the legacy of earlier conflicts played a large role in shaping wartime industrial relations in some sectors of engineering, in the coalfields they overshadowed everything. The mining towns and villages—many of them small, isolated, single-industry communities—were steeped in tradition. With their brass bands, embroidered banners, choirs, and rugby teams, the colliery districts had a folk culture and a texture of social relations all of their own. At the peak of Britain's steam-driven industrialization one in ten of the male workforce, over a million men, worked in the mines; they still numbered three-quarters of a million in 1939. No group had suffered more from mass unemployment, poverty, and industrial conflict in the interwar decades; indeed, the troubled industry came to symbolize depression and class confrontation. Between 1928 and 1936 the percentage of miners wholly or partly unemployed never fell below 24 per cent and in five of those years it was above 30 per cent.[88] Destitution and despair were rife not only in the coalfields of South Wales, Scotland, and the north-east, but even in the Midlands, where miners were commonly thought to be better off; there, too, short weeks and seasonal underemployment were a persistent curse. But while social analysts like Orwell were drawn to the collieries and popular films like *The Citadel* (1938) and *The Stars Look Down* (1939) depicted miners as the archetypal proletarians, experiences in the interwar decades had, if anything, made mining districts more inward-looking and had strengthened miners' sense of being distinct and separate from the rest of labour.[89]

Wartime brought many changes to the coal districts. Some miners volunteered for the forces, others quit the pits for better pay and conditions in the new factories that were springing up as part of the rearmament boom. But very soon that option was closed off. For most of the war miners were exempted from conscription and tied to their jobs; school-leavers in those areas, whether they liked it or not, were also directed into the mines. More families remained intact, since fewer husbands and sons were suddenly drafted or transferred than in other industrial communities.

---

[86] Donnelly and Thoms, 'Trade unions, management, and the search for production in the Coventry motor car industry', p. 104.

[87] e.g. the Birmingham Trades Council petitioned the MoL to 'take immediate steps to stop the growing tendency by provocative employers to use redundancy as a method of removing active shop stewards and trade unionists from their jobs'. NA: LAB 10/444, 14 April 1944.

[88] B. Supple, *The History of the British Coal Industry*, IV: *1913–1946: The political economy of decline* (Oxford, 1987), p. 448. Also, W. H. B. Court, *Coal* (London, 1951); R. Page Arnot, *The Miners in Crisis and War* (London 1961); *idem, The Miners 1939–46* (London, 1979); W. Paynter, *My Generation* (London, 1972); and F. Zweig, *Men in the Pits* (London, 1949).

[89] George Orwell, *The Road to Wigan Pier* (London, 1937); James Hanley, *Grey Children* (London, 1937); also J. B. Priestley's depiction of the mining villages of the north-east in *English Journey* (London, 1934), ch. 13.

Wages and living standards also rose, although there were fewer outlets for miners' new purchasing power. After years, even decades, of uncertain employment, work soon became plentiful and leisure time was reduced to a bare minimum. Miners now had to put in five or six shifts a week continuously for six years, while the war brought new opportunities for their wives and daughters, for whom there had often been few jobs available before. 'My journey to work', one woman recalled, 'used to be one and a half hours there and the same coming back—that was in 1936. When the war came in 1939 everything changed—you didn't have to work far away because the jobs were on your doorstep. If they weren't, there would be transport laid on to take you there.'[90]

But female employment could also arouse male dissatisfaction, as a young Mass-Observation researcher, Mollie Tarrant, found when she visited the South Wales villages of Blaina and Nantyglo in 1942. Young women, with more freedom and money than before, easily set tongues wagging, especially if they broke existing customs. The special trains that took munitions girls to an aircraft factory thirty miles away (nicknamed 'budgies' trains') triggered a whole crop of fantasies: 'Some people are amused by the stories, others are shocked and the whole subject arouses lively curiosity.' But most of all, it was women's wages that irked their men, especially if they exceeded those of an experienced pitman. 'A man underground works like a slave' commented one miner's representative. 'At the end of the week he gets a matter of £3. 15s. In some houses where the wife is an R.O. [Royal Ordnance] worker, she'll bring home between £4–£5. Then you have the psychological effect in the house . . . I know of five cases where the woman brings home more than the man. In one case they've parted.' A Welsh writer who toured the Welsh mining areas for the MoI commented that this 'new kind of indignity' had inflamed old grudges: 'We've had about enough of it. There's no workers' playtime down there where we work, Jack, but there is where my daughter works and earns more money than I do.'[91]

The war, or rather government pressure, brought welfare improvements such as pithead baths to many collieries and, since Bevin had placed the industry under an Essential Works Order, employers lost the power to dismiss workers arbitrarily. The harsh discipline that had characterized many pits before the war was relaxed and there were even attempts to promote joint consultation between workers and managers. But past enmities proved inescapable and neither labour nor employers showed much sign of observing a wartime truce in this industry. Coal accounted for 46.6 per cent of all recorded stoppages 1940–4 (55.7 per cent of all working days lost and 58.5 per cent of workers directly or indirectly involved). Even in 1940, the quietest year of all, when only two disputes in the nation involved more than 5,000 workers, both were in coal. The industry's share of the days lost to strike action

[90] Tina James, 'The experiences of employment for women in mining communities: Then and now', *Labour History Review*, 60(2) (Autumn 1995), 101.

[91] B. Roberts, 'A mining town in wartime: The fears for the future', *Llafur*, 6 (1992); M-OA: FR 1498 'Mining Town—1942' (Tarrant's report); Welsh writer quoted in Mari A. Williams, 'Where *is* Mrs Jones going? Women and the Second World War in South Wales', University of Wales Centre for Advanced Welsh and Celtic Studies, Research Papers 1, Aberystwyth, 1995, p. 6.

dipped a little in 1941 and 1943 (31 and 49.2 per cent of the days lost respectively), but in the crisis year of 1944, coal contributed a whopping 66.8 per cent.[92] In mining, as in engineering, most strikes were brief and affected a single colliery, but by 1943 disputes were much more likely to produce sympathetic actions at neighbouring pits and even to spread across whole regions.[93]

There were many factors that contributed to the persistent guerrilla warfare in the industry, but most important was the bitter legacy of the interwar years when miners' earnings, even in periods of employment, fell sharply in relation to those of other industrial groups. By 1929 miners' earnings were 12 per cent below the level of 1924 and though there was a recovery in the 1930s this helped only those fortunate enough to be working. Wartime militancy reflected a determination to regain the relative pay position that miners had enjoyed prior to the 1921 slump and a conviction that the war emergency was their only opportunity. 'It's our only weapon', commented a Welsh miner. 'Did you ever know the time when we got anything without striking for it?' Many miners pointed angrily to higher company profits—indeed, despite the low output and poor productivity that bedevilled the industry, many leading companies experienced wartime gains in share prices of 20–50 per cent. They also lived in fear of a post-war slump and closures: 'The miner is a big man when it comes to winning the war, but he will not be any use after it.' 'Things'll go back the same as before . . . They're just waiting for the time and then they'll say "all out" again. The war's brought no better conditions in my opinion.' As for company officials, in the view of one trade unionist, they 'were looking forward to the day when peace comes, and they'll have the whip hand again, I think they'll get their chance.' 'War Savings?' one South Wales local councillor responded to an interviewer: 'Yes, we do well here . . . People know what they are saving for. They know what happened after the last war.'[94]

These anxieties had been strongly reinforced by the course of events early in the war. At first accelerating rearmament had sharply increased both domestic need for coal and export demands. The boom lasted until the fall of France which suddenly shut off Continental markets, disrupting the normal flow of trade so that unsold coal piled up at the pitheads and many collieries began to close down. At the very moment when the nation faced the possibility of invasion and defeat, many miners found themselves laid off or on short time. Some joined the armed forces, others found jobs in munitions. There were protests and mining districts gave considerable support to the communist-led People's Convention. But this contraction in the demand for coal was temporary and by late 1941, with war mobilization

---

[92] Wrigley, 'The Second World and state intervention in industrial relations, 1939–45', pp. 29–30.

[93] The Scottish coal industry was by far the most strike-torn. There were 3,182 strikes in Scottish mines during 1939–45 (2,125 during 1940–4). In each of the war years over 50% of the mining strikes took place there. Nothing, it seems, could reduce the level of hostility and suspicion between autocratic owners and militant miners. Knowles, *Strikes*, p. 310.

[94] Quotes are from: B. Newman, *British Journey* (London, 1945), p. 60; Roberts, 'A mining town in wartime', pp. 83–4, 92. On company profits: P. Howlett, 'British business and the state during the Second World War' in J. Sakudo and T. Shiba (eds.), *World War II and the Transformation of Business Systems* (Tokyo, 1994), pp. 139–40.

moving into higher gear, pressure for higher output once again became intense. Now the men were told they must forgo weekends and holidays; extraordinary measures were taken to compel ex-miners to return to the pits, and those who resisted were accused of being unpatriotic. The layoffs of 1940 were short-lived, but they did much to depress morale and reinforce the conviction that miners must use whatever leverage society's increased dependence upon coal might bring.[95]

From late 1941 until the war's end the coal industry proved unable to meet the nation's demands for higher production. Despite continual government exhortations to miners and mine managements that they possessed the key to victory, annual production fell throughout the war so that by 1943, 9 million fewer tons were mined than in 1942 and 30 million less than in 1940. There were many reasons for this failure—among them the small size of most collieries, lack of mechanization, the closure of many pits between the wars and the depletion of the labour force through migration and a dwindling intake of new recruits. Even during the war constant recruitment efforts could not prevent a decline in the number of miners from 773,000 in early 1939 to 701,000 at the end of 1944 with the most serious shortages among underground workers and apprentices. It took almost two years before the government recognized the magnitude of the manpower crisis in the industry, but by then it was hard to find a solution. Young men registering for military service were given the option of underground work in the mines, but fewer than 3,000 accepted the offer. Finally, in January 1944, the so-called 'Bevin Boy' scheme was introduced which drafted men of military age (regardless of social background) into the mines.[96] They were chosen by ballot and very few exceptions were permitted. Not surprisingly, the scheme was highly unpopular and many recruits launched appeals. In the end only 21,800 recruits[97] were allocated to the mines and their contribution to output was probably insignificant—or, at least, that was the verdict of many experienced miners. The scheme also damaged production in another vital economic sector by precipitating widespread strikes among engineering apprentices on Tyneside and the Clyde who demanded that they be exempted from the ballot.[98]

Not only did the numbers of miners decline but their average age increased, accident rates rose sharply, and the fatigue and strain of long periods of intense effort began to show in high rates of sickness and absenteeism. Statistics indicating a drop in a miner's average output per shift are somewhat misleading since men now worked increased numbers of shifts, while the deteriorating condition of the pits

---

[95] In addition to B. Supple see S. R. Broomfield, 'South Wales during the Second World War: The coal industry and its community', PhD Diss., Univ. of Wales, Swansea, 1979, chs. 1–2.

[96] 'Bevin Boys' have written several memoirs: D. Day, *Bevin Boy* (Warwick, 1975); D. Agnew, *Bevin Boy* (London, 1947). Also M-OA: FR 2133, 'Training for the mines'. Those selected by ballot could appeal, but the only grounds for exemption were medical or exceptional personal hardship; almost 40% of those selected lodged appeals but the overwhelming majority were rejected.

[97] The statistics are confusing. Alan Bullock gave this figure for the numbers directed into the mines. The Bevin Boys Association and other sources cite 48,000 which seems to include the period until 1948 and those who volunteered instead of going into the forces. They were trained for six weeks and then worked underground. Pressure for their war service to be recognized officially finally resulted in government action in June 2007 and a special badge has now been issued.

[98] NA: LAB 10/445, 31 March 1944.

and equipment also reduced efficiency. The absentee rate per manshift, which in 1939 was around 6.5 per cent, rose to 9 per cent in 1941, over 12 per cent in the next two years, and a peak of more than 16 per cent in 1945. The highest rates were among younger face-workers, who were particularly discontented over pay and conditions; but there is no way to assess how much of the absenteeism was voluntary and avoidable. These were men required to do heavy physical labour for years on end with few breaks—'nothing to do and nowhere to go except work', as one union leader put it.[99] Internal colliery correspondence among managers bluntly blamed higher absenteeism on the removal of the threat of dismissal. Coal output, complained a government inspector, depended on 'thousands of individual miners, each of whom has the power to temper his efforts to suit his own convenience'.[100] Fines had little effect. The same was true of the often condescending pep-talks of politicians and other dignitaries who toured the mines. Press stories that they were unpatriotic, work-shy, and irresponsible only deepened miners' anger. For their part, poor morale and low productivity resulted from antiquated, unmechanized pits, low pay, and the government's failure to commit itself to public ownership of the industry.

Persistent failure to meet production targets did result in increased control over the industry. By early 1942 there was growing dissatisfaction within the labour movement as a whole at the government's failure to take over coal, the railways, and war production, and the left wing of the Labour Party accused Attlee and Bevin of missing a golden opportunity to extract concessions. But, though Labour ministers pressed for nationalization within the War Cabinet, Churchill threatened that the issue would break up the Coalition. In the event, a Ministry of Fuel and Power was set up in 1942 and a system of 'dual control' or limited state direction was adopted with trade union representation on national-, regional-, and district-level advisory boards. In addition, workplace committees—a counterpart to JPCs in engineering—were also set up. Pit Production Committees (PPCs) had been created in 1940, but few survived for long. The second experiment in 1941–2 fared little better since the committees were widely viewed as a means of disciplining absentees; later, when they were relieved of this responsibility and focused exclusively on improvements in output and work organization, it was the turn of managements to become obstructive in an effort to safeguard their prerogatives. In many instances mistrust between workers and colliery owners ran so deep that the committees tended to become an alternative site of conflict rather than a vehicle for cooperation. And when the executive committee of the South Wales Miners union, a staunch advocate of PPCs, questioned local union lodges in 1943 about the way the committees were operating, less than half bothered to respond.[101]

---

[99] For absentee statistics, see Supple, *The History of the British Coal Industry*, IV, pp. 565–6. The union leader was Arthur Horner, speaking at a Conciliation Board meeting in August 1943: H. Francis and D. Smith, *The Fed: A history of the South Wales Miners in the twentieth century* (London, 1998 edition), p. 407.
[100] Supple, *The History of the British Coal Industry*, IV, p. 564.
[101] NA: CAB 102/400; INF 1/292, 20 August 1942; LAB 10/363, 13 June 1942; M. Heinemann, *Britain's Coal* (London, 1944); Francis and Smith, *The Fed*, p. 403.

With the exception of Scotland where miners seemed from the start engaged in a war with the bosses,[102] coal mining experienced few strikes in the first two years of the war. But things changed early in 1942 as the pressures on the industry to raise production increased and the miners became more and more dissatisfied with both the arduous conditions of their job and their low pay relative to many other groups. Anger overflowed in a rash of strikes, the most publicized of which was in January at the Betteshanger colliery in Kent. Here a strike of almost three weeks occurred after government arbitration found against the miners in a minor pay dispute. It was, however, a decision by the Ministry of Mines (against Bevin's advice) to prosecute the strikers under Order 1305 that gave this stoppage wider importance. The imprisonment of three men and the conviction and fining of 1,050 others simply increased the miners' intransigence. 'Bands played and women and children cheered the procession on its way to court.' Pits in other regions called one-day sympathetic strikes and the Betteshanger men remained out until their leaders were released. 'I'll be eating the bloody table legs', commented one, 'before I go back to bloody pit at 7s a shift... What are we fighting for, to help Russia win the war or keep the bloody owners rich?' It was the government that yielded, giving the men what they wanted coated with a few face-saving words. Only nine men had paid their fines. Though small, the dispute showed clearly the difficulty of enforcing a strike ban in the face of large-scale collective disobedience.[103]

Amid news of military reverses in North Africa and the Far East and an acrimonious debate over production failures in engineering, trouble continued to grow in the coalfields in the spring of 1942. In May alone there were ninety-five separate coal stoppages, involving 75,000 workers and a loss of 250,000 working days.[104] Leaders of the miners' unions tried to contain the discontent, urging workers to redouble their efforts to defeat fascism; so did the CP which had a considerable following in South Wales and Scotland. But even Arthur Horner, communist leader of the South Wales miners, found himself under attack in public meetings. Among the most disaffected groups were the pit apprentices. Unable to leave the pits for cleaner, more lucrative jobs, and suffering the highest accident and absentee rates, they were responsible for a wave of strikes in the Welsh pits in spring 1942 and again at the end of the following year. Already bitter in their teens, often undisciplined and difficult to work with, they were, wrote Bert Coombes, the chronicler of mining life, victims of the depression just as much as the older generation: 'the years in which these lads saw their relatives idling about the street,

[102] J. McIlroy and A. Campbell, 'Beyond Betteshanger: Order 1305 in the Scottish coalfields during the Second World War. Part 1: Politics, prosecutions and protest'; *idem*, 'Part 2: The Cardowan story', *Historical Studies in Industrial Relations*, 15 (Spring 2003) and 16 (Autumn 2003).
[103] On Betteshanger see M-O, *People in Production* (London, 1942), pp. 337–3 (miner quoted on p. 339). Also Clegg, *A History of British Trade Unions*, III, p. 254. Sir Harold Emmerson (formerly of the MoL) described the bands and processions as the miners went to court in his evidence to the Donovan inquiry: Royal Commission on Trade Unions and Employers' Associations, Cmnd 3623 (London 1969). A. Tyndall, 'Patriotism and principles: Order 1305 and the Betteshanger Strike of 1942', *Historical Studies in Industrial Relations*, 12 (Autumn 2001).
[104] NA: LAB 10/434 ('Report on Industrial Relations in Great Britain, 1939–1942').

or watching each hapless day recede before the misery of the next, has left an imprint on their minds which is difficult to erase'.[105]

While pit apprentices achieved few of their demands, adult miners made significant gains when in June 1942 a government board of inquiry under Lord Greene recommended a uniform national minimum wage and substantial pay increases. The Greene award raised miners from fifty-ninth to twenty-third in the government's 'league table' of average industrial earnings and began the process that radically altered their wage position by 1945. Dissatisfaction abated and for several months the coalfields remained quiescent, untroubled by major strikes. Yet war-weariness and overwork still made for a volatile situation in many mines, where minor disputes could easily spiral out of control. 'The men have got the upper hand and they know it', complained one manager: 'Trouble seems to be simmering in the background all the time and it only wants a small thing to set it off.' In October 1943 the government's Industrial Relations Officer for the Durham coalfield cited a string of 'trivialities' as typical. Some men had refused to work because their bus driver (afraid of scratching his bus on some trees) had halted 200 yards short of the pit and others stopped work in sympathy; an alleged short pay packet of one miner brought a walkout of 250; and another occurred at a colliery where management stupidly docked the pay of miners who had left the pit without formal permission following a fatal accident.[106]

Fatigue and frustration after four years of war underlay these outbursts, but in addition miners feared the return of hard times and were determined to protect and extend the gains they had made. With the military situation improving and public debate focusing more and more on post-war reconstruction, workers and trade unions argued that only nationalization could give them due recognition and security and the country the coal production it required. 'In Blaina, at least', wrote Mollie Tarrant, 'there can be no mistaking the sincerity of this demand for State control.' She added, it 'appears as the final and the only all-embracing security'. Churchill's refusal to take up the issue and miners' scepticism about promises of post-war social reform reinforced what Will Lawther, president of the Miners' Federation, described as 'a mood of sullen resentment and anger'. Without pledges that the coal owners would no longer be in charge, miners insisted that they must look to their own interests.[107]

Beginning in January and continuing until the end of April 1944 anger turned to action, producing the most serious industrial crisis of the war and the largest

---

[105] S. Broomfield, 'The apprentice boys strikes of the Second World War', *Llafur*, 3(2) (Spring 1981). B. L. Coombes, *Those Clouded Hills* (London, 1944), p. 65; also, *The Miners' Day* (Penguin Special 1945), p. 7; B. Jones and C. Williams (eds.), *With Dust Still in His Throat: An anthology of writings by B.L. Coombes* (Cardiff, 1999).

[106] R. J. Waller, *The Dukeries Transformed: The social and political development of a twentieth century coalfield* (Oxford, 1983), p. 215; NA: LAB 10/394 (8 October 1943). A growing number of prosecutions of strikers in the Durham coalfield and Scotland also exacerbated the situation: NA: LAB/446, 21 January 1944.

[107] M-OA: FR 1498, 'Mining Town—1942'; B. Jones, B. Roberts, and C. Williams, '"Going from the darkness to the light": South Wales Miners' attitudes towards nationalization', *Llafur*, 7(1) (1996); W. Lawther in an introductory comment to Heinemann, *Britain's Coal*.

walkout since the General Strike of 1926. At issue was a claim by the Miners'
Federation for higher national minimum wage rates for underground and surface
work. Not only was the recommendation of a government-appointed tribunal,
chaired by Lord Porter, significantly lower than the miners demanded, but raising
the minimum wage in some low-paying coalfields without touching piece-work
rates eliminated the jealously guarded differentials between unskilled and skilled
men. The only solution was to raise piece rates locally, but individual employers did
not want to foot the bill. When the government announced that it would not
guarantee the funds for rate increases negotiated at the district level, strikes and go-
slows spread spontaneously across South Wales, Scotland, the north-east, and
Yorkshire. The equivalent of 1.6 million workdays were lost before the strike
wave ended in late April with the miners achieving most of their demands. Taking
place against the background of the bloody Italian campaign and preparations for
the landings in Europe, these strikes produced a wave of criticism against the
miners. The TUC General Council called them 'a blow in the backs of their
comrades in the forces'.[108] A South Wales striker's wife, quoted in the *Aberdare
Leader*, replied: 'I don't like to think that we are letting the men in the forces
down...But...we have seen very hard times and we don't want to go back to
them. Perhaps, it sounds a bit like blackmail in wartime, but I have had eight years
on the dole, and you don't realize how that memory keeps cropping up.'[109]

This crisis, coming during the build-up towards D-Day, convinced Bevin of the
need for additional punitive powers. Under pressure to deal more severely with
strikers, he demanded a new draconian regulation (1AA) that made it an offence
(punishable by up to five years in prison) to incite or instigate strike action among
workers in essential services. This was a sharp reversal of the policy of restraint
followed until now and it was deeply unpopular among many trade unionists and on
the left-wing of the Labour Party. Bevin's insistence that the rising incidence of
strikes in coal and engineering was the work of Trotskyites and political agitators also
flew in the face of all the evidence being supplied to him. Perhaps, as some
contemporaries argued, he was obsessed with subversives; perhaps, strain and
frustration had caused him to lash out. More likely it was a bluff, a political move
calculated to restrain militants with the threat of harsh penalties while deflecting
blame from the trade unions themselves. In fact, the regulation was never used and
in the final months of the war concern about strikes was overtaken by excitement at
the liberation of Europe and plans for peacetime reconstruction.[110]

---

[108] The Miners' Federation requested a minimum wage of £6 and £5 10s a week respectively for
underground and surface workers. The government arbitration committee, chaired by Lord Porter,
awarded £1 less in each case. In Yorkshire there were additional problems over 'home coal' allowances.

[109] Broomfield, 'South Wales during the Second World War: The coal industry and its
community', p. 520.

[110] On 1AA see the works by Bullock, Croucher, Clegg, and the article by Brian Boyd, mentioned
above. Also, N. Stammers, *Civil Liberties in Britain during the Second World War* (London, 1983). Also
MSS 292/250/5, TUC Archive, MRC (Warwick); IWM: 85/31/1, Mrs A. R. E. Keen letters (a
Trotskyite, the letters refer to her arrest and imprisonment April–September 1944 under the
Trades Disputes Act).

Coal was the conspicuous failure of Britain's wartime economy and the greatest threat to the compact that Bevin and the TUC had forged since 1940. The industry had further burnished its reputation for being the most strike-torn in the country. The press was particularly bitter, but public opinion—hitherto fairly sympathetic— also turned noticeably more negative, although there was little sympathy for the mine owners who seemed as stubborn and intractable as those who cut the coal. One result was that a growing proportion of the nation began to conclude that only public ownership and complete reorganization could resolve this vital industry's problems.[111] Another was that miners ended the war more unified than ever: in January 1945 the numerous separate regional and craft organizations were replaced by a centralized National Union of Mineworkers, more capable of mounting a campaign for nationalization. They also finished the war among the highest paid workers, having advanced to fourteenth in the 'league table' of industrial earn- ings.[112] In 1930s popular culture the miner was the symbolic victim of capitalism, the quintessential indomitable proletarian. He retained that aura in the war years and after, in part because of vast numbers, the nation's continuing reliance on coal as fuel, and miners' legendary status in the labour movement and Labour Party politics. When one group of post-war sociologists wished to examine working-class culture and community, they selected an insular West Riding mining village for their case study.[113] But in reality miners' communities were not typical; if anything, the war underscored the differences between them and other workers. They might see themselves as the vanguard of the workers' movement, but this was already an idle boast, although, ironically, their defeat in 1985 symbolized a larger collapse of trade unionism as much as it had in the 1920s.

Wages and Workplace Conditions

Most workers earned more during the war years than ever before. Average real wages for workers rose by roughly 25 per cent during the war—less than estimated at the time, but then government cost-of-living statistics were based on faulty and outdated assumptions. Both wage rates and earnings increased, but much of what workers gained came from much longer hours. The percentage increase varied by industrial sector and region (earnings in the Midlands were among the highest). In some areas the upward trend began several years before 1939 with accelerating

[111] In March 1944 the Gallup organization polled its national sample on whether coal mines should be nationalized: 60% said 'Yes'; under 16% said 'No'; 24% answered 'Don't know'. The percentage of 'Yes' votes among miners was almost 90%. Among professional, executive, and salaried groups 63–65% were in favour. The lowest support (i.e. under 55%) was among farmers, small businessmen, agricultural labourers, housewives, and retirees. Yet, even among these groups the percentage who opposed nationalization was low (e.g. farmers, small business 27%, agricultural workers 19%, and housewives under 12%). BIPO polls March 1944, UK Data Archive Essex.

[112] In the autumn of 1943 they had been 41st. While the cost of living had risen by about 30% in the war, miners' earnings had grown by 90%. They also achieved such long-range goals as holidays with pay, a national wage structure, and the closed shop.

[113] N. Dennis, F. Henriques, and C. Slaughter, *Coal is Our Life* (London, 1956). One of the authors, Cliff Slaughter, worked as a Bevin Boy during the war.

rearmament, although in the first year or so of the war higher prices cut into these gains. But by 1942 a combination of subsidies, price controls, and rationing had stabilized the cost of living, especially for working-class families, and real earnings rose.[114] The efforts of trade unionists were instrumental, but so were the government's costs-plus-10 per cent contracts, and the ethos of 'fair shares' also greased the wheels. Some of the gains in earnings resulted from negotiated rate increases, others came from long hours and plentiful overtime. Government intervention also raised the minimum wages of dockers and the badly paid and largely unorganized workers in agriculture and the catering industry; indeed, the Catering Wages Bill provoked a major revolt of backbench Conservatives who viewed it as yet another attempt to impose socialism by stealth. Average wages for adult men rose from roughly £4 10s in July 1940 to £6 6s 4d in July 1944. Skilled craftsmen in engineering and shipbuilding, especially sheet-metal workers, tool-makers, and boilermakers, earned substantially more. Women's earnings also rose sharply, although very rarely did they obtain parity with men. Even so, their pay in war production—averaging about £3 10s—was often far more than they had received in pre-war jobs in other sectors. 'Wages were good. I'll say that for them', a woman who worked at Lines Bros in South Wimbledon commented to historian Sue Bruley: 'I was previously earning thirteen shillings and sixpence . . . then I went to Lines. I got three pounds . . . it was a lot of money.'[115] Women filling shells in government ROFs were paid a little over £4.

Of course, household income depended heavily upon the number of adult wage-earners. Where a skilled craftsman, his wife, and perhaps a son or daughter all worked in munitions, family income rose sharply and workers could amass considerable savings.[116] In cases where sons and daughters who had previously contributed to the household budget were serving in the forces, the family would be worse off. Already in cities like Coventry, skilled workers were well paid in the 1930s and had begun to enjoy a more affluent lifestyle, many moving to new council estates or purchasing their own homes. The economic changes of the war years were less striking here. It was in the old centres of heavy industry, in Scotland, Wales, and

[114] The official history states that by July 1941 average earnings were 43% above the level of October 1938, while wage rates had risen about 18% in the same period, i.e. the difference was bonuses and overtime. Overtime pay for many workers was 25–30% of their wages; sometimes it was more than half. As a group the highest-paid women workers were on the railways and buses (i.e. c.£4 a week) where they were more likely to get the male rate for the job. Before the war under 1 million workers paid any income tax (and for most it was under £3 a year). By 1943–4 some 7 million were paying (averaging £28 per capita): W. K. Hancock and M. Gowing, *The British War Economy* (London, 1949). Regional differentials continued: engineering wages were highest in the Midlands and especially Coventry; for shipbuilding it was Southampton and London.
[115] Quoted in Sue Bruley, '"A very happy crowd": Women in industry in south London in World War II', *History Workshop Journal*, 44 (1997), 64.
[116] Little is known about wartime savings. Historians often point to the work that Charles Madge did for Keynes: *War-Time Patterns of Saving and Spending*, National Institute of Economic and Social Research Occasional Papers, 4 (Cambridge, 1943). But Madge's view that increased wages did not necessarily translate into higher savings relied upon research done in 1940, with a little additional evidence collected in Leeds in 1942. Madge argued that there were 'cultures of saving' which had little relationship to earnings but his research says nothing about savings rates at the war's end, i.e. after a longer period of increased income.

the north, which had been hardest hit by the interwar depression that the contrast was most dramatic as inactive shipyards and mines suddenly sprang to life while local women found well-paying jobs in new government ROFs.

While all wages rose, in percentage terms unskilled workers did better on average than skilled (average unskilled wage rates climbed from about 70 to 80 per cent of skilled). This was probably inevitable in a tight labour market where so many skilled jobs were subdivided, but it accounts for some of the grievances of crafts-men. This narrowing of differentials was noted in the war years; early post-war studies corroborated the trend, but revisionist scholars disputed the findings, arguing that the underlying data paid inadequate attention to gender, age group, and the specific conditions of local labour markets. Ian Gazeley's recent re-exami-nation of the statistics shows convincingly, however, that pay differentials did narrow significantly—even taking into account age and gender—and that the compression was greater in sectors like engineering which had previously had more rigidly hierarchical wage structures. There were a few exceptions, notably apprentices in shipbuilding whose gains were relatively modest which undoubtedly helped to fuel their unrest during the war.[117] Some scholars have equated this erosion of differentials with the breaking down of intra-class skill barriers and the creation of greater working-class solidarity. Bernard Waites, for example, has argued that wage compression and common living standards strengthened class unity in the First World War, while Mike Savage and Andrew Miles have emphasized the narrowing of differentials as one factor in a larger argument about intra-class mobility and working-class integration.[118] The claim is difficult to substantiate, especially for so brief a period as the six war years, but greater equality in pay and common living standards, coupled with the other social and cultural aspects of war experience, probably did reinforce the sense of a common identity. Certainly, by the late 1940s the combination of higher taxation, narrowing differ-entials, and the sense that their living standards had declined sharply relative to workers strengthened the cohesion of different middle-class strata.

The upward pressure of manual workers' earnings improved their economic situation relative to many groups normally defined as middle class, especially clerks, school teachers, technicians, and lower-paid professionals. Though it is not without flaws, the best data on this is the work done by Dudley Seers and researchers at the Oxford Institute of Statistics; they concluded that the war produced a significant shift away from profits and salaries towards wages in the composition of the

[117] I. Gazeley, 'The levelling of pay in Britain during the Second World War', *European Review of Economic History*, 10(2) (August 2006). Among older works, see K. Knowles and D. Robertson, 'Differences between the wages of skilled and unskilled workers, 1880–1950', *The Bulletin of the Oxford Institute of Statistics*, 13(4) (1951); idem, 'Earnings in shipbuilding', *The Bulletin of the Oxford Institute of Statistics*, 13(11–12) (1951). R. Penn, 'The course of wage differentials between skilled and non-skilled manual workers in Britain between 1856 and 1964', *British Journal of Industrial Relations*, 21(1) (March 1983). Also G. Routh, *Occupation and Pay in Great Britain, 1906–79* (London, 1980).
[118] B. Waites, *A Class Society at War: England 1914–1918* (Leamington Spa, 1987); M. Savage and A. Miles, *The Remaking of the British Working Class, 1840–1940* (London, 1944).

national income.[119] Using 1938 as a base year, Seers estimated that by 1947 average real income had risen 9 per cent for the working class and had fallen over 7 per cent for the middle class. This should not be confused with a 'levelling of class' in a wider cultural sense; indeed, wartime changes provoked marked status fears and a backlash in the late 1940s when the press was full of stories about confiscatory rates of taxation, 'the new poor', and the 'plight of the middle class'. In life-style, patterns of expenditure, cultural preferences, levels of taxation, and mutual perceptions working and middle classes remained sharply divided. And while working-class frustration over continuing austerity in the late 1940s was vocal, it was the middle classes that increasingly viewed Attlee's post-war Britain as an assault on their living standards.

Workers' economic gains came at a price. Wage rates improved but a large proportion of their higher earnings resulted from longer hours and overtime. Twelve-hour shifts were common, so were tight deadlines and speed-ups to fulfil targets that were urgently required. As official reports make clear, fatigue and overstrain were a constant problem in these years, reflected in high rates of injury, absenteeism, nervous depression, tuberculosis, and lung and heart diseases. Years of hard, physical labour permanently undermined the health of some miners, steel workers, dockers, and men in heavy engineering. Workers were frequently exposed to disabling chemicals and the danger of explosions in government shell factories was ever-present. Asbestos was also widely used—for insulation and shell casings and simply sprayed onto ships' boiler pipes and bulkheads—with few precautions. Accident rates rose especially in the early war years and for women in particular, large numbers of whom had moved from relatively safe employment in shops and domestic service into jobs with higher health risks. In 1942, one in twenty-three workers was involved in an accident and the number involving adult women was five times what it had been in 1938—and yet at the peak of war production men, given their preponderance in heavy industrial sectors, still had double the injury rate of women. Unquantifiable though it may be, the costs of these years in terms of poor health and early deaths through cancer and other diseases should not be forgotten, and these were borne almost exclusively by manual workers.[120]

While fatigue and higher injury rates were one side of the wartime balance sheet, another was the improvements made to welfare services and the MoL's more interventionist policy to expand factory canteens, workplace recreation, housing, crèches and medical services. The ethos of a 'People's War' encouraged this and Bevin's strategy of controls and joint consultation gave him plenty of leverage with employers. Ironically, then, while occupational health suffered from the intensity of war production, these same years were also important in the spread of welfarist

[119] D. Seers, *The Levelling of Incomes since 1939* (Oxford, 1951); *idem, Changes in the Cost of Living and the Distribution of Income since 1938* (Oxford, 1949).
[120] H. A. Waldren, 'Occupational health during the Second World War: Hope deferred or hope abandoned?', *Medical History*, 41(2) (April 1997); R. Johnston and A. McIvor, 'The war and the body at work: Occupational health and safety in Scottish industry, 1939–1945', *Journal of Scottish Historical Studies*, 24(2) (2004). Also, K. Price, 'Women of steel: Health and safety issues during World War II', *North East Labour History Bulletin*, 27 (1993).

attitudes in British industry. Prior to the war some private firms—for example, Cadburys, Rowntree, Singer, and ICI—had taken the lead, believing that better welfare services and amenities were critical to improved labour relations and industrial efficiency. But full-scale mobilization of the economy and the recruitment into war production of large numbers of inexperienced workers gave workplace welfare much higher priority than ever before. The numbers of factory inspectors, medical officers, and welfare supervisors multiplied rapidly; canteen services were vastly expanded; and, after a slow start, the capacity of public nurseries went from virtually nothing to over 112,000 places. Hostels were provided for many workers directed to jobs away from home, washrooms and sanitary facilities were upgraded for factories and mines, and, since workers were spending so much longer in the workplace, entertainment programmes were arranged through ENSA and CEMA.[121]

Bevin intended these changes to become permanent after the war, part of a new deal for workers. The best workplace conditions were to be found in large, modern factories, such as the shadow aircraft factories around Coventry or the big Castle Bromwich aircraft factory near Birmingham which figured in the film *Millions Like Us*. Progress was uneven, however. It was difficult to upgrade small manufacturing firms occupying Victorian buildings with poor ventilation, cramped space, and primitive sanitary facilities, while in many ports dockers worked under conditions that had changed little in fifty years. Nonetheless, as a result of the war, workers' welfare had a much higher profile and through the plant-level JPCs workers' representatives for the first time were empowered to discuss the whole range of health, safety, and welfare arrangements.

TRADE UNIONS, WORKERS, AND CLASS CONSCIOUSNESS

Bevin and Citrine sought to maximize the mobilization of labour for the war effort and in the process reshape social attitudes and permanently alter the status of working people. Vital to the strategy were the spread of trade unionism and a strong partnership with government and by the late 1940s labour's gains were unmistakable.[122] With over 9 million members in 1947 unions were stronger, richer, and enjoyed higher public esteem than ever before. 'Gone', wrote the *Times* labour correspondent, 'were the days when [the TUC's] representatives went to Whitehall' clutching their resolutions 'leaving them at the door, extremely happy if they saw a Permanent Secretary, and most handsomely flattered if by accident they stumbled across a Minister.'[123] Unions had been involved in every aspect of the planning and

---

[121] See ch. 6 below.

[122] TUC's representation on official government committees increased from 12 in 1939 to 60 in 1949 dealing with a wide range of themes: productivity, technical education, regional policy, rationing and prices, etc. A. J. Reid, *United We Stand: A history of Britain's trade unions* (London, 2004), p. 379.

[123] J.V. Radcliffe for *The Times* quoted in S. M. Beer, *Modern British Politics* (New York, 1982 edition), p. 214.

implementation of wartime policy and they played a central role in reconstruction planning and Labour's electoral victory. The sea-change was also evident among employer associations whose dominant mood in 1945 was defensive and apprehensive. At first many employers had little appetite for challenging the unions.[124] Only after 1947 did they regain their collective voice in a massive campaign against further nationalization of industries. As we have seen, the war had strengthened corporatist ties between unions, government, and business, but these arrangements were a necessary exercise in compromise and cooperation rather than an expression of some underlying consensus or convergence of outlook.[125]

In fact, organized labour's new prominence was fraught with potential contradictions. The war increased popular support for comprehensive planning and state activism in the economy, but Bevin's policies had also reinforced public faith in traditional structures of voluntary collective bargaining. 'Compulsory arbitration' had always been a deeply ambiguous concept requiring a good deal of smoke and mirrors to make it work. Both sides of industry continued to believe in a self-regulating system that preserved their autonomy and gave the state only a limited role. The national emergency of war made both capital and labour willing to accept temporary restraints on their independence, even though the government's machinery for enforcing compliance (either in making the parties abide by agreements or in preventing strikes) was in reality very limited.[126] But reverence for free collective bargaining as a basic right set limits to any socialist programme of centralized planning. Employers regarded such central controls as unwarranted interference in peacetime and, while the TUC supported a strong, activist state in some areas (e.g. tripartite consultation, social welfare, nationalization, and intervention to ensure full employment), it fiercely resisted any suggestion of state regulation of wages or restrictions on trade union autonomy. This helps to explain the paradoxical gap between the effusive rhetoric of planning in the late 1940s and the limited nature of the plans actually put forward. There never existed the same willingness to pursue a *dirigiste* industrial policy or to accept subordination to government plans as in France or Scandinavia. By 1950, indeed, 'planning' had

---

[124] They accepted, for example, the extension of Order 1305 and much of the wartime system of controls into peacetime fearing that the Labour government might come up with something less tolerable. The trade unions, for their part, supported a renewal of 1305 both because of the power it gave to trade union officials and because they feared a post-war slump like that which followed the First World War.

[125] Even wartime discussions between trade union advocates and moderate employer groups revealed fundamental disagreements. D. Ritschel, 'The making of consensus: The Nuffield College Conferences during the Second World War', *TCBH*, 6(3) (1995).

[126] Stammers, *Civil Liberties in Britain during the Second World War* emphasizes (excessively in my view) the coercive aspects of Bevin's regulatory system. Nina Fishman has also argued that Order 1305 shifted the balance in the 1940s away from voluntarism towards state regulation, more than is usually acknowledged. More convincing is James Jaffe's complex analysis of the continuing priority of voluntarism and of the limitations, ambiguities, and tensions inherent in the very notion of compulsory arbitration. N. Fishman, ' "A vital element in British Industrial Relations": A reassessment of Order 1305, 1940–51', *Historical Studies in Industrial Relations*, 8 (Autumn 1999); James A. Jaffe, 'The ambiguities of compulsory arbitration and the wartime experience of Order 1305', *Historical Studies in Industrial Relations*, 15 (Spring 2003).

come to mean Keynesian correctives to market forces—fiscal demand management rather than state-directed modernization. Though widely agreed to be a pressing necessity, the modernization of Britain's industrial base faltered and lagged behind.

Thus, on the one hand, the war experience seemed to move the country closer to a regulated economy, on the other it underscored traditional voluntarism. In his valedictory address to the TUC Congress in 1948, Citrine announced: 'We have passed from an era of propaganda to one of responsibility.' What this meant for the TUC as a 'governing institution' in partnership with a Labour government was a constant struggle to get workers to be patient over continuing austerity and after 1948 growing difficulty in enforcing voluntary wage restraint. The TUC accepted continuance of the official ban on strikes until August 1951, but it proved hard to contain the tensions between national policy and sectional interests, especially with the onset of the cold war which deepened divisions within the labour movement. The war had revitalized workplace networks, institutionalizing what the Donovan Commission (1965–8) called the 'dual nature' of Britain's industrial relations system—a formal system of union leaders and employers' organizations negotiating industry-wide agreements *and* alongside it a highly decentralized system of company-level bargaining between shop stewards and managers which exercised increasing power.[127] In the circumstances of the late 1940s union leaders found it difficult to maintain discipline—this was especially true of Bevin's old union, the TGWU, which faced repeated rebellions from militant dockers.

Moreover, while union leaders faced grass-roots pressure, the TUC tried to speak for trade unionism as a whole while respecting the cherished independence of individual unions. Its authority was always more apparent than real; the war had strengthened the largest unions who exercised some control over Congress through their bloc votes, but they did not always agree. Part of the problem was the multiplicity of British unions and their rivalries and competing interests, but efforts to reorganize trade union structure—revived in 1944 after a long hiatus—got nowhere. Notions of replacing the existing system with industrial unions covering a whole industry both contravened the interests of big general unions like the TGWU which had so successfully recruited workers in diverse industries and they had little appeal for the craft fraternities, determined to defend their sectional interests. Thus, for all the appearance of unity and direction under Citrine, Bevin, and later Deakin, the war had done little to alter the fragmented and decentralized character of the British industrial relations system. If anything, the labour movement's triumphalism after the war reinforced its basic conservatism and made change an even remoter prospect. Finally, the revitalization of the old heavy staple industries—coal, textiles, heavy engineering, and shipbuilding—also strengthened the cultural conservatism of the union movement, both its male-dominated and male-oriented character and its focus on the big manual unions that had created and still dominated the TUC; not only did this perpetuate the manual–non-manual divide, but it meant that the movement adapted only slowly and

[127] Cmnd 3623, Report of the Royal Commission on Trade Unions and Employers' Associations (HMSO, 1968), p. 261.

reluctantly to the expansion of white-collar unionism which was to be the main area of membership growth in the thirty years after the war.

'Without our people', Bevin declared in 1940, 'this war cannot be won nor can the life of the country be carried on.'[128] From the first, upon becoming Minister of Labour, he phrased the situation in class terms—*'our people'* and more personally *'my people'* for he saw himself as symbolizing labour and a standard-bearer for the working class. Bevin's pride, his coupling of class consciousness and patriotism, also found an echo among workers more generally. As this book has emphasized, for all its powerful imagery of cross-class national unity, the Second World War was a period when considerations of class permeated every aspect of social and political debate. Debate about the working class inevitably implied claims about its position in the nation; the two were interdependent and reciprocally redefined. Workers and labour gained collectively in status and power; they were 'nationalized' both in a patriotic sense and in creating greater class unity, reinforcing the sense of belonging to a *national* class. Recently, historians have emphasized those factors which divide and differentiate workers—differences, for example, of gender, age, religion, skill-levels, and region—rather than the cultural patterns and economic circumstances that they share. But at any given time tendencies towards class fragmentation are in constant contention with processes that draw a class together. In the 1940s a conjunction of material conditions, wartime social patriotism, powerful imagery of the depression years, and a realignment in national politics, all provided the basis for a more cohesive sense of class. Public debate (whether debate about evacuation, poverty, family dissolution, or the Beveridge Report and social reconstruction) played an important role, so did the symbolism of a 'People's War' omnipresent in the media and public discourse. Another powerful factor in promoting a sense of class unity was the expanding power and visibility of trade unionism and the presence of Labour ministers in Churchill's coalition. Men like Morrison and Bevin were representatives of the working class as well as servants of the nation; their speeches both echoed popular dissatisfaction with the elite and depicted workers as belonging to a single class with a common set of interests. And if at times the Labour Party's popularity sank low, this was often because it was viewed as inadequately representing those interests.

The wartime reshaping of working-class identity and the general enhancement of labour's status had, then, many interacting and mutually reinforcing facets (ideological, cultural, material, institutional, and rhetorical). In conclusion, two further points should be underscored. First, in Britain between the wars one can identify aspects of a shared working-class culture—in patterns of family life and consumption, neighbourhood networks, and leisure pursuits.[129] And yet the salient fact of those decades was the sharp disparity in the social experience of workers produced by markedly different regional economies and the geographical concentration of

---

[128] Quoted in Weiler, *Ernest Bevin*, p. 101.
[129] R. McKibbin, *Classes and Cultures in England, 1918–1951* (Oxford, 1998); J. E. Cronin, *Labour and Society in Britain, 1918–1979* (London, 1984); N. Kirk, *Change, Continuity and Class: Labour in British society, 1850–1920* (Manchester, 1998).

mass unemployment. The stark contrast between north and south, between the old industrial regions and the new expanding industries of Greater London and the West Midlands, was the central theme of a whole crop of writers who set off in search of Britain, or more usually England, in the 1930s. While for most people the quintessential manual worker of this period was a northerner, too often he was a northerner without work. Persistent unemployment and poverty had a shattering effect on entire communities, once vibrant but now derelict and haemorrhaging their younger population. War changed all that. Old basic industries like coal, shipbuilding, and heavy engineering became critical once again; the workplace cultures associated with these industries regained their strength; and full employment brought a measure of prosperity and hope for the future. Hard times and past conflict were still very much in people's minds: 'In my inquiries', Ferdynand Zweig wrote, 'I came to realize that the past is something still alive and potent.'[130] But the deepest fault line within the working class—the one that divided employed workers from those who suffered years without a job and whose everyday life was defined by the Means Test and the dole—was gone.

The second point concerns the 'local cultures of solidarity'[131] that developed among war-workers. More than usual, people's lives were work-centred. Many lived in hostels or billets away from their families; for many the day began with long train or bus rides along with fellow workers. And since so much time was spent in workplaces, they became important sites for communal and morale-raising activities: firm dances, concerts, sports events, and clubs. Closely integrated networks were well-established among male skilled craftsmen—among tool-room workers and shipwrights—but many of those who entered the war industries were new recruits, including many women, with no experience of factories. Memoirs and oral testimonies, like those undertaken by Sue Bruley with female war-workers in south London, describe a process of socialization—loyalty to the group was strong and sometimes persisted for years afterwards. 'I loved it', one worker told Bruley, 'there was such an atmosphere...Everybody got on with everybody else. There was no one any better and no one any lower.'[132] To be sure, such comments are nostalgic reflections upon youth from the perspective of old age. But they also recapture a solidarity that grew from shared work and leisure time, 'skylarking' and playing tricks, experiences of raids, and shared worries like trying to arrange childcare or finding time to shop for food. And while some workers in war factories came from middle-class backgrounds they were a small minority, often in supervisory positions or in offices. In big firms or government ROFs with tens of thousands of workers the tone of workplace culture was overwhelmingly and assertively working class. A Scotswoman sent to work at Ford's in Manchester recalled: 'No, you would not have got a doctor's daughter going to Ford's... I never met anyone what we call

[130] F. Zweig, *The British Worker* (London, 1952), p. 87.

[131] R. Fantasia, *Cultures of Solidarity: Consciousness, action and contemporary American workers* (Los Angeles and Berkeley, 1988).

[132] S. Bruley, '"A very happy crowd"', p. 65. Also similar comments about 'community' by women who worked in the Consett steel works, County Durham in K. M. Price, 'An alternative "Consett" story', PhD Diss., Open University, 1986.

middle class . . . No it was all working-class girls and women there. We were all from the same class.'[133] There were divisions and petty rivalries, of course, between workers in different trades and different workshops, but these were nothing compared to the fissure that separated managers and workers, the office and the shop floor.

War factories were also social spaces where political identities were formed. The degree of 'political' activity varied enormously, even within different sectors of large firms, but where there were groups of activist shop stewards they were often a catalyst. Lectures and discussion groups were organized, newspapers and pamphlets circulated, and campaigns mounted to mobilize workers on such issues as air-raid protection, provision of nurseries, control over canteen space, the government's decision to release fascist leader Sir Oswald Mosley from jail, and demonstrations in favour of launching a Second Front. To be sure, at least until the middle of the war, surveys showed that many workers had little faith in conventional party politics. But labour disputes within firms had a politicizing effect—using the word in a broader sense—underscoring group loyalty and a sense of collective rights and common interests. The fact that some 3 million additional people joined unions, more than a million of them women, is scarcely insignificant whether or not they attended meetings and became actively engaged; the solidarity of new workers in support of job actions began to trouble government officials by 1943. Involvement on works' committees or in organizing strikes and job actions also provided some workers with an education in labour politics which led to activity in local trades councils and party politics. Admittedly, in some firms the workforce was quieter and more passive than others, but by 1943 reports from across the country captured a growing sense of entitlement among workers that expressed itself in a gut feeling that they should be consulted, that they deserved a voice. And the discursive environment of the time, with constant references to citizenship and equal sacrifice, reinforced this. As Ferdynand Zweig noted: 'I have no hesitation in stating that factories are the most important schools for education in citizenship . . . and that much more attention should be paid to this aspect of factory life.'[134] Focus on a few texts, written from the outside, has led some historians to magnify workers' apathy, their indifference to war news and cynicism about post-war reconstruction.[135] Workplaces and trade unionism were not the only formative influences upon working-class political attitudes in these years, but they were important ones.

[133] P. Goodman, *Women, Sexuality and War* (Basingstoke, 2002), p. 48.

[134] F. Zweig, *Women's Life and Labour* (London, 1952), p. 59.

[135] S. Fielding, P. Thompson, and N. Tiratsoo, *England Arise! The Labour Party and popular politics in 1940s Britain* (Manchester, 1995); see the critique by J. Hinton, '1945 and the Apathy School', *HWJ*, 43 (Spring 1997).

4

The Mobilization of Women

In one sense women's labour was mobilized at the start of the war, since the government's evacuation scheme required hundreds of thousands of housewives to assume additional burdens. Women's recruitment for jobs outside their homes developed more slowly. Indeed, in the last months of 1939 female unemployment actually rose as non-essential services and consumer industries contracted or made preparations to shift over to war production.[1] At first the government relied entirely upon volunteers; Bevin, like most of the Cabinet, preferred to rely on persuasion. But by July 1940 only 320,000 additional women had joined the nation's workforce and the Manpower Requirements Committee estimated that an additional 2 million industrial workers would be needed, far more than voluntary recruitment drives could ever produce.

The first step was to register women with local employment panels, but this alone did little to increase the labour force so long as the panels relied on persuasion. Parents were often opposed to daughters signing on for the armed forces and prejudice against factory work was strong among many women. Patriotic speeches and recruitment parades of trucks displaying aero-engines and other items of war production also elicited a lower response with married women than expected, many of whom had a negative view of factory work and anyway protested that they were fully occupied with their families. One survey of 600 wives in early 1941 found, for example, that over 46 per cent refused under any circumstances to engage in factory work, while almost 43 per cent declined unless the problems of childcare, shopping, poor transportation, and spouses' objections could be overcome.[2] At the same time many employers were reluctant to employ women, arguing that they were expensive (requiring separate and better washroom facilities etc.), lacking in factory discipline, and prone to absenteeism. Starting in January 1942, however, young single women and childless widows aged between twenty and thirty were designated 'mobile' and conscripted into war work. Given the national crisis, there were few public objections to the drafting of single women, but the extension of compulsion to wives caused greater concern. Officials soon found themselves debating the meaning of a 'home' and trying to define what level of domestic responsibilities constituted grounds for exemption from war work. There was general agreement that mothers with children under fourteen years

---

[1] H. M. D. Parker, *Manpower: A study of wartime policy and administration* (London, 1957).
[2] NA: INF 1/292, 5–12 March 1941.

should be exempt, but the 'Household R' exemption granted to women keeping house for a husband or male relatives indicated the government's priority, wherever possible, to strike a conservative balance between women's domestic obligations and the nation's labour needs.[3]

With 'mobile' women fully occupied, by mid-1942 official attention turned increasingly to the pool of childless wives and older women; it became harder to get exemptions and more married women were directed to take up war work.[4] Statistically the results were impressive. The total number of women in paid employment rose from about 6.2 million in 1939 to around 7.7 million in 1943. In vital sectors of war production, the proportion of women rose rapidly: from 10 to 34 per cent in engineering; 27 to 52 per cent in chemicals; and 32 to 46 per cent in miscellaneous metal industries. Sectors such as textiles, clothing, domestic service, and retail shrank in size as women were 'combed out' for war-related work, while the number of female clerical employees, both in private business and governmental offices, rose rapidly continuing a trend underway prior to the war. In addition, half a million women, mostly young and single, joined the armed forces and another 80,000 worked on farms as members of the Women's Land Army. Eventually in mid-1943 the government began directing housewives into part-time work, usually thirty hours a week, many of them organized in 'paired' or 'split' shifts, so that two women kept a job filled. As a result the rate of employment outside the home increased from 34 per cent to 44.5 per cent among all women aged fourteen to fifty-nine years in the war years, while the figures for married women jumped from 16 per cent in the 1931 census (19 per cent, perhaps, at the war's outbreak) to around 43 per cent at the peak of the war effort. Finally, scores of thousands of women billeted evacuees, servicemen, and war workers while well over a million undertook some recognized form of voluntary activity. In the fourth year of the war, there were very few single women and relatively few married women, apart from those with young children, who were not contributing in some way to the national effort.[5]

Official publicity depicted women's mobilization as blind to social difference, but there emerged a definite stratification in the types of war work undertaken. Thus, while contemporary publicity and later myth emphasized social mixing in factories, imagining them as social melting pots where the daughters of industrialists and aristocrats rubbed shoulders with their proletarian sisters, female recruits to war factories were overwhelmingly working-class and the majority were already at

---

[3] P. Summerfield, *Women Workers in the Second World War* (London, 1988). M. Allen, 'The domestic ideal and the mobilization of womanpower in World War II', *Women's Studies International Forum*, 8(4) (1983); V. Douie, *Daughters of Britain* (London, 1949).

[4] 3,067 women who refused to comply with war directives were prosecuted and 199 were sent to prison for a variety of offences including refusing to work.

[5] Only the Soviet Union mobilized a higher percentage of women for the war effort. Summerfield, *Women Workers in the Second World War*, *idem*, 'Women, war and social change: Women in Britain in World War II' in A. Marwick (ed.), *Total War and Social Change* (London, 1988). Also, C. E. V. Leser, 'Men and women in industry', *Economic Journal* (June 1952); G. Beck, *Survey of British Employment and Unemployment 1927–45* (Oxford, 1951); M. Harrison, 'Resource mobilization for World War II: The USA, UK, USSR, Germany, 1938–45', *Economic History Review*, 50 (May 1988).

work when the war began. Most middle-class women ended up in clerical or administrative work or joined the uniformed services; those in war factories were mostly in supervisory positions as welfare officers or work inspectors causing Labour MP Ellen Wilkinson to caution Bevin about preferential treatment and urging him to take a 'very strong line on the point that working-class women should not be pushed on one side to make room for women of the upper classes'.[6] Even in the forces, as will be seen, there was a distinct pecking order with the army auxiliary the most unpopular and often disparaged as attracting lower-class recruits. Those with more money and education had greater choice in how they might contribute to the war effort; poor women had fewer options. This did stir up anger in the early war years when Home Intelligence reported rumours circulating about officers' wives living idly in garrison towns and wealthy women holed up in the peaceful comfort of West Country hotels; there was also a widespread suspicion that volunteer work was a convenient soft option for the better-off. Indeed, one of the claims of those advocating tighter restrictions on married women was that it offered the best means of equalizing the burdens of rich and poor.[7]

WOMEN AS HOUSEWIVES

Women in war factories and the auxiliary services gained most attention in the media, although the majority of adult women (about 55 per cent or 8.8 million) were full-time housewives and mothers even at the height of the mobilization in 1943. Not that their daily routines had much in common with the pre-war years; being a home-maker was radically different when families were separated by conscription and evacuation, basic goods were rationed, schools closed or on shortened hours, and air raids and dangers to loved ones were a persistent threat. In addition, the distinction between women in factories and women in the home is in many ways artificial and misleading. Wives not only moved in and out of the paid labour force with some frequency, but those in war production continued to run their homes and, as surveys made clear, still shouldered the lion's share of domestic chores.

The greatest challenge and an unending worry for wives and mothers was food. Wartime diaries and letters reveal a continual preoccupation with its cost, availability, quality, and variety. 'Most of my worry this week', runs a typical entry by a Wembley housewife, 'has been about food not raids, but I did manage to get 1/4 lb of cheese just enough for a small cube each.' 'No fish since last June', she writes at a later date, 'except one piece I was allowed at the fish shop for the three of us. This

---

[6] NA: LAB 26/59, E. Wilkinson to E. Bevin, 3 July 1940; H. L. Smith, 'The problem of "equal pay for equal work" in Great Britain in World War II', *Journal of Modern History*, 53 (December 1981).
  [7] NA: INF 1/292, 27 August–3 September 1941. Home Intelligence ascribed the strong public resistance to registering women aged 46–50 to middle-class husbands who feared an erosion of their domestic comforts; indeed, when MPs signed a protest petition, Bevin retorted angrily that nobody had objected earlier when ex-textile workers and nurses were registered to age 50. In fact, the so-called 'grandmothers' call-up' elicited plenty of criticism in workers' households and the TUC's Walter Citrine regarded the move as a serious incursion into workers' private lives.

month we are having two packets each of dried eggs and we have them in one way or another every day. I wish we could have more meat.'[8] Polls found that wives were 'fairly consistently more dispirited and resigned than men'.[9] Some of the pressure on housewives was alleviated by a huge increase in communal feeding. School meal and milk programmes grew (about 40 per cent of schoolchildren took school dinners and 75 per cent received milk by the war's end[10]) but even more striking was the growth of workplace canteens. Only 1,500 were operating in 1939, but by the war's end they numbered over 20,000. Also, in 1940 the Ministry of Food set up British Restaurants, providing modestly priced, off-ration meals to the public at large; by 1943 over 2,000 existed, mostly run by local authorities. Their advocates hailed them as a new kind of social institution, epitomizing the democratic spirit of wartime and places where social solidarity could be forged. Model designs were drawn up for the ideal layout for these spaces; the War Artists scheme mounted exhibitions of photographs and prints in some of them; and nutritionists hoped that they might instruct the public—and especially poor women—in a healthy diet. Economic constraints, however, meant that most were makeshift and basic and the food, while popular, was monotonous and more filling than healthy.[11]

Rationing was introduced only at the very end of the First World War in January 1918 amid growing strikes and demonstrations. For two years popular anger had risen over steep price increases and shortages and hostility towards profiteers was of major significance in sharpening class consciousness.[12] Two decades later, when war again seemed imminent, plans for food rationing were drawn up in advance to prevent malnutrition, ensure more equitable distribution of supplies, and check inflation and profiteering. But though the books and coupons were ready in 1938, rationing was only introduced on five items in January 1940, then gradually extended over the next years. As a result in the first eighteen months of the war, before controls were in place, inflation hit many poorer groups hard. In Bristol, for example, retail prices rose sharply for meat (28 per cent), fish (82 per cent), fruits and vegetables (70 per cent), furniture and household goods (80 per cent), and clothing (51 per cent); increases were also said to be larger in poorer districts and for cheaper quality foods, although it is true that many of the quality items normally purchased by higher-income groups were simply unavailable.[13] The diary entries of Mrs M. E. Creeley, a widow from the London borough of Enfield, repeatedly quote food prices. Already in late October 1939, she complains of price 'ramps':

---

[8] IWM: 88/50/1, Mrs Rose Uttin diary: 23 February 1941, 18 January 1944.

[9] M. Pugh, *Women and the Women's Movement in Britain, 1914–49* (London, 1992), p. 266. Also, NA: INF1/292, 21–28 May 1941.

[10] J. Hurt, 'Feeding the hungry schoolchild in the first half of the twentieth century' in D. J. Oddy and D. S. Miller (eds.), *Diet and Health in Modern Britain* (Croom Helm, 1985).

[11] K. Price, 'Changes on the "kitchen front": The case of British Restaurants in World War II', *North East Labour History*, 22 (1988); J. Vernon, *Hunger. A Modern History* (Harvard, 2007), pp. 187–95.

[12] B. Waites, *A Class Society at War: England 1914–18* (Leamington Spa, 1987).

[13] 'The cost of living in Bristol', *Bulletin of the Oxford Institute of Statistics*, 3(14) (1941); also, 'Liverpool family budgets', *Bulletin of the Oxford Institute of Statistics*, 3(16) (1941). A 1940 Mass-Observation survey of 400 women revealed great concern about declining living standards: M-OA: FR 93 'The housewives' war' (May 1940).

'Foodstuffs are still soaring. The £1 is worth about 17s 6d now... Sugar is now 3 1/2d a lb. Beef has gone up 2d and 3d a lb. Bacon is very scarce.'[14] In the same month 'Lylie' Eldergill, a Bethnal Green woman in her thirties who worked full-time as a machinist and cared for her blind husband, wrote to a friend overseas: 'It is one rush for me from morning till night. The shops are shut at 6 o'clock, so I have to go out in my dinner time to get errands. It is a fight to get a bus in the morning and another to get home at night. The prices of food are going up. I don't know how some people manage. I am glad I haven't any children. It is hard enough to manage on the money.'[15]

The first items rationed early in 1940 were bacon, butter, sugar, meat, and tea. Over the next two years the list grew to include margarine, cooking fats, cheese, eggs, syrup, preserves, soap, sweets, chocolate, dried eggs, and dried milk. The scheme was simple, fixing a minimum quantity of food for every consumer. Special rations and vitamins were allowed to infants and nursing mothers; milk was made available to schoolchildren, and caloric intake was adjusted for some occupations, with additional coupons for those like miners and dockers who engaged in heavy physical labour. Bread and potatoes, regarded as 'buffer' or 'filler' foods, were not rationed nor was fish, although it was frequently unavailable. Beer and tobacco were also not included, but they too were often scarce and rose steeply in price. Since non-rationed goods, including tinned foods, became increasingly hard to obtain, particularly for workers with less time to forage, a second 'points' system was introduced in December 1941. Each person got sixteen points (later twenty) per week and items were ascribed a specific point value. The system ensured that everyone would get a share and gave consumers a measure of choice over 'non-essential' foods. Official manipulation of point values could also be used to persuade the public to buy unfamiliar items. Clothing and footwear were also rationed on a 'points' system from 1941, while the production of furniture and household articles was tightly controlled and priority was given to special groups such as raid victims and newlyweds.

Rationing guaranteed that everyone received a basic minimum; it did not and could not equalize consumption. Periodically, anger erupted over the advantages of the rich who could eat at expensive restaurants (only controlled in June 1942 and then imperfectly) and were able to spend more on better-quality clothes and footwear that lasted longer but carried the same point value. Richer patrons, it was claimed, also received preferential treatment at shops: Home Intelligence reported the common complaint that 'people giving large orders are favoured and the poorer people wanting "little bits" are refused'.[16] Occupational groups like miners engaged in heavy manual labour remained highly critical of their allocation and by early 1943, a survey showed, over 70 per cent of males in heavy manual jobs

[14] IWM: 93/22/1, Mrs M. E. Creeley diary, 22 September 1939, 26 October 1939. She went to work rivet-making for an aircraft firm, then turned to machining parachutes.
[15] IWM: Elizabeth Elkus letters (Elkus lived in California; these are letters to her from friends and relatives in Britain). Eliza ('Lylie') Eldergill to Elkus, 24 October 1939.
[16] NA: INF 1/292, 25 March 1942 (Home Intelligence report: 'Inequality of sacrifice').

(and a rising percentage of female manual workers) were convinced they were not getting enough food to sustain them.[17] Yet, while many might cavil at aspects of the scheme, very few questioned its necessity and a June 1942 poll of 3,000 housewives found that most of them favoured its continuation post-war.[18] Complaints about 'luxury feeding' never disappeared[19] but, compared to pre-war, class differentials and inequities in the type and quantity of food consumed narrowed markedly. The diet was meagre enough and monotonous with lots of 'filler food' and off-ration rabbit stews. But for many working-class families, who had endured long bouts of poverty between the wars, it was tolerable and their consumption in many cases actually rose. As official announcements emphasized, people's diet was also more nutritious and healthier with less animal fat and more milk and vegetables. What was frustrating was that, with wages rising, families could afford more, but could not get it. Queuing in all weathers became a way of life—lasting more than a dozen years. Orwell lauded queues as a marker of British civility, but they were the bane of most women's lives. 'The so-called social life of the queue', one survey admitted, 'which is alleged to outweigh the waste of time and the fatigue of the queuer is 90 per cent a myth.'[20]

By mid-1941, according to official figures, inflation was brought under control and the cost-of-living for the working class was effectively stabilized. Clothing and fuel prices continued to fluctuate, but with rent and food controlled and wages mostly outpacing inflation, the pressure on family budgets eased. One survey concluded that average expenditure on food by working-class families had risen by 35 per cent from May 1940 to June 1943, while the price of most rationed foods, potatoes, and bread increased by about 6 per cent.[21] Much of the extra outlay went for costly 'points' items and workers' savings grew as did their expenditure on beer and tobacco. Aggregate statistics, however, provide only a partial view of the situation. They tell us little about the regional scarcities of food and basic goods or the different circumstances of households. As sociologist Ferdynand Zweig put it: 'Yes, "economic man" exists, but "he" is a female . . . They are the ones who are responsible for the survival of their families.'[22] A middle-aged woman with a husband and adult sons or daughters working in war factories often

---

[17] Ina Zweiniger-Bargielowska, *Austerity in Britain.: Rationing, controls and consumption* (Oxford, 2000), pp. 73–5. In February 1943, according to a government survey, 50% of all male manual workers believed their diet was insufficient to maintain health (with an additional 11% 'doubtful'). Women were less dissatisfied.

[18] NA: RG 23/9A, Wartime Social Survey, Food during the War (June 1942).

[19] 'Cassandra', 'Stop this food scandal', *Daily Mirror*, 8 January 1941. Lord Woolton's diary, 25 March 1942 (Woolton Papers, Bodleian Library, Oxford), comments on the press outcry about 'luxury feeding' in hotels and restaurants.

[20] George Orwell, *The English People* (London, 1944); O. A. MacIver, 'Family life in wartime 1939–45', *Social Work*, 3(10) (April 1946), 234. Also, NA: INF/192, 4–11 June, 16–23 July 1941.

[21] 'Working-class income and expenditure', *Bulletin of the Oxford Institute of Statistics*, 6(6) (1944), 3–4. See also C. Madge, *War-Time Patterns of Saving and Spending* (Cambridge, 1943); Madge's data on Bristol, Leeds, and Glasgow cover the period 1940–2. Local newspapers provide a detailed commentary on changes in the cost of living, shopping difficulties, fuel shortages, and the work of local food control committees, e.g. the *Islington Gazette* provides a good analysis for that London borough 1940–2.

[22] F. Zweig, *Women's Life and Labour* (London, 1952), pp. 9–10.

had more cash than ever before, although feeding them was difficult and she might go short herself to provide for the others. An army wife with several small children faced much tougher choices, especially if she could not take a job. A Leeds survey of a thousand families in 1942 concluded that being a soldier's wife was a principal cause of poverty and many were in debt to friends and relatives.[23] For wives of better-paid workers, used to higher living standards and higher rents or a mortgage, army allowances could bring a sudden descent into poverty. Another hard-pressed group was old-age pensioners, who applied to the Public Assistance Board for supplementary allowances in record numbers in 1940, undeterred by its Poor Law stigma.

Government statistics also obscure price gouging and abuses by traders, wholesalers, thieves, and black-marketeers. Stories about this were legion, but official pronouncements were relatively rare at least until May 1941 when the price regulation committee for the North Midland Region (thirteen such committees were set up in November 1939 to examine complaints of profiteering) decided to go public with a damning indictment of rampant speculation and self-enrichment at the expense of the consumer by 'people who render no services in distribution'. The committee, its secretary wrote, had found 'racket after racket' affecting the price of all kinds of goods, some of them 'changing ownership many times like stocks and shares without even leaving the warehouse'. The head of the Central Price Regulation Committee complained in February 1942 that 'price control work is falling dangerously into arrears' and hinted that regional committees were being used more as a front to appease public discontent than as active watchdogs.[24]

It is difficult to know how widespread trading violations were or how extensive the black market. An early study concluded that illicit trade was small-scale and not very significant, but it relied heavily upon newspaper reports and prosecutions, which represented a small fraction of actual dealings.[25] But, despite the army of inspectors employed by government departments, a well-organized black market appears to have developed, especially after the proliferation of American bases brought in a cornucopia of scarce goods.[26] 'It was possible', recalled a Merseyside man, 'to buy, at a price, almost any foodstuff in short supply... It was all very much *sub rosa*, the quiet whisper in the pub or some place where men congregate.' A Hackney woman remembered going to a butcher in Hoxton: 'If we gave him

---

[23] V. Douie, *The Lesser Half* (Women's Publicity Planning Association pamphlet, London 1943), p. 45.

[24] IWM: 86/24/1, Craven-Griffiths Papers (secretary of the North Midland Price Regulation Committee): Craven-Griffiths to Editor, 28 April 1941 (a general letter to the press), plus the report issued by Sir Douglas McCraith (chairman of the North Midland Price Regulation Committee); Sir R. Evershed (head of Central Price Regulation Committee) to Sir Arnold Overton, Board of Trade, 19 February 1942.

[25] E. Smithies, *Crime in Wartime: A social history of crime in World War II* (London, 1982); *idem*, *The Black Economy in Britain since 1914* (Dublin, 1984).

[26] D. Thomas, *An Underworld at War: Spivs, deserters, racketeers and civilians in the Second World War* (London, 2003); William Hill, *Boss of the Underworld* (London, 1955); R. Samuel (ed.), *East End Underworld: The life of Arthur Harding* (London, 1981).

some extra money he would give us extra meat...There was a lot of thieving going on, lots of goods for sale.'[27] Public indignation about unpatriotic trading, often laced with anti-Semitism, was rife. Yet, low-level black-market activity was widely aided and abetted, while the illegal sale or sharing of clothing coupons, mostly between friends and relatives, was endemic. People argued that their minor transactions—getting a bit more on the side—harmed nobody and acted as a useful safety valve, providing extras for special occasions: a birthday, a wedding, or leave for a relative in the forces. As one person put it, 'We could never have survived on rations during the war; the bit extra we bought on the black market kept us going.'[28]

Aside from food, the other problem that plagued many families was housing. A good deal of inner-city working-class housing was in a deplorable condition. German air raids devastated large portions of British cities drastically reducing the supply of habitable dwellings and creating a growing number of homeless raid victims. Towns with booming war industries had to house thousands of additional workers largely in existing accommodation. New construction by speculative builders and local authorities came to an end and only minimal repairs were made to existing stock: leaking roofs, windows shattered by the blast, broken gas and water pipes were an everyday experience.[29] Newly married young couples found it almost impossible to get a place of their own and ended up sharing with parents or relatives. 'I've nearly walked my feet off looking for a decent flat', declared a factory worker, married in 1942:

> but I just can't get any. I hope I'll have a home of my own. I've only a few things, and they're stored at the furniture firm, where we bought them, because we've nowhere to put them. First, my husband was in the Army, and then he was discharged, and now he's in the mines. And my in-laws are terrified of me having another baby and thrusting more work on them. It's awful. I eat at mother's and sleep at my in-laws because mother's got no room; she's only got a small place.[30]

With the end of the war in sight, things seemed to deteriorate even further, especially in the south where the V1s and V2s wreaked havoc, destroying 23,000 homes and damaging almost a million.

Women who took up war work, but still had to shop and cope with children, were doubly burdened. Factory shifts often made it impossible to get to the shops when there was much left to buy. A great many women dashed out at lunch times, which left them no time to eat. Demands that retail hours be extended met with resistance from retailers' groups who feared additional staff costs, especially when

---

[27] IWM: DS/Misc/49, N. F. Ellison MS, p. 17; J. Golden, *Hackney at War* (London, 1995), p. 7. Also IWM: 90/10/1, Mrs A. Chalmers MS.

[28] E. Smithies, *The Black Economy in Britain* (Dublin, 1984), p. 65; Tony Kushner, *The Persistence of Prejudice* (Manchester, 1989); M. Roodhouse, 'Popular morality and the black market in Britain, 1939–45' in F. Trentman and F. Just (eds.), *Food and Conflict in Europe in the Age of the Two World Wars* (London, 2006).

[29] An estimated 218,000 properties were destroyed, another 250,000 were made uninhabitable, and almost 3 million damaged to some degree. Alan Holmans, *Housing Policy in Great Britain* (Beckenham, 1987), estimated that there was a shortfall of 2 million housing units at the war's end.

[30] M-O, *Britain's Birth Rate* (London, 1945), p. 139.

they had little to sell; and shopworkers' unions also protested that their members had homes too and children to care for.[31] Many women relied on relatives or neighbours for help or they simply 'went sick' for a day and shopped. Government officials urged women to help one another and set up neighbourhood shopping leagues but by 1943 few women were available to organize and run them. Some firms organized their own stores or took workers' orders and arranged for group deliveries from local merchants to the factory. Experiments were also tried with priority cards that enabled factory workers to get served first but these were ineffective and caused angry exchanges with other customers. 'You haven't got time to queue . . .', one explained. 'Even if you leave your coat open in the shops to show you're a worker, they don't take any notice.'[32] Neither government, nor employers, nor retailers, Summerfield writes, 'were willing to accept responsibility for women's shopping problems'.[33] But whether more bloc-buying by firms or greater central government pressure in the already highly regulated and complex food retailing business would have improved women's lot or simply produced additional confusion is anyone's guess. Entrenched gender assumptions and official reluctance to shoulder the responsibility were undoubtedly important, but there was also no obvious or easily adopted solution, although by 1943 the food committees established by municipal authorities had achieved some success in pressuring retailers to adopt more flexible hours.

Childcare was another continual problem for working mothers and yet it took almost three years before public nurseries were set up in significant numbers. The delay resulted in large part from continuing dispute between MoL and the Ministry of Health over whether this was a legitimate sphere for government intervention and concern about the possible risks of infection and psychic damage. And while the number of public nurseries increased rapidly by 1943–4, it never caught up with spiralling demand and in many instances hours were ill-suited to local factory shifts.[34] Children's play centres were set up and some elementary schools took under-fives, but too often childcare was largely thrown back into the laps of mothers, most of whom made their own arrangements with relatives, neighbours, and paid 'minders' who were mostly unregistered, although some local authorities like Leeds and Birmingham did begin to monitor standards. A young mother with two small babies and a husband in the Far East had her sister mind the kids while she worked twelve-hour shifts: 'I never seem to see my babies now. I miss it, dressing them and feeding them, and I sort of feel they'll forget I'm their

---

[31] For the attitude of the Shop Assistants' Union, see the discussion in the Glasgow Trades Council Minutes, 4 and 17 March 1942 (microfilm, Mitchell Library, Glasgow).

[32] M-O, *People in Production* (London, 1942), p. 228.

[33] Summerfield, *Women Workers in the Second World War*, p. 118.

[34] The *Liverpool Daily Post*, 18 July 1944 reported that 700 children were still on waiting lists in the city. Provision was also extremely uneven, sometimes because of the hostility of local councillors and officials: e.g. by the end of 1941 not one full-time public nursery had been opened in South Wales, although 1942 saw rapid growth there: M. A. Williams, *A Forgotten Army: Female munitions workers of South Wales* (Cardiff, 2002), p. 147. Also NA: CAB 102/776 ('The Ministry of Labour and the woman worker's child. Provision of nurseries'). A. Day, 'The forgotten "mateys": Women workers in Portsmouth dockyard, England 1939–45', *Women's History Review*, 7(3) (1998).

Mummy . . . all I see of them is when they're asleep.'[35] Parents' petitions to have children evacuated illustrate the problems: 'Father is working on munitions and the mother states that her head is so bad she cannot attend to her children when she returns home from work . . . the children are left in charge of a neighbour who states she cannot do with them any longer.'[36] Yet, despite the complaints of some rural women that evacuation freed mothers to make big money in factories, the children of most war-workers were at home. A 1942 survey of a sample group of workers revealed that 32 per cent of their children (under 14 years) were at school, 48 per cent were 'minded' by relatives, principally grandmothers, 14 per cent by friends and neighbours, and only 6 per cent were evacuated.[37]

Trying to keep their families supplied and coping with the raids wore women down. Chronic shortages of fuel and basic items like cooking pots, utensils, soap, and bedding made everyday tasks far more onerous. Women pieced together rag rugs, made blackout curtains, sheets, and blankets and found themselves perpetually sewing, knitting, and mending, especially if they had several children. It fell to them to make do and stretch rations, look after elderly relatives, and watch out for children who spent fewer hours in school. Many were lonely, many suffered from fatigue. To meet these challenges they relied heavily on one another. The kinship ties and neighbourly exchanges of services that traditionally operated in poor districts were of vital importance. In some cases pre-war tenants' groups became a source of mutual help; elsewhere it might be a church or chapel or the Women's Institute. On the large St Helier estate in south London, women war-workers' desperate need for public nursery places was the catalyst that created community organization.[38]

As the 'People's War' became the overarching theme of official propaganda, managing the home was redefined as patriotic work, crucial to the nation's struggle. A barrage of posters, press stories, and official bulletins reminded women that food was 'a munition of war', that morale and food were intimately linked, and it was up to them to do more with less. Magazines and newspapers published austerity recipes and Gert and Daisy, the demotic voices of radio's *Kitchen Front*, tried to mix humour and nutritional guidance six days a week. But often food tips turned preachy and pestering: 'A true woman is a good housewife. Remember that, especially in wartime, it is your feminine duty to be thrifty.'[39] For women juggling housework and factory shifts, such injunctions could be more than irritating. Local food advice centres also got a mixed reception from working-class women who mostly lacked time to attend the sessions; and those who did go, often criticized the recommended dishes as too finicky and time-consuming and sometimes too expensive. What is striking, however, about official propaganda about the 'kitchen

---

[35] M-O, *War Factory* (1943; Cresset edition 1987), p. 36.

[36] Leeds Education Papers, Box 377: M.O. Calder to Guest, 18 August 1942; F. B. Lodge to Guest, 27 January 1942.

[37] NA: RG 23/16 Wartime Social Survey: 'Workers and the war, May 1942–October 1942'.

[38] S. Bruley, ' "A very happy crowd": Women in industry in south London in World War II', *HWJ*, 44 (Autumn 1997), 68.

[39] *Daily Mirror*, 5 October 1939.

front' is its tendency to categorize women as housewives *or* war-workers when in reality many were both. This discursive separation, down-playing the multiple demands made upon them, points to prevalent anxieties about the way women in uniform and overalls were challenging conventional gender roles. 'Nationalizing' the housewife underscored her primary responsibility for home and children in normal times. Not official publicity but commercial advertising was most likely to provide frank recognition of the multiple burdens that many women shouldered by marketing products as things that would save time and enable the housewife *and* war-worker to fulfil both roles.

WOMEN IN THE WAR FACTORIES

The great majority of women recruited into war factories were young, mostly in their twenties and thirties, and from the working class. Some were volunteers influenced by patriotism, higher wages, or the prospect of escaping tedious peace-time jobs and routines they hated. Others were reluctant conscripts who within weeks of getting their call-up papers found themselves boring holes in metal, assembling components, and domiciled in hostels or lodgings far from their homes. Many 'mobile' women had never been apart from their families and many girls, anticipating call-up and hoping to avoid being sent away, quit their existing jobs and sought positions with local firms engaged in war work; indeed, in some places like the Wearside shipyards and the Consett steel works near Newcastle, these kinship ties greatly eased the social integration of women into industries that had been exclusively male.[40] Many war-workers had previous experience of factories and for them adaptation was often easier, but for vast numbers of this reserve army of labour, who were transferred from other 'non-essential' economic sectors, conscription meant entry into a totally unfamiliar world.[41]

It should be said at the outset that there were many types of war factories and conditions in them varied widely. In some places women entered small, old-fashioned engineering firms with outmoded equipment and dreadful working conditions; elsewhere they went into modern purpose-built ordnance, aircraft, or vehicle assembly plants whose thousands of workers had access to good canteens, welfare services, and a full programme of entertainments and clubs for leisure

[40] I. R. Roberts, 'A question of construction: Capital and labour in Wearside shipbuilding since the 1930s', PhD Diss., Durham University, 1988, pp. 208–27; K. M. Price, 'An alternative Consett story: An investigation of the visibility and invisibility of women in a town's history in the 19th century, the Second World War, and the "Save Consett Steel" Campaign of the 1980s', PhD Diss., Open University, 1986, ch. 2.

[41] This section examines women in munitions. Similar patterns are evident in other job areas with respect to unequal pay, trade union resistance to female recruitment, camaraderie among women workers, childcare problems, and the difficulties of balancing home and work: e.g. the number of women working for the railways rose from about 25,000 in 1939 to almost 89,000 by 1943. Most were engaged as porters, cleaners, catering, clerks, and booking office staff, although a few managed to rise into higher grades as guards and some worked in railway engineering workshops. For all aspects of their experience: Helen Wojtczak, *Railwaywomen: Exploitation, betrayal and triumph in the workplace* (Hastings, 2005).

periods. Some factories were situated in long-established industrial regions with a pre-existing culture of work and trade unionism; others, like the one that Mass-Observer Celia Fremlin described in *War Factory* (1943), were wartime creations assembled almost overnight in rural areas. And while in areas like Coventry or London, the number of women in manufacturing had grown rapidly between the wars, elsewhere—in the mining villages of South Wales or the north-west, for example—female unemployment and underemployment had been extensive with few jobs available outside domestic work, retail, and other services. Most resistant to female conscripts were the older craft-dominated sectors of heavy engineering, shipbuilding, and ship repair: Rosie the Riveter was rare enough in American shipyards, in Britain she could never have emerged as the heroic symbol of women's war work. Even the few women who entered the nation's shipyards were largely confined to the shops and sheds, well away from the ship berths.[42]

Some forty government munitions plants or Royal Ordnance Factories (ROFs) were constructed to supplement the original three in the London area. Built at a distance from major population centres, they employed over 300,000 people including, as in the First World War, large numbers of women.[43] ROF Chorley, for example, which consisted of 1,500 buildings spread over 1,000 acres, drew its 30,000 workers from all over south Lancashire. The majority of the workforce at the ROFs at Spennymoor and Newton Aycliffe in County Durham were married women, often with small children; their husbands worked in the local pits while they tried to juggle long working weeks and manage their homes. In the coal-mining area of South Wales, three ROFs at Bridgend, Hirwaun, and Glasgoed, employed over 60,000 people, three-quarters of them women. The numbers of women in all areas of engineering increased rapidly reaching over a third of the total workforce. Among the largest employers were firms manufacturing aircraft and aircraft components. Only 7 per cent of workers in this sector were women in 1935, but that figure ballooned to 40 per cent in 1944—at which time the industry employed over three-quarters of a million women. Most contemporary attention focused on the influx of women into firms that were previously exclusively male, but numerous factories that relied heavily on women's labour before the war—for example, the food, clothing, and light engineering and appliance plants of the Greater London—also converted to munitions work and continued using their original labour force.

For all the diversity of firms and trades, however, there was also much that was common in the experience of women war-workers. A great deal of their work consisted of basic, repetitive tasks such as boring, drilling, sewing, and assembling small components. Certainly, some women drove trucks, operated cranes, or were trained for highly skilled welding and machining, but they were a minority. In engineering, jobs that a skilled craftsman would normally have done alone were

---

[42] H. Murphy, ' "From crinoline to the boilersuit": Women workers in British shipbuilding during the Second World War', *Contemporary British History*, (13)4 (Winter 1999); F. Ennis and I. Roberts, ' "The time of their lives?": Female workers in north east shipbuilding, 1939–45' in A. Potts (ed.), *Shipbuilders and Engineers* (Durham, 1987).

[43] P. Inman, *Labour in the Munitions Industries* (London, 1957).

subdivided; male setters mostly set up the lathes and milling machines while women performed simpler, routine operations for which, some experts suggested, the nimble fingers of women were specially suited. They worked long shifts and were often under great pressure to meet production targets. While the MoL insisted that excessive hours in the end reduced productivity, the supply departments were reluctant to intervene and many women continued to work fifty-five hours or more. This was especially true of ROFs where in July 1942 an official enquiry found women working over fifty-five hours a week in two-thirds of them. And since most were situated in remote places and drew their labour from far afield, women found themselves travelling an additional two and sometimes three hours daily on crowded buses and trains. By the time they got home, they often complained, they were too tired to eat. Large numbers of hostels were built to house these workers, but they were never full. Even women who were single, preferred to travel from home—either because they disliked the idea of communal living, thought it too costly or too regimented, or had additional family responsibilities. Not surprisingly, the exhausting routine undermined women's health: 'The girls are getting run down', a Welsh local councillor commented to Mass-Observation: 'Some of the young women are looking quite old. And what can you expect when they're up at 4.45 in the morning and not back here again until 4.30. And then they've got their bits of shopping and housework to do.'[44]

Fatigue also increased the chance of accidents. In shell factories they risked exposure to dangerous chemicals and, although far more precautions were taken than in the previous war, many suffered from skin rashes, nose-bleeds, sore throats, and respiratory ailments. Working carelessly or too swiftly with fuses and detonators could result in death or the loss of a hand or eye; explosions were fairly frequent, although under-reported in local newspapers because of the secrecy surrounding the factories. While the danger of large-scale accidents was far smaller in most sectors of engineering, here too the hazards were considerable as illustrated by a small collection of letters written by a group of welders (all in their twenties) employed at a Huddersfield factory. Covering only five months, from July to November 1942, they contain repeated references to colds, rashes, menstrual problems, burns, and 'arc eye', which was caused by the intense light of the welding flame. A typical letter relates: 'Emily has burnt her face with slag so the nurse has plastered it up. Also your pal Aimee is suffering once again with half my face red . . .' One week Amy listed her hours as over sixty-six; a little later, she writes: 'I think I must have strained myself with lifting . . . I have been getting 160 plates out per day and now I have to get 205 plates out per day and I get 8s a week extra. It's bleeding horse work . . . Believe me, I have come home at 7.30 half dead. I have just washed me and looked at the evening paper and gone straight to bed, buggered.' Several of them spent time off sick or were forced to quit. By November Amy's vision was seriously impaired, despite the goggles and protective masks she wore, and factory doctors told her to stop welding: 'I am *very upset* about this', she

---

[44] Williams, *A Forgotten Army*, p. 122. On resistance to living in hostels: S. T. Dawson, 'Busy and bored: The politics of work and leisure for women workers in the Second World War', *TCBH*, 21(1) (2010).

writes, 'because I don't want to leave the girls. In fact, I am going to risk it till Christmas I think.'[45]

While the pressures of war work were taxing enough for single women, they were still more burdensome for wives and mothers with young children to take care of. Government publicity and the media focused heavily upon young 'mobile' women, but mothers with young children were the guilty secret of Bevin's labour policy— an estimated three-quarters of a million women with children under fourteen worked in industry. For them childcare and shopping were a perpetual nightmare. 'I used to have good health', said one woman when asked about her absences, 'but now I can't eat or sleep properly on the night shift. I have to look after the men folk [a husband and father]. My husband has been badly brought up and won't look after himself.' Some favoured night work because it allowed more time for domestic chores, but the price was high: 'I get up at mid-day to shop', another commented. 'It makes me very tired and depressed, and I go to sleep at the bench. I have no appetite and I don't eat much at the canteen for fear of getting too sleepy. Often I have a night out.' Compulsory overtime exacerbated these problems. The most telling indicator was the absentee rate among women, which remained roughly double that of men, i.e. 10–15 per cent as compared to 6–8 per cent, and an even higher 15–21 per cent in ROFs.[46] Employers and supervisors focused their criticism on young women who took time off to shop, missed the bus after partying late, or took advantage of minor colds and ailments to stay home. But, as surveys of the Industrial Health Research Board made clear, sickness and domestic problems accounted for the lion's share of absences and the problem was most acute among married women in their late twenties and thirties, precisely the age groups with proportionately more young children and husbands away in the forces.[47] Especially on weekends, despite overtime rates of pay, many married women were absent in an effort to 'get straight' at home and salvage some semblance of family life.

Conditions in war factories varied greatly. They were primitive in many older firms, built in the Victorian era without adequate ventilation or sanitation. 'There are', a female shell inspector wrote of her factory in 1942, 'one thousand women on three shifts, and three lavatories and no water. There are cisterns but no water. Two towels every three weeks. Two wash bowls but no soap . . . we have to eat our dinner with dirty and greasy hands.'[48] But pressure from the MoL resulted in improvements. The best conditions were in the large aircraft factories and newly built ROFs; they were brightly lit, had ample washrooms and large canteens, appointed welfare officers, and

---

[45] M. Jolly (ed.), *Dear Laughing Motorbyke: Letters from women welders of the Second World War* (London, 1997), pp. 119, 108, 130.

[46] S. Wyatt, *A Study of Women on War Work in Four Factories* (London, 1945), pp. 36, 24, 22. Also NA: LAB 26/131, Appendix, National Averages of Absenteeism.

[47] S. Wyatt, R. Marriott, and D. E. R. Hughes, *A Study of Absenteeism among Women* (London, 1943); S. Wyatt, *A Study of Certified Sickness Absence among Women in Industry* (London, 1944). The Industrial Health Research Board's investigation of 20,000 female workers in 1944 found that over half of absences were due to sickness and accidents. If young children were sick and could not go to school or to a minder, then mothers had little choice but to stay home.

[48] M-O, A Topic Collections 'Industry', quoted by R. Croucher, *Engineers at War* (London, 1982), p. 262.

8. Women riveting a rear fuselage, Fairey Aircraft Co., *c*.1941.

laid on a wide range of entertainments, including factory dances, concerts, and ENSA lunchtime shows. Newsreels and official publicity showed women operating lathes and assembling components while singing to the BBC's 'Music While You Work' piped in over Tannoy loud speakers.[49]

The classic film depiction of munitions work, *Millions Like Us* (1943), shot on location at Birmingham's huge Castle Bromwich aircraft factory, took great pains to counter negative assumptions about life in industry. The film's purpose was to aid recruitment, dispel public rumour about the loose morality of 'mobile' women, and reassure audiences that they had lost none of their femininity. The factory is light and spacious, the hostel well-appointed and run by a motherly type, and the organized leisure activities are scenes of collective fun. There is no hint of exhausting work shifts, nobody seems tired or bored stiff, and work on the milling machines seems to leave the girls fresh and without a spot of grease on them. No

[49] Singing helped to relieve boredom and aided the social integration of women entering factories for the first time, helping to build community. Popular songs, like films and radio, provided a common frame of reference for young women recruited from different parts of the country. Employers favoured fast-tempo tunes which quickened the pace of production rather than music that encouraged hand-clapping or dancing and interrupted its flow. Workers invented their own lyrics, often mildly indecent, and specific songs were also used as warning signals to alert fellow workers that supervisors or rate-fixers were on the shop floor. See M. Korczynski *et al.*, ' "We sang ourselves through that war": Women, music and factory work in World War II', *Labour History Review*, 70(2) (August 2003); M. Korczynski and K. Jones, 'Instrumental music? The social origins of broadcast music in factories', *Popular Music*, 25(2) (May 2006).

industrial accidents or strikes occur, there is no mention of trade unions or works' committees, and when the factory is bombed, the workers go in orderly fashion to the shelters and nobody is hurt. The overarching theme of *Millions* is the nation's unity; the factory is a microcosm of Britain with women of all classes brought together by the war effort who develop into a community, a substitute family; indeed, the outsider is a stylish upper-class socialite, who starts out rebellious and aloof but is socialized into the group and in the final scene joins in the canteen communal singing as a fleet of bombers roars overhead on their way to Germany.

The film's depiction of industrial production was so sanitized as to be almost unrecognizable, but its theme of community and camaraderie is echoed in memoirs and oral histories, most of which paint a positive picture of war work. 'I had a rip-roaring time', one woman remembered. 'Life at home was restricting. There was a lot of domestic responsibilities because we had a big family.'[50] Workers were encouraged to 'muck in' and make the workplace a genuine community and many formed close friendships and support networks that lasted for years after the war. Workers were billeted together; went in groups to pubs, dance halls, and roller-skating rinks; and consoled each other in times of personal crisis and anxiety over families and loved ones. 'We really lived it up', recalled a Glasgow girl who was sent to an engineering factory in Manchester. 'We were out at night, worked in the day and spent our money.' 'We did get away with a lot of things during the war . . . they couldn't sack you, you see.' 'I loved it . . . there was such an atmosphere there you couldn't help love it', commented a south London woman. 'Everybody got on with everybody else . . . They were all the same. There was no one any better and no one any lower.'[51] Such memories are not false; the passage of years sifts out and edits more negative and divisive facets of shop-floor experience, while those who loathed the whole experience are less likely, perhaps, to volunteer for oral history projects.

In reality, war factories replicated the social and regional divisions of the nation. Working in the finishing shop of an aircraft factory at Wolverton, Doris White remembered: 'How we rowed with each other. Country girls versus Londoners. In one corner the plain types with simple hair styles, in the other bleached blondes with lipsticked mouths . . . A trip over someone's handbag, or the accidental knocking of someone's coat off its hook would result in "Bloody Londoner, go back where yer came from." I kept quiet while my pals returned the verbal fire . . . ' A Manchester woman took exception to the foreman at ROF Risley: 'a bleedin' cockney . . . and lots of London girls, cheeky sods they are too.'[52] In some firms the target of abuse was the large number of Irish recruits: 'The Irish girls stick together and they've only got to open their mouths to get any money they want. They've got all the best jobs in the factory—you never hear of an Irish girl being put off a job to

---

[50] P. Grafton, *You, You, and You* (London, 1981), p. 81.

[51] P. Goodman, ' "Patriotic femininity": Women's morals and men's morale during the Second World War', *Gender and History*, 10(2) (August 1998), 286; Bruley, 'A very happy crowd', 61, 65.

[52] D. White, *D is for Doris, V is for Victory* (Milton Keynes, 1981), p. 70; M-OA: FR 839 'Manchester industrial atmosphere' (August 1941).

make room for a Birmingham girl.'[53] Elsewhere it was the system of labour transfers that aroused anger. Some Home Intelligence reports noted 'bad feeling' between the Scots and English girls, adding that the Scots, who considered themselves in 'furrin parts', were highly receptive to communist propaganda, often sporting hammer and sickle badges. In Scotland the direction of Scots girls into English war factories raised loud objections, while Welsh nationalists protested Welsh women being sent to jobs in the Midlands, arguing that English recruits in South Wales should leave first and citing their pub-going, trousers, smoking in public, lipstick, and dyed hair as conclusive proof of low morals. When Yorkshire girls were sent to jobs away from home, local people demanded 'to know why the Midland girls can't be sent back home before the Bradford girls are exiled'.[54]

As for class tensions, these were mitigated by the overwhelming working-class composition of the workforce in munitions. The Wartime Social Survey reported that 86 per cent of all women in engineering and metals had only an elementary school education and the same was true of 94 per cent of those in assembly and unskilled repetitive jobs and 96 per cent of machinists and hand-tool operators.[55] Middle-class conscripts into industry were few and they usually moved quickly to supervisory positions. The association of factory work and 'common', low-class women remained a recruitment problem throughout the war. 'I started my real war work today', wrote a lower-middle-class diarist, working in a Wembley aircraft factory. 'First of all I loathe and hate it . . . talk about working with a motley crew . . . They were all friendly and tried to help me, but the language from some of them. I must try to get used to it; for I shall be two months in this learners' shop.' Five months later she obtained a medical release—'had to leave as I felt I was heading for a break-down'. 'I *can't* make friends with the girls', wrote another. 'They have been in a factory of one sort or another since they left school at 14 years, and they resent me . . . We hardly speak the same language.'[56] At Celia Fremlin's factory women in the assembly department, mostly from the upper working class (she conjects), viewed the machine shop girls as a rough crowd: 'it's a very low class of girls you get there', 'very low—real nasty some of them', 'machine shop scrubs'.[57]

A survey at the end of the war pointed to 'the lack of social unity between different levels of the factory society and to the remote or non-existent contact between workers and . . . supervisors and, in particular, managers'.[58] Women

[53] K. Lunn, ' "Good for a few hundreds at least": Irish labour recruitment to Britain during the Second World War' in P. Buckland and J. Belchem (eds.), *The Irish in British Labour History*, Conference Proceedings in Irish History, No. 1 (Liverpool University, 1993), p. 107.

[54] On Scots girls: NA: INF 1/292, 30 June–7 July 1942; also 22–29 September 1942; the Glasgow Trades Council vigorously protested the 'iniquitous practice' of sending Scottish girls to England: Minutes, 15 and 22 September 1942 (Mitchell Library Glasgow). For Welsh transfers: Williams, *A Forgotten Army*, pp. 178–94. For the Bradford girls: M-O, *People in Production*, p. 150.

[55] Summerfield, *Women Workers in the Second World War*, p. 57 (Wartime Social Survey, 1944, p. 6).

[56] IWM 88/50/1, Mrs R. E. Uttin diary: entries for 22 October 1942, 7 April 1943; M-O, *People in Production*, p. 156.

[57] M-O, *War Factory*, p. 50.

[58] S. Wyatt, *A Study of Variations in Output*, Industrial Health Research Board, Report No. 5 (London, 1945), p. 1.

supervisors were often unpopular, especially if they were seen as strict, school-mistress types who reported you for smoking or wasting time in the lavatory. Age and class differences added to the friction. The same applied to welfare officers if they commented on the dress, language, private lives, and boyfriends of their charges. Any attempt to act as moral guardians was resented as exceeding the bounds of their position. The welfare officer of a munitions plant near Reading, whose charges included almost 800 Irish women, remembered: 'Some of the girls were exasperating in their complete indifference to authority. To my question "How old are you?" the reply could be "Why should I tell you?"'[59] Supervisors had their own biases and were apt to stigmatize young workers especially if they were assertive and stuck up for themselves. Questioned in December 1943 for a survey on mental health in the workplace, the Labour Manager of a Birmingham firm volunteered a whole catalogue of preconceptions. She declared, among other things, that:

> she never put red-haired girls onto complicated machines because they were always putting their fingers in. She had noticed as a group, single women about 48 years of age, who seemed to have no interest in anything. They were women whose lives had been extremely restricted in the past. A group which she described as 'unbalanced' were what she called 'communist', always grumbling and not willing to take responsibility.

With marvellous understatement, the interviewers noted parenthetically: 'some prejudice evident here'.[60] Even where there was a great deal of affection for a supervisor, which was the case with the Huddersfield welders mentioned earlier, social class interposed barriers. The trainee welders' letters to their youthful female instructor, whose father was the managing director of an engineering firm, are full of humour, teasing, confidences, and sexual innuendo between friends. But, as Margaretta Jolly points out, when the girls address their instructor who was roughly their own age 'familiarity jostles uneasily alongside formality', intimacy alternates with deferential correctness. Teasing was a way of diminishing social difference but it also revealed a certain lingering awkwardness as when they resorted to nicknames, avoiding use of the instructor's Christian name.[61]

Unlike most women drafted into war factories who learned on the job, the Huddersfield welders went through an exacting training process of six months—far longer than most because their factory was not ready for production. A small minority of women workers went to special Government Training Centres (around 94,000 in all) and achieved a higher level of skill, but they often encountered suspicion from skilled workers and foremen, while employers preferred on-the-job

[59] IWM 87/14/1, Miss N. O'Connor MS; M-O, *People in Production*, p. 127 reported that many girls 'resent the almost maternalistic attitude of the forewomen and are irritated when judgments are passed about their private lives, their dress, their language and their boy friends'.
[60] Assoc. of Psychiatric Social Workers Papers, Birmingham 16/5, 11 December 1943. Report on a Midlands research group examining 'fitness for work'. (These papers have now been moved to MRC, Warwick University.)
[61] Jolly (ed.), *Dear Laughing Motorbyke*, pp. 26–35.Valentine Pearson, the instructor, was also a Mass-Observer, which is how the letters were preserved.

training which made it easier for them to deny claims for higher pay at the skilled rate.[62] When the Huddersfield group began work, for example, they were put on jobs well below their capacity and only began welding after some weeks. The sex-typing of jobs was deeply entrenched throughout British industry and remained the norm throughout the war. Specific tasks were labelled 'men's' and 'women's' work and unions were watchful that gender distinctions be maintained. Under the dilution agreements negotiated between Bevin and the engineering unions, there were two kinds of work performed by women: they were officially classified as doing women's work or as 'women doing men's work'. The first group were paid according to a lower women's wages schedule. The second group who replaced men were subject to a probationary period of thirty-two weeks, during which they were paid on an increasing scale and after which they were to get the same basic rate and bonus as men—provided they could do the job without special assistance or supervision. Roughly 75 per cent of women in engineering were paid according to the women's schedule. Few were paid the full male rate even if they did male jobs—employers argued that they required extra supervision and were less versatile and incapable of carrying out a variety of tasks. Employers' strategies to reclassify work provoked stiff resistance from male workers,[63] but the practice of denying women the full rate aroused less opposition—at least until 1943 when the AEU, wishing to position itself for post-war and protect male jobs from undercutting, began a determined campaign to ensure 'the rate for the job'.

Recent scholarship has focused heavily upon male hostility to women's entry into traditionally male occupations. But while there is no dearth of examples of resentment and exclusionary practices, there is a danger of exaggerating gender antagonism and male defensiveness.[64] Compared to the First World War, there was less alarm about safeguarding men's jobs and more confidence in the power of organized labour to protect their interests. In part, this reflected Bevin's skill in negotiating agreements with employers and unions and the rapid spread of joint consultation. Guarantees about the temporary nature of wartime changes were also formalized in the Restoration of Pre-War Practices Act in 1942. To be sure, some men saw dilutees as a threat to wage rates and their continued exemption from the

---

[62] P. Summerfield, 'What women learned from the Second World War', *History of Education*, 18(3) (September 1989); *idem*, 'The patriarchal discourse of human capital: Training women for war work, 1939–45', *Journal of Gender Studies*, 2(2) (1993).

[63] e.g. in November 1942 the management at the Clydeside engineering firm of Barr and Stroud tried to insist that 'if girls carried out certain operations in one department that could be regarded as the firm's practice in all other departments'. Immediately, the union (TGWU) voiced its objection, demanding that 'steps should be taken to ensure that the ratio of men employed prior to the war should be reverted to after the war'. North West Engineering Employers' Assoc. Records, Mitchell Library, Glasgow, TD 1059/7/31, Report on Works Conference between Barr and Stroud and TGWU, 23 November 1942. Employers also tried to classify jobs according to the custom of the area: thus, in January 1941 AEU officials in Coventry complained when local employers claimed that 'if women have been employed on specific work by other employers in the district, firms who have previously only employed males on the same work are entitled to employ women without registering them and at the women's schedule of wages'. C. Wightman, *More than Munitions: Women, work and the engineering industries 1900–1950* (London, 1999), pp. 138–9.

[64] P. Goodman, *Women, Sexuality and War* (London, 2002).

draft, but many also benefited by being raised to supervisory positions. Over-emphasis upon the 'soldier hero' as the hegemonic form of manhood has also led historians to suggest that civilian males saw their masculinity as somehow ques-tioned, 'in deficit' or 'impaired'. But there is very little evidence in *contemporary* sources (as opposed to later oral histories) to suggest that male workers were seen or saw themselves as somehow lesser men or 'doing something trivial'.[65] Indeed, the whole thrust of 'People's War' publicity was to emphasize the vital contributions of air-raid wardens, coal miners, engineers, ships' riveters, firemen, and heavy rescue squads—all were depicted as in the 'front line' of the nation's struggle. Moreover, they were frequently in greater danger than large parts of the army which spent much of the war at remote bases where raids were rare. In addition, male concep-tions of masculinity which were certainly closely linked to work were not defined solely in relationship to women. Another important reference point was the unemployment and job insecurity of the interwar decades and their consequences for men's self-esteem and position within the family.[66] In contrast, the war years ushered in a sustained period of full employment that enhanced the power and status of labour and revived the old industrial regions; if anything, traditional masculine work cultures and confidence were bolstered and reinforced.[67]

There was also by 1940 a consensus that reducing the proportion of work done by skilled labour in engineering and metals was absolutely necessary if Britain's production were to meet its wartime needs. In some firms the number of women employed had already been growing before the war; in others the recruitment of local women—wives, sisters, daughters, and cousins of men working for a firm—facilitated acceptance. Also many workplaces were effectively segregated by gender with large numbers of unskilled or semi-skilled women working alongside one another, supervised by men, separate from the highly skilled tool makers and sheet-metal workers whose workshops remained exclusively masculine. Attempts to breach these sanctums, however, were likely to produce trouble. For example, at the Woolwich Arsenal strongly craft-conscious men of the Heavy Gun division

---

[65] S. Rose, *Which People's War? National identity and citizenship in wartime Britain, 1939–1945* (Oxford, 2003), pp, 182–96; *idem*, 'Temperate heroes: Concepts of masculinity in Second World War Britain' in S. Dudink, K. Hagemann, and J. Tosh (eds.), *Masculinities in Politics and War* (Manchester, 2004). On 'impairment' in oral histories: P. Summerfield, *Reconstructing Women's Wartime Lives: Discourse and subjectivity in oral histories of the Second World War* (Manchester, 1998), pp. 121–43. Rose also states that throughout the war men out of uniform were subject to 'white feather campaigns'. My work indicates that this was very rare and generally disapproved of as contradicting the whole ethos of a 'People's War'. Where it occurred it seems to have resulted from specific and local antipathies or to have been fomented by sections of the press opposed to the system of job deferments.

[66] The impact of interwar unemployment on masculine identity can be seen in contemporary novels: Walter Greenwood, *Love on the Dole* (1933) and Walter Brierley, *Means Test Man* (1935).

[67] R. Johnston and A. McIvor, 'Dangerous work, hard men and broken bodies: Masculinity in the Clydeside heavy industries, *c.*1930–1970s', *Labour History Review*, 69(2) (August 2004); Nick Hayes, 'Did manual workers want industrial welfare? Canteens, latrines and masculinities on British building sites, 1918–1970', *Journal of Social History* (Spring 2002); Pat Ayers, 'The making of men; Masculinities in interwar Liverpool' in M. Walsh (ed.), *Working Out Gender: Perspectives from Labour History* (Aldershot, 2000); M. Savage, 'Class and manual work cultures 1945–70' in A. Campbell, N. Fishman, and J. McIlroy (eds.), *British Trade Unions and Industrial Politics: The post war compromise 1945–1964* (Aldershot, 1999).

tried unsuccessfully to exclude women altogether. Irked at an unpopular manager's claim 'that he could teach a woman to do anything a skilled man could do in six weeks', they also refused to complete the assembly of guns on which women had worked so that the latter were soon limited, one worker wrote, to 'fettling and a few small sub-assemblies'. Skilled finishers also complained of being underpaid compared to female dilutees, saying that rate-fixers 'could see a pile of swarf but not the skill needed to finish the job'. The manager's favourite response to complaints about a job was 'that he could do it with his prick', which soon became a standard catchphrase round the shop.[68] Where men and women worked in teams there were also problems over bonuses: in September 1942 at the North British Locomotive Works in Queens Park, Glasgow, when management argued that women in the work gangs share the group bonus, male tank assemblers refused and threatened to walk out, arguing that the women 'were not of assistance to the men but rather the reverse' and 'were, in fact, reducing the earnings of the men in the squads'. Ironically, the same AEU shop stewards, who at that very moment were pushing to admit women into their union, found themselves forced to support their exclusion from the bonus. In the end women had to settle for a percentage—the same thing happened with gang earnings at Standard Motors in Coventry.[69]

Many male workers were patronizing or reluctant to teach women their techniques or complained that slow-paced helpers cost them money. Quick and proficient women could also be a blow to male pride and existing rates, but women's skills also earned appreciation. Coventry shop steward Ernie Roberts admitted: 'After training they became as good as the men. I must admit that many of us thought they weren't capable of it because they hadn't the industrial background we had had all our lives. But it was surprising the adjustments they made, very quickly, to highly skilled work, in a standards room, for instance, checking very precise gauges.'[70] The most prevalent male response, however, seems to have been one of amused condescension and a belief that women were basically un-mechanical and unsuited to the shop floor. Teasing, pranks, and sexual clowning were more common responses than overt hostility and spitefulness. Doris White recalled the 'caterwauling and whistling' that greeted any woman who ventured into the lathe shops at Wolverton, while age-old antics like nailing bench drawers shut and sending assistants for left-handed screwdrivers were commonplace.[71] Women workers, many of whom were no strangers to factory life, often joined in—answering back and making fun of male co-workers. Inevitably, there was a lot of gossip and rumour about sexual misconduct between workers on the night shifts and some factories got a reputation—usually on the outside among those in nearby communities—for having a 'rough', 'low-class', promiscuous female workforce. As a worker at ROF Chorley recalled:

[68] IWM: H. A. Baker MS, 'Forty-six years in the Royal Arsenal'.
[69] NA: LAB 10/363, 1 and 8 August 1942; and North West Engineering Employers' Assoc. Records, TD 1059/7/31, Report on Works Conference between North British and AEU, 9 September 1942 (Mitchell Library, Glasgow).
[70] E. Roberts quoted in P. Lewis, *A People's War* (London, 1986), p. 119.
[71] White, *D is for Doris*, p. 16.

'They'd say: "Oh, you work at Euxton?" and give you the eye.'[72] Allegations about the loose morals of young 'mobile' workers living in hostels and free of parental guidance were routine; far less attention was paid to sexual harassment and unwanted advances by male supervisors and co-workers, many of them married.

As mentioned, most women in war factories received wages according to a separate women's pay schedule; even those who performed 'male' jobs rarely got the full rate: Croucher estimates about one in six in engineering. The highest-paid sectors for women were aircraft, vehicles, chemicals, and ordnance where wages could amount to £5 or £6 a week with overtime, and in ROFs women on especially dangerous jobs received extra pay. The highest pay rates, however, were in the transport sector for the simple reason that there women mostly received the male rate. Most women in munitions earned about £2 to £3 a week—far more than many had received before but a far cry from the bonanza that rumours about them buying fur coats and other luxuries implied. After paying for transport, canteen meals, rent, or childcare, many had little enough left over. As a group, those who did best were single women in the high-paying sectors who lived with their parents. With good reason most historians have concluded that women made very little progress towards equality of pay in the war years. In his official history, for example, Parker estimated that women's average weekly earnings rose only slightly compared to men—from 47 per cent of a man's in 1938 to 53 per cent in the war. But this picture requires some qualification. The figures given (originally in Parker's official history[73]) relate to average weekly earnings in all industries. In fact, men regularly worked more overtime than women (who often had a heavy burden of work in their homes), while the averages also mask the fact that in certain sectors the improvement in women's relative *hourly rates* of pay was 10 per cent or more. Just as the market pressures of the wartime labour famine squeezed the differentials between skilled and unskilled men, so those between men and women narrowed—although not in non-vital industries like textiles and clothing which remained unchanged.[74]

In this war, as in the previous one, trade unions regarded the replacement of male workers as temporary, 'for the duration' only, and their actions gave priority to protecting male jobs and rates rather than advocating for women's needs. And yet the war years (as was also true in 1914–18) saw a rapid increase in the organization of women. Union membership increased from about 1 million in 1939 to 1.9 million at the peak of mobilization in 1943, while female trade union density almost doubled—from 15 per cent in 1938 to almost 30 per cent in 1943.[75] Much of this growth was in the engineering and metals sector, even though the AEU excluded

[72] Grafton, *You, You, and You*, p. 61.
[73] H. M. D. Parker, *Manpower* (London, 1957), p. 503; also Summerfield, *Women Workers in the Second World War*, p. 170.
[74] I. Gazeley, 'Women's pay in British industry in the Second World War', *Economic History Review*, 61(3) (2008); R. A. Hart, 'Women doing men's work and women doing women's work: Female work and pay in British wartime engineering', *Explorations in Economic History*, 44 (2007). Comparing 1938 and 1943 women's wages moved from 52–64% of men's in engineering, 48–58% in shipbuilding, 53–77% in transport.
[75] S. Lewenhak, *Women and Trade Unions* (London, 1977); S. Boston, *Women Workers and the Trade Union Movement* (London, 1980); N. C. Solden, *Women in British Trade Unions, 1974–1976*

women until January 1943 and union officials were apt to see them as a stopgap source of dues and often paid little attention to issues like shopping and childcare of vital importance to them. Several factors encouraged the rise in membership. The growing power of organized labour and the spread of joint consultation weakened employer opposition to union recruitment. Also, the very nature of engineering work processes meant that there was constant shop-floor negotiation and revision of job rates which affected women's pay. More generally, despite the masculine and uninviting ethos of many skilled union branches, the radicalization of popular opinion and labour's growing success in pushing up wages encouraged more women to join; the pressures of shop-floor activists, hopes of furthering their own pay demands, and a growing solidarity with labour organizations all played a role. This was especially true of large factories with strong shop-steward networks and an array of work-related leisure activities that helped build community.

It was the general unions—Bevin's Transport and General Workers' Union (TGWU) and the National Union of General and Municipal Workers (NUGMW)—that recognized the opportunity presented by the expansion of the female workforce and moved quickly to take advantage of it. By the end of 1943 the TGWU could boast almost 307,000 women members. Indeed, it was the advances made by the general unions that induced the male craft unions to open their doors at least a crack. Eventually, despite significant opposition among its rank and file, the AEU decided after a special postal ballot to admit women in January 1943.[76] Within a year 139,000 had joined, receiving special temporary cards. Prior to this, AEU shop stewards in some factories had assisted the TGWU in its efforts to recruit women, in others they agreed to represent women unofficially for a nominal subscription—sometimes to deter them from enrolling in a general union. Now rivalry between the unions intensified and there were accusations of 'poaching' as AEU organizers made every effort to get women to switch to the craft union.

In the middle war years there were signs—worrying to MoL officials—of a growing propensity to strike among women workers. Officials argued that the strain of long hours, workplace inexperience, and lack of discipline were leading women to ignore their union officials and down tools at the slightest provocation. Recent historical studies have focused especially upon women's efforts to secure equal pay with men. But the majority of job actions were triggered not by gender inequality but by a variety of issues connected to pay and working conditions on which male and female workers often took action together. Some disputes also

---

(London, 1978); G. S. Bain and R. Price, *Profiles of Union Growth: A comparative statistical portrait of eight countries* (London, 1980).

[76] Other craft unions were equally slow to adapt. The Vehicle Builders (NUVB) took very tentative steps to recruit women in Coventry and elsewhere; the Woodworkers (ASW) refused to admit them but agreed to provide union services if they paid the district levy; and the Electricians created a special women's section. In some firms even the Foundry Workers (NUFW) found it expedient to bend a little, especially if they were competing with rival unions like the TGWU for members. T. J. Claydon, 'The development of trade unionism among British automobile and aircraft workers, 1914–46', PhD Diss., University of Kent, 1981, pp. 448–64; H. A. Clegg, *A History of British Trade Unions*, III: *1934–51* (Oxford, 1985; 1994), p. 216; B. Knox and A. McKinlay, '"Pests to management": Engineering shop stewards on Clydeside 1939–45', *Scottish Labour History Journal*, 30 (1995), 17.

arose from the fact that the earnings of groups of women doing almost identical jobs might be quite different because of their different skill classifications. Different adjustments for skill levels and complicated formulae for bonuses, to say nothing of frequent revisions in piece-work rates, also produced sharp and sometimes poorly understood fluctuations in a woman's weekly pay packet. At times unrest focused on wage differentials between local firms, while among Lancashire cotton workers, who were tied to their industry, it was often the higher wages in local munitions plants that spurred wage demands. Thus, in 1941, women workers at John Lucas Ltd and at Guest, Keen, and Nettlefolds Ltd in the West Midlands protested because their wages were below those of aircraft firms in the area; in the London region, the radio and light engineering firms, Cossors Ltd and Gramophone Company, were threatened with strike action by women workers demanding a minimum rate equal to the wages in nearby government ordnance factories. At the Players' Cigarette factory in Nottingham in 1943 hundreds of women staged a sit-down strike in opposition to a compulsory incentive bonus scheme which trade union officials had already accepted.[77]

But underpayment compared to men did become a growing cause of unrest by 1943. Heightened trade union agitation at the national level to ensure the 'rate for the job', even if it was rooted in unions' desires to protect male jobs, was undoubtedly an important factor and possibly the highly publicized national campaign to gain women equal compensation for war injuries played a role. Sometimes protests originated in the common practice of giving men more choice of jobs and allocating the worst tasks to women. At the Rootes Shadow factory at Ryton in Coventry, for example, women complained that in their section they were routinely assigned the most boring and finicky jobs that paid least; also they were not receiving the rate for the job. Getting nowhere with the foreman and the union convener, they went directly to Jack Jones, the TGWU's district organizer. After that things improved, but their actions left lingering bitterness among the men. At Fairey Aviation Co. in Lancashire in September 1943, when women working on heavy milling machines were granted equal wages with men, this sparked discontent and wage demands by other women throughout the machine and assembly shops. By November 1943 a high official at the MoL wrote that women's pay disputes were 'proportionately more prone to result in strike actions than where men are concerned'.[78]

On the matter of equal pay the strategies adopted by the two leading unions, the AEU and TGWU, were quite different. Both unions were concerned that women

---

[77] N. Nakamura, 'Women, work and war: Industrial mobilisation and demobilisation. Coventry and Bolton, 1940–46', PhD Diss., Warwick University, 1984, pp. 53ff.; J. Lucas etc.: NA: LAB 10/ 351, 8 November 1941; Cossors: NA: LAB 10/358, 27 June, 18 July 1942. For the Players' factory: Lewenhak, *Women and Trade Unions*, p. 241.

[78] On Rootes: L. Grant, 'Women in a car town: Coventry, 1920–45' in P. Hudson and W.R. Lee (eds.), *Women's Work and the Family Economy in Historical Perspective* (Manchester, 1990), pp. 234–5. On Fairey Aviation: Wightman, *More than Munitions*, pp. 167–8. By 1943 the Works Councils at Vauxhall revealed growing agitation among women over the differentials with men's pay: L. Holden, *Vauxhall Motors and the Luton Economy* (Luton, 2003), p. 158; H. A. Emmerson (Chief Industrial Commissioner 1942–44), 'Causes of industrial unrest', 3 November 1943, NA: Lab 10/281.

might become a cheap labour alternative to men after the war. But the AEU's priority was to preserve male jobs rather than challenge the low pay of women. In the early war years it focused entirely on protecting the male 'rate for the job'; from 1943 it advocated a comprehensive system that would grade all jobs by skill irrespective of the sex of the worker and the abolition of a 'women's pay schedule'. However, since employers were deeply resistant to such a scheme, the AEU's energies focused almost entirely on securing equal pay for women who actually replaced men. This did nothing for the vast majority whose jobs were traditionally classified as 'women's work'. Viewing women as temporary workers, it wanted to protect the position of its skilled male members for the future. The AEU did not believe that there would be enough jobs for women as well as men at the war's end. By contrast, the TGWU, which had worked hard to unionize women between the wars, saw them as a permanent constituency; it advocated both the rate for the job (though with less persistence than the AEU) and a new national agreement that would revise the pay rates of all women in the engineering industry. Put simply, while it accepted the notion of a 'woman's rate', the TGWU was more consistent and straightforward in its efforts to raise women's status and pay across the industry.

These divisions were central to the most serious and most widely publicized wartime strike over women's pay, which occurred in November 1943 at the Rolls-Royce aero-engine plant at Hillington outside Glasgow. Custom-built with government funds, Hillington employed some 18,000 workers; most were semi-skilled and 7,000 (i.e. 39 per cent) were women, recruited from the Glasgow-Clydeside region and the rural areas of West Scotland. There had been numerous labour skirmishes since the plant opened in 1940 with management trying to impede the spread of unionization and the bid by a large contingent of communist shop stewards to expand their power over the shop floor. In addition, as the Industrial Relations Officer reported, labour relations across the whole Clyde region also seemed to deteriorate markedly in 1943. Shipbuilding and engineering firms were plagued with frequent stoppages and threats of strikes and, while aircraft production remained an urgent priority, workers in other sectors were already beginning to feel the effects of lower demand with increased numbers of transfers and cutbacks in overtime. In the early autumn, for example, over 2,000 workers were transferred from the government ordnance factory at Bishopton, including 360 women who were sent to Hillington and another 480 in their early twenties who were directed to firms in England. Worries about the region's economic future began to preoccupy both employers' associations and local trades councils. At Hillington itself, long-festering unrest over women's pay reached a crisis point as negotiations dragged on without result.[79]

[79] NA: LAB 10/364 reports of November–December 1943; Glasgow Trades Council Minutes, Mitchell Library, October–December 1943; for Bishopton transfers 12 October 1943. P. Bain, ' "Is you or is you ain't my baby?": Women's pay and the Clydeside strikes of 1943', *Scottish Labour History Journal*, 30 (1995); Summerfield, *Women Workers in the Second World War*, pp. 171–3; P. Summerfield and G. Braybon, *Out of the Cage: Women's experiences of two world wars* (London, 1987), pp. 176–7; Croucher, *Engineers at War*, pp. 285–95; Clegg, *A History of British Trade Unions*, III, pp. 201–2; Wightman, *More than Munitions*, pp. 147–9.

While the TGWU had been trying to reach agreement about a new grading structure for all women's jobs, the AEU had decided to make Hillington a test case of 'equal pay for equal work'. Women at this time were paid 47s for a 47-hour basic week while men got 73s 6d for the same job; gender differences in bonuses and overtime further widened the differential. Rolls-Royce insisted that the women were mostly employed on new machinery at tasks designed for them, different from work previously done by men. Disagreements between the two unions helped to stall negotiations, but after an official court of enquiry found that the company had violated the MoL's dilution agreements, all three parties agreed on a plan that graded every machine in the factory irrespective of the sex of its operator. Rank-and-file frustration was high after a year of bargaining; it boiled over in late October 1943 when the women discovered that under the proposed scheme they were still mostly in the bottom grades and would receive only small pay increases. Union officials and most shop stewards were eager to avoid a strike, but it was too late. Women shop stewards called their own mass protest meetings and by early November some 16,000 workers (including many men) had struck and the walkout spread to Rolls-Royce's two other factories in the area. Newspapers condemned the women for taking action at a critical point in the war and letting down the men in the forces, but the Trotskyite Clyde Workers' Committee and the Catholic Guild, which was influential among Irish women at Hillington, championed the strikers.[80] It took almost a month to get a resumption of work and the acceptance of a revised grading formula. What the strike revealed was both the women's strong conviction that they were being treated unfairly and their anger and frustration at trade union officials who neither called a mass meeting to discuss the original offer nor balloted the workforce on its adoption.

The Hillington strike, the largest in the war over women's pay, raised serious concerns in official circles. For the first time large numbers of men had also taken strike action over women's pay and the MoL worried that the agitation might spread not only across Clydeside, but to other industrial regions and impede the build-up for the invasion of Europe. There were signs of trouble at several firms in the Glasgow area, but women withdrew their labour only at Barr and Stroud's Anniesland factory, another plant with a record of persistent labour conflict. And though it took almost a month to settle the strike, on this occasion male workers decided not to participate, although they refused to take over women's jobs and contributed to a hardship fund. But while unrest over unequal pay continued, it did not produce mass action elsewhere. By 1944 large numbers of women were leaving their jobs and, for those who remained, redundancy soon became the chief priority. To this extent the Hillington walkout was untypical. It marked the end not a beginning of a trend; it also reflected the special conditions of the Glasgow region, where the labour movement was strong and disputes were common in all the major industries. By contrast, in South Wales, women's pay scales produced little strike action in ROFs. The region had a militant trade union record in the coal industry, but no pre-war

---

[80] NA: LAB 10/281, Galbraith to Gould, 9 November 1943.

tradition of women's industrial employment. Not only were female munitions workers earning far more than they could pre-war, but their husbands and brothers in the mines were often deeply resentful of women's wages and working conditions, seeing them as undermining male authority and further proof that miners were badly treated and taken for granted. Women's work might cause marital tensions, but the infusion of cash also 'for the first time in years' allowed people 'to pay off arrears of rent, get new curtains, and feed their children properly'.[81]

Thus, while the war did little to change women's unequal pay rates, the sex-typing of industrial jobs, or conventional assumptions about the priority of family and motherhood in women's lives, it did provide employment to women in areas like Wales and the north-east where previously very few opportunities existed. Also, in ways difficult to document, many women achieved greater independence, personally and financially, bolstered by a sense of their contribution to the nation's struggle. Their growing participation in strikes and labour disputes in some sectors illustrates this. It was, as many officials argued, a sign of war fatigue, but it also indicates a growing sense of solidarity and recognition of the importance of their contribution—and a determination that it should not be undervalued.

DOCUMENTING WAR PRODUCTION: A FORM OF SOCIAL EXPLORATION

While manual work in munitions was done overwhelmingly by working-class women, a few middle-class women who volunteered or were directed into work in war factories wrote accounts of their experiences. Just as London's mass shelters, examined in chapter 2, became sites for social exploration, so munitions production allowed middle-class women to navigate daily a normally closed industrial environment, permitting close contact with workers without arousing suspicion.[82] Their narratives explore the themes of class and community but, compared to the patriotic populism of *Millions Like Us*, these accounts are darker, more diffident, and less optimistic about the war as an agent of social levelling.[83] Companionship and acceptance is elusive and class barriers too often seem insurmountable.

Among the earliest and best-known was Inez Holden's *Night Shift* (1941), a fictional work which traces a week in the lives of the night shift at a small aircraft factory during the London Blitz. Holden, a socialist and close friend of George Orwell, had been a journalist for the Beaverbrook press and travelled in literary circles. Early in the war she volunteered for work in an engineering firm and later spent time in a Royal Ordnance factory. The novel investigates whether authentic

---

[81] Williams, *A Forgotten Army*, p. 115. Brian Roberts, 'The budgie train: Women and wartime munitions work in a mining valley', *Llafur*, 7(3–4) (1998–9).

[82] There were a few First World War precursors: Monica Cosens, *Lloyd George's Munitions Girls* (London, 1916); Agnes Kate Foxwell, *Munition Lasses: Six months as principal overlooker in danger buildings* (London, 1917).

[83] See J. Hartley, *Millions Like Us: British women's fiction of the Second World War* (London, 1997), ch. 4.

community can develop among a disparate collection of men and women. They include a girl from the upper class: 'sleek and well brushed', 'the sort . . . who would have been "ladying" it at a First Aid Post'.[84] But the author's chief interest is social gradations within the working class, including the division between female clerks and machine-shop women. Conditions are filthy and primitive, while the work is boring, repetitive, and exhausting. Workers feel trapped, gripe about their pay and have no patience with the patriotic 'yapping' of one of their number. Outside work they all go their separate ways, but when one is sacked, the others rally round. Holden provides little evidence of a real community in formation, but in this book is not ready to abandon hope. It ends when the factory and its workforce are blown to bits in a raid. The narrator escapes (she was fire-watching at her block of flats) and in her curiously detached, understated way thinks about her co-workers, reflecting that 'each one of them had been worth a second chance'.[85]

Three years later Holden produced a second and much harsher novel *There's No Story There* (1944) set in a huge ordnance factory ('Statevale'). With 30,000 workers from all over the country, many of them living in hostels, the plant resembles a vast prison camp with daily security checks and officious police. The atmosphere is more like a fascist state than the 'People's War'. Dressed in asbestos suits and white-flannelled trousers and their faces covered with protective creams and powder, the workers seem surreal, 'scientific, robotic, serious and aseptic'. They are also a cross-section of society's casualties and misfits. Even the plant's superintendent and management seem hopelessly trapped and beleaguered. There are welfare officers, time-and-motion experts, regular fruitless sessions of a Joint Production Council, a whole staff that arranges film shows, well-equipped hostels, and endless committees to facilitate communication. But nothing can change the pervasive fragmentation and impersonality of the place. There is no hope of community here—the workers are completely atomized, only their complaining humanizes them. When a heavy snowfall cuts off the plant, forcing the day shift to sleep in the factory, morale suddenly improves and nature forces people to cooperate and work together; even the gulf between supervisors and workers shrinks. But this is ephemeral. The same snow brings anger among those left in the hostels and a vicious, unexplained fight between women workers. Nothing can develop from such an unnatural place—no friendships, no ties, no 'story' or larger whole. The one character who strives to make something of these fragments is a young manager, a Mass-Observer, forever scribbling down notes about workers' conversations and opinions. In the end he loses his notebook in the snow and is left searching for it frantically with 'a mass of workers observing him'.[86]

---

[84] I. Holden, *Night Shift* (London, 1941), p. 13; *idem, It Was Different at the Time* (London, 1945).
[85] *Ibid.*, pp. 13, 110, 126.
[86] I. Holden, *There's No Story There* (London, 1944), p. 13 (for the quotation) and ch. 10, 'Snowed In'. See also: K. Bluemel, 'There's no story there: Inez Holden's lost war literature' in S. Dean (ed.), *Challenging Modernism: New readings in literature and culture, 1914–45* (Aldershot, 2002). Bluemel's interpretation of the novel differs from the one given here: she views the title, 'There's no story there', as a commentary on workers' exclusion from traditional literary narratives rather than a statement about workers' lack of community, their alienation from each other as well as from the factory.

No narrator is present in Inez Holden's 'Statevale' and even in *Night Shift* she is almost entirely effaced, an observer about whom we learn almost nothing. A different approach was taken by Diana Murray Hill, who worked for a large aircraft firm for two years until her health gave way. Her novel, *Ladies May Now Leave Their Machines* (1944), combines documentary reportage of factory work, fictional stories about other women workers, and detailed observations about her own physical and psychological responses to industrial work. Subtitles break up the text and lengthy sections are devoted to work processes, daily routines, wages, and household budgets. The result is an inferior, fragmented novel—indeed scarcely a novel at all– but a mine of interesting detail. Ties between workers are closer than in Holden, but there is not much warmth and ethnic divisions are evident: 'As a race the Welsh were heartily disliked and were referred to as twisters, grabbers, creep-arses etc. They were very good workers and very clannish.'[87] Interaction between male and female workers runs the gamut from friendly assistance to outright hostility; sometimes work practices divide them, the bonuses of male 'setters' depending on the output of women in their group. As was the case in Holden's 'Statevale', the Joint Production Committee, along with management, dream up endless regulations to chivvy workers; even the Christmas show is cancelled because it might lower production. Trade unionism is a real presence in this factory, protesting bottlenecks and mismanagement during the production crisis of 1942, whipping up enthusiasm for Soviet Russia, and towards the war's end pressuring women workers to demand equal pay—but 'the girls are too dumb about their own fates' and equal pay, Hill recognizes, is a union strategy to protect males rates and preserve jobs for returning servicemen.

The narrator (Hill presumably) records meticulously her own responses to industrial work, beginning with the first bleak impressions: 'Each day, returning, the shock of the dead yellow haze with the stale smell of oil and machinery, struck you again and brought you down to flat level.' It was, she said, a reminder of her loss of freedom, like 'walking straight into a tomb'. Along with most other workers, she moves through a cycle, quickly reaching a peak of productivity ('tear-arsing') and good bonus earnings, followed by a long decline and sickness. She slows down, loses concentration, breaks drills repeatedly, her pay packets shrink, and depression sinks in. 'Browned-off' was the contemporary phrase she and other women gave to their condition:

> Scarcely perceptible at first, and then steadily and more steadily growing till, aided by other factors like lack of sleep, petty illnesses, and factory disturbances, it permeates and then predominates your whole life . . . the browned-off man has his fingers on you, and after . . . a year, two years or more, unless your morale and health are very sturdy, he can make you very poor shadows of the War Effort girls.

For Hill and her co-workers patriotism and the war seemed 'a very remote thing, hardly connected with our work at all'. The walls were plastered with slogans: 'It all depends on me' turned up everywhere, on the back of time cards, even 'inside our

---

[87] D. Murray Hill, *Ladies May Now Leave Their Machines* (London, 1944), p. 27.

pay packets'. But the mood was more selfish: 'Everybody in the factory had money on the brain . . . they grumbled and groaned, and their whole lives were confined by it.'[88] Like Holden's novels and most others of this genre, Hill's story does not develop incrementally but remains a mass of fragments; war work is refracted through the lives of the narrator and her two working-class companions. Again, the story also ends abruptly when the narrator's health breaks down and she leaves the factory. The other two also obtain releases soon after and go their separate ways. What is lacking is a sense of empathy between them; they remain disconnected, detached, unable to form deeper relationships. There is also no sense of better times to come, no hopes for a better Britain once peace returns.

These stories, really disguised documentaries, capture their authors' growing alienation from both factory environment and working-class co-workers. A more positive, direct, and unedited account of factory life, but one which has some of the same themes, is the war diary written jointly by two close friends, Kathleen Church-Bliss and Elsie Whiteman. The two women met through their active involvement in the English Folk Dance Society and before volunteering for war work had owned a tea shop together in Surrey. Both were in their forties, came from affluent upper-middle-class families, had private incomes and connections to London society. The diary describes their experiences first at a government Training Centre in early 1942 and then at Morrisons near Croydon, a subcontractor making aircraft components for Vickers at Weybridge; they remained at the factory until April 1945 but the diary ends in November 1944.[89] Morrisons employed about 500 workers, over half of them female. Their decision to take up engineering was motivated both by a strong desire to contribute to the war effort and—the diary hints in some entries—by a spirit of social exploration: it was an adventure, something quite new, a chance to mix with 'the people' at large. Soon after starting their training course, they write: 'We haven't heard one educated voice, trainees, teachers or office staff and mercifully our own Kensington voices don't seem to have excited comment. They think we are sisters because we speak alike. We think they are all an extraordinary nice crowd and we are rapidly getting used to their abrupt and terse phraseology.'[90] 'Els didn't learn much today of the engineering', another entry declares, 'but she can do Joyce's [a fellow trainee] accent and delivery quite a treat.'[91] Recognizing that hyphenated surnames were a clear indicator of social class, Kathleen shortened hers to Bliss and they were careful in conversations with fellow workers not to mention places like the Café Royal that they had frequented before the war.

[88] Murray Hill, *Ladies May Now Leave Their Machines*, pp. 18–19, 50, 103, 58, 118.
[89] Church-Bliss/Whiteman diaries IWM 91/34/1. The diary with some omissions has now been published with an excellent introduction and notes by S. Bruley, *Working for Victory: A diary of life in a Second World War factory* (Gloucestershire, 2001). At Morrisons they earned around £4–5 per week which they referred to as a 'charwoman's wage' but they paid close attention to their weekly earnings and were frequently angry when they were lower than expected or the firm delayed in paying out bonuses.
[90] Church-Bliss/Whiteman diaries (21 February 1942); Bruley (ed.), *Working for Victory*, p. 4.
[91] Church-Bliss/Whiteman diaries (27 February 1942); Bruley (ed.), *Working for Victory*, p. 6.

The diary is a trove of information about factory life, recording the different jobs and machines on which they were employed, their responses to the work, exhaustion at the long hours, and their detailed observations of fellow workers.[92] They were shocked at the time wasted through bottlenecks and machine break-downs as well as boredom and trips to the women's cloakroom; they also tended to view older women as better, more reliable workers:

> There is an odd assortment of women at Morrisons. A bunch of nice middle-aged grannies with kindly worn faces and amiable manners. Then there is a horde of ghastly looking wantons with long golden locks and buffon erections on top and enamelled faces. Sometimes they bulge out of trousers, at others they sprout out of skintight jumpers. Always they are conscious of one thing only—their exceeding beauty, charm, and glamour.[93]

They adopted names for many of them—'Wax-Doll', 'the Gaudy Image', 'Little Wolatile', Helen who had 'a most peculiar allure' and 'reminds us of a spaniel bitch puppy', and the 'coquettish' 'Peccadillo' caught 'canoodling' in an air-raid shelter with one of the lads. Their diary displays prejudices common to their class and time in sprinkled references to 'dago-type little twerp', 'Peter Joseph, the new little Jew inspector', and 'the awful little Mrs Israel who was set to work on a small lathe next to Elsie' who smoked, did little, and frequently 'drawled': 'I think I'll go to the lav.'

Kathleen and Elsie were avid collectors of gossip about workplace liaisons—'scandal rushes round the factory like a wind'—and the rows, petty jealousies, and 'rumpuses' that erupted between workers enlivening the long hours of labour. But while they viewed fellow workers with an anthropological eye, they were not unsympathetic towards their workmates and formed friendships, at first with male instructors and charge-hands, but then with some of the women, occasionally seeing them outside the factory and exchanging gifts of food. Since they remained in the machine shop for a long time, they were more fully integrated into the workplace than Holden's narrators and became deeply involved in efforts to improve working conditions. They joined the NUGMW in November 1942 and later transferred to the AEU when it permitted women to join, although somewhat alarmed by the radicalism of some of the branch members. Elsie worked hard on a committee that handled the workers' sick-benefit fund and the canteen committee, while in March 1943 when Morrisons established a Works Council, Kathleen was elected as one of two female members. 'We are both amazed (and very proud)', they write, 'that we find ourselves representing the workers on their committees. We always thought we cut absolutely no ice whatsoever and see ourselves as a couple of old "Squeak Aunts" in our dirty old caps and overalls... trundling slowly along on our upright bicycles.'[94] For a long time both women had been critical of the firm's

---

[92] They read Inez Holden's *Night Shift* and Mass-Observation's *People in Production*. Reading Holden while at the Training Centre, they found it 'a very clever book, particularly poignant to us at the moment' but they did not 'think it rings quite true'. 'We should judge', they add, 'the authoress to be a middle-aged woman, and with the inevitable mental aloofness of a woman working outside her own class': Bruley (ed.), *Working for Victory*, p. 13.

[93] Church-Bliss/Whiteman diaries (25 July 1942); Bruley (ed.), *Working for Victory*, p. 56.

[94] Church-Bliss/Whiteman diaries (20 March 1943); Bruley (ed.), *Working for Victory*, p. 121.

petty meanness over wages issues, its substandard tools, delays in providing stools for women to sit down, and its 'petty tyranny' in removing cloakroom mirrors except for the lunch period and clocking-off time. Now with growing involvement on committees their dissatisfaction grew and Kathleen especially became deeply antagonistic towards the management. Even though she won several victories over wage rates and workplace improvements, Kathleen became convinced that Morrisons' managers had no interest in cooperating or agreeing to workers' requests but saw the Works Council as simply 'a safety valve to keep [them] quiet'.[95] At times the diary expresses disappointment at the 'great dearth of women willing to take an active part in factory affairs', but more often the target of their criticism is the firm's 'awful collection of bosses' who were remote and had little personal dealings with the workforce—directors are described as 'a group of vultures', while the nickname dreamed up for the Managing Director was 'the Well Scrubbed Pig'. The firm's managers were closer to them socially, but Kathleen and Elsie identified with their fellow workers in the machine shop. The clothes, make-up, and demeanour of some of the younger women might shock them but they liked the way they asserted their rights and stuck up for themselves.

The diary entries in the final year reveal how many months of continuous work had sapped their earlier enthusiasm and sense of adventure. There are repeated references to exhaustion, depression, and deteriorating health; both suffered from bouts of sickness—'flu, pneumonia, and shingles—and, after a period of sick leave and convalescence in early 1944, they write more and more of 'getting a release' and leaving Morrisons. On weekends they were glad to get away to family and friends or to renew their London contacts in folk-dancing circles. By this time they longed to escape the tiring shifts, dirt, and noise of the factory—all made worse by many nights spent cooped up in uncomfortable shelters during the V1 and V2 raids. There is less humour and liveliness to their descriptions, their 'browned-off' mood resembles the later stages of Diana Murray Hill's narrative. Kathleen and Elsie made real efforts to get along with their co-workers and fit in; age and class, however, set them apart.

Finally there is Celia Fremlin's *War Factory*, a book that historians frequently cite as an accurate description of munitions work, although the author warned that her chapters 'must not be regarded as describing a typical *industrial* life at all; for there are none of the industrial traditions and background with which the true industrial worker is surrounded'.[96] Fremlin, an Oxford graduate and later a writer of detective novels, had tried her hand at social reportage before the war when she worked as a domestic servant, documenting her experiences in *The Seven Chars of Chelsea*.[97]

---

[95] Church-Bliss/Whiteman diaries (12 June 1944); Bruley (ed.), *Working for Victory*, p. 187.

[96] M-O, *War Factory* (1943; reissued by Cresset Library, 1987), p. 18. She continued: 'Rather it is a study of rural adaptation (and failure of adaptation) to a new and startling industrial situation suddenly forced upon them. For the factory has no roots in the place; it has no history or natural growth and development.' Wightman, *More than Munitions Women*, ch. 8 relies heavily upon Fremlin's account to demonstrate women's passivity and uninterest as war-workers.

[97] *The Seven Chars of Chelsea* (London, 1940) documented the huge gulf between mistress and servant which, Fremlin argued, made real understanding between them impossible.

That book caught the eye of Tom Harrisson who recruited her for several Mass-Observation projects including the large survey of wartime industry, *People in Production* (1942). In early 1942 she was called up for war service and directed to a small factory in rural Gloucestershire that made top-secret components for radar.[98] Harrisson, without Fremlin's knowledge, had a hand in her posting to the factory and he arranged for her to secretly document her fellow workers, disguising her furious note-taking during tea-breaks and slack periods by pretending to be an obsessive letter-writer. Her observations were sent by Harrisson to the firm's management for comments and he wrote an introduction and collected them into a book (published anonymously) which was widely reviewed and discussed.

Fremlin's factory was newly established, partly in a converted mansion. Its workforce of about 1,000 was mostly composed of local country girls and former domestics, some 200 textile workers who were transferred when their mill was closed, and conscripts drawn from further afield. Most were housed in hostels or lodgings in the town and very few had prior experience of industrial work ('or indeed of any organized work in a community', Fremlin writes[99]). On arrival at the factory, Fremlin was sent first to the machine shop, where unskilled women workers were employed at simple, routine drilling tasks. Later she moved on to the assembly department where, she indicates, the jobs were more complicated and the women more motivated; in this section the social composition was mostly upper working class with a sprinkling of middle class, including female supervisors. A good deal of ill-feeling existed between the two departments—assembly women made no secret of their view that machinists were coarse, low-class types, while the machine shop felt 'looked down on': 'They're terrible snobbish over there. Turning up their noses... I'd like to ask some of them where *they* come from.' The girls in the machine shop showed a 'quite surprising degree of regard' for managers and 'higher-ups' and were thankful for small attentions: 'He's very nice, the way he speaks to you, isn't he?' By contrast, those in the assembly shop were far more critical with 'something', Fremlin notes, 'of the more sophisticated worker versus boss attitude'.[100]

Most of *War Factory* is devoted to women in the machine shop; Fremlin provides details about their backgrounds and selectively reproduces their conversations. She describes the boredom of the young women, incarcerated in the factory for twelve-hour shifts with few breaks and deployed on the most repetitive, monotonous tasks. They watched the clock, drifted out to the cloakroom, discussed films and cosmetics, checked their astrological signs—anything to pass the time. 'It's funny', commented one, 'when you're in there [machine shop] the time goes so slow... but somehow when you look back the weeks seem to fly by. I've been here two

[98] The factory worked for the RAF to develop radio aircraft detection systems to detect enemy bombers, ships, and submarines. The Ecko company was developed by M. I. Lipman, a socialist businessman, who contacted Mass-Observation in an attempt to cope with what he considered morale problems among the female workforce. M. Lipman, *Memoirs of a Socialist Businessman* (London, 1980).
[99] M-O, *War Factory*, p. 31.
[100] *Ibid.*, pp. 55, 69.

years, but I sometimes feel I've only been here a few weeks. It gives me quite a nasty sort of feeling, like it's running away with my life, you know what I mean?' 'Between three and five in the afternoon', Fremlin writes, 'more slacking and idling goes on than one would have thought possible... Sometimes one can look along the bench and see not one girl in four actually working.' They seemed to know and care little about the war and saw little connection between it and their work. Appeals to patriotism, she adds, were 'almost valueless' with these workers: 'The patriotic posters... which plaster the walls of every room in the factory might as well be so much ornamental scroll work for all the notice that is taken of them.' There were small cliques, but no deeper sense of community; the communal singing, so central to *Millions* and wartime newsreels, is confined to isolated groups: 'indeed, different parts of the room will be singing different songs at the same time'. Life in the hostels is described as a continual round of backbiting and tale-bearing, a 'welter of ill-temper and discontent'. Especially in the last section on Leisure, the report turns into a critique of the women's cultural poverty and apathy, their shallowness and lack of initiative. While they complain of boredom, the manage- ment-sponsored social centre is poorly attended ('Well, you have to be a bit posh to go there, don't you', 'I wouldn't go in there with all them snobs from the office. I'd rather go to an ordinary dance'). There is no 'lively demand' for 'dramatic groups, cycling, or walking clubs'. The girls have no connection to Works Committees or trade unionism. 'They regard their new lives', Fremlin writes, 'not as an exciting adventure, but as something to be put up with.'[101]

Fremlin herself remains almost entirely absent from the text. This tactic, the invisible spectator, means that all social interaction or verbal exchanges between the author and other workers are excluded. What the other girls thought this upper- middle-class Oxford recruit was doing in their midst remains a mystery. Few, one can be sure, thought she would stay in the machine shop very long. Could she hope to get close to these women, penetrate the daily buzz of chatter, and get to know them? In one sense, the question is irrelevant for Fremlin was simply recording her observations about work and morale; but in other ways the issue of empathy is crucial since the book has been so widely cited as a reliable picture of munitions workers. These comments are not meant to minimize Fremlin's remarkable achieve- ment in the book which contains acute sketches of women in the factory—their jokes, complaints, family worries, daily expenses, and social activities—much of it in their own expressive rhetoric. But the author's sense of personal and social distance is always present. Her irritation with many of the workers is evident throughout—this extends to their gripes and idle chatter, their 'carefree irresponsibility', and their sense of the war as an endurance test, 'not as something to be plunged into with zest and enthusiasm'. This made it 'difficult for real social units to be formed in or out of work'.[102]

The book criticizes the long shifts, repetitive jobs, and the authorities' failure to explain to the women the significance of their labour. But negative tones surface

[101] M-O, *War Factory*, pp. 42–3, 30, 48, 49, 113, 121, 106, 84–5, 120–2.
[102] *Ibid.*, *War Factory*, pp. 120–1.

more and more. Of workers living in hostels, Fremlin writes: 'at the root of the trouble is the fact that these girls are leading irresponsible lives... All day in the factory they are doing (most of them at least) easy and quite irresponsible work. When they get home in the evening everything has been done for them... Their attitude is, in fact, almost the same as that of a child who feels himself shielded from the outside world by grown-ups of infinite power and varying goodwill.'[103] She seems to forget that they put in a minimum of sixty hours a week and that many had family ties that took them away on weekends. What began as an enquiry into morale, excessive work hours, and repetitive labour ends on a different note: the girls' failings and their apathy. This was underscored in Tom Harrisson's short preface for the book which compared it to 'other recent work... on political apathy, passive leisure, youth morality'. The 'aimlessness, irresponsibility, and boredom' of the machine-shop girls, in Harrisson's view, was symptomatic of a *dangerous decline in positive citizenship* that 'subtly threatens the health of all democracy'.[104]

Fremlin's account offers a startling contrast to the anodyne communalism of *Millions Like Us*. Unlike the social explorers who saw in London's mass shelters an embryo of active democracy, all the middle-class observers examined here had their illusions severely tested. They were in the factory but not of it. To varying degrees they felt dispirited and alienated, unable to penetrate the group culture and disappointed by their co-workers. In a short essay, Inez Holden reflected upon social difference and the limits of her understanding: 'I began to feel rather isolated... I thought about the effect of factory life on the pampered bourgeois.' For Holden, the low pay, exhausting work, and monotony was temporary; for the others, she wrote, fatigue and unending poverty were normal and blunted perception, except when some misfortune to one galvanized a 'counter poetry of comradeship and generosity'. Behind the fatigue, she concluded, was endurance: 'there is a great strength, an unorganized strength but a strength all the same'.[105]

WOMEN IN THE FORCES AND LAND GIRLS

One alternative to factory work was service in the women's auxiliaries. Founded in the First World War, they were quickly disbanded when peace returned. After the Czech crisis of 1938, with another war on the horizon, they were re-established, although only 43,000 volunteers had joined by the end of 1939. Once conscription was introduced, the auxiliaries grew rapidly, reaching a peak strength of around half a million. Women who opted for the forces gave various reasons for their choice: patriotism, the glamour of the uniform, a thirst for new experiences, and a desire to escape their homes were among the most common. Virginia Cole, a shop assistant, enlisted in the Auxiliary Territorial Service (ATS) to get free of the sexual advances of her stepfather. Joan Welch, who gave up her secretarial job with the Co-op to

---

[103] *Ibid.*, pp. 109–10.   [104] *Ibid.*, p. 9.
[105] I. Holden, 'Fellow travellers in factory', *Horizon*, 3(14) (February 1941).

join the Women's Auxiliary Air Force (WAAF), admitted: 'I wasn't very happy at home because my father had such a strict regime...and I thought it would be better to go into the services.' Another woman reflected that she had 'wanted to do something totally different because I came from an ordinary working background...the ATS came as something whereby I could sort of leave home and be an adventurist'.[106]

The Women's Royal Naval Service (WRNS), was socially the most exclusive, the smallest, and the hardest to get into. It consisted entirely of volunteers who provided letters of reference with their applications. Next in popularity came the WAAF, while the ATS was widely viewed as having the least status: less glamorous, less educated (only 7 per cent of recruits had a high-school certificate), more working-class, and having the most dowdy and unflattering uniform.[107] Women who voiced a preference for the forces picked the navy and air force over the army by a ratio of 4 to 1. In part, the ATS suffered from the fact that, at least until the end of the war, the general public had a higher regard for the air force and navy. But the major problem was the perception that lower class and morally questionable girls went into the ATS. *The Times* warned of 'a general impression that the ATS is not the sort of service a nice girl goes into'.[108] A Mass-Observation survey emphasized male convictions that ATS were little better than amateur prostitutes, while potential recruits worried that their reputations would be irreparably damaged: 'Oh, I couldn't join the ATS. All my friends would think I was one of those.'[109] Told to report to Wrexham for training, one girl admitted: 'By the time I arrived...I was feeling very apprehensive about what lay ahead, niggling at the back of my mind were malicious rumours I'd heard about the moral qualities of the ATS.'[110] A December 1941 survey indicated that 59 per cent still believed that the general public held them in low esteem, while another 16.5 per cent felt their reputation was 'mixed'.[111] Official efforts to combat this negative image, including the enlistment of Churchill's daughter and Princess Elizabeth, never entirely removed the unpopular 'Cinderella' stigma.

[106] IWM: 86/61/1: V. C. Cole MS; *What Did You Do in the War Mum?* (Age Exchange, 1993), p. 17; G. DeGroot, '"I love the scent of cordite in your hair": Gender dynamics in mixed anti-aircraft batteries during the Second World War', *History*, 265 (January 1997), 77.

[107] D. Parkin, 'Women in the armed services, 1940–45' in R. Samuel (ed.), *Patriotism: The making and unmaking of British national identity* (London, 1987), II. On ATS uniforms see NA: INF 1/282, 26 September 1941; M-OA: FR 757 (25 June 1941). One medical officer called the ATS uniform 'the best maternity garment ever invented', NA: CAB 102/771. By 1943 the WRNS numbered 60,400; the ATS, 212,500; and the WAAF, 180,300.

[108] *The Times*, 15 January 1942, reporting a speech in the Commons by Henderson Stewart MP for East Fife.

[109] M-OA: FR 955, 'Attitudes to women in the ATS' (1941). Also, NA: INF 1/282, 2 and 29 December 1941. NA: RG 23/5, 'An investigation of the attitudes of women, the general public and ATS personnel to the Auxiliary Territorial Service', Wartime Social Survey, October 1941. Also INF 1/292, 22 September 1941 ('Scottish women in National Service').

[110] IWM: 88/50/1, J. W. M. Burchell MSS, quoted in G. De Groot, 'Whose finger on the trigger: Mixed anti-aircraft batteries and female combat taboo', *War in History*, 4(4) (1997), 79.

[111] NA: INF 1/292, 1 December 1942. Also, INF 1/292, 10, 22–9 December 1941: 'In appearance they incline to be a sloppy and frowsy lot, altogether rather a "bitchy" crew.'

Dame Helen Gwynne-Vaughan, a professor of botany who had commanded women's auxiliaries in the previous war, led the ATS in the first two years. As officers she recruited upper-class women, especially those from army families, and the whole ethos of the service seemed outdated, harking back to the previous war; the service's publicity which advertised its role as one of supportive services to the army and offered conventionally feminine work like cooking, cleaning, or managing stores did little to encourage volunteers. By the summer of 1941, with the growing need for a much larger intake of recruits, Gwynne-Vaughan was replaced and a series of reforms were set in motion: the uniform was restyled, officer selection made more inclusive and meritocratic, and a new publicity campaign endeavoured to allay the moral concerns of parents and recruits and depict a wider and more exciting range of opportunities open to those who joined. With conscription the ATS expanded rapidly, reaching 212,000 at the peak, but it never lost its public image as the least popular auxiliary service.[112]

Echoing the theme of a 'People's War', publicity about the women's auxiliaries—like that about war factories—stressed class levelling and the ways that the war effort brought together women from all social strata and walks of life. This was the gist, for example, of the popular feature film, *The Gentle Sex* (1943) which depicted the basic training of a group of ATS before they took on their roles as truck drivers, mechanics, ack-ack gunners, and mess orderlies. The characters range from a colonel's daughter to a cockney waitress whose class and individual differences are nullified as they bond into an efficient unit of citizens in uniform and a microcosm of the nation at war.[113] There is some truth in this, and certainly memoirs by middle-class recruits stress their experience of a much wider range of women than they would have met in peacetime; nonetheless in practice social mixing was limited by structural factors as well as individual choice. Middle-class recruits still had a far better chance of being selected for officer training and for jobs in such areas as signals and administration. Virginia Cole remembered two 'posh girls' who for no other discernible reason were immediately sent on a course for potential officers 'much to the disgust of most of the girls in the hut'.[114] As more and more men were replaced by auxiliaries, so the range of jobs and specialized trades expanded rapidly, but the early division of recruits in training into S. and G. ('Specialized' and 'General') classes meant that working-class girls were more apt to be steered into the latter group which included the more menial occupations like cooks, messengers, and orderlies.[115] Patriotic populism may have been the public image of the service, but the culture of command and the relations of ordinary recruits and officers were buttressed by class difference.

---

[112] Lucy Noakes, *Women in the British Army: War and the gentle sex 1907–1948* (London, 2005); S. Bidwell, *The Royal Army Corps* (London, 1977); R. Terry, *Women in Khaki: The story of the British woman soldier* (London, 1988); E. Taylor, *Women Who Went to War, 1938–1946* (London, 1988).

[113] A. Lant, *Blackout: Reinventing women for wartime British cinema* (Princeton, 1991), pp. 89–113.

[114] IWM: 86/61/1: V. C. Cole MSS, p. 9.

[115] Hilary Wayne, *Two Odd Soldiers* (London, 1946); compare on the WAAF: M-OA: TC 32 (Women in Wartime, Box 3, File E, comments by Nina Masel, 25 April 1941).

There were very few disciplinary problems in the women's services—aside from minor cases of insubordination or drunkenness or going AWOL—and female auxiliaries were never subject to the full code of discipline. The penalties they faced ranged from 'fatigues', loss of rank, or a maximum of fourteen days confined to barracks and loss of pay. A small number of women deserted, usually fleeing to London or another big city where—having no ration cards or papers—they were likely to end up in prostitution or low-level criminality. More of a problem for camp commanders were the occasional incorrigible troublemakers who stayed in the services and flouted authority; here the policy was to discharge them as quickly as possible after which they would be directed into war factories.[116] Auxiliaries who got pregnant were discharged as quickly as possible; in the case of single girls who could not or refused to return to their families, arrangements were made with voluntary organizations to provide accommodation before and after confinement and spaces in maternity wards.

As more and more men were needed for service abroad, so the ATS replaced them in growing numbers on anti-aircraft batteries—eventually some 57,000 were employed on gun sites. Widely publicized in the press, at first in the summer of 1941 the presence of women at these sites attracted crowds of onlookers but over the next year they became a familiar part of wartime life. It was a popular form of service with recruits, being closer to a combat role and more directly linked to a military function than the office work and other support roles with which many ATS were occupied. Women worked alongside the Royal Artillery who ran the sites, but they had their own officers and were subject to a separate code of discipline. Moreover, since the War Office remained opposed to the idea of women in combat positions they could act as radio operators, adjust shell fuses, locate enemy aircraft, and set height finders—do everything, in fact, except actually fire the guns. They also received two-thirds of the male pay rate and were not eligible for combat medals.

The nation's growing reliance upon mixed batteries where men and women lived and worked closely together also fuelled public debate about alleged promiscuity and drunkenness among women in the forces. The level of anger and anxiety generated was well illustrated by a Mass-Observation survey of November 1941; the men interviewed not only objected (84 per cent of a sample of soldiers[117]) to their wives or girlfriends joining the ATS but they offered up a whole litany of charges about their being hard-drinking, rough types, little better than whores. At first, to allay moral concerns, middle-aged men, father figures, were posted to these units, but because of generational tensions the practice was discontinued. The arrival of younger men improved morale but also increased public gossip.[118] The 'ack-ack' girls illustrate well the contradictory discourses provoked by women in uniform. As Noakes, Summerfield, and others have argued, women in uniform, particularly

---

[116] NA: WO 277/6, J. M. Cowper, 'The Auxiliary Territorial Service 1939–45' (London, 1949).
[117] INF 1/292, 2 December 1941 ('ATS Campaign').
[118] F. Pile, *Ack-Ack* (London, 1949), p. 189. Also, DeGroot, 'I love the scent of cordite in your hair'; *idem*, 'Whose finger on the trigger'.

those working closely with men, concentrated fears about the war's impact on moral standards and conventional gender roles; at one and the same time they found themselves celebrated in the media for their courage and patriotism and disparaged as unfeminine or immoral. General Sir Frederick Pile, Commander of Air Defence, recalled: 'There were good and bad girls... Occasionally one of the bad ones achieved some embarrassing publicity, but by this time we had a Public Relations Department capable of retaliating with an inspiring photography of some smart, sturdy ATS in military postures.'[119]

As Tessa Stone's research has shown, conditions in the WAAF were somewhat different; recruits were on average better educated, with more coming from middle-class and upper working-class backgrounds.[120] The WAAF was more full integrated into the military structure with women serving not as part of all-female units but in regular RAF commands under the authority of male and female officers. They lived and worked alongside men at RAF bases, substituted for men in a growing number of skilled, technical trades, and in general enjoyed a wider range of opportunities than women in the other services. By the end of 1943 WAAFs constituted 16 per cent of all air force personnel and 22 per cent of those in Britain; they were trained as drivers, fitters, electricians, aircraft ground crew, signal and wireless operators, plotted aircraft, and staffed barrage-balloon posts. They moved into what were previously exclusively male positions but, unlike in civilian industries, substitution caused few problems. This was partly because of military discipline and because the vast majority of men were also in the forces for the war's duration and did not view women as direct threats to their livelihoods. Also, in a larger sense the military, with its emphasis upon male combatants, reaffirmed conventional gender patterns.[121] Stone emphasizes that, while gender was always an inescapable factor in women's lives in uniform, the military context itself also shaped their sense of identity and status; the prestige attached to various jobs in the WAAF, for example, had less to do with gender than with the status that came from proximity to air operations. Similarly, women recruits' emphasis upon their looks and smart uniforms was an expression of individuality in a military structure that accented uniformity as much as it was an assertion of femininity, jeopardized by public claims that uniformed women were somehow de-feminized.

The moral panic about service women drinking and engaging in promiscuous affairs extended to all women in uniform, although the WAAF and WRNS never attracted the same level of negativity as the ATS. Tales circulated of drunkenness, rising VD statistics, numerous pregnancies, and specially built ATS maternity homes. In an effort to quell such derogatory rumours the government decided at the end of 1941 to appoint a parliamentary committee ostensibly to examine the amenities and welfare conditions of the three women's services. Composed of five

---

[119] Noakes, *Women in the British Army*; Pile, *Ack-Ack*, p. 193.
[120] T. Stone, 'The integration of women into a military service: The Women's Auxiliary Air Force in the Second World War', PhD Diss., Cambridge University, 1998; *idem*, 'Creating a (gendered?) military identity: The Women's Auxiliary Air Force in Great Britain in the Second World War', *Women's History Review*, 8(4) (1999). Also, B. E. Escott, *Women in Air Force Blue* (Guildford, 1989).
[121] Summerfield, 'What women learned from the Second World War', p. 227.

women and three men, the committee was chaired by the Liberal social activist
Violet Markham, who had participated in a similar investigation into servicewomen's conduct in 1918, and it included the outspoken Labour feminist Edith
Summerskill. The committee toured large numbers of camps and took evidence
from a wide range of organizations. It recommended a series of changes in food,
welfare, educational, and medical services, including the hiring of more female
gynaecologists. It also called for lectures on sexuality and stable family relationships;
'not', the report was careful to say, 'because the sex morals of the forces are more
precarious than those of civilians but because... life in the forces presents new
educational opportunities'. As to the rumours about drink and immorality, the
committee concluded that, while women generally were consuming more alcohol
in wartime, there was no evidence that those in uniform were more promiscuous. A
woman in uniform seemed to arouse 'a special sense of hostility, conscious and sub-
conscious, among certain people who would never give two thoughts to her
conduct as a private citizen'. Statistics on ATS women discharged for pregnancy
showed that most were married recruits, while the pregnancy rate among single
ATS was about 1.5 per cent—lower than for comparable age groups in the civilian
population. This was also true of the incidence of VD. 'Virtue', the report
admonished, 'has no gossip value' and 'a vast superstructure of slander had been
raised on a small foundation of fact'.[122] As Summerskill observed, the public
seemed far more concerned about servicewomen's moral welfare than their material
conditions or the fact that their pay and disability allowances were far below those
of men in the forces.[123]

While the mass recruitment of women into the armed forces did much to stir up
old anxieties about declining sexuality morality and the erosion of traditional
gender roles, its impact on the women themselves—as numerous memoirs and
oral histories indicate—was profound and overwhelmingly positive. Life in the
military came as a severe shock to many young women, especially those who had
lived sheltered lives or had never been away from home. 'You had', wrote one
WAAF, 'to learn to live in a small space with all sorts and kinds. Although we didn't
have much room at home, we were brought up with a little bit of privacy. You
could do your own thing. There was no privacy in a Nissan hut.'[124] For some, the
rigours of basic training, the discipline and pressures of communal living were
intolerable, but most young women remember it as a broadening experience; they
met a broad cross-section of people, formed friendships, learned new skills,
shared confidences, and matured rapidly: 'The barrack room', in Gerard DeGroot's

[122] *Report of the Committee on Amenities and Welfare Conditions in the Three Women's Services*, Cmd
6384 (1942), pp. 30, 49, 52. Contraceptives (hard to get in wartime) were not made available to servicewomen and an unmarried female officer who contracted VD automatically lost her commission. At the
start of the war the Family Planning Association urged that army doctors give contraceptive advice to
married women in the forces and offered its help with teaching techniques. But the War Office was
distinctly negative and, as chance would have it, the head of ATS medical services was the well-known
opponent of birth control, Dr Letitia Fairfield. Her successor was more sympathetic but also wanted no
adverse publicity. A. Leathard, *The Fight for Family Planning* (London, 1980), pp. 70–1.
[123] E. Summerskill, 'Conscription and women', *The Fortnightly*, 157 (March 1942), 212.
[124] *What Did You Do in the War Mum?* (Age Exchange, 1993).

words, 'was a great melting pot; the experienced and the innocent mixed in a sometimes volatile dynamic.'[125] Summerfield's oral history research indicates that most women, looking back on their service, concluded that they had been significantly changed by their experiences.[126] Usually this was framed in terms of losing their shyness, being exposed to discussion about sexuality, becoming more competent and self-confident. This extended to a sense of commonality with other people which included for middle-class recruits encountering working-class women for the first time and for working-class a sense of being as good as anyone else. For many working-class daughters, who had never been away from home or their local neighbourhood, it may have helped loosen the close ties to their mothers—whereas for war-workers living at home the tie often became even stronger, especially if they depended on Mum for meals, shopping, and even childcare. For many, military service was also closely connected to the meaning of citizenship; most had been too young to vote pre-war, but war service created a direct link between them and the nation. Looking back, this was a period of concentrated living when life was shaped by larger national circumstances, in contrast to later years, preoccupied for most with marriage and children.

Another form of war service that recruited a large number of young working-class women was the Women's Land Army (WLA). It too was a revival of a much smaller force that had been raised in the First World War. Producing only 40 per cent of its food in 1939, it was clear that Britain would need increased production and an expansion of acreage and women were seen as one answer to the shortfall of agricultural labour. In fact, the Land Army was not an army at all, but a semi-private organization, administered by Lady Denman. There were no ranks or military discipline. And while it had a uniform—the famous jodhpur-like breeches, a green sweater and tie, leggings, and a brown slouch hat—shortages meant that many recruits never got all their kit. At its peak in 1943 the WLA numbered 87,000.[127] About a third were from London and other large cities. Some were middle class, but most came from poor backgrounds and had left school at fourteen to work as shop girls, hairdressers, waitresses, and clerks; others came from factories and the Lancashire mills.

Much photographed for magazines and a favourite subject for press cartoonists, the WLA was neglected and unfairly treated, despite the vital importance of the work it was doing. After a month's basic training, recruits were sent to farms and were billeted singly or in pairs with farmers and villagers; later more and more were organized into gangs of twenty to forty women and housed in hostels, presided over

---

[125] G. DeGroot, 'Lipstick on her nipples, cordite in her hair: Sex and romance among British servicewomen during the Second World War' in G. J. DeGroot and C. Peniston-Bird (eds.), *A Soldier and a Woman: Sexual integration in the military* (Harlow, 2000), p. 102.
[126] Summerfield, *Reconstructing Women's Wartime Lives*.
[127] V. Sackville West, *The Women's Land Army* (London, 1944); N. Tyrer, *They Fought in the Fields* (Arrow edition, London, 1999). Among the many memoirs are S. Joseph, *If Only Their Mothers Knew* (London, 1946); A. Hall, *Land Girl* (Bradford-on-Avon, 1993); J. Knighton *Land Army Days* (Bolton, 1994); C. Twinch, *Women on the Land* (Cambridge, 1990); G. Clarke, *The Women's Land Army: A portrait* (Bristol, 2006).

by a Warden, often an elderly spinster or widow. On large, prosperous properties conditions could be good, but the harshness of life on small, isolated farms often shocked Land Girls; many had no indoor water or sanitation, evenings were spent in candlelight, and there was nowhere to go and nothing to do after work. Hostel life was a good deal better and there was more social life, although the curfews and house rules could be irksome. Wages were paid by the farmers and varied a good deal. But the general level was low and there were many complaints of farmers paying late or underpaying, forcing County Agricultural Boards to intervene to ensure that wage minimums were met—in 1939 minimum pay was 38s (out of which about 20s went for room and board) and while this had risen to 48s by 1944, it was still far below the going rate in industry for a 48–50 hour week.[128]

Asked why they had chosen the WLA, most recruits replied that they would have hated being shut up in a munitions factory all day and disliked the saluting, parading, and discipline of the military services. Many were also attracted by the prospect of rural life, though they had little understanding of what it would be like. Official posters cultivated popular images of the countryside, depicting brilliant skies, hayricks, and smiling, wholesome girls stacking sheaves of corn or driving tractors. In fact, much of the work was back-breaking and monotonous, carried on in all weathers: they dug ditches, hoed, ploughed, drove tractors, harvested crops, killed rats, looked after animals, and threshed the grain. Many also complained of attempts to have them do domestic chores and child-minding. Land Girls felt, with some reason, that their status was inferior to the military auxiliaries; they were also treated differently. They got one week of paid vacation per year instead of four; no medical attention or insurance; and fewer travel warrants and clothing coupons, despite the wear and tear involved in their work. They were not even allowed at first to use the cheaper forces canteens on railway and bus stations. In many areas they were well received and well treated, but elsewhere conservative rural prejudices were easily aroused by women going into pubs, smoking in public, or walking out with soldiers. Working closely with male farm workers, they became the butt of sexual rumour and allegations of immorality similar to the women's auxiliaries. By the summer of 1943 some 37,000 POWs, mostly Italians, were also employed on the land—they too acquired a reputation for lechery, not least among Land Girls. The War Office cautioned that 'troops in the Middle East who had seen pictures in illustrated papers of British womenfolk consorting in familiar fashion with Italian POWs, had expressed great indignation'.[129]

Inferior treatment of the Land Girls even extended to demobilization; once again the relative weakness of the Ministry of Agriculture and the WLA's odd position as a non-governmental service served them badly. They were excluded from demobilization gratuities and training schemes which were available to women in the

---

[128] *The Land Worker* (publication of the National Union of Agricultural Workers) contains detailed information on wages. The August 1943 issue wrote that there were 47 wage areas in England and Wales supervised by committees, but only 5 women serving on them.
[129] L. Sponza, *Divided Loyalties: Italians in Britain during the Second World War* (Oxford, 2000), pp. 213–14.

forces, nurses, and civil-defence workers; they were also not covered by the Reinstatement of Civil Employment Act which would have guaranteed them their old pre-war jobs. The government insisted on treating them the same as industrial workers (fearful of opening up demands from that quarter), although their pay and circumstances had been very different. Lady Denman resigned in protest against these exclusions and efforts were made in Parliament, the press, and in some farming regions to publicize the issue and reverse official decisions. Meantime the WLA counselled patience, although in some areas Land Girls who had joined the agricultural workers' union began to hold demonstrations and some took strike action.[130] They organized regional meetings and a rally in Trafalgar Square and drew up a Charter of demands that included war gratuities; pensions for sickness and injury; a guaranteed job after leaving the WLA; and even equal pay with male farm workers. What they received was a one-time government payment of £150,000 to the WLA Benevolent Fund and permission to keep part of their uniform. Their poor treatment continued to be a source of resentment decades later.[131]

In general, when the war ended, far less attention was given to the return of uniformed women to civilian life than men. Married recruits were given priority and the rest were released on the basis of their years of service. Few had ideas of re-enlisting and many were eager to get on with their lives, but found themselves waiting around in boring, routine work until their papers came through. Lectures and vocational programmes were organized, ostensibly to prepare them for post-war life, but they focused mostly on domestic skills, dressmaking, and household budgeting rather than career choices. In fact, few had jobs to reclaim and few, apart from clerks and secretaries, had acquired skills which they could hope to use as civilians. Concerns about them usually took the form of anxiety about whether, after the upheaval of wartime, servicewomen would settle quickly into marriage and child-raising. Little action was taken, however, to ease their transition to peacetime.

As for the women themselves, how did they view their experiences in the women's auxiliaries and the Land Army? Once again, in the case of working-class women, this is very difficult to document. Memoirs and oral histories underscore several themes. The war years are seen as a catalyst, a period of concentrated living, when recruits matured rapidly, met a broader cross-section of people, and gained more confidence in themselves and their abilities. Land Girls often cite their experiences as the beginning of a long-standing appreciation for rural life and some settled permanently in the countryside. There were servicewomen who found their future spouses from distant parts of the country, whom they would not otherwise have met; some travelled overseas, while for many entry into the forces was their first time away from home—helping, perhaps, to loosen some kinship and neighbourhood bonds. Pride in having served the nation coupled with memories of companionship were often contrasted to later years, preoccupied with

---

[130] *The Land Worker*, April 1945, p. 5. Early on the union's journal had ridiculed WLA labour, but then began to actively recruit among them.

[131] Tyrer, *They Fought in the Fields*, pp. 214–36; also *Daily Herald*, 23 April 1945, p. 3, and 17 May 1945, p. 3; *The Land Worker*, June 1945.

marriage and children. These narratives, often composed three or four decades later, foreground individual adaptability to new ways of life rather than broader questions about class or gender roles. In this respect the accounts published by middle-class recruits soon after the war offer a striking contrast, being far more consumed with class differences. Shirley Joseph, for example, who was in the WLA for a year before joining the WAAF, writes of the initial 'strange unfriendliness' of the working-class girls in her WLA hostel; she says repeatedly that she got 'an education' (meaning in class relations) and was warned at the start: 'it's a rough life among some very rough girls'. 'My companions', she wrote, 'just said what they thought and if I didn't like it, I could just lump it.'[132] Similarly, Hilary Wayne who enlisted in the ATS with her daughter wrote of the impassable gulf that accent, tastes, and background created; while the army, she believed, had 'a rare opportunity' to reduce class distinctions, it merely bolstered them with the privileges and selection of officers. The American novelist Mary Lee Settle who enlisted in the WAAF echoed these criticisms and engaged in her own kind of social exploration; she dedicated her book to the 'other ranks'. 'For the first time in my life', Settle wrote, 'I had known the underworld . . . the great moving mass we live in . . . In a more responsible, romantic job I would never have known it.'[133]

NOW THE WAR IS OVER: DEMOBILIZATION

The end of the First World War came abruptly and unexpectedly. Until five months before the armistice Allied armies in the West had been under severe pressure from a massive German offensive and the German High Command's sudden capitulation threw British demobilization planning into some confusion. In 1918 female war-workers were quickly laid off, many of them receiving only a rail ticket and a week's pay for their efforts.[134] By contrast, in 1945 the war's end had been anticipated, often quite unrealistically, for two years. Plans for post-war reconstruction had been debated by numerous committees and widely publicized in the press, while opinion polls monitored public attitudes towards demobilization. Early on, government officials worried that peace would bring a sharp contraction in the labour market. But by 1944, although many workers still feared the return of unemployment, official reports predicted continuing high demand, even suggesting that the voluntary withdrawal of many women from the workforce might create a serious labour shortage in many sectors. This time, it was assumed, jobs would be available for women who wanted them.[135]

---

[132] Joseph, *If Only Their Mothers Knew*, p. 51.

[133] Wayne, *Two Odd Soldiers*. Mary Lee Settle, *All The Brave Promises: Memories of Aircraftwoman 2nd Class 2146391* (New York, 1966), p. 153. Juliet Gardiner, *Wartime Britain, 1939–45* (London, 2004), pp. 448–55.

[134] G. Braybon, *Women Workers in the First World War* (London 1981), chs. 7–8; A. Woollacott, *On Her Their Lives Depend* (Berkeley and Los Angeles, 1994), pp. 105–12.

[135] R. Pope, 'The planning and implementation of British demobilisation 1941–46', PhD Diss., Open University, 1986.

But did they want them? Historians have given several answers to this question, pointing to sharply opposed conclusions about the war's overall impact on gender inequalities and women's perceptions of themselves. Some scholars have argued that many women would have liked to remain in the workforce but were discouraged from doing so by the exclusionary practices of trade unions, the government's decision to close public nurseries in 1945, and more generally by an ideological 'backlash', namely the prevailing view among family experts, the media, public officials, and the public at large that family life had been seriously undermined during the war and mothers had a vital role to play in its reconstruction. Summerfield, for example, has emphasized how many women war-workers wanted to remain in paid employment, although they had doubts as to whether it would be possible. She points to the diversity of women's responses and their ambivalence: most accepting the priority of home and motherhood for women but many feeling frustrated or equivocal about leaving the labour market. Other historians have described women as eager to quit their war jobs, either to resume work in sectors more traditionally feminine or to devote themselves fully to domestic labour and child-raising. Harold Smith, for example, concluded that the most important effect of the conflict was in reinforcing sexual difference. After six years of war, he argued, most women were impatient to get back to their pre-war way of life and to traditional home-centred roles.[136]

Women's views about demobilization were subject to much debate at the time and several attempts were made to gauge opinion, although these surveys have drawbacks and it is dangerous to read too much into them. There is a paucity of comparable pre-war data on which to base assumptions about changes in attitudes and, given the sharp contrasts in regional economies in the 1930s and therefore the different impact of the wartime changes, it is highly likely that there were sharp geographical divisions in women's expectations and preferences.[137] Moreover, survey questions were sometimes vaguely framed resulting in confusion between what women hoped and what they expected would happen after the war. The immediate context in which a survey was taken could also shape responses. In January 1944, for example, a BIPO poll showed that over a third of miners and factory workers anticipated difficulty getting work post-war; at such a time women may have been more reticent about wishing to remain in previously male industrial jobs;[138] this may also have been the case when

---

[136] Summerfield, 'Women, war and social change: Women in Britain in World War II'; *idem*, 'Approaches to women and social change in the Second World War' in B. Brivati and H. Jones (eds.), *What Difference Did the War Make?* (Leicester, 1993); H. L. Smith, 'The effect of the war on the status of women' in *idem* (ed.), *War and Social Change: British society in the Second World War* (Manchester, 1986).

[137] M. A. Williams, in *A Forgotten Army*, emphasizes the distinctive regional characteristics of the South Wales labour market. P. Ollerenshaw, 'War, industrial mobilisation and society in Northern Ireland, 1939–45', *Contemporary European History*, 16(2) (2007), also details the area's distinctive characteristics.

[138] NA: INF 1/292, 32% of factory workers and 31% of miners in the sample thought they would have difficulty finding work after the war, compared to 12% of clerical workers in the sample. 'It's not so much what's going to happen to us as what's going to happen to the men who come home. Will there be jobs for them?' (Woman, 25 years old, always in factory work).

young men were fighting and dying in Italy and Northern Europe. The two most important contemporary sources of survey information about women war-workers' intentions and expectations were the Wartime Social Survey (carried out by Geoffrey Thomas in the autumn of 1943) and a series of reports by Mass-Observation which formed the basis for the organization's book, *The Journey Home* (1944), which is the most nuanced account of male and female opinion about demobilization.[139]

For its report the Wartime Social Survey (WSS) polled the opinions of 2,609 women in various kinds of employment. Roughly half were married and 28 per cent had not been employed immediately before the war; in addition, it should be noted, over half the single women and 36 per cent of wives in the sample were in the same jobs as pre-war. The survey found that 60 per cent of the women wanted to work post-war, although in engineering and metals the proportion was lower. Those most inclined to leave work were married women under thirty-four years and those expecting to marry soon—in other words the group most likely to have postponed home-making and child-rearing during the war. Women over thirty-five years were generally more eager to continue working, mainly for the extra cash, but they also expressed a desire to escape the boredom and drudgery of full-time housework. Asked directly if they approved of women's work after marriage, 58 per cent of the WSS conceded that a woman's place was at home except in cases of financial necessity, although 19 per cent added that, if home and family were not neglected, an extra wage packet helped enormously. But when asked if a vacant job should go to a qualified man or to the best qualified applicant, 52 per cent of wives in the sample said the man should have the job anyway, as compared to 29 per cent of single women.[140]

The evidence collected by Mass-Observation, much of it gathered at a large, modern engineering factory on the outskirts of London with generally good working conditions, largely agreed with the WSS report. Both concluded that large numbers of women could be expected either to leave the labour market altogether or to transfer to traditionally female jobs in the retail and service sectors. Many of the young single women expected to move into some other paid job at the war's end, while young wives and those planning weddings were most impatient to leave: 'I'm only in the job for the duration. Then my only job will be

---

[139] NA: RG 25/50; Geoffrey Thomas, *Women at Work: The attitudes of working women toward post-war employment and some related problems* (WSS, London), June 1944; M-O, *The Journey Home* (London, 1944); M-OA: FR 2059, 'Will the factory girls want to stay put or go home?' (March 1944). The question that Mass-Observation put to its panel members in January 1944 was: 'Should married women be able to go out to work after the war?' Another survey, cited by Summerfield, was taken by the AEU in 1945. It suggested that a majority of women wanted to stay in paid work post-war. In this group 66% wanted to remain in their jobs, including 86% of those over 40 years. But the survey was small, many other women had already left the workforce, and the replies represented only a small percentage of women in the union (and presumably the most active). The AEU used these findings to bolster its case for equal pay (which, as we have seen, had an ulterior motive of excluding women from many jobs). The survey has limited value as a reflection of women's attitudes more generally. Summerfield, 'Women, war and social change', p. 107.

[140] NA: RG 23/50; Thomas, *Women at Work*, p. 28.

running my home properly.'[141] Older women, often part-timers, were more likely to agree with a worker who responded:

> I've been here more than twelve months now. It brightens your mind and gives you something to think about. I'd really like to continue after the war. It makes you feel younger and gives you more interest in life... You see, to me it's freedom... I can do my housework and shopping in the morning... My husband comes home at night and I give him a proper dinner. And now I don't have to scrape every penny together.[142]

And yet the underlying data reveals a good deal of uncertainty and ambivalence. Many women's replies were qualified, contingent on such factors as the general economic picture and a spouse's employment situation. 'It all depends', commented one woman. 'It's very hard to say. I was here before the war, and you don't know how things will turn out at all... Perhaps I might have a baby after the war... and we might be selling matches in the streets—you never know.'[143] In Mass-Observation's sample of factory women 89 per cent endorsed equal pay for equal work, but when asked if women should 'go on doing men's jobs', only 25 per cent said yes, 28 per cent thought it would depend on post-war circumstances, and 43 per cent answered negatively.[144]

What all this suggests on the part of women workers is neither a headlong dash into domesticity nor deep resentment if their wartime jobs disappeared or returned to men. That many women wanted to leave their dirty, exhausting, monotonous, industrial jobs and shift work is hardly surprising. Before the war the work that carried most status and seemed most attractive to working-class women was defined less by skill or even pay and more by cleanliness, security, and 'respectability'—a job where one mixed with 'a better class of people' and wore decent clothes.[145] Women in better-paid, more skilled industrial work and those in administrative or supervisory positions were, perhaps, more likely to want to stay on—even though some considered it unlikely they would be allowed to do so. 'The boys will come back and want the jobs', an unmarried aircraft worker said, 'I think it's going to be just as bad as the last time, or even worse.'[146] Oral histories taken decades later include cases of women who would have liked to have stayed on as engineers, electricians, or mechanics; but the majority seem to have accepted that their status was temporary, 'for the duration'. 'We enjoyed all the different jobs', a former lathe operator from Vickers at Barrow recalled, 'but I don't think it was really a place for girls, no.' 'We had to go really to let them [servicemen] have their jobs back, you see... we were told. We went under those conditions really, that it was just while the war was on.'[147] Women from the St Helier housing estate in south London

---

[141] M-O, *The Journey Home*, p. 54.
[142] *Ibid.*, p. 58.
[143] M-OA: FR 2059, 'Will the factory girls want to stay put or go home?' (March 1944).
[144] M-O, *The Journey Home*, p. 64.
[145] S. Todd, *Young Women, Work and Family in England, 1918–1950* (Oxford 2005), ch. 4.
[146] M-OA: FR 2059.
[147] E. Roberts, *Women and Families: An oral history 1940–1970* (Oxford 1995), pp. 116–17. Also Goodman, 'Patriotic femininity', pp. 290–1.

who had worked in nearby factories also recalled few tensions as men returned from the forces; their firms, which had employed many women before the war, went back to processing foodstuffs or producing toys and household electrical goods. The distinction between 'male' and 'female' work remained as clearly defined as before the war and returning soldiers were often appointed as supervisors.[148] Compared to the First World War, demobilization was also spread over a long period. After D-Day, production targets were lowered in some sectors of industry and there were reductions in overtime; many women began to leave their jobs or were transferred from shell factories, for example, to aircraft firms where demand was still high. By May 1945 around 300,000 women had already left the engineering trades. 'No one asked us to leave work', wrote Doris White of her aircraft factory at Wolverton. 'But, as the men filtered home there were weddings and homes to set up . . . We had managed to find a house to rent, although in a run-down condition, and with my man away, it was left to me to get it in shape. Although I had not been given my cards, I asked for a week off, but I never did go back.'[149]

The national debate about 'demobilization' and readjustment to peacetime life focused overwhelmingly upon men in the armed forces returning home. Large numbers of books, pamphlets, and press articles examined the likely difficulties for men returning from war and offered advice to wives and mothers about what to expect and how to alleviate the pains of transition.[150] By comparison there was little discussion of the difficulties that might be encountered by women in the war industries or, for that matter, about the 350,000 women 'demobbed' from the armed services by the end of 1946. Women in the forces, many of them young and recruited soon after school, often expressed a restlessness and desire to travel or felt that civilian jobs would be humdrum and hard to take; many anticipated with pleasure wearing civilian clothes and getting free of the regimentation and petty rules of service life, but—as one WAAF put it—'I'll miss the companionship and camaraderie of camp life.' Others, who enlisted straight from school, felt that they were not trained for anything: 'I'd like to get out and not be at anybody's beck and call, and wear my own clothes again. Yet I feel . . . I feel nervous about what will happen. If it's just to go on the dole, I'd sooner stay in the army and go abroad . . .'[151] The press speculated about the difficulties that some would have 'settling down', but official action to ease their re-entry was minimal.[152] Images in magazines of their home-coming tended to emphasize a return to normality, symbolized by family and domesticity.

---

[148] Bruley, 'A very happy crowd', p. 71.

[149] White, *D for Doris*, p. 81. On the decreasing numbers of women in engineering, see NA: LAB 8/1117. This also contains figures on the age composition of the workforce 1939–45.

[150] P. D. and L. Bendit, *Living Together Again* (London, 1946).

[151] M-O, *The Journey Home*, p. 61.

[152] While awaiting demobilization many ATSs and WAAFs attended classes and some got vocational training. The classes were often on housing, cooking, making clothes, and domestic skills, stressing their future roles as wives and mothers rather than citizenship education. Behind this was concern that war work had disrupted the normal domestic education that young women would have received from their mothers.

Demand for women's labour remained high in many economic sectors after the war, but the total number of women in paid employment decreased by around 1.7 million between 1943 and 1947, while about 86 per cent still worked in occupations that were dominantly female and their average earnings amounted to around 53 per cent of male wages. Viewed in these aggregate terms, the war's impact on women's employment patterns seems very limited. Yet closer examination does reveal significant changes, although some of them represented an intensification of pre-war trends rather than new developments. Female employment in clerical work, which had been growing steadily for some decades, rose sharply during the war years and then remained at a level far above pre-war; the same was true of engineering whose female workforce (10 per cent of the total in 1939) shrank with the return of peace but still constituted 21 per cent of the total in 1950.[153] Thus, although jobs in Coventry's shadow aircraft factories contracted, openings in the town multiplied at General Electric and at Courtaulds manufacturing synthetic fibres.[154] Similarly, in South Wales employers were quickly drawn to the pool of trained female workers who had worked in munitions, establishing a variety of new industries at the Trading Estates that superseded the big ROF complexes at Bridgend, Hirwaun, and Newport. In South Wales the employment opportunities for women were transformed by the war, while the Labour government's industrial relocation policies ensured that these expanded prospects continued. The number of married women in paid employment also grew: in 1931 the percentage of married women in England and Wales in the formal labour market was 16 per cent; this grew to 43 per cent in 1943 and after a brief decline rose again to over 40 per cent by 1951. In some areas, the rise was even larger: in South Wales, for example, the figures were 3 per cent in 1921, probably not much more in 1931, and then around 30 per cent in 1951.[155]

In two traditional areas of female employment—domestic service and textiles—the war marked a dramatic downturn. Domestic service which had still employed large numbers of women in the 1930s ceased to be a major source of employment. Women moved out of these jobs (especially service in private homes) during the war and never came back. Not only were the long hours, isolation, and low pay associated with such employment unpopular, but young women increasingly viewed service as menial work of low esteem that placed them in a subordinate and demeaning position. After the war there was much public debate about 'the servant problem' which became a metaphor for the erosion of middle-class living standards. There were also efforts to professionalize and enhance the status of domestic work, thereby making it more attractive, but the results were negligible

---

[153] Summerfield, 'Women, war and social change', p. 98. Among transport workers there was also a permanent percentage increase of women: 1939, 5%; 1943, 20%; 1950, 13%, while in metal manufacturing the figures were: 1939, 6%; 1943, 22%; 1950, 12%. White-collar jobs for women in local government work also increased dramatically: 1939, 17%; 1943, 46%; 1950, 38%.

[154] Nakamura, 'Women, work and war', ch. 8.

[155] Williams, *A Forgotten Army*, chs. 1 and 5. The boom in marriages after the war and the lowering of the average age at marriage since the 1930s was also a factor.

and in this sector the war marked the end of an era.[156] The other area of permanent contraction was textiles. Here the industry's demands for labour post-war and the government's eagerness to boost exports resulted in extraordinary measures to force former textile workers back into the mills. Munitions workers had little desire to return to the primitive conditions, poor pay, and rigid discipline of the cotton mills and resented the continuation of government direction of female workers into the industry after 1945. Official publicity campaigns proclaimed the vital importance of such work and tried to project a more glamorous and stylish image of mill girls than the shawls and clogs of the 1930s, but they convinced few and many reacted bitterly—sometimes through group protests, more often by high rates of absenteeism—to official compulsion. A woman who had become a shop steward in a Manchester engineering factory declared: 'I'd rather go to prison than back in a mill.'[157] Government targets for the industry were never achieved and once official controls were lifted, women migrated to other jobs in large numbers.

Thus, despite the clear continuities in women's employment patterns, there were also significant differences, especially when we take into account regional variations. Many women who had postponed marriage and children were quite clear that they wanted a break and looked forward to making a home and raising a family. Others were uncertain, both about their own future and whether a domestic role would satisfy them. Public debate about the war's destructive effects on families focused heavily upon absent and working mothers, helping to strengthen conservative discourses about women's primary role as mothers in the home. But H. L. Smith's claim that most married women wanted to return to their pre-war way of life and that the war's 'most important legacy was a strengthening of traditional sex roles' minimizes the complexity of the situation.[158] There were clear signs—already in the 1940s and even more in the 1950s—that working-class women expected more materially and emotionally out of marriage than previous generations and far more began to combine marriage and paid employment.[159] In the late 1940s continuing austerity placed heavy demands upon them as household managers and provisioners in an era of scarce resources, but increasingly in the 1950s aspirations for

---

[156] In 1931, 1.3 million women were listed as employed in domestic service; the category included women employed in hotels, hospitals, and other institutions as well as private homes. In 1939 domestic service still employed 24% of the female labour force; by 1951 the figure was 11%. Cmd 6650, *Report on Post-War Organisation of Private Domestic Employment* (June 1945, Markham/Hancock Report) *Parliamentary Papers*, 1944–45, vol. 5, June 1945; P. Horn, 'Experiment or anachronism? The role of the National Institute of Houseworkers', *Labour History Review*, 66(1) (Spring 2001); J. Giles, 'Help for housewives: Domestic service and the reconstruction of domesticity in Britain, 1940–50', *Women's History Review*, 10(2) (2001).
[157] *Manchester Guardian*, 5 May 1945, p. 6 ('Girls redirected to cotton mills'). Women who refused redirection back to a textile mill were subject to penalties, even imprisonment. For one protest against redirection into cotton: *Oldham Chronicle*, 12 May 1945. On the official campaign: W. Crofts, *Coercion or Persuasion? Propaganda in Britain after 1945* (London, 1989).
[158] Smith quotes approvingly Mary Goldsmith's 1943 comment that married women 'fervently wish themselves back in their pre-war home routine...': Smith, 'The effect of the war on the status of women', p. 225.
[159] J. Finch and P. Summerfield, 'Social reconstruction and the emergence of companionate marriage, 1945–59' in D. Clark (ed.), *Marriage, Domestic Life and Social Change* (London, 1991).

higher living standards and the availability of work brought increasing numbers of married women into the workforce, creating a new employment profile: women worked after leaving school, left the labour market at marriage or after the birth of a first child, and returned to employment (full or part-time) after their children went to school or grew older. In particular, part-time work enabled wives to balance domestic work and paid jobs, contributing to the greater material 'affluence' of working-class families. This left unchallenged women's primary responsibility for home and family and reinforced the low status and low-wage nature of most jobs open to married women. Indeed, Dolly Wilson has suggested that by the late 1950s in many areas the old definition of a 'good mother' as someone exclusively engaged with her family had lost support; women who worked so that their children could enjoy better living standards were more likely to criticize those who stayed home for neglecting the opportunity to improve things for their families.[160]

***

Recent writing about the war's impact on women has centred upon whether the conflict was a catalyst of gender change. Scholars have largely concluded that continuities with pre-war outweighed the changes and few now regard the war as a 'watershed' for women. While wartime mobilization of women helped to fore-ground such issues as pay inequality, childcare, and women's responsibilities for shopping and home-making, little tangible progress was made in these areas. Equal pay became a more prominent issue late in the war, but in part because male-dominated unions gave it priority for their own reasons. Arguably, support for it was stronger and better organized among women in teaching and the civil service than in industry. Public crèches and nurseries were never sufficient to meet demand and most closed when peace returned. The war did allow women's organizations and female members of Parliament to play a role on the home front and in debates over post-war reconstruction. But the most conspicuous victory over sex-based differentials was the national campaign for equal compensation for war injuries. Under government regulations women disabled through enemy action were com-pensated at only two-thirds of the male rate and housewives were originally omitted from the scheme altogether as not being 'gainfully employed'.[161] Feminists saw it as a perfect, galvanizing issue: conspicuously unfair, and reducible to a simple credo— that no life was worth more than another. It was hard to defend the idea that a woman fire-watching or working in a bombed factory should receive less for the loss of a limb than a man next to her. But while the public supported equal injury compensation by 84 per cent to 11 per cent in 1941, it is doubtful that most viewed it as a specifically feminist issue or that it helped build support for other parts of a

---

[160] D. Wilson, 'A new look at the affluent worker: The good working mother in post-war Britain', *TCBH*, 17(2) (2006). Also Zweig, *Women's Life and Labour*.

[161] 'Wives are cheap', October 1939; 'War injuries—housewives demand compensation', November 1939; 'When the housewife is injured', December 1940; 'Compensation for war injuries', January 1941. All these articles appeared in *Labour Women* the month and year given.

feminist agenda.[162] And with the government fearful that injury compensation might become a wedge for wider demands for equal pay, it took three years (until 1943) and a threatened revolt of backbenchers before the campaign was victorious.

Certainly the war helped to revive organized feminism, but this should be placed in the context of the broader movement of middle-class radicalization in these years. Women in the labour movement were often suspicious of the feminist agenda, viewing it as chiefly concerned to advance the career goals of a middle-class and professional minority. They were sensitive to feminist criticisms of trade unionism and working-class men and frequently criticized middle-class feminists as ignorant of the realities of working-class life. Though many women were happy to pass equal-pay resolutions at annual union conferences, most felt that the issue should be addressed gradually via trade unionism and collective bargaining not legislative action. When an Equal Pay Campaign Committee was formed in 1943, labour women's organizations refused to participate and they also rejected the Six Point Committee's proposal for a blanket bill to outlaw all forms of discrimination.[163] The middle-class blue-stocking image remained strong and young working-class women were generally reluctant to identify with feminism. Yet, at the same time, as Selina Todd has argued, a new cohort of young working-class women was emerging in the 1930s and during the war whose outlook was more confident and modern. In more prosperous areas pre-war they benefited from expanding employment opportunities; they could vote, and their ideas and wants were shaped by the mass media, mass advertising, and a growing range of consumer goods and commercial leisure pursuits.[164] As families became smaller, a daughter's contribution to the household economy also grew, adding to her independence and sense of worth. The lives of this same group and their younger sisters were soon transformed by mobilization into war work which further shaped their responsibilities and aspirations. Asked what they hoped for after the war, their answers were couched more in materialist than feminist terms—although the two were not mutually exclusive. They wanted better homes, more space and privacy, a bathroom, less domestic drudgery, and opportunities for their children. Living in hostels many had enjoyed better conditions and more amenities than in their own homes. Questioned about their view of marriage, they spoke of the need for more sharing, more of an equal partnership; but most often when they voiced their hopes, they compared themselves less with men than with the hard lives of their mothers and grandmothers. A sense of class exclusion as much as sexual discrimination informed their outlook. Most saw themselves as eventually marrying and raising a family, becoming primarily home-makers. But their goal was not a 'return' to domesticity—at least not a 'domesticity' as most had experienced it. What they wanted was precisely what they had previously lacked—a life that had been

---

[162] *Gallup International Polls: Great Britain*, October 1941.

[163] There were exceptions: the Women's Parliaments, for example, took feminist stands on a range of issues including public nurseries, equal pay, and women's representation in the trade union movement.

[164] Todd, *Young Women, Work and Family in England*; S. Alexander, 'Becoming a woman in London in the 1920s and 1930s' in *idem, Becoming a Woman and Other Essays* (London, 1994).

unattainable in overcrowded tenements, insanitary housing, and unemployment-ravaged areas between the wars. They articulated a 'modern femininity' which fused gender and class—they wanted a decent home and a smaller family than the previous generation and saw these as the route to a space in which they could exercise skills, feel more independent, be secure from poverty, and achieve a sense of dignity and social mobility.[165]

And while this outlook may be apolitical, it is not inevitably so, nor does it necessarily exclude a strong consciousness of class. One example will suffice—the diary of Louie White of Leeds. Born in 1918, she left school at thirteen and worked as a shop assistant for ten years before the war. Her husband Jack whom she married in July 1941, worked at Holbeck swimming baths before going into the RAF as an air gunner. Called up for war work, Louie spent three years at the Leeds division of the Blackburn Aircraft Company, employed first on milling machines, then moving on to become an inspector. Her short, hastily written entries provide only the barest outline of her life but one that evokes a vivid sense of the author. She often worked nights, arriving at 7.30 p.m. and returning home at 7.00 a.m.; on this shift she slept till early afternoon and then shopped and did housework before returning to the factory. At the factory Louie volunteered for a first-aid unit and joined the local section of the Women's Home Guard; she went on manoeuvres, learned map-reading, and even received firearms instruction with a sten gun, though this was contrary to government regulations. In June 1943 her husband was listed as 'missing' and then reported dead. A widow at twenty-five she remained at the factory and kept as busy as possible, visiting her mother-in-law, reading, and volunteering for a farmwork vacation. There is no mention of her being active in a trade union, but she was politically on the left and her library choices mirrored public interest in the Soviet Union. 'Had so little to do all night', she writes in September 1942, 'that I actually read one book before I went home next morning. I can't understand why we are doing nothing at work, an aircraft factory—while the Russians are fighting like mad. Any way what can one expect with our government.' Finally, when the European war ended, she made a red flag but noted 'as I won't be at work tomorrow, I shan't be able to use it'. She left Blackburn's in July 1945—commenting that her time there had been happy, but expressing no regrets at leaving; she also noted the election result in capital letters: 'LABOUR IN GREAT !!!'[166] Louie comes through as patriotic, political, a doer, and a joiner—she may not be typical, but she underscores the dangers of taking too literally contemporaries' generalizations about frivolous young working girls.

---

[165] J. Giles, *The Parlor and the Suburb: Domestic identities, class, femininity and modernity* (Oxford, 2004).
[166] IWM: 86/54/1, Diary of Mrs Louie White (3 volumes). Quotes from 28 September 1942, 7 May, and 26 July 1945.

5
Family in Trouble

The war years were characterized by a constant tension or counterpoint between rhetoric that stressed the nation's unity and solidarity and perpetual reminders of society's divisions and inequities. Not only was class consciousness strong in these years, much stronger than subsequent mythology allows, but the strains of wartime life and the requirements of full-scale mobilization had the effect of continually pushing social divisions to the forefront of public discussion. This was evident in the furore over evacuation, the shelter crisis, the mobilization of women, and debates over the efficiency of war production. The social relations of class were similarly inescapable in the organization of voluntary work, which, as James Hinton has shown, contributed to the continuities of middle- and upper-class social power.[1] Even official publicity about a 'People's War' and 'fair shares', which carried the implication that Britain was becoming less class-bound, focused attention on past and existing unfairness. This interplay between national community and social difference was equally pervasive in wartime debate about the family. Starting with the evacuation scheme, the war's destructive effect upon families became a growing preoccupation of government officials, journalists, and a growing phalanx of family and social-work organizations.

Wartime propaganda commonly depicted Britain as one big family: weakened in the 1930s by class division and mutual suspicion (or, as Orwell put it, with the wrong relatives in control) and reunited in the 1940s by common danger and invigorated by a spirit of greater egalitarianism and social compassion. In later years, popular memory, reinforced by books, broadcasts, and films, also emphasized family, both as a social metaphor and as the key institution that enabled Britons to surmount the crisis. The pluck and self-sacrifice of wartime mothers, close family and kinship networks, and cross-class solidarity are all basic to this positive view. Closer examination of these years, however, conjures up another, more complicated picture—one of widespread alarm about the effect of wartime dislocations on the institution of the family, much of it illustrated by class-freighted images: neglected evacuees, delinquent youths and 'good time girls' running wild in the blitzed cities, unfaithful wives, and incompetent mothers. To a striking degree, arguments about the 'crisis' of family problematized poor and working-class families. Admittedly, it is sometimes difficult to separate genuine alarm from the tactical hyperbole of social policy groups aimed at creating a larger constituency for specific reform proposals;

[1] J. Hinton, *Women, Social Leadership, and the Second World War: Continuities of class* (Oxford, 2002).

but the 'traditional' working-class home, enshrined in wartime myth and depicted by academic sociologists in the 1950s as the bedrock of urban communities, was viewed as anything but secure, stable, and unchanging just a few years before.

THE WELFARE OF CHILDREN

There is a broad consensus among historians that the social construction of childhood changed dramatically between the 1880s and the 1940s. In a somewhat schematic but very helpful analysis Harry Hendrick has distinguished several major strands of this change.[2] Prior to the First World War, he argues, public debate focused primarily upon the 'bodies' of poor and working-class children—their physical health, hygiene, nutrition—and the impact on them of labour exploitation, poverty, and substandard urban environments. By the interwar decades, with the emergence of new theories of child development and the growth of psychometrics, the balance shifted more to children's 'minds' and to the family, not as simply an economic unit, but as the chief site of a child's mental development and psychological adjustment to society. The spread of mass unemployment in the 1930s, of course, re-energized debate about the health consequences of child poverty, but this was within the context of an emerging social, medical, and psychiatric consensus about the problems of poor families.

This emphasis upon the family as a psychological entity, in which the quality of mothering was especially important for a child's welfare, gained enormous impetus during the war years. But while we can speak of a growing consensus about children's physical and mental needs, this did not preclude heated dispute over specific issues of policy. Indeed, perhaps the best way to conceptualize wartime debate is in terms of several broad polarities or dichotomies which were ascribed varying importance. These included delineating the state's as opposed to the family's responsibility for the child; the role of environment versus heredity and natural intelligence in determining behaviour; and what we might call a constant oscillation between imagery of children as 'victims'—of physical and mental cruelty, poverty and war—and as potential dangers or threats to social order and the nation's future if their sufferings and needs were left unaddressed. Children were increasingly described as the nation's most precious resource, a form of social capital, but like any investment they could turn out badly. In addition, as many scholars have noted, discussions of childhood assumed a middle-class model as a yardstick against which deviant or abnormal behaviour and experience was measured; the focus of debate and concern was the working-class family seen as most vulnerable and in need of support and improvement. Social class, both explicitly and implicitly, permeated every facet of child welfare.

---

[2] H. Hendrick, *Child Welfare: England 1872–1989* (London, 1994); *idem, Children, Childhood and English Society 1880–1990* (Cambridge, 1997). Also, G. K. Behlmer, *Friends of Family: The English home and its guardians 1850–1940* (Stanford, 1998).

In the first months of the war, it was the evacuation scheme that dominated debate about children. As we have seen, public responses to the government scheme focused overwhelmingly upon the poverty, deviant behaviour, and poor physical condition of so many city children. The country, reported the Commission of Churches, was 'electrified to discover the dirt, poverty, and ignorance, particularly of home hygiene, that still exists in large towns'.[3] Evacuation revealed beyond question the unevenness of local authority provision, the inadequacy of school medical inspections, and an urgent need for more government services. Scarcely consulted in the early stages of evacuation planning, psychologists, nutritionists, and child-welfare experts were now heavily recruited; the numbers of child guidance clinics grew steadily, aided by funds from America, and an ever-expanding number of hostels, residential and camp schools, and war nurseries brought more children than ever before within 'the gaze of the experts'.[4] Initially public attention focused heavily upon the poorest evacuees, rekindling pre-war controversy about the extent of child poverty and malnutrition and the degree to which deficient parenting, ignorance, and poor household management were to blame. The weight attached to good mothering also meant that poor women became society's prime scapegoat for the scheme's initial failure and the key figure in 'problem families'.[5] In theoretical terms evacuation reinforced the significance attributed by experts to the mother–child bond and the emotional dangers of maternal deprivation; it also helped to resurrect the older concept of 'problem families'—or the existence of a large social residuum or underclass whose poverty, ignorance, and low moral standards locked them into an unending cycle of deprivation.[6] The concept was not new, but whereas earlier versions had emphasized heredity and mental deficiency as the cause of this maladjusted minority, writers in the 1940s stressed the possibility of rehabilitation through the intervention of trained social workers and by changing the social environment. This catch-all category of 'problem family' remained central to the practice of local public health services for the next thirty years.[7]

---

[3] Quoted in Bob Holman, *The Evacuation* (Oxford, 1995), p. 140.

[4] N. Rose, *Governing the Soul: The shaping of the private self* (London, 1989), p. 161. The Commonwealth Fund Archives (Rockefeller Archives, Pocantico, New York) contain detailed reports on the effort to introduce the American model of Child Guidance and Mental Hygiene into Britain, beginning in the late 1920s. By 1944 there were over 70 affiliated clinics in Britain, 17 in London alone. Since the 1944 Education Act required local education authorities to establish some kind of child guidance service as part of the school medical service, the numbers grew rapidly in the late 1940s.

[5] P. Starkey, *Families and Social Workers: The work of the Family Service Units 1940–1985* (Liverpool, 2000); *idem*, 'The feckless mother: Women, poverty and social workers in wartime and post-war England', *Women's History Review*, 9(3) (2000).

[6] J. Macnicol, 'In pursuit of the underclass', *Journal of Socal Policy*, 16(3) (July 1987); *idem*, 'From "problem family" to "underclass"' in H. Fawcett and R. Lowe (eds.), *Welfare Policy in Britain: The road from 1945* (London, 1999); J. Welshman, *Underclass: A history of the excluded, 1880–1920* (London, 2006).

[7] Wartime estimates of the number of 'problem families' were much larger than those identified by local authorities post-war, when they usually amounted to about 0.5% of families in many localities. Part of the reason for the resilience and longevity of the concept was the professional interests and identity of Medical Officers of Health who lost several of their local functions with the creation of the National Health Service. For a local study, which shows how 'problem families' became linked to the

In general, evacuation and German air raids drew attention to the possible psychological damage that children could suffer as a result of modern war. As the dangers and disruption of family life continued, the distinction between normality and maladjustment became more blurred, increasing concern about the emotional fragility of 'normal' children.[8] Already in 1939 several psychiatrists had warned that permanent damage might result if young children under five were evacuated without their mothers.[9] The issue achieved much greater importance, however, with the massive recruitment of women into war production in 1942 and growing pressure for the government to fund a major expansion of nurseries. In 1939 there were only about 6,000 places in public nurseries in England and Wales. Many of them were residential facilities for destitute children or those in need of rescue; local public assistance departments had no desire to expand them and mothers working in factories did not want their children in Poor Law institutions. During the First World War the government had set up special crèches for the children of munitions workers, but it mostly relied on women finding their own childcare solutions. In this war the Nursery School Association (NSA) and the National Society for Children's Nurseries (NSCN) called upon the government to take decisive action, but they made little headway until Bevin's MoL and various business groups joined the fight to loosen Treasury purse strings.[10] Of course, women with children under fourteen years were officially exempt from war work, but many needed to work to make ends meet and in reality government policy depended upon their volunteering to ease the labour shortage.

There were three types of public nurseries. Nursery schools and nursery classes provided educational and play facilities for children aged two to five years. Staffed by teachers and volunteers, their hours roughly coincided with elementary schools which made them of limited use to war-workers on long shifts. Day nurseries, run by trained nurses, catered for children under five whose mothers were in war industries; they remained open for long hours to accommodate twelve-hour factory shifts. And, finally, there were residential war nurseries, again staffed by professionals, for infants whose mothers worked around the clock or who because of illness, confinement, or accident could not have them at home.[11] Some private

professional status of local Health Departments, see B. Taylor and B. Rogaly, '"Mrs Fairly is a dirty, lazy type": Unsatisfactory households and the problem of problem families in Norwich 1942–1963', *TCBH*, 18(4) (2007).

[8] Rose, *Governing the Soul*, pp. 159–60.

[9] J. Bowlby, E. Miller, and D. Winnicott, letter to *British Medical Journal*, 16 December 1939. In fact, very few 'under fives' were evacuated without their mothers.

[10] National Society of Children's Nurseries and the British Association for Early Childhood Education (for the Nursery Schools Association) papers and minutes, located in BLPES (London School of Economics). Additional materials on nursery schools can be found in Lady Allen of Hurtwood Papers, MRC Warwick.

[11] Statistics on the different categories of nurseries: S. Ferguson and H. Fitzgerald, *Studies in the Social Services* (London, 1954), p. 190. These included in September 1944: 1,450 whole-time nurseries with a population of 68,181, 109 part-time nurseries with 3,625 places, 62 nursery schools with 6,227 places, and 784 nursery classes with 28,650.

9. London County Council residential school for evacuees ('under fives') near Windsor, 13 February 1941.

firms also organized crèches for their own workers; but most women ended up relying on family or paid 'minders' to look after their children. Eventually the number of places in government facilities grew to 107,000 amid a good deal of opposition, especially towards the war's end when a campaign got underway to continue nursery provision when peace returned.

While MoL officials pushed for more nurseries, they met with stiff resistance from the Ministry of Health, local Medical Officers, and some local authorities. Underlying these concerns was a basic belief that young children should be at home with their mothers and a fear that proponents would use the war as a wedge to achieve an open-ended commitment. As Shrewsbury's Medical Officer of Health put it: 'scheming spinsters are fervently hoping to convert wartime nurseries into a permanent peace-time part of social service'.[12] Different arguments were marshalled against nurseries. Some local authorities dragged their feet, arguing that it was impossible to meet the need for trained staff and repudiating claims that nurseries would free up large numbers of women workers. Other opponents emphasized the risks of infectious diseases and dangers to physical health, while

[12] Dr A. D. Symons quoted in the *Sunday Express*, 5 December 1943. NSCN Papers, Minute Books, no. 6, report for 18 November–15 December 1943.

still more warned of the emotional and psychological damage that could result from prolonged separation of mothers and infants.[13] For this reason residential nurseries attracted the greatest criticism; day nurseries raised fewer objections and were more likely to be seen as a lamentable wartime necessity. As one MoH official wrote: 'Once a child is taken from its parents for the night as well as the day, the family tie is apt to be completely loosened, and before long a neglectful parent would probably cease to take responsibility for her child altogether.'[14] Even MoL officials, under heavy pressure to recruit married women, were reluctant to portray nurseries as a good thing in themselves, defending them only as an emergency measure. Much stronger champions of large-scale provision were found among women trade unionists, the women's sections of the Labour Party, and a range of other women's organizations. Also, towards the end of the war the London Women's Parliament devoted much of its energy to the campaign to keep nurseries open and collaborated closely with the NSCN.[15]

Nursery advocates carried on an extensive campaign in the press, launched petition drives, organized conferences, and lobbied hard with government agencies. They championed them as a way of reducing the burdens on working mothers and (like infant welfare clinics) as sites for instruction in mother-care. Far from spreading contagious diseases, they argued, nurseries were a means of improving the health, hygiene, and nutrition of children who did not otherwise get regular medical attention and of implanting professional expertise into the private sphere of the family. In a 1943 lecture to the armed forces, Lady Allen of Hurtwood, a leading figure in the NSA, declared: 'Probably not one mother in ten thousand knows her job as she should know it and yet it is the most important job in the world.' Neglect of the 'under fives', she believed, had 'resulted in a sorry harvest of ill health, permanent illness, and a pitiable army of ill-adjusted children'.[16] To those who insisted that full-time motherly care was indispensable for mental stability, the NSCN's Secretary responded: 'It is useless to say "mother and child must not be separated" unless we see to it that mother is equipped in every way to care for her child'; she continued: 'Ignorance repels, separates,

[13] For criticism of nurseries as unhealthy with a high incidence of infection: Helen Mackay's article in the *British Medical Journal*, 8 January 1944. In response MoH invited Mackay and other critics to visit any of its nurseries 'unescorted and unannounced'. Journalist Hilde Marchant accepted the offer and wrote (*Daily Mirror*, 13 January 1944): 'As I watched the children at their games, I found them coming up with confidence and showing what they were doing... There was no hooliganism, no savagery—and after having had complete access to the health files, I can say that the medical control had checked child ailments in an impressive way... On the whole I think that Dr Helen Mackay's generalisation that war-time nurseries have a high incidence of infection and a low incidence of happiness is sweeping and unfair.'

[14] Miss Puxley, Assistant Secretary MoH, quoted by P. Summerfield, *Women Workers in the Second World War* (London, 1984), p. 81.

[15] The NSCN minutes etc. contain numerous references to collaboration with the London Women's Parliament, Minute Books 1941–5. They published pamphlets, sent letters to two hundred MPs, and in 1945 called upon women voters to confront prospective parliamentary candidates on the issue.

[16] Lady Allen of Hurtwood Papers (MRC Warwick): MSS 121/NS/3/2/71 (speech to ABCA, 1943). For pre-war: J. Lewis, *The Politics of Motherhood: Child and maternal welfare in England 1900–1939* (London, 1990); NA: MH 55/1571, Interdepartmental Committee on Parentcraft.

especially when it causes failure to carry out responsibility.'[17] Similarly, *Our Towns*, the highly publicized report by the Women's Group for Public Welfare, asserted: 'We cannot afford not to have the nursery school; it seems to be the only agency capable of cutting the slum mind off at its roots and building the whole child while there is yet time.'[18] Angered by the way the nursery debate stigmatized working-class women, the chief women's labour organization, the Standing Joint Committee of Working Women's Organisations (SJCWWO), reminded the MoH to 'avoid generalisations about "the ignorance of parents" which are often loosely made, and which often suggest, quite unjustifiably, that in general it is poor parents who are ignorant'. 'The line of approach', it added, 'should be that the community is at last recognizing its duty to help young parents, whatever their circumstances.'[19]

Nurseries were defended 'as an extension of the home and its amenities, not a substitute for them'. Far from diminishing family life, they were urgently required for rebuilding it after the strains of the war years. They also helped to encourage larger families and could contribute to reversing the nation's low fertility rate—a growing source of concern, as we shall see. 'Motherhood must be made less of a drudgery and anxiety', Sir Drummond Shiels, a prominent physician and Labour politician, wrote to *The Times*, 'if we are to secure the birth rate figures upon which our national welfare and status depend.'[20] Finally, public childcare was also advocated as a safety-valve against marital collapse and family tension, by easing the strains caused by housing shortages and severe overcrowding. What is significant here is that nursery supporters, like their opponents, formulated their case almost exclusively in terms of the welfare and cohesion of families and the national interest, not the freedom, independence, and sexual equality of women. Only a minority began with what today would be regarded as feminist arguments and very few (the left-wing London Women's Parliament is an exception) demanded class parity of access to childcare. Though split over whether women with infants under two years should work outside the home, they argued that critics of women's paid employment were simply blind to the fact that male wages were often too low to support a family.[21]

---

[17] Hon. Secretary's report in NSCN Papers, Minute Books, no. 7, report for 16 November–20 December 1944; NSCN, *A Four Years Plan for Children's Nurseries* (London, 1943) called for at least 300,000 public nursery places for post-war Britain; L. de Lissa, 'The care of the pre-school child: The basis of social reconstruction', *International Women's News*, 35(9) (July 1941).

[18] WGPW, *Our Towns: A close up* (Oxford, 1943), p. 105. A Medical Officer of Health who advocated nurseries as essential for children of 'degraded' parents was reported as saying that: 'there were probably more sluts in England than in any other civilized country': NSCN Papers, Minute Books, no. 5, report for 22 April–19 May 1943.

[19] Labour Party NEC Minutes, 27 October 1943 (SJCWWO Report to MoH, 'Instruction in parentcraft'). The SJCWWO wrote about welfare clinics: 'the idea still persists that these and kindred services are a form of Public Assistance to the poorest mothers and not a public service available to everyone' (Memorandum to the Royal Commission on Population, NEC Minutes, 28 February 1944).

[20] Sir Drummond Shiels to *British Medical Journal* (*BMJ*), 11 August 1945; H. Mackay-Drummond Shiels exchange in *BMJ* (January–February 1944). Also, NSCN, *Memorandum for the Royal Commission on Population* (London, 1945).

[21] 'Personal Memorandum, Lady Allen of Hurtwood', 8 September 1943, NSCN Papers; copy in Lady Allen of Hurtwood Papers. Many nursery school advocates, like Lady Allen, were strongly opposed to nursery care for infants under two years except in the most exceptional circumstances.

But the campaign to keep public nurseries open failed. When the European war ended, Exchequer funding for them was cut in half and few local authorities were willing to make up the difference. Nurseries began to close as more and more women left their jobs in munitions. The closures were once interpreted by historians as the result of a powerful official campaign, legitimated by new theories of child psychology, to push women out of the labour force and back into the home. The truth, as Denise Riley has argued, was more complicated and less coherent.[22] The government's commitment to childcare provision had always been very limited; different ministries were divided over the issue and there was never a single clear-cut strategy. On balance, new psychological theories, strong pronatalist concerns, and a widespread belief that wartime had left family life in disarray, worked against those who advocated permanent funding for nurseries. But there were other factors too. While a vocal minority of women felt strongly about public provision of childcare and publicly demonstrated against closures, the majority of mothers had not used nurseries in the war years and—even if generally supportive—were not disposed to campaign actively for them once peace returned. Play centres and nursery classes attached to schools were sufficient for many women workers and many continued to rely on relatives and minders. Some supporters organized public protests against nursery closures, but they were unable to push the issue to the forefront of the debate during the 1945 election campaign. There were also divisions in their ranks: nursery-school supporters believed that they had gained a good deal under the recent Education Act (although its provisions for nursery classes were never implemented), while the NSCN viewed nursery schools with their shorter hours and lower staff to children ratio (1: 25 or 35 instead of 1: 12) as a cheap, poor substitute that did not solve the needs of working women. Overall the war experience neither reversed the traditional paucity of public childcare provision in Britain, nor did it weaken the old distinction between childcare (all day) and nursery education classes (part-day); as a result, public childcare continued to be largely represented as a service for children in special need whose mothers were somehow deficient or had no alternative but to work full time.

Child welfare advocates were divided over the wisdom of large-scale nursery provision, but they were firmly united in support of another issue that achieved national publicity towards the war's end. This was the plight of the 'deprived child'. The expression denoted children who had no family, who were orphaned, abandoned, destitute, in correctional institutions, or whose parents were chronically incapacitated or too cruel and abusive to care for them.[23] Some were in foster care,

---

[22] D. Riley, *War in the Nursery: Theories of the child and mother* (London, 1983). About a quarter of public nurseries had already closed down by mid-1946 and almost half by the end of 1947.

[23] Prosecutions for child cruelty and neglect increased, although this may have reflected more vigorous policing than changes in behaviour. The number of persons found guilty of cruelty to children rose, especially women. The figures were: for 1940: 261 male, 418 female; 1942: 493 male, 928 female; 1944: 505 male, 1,239 female. There was also a tendency to ascribe children's higher accident rates in and outside the home to parental shortcomings, rather than to the more dangerous environment of wartime cities. WGPW, *The Neglected Child* (Oxford, 1948). Article in Lady Allen of Hurtwood Papers (MRC Warwick): MSS 121/CH/3/4/3 'Punishment or training? Treatment of neglectful mothers' (2 April 1945).

others lived in barrack schools established by the Poor Law authorities or homes run by voluntary and church groups. Estimates of their numbers varied: at the war's end there were 125,000 children and young adolescents in care in institutions and foster homes, although calculations ran much higher when the children of 'problem families' were included.[24] It was also predicted, quite falsely, that many evacuees who had not yet gone home might be deserted by their parents. In contrast to public nurseries, the 'deprived child' did generate sufficient momentum to mobilize Parliament to pull together the various elements of wartime childcare into a new, more comprehensive structure.

Deprived children were the subject of discussion at various stages of the war, usually in reference to the larger issue of institutional versus foster care. With growing public concern about the break-up of families, it was feared that large numbers would need some form of care outside their own birth families at the war's end. One problem was bureaucratic. Children's welfare was divided between several government agencies (principally, Health, Education, the Home Office, and Public Assistance). There were obvious advantages to unifying some of these programmes and it was generally felt that homeless children should not be placed in the hands of public assistance with all the stigma of the old Poor Law. As between foster homes and residential institutions, there was an overwhelming agreement among childcare professionals in favour of the former. Work with difficult evacuees in hostels and the growth of residential nurseries had stimulated research and provided a wealth of information about methods and organization. After the first evacuation, when little or no heed had been paid to the age, religion, social background, or family type of billetors, often with disastrous consequences, expertise in supervising placements and in making appropriate fostering choices developed rapidly. The goal wherever possible, it was argued, should be to keep families intact, providing counselling and psychological services, but when this proved impossible the first alternatives should be adoption or foster care. If a child were sent to an institution, small group homes that could reproduce some semblance of a family environment were deemed far superior to larger institutions.

But while the war had aroused great interest in the methods of caring for separated children, very little official attention had been paid to conditions in existing institutions run by voluntary societies (many of them religious groups) and by public assistance authorities.[25] They soon became the focus of intense national concern, however, after Lady Allen intervened with a letter to *The Times* in July 1944 demanding a public inquiry. Impatient with the lack of response from government officials, Allen had begun to conduct her own investigation. Her letter

---

[24] The 125,000 estimate comes from the Curtis Committee (there were a further 18,000 in Scotland). A higher estimate of 320,000 is given by C. Fraser Brockington, 'Problem families', British Hygiene Council Occasional Paper, no. 2, London 1948. J. Bowlby, *Child Care and the Growth of Love* (London, 1953), wrote: 'Deprived children, whether in their own homes or out of them, are the source of social infection as real and serious as are carriers of diphtheria or typhoid.'

[25] e.g. the Barnardo and Waifs and Strays homes. In general, these institutions put little emphasis on restoring families or maintaining contact with natural parents; rather, it was believed that separation was preferable.

described a forgotten 'army of unhappy children', brought up in largely unregulated institutions 'under repressive conditions that are generations out of date', whose fate had been ignored in national reconstruction planning. Staffs were overworked, poorly paid, and largely untrained; children were being kept 'isolated from the mainstream of life and education' without 'the comfort and security of individual affection'.[26] The response was sensational with numerous educators, psychologists, children's magistrates, and officials of children's homes entering the debate, which spread quickly to the rest of the press. The public outcry was in some ways reminiscent of the shocked reaction to the first evacuation; it served to release the collective conscience about impoverished children whose lives had been ruptured by war or whom society had forgotten. Horror stories abounded. 'I have seen normal children, younger than three, in the care of mentally defective women', wrote Gwen Chesters of the Tavistock clinic; 'I have seen a boy of four, crouching in terror in his bed in the afternoon, left in the dark room with completely bricked up windows, because he had wet his bed the night before.' Before long the *Daily Mirror* began printing letters from those who had grown up in children's institutions beneath the headline: 'You accuse'.[27]

Lady Allen followed up her letter with a pamphlet, *Whose Children?* This graphically illustrated the dreary conditions, ill-trained staffs, and regimentation that, she wrote, often warped these children 'beyond recovery', leaving them unfit for normal, independent life. She described infants who were forced to sit in silence at mealtimes, who were caned, deprived of food or publicly ridiculed for bed-wetting, and who lacked the most basic toys and opportunities to stimulate their minds.[28] It was not Lady Allen's deeds alone that set political wheels in motion; she had, however, helped to ignite concerns about children that had been building throughout the war. As a result, the Home Secretary, Herbert Morrison, announced in December 1944 that he would appoint a committee of inquiry. The following month, however, public opinion was further inflamed by the murder of Dennis O'Neill, aged thirteen, who had been taken from his parents because of neglect and was then brutally mistreated and beaten to death by his foster parents.[29] His case further reinforced the picture of minimal coordination and supervision between the various children's services. Soon after, a committee chaired by Dame Myra Curtis, the principal of Newnham College, Cambridge, began a detailed investigation of the condition of deprived children. Allen was excluded although she was called before the committee, as were the major childcare organizations,

---

[26] Lady Allen's letter appeared in *The Times*, 15 July 1944. She received over 600 letters (including ones from Anna Freud, Susan Isaacs, G. B. Shaw, and Nancy Astor) and 60 were reprinted in *The Times*: Lady Allen of Hurtwood Papers. Also, M. Allen and M. Nicolson, *Memoirs of an Uneducated Lady* (London, 1975).

[27] Gwen Chesters in *The Times*, 19 July 1944; 'You accuse', *Daily Mirror*, 28 May 1945.

[28] M. Allen, *Whose Children?* (London, 1945), pp. 5–11, 21–3.

[29] A detailed report on the O'Neill case (Cmd 6636, HMSO) by Sir Walter Monckton was published by the Home Office in May 1945. The lesson drawn from this case was not that foster care was less desirous, but rather than supervision of foster homes must be improved. The case inspired Agatha Christie's radio play *Three Blind Mice* and later *The Mousetrap*. T. O'Neill, *Someone to Love Us* (London, 2010) by the boy's brother.

women's groups, and psychologists such as D. W. Winnicott, John Bowlby, and Susan Isaacs. The Curtis Report of September 1946 largely vindicated Allen's charges, although it was less vehement than she had been, particularly about the homes run by voluntary societies, preferring circumlocutions like 'unimaginative methods' to detailing cases of harsh discipline and regimentation. Still, the emotional impairment suffered by many children as a result of their treatment came through clearly enough.[30]

Two years later, the Curtis committee's recommendations were embodied in the landmark Children Act (1948), which created a new relationship between the state and the family. It reaffirmed the importance of keeping children with their natural parents if possible and where that was impossible strongly recommended family nurture (boarding-out in foster homes or adoption) as preferable to residential institutions. The Act also brought greater administrative unity to the system of childcare, reversing the fragmentation that had evolved over generations. It mandated that local authorities establish Children's Committees and appoint qualified Children's Officers whose responsibility it was—along with their trained staffs—to evaluate the standards of care provided by parents, social-work professionals, local schools, and other institutions. These changes accelerated the professionalizing of childcare and the spread of psychological and social-work expertise; they also reduced the divide that had separated those who studied children's physical needs and those concerned with their mental development and emotional adjustment. In the first four years the number of deprived children in care rose by 18 per cent; however, in contrast to earlier, many were discharged after short periods.[31] John Stroud, a young Children's Officer at the time, captured the euphoric mood in his autobiographical novel, *The Shorn Lamb*: 'There was a tremendous crusading atmosphere about the new service. Our impression at the university was that the country outside was dotted with castle-like institutions in which hundreds of children dressed in blue serge were drilled to the sound of whistles. We were going to tear down the mouldering bastions. We were going to replace or re-educate the squat and brutal custodians.'[32]

The Children Act did not, of course, stand alone: it should be viewed in the context of the other social reforms of the late 1940s dealing with family allowances, education, national health, national insurance, and public assistance. Taken together this cluster of legislation redefined the state's role in children's welfare and the family. Whereas before 1914 official perceptions focused heavily upon approaches to the family that stressed male work incentives and economic viability, attention

---

[30] *Report on the Care of Children Committee*, Cmd 6922 (London, 1946). Allen was excluded because she was judged to have already made up her mind about the deficiencies of many organizations. She had also been criticized by Lord Latham of the London County Council. For her evidence to the Curtis Committee see Lady Allen of Hurtwood Papers MSS: 121/CC/3/4/53; also her article, 'Some criticisms of the Curtis Report', *Fortnightly* (March 1947). A 1946 Scottish investigation into homeless children came up with almost identical findings: J. Stewart, '"The most precious possession of a nation is its children": The Clyde Committee on Homeless Children in Scotland', *Journal of Scottish Historical Studies*, 21(1) (2001).

[31] Hendrick, *Child Welfare*, p. 218.

[32] John Stroud, *The Shorn Lamb* (London, 1960) p. 8.

now focused heavily upon the mothers' nurture and their role in the moral and behavioural development of the child. A happy, well-adjusted child was on the path to becoming a 'pillar' of the state, while the troubled, neglected one was a social menace—this dichotomy, as the next section shows, was pervasive in debates about lawless youth. By the war's end, as suggested earlier, a remarkable professional consensus had developed about what was best for children. Many of its underlying assumptions (about delinquency, problem families, maternal deprivation, and so on) came under withering attack in the 1960s and beyond, but today most striking perhaps is what Nicholas Rose has called 'the powerful simplicity'[33] of child welfare in that era: the conviction that the major issues were understood and were soluble through planning and progressive social engineering.

MORAL PANICS: YOUTH 'RUNNING WILD' AND SEXUAL STANDARDS

Among the chief worries, already apparent in the early years, was that dislocation of normal life in wartime would result in a weakening of parental discipline and much higher rates of juvenile crime. This was predicted beforehand, based on the experience of the First World War, and official figures soon seemed to justify these fears. In the war's first year the number of children (under fourteen years) convicted of indictable offences increased by 41 per cent. Among young persons (fourteen–seventeen years) the rise was 22 per cent, and for those seventeen–twenty-one years about 5 per cent. By March 1941 the Home Office was receiving complaints from all sides about a wave of crime and hooliganism and conferences of police, probationers, social workers, and volunteer groups mushroomed across the nation.[34] In retrospect, it is unclear whether the statistics reflected a quantum leap in actual crime, more zealous enforcement, or a rising trend in indictments already underway since the legal changes introduced by the 1933 Children and Young Person's Act.[35] The vast majority of offences were of a petty nature. After 1942, not least because approved schools were overflowing, minor offenders were mostly cautioned rather than prosecuted by the police, and the statistics declined somewhat. The gap between public perception and recorded crime was often wide. Thus, a letter from the Catholic Archbishop of Liverpool to Labour Home Secretary, Chuter Ede, in October 1945, painted a picture of a town under virtual mob rule with church and private property subject to malicious damage and women afraid to go out at night. Yet the Home Office noted that Liverpool's

---

[33] Rose, *Governing the Soul*, p. 176.

[34] H. Mannheim, *War and Crime* (London, 1941). The totals were still quite small and the figures for 1942–4 were below those of 1941. NA: ED 138/92 (Bristol Report, 4 November 1941 and 25 February 1943; Norfolk Report, March 1942); HO 45/20250; CAB 102/790. On the First World War, see D. Smith, 'Juvenile delinquency in Britain in the First World War', *Criminal Justice History*, 9 (1991).

[35] V. Bailey, *Delinquency and Citizenship: Reclaiming the young offender, 1914–48* (Oxford, 1987); Hendrick, *Child Welfare*, ch. 6.

official statistics were neither excessive nor dissimilar from other major cities.[36] Like the troublesome evacuee, 'lawless youth' running wild in the blitzed cities and reception areas became a fixed image in debates about the war's impact on the working-class family.

The immediate causes of the rise in juvenile crime were generally agreed upon. It was commonly asserted that evacuated schoolchildren played a large role, visiting an urban scourge upon the countryside,[37] while in the cities the closure of schools and youth clubs and the reduction of teaching hours were blamed for leaving large numbers of young people with excessive free time. Unoccupied or blitzed houses, shops, and factories facilitated larceny and looting; public shelters provided convenient refuges for truants and runaways; and the blackout afforded increased cover for hooliganism, gambling, and sexual licence.[38] Some politicians and chief constables argued that cinemas and dance halls loosened moral values. Hollywood's harmful influence was a well-worn theme before the war; but other observers insisted that film-going kept youths out of pubs and worse forms of mischief. Some blamed high wages and abundant employment for making youth difficult and undisciplined. In contrast to the depression years when juvenile crime was widely linked to poverty, unemployment, and boredom, greater affluence was now often seen as the culprit. 'Raising the wages of adolescents from £3 to £6 a week', argued a probation officer at Southwark Juvenile Court, 'gave boys far too much money to spend and drunkenness was increasing.' 'To shower inflated wages upon an adolescent entirely unaccustomed to them', German *émigré* criminologist Hermann Mannheim concluded in 1942, 'may easily upset his mental and moral balance, give him an equally inflated sense of his own importance and impair his relations with his family.' Yet, this hardly explained the fact that the largest proportional increase in convictions concerned school-age children. Bevin's assurance in Parliament that youth wage levels were not excessive did little to stanch the flow of letters to *The Times* and other papers and unrest and strikes among mining and engineering apprentices probably added to this anger.[39]

The larger theme that pervaded most explanations was the failure of family to provide a suitable environment for social and psychological growth in infancy and adolescence. The absence of fathers in the services and the recruitment of mothers for work in factories had, it was argued, vastly accelerated the collapse of normal family relationships. But a strong accusatory tone was common. Local educational

---

[36] NA: HO 45/25144 ('Juvenile delinquency in Liverpool, 1943–45'). H. D. Willcock, *Mass-Observation Report on Delinquency* (London, 1949). For a French example of this readiness to blame family break-down and the absence of fathers for higher wartime delinquency rates, see Sarah Fishman, *The Battle for Children: World War II, youth crime, and juvenile justice in twentieth century France* (Boston, 2002).

[37] In contemporary fiction: Joyce Cary, *Charlie is My Darling* (London, 1940).

[38] M-OA: FR 553 (24 January 1941); NA: INF 1/292 (4–11 November 1940; 9–16 July 1941); CAB 102/270, 790; J. A. Watson, 'The young offender', *The Fortnightly*, 157 (January 1942).

[39] H. Mannheim, 'Some reflections on crime in wartime', *The Fortnightly*, 157 (January 1942). Also NA: INF 1/292 (Reports for 19–24 May, 2–9, 9–16 July 1941; 9–16 March, 6–11 July 1943); INF 1/282 (14, 28 October 1943); M-OA, File Report 553 (24 January 1941); M-O, *Report on Juvenile Drinking* (June 1943); M-OA, Youth Box 2, file C.

committees, magistrates, and chief constables blamed parental indifference or low moral standards, asserting that 'the sense of parental responsibility has notoriously declined'.[40] Even the proliferation of wartime services was not without risks: 'Our problem', a Basingstoke evacuation officer wrote in 1943, 'is to revivify the consciousness of parents so that they can use the social welfare services for advice and guidance, but not as a means of evading duty and responsibility.' At the war's end a widely circulated London report emphasized 'the apparent lack of parental control which prevailed in many instances', and added, 'such parents appear to have little or no idea of how to deal with such misdemeanours—quite willing and even anxious to shift their responsibility onto anybody willing to undertake it and when given advice, more often than not, fail to take advantage of it'.[41]

Even before 1939 there had existed considerable agreement about the aetiology of juvenile crime and wartime developments were seen as vindicating these ideas. Thus, though several major studies on youthful offenders appeared during the war, they relied heavily on earlier research.[42] Between the wars the older, rather deterministic, theoretical focus on the social and economic environment of young offenders was modified to give more weight to recent psychological theory. Widely publicized by the press and radio, the new penology reflected the growing influence of the child-guidance movement in Britain; it rejected single-cause explanations of crime, whether environmental or hereditarian, focusing instead on the complex interplay of individual psychology and physical surroundings. For Cyril Burt, one of the leading experts, naughtiness and delinquency were not inherently different, but points on a spectrum; some children, especially those who were backward or of low intelligence, were more predisposed to engage in criminal behaviour—less because of poverty than family relationships and the nature of the home.[43] Penologists assigned varying weight to social and psychological causes, but what is striking is their shared confidence that delinquency could both be understood scientifically and overcome by appropriate rehabilitative measures.[44] A loose

[40] E. Smithies, *Crime in Wartime: A social history of crime in World War II* (London, 1982), pp. 169–85 (p. 173 for quote on decline of parental responsibility); E. Younghusband, 'London's children under fire', *The Howard Journal*, 6 (Autumn 1941).

[41] For the Basingstoke officer, see LCC: PH/GEN/3/10, P. S. Lean to D. E. Sharp, 11 February 1943; LCC: EO/HFE/1/159 ('Juvenile delinquency July 1946–October 1948', Report by the Borough of Finsbury Youth Committee), London Metropolitan Archives, Clerkenwell. Views about juvenile crime were essentially the same in Scotland: D. Smith, 'Official responses to juvenile delinquency in Scotland during the Second World War', *TCBH*, 18(1) (2007). Also, J. Watson, 'The child and the aftermath of war', *The Fortnightly*, 167 (April 1947).

[42] A. M. Carr-Saunders, H. Mannheim, and E. C. Rhodes, *Young Offenders: An inquiry into juvenile delinquency* (Cambridge, 1943); W. Norwood East, *The Adolescent Criminal* (London, 1942); J. H. Bagot, *Juvenile Delinquency* (London, 1941).

[43] C. Burt, *The Young Offender* (London, 1925); P. Rose, *The Psychological Complex: Psychology, politics and society in England 1869–1939* (London, 1985).

[44] Advocates of a more punitive approach were not entirely silent and, despite the Home Office's repeated opposition, magistrates ordered an increased number of birchings for juvenile offenders (from 58 cases in 1939 to a high of 546 in 1941). The issue received national publicity in early 1943 after two boys of 11 and 13 years were beaten at Hereford for theft and burglary before a parent had a chance to appeal the sentence. *PP*, 1942–3, Cmd 6485 ('Hereford Juvenile Court Inquiry'); also NA: CAB 102/790; INF 1/292 (18 November 1943); Editorial in *The Howard Journal*, 6(3) (1943). Birching

coalition of liberal progressive reformers such as the Howard League, the Children's Department of the Home Office, the juvenile courts, and probation services emerged prior to the war. They lobbied long and hard for a system that would give priority to prevention and 'treatment' rather than punishment, blurring earlier distinctions between delinquents and maladjusted or neglected children. Their ideas were influential in shaping the Children and Young Person's Act of 1933, which among other things, replaced the old segregated system of reformatories and industrial schools with all-purpose Approved Schools. They were also of central importance in the organization of local Children's Departments in 1948, emphasizing family involvement or foster care in the process of reclamation with institutionalization as a last resort. One result, it should be noted, was to bring within the jurisdiction of the courts many more children who were not offenders but simply in need of care and protection—that is, 'at risk' of becoming delinquents.[45]

Two themes already present in pre-war research were reinforced by wartime experience and evacuation. First, as we have seen, the concept of 'problem families' came to enjoy wide currency and was soon a mainstay of enquiries into causes of delinquency, repeatedly invoked despite its lack of clarity. As J. H. Bagot stressed in a 1941 study: 'Juvenile delinquency is concentrated in one section of the population, the very poor, and even within this section, minor subnormal groups are responsible for a large proportion of the total number of cases.'[46] Secondly, the war underscored the causal connection drawn between criminality, family break-down, and prolonged separations, particularly early rupture of the child–mother bond. The most influential work in this vein was John Bowlby's *Forty-Four Thieves*, which, while not published until 1946, derived from work done at the London Child Guidance clinic before the war.[47]

The typical youthful offender in most pre-war sociological and psychological studies was not only working-class but almost always male. Female delinquency concerned sexuality almost exclusively and was traditionally viewed as a lesser problem. But beginning in 1942, sexual promiscuity, prostitution, and drunkenness

---

was banned in 1946, although within two years a campaign got underway to bring it back. As one supporter put it, 'Young people are like Germans, unless they are kept in their place they soon become a nuisance and . . . cough up leaders who disturb our sleep': LCC: EO/HFE/1/161 (Conference on Juvenile Delinquency; Memorandum submitted by the Fellowship of St Christopher, August 1949). The foremost medical journal, *The Lancet*, commented, 'If war is brutalising, its effects are not confined to one section of the community . . . A taste for the use of the cosh and a taste for the use of the cat may both have been fostered by five years of violence': 'Crimes of violence', *The Lancet* (8 April 1950). On corporal punishment in Scotland: L. Mahood, ' "Give him a doing": The birching of young offenders in Scotland', *Canadian Journal of History*, 37(3) (2002).

[45] Bailey, *Delinquency and Citizenship*. Also, Abigail Wills 'Delinquency, masculinity and citizenship in England, 1950–70', *Past and Present*, 187 (May 2005).

[46] J. H. Bagot, cited in T. Stephens, *Problem Families* (Liverpool, 1947), p. 7. Interwar surveys viewed the so-called 'social problem group' as a prime breeding-ground of criminality: 'the source', so the Liverpool sociologist, D. Caradog Jones, wrote, 'from which the majority of criminals and paupers, unemployables and defectives of all kinds are recruited': D. Caradog Jones, *The Social Survey of Merseyside* (London, 1934), III, quoted by J. Macnicol, 'In pursuit of the underclass', p. 311.

[47] J. Bowlby, 'Forty-four juvenile thieves: Their characters and home lives', *International Journal of Psychoanalysis*, 25 (1944).

among adolescent girls became an increasing preoccupation. The wartime environment—with parents often absent, schooling disrupted, and men in uniform everywhere—coupled with feminine desires for romance and glamour had, it was argued, produced a tidal wave of immorality. The number appearing in court who were 'beyond parental control' and 'in need of care and protection' had risen sharply (in some central London areas the figures for 1945 were five or six times higher than 1939), while waiting lists lengthened for female vacancies in Approved Schools.[48]

The press was full of articles about teenagers besieging army camps, runaways hanging out in the shelters, and young women flocking to dance halls and pubs in search of excitement. As indicated in the last chapter, the women's military services became the focus of a flood of offensive humour and insinuations about their drinking and sexual conduct, resulting in 1942 in an official inquiry, chaired by Violet Markham. It concluded that the claims had no foundation, and that a few cases of loose behaviour were multiplied many times over by malicious gossip. The growing numbers of female war-workers, living away from home in hostels, fuelled similar speculation. In the South Wales mining town of Blaina, Mass-Observation's Mollie Tarrant was told lots of stories about 'goings-on' on the trains that took local munitions workers to a nearby factory; but she also uncovered nothing to substantiate them.[49] Similarly, newspapers reported a 'grave peril to youth' at Blackpool in 1941 where, according to one local alderman, girls between thirteen and sixteen were having sex with soldiers and VD rates were spiralling. Subsequently an inquiry found that VD rates were very low among Blackpool teenagers, while claims of swarms of pregnant girls were contradicted by an illegitimacy rate that was actually lower than pre-war.[50] In retrospect, what is particularly noteworthy is the severity of the punishments often meted out to young women. One example of a girl 'at risk' from 1943 will suffice. A fifteen-year-old office worker (with no previous court appearances) was picked up by the police at Hyde Park Corner for being intoxicated and in the company of soldiers. No action was taken against the soldiers. She was sent by the magistrate to a remand home to undergo a medical examination and was then placed on probation for a year and sent away to a rural hostel for women in the Land Army where she had to work in the canteen. What was notable about her case and led to a heated parliamentary exchange was not the severity of the sentence, but allegations that while in the hostel she had been improperly

---

[48] Ferguson and Fitzgerald, *Studies in the Social Services*, p. 97; British Medical Association, *The Problem Girl* (London, 1946); Pamela Cox, *Gender, Justice and Welfare: Bad girls in Britain 1900–1950* (Chippenham, 2003); *idem*, 'Girls in trouble: Defining female delinquency, Britain 1900–1950' in M. J. James, B. Soland, and C. Benninghau (eds.), *Secret Gardens, Satanic Mills: Placing girls in European history, 1750–1960* (Bloomington, 2005).

[49] M-OA: FR 1498 ('Mining Town 1942'—Mollie Tarrant's report on the South Wales mining communities of Blaina and Nantyglo).

[50] NA: ED 124/6; ED 138/92; P. Tinkler, 'Sexuality and citizenship: The state and girls' leisure provision in England, 1939–45', *Women's History Review*, 4(2) (1995), 201–4. For the gap between public perceptions and statistics in the Blackpool case and the difficulties (even impossibility) of arriving at accurate statistics, see Andrew Hobbs, 'It doesn't add up: Myths and measurement problems of births to single women in Blackpool, 1931–1971', *Women's History Review*, 17(3) (July 2008).

supervised by the probation service.[51] Girls considered 'at moral risk' could be placed under the guidance of the probation authorities or even sent to an Approved School, even though they had broken no law and might be over sixteen, the legal age of consent.

Derogatory rumour proved impossible to quell. Even before war was declared, women's groups and moral-welfare organizations had urged precautionary measures against 'khaki fever', including the recruitment of women's police auxiliaries to monitor the situation.[52] Symbolizing these fears about declining morality was the 'good time girl', a common parlance in press articles, official reports, and public conversation. She might be a young wife with a husband serving overseas or a young mother with home responsibilities, but more often the term was applied to schoolgirls 'out of control' and single factory workers or recruits to the uniformed services. And while it did not specify social background, most often the label implied a girl of the working class. The 'amateur prostitute' as she was also called, became a focus for pronatalist anxieties about family stability and the quality of the next generation of mothers. Her sexuality outside marriage was viewed as deviant, a threat to the moral and physical health of the nation, and the principal cause of spiralling VD and illegitimacy statistics.[53] Throughout all this, a double standard remained firmly in place. Masculine sexuality was tacitly assumed to be natural and inevitable; young women were the problem and their disruptiveness needed to be contained.

Above all, it was the presence of huge numbers of soldiers and airmen on British soil that raised public anxiety to new levels, especially the arrival of hundreds of thousands of fun-loving, well-paid GIs. By May 1944, 1.7 million Allied and Commonwealth troops were stationed in Britain. A probation officer in Bath, the focal town for a number of US bases, complained: 'there are girls . . . whose only ideas in life are men, lipstick, and showing as much of their bodies as they can'; some, she added, 'were undoubtedly suffering from sexual mania'.[54] Another probation officer working in the London dock areas emphasized the vulnerability of young girls of fourteen years or so 'who are misfits at home or at work or who feel inferior' and sought 'compensation for the dullness, poverty, and, sometimes, unhappiness of their home life'. Brought up on Hollywood and cheap romance magazines, he wrote, they were easy victims to 'the

---

[51] *PD* (Commons), 5 November (cols. 1032–56), 11 November (cols. 1383–404), 1943.

[52] A. Woollacott, '"Khaki fever" and its control: Gender, class, age and sexual morality on the British homefront in the First World War', *Journal of Contemporary History*, 29 (1994). Members of the Women's Auxiliary Police came from various social backgrounds, including many from the upper working class or lower middle class: L. A. Jackson, *Women Police: Gender, welfare, and surveillance in the twentieth century* (Manchester, 2006).

[53] British Medical Association, *The Problem Girl*; Lucy Bland and Frank Mort, '"Look out for the good time girl": Dangerous sexualities as a threat to national health', *Formations of Nation and People* (London, 1984); '"Good-time" girls of 14 are running wild' (Headline), *Daily Herald*, 23 March 1943, p. 5. For some critics, women in pubs, wearing make-up or trousers, were sufficient indicators of sexual promiscuity. 'Years ago', commented an elderly Scot, 'you could tell a respectable lassie by the way she dressed. Now you can't tell at all. They all dress alike, they paint and powder the same' (quoted in L. Stanley, *Sex Surveyed, 1949–1994: From Mass-Observation's 'Little Kinsey' to the National Survey and the Hite Reports* (London, 1995), p. 170).

[54] E. Smithies, *Crime in Wartime*, p. 183; NA: INF/282, 28 October 1943; INF 1/292, 9–16 March, 19–26 October 1943; *PD*, House of Commons, 415 (2 November 1945).

American attitude to women, their proneness to spoil a girl, to build up, exaggerate, talk big, and to act with generosity and flamboyance'.[55] Home Intelligence surveys recorded growing criticism of the behaviour of GIs, but public anger placed the heaviest blame on 'predatory' young women who, it was said, 'ran riot' and 'threw themselves' at the soldiers. Press accounts and official statements echoed this, in part because they were disposed to minimize tension with the American authorities. 'These servicemen', a Home Office summary concluded, 'showed up weakness in family life, lack of control, instability, lack of moral or intellectual balance.'[56] Public disapproval was even stronger when the men involved were black. By the last stages of the war, there were over 100,000 black GIs in Britain and around 10,000 black servicemen and contract workers from the empire. While the segregationist practices of the American military were widely deplored, interracial sex, as David Reynolds has written, was where most British people drew their colour line.[57] A variety of initiatives were undertaken to discourage such relationships. A 'whispering campaign' was set in motion by churchmen, women's groups, local government officials, social workers, and probation officers to warn young women about unwanted 'half-caste' babies and the dangers of venereal disease. Local police constabularies recruited more women and stepped up their surveillance of girls under eighteen years; they also routinely reported women in the armed services found in the company of black men. Young girls were also more likely to land in juvenile court, Sonya Rose has argued, 'if the soldiers with whom they were associating were black Americans'.[58] If anything, in the last eighteen months of the war, with foreign troop concentrations growing rapidly in preparation for the invasion of Europe, complaints about adolescent girls overshadowed earlier alarm about the criminality of teenage boys.

Public anxiety about the 'youth problem' did not subside after 1945; indeed, in the early post-war years, public debate at times seemed even more obsessed than in wartime with panic about pre-marital sex and what was described as a wave of lawlessness. Youth committees set up by local authorities reported on the situation in their areas; advocates of youth clubs pointed to a growing crisis which required more recreational outlets for young people; and in educational curricula there was a strong push for providing girls with more instruction in childcare and housecraft. Post-war cinema also fanned these concerns, releasing a cluster of films about 'spivs', 'good time girls', and violent young criminals. They included *The Blue*

[55] NA: HO 45/20730, Regional reports: London. Also, Ferguson and Fitzgerald, *Studies in the Social Services*, pp. 97–8.
[56] NA: HO 45/20730, 'Summary of Probation Officers' reports on social work during the war'. Also, NA: INF 1/292, 6 July–11 July 1943 reports on Eastern and N. Midland regions; 19 October–26 October describes a 'wave of moral delinquency', calls for more police supervision of 'young girls who fling themselves at soldiers', and anxiety over the 'growing number of enthusiastic amateur prostitutes'.
[57] D. Reynolds, *Rich Relations: The American occupation of Britain, 1942–1945* (New York, 1995), p. 308. Also Mica Nava, 'Wider horizons and modern desire: The contradictions of America and racial difference in London, 1935–1945', *New Formations*, 37 (1999).
[58] S. Rose, 'Girls and GIs: Race, sex, and diplomacy in Second World War Britain', *International History Review*, 19(1) (February 1997), 157; *idem*, 'Sex, citizenship, and the nation in World War II Britain', *AHA* (October 1998). Also Nuffield College Reconstruction Survey 1942 (Oxford) Folder A-16 Area Report for Merseyside.

Lamp (1950), featuring Dirk Bogarde as a young killer, Riley, who guns down a policeman and is then hunted by both the police and the professional underworld. Riley is the maladjusted product of war: neurotic, repressed, sexual, and deeply dangerous. Popular memory, then, that all was calm and quiet until the Edwardian jackets and drainpipe trousers of Teddy Boys captured the headlines around 1954 is wide of the mark. The ground was well-prepared for panic over the Teds; all that was lacking was the sartorial signifier. Based on statistical research conducted for the Home Office, Leslie Wilkins claimed that children born 1935–42 were more prone to crime than those born in any other seven-year period, while Josephine Bell, in a more popular account, interpreted post-war teenage crime figures in terms of two waves (1948–53 and 1958–62) the first being caused by those who as young children experienced the separations of wartime and the second by those who were born during the war and 'spent their earliest lives in chaotic conditions'.[59] Anxiety about delinquent youth encapsulated a whole array of fears about society and the nation, but prior to the mid-1960s at least, this disruptive agent was virtually synonymous with working-class youth.

As the war lengthened and marital separations became more prolonged, so debate also focused upon the sexual and moral standards of wives and mothers. 'Infidelity is not yet taken for granted but it is losing its social stigma', a probation officer wrote to the Home Office.[60] Women were viewed as the chief culprits. 'The sexual excitatory effect of war', warned the psychologist George Ryly Scott as early as 1940, 'is known to every student of psycho-pathological problems. Woman, granted a new-born partial freedom simultaneously with the means of avoiding the consequences of illicit love, has become drunk on sex.'[61] A Mass-Observer answered a 1945 inquiry about sexual morality: 'No one seems to see any value in fidelity to one and the same partner'; another complained of the casualness and bravado of teenage mothers who returned to school 'flaunting their babies with pride'; while a third, the headmistress of a London school, now in the country, detailed several cases of evacuated working-class mothers who had 'gone astray'.[62]

Underlying this alarm were several basic facts. Vast numbers of males under thirty-five had been called up and separated from their wives, fiancées, and girlfriends; by 1944 an estimated 55 per cent of men in the armed forces were married (i.e. over 2.5 million) and many were posted overseas for long periods.[63]

---

[59] L. T. Wilkins, *Delinquent Generations* (London, 1960); J. Bell, *Crime in Our Time* (London, 1962). Also, M. Fry *et al.*, *Lawless Youth* (London, 1947); T. R. Fyvel, *The Insecure Offenders* (London, 1963). A minority, like Dr Peter Scott, a psychiatrist attached to the LCC's remand homes, found public concern 'out of all proportion to the relatively small increase in juvenile crime' (LCC archives EO/HFE/1/161).

[60] Probation officer (G. W. R. Searle, Leicester City): NA: HO 45/20730.

[61] G. R. Scott, *Sex Problems and Dangers in Wartime* (London, 1940). During the war, public debate focused upon heterosexual relationships. Police surveillance of homosexuals decreased and the numbers of arrests dropped sharply. This changed dramatically in the post-war years when the campaign against homosexuality was integral to the larger theme of reconstructing family life. M. Houlbrook, *Queer London: Perils and pleasures in the sexual metropolis 1918–1957* (Chicago, 2005).

[62] M-OA, File Report 2205, 'Sex, morality and the birth rate' (January 1945). Also, Anon., 'The problem presses', *Social Work*, 3 (January 1944); M-O, *The Journey Home* (London, 1944), 47.

[63] Ferguson and Fitzgerald, *Studies in the Social Services*, p. 3.

Worries about female chastity and fidelity, always rife in such situations, were compounded by the mass recruitment of women into war work and the huge build-up in Britain of foreign troops. Many older men believed that industrial workshops were no place for respectable women, while some workers' wives, unhappy at their spouses working alongside women, were quick to suspect female co-workers of sexual licence. Women were subject to a range of contradictory messages: to participate, be social, look attractive, and keep up morale, but also to remain chaste and avoid giving alarm to absent males serving in the forces. Public anxiety was, of course, also coercive. Much was made of the alleged wider social freedom of women in wartime, but fear of spiteful neighbours or relatives also prevented many from experiencing it—for many lonely women, it was the female comradeship of the working day that enabled them to get through these years.

What were viewed as the chief indicators of declining sexual standards? Among the most commonly cited barometers was the incidence of venereal disease. Statistics were notoriously unreliable, especially in the case of gonorrhoea, but by all accounts the number of cases had risen sharply by 1941. Most affected were the nineteen–twenty-three age group; cases in men decreased somewhat after 1942, but those for women continued to rise. Dr Sydney Laird, the author of a widely read Penguin Special on the subject, estimated that by the end of 1941 the number of early syphilis cases exceeded the 1939 figures by 50 per cent for civilians and 70 per cent for the uniformed services.[64] Many cases certainly went unreported, but even so, the aggregate numbers (as opposed to the percentage rise) do not seem alarming. VD was, however, a powerful symbol that crystallized other anxieties: about the long-term drop in the national birth rate (the risks of sterility and birth defects were strongly emphasized); the dangers of physical deterioration; the collapse of religion; the loosening of family bonds; and, for feminists, the persistence of a double standard of morality. From the autumn of 1942 the government mounted an intensive publicity campaign to combat the spread of VD. The Chief Medical Officer of the Ministry of Health addressed the issue on radio, press coverage expanded dramatically, and government-sponsored films and lectures were prepared for factories.[65] A remarkably explicit poster campaign warned men of the dangers of prostitutes and easy girlfriends. Sex-hygiene classes for the uniformed services became less perfunctory, although contraceptives were made readily available only to male recruits. In general, the public welcomed this educational

---

[64] S. M. Laird, *Venereal Disease in Britain* (London, 1943), p. 34. Official figures showed that for women the percentage increase in early syphilis cases 1939–41 was 63%; for men, 113%. The percentage increase in gonorrhoea for the same period was 85% for women, 90% for men.

[65] R. Davenport-Hines, *Sex, Death and Punishment* (London, 1996), pp. 260–75. A. Bingham, 'The British popular press and venereal disease during the Second World War', *Historical Journal*, 48 (4) (2005). NA: INF 1/293, 'Public reactions to the venereal diseases campaign' (26 March 1943); RG 23/56, P. J. Wilson and V. Barker, 'The campaign against venereal diseases' (January 1944); RG 23/38, 'The campaign against venereal diseases' (March–April 1943). Also M-OA: FR 1573 and 1579; M-OA A9, 'Sex surveys' Box 1. Pressure for more vigorous government action to deal with VD also came from the American and Canadian military authorities, frustrated by British reticence and resistance to compulsory notification of VD cases and tougher penalties for infecting others. British authorities complained that many GIs were already infected with VD when they arrived in England.

campaign, although a minority claimed that it over-emphasized medical rather than moral prophylaxis.[66] There were also demands for compulsory notification (as with other contagious diseases) and for tougher legal penalties against those who infected others. But social purity groups remained mostly opposed to anything that suggested state regulation and therefore tacit acceptance of vice while most politicians and doctors resisted steps that would criminalize sexual diseases and promote greater secrecy. After November 1942 (under s. 33B of the Defence of the Realm Act), Medical Officers could compel treatment for anyone reported to have infected two or more people. Significantly, between January and September 1943 information was lodged against 3,344 women, compared to only 213 men, although male VD rates were always substantially higher.[67]

Established courtship and marriage rituals proved impossible to sustain in wartime. Courtships and formal engagements became shorter; weddings were generally smaller and more hasty, designed to fit in with leave and postings and with wartime scarcities. Elaborate white weddings gave way to small ceremonies with couples in uniform or everyday dress. Not surprisingly the war, as was true 1914–18, had a marked effect on nuptial rates: there was a fairly dramatic rise in late 1939 and 1940 as couples expecting to be separated got married; then came a sharp drop until the end of 1943, after which the figures began rising again, slowly at first but then much more rapidly in 1945. The increased geographical mobility of people in wartime removed young people from their families and neighbourhoods, opening up a larger range of contacts and potential partners. By the war's end more people were marrying and their average age grew steadily younger.[68] Though this trend might well have been taken as proof of the resilience of matrimony, it was overshadowed by the higher incidence of divorce and separation.

In contrast to the First World War, both the numbers of petitions filed and the divorce rate rose significantly during the Second World War. In part the increase resulted from a widening of the admissible grounds in 1937, accompanied by administrative changes that expanded the numbers of courts with jurisdiction in such cases. Even more important, however, was the 1942 decision of the War Office and the Treasury—bowing to pressures within the military—to make divorce simpler, cheaper, and more widely available to servicemen, although lengthy delays were still common.[69] In most cases divorce was followed by remarriage. These changes

---

[66] Letter of Archbishop Temple of Canterbury, *The Times*, 24 February 1943.

[67] C. Haste, *Rules of Desire. Sex in Britain: World War I to the present* (London, 1992), p. 134; F. A. Iremonger, *William Temple* (London, 1948), pp. 448–50: Temple threatened to resign as president of the Central Council of Health Education over s. 33B, believing that it reduced a moral problem to a purely medical one and threatened to make fornication safe. Also, *PD* (Commons), 15 December 1942, cols. 1807–79.

[68] Ferguson and Fitzgerald, *Studies in the Social Services*, p. 18; J. M. Winter, 'The demographic consequences of the war' in H. L. Smith (ed.), *War and Social Change: British society in the Second World War* (Manchester, 1986). Also, C. Langhamer, 'Love and courtship in mid-twentieth century England', *HJ*, 50(1) (2007).

[69] In April 1943 the Poor Persons' Committee of the Law Society reported 3,500 cases of divorce concerning soldiers pending formal hearing and another 5,000 cases under consideration; by May 1946 some 43,000 service cases had still not been dealt with. R. J. Morgan, 'The introduction of Civil Legal Aid in England and Wales, 1914–49', *TCBH*, 5(1) (1994).

made divorce widely available to the working class for the first time. In 1939 the total number of divorce petitions was 8,517; in 1942, 11,613; in 1944, 18,390; and they rose again to 24,857 in 1945. The divorce rate in the war years climbed from 1.5 to 3.6 per 10,000 of the English population, cresting at 13.6 in 1947 (which reflected a considerable backlog of earlier petitions).[70] Another highly publicized aspect of the figures was the fact that for the first time more men than women were filing for divorce which was widely interpreted as proof of widespread infidelity among wives of servicemen. In fact, divorce initiated by a man through the army welfare scheme was much cheaper and quicker than if a civilian wife brought the action.

The legal grounds for divorce remained unchanged: adultery, desertion, and cruelty; but popular opinion, while stressing 'the desirability of unbroken, lifelong marriages', viewed unhappiness and mutual incompatibility as sufficient cause, especially if there were no children. 'If they're not happy', one woman replied, 'it's no use living together. Life is too short. You don't know when you marry what they are like.'[71] Also, pre-war statistics are misleading as an index for marital break-down among workers, since in that period unhappy spouses simply moved out—only a minority paid for formal separation agreements—and formed other relationships, often long-term, outside marriage.[72] Given the extraordinary conditions, and compared to post-1965 trends, wartime divorce rates do not seem very high, but they were alarming to many at the time. In response, the government took steps to bolster marriages in trouble, both through the Army Reconciliation Scheme which employed local army welfare officers to reconcile estranged servicemen and their wives and through funding the expansion of marriage guidance centres, staffed by mostly middle-class female volunteers.[73]

If the collapse of marriages was taken as proof of deteriorating moral standards, the increase in illegitimacy was viewed with even greater alarm. The Registrar-General's figures for England and Wales show 255,460 illegitimate births for the years 1940–5—some 102,000 more than in the period 1934–9. They represented 4.2 per cent of all live births in 1939 (6 per cent in Scotland) and 9.3 per cent of a much larger total in 1945 (8.7 per cent in Scotland).[74] Contrary to popular belief, however, which made young single women the chief target of public opprobrium, the illegitimate birth rate for unmarried women under twenty-five years was lower

---

[70] *Statistical Digest of the War* (HMSO, 1951), table 52; G. Braybon and P. Summerfield, *Out of the Cage: Women's experiences in two world wars* (New York, 1987), p. 212. Also, O. R. McGregor, *Divorce in England: A centenary study* (London, 1957).

[71] Liz Stanley, *Sex Surveyed, 1949–1994* (London, 1995), p. 127. A 1951 Gallup Poll showed that 60% of the population thought that after 7 years' separation a couple ought automatically to be able to get a divorce.

[72] J. Klein, 'Irregular marriages: Unorthodox working-class domestic life in Liverpool, Birmingham, and Manchester, 1900–1939', *Journal of Family History*, 30(2) (April 2005).

[73] J. Lewis, D. Clark, and D. H. J. Morgan, *'Whom God Hath Joined Together': The work of the Marriage Guidance Council* (London, 1992). At the war's end the Citizens' Advice Bureaux run by the Charity Organization Society also incorporated marriage counselling into their work.

[74] *Registrar-General's Statistical Review of England and Wales, 1940–45* (London, 1951); Ferguson and Fitzgerald, *Studies in the Social Services*, p. 90; *National Council for the Unmarried Mother and Her Child. Annual Reports* (London, 1938–46); L. Fisher, *Twenty-One Years and After* (London, 1946).

than pre-war, while that of the over twenty-five group rose. These 'irregularly conceived maternities' increased in the war years over the 1938–9 period by 24 per cent for those twenty-five–thirty years of age; 41 per cent for those thirty–thirty-five; and around 20 per cent for those thirty-five–forty-five. It was those who would usually have been producing children in marriage who were doing so out of wedlock.[75] Some evidence suggests that public attitudes towards illegitimacy became a little more sympathetic; certainly, unmarried mothers were far less conspicuous than in peacetime because of expanded childcare and the absence of so many husbands. But the stigma of single parenthood remained heavy in many communities and the plight of many women was desperate. Many lost their jobs or were thrown out of workers' hostels and private billets. Official attitudes at every level were predominantly moralistic and condemnatory, few babies were covered by affiliation orders, and the central government preferred to delegate the matter to voluntary associations. A scheme to assist munitions workers was so poorly publicized that many social workers and factory welfare officers were unaware of its existence. Single mothers were often left to cope for themselves, aided by family and friends; women in uniform were somewhat better served, largely because of pressure from the military authorities.

Indeed, the most striking feature of the official statistics was the sharp drop in the number of maternities subsequently regularized by marriage. In wartime, extra-marital conceptions remained fairly constant; indeed, estimates were below the pre-war figures in five of the six years.[76] But the proportion later regularized by marriage fell from 70 per cent in 1938 to 37 per cent in 1945 (and then rose again to 44 per cent in 1946 and 56 per cent in 1947). Forced separations produced by total mobilization, sudden transfers, the shift to more transient relationships, and a reduction perhaps of parental and community controls meant that couples were less likely to marry and legitimize their offspring. But efforts to introduce legislation permitting servicemen to marry by proxy were defeated in the Commons, largely out of fear that troops would be taken advantage of and ensnared by 'designing women'.[77]

'Irregular' births to married women also produced growing anxiety as symptomatic of moral decay. Unless the father was formally registered as someone other than her husband, official statistics showed the children of a married woman as legitimate; thus, we possess only very crude estimates. A survey conducted by the Birmingham Public Health Department suggested that such 'irregular' pregnancies to married women tripled between 1940 and 1945, though in some cases the marriage had foundered well before. Over half involved servicemen's wives. In the last two years of the war married women accounted for about one-third of 'illegitimate' conceptions in Birmingham. Comparable statistics are, however, lacking for other regions.[78]

[75] Ferguson and Fitzgerald, *Studies in the Social Services*, p. 91; NA: CAB 102/771.
[76] The Registrar-General's report of 1938–9 had estimated that 'nearly 30% of all mothers today conceive their first-born out of wedlock' (for those under 20 years the figure was 42%).
[77] *PD* (Commons), 30 June 1943.
[78] Birmingham: Public Health, Maternity and Child Welfare Committee, minutes for 10 November 1944–30 October 1945 (Birmingham City Archives, Birmingham Central Library). NA: MH 55/1654 contains fragmentary figures for other areas. On the problematic nature of 'illegitimacy' as a category and

Public opinion had little sympathy for these women who were viewed as having 'failed' their husbands and society. Fidelity and constancy were at the heart of the patriotic femininity idealized in wartime.

The disruption of total war produced exaggerated fears that gender roles had been subverted, the family seriously weakened, and sexual morality undermined. Already in 1941 a committee of psychiatric social workers, having gathered evidence from many regions, warned of 'a break-down in moral and social values'.[79] 'The moral situation of the country today', Archbishop Temple declared in 1943, displayed 'two apparently contradictory features': first, 'splendid endurance, mutual helpfulness and constancy, which, during the Blitz, reached heroic proportions', and secondly, 'a really alarming collapse in respect of honesty and sex morality'. 'The family itself', he warned, 'has been largely disintegrated . . . old conventions fail and nothing takes their place.'[80] At a time when official propaganda resorted more and more to the family as a symbol of what the nation was fighting for, that same family seemed at greater risk. The separations of wartime and the dramatic changes in every facet of people's lives undoubtedly affected behaviour, but public alarm was disproportionate. Moreover, prevailing attitudes *about* sexual behaviour and the family seemed little altered.[81] Contemporary surveys continued to indicate strong disapproval of pre-marital sex, especially among the working class. Marriage and monogamy were considered the basis of a stable society. Anthropologist Geoffrey Gorer's survey of 10,000 respondents for the Sunday newspaper, *The People*, found that the sexual experience of half the married participants in the sample was limited to their spouse (the proportion was even higher among the working class). Further, more than half of men and two-thirds of women preferred that neither partner should have sexual experience before marriage.[82] As for divorce, there is evidence of a hardening of official attitudes and a growing campaign against what an Anglican report on *Home and Family Life* in 1944 called 'the limited liability' notion of marriage.[83] Divorce was still widely associated with matrimonial 'offence' and Geoffrey Fisher, who succeeded Temple as Archbishop

its measurement: Gail Reekie, *Measuring Immorality: Social inquiry and the problem of illegitimacy* (Cambridge, 1998).

[79] Papers of the Association for Psychiatric Social Workers, Birmingham (now at MRC, Warwick), 16/5, 'Social changes due to the war and their significance' (texts for talks and papers to the Association for Psychiatric Social Workers, January 1942). For the individual reports see 20/7 ('Mental Health Emergency Committee: Statements for report on changes in social conditions', November 1941).

[80] Quoted in *Quarterly Leaflet of the Church of England Moral Welfare Council* (August 1943), p. 4 (copy in NA: MH 55/1653). Also, E. Urwin, *Can the Family Survive?* (London, 1944).

[81] Stanley, *Sex Surveyed, 1949–1994*. The 1949 study by Mass-Observation (dubbed the 'Little Kinsey' report) also revealed that public opinion was divided about whether sexual standards of behaviour were falling. While 44% (of over 2,000 questioned) said they were declining, 29% felt they were much the same as ever, while another 17% thought things were improving after a wartime loosening of standards. Most agreed that the war had produced more frankness and less furtiveness in sexual behaviour. Also, E. Chesser, *The Sexual, Family, and Marital Relationship of the English Woman* (London, 1956).

[82] G. Gorer, *Exploring English Character* (New York, 1955), p. 87. The data for Gorer's study were gathered in 1951. Also, C. Langhamer, 'Adultery in post-war England', *HWJ*, 62 (Autumn 2006).

[83] *The Listener*, 27 January 1944, p. 96.

of Canterbury, described it as 'always the outcome of human sin . . . an area of poison and a centre of infection in the national life'.[84] Remarriage in a church remained almost impossible.

THE ELDERLY

The war years belonged to youth. Pictures in wartime magazines teem with young faces: uniformed men, scarcely out of their teens; female conscripts learning how to operate lathes; infants in nurseries and young mothers with evacuee children. Youth was heroic, dynamic, romantic, tragic, and photogenic. It was the victim of war but also, as we have seen, a cause for alarm. Elderly air-raid wardens, WVS volunteers, and members of 'Dad's Army' were also news, of course, but youngsters dominated. In 1945 Humphrey Spender's film, *Diary for Timothy*, asked what kind of a world a one-year-old infant would inherit; there was no equivalent for 'Darby and Joan', although people of pensionable age constituted 12 per cent of the population. In retrospect, however, the war years were critical in defining and standardizing what we mean by 'old age'.

For the working-class elderly, as much as any other group, wartime life was diverse and one must be cautious when making generalizations. Health, geography, employability, and the proximity of relatives were key determinants of experience. For many men and women in their sixties who were in reasonably good health the war brought new possibilities of employment, especially if they had valuable skills and work experience. Some who had previously suffered prolonged unemployment in depressed local economies were now reabsorbed into their old jobs; others were recruited for new tasks, sometimes on a part-time basis or even working at home and at local centres, assembling and sorting parts for a variety of war industries. Many older men and even more women also gained a renewed sense of their own worth through voluntary activity—as wardens or fire-watchers, preparing meals for the WVS, minding infants and evacuees, or helping out at the Women's Institute and the Red Cross. Surveys indicated that elderly women, especially those in part-time employment, were often very happy, enjoying the company of fellow factory workers as well as the pay, and some were sad about the prospect of leaving once peace returned.

For older pensioners, however, and especially those who were frail or sick, wartime conditions could be extremely hazardous and disorienting. In the first weeks of the conflict, large numbers of elderly patients were discharged from hospitals to make room for anticipated air-raid casualties—unnecessarily so, as it turned out, since major raids did not materialize for months and many hospitals

---

[84] *PD*, House of Lords (28 November 1946, col. 483). Fisher led the opposition in the House of Lords to proposals for making divorce easier. The Royal Commission on Marriage and Divorce (1951–5) rejected any significant change in the law and admonished that people should expect less of married life and take its responsibilities more seriously. The final report blamed both modern psychology and women's 'emancipation' for encouraging an atmosphere in which self-gratification was given priority over self-discipline and social obligations. McGregor, *Divorce in England*.

had beds to spare.[85] Many were chronically sick or bedridden, including some suffering from TB or cancer. Some, to their horror, ended up in already over-crowded public-assistance institutions; others were a heavy burden on their families and neighbours. When the Blitz came, many old people faced serious difficulties getting to shelters after the alarm had sounded, negotiating blacked-out and often rubble-strewn streets, to say nothing of spending nights in cold, damp shelters on hard benches and campbeds which increased their risks of illness. Shopping was another nightmare, requiring more time on one's feet in long queues and travel over greater distances when local grocers and butchers' shops were damaged or de-stroyed. Public transport was also slower and less predictable, while basic household chores became much harder, given the grime, soot, and broken glass that blanketed blitzed localities. Moreover, the accelerated movement of younger people—because of evacuation, conscription, work transfers, or the raids themselves—fragmented and depopulated old, settled neighbourhoods like London's East End, leaving many elderly more isolated and lonely and depriving them of local support systems.

Not surprisingly, reports of disorientation and neglect grew more numerous. Old people were found to have virtually moved into some of the public shelters; they also became more-or-less permanent residents of many rest centres, originally conceived as temporary havens for homeless raid victims. Official efforts to evacuate them also met with limited success. They often resisted attempts to separate them from their normal surroundings and, in any case, there were few places for them in hostels and, despite public appeals, few private billetors were willing to take them in.[86] Some were sent to provincial hospitals, others were housed in former work-houses, although they dreaded these drab, poorly appointed dormitories, with the attached stigma of ending their days on public assistance. 'The fear of being treated as a pauper', Titmuss wrote, 'was much more real than the fear of bombs' for many.[87] As a letter in the *Manchester Guardian* made clear, conditions in public-assistance institutions were often dreadful: 'On each chair sat an old woman in workhouse dress, upright, unoccupied. No library books or wireless... No easy chairs. No pictures on the walls... None was allowed to lie on her bed at any time throughout the day, although breakfast is at 7 a.m.... three had crashed forward, face downwards, on to their immaculate bedspreads and were asleep'. These women, the writer added, were not victims of 'conscious cruelty' but of 'official rigidity, parsimony, and lack of imagination'.[88] Growing public pressure and a

---

[85] R. Means and R. Smith, *The Development of Welfare Services for Elderly People* (London, 1985), ch. 2. 140,000 patients were discharged from hospital in just two days; many were elderly, although exactly how many is impossible to calculate. Others were removed from hospital waiting lists to make way for expected bombing casualties.

[86] NA: HO 199/442, Rest Centre report on Manchester, 6 January 1941: 'Old and infirm people suffering from shock, cripples and blind people had to sit all night in the crowded hall... The lavatories were up steps which were very dark; later in the week these were painted, on the initiative of the users of the centre.'

[87] R. M. Titmuss, *Problems of Social Policy* (London, 1950), p. 451. The daily press ran appeals for billetors to take in the elderly, e.g. 'Can you give them shelter?', *Daily Herald*, 17 December 1940.

[88] *Manchester Guardian*, 6 March 1943. The letter provoked a considerable correspondence. See also, E. D. Samson, *Old Age in the New World* (London, 1944), esp. pp. 47ff.

highly critical investigation in 1944 by the Nuffield Foundation did bring improvements and greater sensitivity to their needs. Local authorities and voluntary groups, including the WVS and local Old People's Welfare Committees, set up more hostels and helped coordinate local services, including in some cases home-helps and mobile meals services. But official reaction was slow and too often guided by the concern that 'they should not block facilities which might be required by others'.[89]

While the weak and infirm suffered most, even the elderly who were comparatively healthy faced new burdens during the first two years of the war—including additional financial hardship. The poverty of old people was nothing new.[90] Anyone who had to pay rent and live on 10s a week pension or received no support from relatives fell well below most 'poverty lines' constructed by social investigators. And fewer pensioners could hang on to their jobs in the labour market of the 1930s. Only 275,000 pensioners claimed means-tested public assistance, but that was more a reflection of the intrusive character of the system than the true state of affairs. Price inflation in the first eighteen months of the war, particularly for basic foods, hit old people especially hard. Indeed, when supplementary pensions were introduced in June 1940, some 1.27 million applications were received in the first two months alone, more than three times the number officials had anticipated.[91] This unexpected deluge of claimants was the result of need, testimony to the extent of destitution; but it also pointed to a growing sense of entitlement and of grass-roots mobilization among the elderly which began before the war and grew as inflation diminished their resources still further. The country's mood in late 1940 was also more radical and assertive, and this too was a catalyst for organization.

The largest and most important rank-and-file organizations campaigning for changes in the pension system were the National Spinsters' Pensions Association (NSPA) and the National Federation of Old Age Pensioners Associations (NFOAPA).[92] Founded in Bradford in 1935, the NSPA won a large following

---

[89] H. Jones, *Health and Society in Twentieth Century Britain* (London, 1994), p. 104. For the Nuffield survey, see Means and Smith, *The Development of Welfare Services for Elderly People*, pp. 81ff.

[90] In the interwar years roughly one-third of those over 65 years (more women than men) lived alone. Rowntree's 1936 survey of York estimated that 31% of the working-class population in the city were 'in poverty' while the figure for those over 65 years was 47.5%. And yet this was a considerable improvement over the situation 30 years before.

[91] The number of applications rose far above expectations in some places like Bristol (24 times the number anticipated as opposed to 2 times for Glasgow) where previously the Poor Law stigmata had acted as a formidable deterrent: 'Budgets of old age pensioners and households on public assistance', *Bulletin of the Oxford Institute of Statistics*, 3(4) (1941). On the interwar decline in employment for older men, see S. M. Riddle, 'Age, obsolescence, and unemployment: Older men in the British industrial system, 1920–39', *Aging and Society*, 4(4) (1984). For familial support pre-war: C. Gordon, 'Familial support for the elderly in the past: The case of London's working class in the early 1930s', *Aging and Society*, 8 (1988). By 1941 one-third of pensions were being supplemented by the Assistance Board, although there were still many who refused to seek assistance, linking it with Poor Law charity. An Assistance Board inquiry of 1942 found that many pensioners lacked clothes, cooking equipment, and blankets: Pat Thane, *Old Age in English History: Past experiences, present issues* (Oxford, 2000), pp. 355–63. The Assistance Board transformed its public image in the war by becoming a strong advocate for poor pensioners.

[92] J. Macnicol, *The Politics of Retirement in Britain, 1878–1948* (Cambridge, 1998); Thane, *Old Age in English History*; J. Macnicol and A. Blaikie, 'The politics of retirement, 1908–48' in M. Jefferys (ed.), *Growing Old in the Twentieth Century* (London, 1989).

among working-class women in the textile towns of Lancashire and Yorkshire; indeed, it boasted a membership of 150,000 at the outbreak of war. Spinsters felt particularly badly treated by the existing law which provided pensions for insured women at sixty-five years (reduced to sixty years in 1940). Unmarried women, they pointed out, were much more likely than men to lose their jobs in their fifties, either through ill-health or dismissal; they then became ineligible for a non means-tested pension, although they had contributed for years to the insurance fund. The NSPA called for a pension for single women at fifty-five years which would give them the same rights as widows. The second organization, the NFOAPA, grew out of a coalition of pensioners' groups in 1938. Demanding £1 a week non-contributory pension for men and women (double the existing level), it soon spearheaded political activism among the elderly. Largely working class, the movement was radical both in style and politics, with many of its sections originally linked to branches of the Independent Labour Party. Its publication, *The Pensioner*, had an acerbic turn of phase, pointing out the generous pensions that MPs and other officials had secured for themselves, exhorting readers to force local politicians to pledge their support or be punished at the ballot box. Membership figures for NFOAPA are vague and unreliable, but it sent a monster petition to parliament in 1939, claiming 5 million signatures, while by 1944 it had, according to some estimates, as many as 600 branches, many of them boasting 5,000 members and some over 10,000. In brief, the war years saw for the first time the emergence of a large, grass-roots movement asserting the right of pensioners to a fair deal. 'Wherever you go now', commented one politician in August 1943, 'in every constituency you are met by the aged people and their organizations.'[93]

But while these years saw the first significant attempt of pensioners to exert political pressure, results were decidedly mixed. The Old Age and Widows' Pensions Act of 1940, it is true, reduced the pensionable age for insured women and the wives of male pensioners from sixty-five to sixty. This helped women who were no longer able to work past sixty; it also alleviated the distress of couples who, because the husband was older, had been forced to get by on one pension until the wife became eligible. But while these changes and the introduction of supplementary pensions in cases of proven need were a response to growing agitation in the constituencies, they were also a calculated response, designed to obviate larger concessions and a more costly across-the-board hike in pension rates. As for a spinster's pension at fifty-five, officials feared that any such concession would soon escalate pressures for an age reduction for all women. In fact, the situation in the war years was far from being congenial to a new deal for the elderly, notwithstanding the NFOAPA's claim that the fabulous sums spent on the war made nonsense of assertions that more generous treatment was financially impossible.[94]

Several factors limited the pensioners' impact. For one thing they lacked an articulate, forceful, and continuous parliamentary advocate for their campaign.

[93] A. Blaikie, 'The emerging political power of the elderly in Britain, 1908–48', *Aging and Society*, 10 (1990), 31.

[94] H. L. Smith, 'Gender and the welfare state: The 1940 Old Age and Widows' Pension Act', *History*, 80(260) (October 1995).

Many old people also remained unorganized and either felt impotent to change things or were not inclined at this time of national danger to assert priority for their sectional interests. The NFOAPA's abrasive campaigning style was itself a hindrance in some circles and its ability to put pressure on politicians was limited in a period when party competition was muted if not on hold. Above all, however, policy debate about old people was governed by a combination of financial stringency which cut across the political spectrum and, in proposals for post-war welfare reform, a strong ideological emphasis on the health and security of children and young, working parents. Not only was concern about the plight of the old shaped by anxiety that higher pensions and other social spending would constitute a dangerous drag on the post-war economy, but national preoccupation with rebuilding families, raising the birth rate, combating delinquency, and safeguarding poor children had the effect of marginalizing the needs of the elderly. In the prevailing rhetoric of 'social capital', they came up short.

Thus, while the Beveridge Report on social insurance was welcomed enthusiastically in November 1942 as providing 'cradle to grave security', it looked a good deal less lavish and revolutionary from the vantage point of those closer to the grave—'for all practical purposes...useless' was the way *The Pensioner* described it.[95] Apprehension about low birth rates and statistical predictions of a rapidly aging population, coupled with a determination to make the scheme seem economically feasible, were decisive in shaping the proposals. The thrust of the debate emphasized the burden that the elderly constituted for society and the right to a subsistence level pension, without a means test, was denied. The report recommended that pensions be universal (removing the stigma of being only for the poor), but it endorsed only modest increases and suggested that these be phased in over a twenty-year period. Wartime evidence of poverty among the elderly took a back seat to reducing the plan's costs and giving priority to children and active producers. In the event, the deferral of pension increases was deemed not only unreasonable but politically unacceptable and the post-war Labour government's National Assistance Act of 1946 included higher rates immediately, but at 25s a week for individuals and 42s for married couples it was well below what NFOAPA was demanding by that time (i.e. 30s and 60s). Post-war pensions were said to be at 'subsistence' level but the definition was always tight-fisted and within a few years inflation again brought a re-expansion of old people reliant upon means-tested supplementary benefit. Any possibility that pensions might redistribute wealth between classes in any significant way was contained. Surveys consistently showed that elderly working-class women were the largest group in poverty.

The other crucial feature of the Beveridge Report and the legislation that followed was a retirement qualification. After the war, for the first time, eligibility for a pension meant giving up work—something that advocates for the elderly

---

[95] Blaikie, 'The emerging political power of the elderly', p. 33; Beveridge wrote in his 1942 report on 'Social insurance and allied services': 'It is dangerous to be in any way lavish to old age until adequate provision has been assured for all other vital needs, such as the prevention of disease and the adequate nutrition of the young.' Thane, *Old Age in English History*, p. 8. There was a revolt of back-bench Labour MPs over pensions in July 1942 and when the Beveridge Report was published public criticism focused on its parsimony towards pensioners.

remained divided over. The TUC supported mandatory retirement before the war as a solution to the problem of excess labour; it argued that the withdrawal of older workers would reduce unemployment, accelerate promotions for younger workers, and prevent employers from using the pension as an excuse for depressing wage rates generally. These fears contradicted the concern of demographers and Beveridge himself that Britain was moving into a period of labour shortage, when workers should be given inducements to continue in their jobs. In the end, Beveridge largely yielded to trade union pressure so that, while higher pension incentives were offered for postponing retirement, they were too meagre to have much impact. Thus, the post-war years ushered in an age of mass retirement. The number of people working in their sixties declined sharply as the vast majority of men retired at sixty-five years and women at sixty—indeed these ages became a new definition of 'old'. Some scholars argue that requiring pensioners to quit work created a 'structured dependence' which further marginalized the elderly, representing them as an unproductive burden regardless of their capacity or desire to continue working. However, as Pat Thane has pointed out, much of the work hitherto undertaken by the elderly (and especially by women) to make ends meet was poorly paid and scarcely reinforced their sense of dignity and worth.[96] Moreover, industrial employers in the 1950s showed little interest in employing older workers, finding plenty of alternatives in the expanding female labour force, immigrants from overseas and, by the decade's end, the entrance of 'baby-boomers' into the job market.

NATION AND FAMILY

The circumstances of war injected a mood of crisis into public debate about the family and forged a broad consensus that this basic institution was in trouble. But war also reinforced older anxieties about Britain's falling birth rate and its potential consequences for the nation's power. Rhetoric about 'rebuilding families' always implied more than just personal relationships; it encompassed larger national fears about the British population's ability to sustain its economy and social services and its vast empire abroad.

Alarm about low fertility began in the late nineteenth century, shaped by the climate of international rivalry and the spread of racialist and Social Darwinist doctrines. Concern escalated rapidly with the enormous death toll of the First World War, while the decrease in the birth rate after 1918, reaching new lows in the early 1930s, produced a spate of warnings of Britain's inevitable decline. Pronatalist concerns encompassed both the overall size of the nation's population

[96] P. Townsend, 'The structured dependency of the elderly: A creation of social policy in the twentieth century', *Aging and Society*, 1 (1981); S. Harper and P. Thane, 'The consolidation of "old age" as a phase of life, 1945–65' and P. Johnson, 'The structured dependency of the elderly: A critical note' both in M. Jefferys (ed.), *Growing Old in the Twentieth Century* (London, 1989). In 1951 there were 6.8 million 'old people' in Britain (i.e. males over 65 years and women over 60 years) and they constituted 13.5% of the population. In 1953 over half of pensioners had no income except for their state pension.

and its 'quality' in terms of the health and intelligence of new birth cohorts, and class differentials in fertility—especially the higher rates of reproduction among the poor and 'less responsible' sections of society. Until the mid-1930s fear about 'under-population' had been largely confined to a small group of demographers, eugenicists, and intellectuals, but now it broke into the mass media and permeated a wide range of social-policy discussions. Improved statistical techniques and widespread intelligence testing made for more elaborate and seemingly more reliably scientific forecasts of future trends. Books such as *The Twilight of Parent-hood* (1934) by Dr Enid Charles, a social biologist at the London School of Economics, attracted widespread attention and references to demographic 'suicide' spread to radio and the national press, especially after an article in *The Times* on 'The dwindling family' generated a large correspondence in the autumn of 1936.[97]

Some contemporaries emphasized the dysgenic effects of smaller families among the wealthier, more educated sections of society and called for policy-makers to encourage them (through tax incentives, for example) to produce more children. A few conservative hardliners like clergyman and publicist Dean Inge still worried that social services were merely subsidizing 'the teeming birth rate of the slums' and some participants in wartime debate continued to stress mental deficiency and genetic inheritance as the cause of 'problem families'.[98] But already in the 1930s, even among members of the Eugenics Society, pronatalism became more and more aligned with a reformist social politics that emphasized the cost of inequality to the nation. Concern about population quality, physical efficiency, and 'the wastage of human assets' took an increasingly environmentalist position, focusing on the urgent need to improve housing, health care, and reduce the poverty in which so many children were being raised. Research also showed that the sharp drop in the birth rate stemmed especially from the smaller size of working-class families; class differences in fertility had diminished, giving way to convergence. If people were choosing to have smaller families, then constructive social engineering, at least in theory, could reverse the trend. With demographers arguing that Britain's population would soon move into sharp decline, the only feasible solution, it seemed, lay in persuading the working class—who represented three quarters of the nation—to have more children and to take better care of those it had.

This was the central message of Richard Titmuss's book, *Birth, Poverty, and Wealth* (1943) and press reviews translated his argument into provocative headlines: 'Poor folks babies stand less chance', 'The babies who need not die', 'Infant victims of capitalism'.[99] In *Picture Post*'s 'Plan for Britain' in January 1941, biologist Julian

---

[97] E. Charles, *The Twilight of Parenthood* (London, 1934); it was reissued as *The Menace of Underpopulation* (London, 1936). *The Times* (London), 28 and 29 September 1936 ('numbers will fall, perhaps catastrophically, in the next fifty years'); R. A. Soloway, *Birth Control and the Population Question in England, 1877–1930* (Chapel Hill, 1982); *idem, Demography and Degeneration* (Chapel Hill, 1990); A. Davin, 'Imperialism and motherhood', *HWJ*, 5 (Spring 1978).

[98] Soloway, *Demography and Degeneration*, p. 332; Inge resigned from the Eugenics Society in 1943 when he learned that Beveridge was to give the Galton Lecture.

[99] On Titmuss and the Eugenics Society: Ann Oakley, *Man and Wife* (London, 1996), p. 190 for the press response to Titmuss's wartime books. Also, Richard and Kay Titmuss, *Parents Revolt* (1942).

Huxley, like Titmuss a prominent figure in the Eugenics Society, insisted that the state must promote 'healthy family planning' and ease the burden of child-rearing for poor families. 'Unwanted children, worn-out mothers, over-large families due to mere ignorance', he wrote, 'are just as bad as too few children.'[100] Mass-Observation also 'lined up with those who do not want the English people to disappear', arguing that 'a social framework' had to be constructed 'where the family of 4–6 deliberately conceived and by intelligent citizens with modern out-looks and modern interests makes some sort of sense'.[101] In this way the population problem infiltrated a wide array of debates, including those about family allow-ances, nursery provision, the Beveridge Report, and the need to provide mother-craft instruction to young women whose normal home life had been disrupted by service in uniform or war factories; it became integral to progressive politics. Already in the 1930s Gunnar Myrdal and Swedish socialists had achieved political success with a strategy that joined pronatalism and progressive family legislation; the war years increased their model's appeal not only in Britain but among social democratic parties across Europe—not least because it enabled socialists to show their patriotic credentials and concern for the nation as a whole rather than simply the sectional interests of labour.[102] As pressure for action built up, the government issued a White Paper on 'The Current Trend in Population' and followed this up by appointing a Royal Commission in 1944, although by the time its report appeared in 1949 public anxiety had largely abated.[103] Ironically, just as pressure for action peaked, the birth rate began to rise significantly—in 1944 there were 20 per cent more births than the annual average for 1935–8.

This chapter has examined the preoccupation of 'elite' groups—doctors, psy-chologists, officials, and social policy groups—with the war's impact on the family and the nation's low birth rate. Certainly, there was no escaping the barrage of radio and press commentary, but workers' voices were seldom heard and these issues seem to have had little resonance with working-class men and women. The separation of families and the hardships of war had produced a hunger for home life and some semblance of normality. But family size was regarded as a personal choice not a national issue. Young working-class couples viewed children as central to a marriage, but they wanted two, or at most three, and not the four being called for by pronatalists. The older generation might be fatalistic about such things—'Just leave

[100] *Picture Post*, 4 January 1941.

[101] M-O, *Britain and her Birth Rate* (London, 1945), pp. 7, 227.

[102] J. M. Winter, 'Socialism, social democracy and population questions in Western Europe, 1870–1950' in M. S. Teitelbaum and J. M. Winter (eds.), *Population and Resources in Western Intellectual Traditions* (Cambridge, 1989); M. S. Quine, *Population Politics in Twentieth Century Europe* (London, 1995).

[103] Most of the Commission's recommendations were quietly shelved. *Report of the Royal Commission on Population*, Cmd 7695 (London, 1949); P. Thane, 'Population politics in post-war British culture' in B. Conekin, F. Mort, and C. Waters (eds.), *Moments of Modernity: Reconstructing Britain 1945–64* (London, 1999); J. M. Winter, 'Population, economists and the state: The Royal Commission on population' in B. Supple and M. Furnall (eds.), *Economic Knowledge and the State* (New York, 1990). See also the analyses of the Commission's Report in *Eugenics Review*, 41(3) (October 1949).

it to chance. 'Ow can you decide?'—but young people favoured reproductive planning and fewer children.[104] Young women especially pointed to the poverty, endless work, and lack of freedom of their mothers. 'My mother's had a big family, and it hasn't given her much of a chance.' 'You can't keep 'em right, not on what the railway pays; and I seen enough of ma's life not to want to do the same.'[105] For many having a small family went with their aspirations for a better life, social mobility, and being modern, while numerous offspring were often seen as proof of irresponsibility, lack of control, a sign of being lower class, and not quite respectable.[106] Having had few opportunities themselves, they wanted more for their children: 'I'd like to give my children a good education and a happier time than I had and if you've got four or five you can't do it.'[107] Suggestions that family allowances might induce larger families brought angry responses. A young London wife declared that '*she* wasn't going to have a baby for five bob a week' and 'I'd like to see *them* keep a baby on five shillings.' Equally adamant was a married woman with two children who wrote to Dr Hill, the popular radio doctor: 'Shall I tell you what an ordinary man's wage is in the mills; just over three pounds and you expect us to have big families. No, I'm finished and I won't be paid to have children . . . Come to Huddersfield and learn how the women have to go out to work—slavery. Let the better class have them; they might spoil their figures. I've no intention of having any more for no government.'[108]

The anger towards *them* is a reminder of the fact that the 'family crisis' in the war years was invariably construed as a crisis of poorer and working-class families. Worries about divorce, delinquency, and sexual licence focused upon them; similarly, concern about infant health and child development centred on working-class mothers, as it had in the interwar decades. There was, however, a noteworthy change in language during the war years. The angry, accusatory tone so loud at the time of the first evacuation receded—although it never disappeared altogether— and was replaced by a language that emphasized equal citizenship and social justice and focused more heavily upon past inequities and the warping effects of class division. Discourse about family was still heavily inflected by class, but framed in a narrative of how the class divisions might be reduced. It was also a language that presumed a large and ongoing role for the state. War had eroded the separation between the private sphere of the family and the public realm of policy; it deepened the realization that human life is social capital: birth, nurturing, employment, even

---

[104] M-O, *Britain and her Birth Rate*, p. 59. Other helpful sources for working-class attitudes: Gorer, *Exploring English Character*; the surveys of BIPO; P. Jephcott, *Girls Growing Up* (London, 1942); idem, *Rising Twenty* (London, 1953); E. Slater and M. Woodside, *Patterns of Marriage: A study of marriage relationships in the urban working classes* (London, 1951). On birth control: Kate Fisher, *Birth Control, Sex and Marriage in Britain, 1918–1960* (Oxford, 2006).

[105] M-O, *Britain and her Birth Rate*, p. 166.

[106] S. Brooke, 'Bodies, sexuality and the "modernization" of the British working classes 1920s– 1960s', *ILWCH*, 69 (Spring 2006).

[107] M-O, *Britain and her Birth Rate*, pp. 124–5. Also, Slater and Woodside, *Patterns of Marriage*, p. 70.

[108] Slater and Woodside, *Patterns of Marriage*, pp. 189–90; M-OA: FR 2111, 'Population problems' (June 1944); the broadcasts were given in March 1943 and January 1944.

death became subject to closer regulation. Older attitudes distinguishing the respectable working class from those who relied on the state for help had already begun to change during the depression years. The posters and propaganda of wartime, war jobs, and service in the forces; rationing; and a whole host of government allowances all strengthened the everyday links between workers and state, eroding older suspicion of state policies and authority. In its place developed a sense of rights and entitlement—the context for growing sentiment in favour of a guaranteed national minimum standard of living and universal benefits by right as envisioned by Beveridge.[109] This was evident in numerous areas: for example, the wartime readiness of the elderly to seek supplemental assistance from Public Assistance, which surprised officials; the numbers of young mothers who went to maternity and infant welfare centres and recognized their right to expanded welfare services; and the avalanche of demand for medical services once the National Health Service was introduced in 1948.

The conditions of war, wrote Jean Heywood in an early account of the post-war children's services, 'rediscovered for the nation the value of the family'.[110] Certainly, by the late 1940s the British people seemed preoccupied with family and children to an unprecedented degree. A similar revival of family life occurred in other European countries, although the specific form of post-war familial ideology differed from place to place. Everywhere in Attlee's Britain the faces of smiling, responsible parents and healthy, carefree children gazed out from advertising billboards and National Health Service posters, symbolic of the nation's 'social capital' and a better future. Widespread concern about low birth rates helped to strengthen domestic and mothering images of women; popular magazines and radio espoused the ideas of rapidly growing numbers of childcare professionals; and government social policy redefined the reciprocal obligations of parents and the state, reflecting a new 'social democratic' conception of family as the basic unit of the nation and the chief incubator of citizenship and community values. Not that everything was splendid. Public anxiety about juvenile delinquency remained high. But claims that the war had disintegrated family, undermined moral values, or created a 'marital crisis' lost their power as the nation settled into the years of the 'baby boom'. Looking back, especially from the vantage point of the late 1960s and beyond, the 1940s and 1950s took on the aura of a golden age when family bonds enabled people to survive the war, when long-lasting marriage was the norm, divorce rates were low, and single parents were rare exceptions. Scholars are acutely aware of silences about many aspects of European experience in wartime. In Britain moral panic about the family was an example; by the 1950s it had disappeared down one of society's memory holes.

[109] P. M. Graves, 'A blessing or a curse? Working-class attitudes to state welfare programmes in Britain 1919–1939', *Labour History Review*, 74(2) (August 2009); J. Harris, 'Did British workers want the welfare state?' in J. Winter (ed.), *The Working Class in Modern British History* (Cambridge, 1983).
[110] J. Heywood, *Children in Care: The development of the service for the deprived child* (London, 1965), p. 133. Also, May Ravden, 'The importance of the family', *Sociological Review*, 34 (1942).

6

Leisure, Culture, and Class

The 'People's War' typically conjures up two seemingly contradictory sets of images. One foregrounds patriotic sacrifice, marathon working hours, destroyed neighbourhoods, separated families, and women tired out from endless queuing and making-do. The second group, equally strong, emphasizes youthful pleasure, wartime entertainment, and collective leisure activities. Indeed, many vivid individual memories of those years are not of work but of play: packed dance halls, shows in factory canteens, cinemas, and pubs, accompanied by a soundtrack of wartime comedy and popular songs. In part, of course, this is because the recent flood of memoirs and oral histories comes overwhelmingly from those who were young at the time and reminisce from the vantage point of their seventies and eighties. But the centrality of leisure and entertainment in wartime iconography also derives from a concerted official effort to raise morale and project community across classes. Imagery of Britain at play, sharing the same jokes, enjoying the same cultural heritage was vital to the whole project of publicizing the nation as more inclusive, democratic, and egalitarian than ever before.

This chapter examines wartime leisure from two perspectives. First it explores how workers spent their often very limited leisure time. Secondly, it focuses upon growing state involvement in organizing programmes for workers and public debate *about* popular leisure. In this sphere, as in so many, the boundaries of public and private life were significantly redrawn: the more the state became engaged in the provision of leisure activities, the more their quality, content, and purpose were debated. Class was integral to these discourses about the forms of mass enjoyment, the connections between recreation and active citizenship, and whether or not a shared 'national culture' existed.

TAKING TIME OFF FROM THE WAR

Age and Gender Differences

The leisure time of the working classes varied considerably depending, for example, on where they lived, their occupation and working hours, whether they were engaged in voluntary activities, individual preferences, and familial responsibilities. But broadly speaking the two most important determinants of how people spent their time were age and gender.

Whether they were evacuees or not, the lives of school-aged children changed enormously in the war years. Evacuated children had to adapt to foster parents, new schools and playmates, and in many cases a suburban or country environment very different from where they came. Those who remained in the cities played in neighbourhoods that were transformed by bomb damage and the departure of neighbours and they often spent long hours in family or public air-raid shelters. The blackout, downed power lines, broken glass and metal, and fire-service water tanks were all potential hazards. There were new games—aircraft spotting and shrapnel collecting, for example—but what changed most was less children's activities than the fact that many had far less supervision because of the absence of parents, either at work or conscripted, and because schools were closed for long periods or operated on reduced schedules. Children lost a lot of school time and truancy remained high even after some semblance of normal schedules returned; tests showed a significant drop in reading and writing skills and while in rural counties harvest camps and the employment of child labour on farms may have offered valuable experiences to some boys and girls, school officials worried that they contributed to lower educational attainment. Shopping, or rather queuing up for food and other necessities, also figured large in the lives of many children of both sexes and regularly absorbed a portion of their 'free' time throughout the 'rationing years'. Teenage girls especially often had to fill in for a mother recruited into munitions, doing housework and minding younger siblings.

The anxiety of government officials and social-service organizations about the war's disruption of children's lives soon crystallized into something of a 'moral panic' about juvenile delinquency. This surfaced when evacuees from the slums were accused of causing crime waves in some reception areas, while in blitzed cities attention focused on children, especially adolescents, who were said to be 'running wild' in air-raid shelters, vandalizing property, and taking advantage of unguarded homes to loot and steal. Sexual promiscuity and drunkenness among adolescent girls also became a growing preoccupation; the number appearing in court described as 'beyond parental control' and 'in need of care and protection' rose sharply while waiting lists lengthened for vacancies in Approved Schools.[1] Aside from more policing and exhortations to church groups and parents to intervene, the remedy most often recommended was the expansion of youth programmes and clubs. Most had closed down at the start of the war, as buildings were requisitioned and many youth leaders were called up for military service or took up war work. By late 1940 it was estimated that the majority of young people aged fourteen–eighteen years had no contact with any organized youth group.[2] Now there was a rush to restart programmes. The chief target group was working-class youths of fourteen–eighteen

[1] S. M. Ferguson and H. Fitzgerald, *Studies in the Social Services* (London, 1954), p. 98.
[2] P. H. J. H. Gosden, *Education in the Second World War* (London, 1976), ch. 10; 'Challenge of youth', Board of Education Circular 1516 (June 1940); P. Tinkler, 'Sexuality and citizenship: The state and girls' leisure provision in England, 1939–45', *Women's History Review*, 4(2) (1995); *idem*, 'Cause for concern: Young women and leisure, 1930–1950', *Women's History Review*, 12(2) (2003); D. Smith, 'Official responses to juvenile delinquency in Scotland during the Second World War', *TCBH*, 18(1) (2007), pp. 99–103.

years, especially those who had recently left school; the same age cohort in the middle class was more likely to be under school supervision and was viewed as far less 'at risk'.

In fact, as early as October 1939, the Board of Education began to lay the groundwork for a national youth service, establishing a National Youth Committee and urging local educational authorities to survey leisure facilities in their areas, open clubs, make contact with factory welfare officers and organize special 'youth weeks'. As outlined by the Board's circular, 'The challenge of youth', the plan had three objectives. First, it saw youth clubs as a way of bolstering the working-class family and compensating for its cultural deficiencies. They could counteract the influence of commercial dance halls and cinema and help complete the socialization of youths who left school at fourteen. Secondly, at a time when young people were spending long hours in cramped shelters and factories, clubs were a way of encouraging physical fitness and personal hygiene. And, finally, supervised recreational activities were viewed as a solution for rising levels of delinquency and a way of monitoring the sexual contacts of young girls.[3] The Board of Education envisioned 'Service of Youth', as it was soon called, as a permanent way of maintaining contact with school leavers and teaching them the responsibilities of citizenship—which in the case of girls, as Penny Tinkler points out, meant an emphasis on domestic skills. As a result, a wide array of clubs and recreational facilities were created by local governments and voluntary organizations, while in some areas groups of young people who were too young to enter the forces volunteered to form local squads to help with civil defence and evacuation. Churchill, who believed that too many young men lacked discipline, floated the idea of some form of compulsory cadet training or required community service for boys between leaving school and being called up. But the response of most officials was tepid, believing that it savoured too much of fascist youth movements. In the end it was decided that all youths (boys and girls) between sixteen and eighteen years should register and then be called for interviews before local youth committees. Large numbers registered but when it became clear that the interviews were purely voluntary the participation rate declined sharply. In addition, while pre-military training organizations (like the sea or army cadets) existed for boys, there were few equivalents for girls and the War Office had no interest in preparing recruits for the women's auxiliaries. Overall these official schemes seem to have achieved little success for at least half of young men and 75 per cent of young women continued to be classified as 'unattached' to an organized, approved form of youth activity.

One thing that the interviews of local youth committees quickly ascertained was how little free time many young people had. The majority of those over fourteen years were working fifty hours a week in war industries and often had long

---

[3] There was heated debate over whether clubs should be sites for sex education. Catholic Bishop Marshall of Salford described the British Social Hygiene Council's plans for a lecture on venereal disease in Blackburn as 'positively injurious to the moral welfare of our youth': Bishop Marshall to Fr. Leycester King (Cardinal Hinsley's representative on the British Social Hygiene Council), 24 September, 11 October 1940, Bishop Marshall Papers, Salford Diocese (Burnley).

commutes in addition.[4] What spare time they had, especially since many were earning good money, they preferred to spend on commercial entertainments in pubs, dance halls, and the cinema. For young male workers this meant little change from pre-war—except that jobs were now easier to get and better paid. By contrast, young working women—especially those living in lodgings or hostels away from home—found that wartime gave them greater freedom and independence and a lot more money so that they could smoke, drink, and go out more often than before.[5] They met new friends, including a wider choice of potential marriage partners, travelled more widely and socialized often in work-centred groups, going to pubs, dance halls and skating rinks. Many nostalgically recalled these years as a time of freedom, concentrated work and play, and mutual support: 'like a big happy family', 'we had a wonderful social life, we were out every night', or 'if we were on nights we used to go to the Ritz in the afternoon, we were knackered by the time we went to work'.[6]

Indoor pastimes such as cards, darts, billiards, and table tennis grew more popular, being well-suited to life in hostels and barracks. But the three most popular activities were dancing, going to the cinema, and drinking in pubs. Dancing was the favourite night out: a chance to dress up, a way to meet the opposite sex, and an escape from routine, fatiguing jobs. 'Everybody danced', remembered one young munitions worker who, even when she was on nights, got up in the middle of the day to dance every other afternoon.[7] Hostels and war factories organized regular dances; so did churches and town halls, but young people in large cities often preferred big commercial halls like the Hammersmith Palais in London or the Ritz and the Plaza in Manchester. Again the wartime 'dance craze' elicited very mixed responses— applauded as a sign of the nation's resilience under stress but also a source of public angst for allegedly contributing to greater sexual promiscuity.[8] Communal dances were especially popular: conga-lines, boomps-a-daisy, the hokey-cokey, and so on, while from 1942 the growing presence of GIs brought excitement, swing music, and jitterbugging to many areas. The Americans, a woman supervisor of a munitions hostel at Reading recalled, 'created endless distractions: dances galore, transport galore, and PX galore'.[9] But sometimes bored, hard-drinking GIs turned violent:

---

[4] A June 1944 Home Office inquiry revealed that 15% of all boys 12–14 years in England and Wales were regularly employed on some work during the day. The figures varied greatly by region— some being as high as 40%; R. M. Titmuss, *Problems of Social Policy* (London, 1950), p. 418. Also, S. Cunningham, 'Reform or recalcitrance? The Home Office and the regulation of child labour, 1939–1951', *Historical Studies in Industrial Relations*, 13 (Spring 2002).

[5] S. Bruley, '"A very happy crowd": Women in industry in south London in World War II', *HWJ*, 44 (Autumn 1997).

[6] *Ibid.*, p. 70; P. Goodman, '"Patriotic Femininity": Women's morals and men's morale during the Second World War', *Gender and History* 10(2) (August 1998), p. 286. Also P. Grafton, *You, You, and You* (London, 1981), pp. 80–1.

[7] C. Langhamer, *Women's Leisure in England 1920–60* (Manchester, 2000), p. 66.

[8] R. McKibbin, *Classes and Cultures: England 1918–51* (Oxford, 1998), ch. 10; see also Christina Baade, '"The dancing front": Dance music, dancing, and the BBC in World War II', *Popular Music*, 25(3) (2006).

[9] IWM: N. Connor MSS 87/14/1. PX refers to Post Exchange, which supplied US bases with goods such as sweets, cigarettes, nylons, etc.

'Things are getting pretty bad in Bedford', one woman wrote. 'The Yankees are molesting and beating up no end of girls . . . I had rather a tussle with one in the High Street the other night.' Another woman in Suffolk, after being dragged to the ground wrote 'My hands, face and legs are all cuts . . . it's my last trip out at night without a male escort, my nerves are gone absolutely.'[10]

The increased presence of women in pubs also gave rise to growing public debate. In the 1930s, female pub-goers were mostly older and married, but 'the war', Mass-Observation reported in June 1943, 'has made revolutionary changes in both the age and sex distribution of public house drinkers'. Young women, especially those separated from their homes and established social networks, found pubs a good place for socializing—here they could joke and talk, meet men, and in the case of lonely newcomers become integrated into a group and a neighbourhood. Of those questioned for a survey in one London borough 45 per cent of women under thirty years old said they were going more often to pubs since war began and only 7 per cent said they went less than before.[11] But regional differences remained: in Wales and parts of the north the stigma attached to females in pubs persisted and evacuated mothers who appeared in a public bar, especially in trousers, were likely to arouse the fury of locals, whereas in the London region pubs were rapidly becoming a 'recognized way of enjoying your free time'.[12] As Selina Todd has shown, a more independent cohort of young working-class women was already emerging in many cities in the 1930s, but in Nonconformist Wales the attitudes and behaviour of munitions workers represented a stronger threat to social and moral conventions.[13] Those most likely to deplore women in pubs were older men, the clergy, and middle-class moralists; but much of the population took the changes in their stride. While drunkenness was deplored, many felt that young people had earned the right to a drink; 'there seems', Pearl Jephcott observed, 'to be a feeling that if women are sharing paid work with men they are entitled to share their pleasures too'.[14] 'All this old-fashioned prudery', a thirty-year-old woman commented, 'it's disgusting. Women are doing just as much in this war as men.' Even in mining areas, as workers' institutes began to function more as centres for voluntary activities, so more women joined their men at the bar.[15]

---

[10] NA: FO 371/34123, Extracts from Army Mail Censorship Reports, 11–31 December 1942 (Bedfordshire), 11–25 April 1943 (Suffolk).

[11] M-OA: FR 1873 (June 1943), 1635 (March 1943); Langhamer, *Women's Leisure in England 1920–1960*, p. 72. Also, M. Jolly (ed.), *Dear Laughing Motorbyke: Letters from women welders of the Second World War* (London, 1997). For Mass-Observation's pre-war research: *The Pub and People* (London, 1943; repr. 1987).

[12] N. Baring, *A Friendly Hearth* (London, 1946); Quotation from P. Jephcott, *Rising Twenty: Notes on some ordinary girls* (London, 1948), p. 146.

[13] S. Todd, *Young Women, Work and Family in England 1918–1950* (Oxford, 2005); M. A. Williams, *A Forgotten Army: Female munitions workers of South Wales 1939–1945* (Cardiff, 2002), pp. 171–6.

[14] Jephcott, *Rising Twenty*, p. 147. Also C. Langhamer, '"A public house is for all classes, men and women alike": Women, leisure and drink in Second World War England', *Women's History Review*, 12(3) (2003).

[15] By 1944, Colin Griffin estimates, over a third of miners' institutes either had women members or made provision for joint activities with groups like the Women's Institutes and the WVS, while a

Another sign, perhaps, of the war's impact on women's self-perceptions was a dramatic rise in smoking. Both sexes smoked more, but the big increase was among young women in factories and the forces. Smoking became more than ever a rite of passage, part of being grown up and moving into new public spaces. Cigarette advertising—abundant in the wartime press—portrayed a smoke as the perfect accompaniment for factory breaks, off-duty periods in canteens and barracks, and also an antidote to boredom, depression, and anxiety. It took your mind off things, was something to do in shelters or shopping queues, a social ice-breaker and part of the encouraged sociability of the time. It was also a 'democratic' habit that all social strata shared; indeed, by the war's end 80 per cent of men and 40 per cent of women over sixteen years of age smoked regularly and roughly 11 per cent of average household expenditure went on tobacco. The result was evident decades later in much higher lung cancer figures for the wartime generation, especially women.[16]

The leisure time of older women probably changed least, although some who entered munitions factories had more money to enjoy themselves and gained new friends. For many, however, war work was exhausting, especially when combined with housework, child-raising, and standing in shop queues. As numerous surveys indicate, working-class mothers had little time to themselves or their 'free time' was at best fragmented—odd moments when they were not busy with something or someone's needs. Their responses suggest that they made little distinction between chores and leisure—sewing, mending, knitting, and baking being quite common answers to what they did in their spare time. Listening to the BBC while darning, reading a library book over their tea, or writing letters to evacuated children and husbands in the forces was about all the break they got. And while writing letters consumed far more of everyone's time during the war—telephones being fairly rare and expensive—wives and mothers probably wrote the lion's share, often acting as the connecting link between dispersed family members. Exhorted as a patriotic duty to write frequently to menfolk in the forces, they engaged in what Jenny Hartley has dubbed a process of 'long-distance mothering'—no easy task for women who had left school at fourteen and often had difficulty putting their thoughts and emotions down on paper.[17]

The leisure preferences of older men also remained much the same, except that most worked far longer hours than in peacetime and many were busy with fire-watching and Home Guard duties. Working-men's clubs and pubs flourished with

quarter had established women's clubs or 'ladies' affiliates: 'Not just a case of baths, canteens and rehabilitation centres: The Second World War and the recreational provision of the Miners' Welfare Commission in coalmining communities' in N. Hayes and J. Hill (eds.), *'Millions Like Us'? British culture in the Second World War* (Liverpool, 1999), p. 267.

[16] M. Hilton, *Smoking and British Popular Culture* (Manchester, 2000); P. Tinkler, '"Red tips for red hot lips": Advertising cigarettes for young women in Britain, 1920–1970', *Women's History Review*, 10(2) (2001). National expenditure on smoking rose from £177 million in 1938 to £690 million in 1947.

[17] J. Hartley, '"Letters are *everything* these days": Mothers and letters in the Second World War' in R. Earle (ed.), *Epistolary Selves: Letters and letter writers 1600–1945* (Ashgate, Brookfield, 1999). In general on women's leisure pastimes: Langhamer, *Women's Leisure in England*. Also, M. Spring Rice, *Working-Class Wives* (London, 1939; repr. 1981).

the higher wage packets of wartime as did traditional pastimes like choral groups and brass bands. Certain hobbies like vegetable gardening or raising chickens and rabbits became more popular as a way of supplementing family rations.[18] But the big change for older men, at least at first, was the closure of sports grounds and race tracks and their conversion to war-related uses. Within a short time the government lifted the ban, allowing racing, cricket, rugby, and football to resume on a reduced scale. But audiences declined sharply. Many players and coaches were conscripted into the forces and football teams were reduced to playing mixed professional and amateur matches.[19] Amateur sports flourished with large numbers of competitions organized by war factories and the armed forces, but by 1945 the nation was hungry for traditional spectator sports which attracted huge attendance in the early post-war years.[20]

Another casualty of the war was the family vacation. By 1939 a brief holiday away from home at Blackpool or the resorts of the Kent coast was within the reach of many industrial workers.[21] But in wartime, with the threat of invasion, many coastal areas were restricted or cordoned off by barbed wire and boarding houses, hotels, and holiday camps were often requisitioned for war personnel. To conserve transport for war purposes government publicity campaigns also sought to dissuade people from 'unnecessary travel'. But it was also clear that some form of organized substitute was necessary to fill the gap and improve morale. As a result, in the summer of 1941 the government launched 'Holidays at Home', encouraging local councils and voluntary groups to plan an array of summer activities that workers could enjoy close to home. What was offered at first was fairly meagre, but the programme grew with some municipalities arranging an impressive array of concerts, sports meets, dances, open-air theatres, beauty contests, dog shows, and children's games and pageants. The LCC Parks Department was the most ambitious, estimating that in 1942 over 1.25 million had attended its events, including some 500 concerts and 100 open-air dances.[22] In addition, miners' welfare institutions and many of the larger, more paternalist industrial firms sponsored weeks of

---

[18] For wartime rabbit-raising in fiction, see Monica Dickens' novel about munitions workers, *The Fancy* (London, 1943).

[19] N. Fishwick, *English Football and Society 1910–1950* (Manchester, 1989); A. Rippon, *Gas Masks for Goal Posts: Football in Britain during the Second World War* (Stroud, Gloucs., 2007); Tony McCarthy, *War Games: The story of sport in World War II* (London, 1989); P. Lanfranchi and M. Taylor, 'Professional football in World War II Britain' in P. Kirkham and D. Thoms (eds.), *War and Culture: Social change and changing experience in World War Two* (London, 1995); N. Baker, 'A more even playing field? Sport during and after the war' in Hayes and Hill (eds.), *'Millions Like Us'?*

[20] Tom Finney, *Football around the World* (London, 1953); D. Birley, *Playing the Game: Sport and British society 1910–45* (Manchester, 1995). Cricketers Len Hutton and Dennis Compton became physical training instructors in the forces, so did footballers Stanley Mathews, Joe Mercer, and Matt Busby.

[21] J. A. R. Pimlott, *The Englishman's Holiday: A social history* (London, 1947); S. Barton, *Working-Class Organisations and Popular Tourism 1840–1970* (Manchester, 2005). No more than 4 million workers took some form of paid holiday in 1937, but by November 1938 it had risen to about 9 million (4.4 million of them under collective agreements). By 1945 some 14 million workers enjoyed paid holidays under collective agreements.

[22] C. Sladen, 'Holidays at home in the Second World War', *Journal of Contemporary History*, 37(1) (January 2002).

special entertainments, sporting competitions, musical evenings, and circus displays. However, as Chris Sladen has shown, such programmes—well-attended though they were—constituted a poor substitute for a real holiday and for mothers, far from providing a break from household chores, they often involved more work preparing picnics and cooking extra meals. Higher wages and growing fatigue meant that in the second half of the war more and more families decided that they were entitled to a proper week's holiday given the pace of work in the other fifty-one. An increasing number simply ignored official injunction, braving crowded trains and buses to get to Blackpool and other resorts. A *Picture Post* photo spread in August 1943 showed crowds of holiday-makers enjoying the beaches and dance halls of Blackpool. As Sladen points out, while memoirs and oral histories frequently repeat the myth that war-workers never got holidays, ticket sales and railway company evidence contradict such claims.[23]

Finally, although studies of the war typically stress middle-class voluntarism, it is also important to remember that a great many working-class men and women devoted their 'spare' time to community and voluntary activities—often through church or chapel groups, Mothers' Unions, or Workers' Clubs. The diary of Kathleen Tipper, a young secretary in a London shipping firm, offers one example. She tried more than once to join the WRNS but was not accepted. After her regular work she volunteered both at a local YMCA canteen and the New Zealand Forces Club in Charing Cross Road. Kathleen and her sister took their turn fire-watching and, after their mother's death, looked after their father and brother. Patriotic, Christian, and a little prim, she was often critical of other women, especially if they drank very much or seemed intent on 'picking up' soldiers. When not volunteering she read widely, went to concerts, and relied heavily on radio for entertainment, especially the drama put on by BBC Playhouse. A doer and a joiner, hers was a very busy existence, informed by a strong sense of duty, and she continued her voluntary work until late 1946.[24]

Reading

'I think there never was a time when there was so much obvious hunger for books, and so few books to satisfy it.' Like many contemporaries this bookseller was convinced that war had increased the amount of reading that people did and this is probably true for most working-class families, although impossible to quantify. To some degree it continued a trend already underway before the war when far more papers, books, and magazines began to enter working-class homes. Wartime conditions were especially conducive to reading. People found themselves with more hours to wile away—travelling on slow trains, sheltering from raids, or confined to homes by the blackout. Those in the armed forces and war jobs living away from their families often turned to reading as a way to pass off-duty evenings

[23] C. Sladen, 'Wartime holidays and the "myth of the Blitz"', *Cultural and Social History*, 2 (2005).
[24] Patricia and Robert Malcolmson (eds.), *A Woman in Wartime London: The diary of Kathleen Tipper 1941–1945* (London Record Society, 2006).

in barracks, hostels, or lodgings; so did civil-defence workers waiting for action and unable to leave their posts. And for spouses and parents, missing their loved ones, a good book was a welcome distraction. 'My two sons are away', commented a middle-aged mother, 'and I read a lot to stop me worrying and thinking about them.' 'I read more now than I ever did', wrote a young typist in her mid-twenties. 'My boy's away in the Middle East and I don't go out much, I expect that's the reason.'[25] Mass-Observation's surveys of booksellers and librarians seemed to confirm the trend. One reported: 'The factory workers are all going mad on buying books, and there's the ARP and demolition squads quite near, and they buy books too.' 'The most unlikely people buy books now', another noted, 'we've extended sales tremendously among the working classes.' 'It's partly the blackout', a librarian explained, 'and the fact that they have to make their own amusements. But it's a direct result of the war too. People's curiosity has been awakened—they want to find out a few facts for themselves—they want to understand the world better, and so they've started to read.'[26]

What kind of books were most popular? As Jonathan Rose makes clear, a sizeable minority of workers who were avid readers had always existed. This self-improving group, seeking access to a book culture that formal schooling had failed to extend to them, read what might be called 'serious' fiction or non-fiction, often in Everyman or Penguin editions that could easily be slipped into a pocket or haversack. Their tastes, Rose has argued, were usually conservative and conventional; few read the 'moderns' and they were more likely to choose Dickens or Hardy than Woolf, Forster, or Lawrence.[27] For the vast majority of readers, however, the most popular genres were crime thrillers, westerns, detectives, and light romance. Mills and Boon's immensely popular romances occupied the spare time of many women and readers generally favoured escapist fiction with war stories, like war films, losing favour as the conflict continued. As the young typist quoted above put it, she liked family stories with happy endings: 'there is enough tragedy in real life' and 'that's one of the reasons I *never* read a war book'.[28] Others enjoyed a bit of spice. 'Barracks, billets, and lodgings', Steve Chibnall suggests, 'meant that "illicit" materials did not have to be hidden from parents or partners.'[29] James Hadley Chase's *No Orchids for Miss Blandish*, a grizzly concoction of sex and violence, sold half a million copies. In the non-fiction category working-class readers chose books

---

[25] M-O survey, cited by J. McAleer, *Popular Reading and Publishing in Britain 1914–1950* (Oxford, 1992), pp. 73–8, 95, 96. M-OA 'Reading' Box 8 File F (October 1943).

[26] M-OA: FR 2018, 'Books and the people' (1944); J. Rose, *The Intellectual Life of the British Working Class* (New Haven, 2001), pp. 233–4. Also D. C. Russell, 'Promotion of public libraries in the Second World War', *Library History*, 15 (May 1999); M-OA: FR 1332, 'Report on books and the public' (1942).

[27] Rose, *The Intellectual Life of the British Working Class*. Also J. Cary, *The Intellectual and the Masses: Pride and prejudice among the literary intelligentsia 1880–1939* (London, 1992).

[28] Cited by McAleer, *Popular Reading and Publishing*, p. 95.

[29] S. Chibnall, 'Pulp versus Penguins: Paperbacks go to war' in P. Kirkham and D. Thoms (eds.), *War and Culture: Social change and changing experience in World War Two* (London, 1995), pp. 141–2. Also George Orwell's essay 'Raffles and Miss Blandish', *Horizon*, October 1944. Also, N. Joicey, 'A paperback guide to progress: Penguin Books *c*.1935–*c*.1951', *TCBH*, 4(1) (1993).

on practical topics like cooking and clothes-making while others began buying Allen Lane's series of Penguin Specials.

Even more than book sales, newspaper circulations rose dramatically. And whereas men and women chose different books and magazines, they read the same newspapers. During the war years for the first time large numbers of workers read national daily papers regularly (as opposed to taking only a Sunday paper). Between 1937 and 1947 sales of the national dailies rose from about 10 million to 15.5 million copies a day.[30] Some of this was at the expense of the local and provincial press, but much of the increase came from new readers. One of the most successful papers in attracting new readers was the *Daily Mirror*, whose meteoric rise and influence on wartime opinion has been closely studied by scholars. The *Mirror*'s tabloid format, snappy prose, bold headlines, and mixture of sport, escapism, and personal stories seemed perfect for canteen breaks and other odd moments. Its petulant, debunking style was best personified by 'Cassandra' (William Connor) whose salvoes were aimed in all directions: against 'fools in high places', bureaucratic red tape, middle-class aesthetes, grasping employers, and slack workers. Above all he railed at 'Blimpery' whether among army 'brass hats' or more generally among politicians, churchmen, administrators, and employers. By the end of the war the *Mirror* developed an astonishing rapport with its readers by perfecting what has been termed a kind of 'ventriloquism'. Addressing readers in their own sceptical, blunt language and giving them the satisfaction of hearing figures of authority confronted in the same idiom, the paper had the feel of democracy and straight-talk. By devoting extensive space to readers' letters and opinions, it became the closest approximation in print to workers' humour and forms of expression. By the end of 1941 it was read by about a quarter of all adults and a third of the armed forces. Labour's *Daily Herald*, despite only minor concessions to tabloid techniques and a dryer, didactic tone, also had a good war, improving its daily circulation from 1.6 to 2 million. Compared to the *Mirror*, it appealed more to older, skilled male workers especially in the Labour heartlands of the industrial north. *Mirror* readers were younger, included far more women, and were more heavily concentrated in the south and the Midlands. What drew younger readers was entertainment, style, and sport more than hard news or political coverage. But that did not prevent the *Mirror* from advancing a reformist political agenda and becoming very influential in the election of 1945 since it spoke to new voters and had developed a loyal following among workers and lower middle-class readers.[31]

Magazines also enjoyed increasing popularity; indeed, a 1947 Hulton survey estimated that over 68 per cent of working-class men and 62 per cent of working-class women read a weekly magazine.[32] Despite paper shortages and print restrictions,

---

[30] P. Kimble, *Newspaper Reading in the Third Year of the War* (London, 1942).

[31] A. C. H. Smith, E. Immirzi, and T. Blackwell, *Paper Voices: The popular press and social change 1935–65* (New Jersey, 1975); M. Bromley, 'Was it the *Mirror* wot won it? The development of the tabloid press during the Second World War' in Hayes and Hill (eds.), *'Millions Like Us'?*; H. Richards, *The Bloody Circus: The Daily Herald and the left* (London, 1997); M. Pugh, 'The *Daily Mirror* and the revival of Labour 1935–45', *TCBH*, 9(3) (1998).

[32] McAleer, *Popular Reading and Publishing*, p. 78.

they achieved record sales and copies were passed around among multiple readers. Some like *Peg's Paper*, *Red Letter*, *Home Chat*, and *Glamour*, which targeted young working-class girls, were already well-established by the 1930s, but *Woman's Own* and *Woman* (launched in 1932 and 1937 respectively) with their focus on marriage, home, and family successfully moved beyond a socially fragmented readership to construct a national clientele that transcended classes. Offering tips about how to manage in wartime, short fiction, the Agony Aunts' letters columns, and comments on contemporary social issues, these magazines developed what has been called a 'code of intimacy' with their readers—speaking to and for them, providing advice, support, and entertainment at a time when the pressures on women had increased significantly. They addressed women as citizens, took positions on issues like childcare and family allowances, and became conduits for government publicity campaigns directed at women.[33] Other popular magazines like *John Bull* and *Picture Post* were illustrated weeklies, the former being more consciously populist while the latter has some claim, in Stuart Hall's phrase, to being the 'social eye' of the era with its unrivalled photojournalism and social democratic slant.[34] Launched in 1938 by the publisher Edward Hulton, *Picture Post* rapidly gained a circulation of over 1,350,000 copies and soon boasted perhaps as many as 5 million weekly readers. They included the middle classes and skilled workers and the magazine became an important platform for discussing social and political reconstruction; like the *Mirror*, *Picture Post* did much to mobilize its readers in support of wide-ranging plans for post-war and to advance a more democratic and egalitarian vision of Britain.

Listening

This was the first radio war; the vast majority of the nation regularly tuned in daily to the BBC and an estimated 17 million listened to the 9 o'clock news each night. For most people the war began with Neville Chamberlain's broadcast on the morning of 3 September 1939 and at every stage between then and victory the 'box on the dresser' was central to their experience. In 1939 about 75 per cent of homes had a radio and just about everyone had access to one; by war's end almost all families had managed to acquire at least a cheap utility receiver and relied heavily on radio for news and entertainment. Churchill's speeches, Priestley's *Postscripts*, BBC Playhouse, and numerous variety programmes became fixtures of the nation's weekly routine.

[33] J. Winship, 'Women's magazines: Times of war and management of the self in *Woman's Own*' in C. Gledhill and G. Swanson (eds.), *Nationalising Femininity* (Manchester, 1996); *idem*, 'Nation before family: *Woman*, the National Home Weekly, 1945–1953', *Formations of Nation and People* (London, 1984); J. Leman, '"The advice of a real friend": Codes of intimacy and oppression in women's magazines, 1937–1955', *Women's Studies International Quarterly*, 3 (1980). On girls and magazines, see P. Tinkler, *Constructing Girlhood: Popular magazines for girls growing up in England, 1920–1950* (London, 1995).
[34] S. K. Smith, '*Picture Post*, 1938–1945: Social reform and images of Britain at war', PhD Diss., Stanford University, 1992; Stuart Hall, 'The social eye of *Picture Post*', University of Birmingham CCCS Working Papers in Cultural Studies, 2 (Spring 1972); 'Plan for Britain', *Picture Post*, 4 January 1941.

However, the war's opening weeks were in many respects a failure for the BBC. While, as Scannell and Cardiff have shown, the BBC was already changing in the late 1930s, introducing more variety programmes, popular records, and dance-band music, it still retained a good deal of its Reithian *de haut en bas* flavour. At first, unsure of what to expect, it deluged the public with a curious mix of light music, patriotic injunction, repetitive news bulletins, and tedious official announcements. There were also daytime periods of silence, when the BBC went off the air altogether. After one week, Mass-Observation reported, 56 per cent of women and 57 per cent of men declared that they were 'fed up with the BBC'. But it recovered quickly, instituting a wide range of changes. Listener Research was expanded to gain more feedback (and incidentally to monitor public morale); a new array of programmes were introduced; and in January 1940 a new Forces Programme was started, aimed at British troops in France, which dropped the goal of educating its public and focused on entertaining them with comedy, variety shows, and popular music. By 1941 over 60 per cent of the BBC's audience was tuned in to the Forces network and its share among young people was considerably higher.[35]

Before 1939 the typical audience in the mind's-eye of programme directors for the National Service was the nuclear family, at home, round the fireside. In class terms they were still inclined to think of the average listener as suburban and geographically located in the Home Counties, although regional programming, especially for the large Northern Region, was more attuned to the preferences of working-class listeners. This soon changed dramatically with many new programmes, some airing before live audiences from munitions factories and military camps complete with current service and factory slang. The accents and humour of the working class, once a rarity, became normal and many of the emerging radio stars were conspicuously working class. These included East London's Vera Lynn and Yorkshire's Wilfred Pickles. Openly unsophisticated Lynn personified a chaste girlfriend or the girl next door and her sentimental ballads made her into a national institution. Pickles gained his start in the Northern Region, became enormously popular through his interviews with ordinary 'folk' and remained so all the way through the 1950s. When, in response to pressures for greater social inclusivity, he was first called upon to read the evening news, his accent drew sharp reaction from sections of the press and cartoonists depicted him with shirt sleeves rolled up and a muffler and cloth cap.[36] Taken off the air, he soon returned by popular demand.

Listening routines were transformed by the conflict; large new audiences developed outside private homes in military barracks, air-raid shelters, workers' hostels,

---

[35] P. Scannell and D. Cardiff, *A Social History of British Broadcasting* (Oxford, 1991), I; S. Nicholas, *The Echo of War: Home front propaganda and the wartime BBC, 1939–1945* (Manchester, 1996); *idem*, 'The people's radio and its audience, 1939–45' in Hayes and Hill (eds.), *'Millions Like Us'*; Tim O'Sullivan, 'Listening through: The wireless and World War Two' in P. Kirkham and D. Thoms (eds.), *War and Culture: Social change and changing experience in World War Two* (London, 1995). The Mass-Observation survey is cited by Nicholas, *The Echo of War*, p. 30. R. Silvey, *Who's Listening? The story of BBC audience research* (London, 1974).

[36] Vera Lynn, *We'll Meet Again: A personal and social memory of World War II* (London, 1944); W. Pickles, *Between You and Me* (London, 1949); 'Pickles mail misled BBC: Why he's back on the news again', *News Chronicle*, 31 January 1942.

and civil-defence posts. The BBC also found a new venue in war factories with daily broadcasts such as *Music While You Work*, *Works Wonders*, and *Workers' Playtime* designed to boost production; relieve the tedium of boring, repetitive jobs; and provide entertainment during canteen breaks and meals.[37] By 1943 over 7,000 war factories (with over 4 million workers) relayed these programmes to their workers over Tannoy loudspeakers. Workers, many of them young women newly recruited into factory work, seemed to have enjoyed these programmes and the distractions they offered, although some found their easily parodied, cheery communalism more than a little patronizing. One worker commented: 'When the chaps in my works get a rotten job... they often mimic these programmes: "Ho yes, I *love* my work." "Ho no, I *never* get fed up." "Ho yes, I would like to work longer hours", etc.'[38] Other programmes targeted the women's auxiliary services or were directed at women in the home (at the 'kitchen front') providing practical tips on nutrition and stretching rations to feed a family or giving advice about evacuees and their social and psychological difficulties. Among the favourite performers was Dr Charles Hill, the radio doctor, who dispensed advice about health and 'keeping regular' and whose voluminous postbag was regularly used by the government to gauge popular morale.

BBC programmers (aided by Listener Research) grasped the segmented nature of the national public and the need to stream entertainment for specific groups, but much of what they did also catered consciously to the task of redefining the nation in broad, inclusive, populist ways. By 1941 radio sounded more like the mass of the nation talking to itself. There was strict censorship, of course, more than people appreciated at the time. Food shortages, labour disputes, the sufferings of raid victims, and the daily hardships of families got little coverage in broadcasts; similarly, the bitterness and anger of troops disembarked after Dunkirk went unreported along with much else in the disastrous military campaigns of the early war years. *Factory Features*, a series of programmes examining the nation's war industries, scrupulously avoided references to labour disputes or production bottle-necks. A producer sent to a gun factory in July 1942 where several shop stewards had just been sacked, found workers 'up in arms and the whole place bordering on revolution'; this, as the factory's manager commented, 'was no time for a sunshine broadcast'.[39] But while the internal culture of those at the top of the BBC was not

---

[37] M. Korczynski *et al.*, '"We sang ourselves through that war": Women, music and factory work in World War II', *Labour History Review*, 70(2) (August 2005); M. Korczynski and K. Jones, 'Instrumental music? The social origins of broadcast music in British factories', *Popular Music*, 25(2) (2006).

[38] P. Scannell, 'Factory programmes for the workers on British wartime radio', unpublished paper given to 'Traditions et classes ouvrières', colloquium held at the École des Hautes Études en Sciences Sociales, Paris, October 1991; the quotation is from p. 21 (LR/1458 'programmes about industry and war workers in industry', December 1942, BBC Written Archives at Caversham). Also, P. Scannell and D. Cardiff, 'Good luck war workers! Class, politics and entertainment in wartime broadcasting' in T. Bennett, C. Mercer, and J. Woollacott (eds.), *Popular Culture and Social Relations* (Milton Keynes, 1986).

[39] Scannell, 'Factory programmes for the workers on British wartime radio', p. 19 (BBC Archives LR/1458, 'Programmes about industry and war workers in industry', Banks to Gilliam, 19 July 1942).

vastly changed, there was a sudden influx of new personnel who were more apt to test the limits of censorship and their own scope for independence. Thus, by the last two years of the war, although it involved constant struggle and compromises, radio did jettison some of its traditional caution and devoted more air time to post-war reconstruction, moderately reasserting its independence which had been eroded during the war.[40]

To the extent that a 'common culture' existed in wartime, by which we mean overlapping interests and shared cultural reference points, then radio was central to it, supplying much of the common pool of information, popular music, even catchphrases and jokes of the time. Comedy was certainly an area where the national audience was regarded as one. Satire, slapstick, the ability to joke when in a tight corner, were represented as basic to national character, quintessentially British. American comics were well known and became increasingly influential during the war, but it was the home-grown variety, rooted in the Music Hall tradition who triumphed. There were cockneys like Tommy Trinder and radio's street-wise barrow boy, Syd Walker, and northerners, especially Lancastrians, like Gracie Fields and George Formby and Liverpudlian gag-men like Tommy Handley, Arthur Askey, and Frank Randle. In the forces, meanwhile, a younger generation also began to emerge, including Charley Chester, Norman Wisdom, Max Bygraves, Harry Secombe, and Peter Sellers who kept Britain laughing long after the war.[41]

Most successful of all wartime comedies, however, was Tommy Handley's show *ITMA* which achieved a weekly audience of 16 million. The title derived from a *Daily Express* headline about Hitler, 'It's That Man Again', suitably abbreviated to echo officialdom's craze for acronyms. Aiming at a laugh every eleven seconds, the result was rather like a cartoon in sound—a madcap patter of puns, malapropisms, parodies, and surreal burlesques which worked in topical references and wartime slang. It was mildly subversive satire that exactly caught the public mood—laughing at authority rather than challenging it, often taking aim at inept bureaucrats, upper-class twits, and funny foreigners through a parade of characters whom Handley encounters. There was Colonel Chinstrap, the bibulous ex-Indian army Blimp; Fusspot, the civil servant; the mysterious Funf, a German agent with feet of sauerkraut; the Cairo Pedlar Ali Oop who sold dirty postcards; Signor So and So, the Italian who tried to get off with all the women on the show; and Mrs Mopp, Whitehall's charlady who made her weekly entry with 'Can I do you now, Sir?' and continued to boom *double-entendres* at her 'civic gentlemen'. *ITMA* catchphrases became part of the nation's daily speech and many lasted well after the war: 'This is Funf speaking'; 'After you Claude, no after you Cyril'; 'I don't mind if I do'; 'It's bein' so cheerful as keeps me goin''; 'I'll have to ask me Dad'; 'What me? In my state of health'. Anyone who grew up in the decade after the war heard them all the time.[42]

[40] In addition to Nicholas, *The Echo of War*, see D. M. Smith, 'Politics through the microphone: BBC radio and the "New Jerusalem", 1940–45', PhD Diss., London University, 1999.

[41] J. G. Hughes, *The Greasepaint War: Show business 1939–45* (London, 1976).

[42] Francis Worsley, *ITMA 1939–1948* (London, 1949).

By most measures the BBC had a good war. It became more important than ever as part of the private, domestic culture of most families and it played a huge role in defining the national community. The most obvious changes in broadcasting reflected the goals of raising morale, pleasing, entertaining, and communicating more effectively with a mass audience. But, while cognizant of the variety of public taste and moving far in the direction of meeting public preferences, the BBC also retained the view that public broadcasting should educate people and improve their cultural standards. Among its most successful 'crossover' ventures, combining entertainment and education, was the quiz programme *Brains Trust* which invited the audience to pose questions and brain-teasers to a distinguished panel of regulars—including scientist Julian Huxley, philosopher Cyril Joad, and world traveller Commander A. B. Campbell—and guest participants. Unscripted and performed live, their discussions of philosophy, science, and the arts had a rare spontaneity and lots of humour, while over time a long list of the country's leading intellectuals and public figures appeared on the programme. At its height in late 1943 *Brains Trust* captured an unprecedented 30 per cent of adult listeners and received over 3,000 letters a week, while the format was copied for entertainments at forces camps, factories, and village halls. It remained enormously popular, even though its organizers' avoidance of controversial political issues drew occasional protests from the panellists and listeners alike, increasingly so as national debate about post-war reconstruction moved into high gear towards the end of the war.[43]

As Sian Nicholas has argued, 'in almost every field of wartime broadcasting old aims and new needs vied for precedence'.[44] Thus, in addition to expanding its light entertainment, the BBC also attached great importance to providing serious radio drama and classical music, lectures, discussions, and adaptations of literary works. Like the Council for the Encouragement of Music and the Arts, which is discussed later in this chapter, BBC programmers believed that the war had created large new audiences for the arts and it strove to shape public taste and define a 'national culture' in which everyone had a stake. Yet, while eager to feature 'ordinary people' and to communicate more effectively with the whole nation, BBC planners invariably thought of society as a pyramid with workers at the base. The aim was to elevate mass taste and thereby invert the pyramid and to create a medium for the people rather than an outlet for their opinions. This placed clear limits on the BBC's populism. As Paddy Scannell comments: 'The working class was accepted for the first time as part of the polity, but not as an active participant in its decision-making processes... "They" have been recognized, brought into the public realm constituted by broadcasting, but in ways that still maintained the space between us and them, the broadcasters and audience.'[45] Internal BBC memoranda illustrate this well. The Corporation's mandarins were deeply troubled when during a transmission from a war factory the announcement of 'Worker of the Week' was greeted by

[43] Howard Thomas, *Britain's Brains Trust* (London, 1944); Nicholas, 'The people's radio and its audience', pp. 84–8.
[44] *Ibid.*, p. 76.
[45] Scannell, 'Factory programmes for the workers on British wartime radio', p. 26.

a burst of ironic laughter from fellow workers, raising unsettling doubts about such programmes' credibility with the working classes. Similar apprehension surfaced when it came to organizing programmes about post-war reconstruction. Thus, Christopher Salmon of the Talks Department argued in July 1941 that 'actual legislative proposals . . . are better discussed by people with administrative experience and a knowledge wider than working people can hope to have of the whole political and economic fabric'. The Director of the Scottish BBC was more blunt. Having listed the topics that workers would want to discuss as 'the war, home politics, industrial grievances, football and the dogs', he added: 'we believe that what they would want to say about the first three could not be broadcast'.[46]

Watching

The other mass leisure activity of the war years was 'going to the pictures'. By the late 1930s few European countries came close to Britain in cinema attendance. Weekly audiences averaged about 23 million with 40 per cent of the population going once a week regularly and 25 per cent twice or more. The entertainment was cheap with 80 per cent of cinema admissions priced under a shilling and 43 per cent under 6d in the mid-1930s, while matinee performances as low as 3d were affordable for children and even the unemployed. Not only were the shows a bargain, but the cinemas themselves with exotic names like the Granada, Rialto, Odeon, or Ritz became increasingly comfortable, even opulent, in their decor with marble staircases, goldfish ponds, and exotic Moorish or Egyptian styling in some, adding to their dream-palace mystique. The cinema-going public included all sections of the urban working class, but women of all ages and young people constituted the largest groups. Fan clubs and movie magazines flourished and the impact of movies on young people's fashion, hairstyles, make-up, and language was immense. For older women, the cinema (like radio) was a favourite form of relaxation, but unlike radio it got them out of the home. This was somewhere cheap and respectable where they could go alone or with friends without causing malicious gossip. Older men went less frequently but films did become a family recreation as well as a collective experience: people queued together and chatted with neighbours and acquaintances; buskers entertained and passed the hat; sweets were purchased; there was clapping, shared laughter and sometimes catcalls during the programme, and a bag of chips on the way home. By 1939, then, going to the cinema had become as much a routine fixture of life as pubs and football and unlike these, something that men and women would do together.[47]

---

[46] For Salmon: Cardiff and Scannell, 'Good luck war workers!', p. 105. For the Director of Scottish BBC: A. Marwick, *Class: Image and reality in Britain, France and the USA since 1930* (Oxford, 1980), p. 228; the original document is in a file labelled 'Reconstruction-Political ("Working man") Talks', Acc. No. 1644, BBC Written Archives at Caversham. Sian Nicholas has used the phrase 'elevated classlessness' to describe the flavour of the BBC's populism.
[47] J. Richards, *The Age of the Dream Palace: Cinema and society in Britain 1930–1939* (London, 1984).

Like other forms of mass entertainment cinemas were closed in the first weeks of the war but the policy was quickly reversed and attendance was soon booming. With full employment and higher wages box-office receipts trebled and average weekly attendances climbed to over 31 million. Young war-workers went at least once a week and many several times, provoking concern among some social analysts who thought a more constructive form of recreation was desirable. Young girls, Pearl Jephcott argued, were especially vulnerable to the 'cheap romance' of popular films and their 'violence, vulgarity, sentimentality and false psychology'.[48] And Mass-Observation feared that this kind of passive entertainment contributed to the decline of active citizenship. 'There is always a lot of talk about films as the weekend approaches', Mass-Observer Celia Fremlin wrote about her co-workers in a munitions factory, 'and going forms a sort of focal point to an otherwise aimless and drifting weekend.'[49] Government agencies like the MoI, however, focused quickly upon the cinema's potential as a powerful instrument for raising morale and bridging the gap between government and people. Aside from its normal censorship role government became increasingly active in proposing desirable film projects and organizing joint ventures with commercial companies. In addition, hundreds of short government films on every imaginable aspect of the war effort were shown in workplaces, army camps, community halls, schools, or as add-ons to commercial cinema programmes. Historians have suggested that these documentaries—many of them made by left-wing film-makers—increased public support for state planning and raised expectations of post-war social reform. Nicholas Pronay, in particular, has compared them to a classic agitprop operation which 'may very well have significantly raised "political consciousness"', although as the years went by many audiences grew resentful of having to sit through official films.[50]

While the majority of films still came from Hollywood, the war was something of a 'golden age' for British cinema both in the quality of the films produced and their success at the box office. Excellent scholarly studies of Britain's film industry exist for this period and only a few general points need be made here.[51] Three

---

[48] P. Jephcott, *Girls Growing Up* (London, 1942), pp. 118–19, 124; *idem, Rising Twenty*, p. 155. Jephcott noted 'the amazing extent to which the minutiae of the clothes and hair arrangement of an American actress may affect the spending habits of a child in a mining village in Durham or a girl in a tenement in Central London': *Rising Twenty*, pp. 62–3.

[49] M-O, *War Factory* (London, 1943; repr. 1987), p. 81. Many wartime diaries carefully record the films seen: e.g. IWM: 86/54/1 Diary of Mrs Louie White.

[50] N. Pronay, '"The land of promise": The projection of peace aims in Britain' in K. R. M. Short (ed.), *Film and Radio Propaganda in World War II* (London, 1973), p. 72. J. P. Mayer hoped that government intervention in the film industry would be extended post-war as a form of citizenship education: J. P. Mayer, *British Cinemas and Their Audiences* (London, 1948); *idem, Sociology of Film: Studies and documents* (London, 1946). The Workers' Film Association also toured factories, hostels, and Co-op branches: A. Burton, 'Projecting the New Jerusalem: The Workers' Film Association, 1938–46' in Kirkham and Thoms (eds.), *War and Culture*. On government documentaries, see N. Pronay and D.W. Spring (eds.), *Propaganda, Politics and Film 1918–45* (London, 1982); T. Haggith, 'Citizenship, nationhood and empire in British official film propaganda 1939–45' in R. Weight and A. Beach, *The Right to Belong* (London, 1998).

[51] A. Lant, *Blackout: Reinventing women for wartime British cinema* (Princeton, 1991); A. Higson, *Waving the Flag: Constructing a national cinema in Britain* (Oxford, 1995); J. Chapman, *The British at*

common themes or motifs running through wartime production were: the projection or redefinition of national solidarity; the war's impact upon family life, women, and gender roles; and what we might call the 'master narrative' of the recent past. Wartime films redefined the nation to be more inclusive and democratic. The stereotypical traits of national character did not change much from earlier renditions—modesty, courage, emotional restraint, decency, and tolerance being among the most prominent—but they appeared in more demotic form. Whether they portrayed the armed forces or factory workers, women or men, films emphasized the ordinary citizen. One way of doing this was through plots that focused on the construction of community, where a socially mixed group of people, thrown together by the maelstrom of war, learn to work together as a team, epitomizing the nation's new-found spirit (*Millions Like Us*; *The Way Ahead*; *Fires Were Started*). In war, so the underlying message went, emotional unity, shared heritage and traditions, transcended class difference and material inequalities. Regional divisions were noted, even celebrated, in stock portrayals of dour Tynesiders, Scottish ships' engineers, ebullient cockneys, and comic Welshmen, but in such a way as to underscore unity. To be sure, the nation was never as unified as films proclaimed and class divisions repeatedly erupt into their plots producing cracks in the facade—although the tensions are usually repositioned in the context of personal relationships where they can be resolved. Social class was never ignored in these dramas, but it was neutralized, although in a few cases—Anthony Asquith's *The Demi-Paradise* or Noël Coward's *In Which We Serve*, for example—it was sympathetically reaffirmed in ways that contrasted with and challenged the dominant populism of the era.[52]

By 1943 film-makers focused more and more upon the home front, trying to address and to a degree relieve public anxieties about women's mobilization and the war's impact on the family, gender roles, and sexuality. As Sue Harper notes, the film industry 'dealt with these changes in an extremely nervous and selective way'.[53] Treatment of such themes as 'mobile women' living in hostels (*Millions Like Us*), the femininity of uniformed women (*The Gentle Sex*), or sexual morality and marital breakup (*Perfect Strangers*; *Love Story*; *Waterloo Road*; *Brief Encounter*) was invariably calculated to allay or defuse public anxieties and to underscore the obligations of women as citizens in wartime. Film-makers largely reaffirmed and nationalized conventional femininity and found strategies for containing the more threatening topics. With female audiences, however, the biggest commercial successes were not these 'social problem' films, but the Gainsborough studio's lush

War: Cinema, state, and propaganda, 1939–1945 (London, 1998); C. Coultass, *Images for Battle: British film and the Second World War, 1939–1945* (London, 1989); Tony Williams, *Structures of Desire: British cinema 1939–55* (Albany, 2000); P. M. Taylor (ed.), *Britain and the Cinema in the Second World War* (London, 1988); A. Aldgate and J. Richards, *Britain Can Take It* (Oxford, 1986); R. Murphy, *British Cinema and the Second World War* (London, 2000); P. Stead, *Film and the Working Class* (London, 1991), ch. 6.

[52] Neil Rattigan, *This is England: British film and the People's War, 1939–45* (Madison and London, 2001) examines the role of class in wartime film.

[53] S. Harper, *Women in British Cinema: Mad, bad and dangerous to know* (London, 2000), p. 30.

costume melodramas which turned Margaret Lockwood and James Mason into leading box-office stars. Set in a stylized Regency or Restoration past with plots revolving around aristocrats, highwaymen, and gypsies, these escapist fantasies featured more flamboyant, sexually aggressive women than the chaste heroines of the dramas about wartime. Here, safely consigned to the past, transgressive women had their fling on screen—usually coming to a bad end but stealing the show in the meantime.[54]

To redefine the nation more inclusively and communicate this message effectively, films also had to confront the interwar past that Priestley's famous 'Postscripts' had outlined: the broken promises of 1918, the yawning social divide between rich and poor, and the 'Hungry Thirties' of mass unemployment. In the 1930s tight censorship had prevented any serious examination of these topics, let alone labour disputes or class conflict, although two films, *The Citadel* (1938) and *The Stars Look Down* (1939), did eventually break the silence. With their fusion of documentary and narrative modes and their undercurrent of radicalism, these films about poverty-stricken coal-mining communities anticipated wartime's social dramas. The war brought a loosening of earlier controls allowing, for example, Walter Greenwood's classic novel, *Love on the Dole*, to be filmed in 1941. The MoI wanted to demonstrate that Britain was a democratic nation committed to free speech and willing to face the most unsettling truths about itself.[55] Although successfully adapted for the stage before the war, the censors had twice rejected proposals for the film as displaying 'too much of the sordid and tragic side of poverty'. Now it could be made, although John Baxter's film altered details of the novel, softening its political radicalism. Most importantly, the slums of Hanky Park and the Means Test were now viewed from across the divide created by the war; the depression was consigned to a past that was over and finished; and at the film's end a statement by A.V. Alexander (Labour MP and First Lord of the Admiralty) flashed across the screen: 'Our working men and women have responded magnificently to any and every call made upon them. Their reward must be a new Britain. Never again must the unemployed become the forgotten men of the Peace.' The same message recurred in innumerable films: that the war and present sacrifices would herald a new dawn and usher in a more egalitarian society and better times. Future expectations were summoned to relieve the burden of the past—Britain was a 'land of promise'.[56]

How did audiences respond to these films? Historians have often interpreted wartime film as a reflection of British society and, in many cases, as an active contributor to the forging of a progressive consensus about post-war reconstruction. Certainly, film-makers produced a steady stream of films depicting the nation's involvement in the war, many of them lavishly praised for their realism—in particular

[54] S. Harper, *Picturing the Past: The rise and fall of the British costume film* (London, 1994).
[55] C. Levine, 'Propaganda for democracy: The curious case of *Love on the Dole*', *JBS*, 45 (October 2006). S. Constantine, '*Love on the Dole* and its reception in the 1930s', *Literature and History*, 8 (1982).
[56] For example, Baxter's *The Shipbuilders* (1943) on the Clydeside shipyards.

their focus on ordinary people with authentic class and regional accents. Today these characters may seem a trifle clichéd or predictable, but to contemporaries they did represent a breakthrough towards greater verisimilitude.[57] But cinematic realism, as Jeff Hill explains, is an interpretive system with its own assumptions and narrative conventions and always comparative, structured in relation to what went before. It was permeated by the cultural construct of a 'People's War' and the need for national consensus; it also omitted or sanitized a great many aspects of people's lives. Workers watching these films neither expected nor wanted an accurate representation of their lives. They liked stars, glamour and romance— entertainment, amusement, and relief from the worries and strains of everyday life. As the war continued, audiences became tired of war films while highly acclaimed 'social problem' films like *Millions Like Us* or *Love on the Dole* were often more popular with suburban than working-class audiences. Evidence about audience responses in working-class areas is sparse, but it reveals a gap between the films that critics (and later, historians) praised most highly and those most successful with the viewing public.[58] The most popular genres remained slapstick comedies, like those of George Formby, or the Gainsborough melodramas, while the latest star-studded releases from Hollywood like *Gone With the Wind* or the romantic sufferings of *Mrs Miniver* were a big hit with all social groups. Working-class letters and diaries demonstrate clearly the recreational importance of film-going but are far less clear about what people took away from these outings. In general, it seems, films reinforced a sense of national unity and common purpose; they presented Britons with a reassuring portrait of themselves, but while they provided a screen for contemporary anxieties and dilemmas, they largely bolstered conservative gender attitudes and communicated popular hopes for social reform in conciliatory and non-adversarial terms.

The war years saw a concerted effort by the BBC and the film industry to be more inclusive of working-class audiences—recognizing their tastes, including more working-class characters and accents, and promoting the ethos a 'People's War'. Both media were important in constructing shared cultural reference points that cut across class divisions and state encouragement, through the MoI and other agencies, was central to this project. In addition, government initiated youth programmes and 'Holidays at Home' which sought to counter the potentially divisive effects of boredom and uplift popular morale. In a larger sense, however, there was no common culture—in the books they read, the music they listened to, and what they did, the middle and working classes lived separate, mostly self-enclosed lives. Yet early in the war important groups saw the conflict as a rare opportunity to further long-standing goals of educating working-class artistic tastes

---

[57] Jo Fox, 'Millions like us? Accented language and the "ordinary" in British film of the Second World War', *JBS*, 45 (October 2006).

[58] J. Poole, 'British cinema attendance in wartime: Audience preference at the Majestic, Macclesfield, 1939–1946', *Historical Journal of Film, Radio, and Television*, 7(1) (1987); J. Richards, 'Wartime British cinema audiences and the class system: The case of "Ships with Wings" (1941)', *Historical Journal of Film, Radio, and Television*, 7(2) (1987). Also, J. Richards and D. Sheridan (eds.), *Mass Observation at the Movies* (London, 1987).

and defining a shared national culture in which all had a stake. It is to this project that we turn in the next section.

CEMA CULTURE: 'THE BEST FOR THE MOST'?

'Everything nowadays becomes a problem', wrote the influential drama critic Ivor Brown in December 1940. 'Even entertainment is a problem. That is because entertainment has come up in the world and joined the ranks of national necessities.'[59] It was quickly recognized for example that after raids cinemas, pubs, and city-centre leisure institutions were vital to public morale which suffered greatly where they were heavily damaged. The government quickly modified its early bans on cinemas, theatres, and sports events. But more was needed and since the civilian population was spending so much time in factories, workers' hostels, civil-defence posts, and air-raid shelters, the state took unprecedented steps to bring leisure programmes to these sites. Paradoxically, at a time when work seemed all-consuming to many workers, their leisure time attracted growing official attention. As Brad Beaven writes, 'Never before had the leisure of the working class been so systematically scrutinized by the state through a network of intelligence officers and researchers.'[60] It seemed natural that in a 'People's War' the arts and entertainment should also be mobilized to provide war-workers of all kinds with a break from their daily grind; recreational and educational programmes also expanded rapidly in the armed forces for exactly the same reasons: to bolster faltering morale, ease the strains of family separations, and give soldiers a better sense of what they were fighting for.

There was no overall plan guiding government intervention. Instead, action developed piecemeal, shaped by voluntary initiatives and outside pressures, which had the effect of stimulating a wide-ranging public debate. For some, the object was to supply popular entertainments, to provide distraction from the harsh realities of life. But very quickly debate about recreational programmes became intertwined with criticism of mass culture and claims, advanced before the war, that leisure should be creative, reinvigorating—a source of recreation rather than mere amusement. Phrases like 'education for leisure' and 'the right use of leisure' abounded. Running through these ideas was a common theme: that recreation should educate, introduce workers to higher culture, and foster social cohesion by defining and providing an appreciation of a shared, national culture. These two contradictory viewpoints were embodied in the two organizations—both of them originating from private initiatives—on which the government relied most heavily for its provision of recreational programmes: the Entertainments National Service

---

[59] I. Brown, 'This entertainment problem', *New Statesman*, 7 and 12 December 1940. Brown became director of drama at CEMA.
[60] B. Beaven, *Leisure, Citizenship and Working-Class Men in Britain 1851–1945* (Manchester, 2005), p. 211.

Association (ENSA) and the Council for the Encouragement of Music and the Arts (CEMA).

By far the larger in size and budget, ENSA was the brainchild of the theatrical impresario, Basil Dean, an autocratic and abrasive but highly talented empire-builder. Dean had organized variety shows and concerts for troops in the First World War. But when, during the Czech crisis of 1938, he outlined his ideas for the War Office he got little encouragement and ended up arranging to work through the NAAFI, the organization responsible for forces' canteens. Things went slowly at first, but Dunkirk altered that with ENSA being brought in to lighten the spirit of soldiers being unloaded off the vessels from France. Soon Dean was active in arranging shows for troops in camps across the country and, as British forces overseas expanded, so did ENSA, eventually employing some 4,000 people and sending its performers to every theatre of the war. ENSA was also active among civilians, entertaining crowds in the air-raid shelters and, with Ernest Bevin's assistance, bringing shows to factory canteens—in some large firms as many as one or two a week during lunchtime breaks. Dean was able to enlist some big stars like Gracie Fields and George Formby but, since demand for performers was high and the talent pool small, many shows were of poor quality. ENSA's staple fare was comedy, popular music, and variety turns, although Dean eventually negotiated co-operative ventures with the BBC, put on plays, and engaged the London Symphony Orchestra and the Halle for evening concerts.[61] Dean's incursions into the world of classical music, however, were poorly received by organizers of the second organization, CEMA, which saw itself as the guardian of 'serious' art and felt that ENSA's function was to cater to popular taste and leave matters of 'artistic integrity' to them. Efforts to broker cooperation between them largely failed and CEMA's officials touring the provinces were happy to funnel bad reports of 'Ensa-tainment' back to their London headquarters.[62] In 1943, eager to underscore the differences between the two organizations, the Council adopted a ruling that prevented any ENSA artist from working for it. The tensions between the two illustrate the split priorities informing the provision of recreation in wartime: to raise morale or improve taste, embrace public preferences or promote 'the best', to entertain or educate?

Though much smaller than its rival, CEMA had a more enduring significance as the forerunner of the post-war Arts Council and the beginning of state patronage of the arts. The ideas behind the organization included several different but overlapping strands of interwar thinking about class and the nation. Sir Kenneth Clark, Director of the National Gallery and one of the founding board members of CEMA, was anxious to sustain the arts and artists at a time when private patrons

---

[61] Basil Dean, *The Theatre at War* (London, 1956); R. Fawkes, *Fighting for a Laugh: Entertaining British and American armed forces 1939–46* (London, 1995). Also, the memoir by C. Wells, *East with ENSA: Entertaining the troops in the Second World War* (London, 2001).
[62] NA: LAB 26/35, Rosetti, 8 February 1941; also T. H. Hull to Rossetti, 3 September 1941; LAB 26/40 and LAB 26/42 contain materials on the friction between ENSA and CEMA. Dean reacted angrily: 'It was irksome to find ourselves regarded as the chain-store of the concert world while CEMA dealt only with the custom-built trade': *Theatre at War*, p. 135.

10. Royal Ordnance Factory, Leeds, works canteen, 17 April 1941.

were dwindling, but he also believed that culture could act as a force of social cohesion, joining together a class-divided nation confronting the threats of fascism and war. For Clark, whose social views were basically conservative and owed much to Matthew Arnold, improving popular taste and appreciation for the arts was linked to civic and moral improvement and the promotion of a national culture. Others who dreamed of upgrading popular leisure and making the arts relevant to the lives of all citizens—Unity Theatre, for example, and the Artists International Association (AIA)—were politically on the left. They denounced the dulling, stultifying effect of mass commercial entertainment arguing that it encouraged manipulation and passivity and drove out authentic folk traditions; they envisioned a shared, democratic national culture which coupled the reform of popular recreation and radical social and political change. The war and, in particular, the inclusive discourse of a 'People's War' gave enormous stimulus to these ideas; the democratization of British culture, it was argued, was a vital part of the struggle for civilization against Hitler.[63]

The immediate origin of CEMA was a series of discussions between a private charitable foundation, the Pilgrim Trust, and the Board of Education in late 1939.

---

[63] The eagerness of publishers and editors in the 1930s to encourage working-class writers also continued during the war years in the magazine *Seven* and John Lehmann's *Penguin New Writing*; C. Hilliard, *To Exercise Our Talents* (Cambridge, MA, 2006); John Lehmann, *I Am My Brother* (New York, 1961).

Before the war the Trust had supported schemes for adult education and efforts to bring art to depressed industrial regions. The Board of Education was concerned about war's impact on voluntary programmes for adult education and was eager to elicit additional funds from a reluctant Treasury for cultural programmes to help sustain the population's morale. At the same time, with private funds drying up, the Arts and Entertainment Council was eager to find other sources of patronage for the arts, while Clark had formed the War Artists Advisory Committee to commission professional artists to create a pictorial record of the war and of historic buildings that might soon be lost forever to enemy raids. From the beginning CEMA was divided over how best to 'encourage music and the arts'. In the eyes of the Pilgrim Trust's representatives and their allies at the Board of Education the essential thing was to take art to the people and encourage local artistic activity, especially in regions without major cultural institutions and with few professional orchestras or theatres. They wanted to promote amateur work and saw popular participation, music-making, and play-acting by ordinary people as an answer to passive consumption of entertainment. For others, like Clark, the chief problem was to ensure the survival of professional artists and high performance standards in spite of the dispersal of audiences and the destruction or closure of theatres and concert halls.[64] CEMA's slogan was 'the best for the most' but the inherent tension between popular commitment and professional standards split the organization throughout the war years.

Initially the main focus was upon amateur performance. Professional Musical Travellers were hired and sent to the provinces where they arranged concerts and helped organize local brass bands and choirs; other advisers were employed to encourage participation in amateur dramatic societies. In the first half of 1940, according to Eric White, CEMA's Musical Travellers established 37 amateur orchestral and 244 choral groups and helped organize 254 concerts.[65] The numbers of local dramatic societies also grew rapidly. Soon this was balanced by efforts to increase the general public's opportunities to enjoy the arts by the provision of professional performances. During the London Blitz CEMA volunteers made their way through the blackout to communal shelters and rest centres giving concerts and recitals. At the same time professional companies benefited from CEMA grants: they sponsored provincial tours by major orchestras such as the London Symphony and the London Philharmonic, and the Old Vic theatre company, its home destroyed by bombing, went to the industrial districts of Lancashire and South Wales. Other drama companies were hired to tour factory hostels with a wide range of plays and they participated in the government's 'Holidays at Home'

[64] A. Sinclair, *Arts and Cultures: The history of fifty years of the Arts Council of Great Britain* (London, 1995). F. M. Leventhal, 'The best for the most: CEMA and state sponsorship of the arts in wartime 1939–41', *Twentieth Century British History*, 1(3) (1990). N. Hayes, 'More than music while you eat? Factory and hostel concerts, good culture and the workers' in Hayes and Hill (eds.), *'Millions Like Us'?* Also, J. Weingartner, *The Arts as a Weapon of War: Britain and the shaping of national morale in the Second World War* (London, 2006).
[65] E. White, *The Arts Council of Great Britain* (London, 1975), p. 30. The monthly *CEMA News Bulletin* (later the *Arts Council Bulletin*) details the number and type of CEMA performances etc.

scheme. The major discussions within the Drama Panel weighed the alternative of 'playing down to the unknowledgeable and giving them the popular items' or 'offering them classics, which might be above their heads, but would excite the imagination'.[66] Very soon a major portion of CEMA's energies was also devoted to sending concert parties to munitions factories, although Ernest Bevin's decision to have ENSA also provide lunch-hour concerts for war-workers troubled CEMA's London headquarters, especially when the Minister hinted that CEMA might be 'too highbrow' for factory workers. As Mary Glasgow (secretary to the Council) advised one organizer: 'We musn't be afraid of being popular and simple in our efforts to avoid being vulgar and sentimental. Above all, we musn't let people call us highbrow.' Often, she wrote about classical music, 'the best stuff "gets across" provided you don't tell listeners what it is beforehand'.[67] CEMA's factory concerts continued to grow; there were more than seventy a week by 1944. In that year over 1.5 million people attended 6,140 CEMA concerts and over 3,500 of them took place in factories, hostels, and on construction sites.[68]

Another CEMA programme was 'Art for the People' which W. E. Williams, a leader in adult education and an editor at Penguin Books, had launched before the war with the aid of private funds. He was also about to become a key figure in the army's ABCA programme. 'Art for the People' brought exhibitions of paintings and sculpture (loaned by galleries and private collectors as well as the War Artists Advisory Committee) to towns and villages which otherwise had little chance of seeing them. Some 300,000 people were said to have visited these shows in 1940 alone. Also closely involved with the programme was the Artists International Association (AIA) which in the 1930s had sponsored the first Surrealist exhibition in London and had organized shows on unemployment, the war in Spain, and working-class life. A product of the Popular Front era, AIA was thrown into some ideological disarray by the Nazi–Soviet pact; but by 1940, in association with CEMA and other government agencies, it began organizing travelling art exhibits which were hung in British restaurants, village halls, and war-workers' canteens across the country—sometimes inspiring factories to mount their own shows of art by staff and workers. One 1941 exhibit in Charing Cross Tube station attracted 150,000 visitors in just three weeks. Everyman Prints, depicting different facets of the war on the home front, were produced by AIA in mass editions, cheap enough for workers to buy and AIA artists were hired to liven up the grim interiors of hostels and factories with murals and posters.[69]

[66] C. Landstone, *Off-Stage: A personal record of the first twelve years of state-sponsored drama in Great Britain* (London, 1953), pp. 53–4.
[67] NA: EL 2/29, 'Factory concerts, general correspondence' (1940–3), M. C. Glasgow to J. Hollins, 1 October 1940.
[68] J. Lindsay, *British Achievement in Arts and Music* (London, 1945), p. 10; Hayes, 'More than music while you eat?', p. 223.
[69] L. Morris and R. Radford, *The Story of AIA: Artists International Association 1933–1953* (Oxford, 1983); Brian Fox, 'Message and medium: Government patronage, national identity, and national culture in Britain, 1939–45', *The Oxford Art Journal*, 14(2) (1991). In 1942 alone, CEMA was responsible for 132 exhibitions of paintings, 120 exhibitions of prints and reproductions, and 62 architectural exhibits.

As time passed, discord grew between the advocates of artistic professionalism and those for whom adult education and the revival of participatory folk traditions and local culture was the highest priority. Both groups were missionaries for the arts; both talked of raising standards of appreciation; both believed that the war constituted an opportunity to make the arts more central to people's lives. The problem was how best to achieve these goals. Early on, there were criticisms from the press and professional arts companies that CEMA's efforts to encourage amateurism were a waste of money and that many of the local groups it sponsored soon collapsed after an initial flurry of activity. Those, like the composer and Council board member Ralph Vaughan Williams, who were strong supporters of encouraging amateur musicians, found themselves on the defensive. Above all, the appointment of J. M. Keynes as chairman in April 1942 greatly reinforced the advocates of cultural standards against what was increasingly called the 'welfarist' approach. An unrepentant elitist and not 'the man for wandering minstrels and amateur theatricals', as Clark put it, Keynes believed that the way to turn art into 'a living element in everybody's upbringing' was to expose audiences to performances of the highest quality. He gradually reversed the anti-metropolitan bias of the early days, channelling more funds to activities in the capital. He also made preparations for post-war, pushing for CEMA to create a string of subsidized theatres (in part as an answer to the monopoly of cinema chains over local theatre spaces) and developing plans both for a National Theatre and for turning Covent Garden into a national opera and ballet theatre. It was his vision above all that informed the transformation of CEMA into a permanent Arts Council in June 1945. The drama advisers scheme was the first to be curtailed; then, in 1943 the number of Music Travellers was reduced and they were renamed as Regional Organizers and their functions redefined. Some quit altogether, believing that, after pioneering work at the local level in developing new audiences, they had been left high and dry. 'Now, having created a demand, mobilised the enthusiasts and built up audiences', one wrote, 'the cut has come without warning.'[70] The Pilgrim Trust withdrew its support, influenced perhaps by the change of direction, but in any case Treasury funds now accounted for the lion's share of funding.

From the beginning, CEMA artistes in the field faced the difficulties of their work with a missionary, pioneer zeal. When the Music Travellers (mostly women) toured London's mass shelters and rest centres, they played 'under appalling conditions... in dark, underground vaults', found 'their way... through bombs and barrage', and were often forced to 'spend the night where they are'.[71] In the provinces they went from one village or factory to the next; the hours were long and the frustrations many, especially where there was no tuned piano or suitable space for performing. One admitted that she 'felt less like an apostle of high art than a

[70] NA: EL 2/47, March 1943; Sybil Eaton; Leventhal, 'The best for the most'. There is also a small cache of papers by Eaton and other travellers at Dartington Hall Archive, Devon.
[71] *CEMA Bulletin*, no. 7 (November 1940). *CEMA Arts Bulletin*, no. 7 (November 1940) reported that, in October 1940, 150 concerts had been held in rest centres for Londoners made homeless by the bombing and they were continuing at the rate of 8 a day.

vacuum-cleaner salesman'. Another wrote: 'There have inevitably been many moments in the last weeks when one has been tempted to chuck the work and go to the nearest ARP post to enrol. The feeling that one may be singing while England is burning is sometimes difficult to bear.'[72] They were invariably middle-class and worried about the reception they might receive. Arranging concerts for a devastated area of Clydebank, an organizer reported: 'I was very nervous about it as I didn't know how the people would react to music after what they had been through.' What made the work worthwhile, all agreed, was the gratitude and enthusiasm of audiences. 'The joy', wrote Eve Kisch, 'lies in "building up" a public; following a vocal piano recital by a violin, then maybe a cello or flute, finally perhaps a string quartet: but it is all important that this "progress" should be directed by the audience's own taste, forcing the pace inevitably leads to reaction.' At times, she adds, she was astonished to find that a complex item on the programme—'something perhaps which the artist had hesitated to risk'—'gave the most pleasure'. On such occasions, 'One feels like embracing the audience.'[73] The work took its toll, especially when audiences were small or inattentive. It could also provoke other, professional worries: 'I realized', wrote a Music Traveller in her resignation letter, 'that this job was not one which any person could keep on doing indefinitely, if they want to be a performing artist.' With all the duties required, she added, performing was compromised though 'I have always considered it a compromise which any artists worth their salt should be willing and glad to make for a time under war time conditions.'[74]

The aim of these artistic missionaries was to foster an appreciation of the arts and to draw social classes together by promoting the sense of a shared national culture. On tour, actors and musicians ate and slept in the hostels where they performed or sometimes lodged with local families, creating new opportunities for social exploration. But, despite the good intentions, such cross-class mixing could easily produce misunderstandings and artists were repeatedly counselled not to appear aloof or too 'highbrow'. The delight of Music Travellers when performances went well—even if people only listened quietly ('one could hear the proverbial pin drop')—reflects their fears of audience rejection. Communist actress Beatrix Lehmann pondered the difficulty of surmounting these social and cultural barriers. Workers with little education and long experience of unemployment, she wrote, wanted 'to laugh, to relax, and to remain intellectually unstirred'; they had little idea of 'how to approach an art (i.e. drama) that wakes up the intelligence rather than putting it to sleep'.[75] And when the going got tough, there was a tendency to

---

[72] NA: EL 3/1, 'Regional directors' reports' (1942–4), Region 10; *CEMA Arts Bulletin*, no. 3 (July 1940).

[73] On Clydebank: *CEMA Arts Bulletin*, no. 13 (May 1941); Eve Kisch, 'Music in wartime', *Our Time*, 2(13) (July 1943), 11.

[74] NA: EL 2/56. Also, D. Sheridan, '"Singing while England is burning": Women musicians as working music travellers in wartime Britain, 1940–43' in K. Cowman and L. A. Jackson (eds.), *Women and Work Culture. Britain c.1850–1950* (Aldershot, 2005), p. 239.

[75] For 'hear the proverbial pin drop': NA: EL 2/28, G. Smith to Miss Crook, 25 November 1940, describing a Leeds factory tour: 'two thousand men fresh from their lathes and machines displaying

resort to generalities about workers' lack of 'mental alertness' or 'inability to concentrate' or to speculate about 'the percentage of workers who might be culturally rehabilitated'.[76]

As wartime cultural programmes expanded, reaching larger and previously untapped audiences, enthusiastic contemporaries began to speak of a 'cultural renaissance'. Dr Reginald Jacques, CEMA's musical director, wrote: 'Hundreds of thousands of people are discovering that music is not merely the prerogative of a few...but a necessary constituent in the life of Everyman...What a land of promise is this vast potential audience!' John Lehmann, the editor of *Penguin New Writing*, recalled: 'It seemed to me—as it seemed to many others—that under the most unlikely conditions, in the middle of a total war, something of a renaissance of the arts was taking place.'[77] Most historians, with a few recent exceptions, have also credited CEMA with a good deal of success in stimulating public interest in serious music, art, and drama.[78] Unfortunately, we have little reliable evidence about audience responses. CEMA organizers submitted reports on the reception of their programmes and these offer some insight into the responses of working-class audiences, although, it must be said, the writers were interested parties, in most cases committed to the mission and eager to promote a continuation of funding post-war. In their impact and popularity CEMA events almost certainly varied a good deal. Performances by well-known companies were highly successful. The London Philharmonic, the Halle, the Liverpool Philharmonic, Sadler's Wells, the Ballet Jooss, and the Ballet Rambert all played to large, appreciative audiences. The Old Vic's tour of the Welsh coalfields was undoubtedly a great success with the actors lodging with mining families. Charles Landstone recalled: 'It was exciting...to stand in this grim mining town and to watch the people in their Sunday best, pouring into the hall. You could see them across the valley...coming down the hill on the opposite side in a long crocodile.' Their silent attention to the play, he added, 'gave me the feeling that all this strain and pressure might really be worthwhile'. Similarly, when a star like the actress Sybil Thorndike gave a reading in the canteen of a Midland aircraft factory 'the silence and attention was extraordinary, and the applause tremendous'.[79] People gathered in mass shelters during the Blitz seemed to have appreciated CEMA's efforts and the same was probably true of war-workers, women's auxiliaries, and Land Girls stuck in remote hostels where there were few other entertainments; similarly

---

such intelligent appreciation of classical music'; Beatrix Lehmann, 'The theatre and the audience', *Our Time*, 2(7) (November 1942), 25.

[76] NA: EL 3/1, 'Regional directors' reports' (1942–4), report of Tom Harrison, 1944; report of Jeanette Jackson, 1944.

[77] Landstone, *Off-Stage*, p. 50; *CEMA Arts Bulletin*, no. 26 (June 1942); Lehmann, *I Am My Brother*, p. 161; J. Minihan, *The Nationalization of Culture* (New York, 1977).

[78] Among those who doubt CEMA's impact: Beaven, *Leisure, Citizenship and Working-Class Men in Britain*; Hayes, 'More than music while you eat?'; J. Pick, *Managing the Arts? The British experience* (London, 1986).

[79] Landstone, *Off-Stage*, p. 54. For Sybil Thorndyke: NA: EL 3/1, 'Regional directors' reports' (1942–4), Region 9, report by Tom Harrison.

concerts in village halls and churches were likely to be well received, drawing as they did self-selected audiences.

Far more difficult to assess is the response to CEMA's regular offerings of concerts and drama in factory canteens and workers' hostels. Workers were sometimes bored or preferred ENSA variety acts and many factory concerts were clearly failures.[80] In some huge canteens in government shadow factories performers could scarcely be heard above the din, while some workers admitted that, tired and dirty on their breaks, they simply did not feel like sitting and listening to a recital. At times, it seems, the managers, directors, and welfare officers of a firm who invited CEMA were much more enthusiastic than the average worker who preferred familiar tunes. The work of local Welfare Officers in preparing for appearances could have a considerable impact on their success or failure. As the Carlisle Regional Officer put it: 'an enthusiastic welfare officer seems the deciding factor, and even where he has no specific musical culture, he can produce an audience as quiet and attentive as in a concert hall even during the lunch hour'.[81] Clearly, much of the talk about a 'cultural upsurge' or dramatic changes in workers' preferences was pure hyperbole; for one thing, concerts were occasional rather than regular events in most factories. In part the exaggeration can be traced to the enthusiasm of progressives who believed that in culture and in other spheres, the war was lowering social barriers. But it is important not to fall into the other extreme: generalizing that workers were indifferent, interested in a pint, a bet, a smoke and little else, thereby lumping them together as an undifferentiated mass rather than collections of individuals.

From CEMA's own files it seems that regional differences were important in audience responses. In South Wales or the north-east, areas with strong traditions of adult education, brass bands, and choral groups, performers could expect a warm welcome. The Shropshire and Staffordshire mining districts were also consistently favourable terrain. After describing a disappointing factory tour where apathy was the dominant response, one violinist felt renewed by four concerts 'organized publicly in mining villages'; these 'met with tremendous success and appreciation which showed that there really is a keen and widespread demand for music among the working people of this country'.[82] Reports from the West Midlands indicate a

---

[80] Hayes, 'More than Music While You Eat?'

[81] NA: LAB 26/35, 'Provision of entertainment for munition workers'. NA: EL 2/21, 'Factory concerts, general correspondence' (1940–3) contains negative as well as positive reports on audience receptivity; for the workers 'tired and dirty' see Rossetti's notes for a Ministry of Labour conference on factory concerts, 3 March 1941. On active welfare officers: see the correspondence of J. A. Harvey, Welfare Officer of the W.T. Copeland, Spode Works, Stoke on Trent in NA: EL 2/30. He did preparatory work before and after CEMA visits: 'Enthusiasm is high; the venture, started as an experiment, now is an accepted fact and when next your artists visit us we shall be an enlightened audience instead of the "raw material".' (August 10, 1941). On the Spode Works see also *CEMA Arts Bulletin*, no. 17 (September 1941). Also NA: EL3/1, 'Regional directors' reports' (1942–4) report of Ms Anne Carlisle for Region 4.

[82] Violinist, 'A tour with CEMA', *Our Time*, 1(7) (September 1941), 18. He was also critical of the way that some managers and directors shepherded the CEMA artists around so that they had little time to meet workers and shop stewards; this he argues erected a 'barrier of distrust and suspicion' *vis-à-vis* the workers.

lower level of interest in canteen concerts and small turn-outs at hostels. In the eyes of CEMA staff members, skilled workers were more likely to be responsive than unskilled, while the toughest audiences of all were thought to be 'poorly educated young girls' recruited in the thousands into government ROFs. Yet even here there were exceptions: at ROF Aycliffe (County Durham) not only were concerts successful but workers formed their own musical groups and put on lunchtime recitals, while at ROF Hooten (Cheshire) the labour officer admitted: 'I was doubtful whether it [the concert] would be appreciated by the majority of our workers' but it turned out to be 'the most popular concert held in these works'.[83] CEMA's success in hostels also varied: in isolated areas (e.g. rural Land Army hostels) where there was little to do outside working hours, concerts and especially play readings were well received, but attendance was smaller if commercial entertainments were easily accessible. A general summary for 1942–3 declared: 'mixed audiences are much the best for all kinds of entertainment. An all-woman audience is often too emotional or hysterical; an all-male audience generally dull.'[84] Few reliable conclusions can be drawn from all this, although CEMA took its own internal reports seriously and tried increasingly to select venues where success could be anticipated. Clearly, a minority of workers were very receptive to CEMA's efforts and may well have continued to develop their artistic interests as a consequence. Admittedly, factory workers were captive audiences who were not exercising choice between classical music and other forms of entertainment. But, at the same time, a crowded lunch-room with tired and hungry workers listening to a three-musician recital was perhaps not the best measure of workers' interest in serious music. In the end what the records do show is how diverse workers' responses to CEMA were and the role of age, gender, factory environment, and local traditions in shaping them.

The expansion of CEMA occurred amid growing concerns about the nation's morale and an outpouring of radical critiques of pre-war society. National morale and social unity would be strengthened, it was argued, if the population had a deeper understanding of its common heritage and cultural roots. But consensus about the desirability of harnessing the arts for the nation's struggle masked disagreements over the definition of a 'common culture' and how to integrate the masses. For Keynes and Clark, maintaining artistic standards and bolstering established cultural institutions was always a major consideration. They regarded cultural policy as a process whereby the masses were invited to participate in elite 'high culture' by people who 'defined themselves as possessing superior sensibilities to which everyone else should aim'.[85] Others in CEMA advocated a more populist and educational approach, viewing the war as an opportunity to rekindle authentic folk traditions and to democratize the meaning of 'national culture'. For them,

---

[83] Criticism of female ROF workers: NA: EL 3/1, 'Regional directors' reports' (1942–4), Region 9, report by Tom Harrison. For ROF Aycliffe, NA: EL 3/1, Region 8, Report of M. Davidson, 1944; also report by Helen Munro, Region 1, May 1944. For ROF Hooten, NA: LAB 26/35, J. W. Brown to Regional Welfare Officer of Merseyside.

[84] NA: EL 1/16, 'Council papers' (1943–4), paper 161, report on year July 1942–June 1943.

[85] B. Foss, *War Paint: Art, war, state and identity in Britain 1939–45* (New Haven, 2007), p. 192.

giving workers access to music, painting, and drama enriched their leisure, provided an alternative to commercial entertainment, and at the same time promoted community and active citizenship. The socialist biologist and popular broadcaster Julian Huxley insisted that recreation (like health and education) should be planned as a 'social service'; the state should establish local civic centres as part of post-war reconstruction: 'art and beauty', he wrote, 'must be made to play their part'. On CEMA's board W. E. Williams also championed arts centres, writing in *Picture Post* in 1943: 'Let us so unify our popular culture that in every town we have a centre where people may listen to good music, look at paintings, study any subject under the sun, join in a debate, enjoy a game of badminton and get a mug of beer or cocoa before they go home.'[86] Williams's vision which, as Richard Weight has written, was an eclectic mix of ENSA and CEMA under one roof, excited the interest of planners and architects who produced some creative designs,[87] but few materialized in the period of post-war austerity.

Finally, CEMA's work illustrates two general characteristics of wartime culture. First, in this sphere, as in others, the early war years opened up a space for radical ideas and an idealism which retreated before more conservative and limited goals by 1943. Secondly, while these progressive intellectuals from the middle and upper classes sought to educate workers and foster a more cohesive nation, their work often had the effect of highlighting or focusing attention on class differences. CEMA's project was populist in the sense of wishing to incorporate workers more fully into the imagined nation. But by assuming that the reformers understood and could represent the good of all sections of society, it was also inherently hegemonic. Workers' needs and interests were recognized, but in ways that maintained the social space between them and those who spoke for them.[88]

At the war's end there was more than a whiff of utopianism about the anticipated future of the arts. ENSA was quickly wound up, but powerful forces, among them Keynes and R. A. Butler, who took over the Board of Education in 1941, had carefully prepared the ground for CEMA's transformation into an Arts Council making state patronage of the arts permanent. In addition, Labour's electoral landslide strengthened the conviction of left-wing groups—those associated with the magazine *Our Time*, for example—that a new era had dawned for the arts. Within a few years, however, the euphoria had passed, a more pessimistic mood set in, and wartime discourse about a classless national culture dissipated.

Contemporaries and historians have given several explanations for this. Some writers have emphasized the role of Keynes and the Arts Council in undermining the populist potential of CEMA and focusing state funding on established arts institutions and support for professionalism. But Keynes died in 1946 and presumably his priorities could have been modified had the will to do so been present.

[86] J. Huxley, 'Economic and social man', *The Fortnightly*, July 1941; *Picture Post*, 2 January 1943. Also *CEMA Bulletin*, no. 55 (November 1944), no. 66 (October 1945); NA: T 227/69 ('Conferences on enjoyment of leisure, 1948–50').
[87] R. Weight, '"Building a new British culture": The Arts Centre Movement 1943–53' in R. Weight and A. Beach, *The Right to Belong* (London, 1998).
[88] Scannell, 'Factory programmes for the workers on British wartime radio'.

Among socialist intellectuals the focus of blame was more often Attlee's Labour Party, whose failure to pursue a socialist agenda for the arts, it was argued, opened the way for cultural conservatives to reassert their agenda; this was the conclusion of communist author Jack Lindsay, who wrote enthusiastically about a wartime cultural renaissance, but described the post-war decade as a 'betrayed spring' (a reference to 1848 and the 'spring-time of peoples', very much in the news at the time).[89] In his Fabian lecture *The Arts under Socialism* (1947), J. B. Priestley also regretted that a golden opportunity was being missed: 'There are too many people in authority here', he argued, 'who fail to appreciate the importance of art to a society like ours.'[90] Andrew Croft's recent writings have also accepted the claim that the war had produced a 'cultural upsurge' whose potential the post-war Labour government neither cultivated nor understood.[91]

Labour had other pressing economic and legislative priorities and by 1947 economic crisis brought sharp cuts in many areas, but in fact it did triple funding for the arts, most of it going to support Covent Garden, Sadler's Wells, the Old Vic, the nation's leading orchestras, and new arts festivals at Aldeburgh, Edinburgh, and Cheltenham. What critics on the left at the time objected to was its failure to nurture specifically socialist cultural organizations, while among historians Ross McKibbin has berated Labour for its narrow, economic conception of socialism, arguing that its refusal to challenge or uncritical acceptance of powerful social institutions or status hierarchies in civil society blunted the potential for radical change.[92] Possibly the government feared a backlash if public funds were allocated for a clearly ideological agenda, but with respect to the arts and cultural policy the party lacked clear aims. Socialist artists and intellectuals debated cultural reform and popular recreation but most Labour supporters in the constituencies and the trade unions, apart from occasional rhetoric on the subject, focused on workers' material needs and the party's electoral prospects. The trade unions, for example, debated leisure mostly in the context of demands for a forty-hour week and paid vacations. As Jeff Hill has pointed out, the dominant discourse in Labour circles was liberal and pluralist. Democratic socialism meant choice among the widest selection of pleasures provided by private business, voluntary action, and the state. The state's role, in other words, was to provide more libraries, sports facilities, and theatres, not to tell workers what they should like. 'The use of leisure', so ran the party's electoral manifesto in 1949, 'is something personal. We do not want exhortation or interference. We do want greater richness of opportunity for the individual.'[93]

---

[89] J. Lindsay, *Betrayed Spring* (London, 1953).

[90] J. B. Priestley, *The Arts under Socialism* (London, 1947), p. 9; also, *Our Time* (March 1947), 171.

[91] A. Croft, 'Betrayed spring: The Labour Party and the British literary culture' in J. Fyrth, *Labour's Promised Land: Culture and society in Labour Britain 1945–51* (London, 1995).

[92] McKibbin, *Classes and Cultures*, p. 534; also *idem, Parties and People: England 1914–1951* (Oxford, 2010), pp. 158–63.

[93] J. Hill, 'When work is over: Labour, leisure and culture in wartime Britain' in Hayes and Hill (eds.), *'Millions Like Us'?*. Election Manifesto quoted at p. 260.

It is also very doubtful whether workers had much interest in the kind of provision that intellectuals on the left advocated. Expectations had been pitched too high and the sense of let-down was equally great. In his memoir Charles Landstone admitted: 'All of us thought that all that remained to be done was to provide new buildings and new theatres for this vast new audience, but, unfortunately, an extraordinary thing happened. The audience disappeared from their hostels, camps and their war centres, and in a flash [they] appeared to have left their interest behind them.'[94] The Arts Council's regional directors reported that while middle-class support for 'high culture' remained enthusiastic and solid, workers were withdrawing in favour of commercial entertainments and familiar pursuits. As peacetime patterns of life re-established themselves, it was workers' traditional pastimes that boomed, now sustained by higher wages and full employment. Pubs, cinemas, and dance halls did well; seaside resorts and holiday camps received huge crowds in the summer months; and the attendances at football, rugby, speedway, horse, and dog racing were at a record high. Aneurin Bevan's Local Government Act of 1948 contained a clause permitting local authorities to levy a special rate for support of cultural activities, including the establishment of local civic or arts centres.[95] But cash-strapped local governments who doubted the centres were even needed chose not to follow through.[96]

But it was not just workers whose interest flagged. There was also a loss of enthusiasm among intellectuals and artists who had joined the war effort in large numbers and embraced the project of unifying the nation through culture as a form of radical action. Some signs of unease were already evident during the war. Cyril Connolly warned in *Horizon*: 'We are becoming a nation of culture-diffusionists... We are not making true art...war artists are not art, the Brains Trust is not art, journalism is not art, the BBC is not art, all the CEMA shows, all the ABCA lectures, all the discussion groups...we are turning all our writers into commentators until there will be nothing left to commentate on.'[97] Working as a reporter V. S. Pritchett visited shipyards and factories and his diary entries echoed Orwell's call for a revolution, but looking back, he reflected: 'I'm not sure that to be so drowned in the mass was good for the act of writing...A writer soon finds himself wondering how large a helping of human beings his talent can manage.'[98] But it was in the late 1940s and early 1950s, with socialism in power, growing criticism of austerity and middle-class 'plight', and the beginning of the cold war, that the prevailing mood shifted.

---

[94] Landstone, *Off-Stage*, p. 60. Also, S. J. Coulson, 'Culture: Boom or slump?', *Our Time* (August 1946).

[95] Weight, 'Building a new British culture'; I. Evans and M. Glasgow, *The Arts in England* (London, 1949), p. 25.

[96] They were more successful in South Wales, though even there the younger generation had less interest in miners' institutes by the 1950s. Griffin, 'Not Just a Case of Baths, Canteens and Rehabilitation Centres'; M. Nicholson, *Clubs for Citizens* (London, 1945); NA: T 227/69 ('Conferences on Enjoyment of Leisure, 1948–50') contains discussions of arts centres and local authority funding.

[97] C. Connolly, 'Writers and society 1940–43' in *idem*, *The Condemned Playground* (London, 1945), p. 285. Also, J. Spink, 'The strategic retreat of the left', *Horizon* (January 1943).

[98] V. S. Pritchett, *Midnight Oil* (London, 1971), p. 242.

Contrasting the left-wing ethos of the 1930s and the post-war mood, American sociologist Edward Shils emphasized the revival of patrician elite culture, evident, among other things, in the iconic status of T. S. Eliot whose *Notes Towards a Definition of Culture* (mostly written during the war) deplored the recent tendency 'to dissimulate social distinctions and to pretend that the highest degree of "culture" ought to be made accessible to everybody'.[99] The defence of cultural and aesthetic standards replaced the democratization of culture and when in 1959 the 'Two Cultures' controversy erupted between C. P. Snow and F. R. Leavis, the phrase denoted the gulf between the Arts and the Sciences; it had nothing to do with the division between 'serious' and 'popular' culture.[100]

The last curtain call for the project of presenting nation and culture as a unitary whole came in 1951 with Labour's Festival of Britain. The idea for a centenary celebration of Queen Victoria's Great Exhibition was suggested as early as 1943 by the Royal Society of Arts but the driving force behind it was Herbert Morrison who wanted to celebrate the nation's recovery from the war and revive the spirit of wartime citizenship and collectivism. Taking a cue from Gracie Fields, Morrison declared: 'I want to hear the people sing.'[101] The Festival pavilions on London's South Bank and related events in communities across the country showcased British culture and traditions, science, and technology. Popular entertainments were featured alongside specially commissioned choral, operatic, orchestral, and artistic works and the bold, clean lines of Festival architecture aligned the whole thing with modernism and the future—an escape from current austerities and drabness. Organized by high-minded, middle-class do-gooders, planners, and progressives, it was—as Michael Frayn observed in a sparkling essay—the splendid swan-song of these 'Herbivores' just before profit-minded 'Carnivores' of the 1950s retook the citadel.[102] The Festival attracted millions of visitors but wartime solidarity was irrecoverable—indeed it had always been fractured and ambiguous. The project of constructing a more democratic national culture no longer had momentum. In the mid-1950s the divide between an elite 'high culture,' increasingly sustained by state patronage, and a largely self-enclosed working-class culture, whose entertainment was commercial and self-financing, seemed as wide and firmly ingrained as ever.

[99] T. S. Eliot, *Notes Towards a Definition of Culture* (New York, 1959), p. 81; E. Shils, 'The intellectuals', *Encounter*, 4(4) (April 1955). R. Hewison, *Under Siege: Literary life in London 1939-45* (Oxford, 1977); and R. Weight, 'State, intelligentsia, and the promotion of national culture in Britain, 1939-45', *Historical Research*, 69(168) (February 1996) follow Shils in exaggerating, in my view, the shift during the war years as opposed to afterwards.

[100] P. Mandler and S. Pedersen (eds.), *After the Victorians: Private conscience and public duty in modern Britain* (London, 1994); P. Mandler, 'Two cultures—one—or many?' in K. Burk (ed.), *The British Isles since 1945* (Oxford, 2003).

[101] Conjuring up Gracie Fields's film, *Sing As We Go* (1934, dir. Dean) and *Let the People Sing* (1942; dir. Baxter).

[102] Michael Frayn, 'Festival' in M. Sissons and P. French (eds.), *Age of Austerity, 1945-51* (London, 1963); M.Banham and B. Hillier (eds.), *A Tonic to the Nation: The Festival of Britain 1951* (London, 1976); B. Conekin, *'The Autobiography of a Nation': The 1951 Festival of Britain* (Manchester, 2003).

7

A Citizens' Army

Despite the huge number of studies of wartime society and an equally rich literature analysing specific military campaigns, the long-standing gulf between social and military historians is still very much in evidence in the historiography of Britain during the Second World War. Most social histories make an explicit or implied equation of 'home front' and 'civilian' which means that servicemen are treated as some kind of invisible 'Other' whose absence and needs shaped the lives of those at home but who otherwise scarcely appear, notwithstanding the fact that the majority spent most of the war in Britain in camps, depots, and bases. On the military side, with a few exceptions, the social history of the armed forces is in its infancy. And yet men (and women) in uniform were integral to every aspect of the war years, whether it was jobs, class-stratification, debates about morality, problems of marital breakdown, family poverty, politics, or post-war reconstruction. Those based in Britain moved back and forth between families and camps and were sometimes drafted into rescue and rubble-clearance in blitzed cities; those abroad were never far from their families' thoughts, while demobilization and reintegration into civilian life defined the early post-war years.

One problem, of course, in writing about the soldier's experience stems from its extraordinary diversity, far more than in the First World War when so many took a one-way trip to the trenches of northern France. Garrison duty on Gibraltar bore little resemblance to training-camp life in Britain or to the conditions of desert and jungle combat in Libya and Burma. What follows, then, is not an attempt at a condensed social history of workers in uniform; this would inevitably be too general or hopelessly kaleidoscopic. Instead emphasis is placed on class relationships as they injected themselves into army life, the clash of citizenship rights and military discipline, and the forms of political expression that surfaced, especially towards the end of the war. Final comments on demobilization and, in particular, the plight of disabled veterans illustrate both the mood and treatment of returning veterans and the fact, often neglected, that for many families the war did not end in 1945 but was a constant and terrible companion for years thereafter. Armies are a special kind of social institution; they reflect the values, priorities, and policies of the societies in which they develop. In the case of Britain the wartime army also illustrates the larger clash in society between the forces of entrenched tradition and those pressing for greater democratization.

CIVILIANS INTO UNIFORM

For the second time in a quarter century the British army, a small, conservative, professional organization, mostly designed for policing the empire, was rapidly transformed into a conscript force ten times its peacetime size and capable of fighting a modern, mechanized war on the Continent and elsewhere. Within two years of the end of hostilities in 1918, the army had shrunk from 3.5 million men to 370,000 and by 1927 its size had been further reduced to 207,000 men, many dispersed in small garrisons overseas rather than large fighting formations. As the international situation deteriorated in the 1930s, the nation found itself caught between well-founded Treasury forebodings about the dangers of large defence expenditures on an economically weak state and military demands for armaments increases. The strategic priority given to the air force and navy, coupled with continuing party political wrangling over conscription, further delayed the reconstruction of the army.

It was only in March 1939, in the panic-stricken atmosphere after the Prague crisis, that the government announced its intention of doubling the Territorial Army and then a month later authorized the first-ever peacetime conscription. This was initially limited to six months' training followed by service in the reserves for men of between twenty and twenty-one years. With the outbreak of war in September military obligation was extended to all males of between eighteen and forty-one years. These sudden moves produced considerable chaos. Registration proceeded slowly affecting only those under twenty-seven years by May 1940 and did not include men of forty until the summer of 1941. Between the war's outbreak and June 1941 the army tripled in size (to 2.2 million men) and reached its peak of just under 3 million men in June 1945.[1] Such rapid expansion produced numerous problems, especially since the RAF and the navy had budgetary priority prior to the war. The existing system for selecting recruits for the army's diverse occupations relied heavily on a brief interview at enlistment, but it soon became evident that this resulted in a serious wastage of skills with many men inappropriately categorized and discontented. Eventually in the summer of 1941 the system of personnel selection became more efficient through wider use of psychological and aptitude testing and by deferring placement until after basic training was completed. The rapid acceleration of recruitment also stretched to the limits the army's capacity to train, equip, and provide adequate officers and NCOs for the force resulting in severe shortages of weapons and primitive, makeshift camps, with many recruits living under canvas for extended periods of time.[2] These problems were further

---

[1] The Royal Navy and Air Force, though smaller in size, also expanded very rapidly. Royal Navy: 180,000 in June 1939, 395,000 in June 1941, and 783,000 in June 1945. The Royal Air Force: 193,000 in June 1939, 662,000 in June 1941, and 950,000 in June 1945.

[2] P. J. Wainwright, 'The National Service debate: Government conscription and the peace movement in Britain, 1936–1942', PhD Diss., Stanford University, 1993. On the assignment of personnel to specific units: J. A. Crang, *The British Army and the People's War* (Manchester, 2000), ch. 1; P. Vernon and J. B. Parry, *Personnel Selection in the British Forces* (London, 1949); IWM: R. K. Ellis, MS microfilm.

aggravated by the massive losses of weapons and equipment suffered in the French campaign and at Dunkirk.

Far fewer troops were engaged in combat than in the First World War. In this more mobile and mechanized war, a British infantry division of 17,000 soldiers had about 4,000 combat troops or around 66–75 per cent in support positions. Over 25 per cent of the army were classified as skilled tradesmen. This accounts in part for the much lower likelihood of death or injury than in the First World War, although among fighting units the statistics remained very high, especially in Normandy in 1944 where the infantry, which represented less than 25 per cent of the total force, sustained the overwhelming majority of casualties. Altogether in this war 145,000 soldiers were killed or died from injuries; almost 240,000 were wounded, respectively 4.6 and 8.7 per cent of the total (the rates for the Western Front 1914–18 were 13.4 and 36.4 per cent). Most of these casualties came in Italy and Northern Europe in the final eighteen months of the war; by comparison the rates for fighting, brutal though it was, in the Western Desert and the Far East were much lower, although in those theatres malaria, dysentery, and digestive diseases were a terrible scourge. Men wounded in battle did, however, have a better chance of recovery than in the First World War, thanks to improved medical services, blood transfusions, sulpha-drugs, and penicillin—the latter being first available in large quantities for the Italian campaign.[3] In addition, some 173,000 soldiers became prisoners of war;[4] those captured in the battle for France endured captivity for five years and those at Singapore for over three years under far worse conditions. A few limited exchanges of seriously disabled prisoners were arranged with Germany and Italy before the conflict was over, but only 4,000 gained early release in this way.

Some men, less than 25 per cent, volunteered, motivated by patriotism or the assumption that they might thereby have a wider choice of service options. But there was no reprise of the war enthusiasm of August 1914; most waited for their induction notices. Few inductees were rejected as 'definitely unfit for service', but an increasing number of later medical discharges raised questions about the validity of initial health inspections. Aside from medical and occupational deferments or exemptions from conscription, provision was also made for conscientious objection to military service. In all 59,000 men (1.2 per cent of those called up by the forces) gained conscientious objector status after appearing at local tribunals: they accounted for about 2 per cent of those registering in late 1939, but from July 1940 the rate had declined to below 0.5 per cent. Some firms and many local councils dismissed conscientious objectors or refused to employ them; sometimes they encountered prejudice from co-workers, but overall the level of persecution was far less than in the previous war, in part because the government had by late

---

[3] John Ellis, *The Sharp End: The fighting man in World War II* (New York, 1980), pp. 156–85; M. Harrison, *Medicine and Victory: British military medicine in the Second World War* (Oxford, 2004). The total of British dead and wounded in the First World War was 2,370,000.

[4] 135,000 were POWs in the European war, another 38,000 were prisoners in the war against Japan.

1940 adopted a much broader concept of national service, which included important and dangerous activities at home.[5]

On entering the army, recruits confronted basic training: an endless round of parades, route marches, drills, saluting, kit inspections, petty harassment, and 'spit and polish' designed to erode individuality and to compel conformity, discipline, and obedience. This process for whipping raw recruits into shape had changed little since the previous war, but efforts to modify drill and introduce new kinds of training met with persistent opposition from regimental commanders, many of whom, David French writes, returned from Dunkirk 'convinced that their troops needed more, not less, training in formal drill and obedience to orders'.[6] But the generation that grew up after the carnage of the Somme was in general better educated; less pliable; and more anti-military, class conscious, and cynical than their fathers. 'After nearly three months in the army', complained one private in December 1940, 'I have not yet fired a rifle, never handled the equipment I am supposed ultimately to use, and possess no more knowledge than I did in civilian life of how to defend myself, let alone defend other people, and have all the time lived in the most miserable conditions under canvas.'[7] 'Last night's orders', reported a Royal Artillery lance-corporal in 1942, 'stated that all woodwork (skirting boards, doors etc.) in barrack rooms were to be washed and everything generally cleaned up for the morning inspection...Our room, however, was among a score or so to be checked for not being up to standard. Apparently we had forgotten to dust the top of the door.'[8] Small infractions resulted in punishments or fatigues: from confinement to barracks and extra guard duty to cookhouse chores, painting, digging, cleaning, and parading in full kit. 'I joined the army because I thought it was the only way to fight fascism', explained a Glaswegian fusilier with a long record of punishments, 'a lot of my troubles came about when...I met the same attitudes in the British army.'[9]

New recruits quickly learned the rules: avoid officers; never volunteer; carry out an order no matter how ridiculous; always walk as though you are on an errand, preferably with a bucket or a piece of paper in hand, so as to avoid being nabbed for fatigues; remain inconspicuous and learn 'the great secret of how to look busy and do nothing'. It was a world sharply divided into 'Them' and 'Us' which promoted cooperation among 'squaddies' and a code of covering for others, for it was only as

---

[5] Of the 20–21-year-olds called up in 1939, the Ministry of Health claimed that only 2.3% were 'definitely unfit' for service (*The Times*, 17 June 1940); Rachel Barker, *Conscience, Government, and War: Conscientious objection in Great Britain 1939–1945* (London, 1982).

[6] D. French, *Raising Churchill's Army: The British Army and the war against Germany* (Oxford, 2000), p. 193.

[7] *Daily Worker*, 10 December 1940. Some 324,000 men were enlisted in the army between June and August 1940, too many for the training system to absorb and before the military could resupply after the crippling equipment losses in the French campaign.

[8] M-OA: FR 1485, 'Basis of political trends in the army' (November 1942). Also, M-OA: FR 836, 'An army depot' (August 1941). Another example: Ellis, *The Sharp End*, p. 15.

[9] P. Grafton, *You, You, and You: The people out of step with World War II* (London, 1981), p. 113. Also, IWM: N. Chaston (microfilm); C. Parker MS; H. Berry (microfilm); L. A. Roebuck MS; R. K. Ellis (microfilm).

part of a team that one could cope. But at a time when morale was battered by repeated defeats, age-old army rituals seemed to confirm a growing perception that the army was a dinosaur, outmoded and outclassed in the modern age of blitz-krieg.[10] Recruits who had never been away from home or had led sheltered lives suffered most from the cramped, primitive conditions, fatigues, and NCO insults; later intakes included older recruits, many with strong trade union ties, who were particularly critical of pointless routines.

With the fall of France most British assumptions about how this war would be fought also collapsed. The immediate task was to rebuild and re-equip the army for home defence and a possible German invasion. Once Russia and the United States entered the war against Hitler, however, Britain's future role as a base for invading the Continent became clear and troops were trained for that campaign. Military historians disagree over the extent to which army leaders learned from their mistakes, undertook a fundamental overhaul of the organization, or revised their basic doctrine. However, in the provision of welfare services there were dramatic changes. Underlying them was a recognition that the efficiency and training of servicemen was impaired by boredom, marital worries, and anxiety about their families, especially those in heavily raided cities. In addition, the army greatly expanded its educational programmes. British soldiers, it was argued, had little sense of what they were fighting for and lacked the zeal and ideological commit-ment of German and Japanese troops. The expansion of these programmes, despite resistance on the part of conservative officers, reflected both the more democratic, egalitarian ethos of Britain's war effort after 1940 and—as the string of humiliating defeats continued in Greece, Crete, Singapore, and Tobruk—recognition that army morale had sunk very low. By the end of 1941 a whole array of welfare services were in place, including voluntary local welfare officers to provide information about families, radio programmes aimed at the forces, and a large increase in organized leisure activities including film shows, CEMA plays and concerts, sports, dances, and educational classes. These changes paralleled a similar expansion of welfare for the vast numbers of male and female civilians mobilized into war production.

These reforms, however, did nothing to reduce deep discontent over low pay and meagre dependants' allowances which, despite gradual improvements, continued to lag far behind civilian wages. At first an army private got 17s a week, out of which 7s was stopped for his wife; he also had to pay for kit-cleaning materials and met any barracks breakage charges out of the remainder. Recruits' boredom stemmed in part from the fact that they could not afford to do much that was not free. Comparison with civilian workers and foreign troops, especially American GIs who received four or five times as much pay and were further subsidized by cheap PX prices, made the poverty of British soldiers all the more intolerable. 'The soldier really begins to grouse', wrote one sergeant-major, 'when he goes into a pub and finds that he can only afford a glass of beer, whilst the munition worker

---

[10] M-OA: FR 836, 'An army depot' (August 1941); M-OA: FR 1105: 'Morale in Donnington' (March 1942); M-OA: FR 747, 'Civilian queries about army life and organisation' (June 1941); M-OA: FR 886, 'Civilian attitudes to the navy compared to the RAF and army' (September 1941).

slaps down a £1 note and asks for a whisky or gin'.[11] Residual Poor Law attitudes seemed also to govern allowances to soldiers' families, which were often insufficient to provide for basic necessities. After considerable pressure and political debate, the rates were raised in 1942 so that an army private got 3s a day or 21s a week from which he made a compulsory allotment of 3s 6d to his wife, leaving him with 17s 6d basic pay. His wife received 18s a week, plus an additional 7s (half from the government and half from her husband's pay) and allowances for their children.[12] Child payments, it should be noted, were set below the rates that had provoked nationwide discontent among billetors of evacuees. An army private's wife and two children received 32s a week in 1939, 38s at the beginning of 1942, and 43s later in 1942 until April 1944, when the rate was raised significantly to 60s. By far the largest group of complaints (39 per cent) in servicemen's letters to John Hilton's popular radio programme in early 1942 were about pay and allowances.

A War Office morale report concluded in 1942: it was 'generally accepted as *axiomatic* that a private soldier's wife and children in an urban area who had no resources other than his pay and allowances simply could not manage'.[13] Surveys showed that many women quickly found themselves in debt and that shopkeepers and landlords were particularly reluctant to extend credit or rent to service wives with young families. Not only were the poorest groups affected, but better-paid working-class families, whose income had sharply contracted, suddenly found themselves unable to keep up with rents, mortgages, insurance, and hire-purchase payments. Many wives took war jobs and since nursery places were few and costly they often relied on relatives or minders to look after their children. Many saved money by moving in with parents or in-laws, although this created strains of a different sort. Far better off were young wives without children, who could live cheaply with parents while receiving both their basic allowance and wages from war jobs.[14] Advised by the Treasury against large flat-rate increases in allowances and reluctant to weaken work incentives for forces' wives, the government established supplementary war service grants to meet special hardships. Large numbers of grants (averaging 15s a week) were eventually made, but critics charged that these means-tested payments carried a stigma that made many of the needy loath to apply. They also did not cover widowed mothers or aged parents whose sons helped them financially before conscription; they had to turn for help to the Public Assistance Board.[15] It is hardly surprising that

---

[11] PRO: WO 32/15772, morale reports for 1942 repeatedly focus on pay grievances in the military. 'Democritus', *What's Wrong with the Army?* (London, 1942); M-OA: FR 827, 'Report on service and civilian pay' (August 1941); M-OA: FR 1418, 'Service pay' (September 1942); also M-OA: TC Armed Forces Box 4. The sergeant's quotation is from NA: WO 163/161, May–July 1942. The Communist Party issued a number of pamphlets advocating for higher service pay, including a basic rate of 5s a day for privates and their equivalents: e.g. *Fair Play for Servicemen and Their Families* (1941); *Army Pay and Allowances* (1942); Frank Lesser, *Service Pay, Allowances, and Pensions* (1942).

[12] *PD* (Commons), 19 December 1941, 19 February 1942, 2 March 1942.

[13] NA: WO 32/15772, May–July 1942.

[14] C. Madge, *War-time Patterns of Saving and Spending* (Cambridge, 1943); R. M. Titmuss, *Problems of Social Policy* (London, 1950), p. 415fn. BIPO polls, conducted in October 1941, August 1942, and March 1944 all showed a high level of public support for higher army pay.

[15] *PD* (Commons), 2 March 1944.

Beveridge's 1942 social insurance report, promising a basic minimum for families, received strong support from servicemen.

In addition to financial worries, War Office morale reports indicate increasing anxiety among servicemen about the stability of their marriages and the fidelity of girlfriends and wives. The war had a marked effect on nuptiality rates with a fairly dramatic rise in late 1939 as couples expecting to be separated got married. Questioning some 200 working-class soldiers and their wives, Slater and Woodside showed how little time many had enjoyed together, particularly those wed just before call-up, often after brief courtships: 'five years married but parted for four'; 'six years married but away in the army for five'; 'happy, what we've had of it', commented one serviceman who had been married for four and a half years with a fortnight being the longest he had spent with his spouse.[16] For those posted overseas the strain of separation was especially difficult: two-thirds of British forces eventually served abroad and among those overseas in 1945 at least 250,000 had been away continuously for five years and many more for two to four years.[17]

For a population that had mostly left school at fourteen, letter-writing was a flawed and unfamiliar means of communication. Opportunities for misunderstandings and uncertainties abounded. Stories circulated freely about 'good time girls', the promiscuity of female war-workers living in hostels away from their home-towns, and the sexual conquests of American and other Allied troops stationed in Britain (esteem for the Red Army was not unrelated to the fact that they were not on British soil).[18] Soldiers overseas often had only a vague sense of the multiple burdens shouldered by wives, especially those who kept their fears and troubles out of letters; similarly, most husbands conveyed only a sanitized version of what army life or combat was really like. Mail deliveries overseas, despite the army's recognition of their importance, could be delayed or lost altogether, especially in the case of forward units whose letters might take months to arrive. Men stationed in Britain were more fortunate, but leaves were brief and infrequent and wartime travel was notoriously difficult, especially for those in isolated areas. Compassionate leave for 'home' troops could be granted in extreme circumstances where an air raid or some

---

[16] E. Slater and M. Woodside, *Patterns of Marriage: A study of marriage relationships in the urban working classes* (London, 1951), p. 215. See also S. Sokoloff, ' "How are they at home?": Community, state, and servicemen's wives in England 1939–45', *Women's History Review*, 8(1) (1999).

[17] S. M. Ferguson and H. Fitzgerald, *Studies in the Social Services* (London, 1954), p. 3.

[18] Few soldiers saw in the same light trips to brothels or flings in Naples or Brussels—a double standard of faithfulness remained firmly in place. IWM: C. G. Beech MS. The army operated a system of regulated brothels in most overseas areas, while trying to crack down on unregulated or 'amateur' prostitution. Pressure from the Church, morality societies, and those concerned about venereal disease led to the Cairo military brothel (the Berka) being placed out of bounds to forces in August 1942; similar measures were taken later in Italy and N.W. Europe. Mark Harrison emphasizes the extent to which debate about brothels was class-based with 'Other Ranks' viewed as more vulnerable, having less self-discipline than officers and 'more limited resources for sublimation through social and intellectual interests'. M. Harrison, 'Sex and the citizen soldier: Health, morals, and discipline in the British army during the Second World War' in R. Cooter, M. Harrison, and S. Sturdy (eds.), *Medicine and Modern Warfare* (Amsterdam, 1999). In a later book Harrison notes that every case cited by a 1942 study of VD in the army was 'drawn from the other ranks, giving the impression that such behaviour was class-based': M. Harrison, *Medicine and Victory: British military medicine in the Second World War* (Oxford, 2004), p. 101.

other emergency had thrown a family into crisis and by 1943–4 requests averaged 8,000 a month reflecting the accumulated strains of protracted separations. For soldiers abroad a posting home on compassionate grounds was very rare.[19]

In official documents blame for marital breakups and deteriorating moral standards focused squarely upon wives; they were chief culprits. 'Many excellent young mothers', a London probation officer concluded in answer to a Home Office survey, 'have been unable to stand the loneliness at home, particularly when their husbands are abroad, with not even spasmodic leave to break the monotony... Hasty war marriages, on embarkation leave, sometimes between comparative strangers, with a few days or weeks of married life, have left both parties with little sense of responsibility towards one another.' A Medical Officer in the Middle East reported that the fidelity of wives 'usually stood two years' separation but that in the third and subsequent years an increasing percentage lapsed'.[20] A much sharper accusatory strain threads its way through the War Office morale reports. In mid-1942 one of these catalogued ways that women lowered morale:

1. Women persuade their husbands to go absent and overstay their leave.

2. Women dissuade husbands for volunteering for overseas and dangerous duties.

3. Women absent themselves from factories—so as to coincide with husband's leaves.

4. 'A worry which is constantly sapping the morale of a great part of the Army is due to the suspicion, very frequently justified, of fickleness on the part of wives and "girls".'

5. 'Women almost invariably prefer the society of R.A.F., civilian workers, U.S. and Dominion troops to that of the British soldier because he has less money to spend on them.'[21]

'The most efficient fifth-column work done out here is carried on by the women of England', commented an army parson in North Africa. 'Wives who should pre-sumably be a source of comfort seem to be in many cases the reverse', concluded another report, adding that 'letters from wives who are not equal to the test of prolonged separation do perhaps more than any other single factor to undermine the soldier's morale... and often persuade the soldier to go absent'. 'Anxiety, indignation and a sort of despairing cynicism', claimed yet another report in early 1943, 'are rife among the First and Eighth Armies in Libya and Egypt, and intense bitterness is felt against the Canadians and Americans, who are supposed, rightly or wrongly, to be the causes of the trouble.' Of an average hundred 'anxiety cases daily', '1/3 are proven infidelity of wives, 1/3 suspected infidelity (in most cases the

[19] Titmuss, *Problems of Social Policy*, pp. 209, 414–15; NA: WO 32/15772, February–May 1944.
[20] Ferguson and Fitzgerald, *Studies in the Social Services*, pp. 99, 23.
[21] NA: WO 32/15772, 'The influence of women' (May–July 1942). Also, Brigadier A. B. McPherson, NA: WO 277/16, 'Army discipline' (War Office, 1950). For similar air force worries: M. Francis, *The Flyer: British culture and the Royal Air Force 1939–1945* (Oxford, 2008), ch. 4.

suspicion proves to have been well founded) and the remaining 1/3, other forms of domestic trouble'. Even the highly publicized anti-VD campaign, mounted by the government in Britain, was said to be construed by troops in India as proof of increased sexual licence among women at home. After a tour of the Italian, Middle East, and Persia-Iraq commands in the summer of 1944, Lieutenant-Colonel J. H. Sparrow, the intelligence officer who compiled many of the morale summaries, argued that no greater enemy of morale existed than these domestic anxieties, especially among long-service men. He added: 'Nine times out of ten it [marital friction] is caused by selfish women', and, though far from paragons of virtue themselves, many soldiers felt badly let down by British women and 'profoundly ashamed of them'.[22] The voices here, it is important to remember, are those of officials and senior officers: quick to blame women, mostly insensitive to their hardships, angered that non-military factors should damage efficiency. Worries about soldiers' fighting spirit and lax discipline were blamed on 'feminine influence' and women's failure to restrain their sexual desires for the national interest.

Many separated couples remained faithful; many did not; and large numbers of marriages went through rocky periods or collapsed altogether. But it is important to note, for example, that the often-cited link between men going AWOL and 'worries about home' also reflected the fact that those claiming domestic troubles generally received more leniency. Bad news from home and a wife's alleged infidelity were accepted as 'mitigating factors' by review boards reviewing court-martial sentences. According to regulations, it was a 'soldier's duty to inform his C.O. immediately he knows, or has strong reason to believe, that normal domestic relations has [*sic*] ceased between himself and his wife and his family'. In a growing number of cases, jealous soldiers caused their wives severe economic hardships by angrily beginning formal separation proceedings. Once the army accepted a husband's claim, administrative practice placed the burden upon the wife. And since the War Office regarded a wife's allotment as an emolument of the soldier, granted to assist him in meeting his family obligation, it insisted that the commitment ended once he disavowed those obligations, even before any legal separation had been concluded. As was pointed out in a Commons debate in 1943, this could be disastrous and demands were made that allowances be continued so long as a soldier remained legally responsible for maintaining his family. Also, once set in motion, perhaps in the heat of anger, many soldiers also found the process difficult to reverse.[23]

Through the Army Reconciliation Scheme, begun in spring 1942, local Army Welfare Officers, in cooperation with a variety of family welfare groups and social work organizations, worked to resolve marital disputes and shore up unions in trouble. Probation officers could also be called in where an illegitimate child had

[22] NA: WO 32/15772, May–July 1942; August–October 1942; February–April 1943; May–July 1943 (8th Army); March–May 1944 (India); NA: WO 163/163, Lieut.-Col. J. H. A. Sparrow, 'Report on a tour of Italy, M.E., and P.A.I.C., June to September 1944'; J. H. Sparrow, *Army Morale* (HMSO London, 1949). A wealthy barrister, Sparrow later served as Warden of All Soul's College, Oxford. The BBC reported in spring 1944 that British troops were concluding from the anti-VD campaign that 'there is a serious breakdown of morals among the womenfolk at home'.
[23] NA: WO 32/15772, February–April 1943; *PD* (Commons), 5 August 1943.

been born to a soldier's wife or he had received no news for a long time. After 1942 there was considerable public debate about 'irregular' births to wives of servicemen overseas, although not even rough statistics exist, and higher illegitimacy rates generally provoked alarm. Many returning servicemen simply accepted as their own children born in their absence. Some wives decided upon adoption, although this required a spouse's consent; still others who wanted to keep their child found that reconciliation with their husband was conditional on giving it up. In addition, divorce petitions filed by servicemen rose significantly. Of a total of 175,000 army cases that legal aid dealt with during the war fully 140,000 concerned matrimonial problems, much to the consternation of commanding officers. National divorce statistics rose from 4,100 in 1935 to 15,600 ten years later and peaked at 60,300 in 1947—which reflected a large backlog of earlier petitions. For the first time more cases were also initiated by husbands than wives. Yet, while public opinion focused blame on unfaithful wives, other factors contributed to the sharp jump in statistics. A 1937 Act had widened the admissible grounds and expanded the numbers of courts with jurisdiction over divorce cases. Even more important was the 1942 War Office decision to make divorce simpler, cheaper, and more widely available to servicemen. Initiated by a man through the army welfare scheme, divorce was far cheaper than if his civilian wife brought an action—then the cost could exceed £100.[24] Divorce was too expensive for most workers pre-war—usually one party simply moved out, sometimes paying for a separation agreement which precluded remarriage, and often workers cohabited with new partners without formal marriage. Thus, the inflated statistics also reflected the fact that divorce had for the first time become widely available to the working class.

By the war's end the army alone had called up over 3 million men, most of whom identified little with the army or its traditions.[25] Clearly, by 1942 not only had many civilians been forced to adapt to the army, but the army had been compelled to adjust to their needs. It did so unevenly, developing an impressive structure of services to meet soldiers' welfare and legal needs and, as we shall see, instituting a whole array of entertainments and educational classes. But the strength of regimental traditions, the decision-making independence they gave to individual commanders, and the failure to make fundamental changes in army doctrine moderated the impact of these democratizing reforms. The upper echelons of the army continued to be regular soldiers, a good many of whom remained doubtful about or paid lip service only to many of the new regulations and programmes. In some respects, faced with its very real failures in the first three years of the war, the army yielded to pressure for institutional changes, but these

---

[24] Crang, *The British Army and the People's War*, pp. 101–5. In April 1943, according to the Poor Person's Committee of the Law Society, there were 3,500 divorce cases concerning soldiers pending formal hearing and another 5,000 cases under consideration. The annual average of divorce petitions for England and Wales 1931–5 had been under 4,800. In May 1946 some 43,000 service cases still had not been dealt with. NA: WO 32/15772, February–April 1943; *PD* (Commons), 10 May 1946.

[25] 3.8 million served in the army during the course of the war. By 1945 some 63% of men aged 20–29 years were in military uniform. About half the men in the armed forces were married at the war's end. HMSO, *Statistical Digest of the War* (London, 1951), p. 13.

were grafted onto an inner core of structures and values that altered little. Nowhere was this tension between continuity and change more evident than in the relations of officers and men.

OFFICERS, MEN, AND MORALE

Every facet of military life underscored the distance between officers and men or 'Other Ranks' as they were called. Officers were explicitly advised not to socialize with ordinary soldiers; they had different food, accommodation, uniforms, clothing coupons, pensions, allowances, pay, medals, first-class (as opposed to third-class) rail permits, a separate mess, servants and—under the Geneva Convention—were segregated as POWs and could not be put to work. To a degree this is true of every army, the goal being to promote sufficient contact and familiarity to win loyalty and respect, but not so much as to endanger unquestioning deference to authority. But in the British army it was particularly rigid, being heavily reinforced by differences of class. 'To describe the services without recognizing their class nature', Richard Hoggart writes, 'would be like describing a vehicle without reference to its main frame.'[26] For working-class conscripts, particularly at the start of the war, the army replicated the class-determined structures of civilian life and, while socially the officer corps changed dramatically with the commissioning of 200,000 new men, much of the old ethos remained.

In 1939 the social composition of the officer corps had changed very little since the pre-1914 era. While the army's massive expansion during the First World War had resulted in large numbers of officers being commissioned from the ranks (some 41 per cent of the total), few of those who survived opted for an army career or, if they did, managed to outlast the cutbacks and retirements of peacetime; by the 1930s once again only 5 per cent of commissioned officers were NCOs promoted from the ranks. Soldiering between the wars was a gentlemanly and not very taxing career, but the pay was bad and promotion slow and, even if they could somehow have surmounted the social barriers, working- or lower-middle-class recruits would have found the costs of being an officer and belonging to a mess prohibitive without a cushion of additional private resources. Of the officers trained at the military academies of Sandhurst and Woolwich 1920–39 some 85 per cent were from public schools (mostly prestigious private boarding schools) and even in 1939 their intake included only 5 per cent from state grammar schools.[27] 'By the 1930s',

---

[26] R. Hoggart, *A Sort of Clowning: Life and times 1940–1959* (Oxford, 1991), p. 6. Also, IWM: N. A. Forde MS, p. 55 etc. For officer–other ranks segregation in hospital wards: K. Douglas, *From Alamein to Zem Zem* (London, repr. 1992), pp. 140–1. For class differences within the RAF, especially between fighter and bomber pilots, officers, and sergeant pilots: Francis, *The Flyer*.

[27] C. B. Otley, 'Militarism and the social affiliations of the British army elite' in J. van Doorn (ed.), *Armed Forces and Society* (The Hague, 1968); *idem*, 'The social origins of British army officers', *Sociological Review*, 18 (1970); *idem*, 'The educational background of British army officers', *Sociology* (May 1973).

David French observes, 'the senior ranks of the army were in danger of becoming a self-perpetuating gerontocracy.'[28]

With its strong regimental traditions and close social ties, this exclusive military caste became the chief scapegoat for Britain's early battlefield failures. Its most effective negative symbol was David Low's cartoon character, Colonel Blimp: a corpulent, walrus-moustached, privileged, and incompetent reactionary, more suited to polo fields and imperial sunsets than modern mechanized warfare—a humorous fossil, but also a downright menace in the crisis of 1940. In radical press and popular parlance Blimp quickly became a convenient shorthand for everything that blocked a more efficient, meritocratic army—far more ingenious at fighting domestic enemies than foreign ones, including Hore-Belisha, whose removal from the War Office in early 1940 was widely interpreted as victory for 'Blimpery'. Battlefield failure also reflected the long history of budgetary parsimony and impossible strategic choices with which the interwar military had been forced to cope, but failures of leadership and the army's whole culture aroused increasing criticism and demands for reform as the list of defeats grew longer. Privately in his diary, Chief of the Imperial General Staff (CIGS), General Sir Alan Brooke, worried that the army's best potential leaders had died two decades before on the Western Front; other senior commanders feared that rank-and-file soldiers had too little training, motivation, or fighting spirit to cope with the Wehrmacht, although such things could not be said publicly in the political atmosphere of 1940–2.[29]

After conscription was introduced, the shortage of officers became acute and large numbers of cadet training schools (OCTUs) were quickly established. Following a mandatory period in the ranks, men nominated by their commanding officers as potential candidates were given a brief interview by a regimental panel and, if found suitable, sent off for an OCTU course. This system rapidly came under attack. Not only was there little uniformity of standards among the regimental panels, but by January 1941 some 25–30 per cent of those selected were failing to pass the course. Politically too the process aroused a storm of criticism. In the brief initial interviews, it was argued, family background, school, accent, and social skills counted much more than intelligence, temperament, or capacity for leadership; regular officers were predisposed to replicate themselves and to judge intelligent workers or capable NCOs as lacking the necessary style and demeanour for a commission. In the autumn of 1940, public schoolboys still had fourteen times more chance of becoming an infantry officer than those from state schools, while the navy reserved half the places in their officer cadet programme for public schools. Indeed, as late as February 1942 Sir Edward Grigg, the Under-Secretary for War, was still contradicting claims in the Commons that interview boards were asking: 'How much money have you got and what does your father do?' In fact, the Army

[28] French, *Raising Churchill's Army*, p. 163. Alan Wood, an Australian journalist, wrote a scathing attack on the officer corps as a public school stronghold which sold over 37,000 copies in 15 months; see 'Boomerang' (pseud.), *Bless 'Em All: An analysis of the morale, efficiency and leadership of the British army* (London, 1942).

[29] A. Brooke, *War Diaries 1939–45: Field Marshall Lord Alanbrooke*, ed. A. Danchev and D. Todman (London, 2001), p. 243, entry for 31 March 1942.

Council made serious efforts to weed out or demote older, incompetent officers, many of them called up from the reserves to fill the extreme shortage of the early months of the war. More systematic reviews were undertaken of officers who were over forty-five years and below the rank of lieutenant-colonel. By the spring of 1942 some 17,600 reviews resulted in about 3,800 officers being transferred to other duties or retired altogether and this helped to make room for the promotion of younger men.[30]

For some, however, things were moving too rapidly. In January 1941 *The Times* published a letter from Lieutenant-Colonel R. C. Bingham, an OCTU commander, which focused the debate in terms of class privilege or the natural leadership qualities of the gentleman. Bingham argued that the 'middle, lower middle, and working classes . . . now receiving the King's commission' had no grasp of 'man management':

> These classes, unlike the old aristocratic and feudal (almost) classes who led the old Army, have never had 'their people' to consider. They have never had anyone to think of but themselves . . . they do not know how to begin. Man management is not a subject which can be 'taught'; it is an attitude of mind, and with the old school tie men this was instinctive and part of the philosophy of life.

Here was Blimp incorrigible, unrepentant.[31] The letter (itself a breach of King's Regulations, for which Bingham was soon sacked) provoked a flood of scathing rebuttals in the tabloids, questions in the Commons, and some sympathetic responses in the conservative press. Eager to dampen the fires, the War Office revealed that 76 per cent of a recent sample of officer candidates came from the state sector and only 24 per cent from private schools; but the *Daily Mirror* quickly retorted that this still gave public schoolboys a ten-to-one advantage. An editorial in *The Times*, while admitting that Bingham's views were 'couched perhaps in terms unnecessarily calculated to excite prejudice', insisted that class was less at issue than whether the state education system inculcated qualities required for good officers. A. D. Lindsay, the Master of Balliol and an active proponent of army education, wrote that often boys from poor homes were so focused on exams that they acquired only 'one qualification for a commission in the Army . . . a university education', while neglecting 'the training of body and character'. 'The quality chiefly required is the ability to command', wrote another correspondent, 'and in this, of course, the public school boy excels.' He added: 'the place of the day school

---

[30] F. I. de la P. Garforth, 'War Office Selection Boards (OCTU)', *Journal of Occupational Psychology*, 19 (1945); B. S. Morris, 'Officer selection in the British Army 1942–45', *Journal of Occupational Psychology*, 23 (1949); 'A new way to choose our army officers', *Picture Post*, 19 September 1942; C. Ponting, *1940: Myth and reality* (Chicago, 1993), p. 143; E. Grigg in *PD* (Commons), 19 February 1942; Crang, *The British Army and the People's War*, pp. 47–9 for efforts to remove older, less competent officers.

[31] *The Times*, 15 January 1941. Bingham had been itching to publish a letter in *The Times* and had received some encouragement from Basil Liddell Hart. R. C. Bingham to B. Liddell Hart, 8 June 1938, 24 May and 2 June 1939, Liddell Hart Correspondence 1/73, Liddell Hart Military Archives, King's College, London University.

boy is to serve: need we be surprised therefore if in any other position he goes to excesses and generally displays the worst characteristics of self-consciousness?'[32]

The claim that soldiers' low morale was the fault of recently commissioned junior officers occurs frequently in official sources, including War Office morale reports for 1942–3.[33] But the dependability of these reports is open to question both because they relied heavily on officers' interpretations of the average recruits' feelings and because they were prepared by commanding officers, mostly older regular army men, and addressed to the Army Council. Parts of the Army Council were probably quite receptive to the idea that rank-and-file discontent derived largely from man-management failures by subalterns who lacked the right background and attitude to their men—a consequence of the officer corps' dilution by 'cadets coming from the smaller universities'. The same point about British forces' morale was made in a March 1942 American intelligence report, although this accused middle-class officers of aping patrician class attitudes. The 'new generation of subalterns', it noted, 'have gone back to the polished cross-straps, swagger canes, long haircuts, and Mayfair moustaches of the traditional British "military gentleman"'. With morale at its lowest after the debacles of Tobruk and Singapore, such affectations of dress seemed especially provocative; 'officer–men relationships' concluded the report 'have become immensely complicated, resolving at times into a class struggle which threatens the whole organization with disunity'.[34] J. H. Sparrow's morale summaries repeatedly cited the failure of inconsiderate officers 'to care properly for their men's welfare and to inspire the men's respect'. Criticisms of officers, he argued in the summer of 1942, 'are almost always followed by references to capitalism, democracy, Russia, and the like'. A year later he asserted that 'one selfish or stand-offish officer produces more potentially disaffected soldiers than six communist agitators'. From the opposite end of the political spectrum, left critics echoed these criticisms of conceited junior officers full of their new status.[35]

In few places, however, was the gulf between officers and men more glaring than on the overcrowded ships that took thousands of troops from England around the Cape to Suez or the Far East. Servicemen's memoirs and letters home describe these voyages at length: not only were they the first journeys overseas for many, but in a ship's confined space military hierarchy seemed all the more oppressive. 'Even after a year and a half's experience of the army's caste system', Richard Hoggart remembered, 'this was a shock.' The contrast between thousands of men herded into airless decks, sleeping wherever they could sling hammocks and eating in

---

[32] *PD* (Commons), 19 February 1942; *The Times*, 24 January, 28 January, 17 January 1942.

[33] The War Office did its best to monitor opinion in the services just as it had in the First World War. Divisional and district commanders in Britain and commanders-in-chief of the various overseas commands prepared quarterly statements, drawing on a range of sources including mail censorship reports; these were then summarized and distributed to the War Cabinet, the Army Council and field commanders.

[34] National Archives (Washington) O.S.S. Research and Analysis Report 617, 'Morale in the British armed forces', 21 March 1942. Also, letter by 'Socialist Subaltern' to the *New Statesman*, 8 March 1941.

[35] NA: WO 163/161, August–October 1942, May–July 1942, cited by D. Englander and Tony Mason, *The British Soldier in World War II*, Warwick Papers in Social History, 1984, pp. 9–10.

batches of 500, often stripped to the waist because of the heat, and the officers' cabins, with waiter service, white table napkins, and printed menus, was so marked as to be almost surreal. John Colville (Churchill's Private Secretary and later a fighter pilot), uncharacteristically roughing it with some 3,000 other rankers on a six-week voyage to South Africa in early 1942, found that they were crammed into the three lowest decks while officers, nurses, and WAAFs shared the 'two spacious upper decks'. Most were bound for Singapore. 'In the evenings', he wrote, 'we watched the dancing on A-deck and listened to the music from a string orchestra. The menus for the five-course dinners for the commissioned ranks were handed round on the mess-decks while we were fed on our unsavoury rations ... It is not surprising that strong and bitter political feeling was rampant ... long before we reached Durban.' A common ditty went: 'Troopships more than Pollitt can, Radicalise the working man.'[36]

Continuing political criticism of officer selection on social-class grounds and abundant evidence that existing procedures were not producing sufficient numbers of suitable candidates for the OCTUs finally led to a revamping of the system in the spring of 1942. Personnel Selection Officers and commanding officers now made recommendations during the early period of a recruit's training. The old panels of senior officers were replaced by War Office Selection Boards (WOSBs), which included a senior officer as president, a psychiatrist, and military testing officers. Candidates underwent a series of written tests, interviews, and practical assignments over a three-day period usually at a country house. The process was widely judged a success: applications for commissions rose 25 per cent above the 1939–41 level and by the war's end out of 140,000 who took the tests, 60,000 were sent on to OCTUs where the pass rate improved significantly (92 per cent).[37] But traditionalists, including Churchill and General Paget, Commander of the Home Forces, remained dubious about psychiatrists and in March 1943, probably because of Churchill's repeated pressure, the proportion of men given psychological tests was reduced to about half.[38] They were also forbidden to ask questions about sex or religion. Overall the changes (coupled with victory at El Alamein) did much to restore public confidence in the system and to undercut charges of unfairness and social elitism, although it was still true that few of those commissioned were working class. 'Socially', wrote Richard Hoggart of his group, 'our central or most

---

[36] Hoggart, *A Sort of Clowning*, p. 29; J. Colville, *The Fringes of Power: 10 Downing Street diaries 1939–55* (London, 1985), pp. 451–2. Also, N. McCallum, *Journey with a Pistol* (London, 1959), pp. 24–5; IWM: C. G. Beech MS; H. Berry MS; R. I. Higgins MS. For a vivid account of the British upper-class social scene transferred to a war zone, and the inevitable sharp segregation of administrative staff, officers, and 'Other Ranks', see Artemis Cooper, *Cairo in the War, 1939–45* (London, 1989).

[37] Vernon and Parry, *Personnel Selection in the British Forces*, ch. 4; de la P. Garforth, 'War Office Selection Boards (OCTU)'; Morris, 'Officer selection in the British Army 1942–45'; NA: WO 277/16, 'The Second World War, 1939–45: Army morale', by Lieut.-Colonel J. H. Sparrow (War Office 1950), mentions that although no comprehensive figures existed for the educational background of officers commissioned during the war, a sample of 1,218 candidates accepted for training for commissions in July and August 1944 included 34% from public schools, 62% from state and state-aided schools; the rest were from independent non-grant aided secondary schools.

[38] Crang, *The British Army and the People's War*, p. 35. On Churchill's pressure: P. Addison, *Churchill on the Home Front 1900–1955* (London, 1992), pp. 352–4.

common point of origin was lower-middle- to slightly middle-class with a very few from the upper-middle-class at one end and a very few from the cleverer among the respectable working-class at the other.'[39] No systematic data, however, were gathered on the social background of officers in the last half of the war.

The War Office introduced other reforms. Changes were made in military training, new instructional manuals were issued about how to lead,[40] and practices like reserving the best bars in an area for the exclusive use of officers and the commandeering of military vehicles for recreational travel were outlawed. Some attempt was also made to reduce the glaring inequality between the living conditions of officers and men on troopships. Moreover, army education was organized so as to encourage more interchange between officers and men and weekly 'request hours' were introduced during which men could speak informally with officers about anything that was troubling them. Many new officers were specialists (camouflage, press, censorship, and embarkation officers, for example) with no time for and little contact with regular army rituals. If some subalterns bought swagger canes and affected patrician ways, more of these new men were critical, in the army but not of it, irritated by rules and regimentation, and politically inclined to the left. Overseas in combat infantry and armoured units where junior officers especially experienced the same danger, suffering, close quarters, and lack of amenities as everyone else, there was more trust and far less friction. It was at rear echelon bases and depots that drills and privileges were likely to provoke continuing resentment between officers and men. Such changes, then, along with gradual improvements in pay, did improve morale but their effectiveness was uneven. Inevitably tension between the autocratic aspects of army life and wartime pressures for democratization was always present and, in comparison with the lavishness of the American services, material conditions remained spartan. Indisputably, the ethos of British forces remained far less democratic than the American, but changes did slowly occur.[41]

One sign of change was the lionizing of General Bernard Montgomery; he had no rivals for the role of People's General in a People's War. Slim, the victor of Burma, an ironmonger's son, who alone of the top British commanders did not go to a public school, was scarcely known until the end of the war. Vain, self-promoting 'Monty' cultivated a populist image: his dress was unconventional; his beret or bush hat with multiple regimental badges seemed to underscore the irrelevance of bullshit and petty rules; his leadership style was personal, tailored to civilians in uniform whom he sought to reach by descending unannounced on units for informal chats or through 'personal messages' to put them 'in the picture'. Curiously, in the 8th Army, his kind of unorthodox dress soon became a marker of rank and social class: Blimp gave way to a new officer stereotype with cravats, suede

---

[39] Hoggart, *A Sort of Clowning*, p. 9.

[40] The most important were *The Soldier's Welfare: Notes for Officers* (1941) and *Comrades in Arms* (1942).

[41] Captain X (William Shebbeare), *A Soldier Looks Ahead* (London, 1944). Also, Tom Harrisson, 'The British soldier: Changing attitudes and ideas', *British Journal of Psychiatry*, 35(2) (1945); *idem*, 'His private war-aim', *New Statesman*, 17 July 1943.

shoes, pullovers, sheepskin coats, corduroy trousers, and inflated accents—all brilliantly captured in 'Jon's cartoons for the forces' press.

Perhaps the best indicator of the army's changing image was in film. In *Desert Victory* (1943), the highly successful feature-length documentary of the Egyptian campaign produced by the Army Films Unit, Montgomery and, even more, ordinary infantrymen are the heroes, advancing steadily from El Alamein to Tripoli through desert sandstorms and the burning wreckage of German tanks. Success in North Africa also removed censorship obstacles to Powell and Pressburger's *Life and Death of Colonel Blimp* (1943). The script was rejected when first put forward around the time of the Singapore disaster. Both the War Office and Churchill insisted that it would damage morale and 'give the Blimp conception of the Army officer a new lease on life at a time when it is already dying from inanition'. Victory in North Africa removed official obstacles, however, and Powell and Pressburger's Blimp turned out far more sympathetic and heroic than the die-hard figure targeted in Low's cartoon and the press campaign. Out-of-touch, more sad than dangerous, he gives way to and ultimately recognizes the qualities of a new breed of officer, raised from the ranks, young, more ruthless, and realistic about the methods of a less gentlemanly age; indeed, the script's first page began with a dedication 'to the New Army of Britain, to the new spirit in warfare, to the new toughness in battle'.[42]

The most important cinematic attempt to represent the spirit of Britain's new army and specifically an officer's relationship to his men was Carol Reed's *The Way Ahead* (1944), starring David Niven as a fair and sympathetic lieutenant who welds eight raw recruits from different walks of life into an efficient combat unit. The film was first proposed in 1942 when public anxiety over the infantry's poor performance was at its greatest; Brendan Bracken at the MoI wanted something that would do for the army what Noël Coward's *In Which We Serve* had done for the navy. Reed's band of recruits is the People's Army, drawn from different occupations and classes, including an employer, a clerk, and a cockney boiler stoker played by Stanley Holloway. The men retain their individuality, but social distinctions lose their significance in military life. The film's press handout commented: 'The honour of the regiment, of the Army is safe in the keeping of the ordinary man.' At first these new recruits resist the discipline, drills, and square-bashing of basic training, but then succumb to the firm, humane, man-management of their officer. Niven may not be fully convincing as a garage mechanic and Territorial soldier promoted from the ranks, but Lieutenant Perry was supposed to epitomize the new officer ideal: capable, fair, trusted, identifying with his men and solicitous of their welfare. Final scenes showed the unit acquitting itself well in North Africa, bravely counterattacking after a German assault and moving steadily forward. Originally conceived as a way of restoring the public's faith in the army, production was hampered by a series of problems. When it was finally released around D-Day, the

[42] A. Kuhn, '*Desert Victory* and the People's War', *Screen*, 22(2) (1981); P. Rollins, 'Document and drama in *Desert Victory*', *Film and History*, 4(2) (1974); NA: INF 1/221 contains extensive materials on the making of the film; 'What a difference a war makes: The *Life and Death of Colonel Blimp*' in J. Richards and A. Aldgate, *British Cinema and Society 1930–1970* (New Jersey, 1983).

nation's mood needed no boost and its box-office success coincided with a revival of confidence in Britain's institutions and values.[43]

DISCIPLINE AND PUNISHMENT

Discipline was the foundation of army life, but most charges resulted from trivial offences such as failure at kit and uniform inspections, getting back late from a leave, petty disobedience, being drunk and disorderly, and falling asleep on duty. Most punishments meted out by commanding officers were correspondingly minor: men were given periods of CB (confined to barracks), fined, assigned to extra guard duties, and ordered to carry out all manner of unpleasant, menial tasks like cleaning latrines or painting fences. Sympathetic forces' columns in the press at times reported stories of exceptional unfairness and printed soldiers' anonymous letters of complaint, but there was little real objection to the punishment system— servicemen and civilians alike accepted it as arbitrary and inevitable, part of the natural military order like bad food or saluting. Serious offences could lead to a court martial, terms of imprisonment and hard labour, even the death penalty, although for ordinary breaches of the civil or criminal law (such as theft or assault involving a civilian) servicemen who were part of the Home Forces came under the jurisdiction of regular civilian courts. Serious crimes included large-scale theft, looting, going AWOL, offences involving military vehicles, desertion, assault, rape, murder, and the graver forms of insubordination, including mutiny and political agitation. Some of these cases raised complex issues about the rights of citizens in uniform. Accused men, ignorant of the law and their own rights and lacking resources for their defence, often found themselves deeply disadvantaged by the system of military justice, while their defending officer might have little expertise and inadequate opportunity to prepare a case. There was also no right of public appeal from a court martial sentence.

As a whole, the British forces in the Second World War were extremely law-abiding and the number of courts martial remained very small.[44] From September 1939 to September 1946 there was a total of 211,684 courts martial for the army, 127,807 taking place in Britain and 83,877 abroad. Violent crimes were rare and, once British forces took up occupation duties in Italy and Northern Europe, so were rapes. The vast majority were AWOL cases: in 1942, for example, 82 per cent of men serving sentences in detention barracks had been convicted of desertion or being AWOL. Theft was the other major problem; indeed, with huge quantities of military supplies constantly being unloaded, the opportunities for large-scale theft of stores became plentiful, and in port areas of North Africa, the Middle East, and

[43] V. Porter and C. Litewski, '*The Way Ahead*: Case history of a propaganda film', *Sight and Sound* (Spring 1981).
[44] Cmd 7608, 'Report of the Army and Air Force Committee 1946', *Parliamentary Papers* (London, 1949).

later in Northern Europe organized black markets began to flourish, closely connected to the surrounding civilian economies.[45]

Among troops in Britain, AWOL cases usually resulted from soldiers' anxieties about their families. Those who deserted altogether were virtually compelled to engage in criminal activity having no registration card or ration book. Overseas, in the Burmese jungles or the North African desert, there were few places for deserters to go, although some managed to disappear in Cairo and some gangs were formed, with names like the Dead End Kids and the British Free Corps, who preyed on base areas in the Middle East.[46] Among combat infantry units the statistics for desertion rose rapidly in North Africa in mid-1942 and again in Italy in 1943 as a result of battle exhaustion and nervous strain. Army commanders were deeply worried, especially after the long retreats in North Africa and the loss of Tobruk, that morale was at breaking-point. Some high-ranking officers recognized the physical and mental exhaustion of their forces, but many believed that too much comfort, lax discipline, and the reaction to the carnage of the First World War had made recruits softer, less willing to fight. Churchill was especially troubled by large forces surrendering to the enemy in Crete, Singapore, and Tobruk and pressed the Army Council to investigate whether regulations justifying surrender needed re-drafting. During the Italian campaign, AWOL cases again rose sharply at certain times, although given the size of the Allied armies and the length of their lines, it was hard to escape for long. But while senior officers called for stiffer punishments as a deterrent, their alarmism seems little justified; as a proportion of the total forces, AWOL cases remained low and disproportionately they involved very young soldiers. Indeed, focus on rank-and-file discipline amid the military defeats of 1942 may have masked a deeper reluctance to confront the army's structural shortcomings and its failure to engage in a serious overhaul of military doctrine. In March 1942 CIGS Alan Brooke confided to his diary: 'Half our Corps and Divisional Commanders are totally unfit for their appointments...they lack character, imagination, drive and powers of leadership.'[47]

Some 300 men had been executed for desertion in the First World War. But in the wake of the studies of shell shock in the 1920s, the authorities became more lenient and showed greater psychological understanding. By 1930 desertion had ceased to be a capital offence, although some senior field commanders urged its reintroduction as early as 1940. Even in the American army, which retained the death penalty, only one deserter was shot. But in May 1942 Commander-in-Chief, Middle East, General Auchinleck cabled London concerned about a growing number of convictions for desertion and the high rate of surrender among British

[45] No systematic study of criminality or black market trading in the forces exists. For some details see D. Thomas, *An Underworld at War: Spivs, deserters, racketeers and civilians in the Second World War* (London, 2003). Also, McCallum, *Journey with a Pistol*; IWM: L. Waller MS; Tony Lane, *The Merchant Seaman's War* (Manchester, 1990), pp. 120–7, 138; S. Longden, *To the Victor the Spoils* (London, 2007).

[46] Ellis, *The Sharp End*, p. 377, fn. 65.

[47] NA: WO 163/51, 'Army Council Minutes and Papers' (December 1942); Brooke, *War Diaries 1939–45*, p. 243.

troops relative to their casualty figures; the death penalty, he asserted, would have been a 'salutary deterrent' in a number of cases of cowardice and desertion. In fact, as David French points out, the chaotic nature of the battlefield in North Africa meant that large numbers of men became separated from their units and simply latched onto others—it was often impossible to distinguish the stragglers and lost from deserters, while lightly-armed infantrymen had little option but to surrender when surrounded by enemy tanks (German forces did the same thing).[48] Auchinleck's request was rejected on the grounds that the general public would not stand for it and that such a move would further impair troop morale. Moreover, any effort to restore the death penalty would have necessitated debate in Parliament and a full disclosure of statistics; few wanted to publicize the issue to this extent or to give Goebbels a golden opportunity for propaganda. In this period, however, in an effort to tighten discipline, sentences became heavier for those convicted. Again in Northern Europe in 1944–5, with more troops than ever engaged in combat, it is hardly surprising that the number of deserters rose. Most were young infantrymen, or sometimes soldiers who had fought well previously but doubted their luck could last. Often they were treated as AWOL and simply returned to the line. Courts martial imposed a sentence of up to ten years for desertion, but reviewing officers regularly reduced these sentences to three years' penal servitude and, since manpower was short, most offenders were returned to active duty after six months.[49]

Two areas where civilian rights and military practice were especially in conflict were first, the conditions of soldiers who were awaiting trial or in army prisons, and second, the small number of cases where men were accused of mutiny. Mistreatment in military prisons or detention barracks first became a public issue in 1940 when questions were raised in Parliament about cruelty towards men who, after induction into the army, declared a conscientious objection to service, often by refusing to put on a uniform. In two Liverpool institutions, for example, it was claimed that conscientious objectors were beaten with rifle butts, fed on a diet of bread and water, kept in solitary confinement, and were kicked and hit as they paraded for exercise. Most of them finally gave in and returned to duty. In this case an officer and six NCOs were court-martialled but their sentences were light.[50] The general public, however, had limited sympathy for pacifists and it was not until spring 1943 with the death of Rifleman William Clayton at Fort Darland, Gillingham that brutality in military prisons became a topic of national concern.

---

[48] D. French, 'Discipline and the death penalty in the British army in the war against Germany during the Second World War', *Journal of Contemporary History*, 33 (October 1998). Also, NA: WO 32/15773.

[49] M. Connolly and W. Miller, 'British courts martial in North Africa, 1940–43', *TCBH*, 15(3) (2004). Also, Ellis, *The Sharp End*, pp. 243ff.; V. Scannell, *Argument of Kings* (London, 1987). On desertion and AWOL in Normandy in 1944 and officer concerns about the low troop morale, see D. French, ' "Tommy is no soldier": The morale of the Second British Army in Normandy, June–August 1944' in B. H. Reid (ed.), *Military Power: Land warfare in theory and practice* (London, 1997).

[50] Barker, *Conscience, Government, and War*, pp. 91–3; Pat Starkey, *I Will Not Fight: Conscientious objectors and pacifists in the north-west during the Second World War* (Liverpool, 1992).

Though suffering from deafness and advanced tuberculosis, Clayton was passed as fit for duty by a medical officer and later died after brutal mistreatment by two warrant officers; they were later convicted of manslaughter by a civilian court. The Clayton inquest, Home Intelligence reported, was 'a main topic of conversation', especially among the working classes and 'those in contact with the ranks'. Many believed that the NCOs and the doctor had been let off too lightly, while others expressed their 'severe shock that cruelty, which was thought to be peculiar to the Gestapo, should be practised on British citizens in an English camp'.[51] Pressure built up for a parliamentary investigation of military prisons, especially when almost immediately a second case came to light, where a serviceman awaiting trial, originally for minor insubordination, had been confined to an unheated and poorly lit cell for eight weeks in winter and that his personal correspondence had been burned by an officer.[52] However, when released in November 1943 the report on military prisons was widely seen, especially by servicemen, as a whitewash and too lenient where officers were concerned. Evidence of continuing sadism and the suppression of basic rights continued and prisoners awaiting courts martial often faced excessive delays.

Certainly, there is considerable evidence of mistreatment in military prisons overseas and of soldiers' rights being disregarded.[53] Some of the 'strikes' at the war's end or 'mutinies', as the army insisted on calling them, offer illustrations of this. In November 1946, for example, after a five-day non-violent work stoppage over the slowness of demobilization came to an end at Tel-el-Kebir, Egypt, the men arrested were placed in detention cells at an abandoned German POW camp nearby. D. N. Pritt, who defended them, described the filthy state of the cells: the latrines were crawling with lice; washing facilities were one tap and a wooden bench; there were no lights, nothing to read, nothing to do and their cigarettes were taken away and none reissued for fourteen days. The goal was to force the men into making 'voluntary' confessions—those who did were removed and put under open arrest.[54] In another case, at the Kalyan detention barracks in India, Private J. M. Johnson, aged twenty-three years, who had gone AWOL in February 1946 after serving five years in the infantry, was held under close arrest for ten months, confined to a small cell in tropical heat, sometimes going for days without visits from an orderly and weeks between visits from a medical officer. At the end of this he was sentenced to a year's hard labour.[55] An ordinary soldier, but not an officer, lost all pay while under close arrest, so that long delays were a punitive hardship to

[51] *PD* (Commons), 30 June, 1 July, 6 July 1943. Home Intelligence comments in NA: INF 1/292, 11–18 May 1943, 29 June–5 July 1943. Also, *Daily Mirror*, 7 July, 23 November 1943; 'Are courts martial unfair?' *Tribune*, 5 November 1943.
[52] Case of Gunner Blunden: *PD* (Commons), 21 September, 12 October 1943. Also *PD* (Commons), 7 and 27 November 1945 (Military detention barracks).
[53] A 1965 film, *The Hill* (directed by Sidney Lumet), dramatized brutality in a Second World War prison in Libya.
[54] D. N. Pritt, *The Autobiography of D. N. Pritt*, II: *Brasshats and Bureaucrats* (London, 1966), pp. 256–65.
[55] R. J. Spector, *Freedom for the Forces*, National Council for Civil Liberties (London 1947), pp. 19–20.

himself and his family. Publicity about such cases did result in a public inquiry into the court-martial system and a series of reforms designed to expedite trials, improve legal representation for defendants, and permit appeals.[56]

A second area where the military code of law seemed completely at odds with soldiers' notions of their basic rights as citizens concerned the definition of 'mutiny'. Officers were supposed to explain to their men the regulations concerning discipline, cowardice, desertion, and mutiny; in practice, this rarely happened and most servicemen, many of whom were trade unionists with a firm belief in the legitimacy of collective action, had little grasp of the breadth of behaviour that constituted mutiny under military law. To most laymen it implied dramatic disloyalty, refusing to go into combat, or rank-and-file soldiers shooting their officers, or rioting and violence of some kind. But the army defined mutiny as simply collective insubordination, a combination of two or more persons to resist or induce others to resist lawful authority. Drawn up in the seventeenth century for a very different era in which brutal methods were judged necessary to compel unquestioning obedience, the military code focused little on safeguarding the rights of civilians conscripted into the forces. Thus, attempts by servicemen to seek redress for their grievances, to question the decisions of officers, or to assert their rights by civilian tactics like peaceful demonstrations or work stoppages, could quickly trigger charges of mutiny, potentially a capital offence.

Very few men were actually tried for mutiny and mutiny in the sense of outright refusal to go into combat was very rare. The most notable case occurred in September 1943 at Salerno among soldiers of the 50th Northumbrian and 51st Highland Divisions. Though still highly controversial today, the protest was rooted in an administrative blunder: a request to reinforce Mark Clark's 5th Army at Salerno was sent to the wrong camp. The men had been convalescing from wounds in a transit camp in Tripoli after going through the desert campaign and the Sicily invasion. They volunteered expecting, as promised earlier, that they were being returned to their original units. In fact, they were put ashore at Salerno. When ordered to join the 46th Division, feeling lied to and tricked, some 300 out of 1,500 men at first refused to leave the beach and sat down 'on strike'. Taught not to allow themselves be drafted into other regiments, they wanted to rejoin their original divisions which, it was rumoured, were being repatriated to Britain to prepare for the invasion of France. Eventually all but 191 men agreed to follow orders; the holdouts were first placed in a prisoner cage next to a group of jeering German captives and then sent to Algeria for trial. The victims of an official muddle, they expected to be cleared. But three sergeants were sentenced to death, later commuted to reduction to the ranks and twelve years' penal servitude, five corporals were reduced to ranks and sentenced to ten years' penal servitude, and the privates received seven years' penal servitude. As in so many cases, after demanding maximum severity the army suspended all the sentences and returned the men to front-line units. But their morale was broken and many subsequently

---

[56] Cmd 7608, *Report of the Army and Air Force Courts-Martial Committee 1946* (HMSO, January 1949).

deserted, ending up in prison. Recent evidence also suggests that some were victimized in their new units, being penalized with almost continuous combat duty without rest or leave.[57]

Insensitive handling of the situation by senior officers played a large role in the Salerno case. This was equally true in several cases where deplorable conditions on troopships provoked servicemen to revolt. Gerry Rubin has made a detailed analysis of one of these shipboard mutinies, showing both the combination of factors that could produce a walkout and the clash between military discipline and civilian-style assertions of rights.[58] It occurred at Durban, a vital transit port for forces bound for the Middle and Far East, in January 1942. A large number of troops, both soldiers and airmen, had arrived in Durban on troopships, some of them modern and fairly luxurious vessels. After a brief stay in a well-appointed transit camp and a warm welcome from the local population, they were re-embarked to be convoyed to Singapore, which was then engaged in a desperate struggle against Japanese forces. On 12 January many of the men who were assigned to a small vessel, the *City of Canterbury*, complained that the ship was 'dirty, bug infested, lousy, old and unseaworthy, and lacking life-saving apparatus and sufficient lifebelts in good condition'. After a night aboard the ship, they became still angrier and many complained of being 'bitten alive and feeling filthy'. Sentries were posted on the gangways but a large group of men left the ship anyway and some 300–400 voiced their refusal to sail on her. An Air Commodore who inspected the ship agreed to make an official complaint about her condition but insisted that the troops must go aboard or be charged with mutiny or desertion. There were some signs that the protest might spread and several other vessels at the port were immediately moved away from the quayside. Around the *City of Canterbury* the scene was one of considerable confusion. Most men re-embarked after threats and discussion, in-cluding some of the original ringleaders; some thought the order to cast off a bluff and were surprised when the ship departed leaving 160 airmen, mostly skilled air crews, and 28 soldiers ashore. Aside from a member of the RAF and an army sergeant, all were 'Other Ranks'.

Afraid that such protests might become infectious at a time when reinforcements were urgently needed, London decided to court martial all 188 men, rather than make an example of the NCOs, or just send them on to their destination. They were tried in three separate groups in February. The first trial, involving thirty RAF men, resulted in an acquittal; there seemed to be some confusion whether formal orders to board had been issued, in any case many of the accused denied hearing them, and numerous witnesses were by this time on their way to Singapore. When the army tried its twenty-eight men, it decided to play safe and add to mutiny a more general charge (Army Regulations, s. 40) of being absent from their place of duty. Here the

---

[57] Saul David, *Mutiny at Salerno: An injustice exposed* (London, 1995). *PD* (Commons), 22 March 2000, has a detailed exchange over the Salerno case with the MP for Aberdeen South, Anne Begg, attempting unsuccessfully to gain a pardon for the men involved.

[58] Gerry R. Rubin, *Durban 1942: A British troopship revolt* (London, 1992); *idem, Murder, Mutiny and the Military: British court martial cases 1940–1966* (London, 2005).

NCO was convicted of joining a mutiny and sentenced to two years' imprisonment with hard labour; the rest got eighteen months with hard labour. This in turn made it difficult for the Air Ministry to avoid trying the remaining airmen, although given the acquittal verdict of the first trial, it opted for the lesser s. 40 charge. They too were found guilty and sentenced to one year's imprisonment with hard labour and the NCOs were reduced to the ranks. Thus, for the same actions, the three groups were given three different penalties and the first thirty airmen escaped punishment altogether, although equally involved in the disturbance. Shortly thereafter, except for the army sergeant who was singled out as the 'worst offender', the protesters sailed for the Far East; their prison sentences were suspended (unless triggered by some later indiscipline) and later remitted altogether. Singapore had by now surrendered and most went to India. Those who had sailed with the *City of Canterbury* were mostly killed or captured by the Japanese at Singapore or Batavia.

Rubin's reconstruction of events makes two things clear. First, the protest concerned the appalling condition of the vessel, all the more unsatisfactory because of the sharp contrast with the men's experience on the voyage out to Durban. There was never any evidence that the men were seeking to avoid going to Singapore. Secondly, as official enquiries made clear, the protest was badly mishandled by officers at the scene. Not only had the ship been improperly inspected, but the lines of responsibility for embarkation were unclear, not least because of the different services involved. Had clear promises been given about cleaning and fumigating the ship, it is likely that the last group of holdouts could have been persuaded to board. As it was, discontent spiralled into sullen refusal. The men, many of them skilled tradesmen, felt they were within their rights to protest non-violently. At the core of the *City of Canterbury* and other similar protests[59] was not political radicalism or class anger, but a more generalized unrest among servicemen over poor conditions, neglect by their officers, sheer frustration at the insensitivity of the military system to basic needs, and lack of channels for voicing grievances.

At the war's end, as we shall see, 'strikes' to protest the slow pace of demobilization also resulted in courts martial for mutiny. But the most publicized case of this period was also sparked by intolerable conditions. It occurred in May 1946 at Muar, Malaya, where the 13th Parachute Battalion of the Lancastrian Regiment had been sent to 'rest' camp after combat service in Northern Europe and Java. There were none of the promised recreational facilities: the men lived under canvas amid heavy rain and flooding, many of them becoming sick. And a new commander and his sergeant-major seemed determined to tighten up discipline by frequent parades and

---

[59] A second walk-off from the *City of Canterbury* occurred at Bombay in April 1942; at Durban in August 1942, 1,000 RAF men 'walked off' the *Empire Woodlark*, claiming that it was unseaworthy. In both cases, however, discontents were defused by negotiations. In December 1945, 9 corporals were tried for mutiny after they 'walked off' the *Empress of Scotland* in Liverpool in protest against lice-infested blankets and a 10-hour wait between meals. Other minor rebellions occurred among naval ratings, e.g. on HMS *Lothian* during its voyage to join a task force for the Philippines in 1944. P. Tatchell, *Democratic Defence: A non-nuclear alternative* (London, 1985); Rubin, *Durban 1942*, pp. 110–13. For indiscipline and collective action on British merchant ships see Lane, *The Merchant Seamen's War*.

drills: 'Men with dirty boots were put on a charge...sometimes getting 7 to 14 days. You only had to walk outside your tent and your boots were thick with mud.'[60] When the paratroopers rebelled and refused to turn out for a parade, some 258 of them were arrested and court-martialled, though the original charge of mutiny was downgraded to 'refusal to obey an order'. Most were young men under twenty-one years and 60 per cent had little combat experience; they were very much 'civilians in uniform' who, now that the war was over, felt entitled to take strike action. Their trial which lasted almost a month and was widely covered in the national press, aroused deep public anger in Britain where protest petitions quickly began circulating. All but three of the accused were found guilty; eight were sentenced to five years' imprisonment and the rest to three years. But the case was becoming a serious embarrassment; the treatment to which the men had been subjected was flatly unjust and indefensible. The Army Command quickly suspended the court-martial sentences and the new Labour government, desperately looking for a way out, quashed them on grounds of procedural irregularities. The main problem, as was true of the troopship protests, was the lack of any basic code of servicemen's rights and a system that provided too few checks against misused authority. At some camps representative Welfare Committees were established as early as the summer of 1945 to provide a formal channel for rank-and-file complaints, but not until May 1947 did they become widespread.

EDUCATION AND POLITICS IN UNIFORM

Immediately after Labour's landslide electoral victory in 1945 it was widely asserted that the forces' vote had played a large role.[61] Political commentators both on the right and the left placed great importance upon the radicalizing effect of service in the armed forces and the Army Bureau of Current Affairs (ABCA), the army educational scheme, was widely seen as an incubator of left-wing views and support for radical reconstruction post-war. Later memoirs and recollections often reinforced this view: for example, historian E. P. Thompson, then a young tank commander in Italy in 1944, recalled a 'resolute and ingenious civilian army, increasingly hostile to the military virtues...anti-fascist and consciously anti-imperialist'. Its soldiers, he added 'were infused with socialist ideas and expectations wildly in advance of today's tepid Labour leaders'.[62] Recent accounts have qualified or contested this view, particularly with regard to the electoral significance of servicemen's votes which accounted for only a small minority of the total in

---

[60] L. James, *Mutiny in the British and Commonwealth Forces 1797–1956* (London, 1987), p. 174. On Muar, see also Richard Kisch, *The Days of the Good Soldiers: Communists in the armed forces in World War II* (London, 1985), pp. 153–7; M-OA: FR 2425 (October 1946); *PD* (Commons), 8 and 22 October 1946. Muar is about 90 miles south-east of Kuala Lumpur.

[61] e.g. R. A. Butler, *The Art of the Possible* (Boston, 1972), p. 129; Woodrow Wyatt, *Into This Dangerous World* (London, 1952), p. 57.

[62] E. P. Thompson, 'A state of blackmail' in *Writing by Candlelight* (London, 1980), p. 131; also 'A question of manners', in the same collection.

1945. But the weight of evidence leaves little doubt that the general leftward trend of opinion in these years was reflected and even accentuated among men and women in the armed forces.

One difficulty in assessing servicemen's political mood is the military's resistance to allowing political expression within the ranks and its often clumsy efforts to prevent it by invoking King's Regulations.[63] The army's own ambivalence about the degree to which politics belonged in a modern, mass conscript system is apparent in its programme for current affairs and citizenship education, begun in the summer of 1941. Already at the end of the First World War the army had initiated current affairs and citizenship programmes as a way of countering low morale and defusing radical discontents that were spreading among the troops. Retrenchment of military budgets in the interwar decades reduced the civic portion of army education to insignificance but the combination of mass mobilization and military disaster provided impetus for a dramatic expansion predicated upon the belief that soldiers would fight better if they had a clear idea of what they were fighting for. At first it was civilian organizations such as the Workers' Educational Association (WEA) and the YMCA that took the lead but their classes and lecture series reached only a fraction (about 20 per cent) of soldiers and were often deemed too academic in nature.[64]

Growing alarm about low morale and lack of ideological commitment among troops widened support for a more comprehensive approach. Within the Army Education Corps, a new department was established to oversee the scheme and issue publications around which discussions could be organized. ABCA was placed under the direction of W. E. Williams, who had been associated with adult education through the WEA and with Allen Lane's Penguin Books. The scheme was heavily oriented towards current affairs, aiming to inform conscripts about the war and the world that gave rise to it; it was also compulsory, scheduled in duty hours; and leadership of discussions and the bulk of lectures fell to regimental officers at the platoon or section level. They were assisted by two carefully vetted publications supplied weekly to units: *War*, covering the latest battlefield events, and *Current Affairs*, which included a broad range of topics but after 1942 became increasingly and controversially concerned with issues of post-war reconstruction.

From the beginning different groups in the army had different priorities for ABCA. More conservative members of the Army Council regarded its purpose as essentially patriotic propaganda; others saw it more as adult education calculated to

[63] King's Regulations no. 541 sanctioned political debate but not where a soldier identified with a political party or circulated party literature; more sweeping was no. 40, which subsumed politics under 'acts, conduct...to the prejudice of good order and military discipline'; in addition, Army Council Instruction no. 1527 of 1944 dealt explicitly with servicemen allowing their names to be published for political purposes, signing public petitions, circulars, and appeals dealing with political matters.

[64] S. P. Mackenzie, *Politics and Military Morale: Current affairs and citizenship education in the British Army, 1914–1950* (Oxford, 1992); P. Summerfield, 'Education and politics in the British armed forces in the Second World War', *International Review of Social History*, 26(2) (1981); T. H. Hawkins and L. J. F. Brimble, *Adult Education: The record of the British army* (London, 1947); N. S. Wilson, *Education in the Forces, 1939–1946* (London, 1949). For the period before ABCA, see also M-OA: FR 686, 'Report on education in the armed forces' (May 1941).

inform and to supplement the limited formal schooling of many recruits or even to give them vocational training for re-entry to the post-war labour market. Some emphasized its role in creating a new and deeper sense of the responsibilities of citizenship, while others hoped that these weekly sessions would draw officers and men closer together and contain more radical political discussion groups that were developing spontaneously among discontented servicemen. At the War Office, Margesson and Lord Croft worried that it might become an outlet for socialism and nurture 'political agitation within the army'. And Churchill, having learned of the scheme, quickly turned against it: 'I do not approve of this system of encouraging political discussion in the army... Discussions in which no controversy is desired are a farce. There cannot be controversy without prejudice to discipline. The only sound principle is "no politics in the army".' Sir James Grigg, at the time Margesson's Permanent Under-Secretary, was more inclined to see ABCA's positive potential and knew when the prime minister's periodic outbursts could be safely ignored.[65]

In addition, the scheme had powerful champions in General Alan Brooke, then Commander of the Home Forces, and General Adam, the Adjutant-General, whom Jeremy Crang describes as the 'key architect of the wartime citizens' army'.[66] Surprised at how little many soldiers knew about their own country and worried about the prospect of a third inactive winter with home forces cooped up in camps, Adam pushed for further expansion and the introduction of the so-called Winter Scheme. Soon known as BWP after the *British Way and Purpose* booklets produced for it, this scheme allotted an additional three hours a week of duty time to classes, but with a more pointed focus on citizenship and facets of British life. Originally planned for November 1942 to the following February, it continued until the invasion of Europe.

In addressing such issues as the role of the state, trade unions, educational opportunity, and the obligations and entitlements of citizenship, BWP sessions inevitably tested the line which the War Office had hoped to draw between education and politics. The most celebrated instance of this came in December 1942 with ABCA's decision to devote an issue of *Current Affairs*, along with a summary by its author, to Beveridge's report which popular opinion in Britain had welcomed as a new 'Magna Carta'. Sir James Grigg raised a firestorm of criticism by forcing the publication to be withdrawn. Lifted after three months, the ban was condemned in Parliament and the press and reinforced the distrust and cynicism of many servicemen.[67] What, it was asked, was the war about, if not a soldier's

---

[65] Mackenzie, *Politics and Military Morale*, p. 100; Addison, *Churchill on the Home Front*, pp. 346, 354. In late 1942 a row developed over an ABCA poster campaign 'Your Britain: Fight for it now!' This included several posters about post-war reconstruction. One, in particular, angered Churchill who called it 'exaggerated and distorted propaganda'. Designed by Lieutenant Abram Games (the foremost poster designer in mid-century Britain), it depicted a poor boy with rickets standing in a ruined building, superimposed on which is the modern Finsbury Park Health Centre.

[66] Crang, *The British Army and the People's War*, p. 140.

[67] NA: WO 32/15772, February–April 1943; NA: INF 1/292, 'Weekly report for December 1–8, 1942'. Also, Hugh Lawson, 'Service regulations must be changed', *Tribune*, 20 August 1943; Lance-Corporal F. G. Hunt, 'ABCA alone won't do', *Tribune*, 12 January 1945.

democratic right to discuss his nation's future? Citizenship education meant instructing troops about making political choices.

How effective were ABCA sessions? Opinions varied widely and so undoubtedly did their quality. Some army commanders had minimal commitment to the programme, regarding it as a waste of time—or worse. And while some junior officers were enthusiastic, others had little relish for conducting seminars and felt woefully unprepared for this new burden. Mass-Observation reported that one officer began by saying: 'I'm not at all interested in this sort of scheme. But you've got to listen to it and I've got to talk about it to you . . . You can sit down, you can smoke, but, by God, if I catch you going to sleep you'll be for it.'[68] The ineptitude of some group leaders quickly became apparent: 'T'want bad', concluded one soldier, 'but why do they bloody talk about what they know fuck all about?'[69] After a session about Beveridge, H. A. Wilson, a payroll clerk in the Royal Engineers, wrote in his diary: 'Very soon the lecture developed into an open discussion and the embarrassed Major was beset by rampant, fanatical socialists holding forth on economics and world affairs, especially Russian affairs.'[70] In some units, especially overseas, there was little time for ABCA classes; in others they became simply a break, a chance to sit down and smoke. But from the end of 1942, as expectations of peace grew and party political debate began to revive in Britain, there were signs of army education's growing popularity, even on bases abroad where regular sessions were often not possible. As Mackenzie shows, a survey of 5,000 soldiers in Britain in late 1943 found that 60 per cent regarded ABCA as successful and 10 per cent as adequate, while of the 8,500 men and women who filled out another questionnaire some 78 per cent found the discussions interesting.[71] To interpret these classes as vitally important in radicalizing soldiers is excessive, but it is also misleading to discount them altogether. They helped legitimize debate in an army structure that was deeply ambivalent about the political rights of 'civilians in uniform'. They also created situations in which lecturers, trade unionists, and committed young officers could act as catalysts, exerting a strong impact on others less politicized.

Small groups of political activists were also the driving force behind the so-called 'forces' parliaments' organized by servicemen at bases overseas in the last two years of the war. Before the war the League of Nations Association and the Association for Education in Citizenship had sponsored mock parliaments to publicize their work, while in wartime Britain the Communist Party founded a series of women's parliaments and the People's Convention of January 1941. These examples probably influenced radicals in the military; the tactic was also an ingenious way of going

---

[68] M-OA: FR 948, 'Report on ABCA' (November 1941).

[69] M-OA: FR 963, 'Report on army education, ABCA scheme' (16 November 1941).

[70] IWM: 80/5/1, H. A. Wilson War Diary, 2 August 1943.

[71] Mackenzie, *Politics and Military Morale*, pp. 184–5. ABCA's Play Unit adapted 'living newspaper' initiatives pioneered by the Unity Theatre in the 1930s and performed a number of political plays. Three full-time companies toured home and overseas bases. D. Watson, ' "Where do we go from here?" Education, theatre and politics in the British Army, 1939–45', *Labour History Review*, 59(3) (Winter 1994).

beyond officially sanctioned debates and, perhaps, a reminder to servicemen that when the House of Commons was last chosen in 1935, many of them had been too young to vote. The best known of the forces' parliaments began in early 1944 at the Music for All Services Club, Cairo, a pleasant, off-base meeting place for Allied servicemen, with reading rooms and inexpensive food, concerts and plays. H. A. Wilson, who often went there to listen to music, called it unique: 'There, for the first time in my life, I had the pleasure of seeing privates, sappers, NCOs and officers of all ranks and of all services... and nationalities mix together without the slightest embarrassment.'[72] Cairo was the permanent posting for several thousand troops on the HQ staffs and the main destination for servicemen on leave in the Middle East theatre. The parliament, which was founded entirely by 'Other Ranks', adopted Westminster procedural rules, although party labels were not used in its first two meetings. In February its steering committee held an election and of the votes cast Labour received 119, Common Wealth 55, Liberals 38, and Conservatives only 17. As a result Labour (really a joint Labour–Communist ticket) became the governing party and presented a radical programme of nationalization and social reforms. Since numerous war correspondents and broadcasters were still stationed in Cairo, these events gained considerable attention; the fighting having shifted to Italy, there was not much competing news.[73]

Troubled by this turn of events, the brigadier in charge of the Cairo area, who had originally sanctioned the parliament, now decided to curb its activities. At the next meeting, on 5 April, when a crowd of about 500 had gathered to hear debate on bills to nationalize the banks and to create a national investment board, an officer gave notification that the assembly was contrary to King's Regulations and stipulated the restrictions that must govern future meetings. After an overwhelming vote of protest and passage of the bill nationalizing the banking system, the parliament was dissolved. In the following months, several of those involved were posted to other areas and Special Branch (SIB) conducted investigations of suspected communists among the forces in Egypt. The press were also prevented from filing their stories in Britain and forces' mail was heavily censored in a misguided attempt to silence criticism. The overreaction merely intensified publicity once the news reached London. Richard Kisch exaggerates when he describes the 'Music for All' affair as 'the most exciting topic of conversation in every barracks, canteen, base, encampment, and foxhole'.[74] But it was indicative of growing activity among a minority of political activists, who were increasingly seen by the Army Council as ringleaders and troublemakers; they were investigated, watched, re-posted, and

[72] IWM: 80/5/1, H. A.Wilson War Diary, 23 April 1942.
[73] On the Cairo and other 'parliaments' see Kisch, *The Days of the Good Soldiers*; B. Davidson, 'The Cairo Forces Parliament', *Labour History Review*, 55(3) (Winter 1990); 'The Troops Parliament by one of its ministers', *Tribune*, 26 May 1944; *PD* (Commons), 4 October 1944; IWM Sound Archives, Sam Bardell interview in 'The People's War'. Kingsley Amis, who served in the Signal corps, wrote a fictional account: 'I spy a stranger' in *My Enemy's Enemy* (London, 1962). B. Moore and G. Barnsby (eds.), 'The Anti-Fascist People's Front in the armed forces: The communist contribution 1939–46', *Our History*, pamphlet 81, February 1990.
[74] Kisch, *The Days of the Good Soldiers*, p. 53.

even discharged from the forces on the flimsiest pretexts. Other mock parliaments, though far less publicized, were organized at the RAF transit base at Heliopolis, just outside Cairo, and in 1945 among occupation forces in the Rhineland; one set up at Deolali, near Bombay, was quickly proscribed in 1946 after it voted to censure the shooting of Indian demonstrators by British troops and then passed a resolution in favour of immediate Indian independence.

No matter where they were stationed, much of army life for most conscripts was monotonous and routine and they developed an insatiable thirst for reading material. Forces at home could obtain civilian newspapers and magazines, some of which like the *Daily Mirror, Sunday Pictorial, Picture Post, Lilliput,* and *Men Only* established regular forces' columns to address the concerns and grievances of those in uniform. With less regularity, the British press was also delivered to NAAFIs, messes, and reading rooms at base camps abroad, but front-line troops could go weeks between parachute drops. The *Mirror* especially viewed itself as the forces' paper (one-third of all servicemen read it). Columnists such as Gerry Allighan and Bill Greig took the stance of wise, older friends, dismissive of petty grievances, but prepared to take the side of the ranker against those in authority. 'Can an OC stop a man having his wife with him in a town which is not a restricted area?' asks one correspondent. Allighan's answer: 'He certainly can't. If he attempts to, send me full particulars, and it will soon be altered.'[75] 'Is it really a fact', wrote an exasperated Churchill to Bracken in July 1944, 'that the only journalists who are any good are the malignant scum of the "Daily Mirror"? I think you are underrating the troops by supposing they only like the garbage on which they are being fed.'[76]

The services' press encompassed several types of publication. A few, like *Parade, The War Illustrated,* and *Soldier* were official in tone and could scarcely be said to speak for the forces. More important and more expressive of servicemen's opinion were numerous small-circulation papers, written by soldiers for soldiers, that developed spontaneously in every theatre of the war—in some cases lasting only a few months. They originated from the ranks as crudely typed divisional and battalion newsheets, wall bulletins, and mimeographed papers of a few pages. They were read by everyone and were a channel for complaints and suggestions, as well as a source of local news. A typical example may be found in the letters that J. Newmark, a young communist and clerk in the ordnance corps, wrote to his wife from the Western Desert in late 1942. He spent much of his time putting out a wall newspaper for his unit, including articles copied from the *Daily Worker,* although the row over ABCA and the Beveridge Report seems to have prompted his commanding officer to exercise closer censorship.[77]

---

[75] A. C. H. Smith, E. Immirzi, and T. Blackwell, *Paper Voices: The popular press and social change, 1935–1965* (New Jersey, 1975), p. 74; P. Kimble, *Newspaper Reading in the Third Year of the War* (London, 1942), p. 6.

[76] S. P. Mackenzie, '*Vox Populi*: British army newspapers in the Second World War', *Journal of Contemporary History*, 24 (1989), 676.

[77] IWM: J. Newmark correspondence, e.g. 24 November 1942; early January 1943. Captain X (William Shebbeare) viewed Wall newspapers as 'a concrete symbol of the new spirit that breathes in our citizen army', *A Soldier Looks Ahead*, p. 27.

These papers appeared wherever British troops were stationed overseas, but they first became significant in North Africa, where Warwick Charlton, who had previously worked for the *Daily Sketch*, began duplicating newsheets and in September 1941 launched what soon became a daily, the *Eighth Army News*. A year later he added *Crusader*, an equally successful weekly. They included service slang, jokes, sports reports, short stories, and regular news items about home and the war. Once their significance for troop morale was recognized, Charlton's papers were officially nurtured, gaining the approval and protection of Montgomery. They won wide readership because they spoke directly to and for the ordinary 'desert rat', voicing his suspicions and distrust of authority, and providing space for his letters about pay, leave, and other aspects of service life. In early 1943, a more formal press unit was established in Tunis, where Hugh Cudlipp, previously the dynamic young editor of the *Sunday Pictorial*, began producing a new paper, *Union Jack*. Later he recruited onto its staff prominent Fleet Street professionals who had been drafted like William Connor ('Cassandra') and Peter Wilson of the *Daily Mirror*. In the same year another well-known figure, Frank Owen of the *Evening Standard*, was enlisted by Lord Mountbatten to edit *S.E.A.C.* for forces in the India and Burma theatres. As civilians these men had been among the most hard-hitting and controversial journalists; their skills brought style and toughness to the army press, but at the cost of periodic heartburn for senior officers and the War Office.[78]

Army newspapers trod a fine line. Controversial and criticized in many quarters for their leftist bias, they tested the boundaries of their independence, while having to submit to intermittent efforts to rein them in. Their strength was their popularity among servicemen; their predicament was that the more faithful they were to their readers' concerns, the more likely they were to attract complaints from senior officers and Conservative politicians in London. From 1943, as soldiers' thoughts turned increasingly to repatriation and post-war issues, so army newspapers, like ABCA, focused more on employment, housing, education, and social security—in short, the shape that post-war Britain should take. With blunt commentary they followed such issues as the Commons debate on service pay in 1944; the miners' strikes in the spring of that year; and the revival of partisan politics in Britain as government critics tested the party truce in a number of by-election contests.

As news about the content and political slant of the army papers reached Britain, they came under increasing fire from disgruntled Conservatives, including the party chairman, Ralph Assheton. It was not only the coverage of specific subjects that was at issue, but the papers' general hostility towards authority and their biting cynicism about government promises and post-war prospects. The effect, critics argued, was divisive and subversive of discipline. But being readable and popular, forces' papers were also considered integral to troop morale, a safety valve for servicemen's need to sound off and talk back to authority albeit vicariously, and a fairly sensitive

---

[78] Mackenzie, '*Vox Populi*'; Michael Anglo, *Service Newspapers of the Second World War* (London, 1977); *Union Jack: A scrapbook, British forces' newspapers 1939–45* (HMSO, London 1989); Hugh Cudlipp, *Walking on Water* (London, 1976). Also, Edward Budd, *A Printer Goes to War* (London, 1975).

barometer of rank-and-file opinion. If some commanders accused them of left-wing indoctrination of troops, others (including Grigg at the War Office) recognized that their brand of radical populism was closely attuned to both the mood of their readers and reflective of trends in the British press as a whole.

What, then, can be concluded about the political mood of ordinary soldiers towards the end of war? Any answer has to be impressionistic. Recent revisionist accounts have challenged the older view of a politicized soldiery, arguing that deep cynicism, apathy, and indifference to politics characterized the outlook of the average soldier or airman. Stephen Fielding, for example, cites as an example an officer's comment on the ABCA sessions he conducted:

> The general line that is always taken is the *We* and *They* line. Here is a typical sort of argument: 'What can I do about it all? I may elect a Labour MP, but as soon as he gets into Parliament he does nothing about the things he says he is going to do. They hold all the power and They always will . . . They have all the money and the newspapers and everything. It always has been like that and it always will.'[79]

For sure the soldier's outlook is cynical and deeply distrustful of party politics and politicians—but the tone is not one of indifference or apathy. Similarly, accounts focusing on the level of soldiers' interest in party politics or what they knew about the Beveridge Plan or other reform proposals often contrast a small 'thinking minority' and a large, ill-informed and apolitical mass, whose horizons rarely extended beyond 'beer, sport, and crumpet'. But a more capacious definition of 'political'—one that embraces a sense of class identity, critiques of authority and 'vested interests', feelings of entitlement and nebulous demands for change—gives a more complex picture than simply disaffection or disengagement.[80] Of course, as many letters and diaries indicate, service in the forces also politicized many recruits. For example, politics dominated the correspondence between Aircraftsman Fred Lightfoot, stationed in India, and his father. A Londoner, Fred left school at fourteen and worked as an office boy in a small engineering firm before the war. While in uniform his political views had moved sharply left and his father, a post-office employee, regularly sent him packets of radical books, copies of *Tribune*, and materials put out by the radical Common Wealth party, which Fred now supported. His father, whose outlook was conservative, anti-union, and generally cynical about politicians, worried that being outspoken politically might get his son into trouble: 'No boy I should lay low as regards anything "political" while your

---

[79] S. Fielding, 'What did "the People" want?: The meaning of the 1945 general election', *Historical Journal*, 35(3) (1992), 629; the quotation comes from M-O, *The Journey Home* (London, 1944), p. 107. Also, Tony Mason and Peter Thompson, ' "Reflections on a revolution?": The political mood in wartime Britain' in N. Tiratsoo (ed.), *The Attlee Years* (London, 1991); S. Fielding, P. Thompson, and N. Tiratsoo, *England Arise!* (Manchester, 1995); R. Lowe, 'The Second World War, consensus and the foundation of the welfare state', *TCBH*, 1(2) (1990).

[80] There was a lively debate about the degree to which soldiers had become politicized; e.g. the correspondence columns of *Tribune* from August 1944 to April 1945, contained many letters from servicemen, some deploring forces' apathy, others describing growing political interest: Private X, 'Politics in the Eighth Army', *Tribune*, 7 May 1943. Also, 'The inarticulate revolution' by a Serving Soldier, *Tribune*, 10 March 1944.

[*sic*] out where you are because I'm sure we've never had and never will get freedom of speech or any other freedoms—there's always someone spying ready to split—so keep MUM.' Party politics saturates their letters especially in the final year of the war with the father disgusted at 'union big mouth leaders, Bevan and the like' and also fed up with the Tories: 'their [*sic*] all throwing S[HI]T at each other now in the electioneering...all sorts of promises...there's not a bit of difference'. Despite Fred's pressure, the father decided to abstain but he cast Fred's proxy for Labour (there being no Common Wealth candidate in the constituency).[81]

Admittedly, the mood of many soldiers was largely negative; it was deeply anti-Tory and in many cases critical of Labour, although that changed as the general election drew closer. Gerry Allighan, who ran the *Daily Mirror*'s forces' column, quoted one correspondent: 'We don't trust the politicians. It's them what bungled or wangled the country into this war...We were fools to trust them before, and we'd be bigger bloody fools to trust them again.'[82] As Mass-Observation's fine survey about demobilization and post-war prospects, *The Journey Home* (1944), indicated: cynicism about the future coexisted with raised expectations and a streak of utopianism. Anxiety about another 'betrayal' like 1918 and fears of unemployment were joined to hopes for social change and firm assertions that the war had made a return to the thirties impossible. The same ambivalence can be found in soldiers' responses to the Beveridge Report. An RAF physical training instructor noted in his diary: 'They are nearly all enthusiastic about it, but a clear majority have expressed doubts as to whether it will be adopted. Typical comments were: "The insurance companies will squash it"; "It's too good to be true, they'll water it down a lot"; "Don't worry they'll never get it past Parliament."'[83] Many, so army morale reports for 1944 indicated, were 'firm in their opinion that the state must assure an improved standard of living for the people'. And while many expected a hard struggle against vested interests which would do 'all they can to prevent sweeping changes', others were more optimistic that 'a better social structure can be erected'.[84] Official analyses found 'deep preoccupation with postwar prospects'.[85] But while soldiers worried about jobs, housing, family, and getting home in one piece as quickly as possible, these were not purely private concerns deflecting their minds away from politics; rather they assumed that solutions required state action. About the rising incidence of strikes at home, opinions were mixed. Some servicemen resented the demands of munitions workers and miners, whose pay seemed princely compared to their own; but others, especially older men with trade union experience, showed little inclination to accept official

[81] IWM: F. Lightfoot 06/7/1, Memoirs and correspondence from his father. Quotes from letters: undated, *c.* 16 June, 23 June.
[82] Garry Allighan, 'Who obstructs the soldiers' vote?', *Tribune*, 30 June 1944. For pro-Soviet feeling among the troops, as reported to the War Office, see NA: WO 32/15772, February–April, May–July 1943.
[83] M-OA: FR 161, 'Some opinion trends among the forces' (March 1943); McCallum, *Journey with a Pistol*, p. 141. Also NA: WO 15772 February–April, August–October 1943.
[84] NA: WO 15772 (March–May 1944, report on India).
[85] NA: WO 15772 (August–October 1942).

censure of industrial action (strikers could be friends and family members) as being at odds with patriotic loyalty. As J. Newmark wrote to his wife on 21 March 1944: 'The recent coal strike was the subject of a heated debate, most chaps condemning the miners. But one lad, an eloquent Welshman, defended them warmly saying they were looking after our standard of living to which we must come back unimpaired.'[86]

As victory moved closer and expectations of a general election grew, the process of registering servicemen to vote attracted increasing attention in the press. But whether the slow pace of registration was a sign of political apathy, as some historians and contemporary observers have argued, is open to question. The procedure was straightforward enough: soldiers had to complete Army Form B2626 to be eligible to vote or to appoint a proxy; but by the summer of 1944 the response had been very low—among many units in the Mediterranean, for example, it was well under 50 per cent. On the left, blame for this reluctance was put on army commanders who, it was said, deliberately gave registration a low priority, hiding announcements on crowded notice boards, or making soldiers go out of their way to pick up the forms in the orderly room. Thus, *Tribune* reported that on one base in Belgium:

> Nearly 1,000 men were assembled on parade and divided into platoons. The O.C. arrived and, without any preliminaries, barked: "All those who don't want to vote fall-out!" It should be noted a) that the parade was timed just before dinner on Sunday, and the men were eager to have their meal and get out, and b) that although it was raining, and there is always ample space for inside parades, this one was held outside. Not surprisingly, about 40% fell out . . . The barest instructions were given on the filling in of application forms.

An NCO, writing to *Picture Post* in May 1944, saw a broader plot of Tory ministers: 'It seems that the Government has selected a psychological moment when the Services are more interested in getting the war over than in their potential political activity; and, presumably, if a time limit becomes operative, the vast majority fighting for a better society will find themselves incapable of shaping it.'[87]

Some commanders, it is true, resented having to find time for this new task that had been thrust upon them, especially during the last stages of the war in Northern Europe. In some cases the forms arrived late or in insufficient quantities. And many soldiers, when interviewed, were cynical about party politics and focused more on when they could return home. But registration also moved slowly because in the summer and autumn of 1944 the end of the war and a general election still seemed

---

[86] IWM: J. Newmark correspondence, 21 March 1945. Also on soldiers' responses to the miners' strikes: *Eighth Army News*, 14 March 1944 ran the headline: 'Right to strike is part of the freedom we fight for'. NA: WO 32/15772, May–July 1944: another debate overseas, mentioned in official morale reports, had 46% of men on the side of the miners and 40% against them, while troops in India were also divided between those who feared victory and repatriation would be delayed and those who argued that the strikers had no choice but to act since they would never get their grievances rectified post-war.

[87] Allighan, 'Who obstructs the soldiers' vote?'; M-OA: FR 2135, 'The forces vote' (19 July 1944); 'Do the forces want the right to vote?', *Picture Post*, 19 August 1944; 'Servicemen's votes', *Tribune*, 8 June 1945 for the base in Belgium; NCO's letter in *Picture Post*, 20 May 1944.

a long way off, especially to troops engaged in France and the Low Countries and even more to units in the Far East or those who expected to be sent there. By early 1945, with party divisions mounting in Churchill's coalition and the home press speculating more about an election, the pace of forces' registration picked up. Eventually it reached roughly 64 per cent, which under the circumstances does not seem a meagre percentage; of these 59 per cent are estimated to have voted, some 66 per cent of them having arranged for proxy votes, mostly cast by their wives. Unrewarded in 1918, the returning soldier was a powerful symbol in this contest. 'Vote for Him!' the *Daily Mirror* election headline urged, invoking at once soldiers abroad and those who had died fighting; this time the soldier's voice must be heard.

During the campaign some units held mock elections, including some on troopships headed for the Far East.[88] Earlier restrictions on political discussion within the forces were no longer really enforceable. 'It's been a revelation to me', wrote J. Newmark to his wife on 20 June, 'how interested the lads have been in the Election Speeches broadcast on the G[eneral] F[orces] programme. Tonight, for instance, there was complete silence when Jim Griffiths, the miners' leader, spoke in impassioned terms of the coal muddle. I only hope the rest of the forces are equally Labour in sympathy—we want to clear out the entire reactionary Tory clique.'[89] And while the forces' vote, altogether about 1.7 million, spread over more than 600 constituencies, played only a limited role in Labour's victory, there is no question that it was heavily pro-Labour. 'Well Fred', Fred Lightfoot's father wrote, 'the election is over and you know you've got what all servicemen wanted—a Labour government and a good, overwhelming majority.'[90] Among the forces, as in the nation as a whole, anti-Tory feeling translated into identification with the Labour Party in the year prior to the general election. After it friction and minor forms of insubordination grew on many bases, as many soldiers spontaneously stopped saluting, reasserting their civilian status against the army and its codes. In Cairo special 'saluting patrols' were introduced to restore discipline, while as late as spring of 1946, the War Office noted: 'in many cases the failure to salute is quite blatant and widespread', amounting to 'a conscious act of disrespect'.[91]

DEMOBILIZATION AND RESETTLEMENT

Demobilization after the war proceeded fairly smoothly. There was no unrest equivalent to the widespread protest strikes and demonstrations over delays in release, hours of work, and army discipline that spread rapidly through bases in

---

[88] 'Troopship votes Labour', *Tribune*, 8 June 1945; 'Another ship goes Labour', *Tribune*, 6 July 1945 (correspondence columns).

[89] IWM: J. Newmark correspondence, 20 June 1945 (see also 5 and 29 July).

[90] IWM: F. Lightfoot 06/7/1, letter of 30 July 1945. Labour MP Tom Driberg complained of 'widespread disenfranchisement of servicemen' because ballots were lost in transit or were disqualified because the forms were made out incorrectly: *PD* (Commons), 22 November 1945.

[91] Sam Bardell in P. Lewis, *A People's War* (London, 1986), pp. 240–1; NA: WO 32/15772, February–April 1946 (Home Army).

Britain and overseas in early 1919, although the precedent certainly affected government plans for the end of the war. After this conflict also the long-term reintegration of veterans was more successful, partly through careful preparations, but mostly because of a buoyant and expanding labour market. The bemedalled veterans, hawking matches on street corners in the 1920s may have troubled the thoughts of many people as they prepared for another peace, but they never reappeared.

Planning for 'demobilization' got underway in earnest in 1943, although Bevin, the chief architect of the policy, did his best to avoid that word until the war was over in the Far East, while Churchill was reluctant to announce details of a release scheme until late in 1944.[92] It was assumed that 'demob' would take place in two phases after victory in Europe and the Far East and that new classes of men would be called up to replace those who had served for long periods. Since it was widely believed that a precipitous jettisoning of wartime economic controls and policy failures in the release of the forces had damaged economic recovery after the First World War, there was strong support for a gradual, staged return of veterans to the labour force within a larger framework of reconstruction policies. Three sometimes contradictory sets of concerns dominated official discussions: the demands of the military and their anticipated requirements for occupation forces and post-war duties; efficient transition to a peacetime economy; and, most influential of all, popular wishes and expectations. After all the rhetoric of 'fair shares' and 'equal sacrifice', it was imperative that the scheme be simple, popular, and easily under-stood and that it should be seen to be fair, even though releases according to occupational priorities might be economically more desirable. Yet, in the forces, as one Royal Engineers' sapper admitted in 1943: 'everyone believes that there will be no early release for himself... but secretly hopes that a chance may present itself for him to get out quickly'.[93]

The underlying principle of the scheme was simple: first in, first out. Over 90 per cent of the forces were released under what was called Class A: according to a combination of age and length of service, where one year of age was the equivalent of two months' service. There was a certain amount of grousing on the part of younger conscripts who felt that this gave too much weight to age, while the scheme did not factor in marital status and length of service overseas as some had wanted. But, as polls showed, initial responses to the scheme, both in the forces and among civilians, were favourable.[94] Clearly, however, there had to be provision for exceptions to the age-service rule to accommodate hardship cases and to release much-needed specialists. These included construction workers, teachers, coal

[92] Rex Pope, 'The planning and implementation of British demobilisation 1941–1946', PhD Diss., Open University, 1986. For the previous war: D. Englander, 'Die Demobilmachung in Grossbritannien nach dem ersten Weltkrieg', *Geschichte und Gesellschaft*, 9 (1983).

[93] M-O, *The Journey Home*, p. 49.

[94] *Ibid.* The Gallup (BIPO) polls of civilian opinion were strongly favourable and consistent: September 1943: 59% approved, 29% disapproved, and 12% did not know. November 1945: 56% approved, 28% disapproved, and 16% did not know. The latter poll showed remarkable agreement irrespective of gender, age, and social class. H. Cantril, *Public Opinion 1935–46* (Princeton, 1951).

miners, and certain categories of skilled workers, but Bevin—ever fearful that accusations of column-dodging could ruin the scheme—insisted that such early releases (Class B) be limited to 10 per cent. In addition, the terms of Class B releases were more stringent and allowances were less, so much so that many eligible men preferred to wait their turn, exacerbating the shortage of certain labour categories.

The first releases began on 15 June 1945. Inevitably, there were some problems with a scheme that treated men by seniority. The release of many officers was delayed because of deficiencies of numbers, while aircraft ground crew, pay clerks, and other groups vital to demobilization could not be sent home on time. Naval ships were at sea throughout the globe, while acute shortages of transportation left many troops waiting in port cities for long periods; prior agreements to assist in repatriating US and Commonwealth forces led to resentment and, in at least one instance, angry British soldiers demolished a cinema after watching newsreels of American GIs going home aboard Cunard liners.[95] What really threatened to unbalance the scheme, however, was Japan's swift capitulation after the bombing of Hiroshima. This fuelled servicemen's hopes for immediate release and intensified business demands for selective demobilization to speed up conversion to a peace-time economy. An avalanche of angry mail to MPs and the press complained of noticeably different rates of release from the three services and a much faster demobilization of workers from war factories at home. The press also speculated that service chiefs were deliberately inflating their estimates so as to retain more men. Among troops in the Far East, who had long been anxious that jobs and opportunities would be snapped up by the time they were brought home, morale was especially low and many of these men felt let down by a unanimous resolution at the TUC annual meeting urging that troops be repatriated as quickly as possible from areas where transport was available (i.e. those in Britain and Europe) and that forces elsewhere should be compensated financially for the delays.[96]

In response to these pressures the Labour government accelerated the rate of release in October 1945 and by January 1946 demobilization had reached 80,000 a week. Around 3.7 million men and women had left the services by July 1946 and at the end of that year the process was virtually completed, some 4.25 million having been demobilized.[97] From a logistical and administrative point of view it was a considerable achievement. But for many men their final months of service were a time of anxiety and frustration. They worried about job prospects, finding a place to live, and about resuming relationships with their wives and families after long absences. Many feared that the war's end would mean the return of interwar unemployment, placing 'very little reliance . . . on the promise that men will be reabsorbed by their employers into their old jobs'. 'Take it from me', one ranker in

---

[95] This occurred in India: M-OA: FR 2283, 'Forces views on demobilisation' (September 1945).

[96] TUC, *Annual Report 1945*. Also, A. Calder and D. Sheridan (eds.), *Speak for Yourself: A Mass-Observation anthology 1937–1949* (London, 1984), pp. 148–50; also, letter by Capt Bellengen, 'I accuse Mr. Amery', *Sunday Pictorial*, 6 August 1944, on low morale in S.E. Asia.

[97] Rex Pope, 'British demobilization after the Second World War', *Journal of Contemporary History*, 30(1) (January 1995), 75.

the Middle East remarked as early as spring 1942, 'it will be the same story after this war as it was after the last one. All the plum jobs etc will be plucked before we get home. If I could believe that things would be better after this war than they were prewar, I wouldn't mind putting up with all this.'[98] Some found themselves with almost nothing to do and with minimal recreational facilities to help pass the time; others—especially if they were part of the release process—were working harder than ever before. Occupation experiences also varied a good deal and some duty, like the struggle against left-wing resistance in Athens or British efforts to restore French and Dutch colonial regimes in Indo-China and Java, was resented by many conscripts.

In such a climate, among troops who increasingly viewed themselves as civilians trapped in the military, petty fatigues and drills, dress codes, poor food and camp conditions, and delays in mail could easily flare into insubordination. Mentally conscripts awaiting their 'demob' papers were already out of the forces. This was evident in the epidemic of non-saluting after Labour's electoral victory; it also surfaced in myriad petitions and a growing number of small-scale 'strikes' protesting conditions and delays in releases. Sympathetic commanders could usually restore calm, but at some bases, and especially in the case of the paratroopers at Muar in Malaya, serious confrontations developed, especially in units where it was believed that regular army officers and NCOs were on a campaign to reassert discipline which they thought had grown too lax.

The peak of these brief and non-violent demobilization 'strikes' came in January 1946 when over twenty RAF bases were affected in the Middle East, India, Ceylon, Burma, and Singapore.[99] For some time station commanders had been warning the Air Ministry to expect trouble, noting that a strong 'trade union spirit' had developed among skilled ground crews; some argued that the loss of experienced NCOs had aggravated the situation. Aircraft technicians and members of Transport Command were crucial to the return of other forces and hence their own repatriation was often delayed—some of them having completed five years of service, almost all of it overseas. At the Dum Dum base near Calcutta, for example, over 1,200 airmen went on strike to protest repatriation delays and to demand BOAC rates for servicing BOAC planes. Other troubles occurred around Karachi, especially the huge maintenance depot at Drigh Road where the spark was the camp commander's insistence, despite the appalling heat and rainy conditions, that the men parade in their blue serge walking-out uniforms rather than the usual light tropical kit. At Dum Dum and at Cawnpore, where some 5,000 RAF personnel quit work, Indian airmen also joined the walkouts. Indeed, a month later, in February, serious mutinies occurred in the Indian navy and air force amid expanding civil disturbances in which hundreds were killed.[100]

---

[98] NA: WO 32/15772, November 1943–January 1944 (India section); May–July 1942.

[99] D. Duncan, *Mutiny in the RAF: The Air Force strikes of 1946*, The Socialist History Society, Occasional Paper Series no. 8 (London, 1999), estimates that the strikes in the Middle and Far East affected some 60 units and 50,000 men. The author was stationed at Drigh Road.

[100] Kisch, *The Days of the Good Soldiers*; James, *Mutiny in the British Commonwealth Forces*, p. 175; *PD* (Commons), 21 November 1945; 27 November 1948; *Daily Herald*, 29 and 30 January 1946. In Bombay 5 days of rioting involved 3,000 Indian forces; other troubles soon spread to Calcutta, Madras, and Karachi.

Once the strike wave subsided, despite the non-victimization pledges that many station commanders had given, Special Branch began interrogations of ring-leaders.[101] Most belonged to trade unions and in Britain fellow unionists launched defence campaigns and questions were raised in the Commons by left-wing MPs. The accused men, it became clear, endured unnecessary hardships in prison, while threats of heavy sentences, delays in repatriation, and of economic penalties against dependants had been made to extract from them and other servicemen incriminating statements. The most publicized cases involved two Communist Party members: Aircraftsman Arthur Attwood, a member of the Electrical Trades Union, who had led the strike delegation at Drigh Road, and Aircraftsman Norris Cymbalist, a leather worker in civilian life, who had been active in the protests at the RAF Seletar and Kallang bases in Singapore. Attwood's court martial was held near Bombay, some 800 miles from Drigh Road, where most potential witnesses for his defence could be found. Acquitted by a first court, he was then re-prosecuted and found guilty; but, with a growing protest movement developing among organized labour in Britain, the verdict was annulled by the Air Council.[102] Cymbalist, who had been in trouble before in Egypt, was less fortunate. Convicted of inciting mutiny, he was sentenced to ten years' penal servitude, later reduced to five; after repeated demands for an enquiry, he too was released in November 1947 but only after serving almost two years in gaol. But, as we have seen, the strongest public reaction came in the case of the Muar paratroopers 'mutiny' in May 1946. Within a couple of weeks of the guilty verdicts, according to Richard Kisch, over 500,000 petition signatures were collected, while MPs and the press were united in their outrage at the trial and the circumstances that had brought it about.[103]

As the months passed, however, vast numbers of servicemen were repatriated, passing through Dispersal Centres where they received ration cards, clothing coupons, a 'demob' suit, a booklet outlining their rights, and a sum of money calculated according to their rank, marital status, and length of service.[104] Many privates emerged with £80–£100, more money than they had ever possessed (£4–£5 a week was a good wage), but there was nothing akin to the 1944 GI Bill of Rights which transformed the lives of so many US servicemen. When the war began, the government had assured returning servicemen that they would be reinstated in their former jobs; but as time passed three or four men might be called up from the same job and it became difficult to see how this principle could

[101] Duncan argues that most station heads and unit commanders adopted a moderate and conciliatory attitude. It was among senior SEAC officers that pressure for court-martialling ring-leaders came, especially Air Chief Marshal Sir Keith Park, in charge of SE Asia Command, who opposed any leniency and wanted to set an example. Duncan, *Mutiny in the RAF*.

[102] The electrical and engineering unions and the London Trades Council were very active, so was the National Council for Civil Liberties.

[103] On Attwood and Cymbalist, in addition to Kisch and Duncan, see Pritt, *The Autobiography of D. N. Pritt*, II: *Brasshats and Bureaucrats*; Spector, *Freedom for the Forces*; J. Saville, *Memoirs from the Left* (London, 2003). On Muar: Kisch, *The Days of the Good Soldiers*, pp. 158ff.; M-OA: FR 2425 (October 1946).

[104] Government Resettlement Advice Centres, set up in the major towns, were heavily used and dealt with a huge volume of enquiries.

be upheld. In 1944 political pressure had actually resulted in a tightening of the language of this pledge. As it happened, however, the labour market was so strong that difficulties rarely arose. Very few contested cases were turned over to Rein-statement Committees, although veterans often resented the fact that men who had not been conscripted had in the meantime advanced in pay and status. Men whose apprenticeships had been interrupted were offered the chance to finish through grants and training courses, while they could get up to a third of it waived for related experience gained while in uniform. There were other schemes to assist those preparing for university or a professional career or wishing to restart small businesses; however, only a small proportion of men used these programmes. The degree to which ex-servicemen opted for new areas of employment or used any skills they had gained in uniform is difficult to gauge, but most who had worked before induction probably returned to the economic sectors, if not the firms, that had employed them.

The worst problem for many ex-servicemen and their families was a drastic shortage of housing. Bombs had destroyed or damaged vast numbers of dwellings and the deferral of regular repair and maintenance had deteriorated much of the nation's housing stock. A London survey, conducted during 1943–6, of 200 soldiers and their wives, found that a quarter were living with relatives, usually the wife's parents, while another half of the sample were accommodated in rooms or lodgings that were mostly cramped and overcrowded. Many had no kitchens, let alone bathrooms, and many with small children were short of beds and bed-rooms and had very little furniture. Relations with landladies were often strained— so were family ties: 'There's no privacy; there's always an audience', admitted one wife. 'You have to restrain yourselves, and the only time you can talk is in bed, and then you're tired. You'd be happier when you're on your own.'[105] For such families housing was a vital concern in the national election of 1945, while in the summer of 1946 angry ex-servicemen and their wives were prominent in the squatters' move-ment that for a while seized unused military camps across Britain and took over empty flats and houses in parts of London.[106]

Beyond finding jobs and suitable accommodation, servicemen and their families had in many cases to make significant psychological readjustments. Couples married during the war had often spent little time together. Soldiers found their wives no longer the young girls they had left behind: they had acquired new interests; they had often grown more independent; many were suffering from years of overwork, anxiety about raids and damage to homes, long hours of queuing for food, worrying about their husbands, and raising children alone. Many men did not welcome their spouses' increased independence; some wives found themselves viewing their husbands more critically; and many children, after long periods of evacuation, found returning to their families traumatic or found the reappearance

---

[105] Slater and Woodside, *Patterns of Marriage*, p. 152. Also, NA: WO 32/11742, 'Houses and employment for ex-servicemen: Effect on morale 1944–49'.

[106] J. Hinton, 'Self-help and socialism: The squatters' movement of 1946', *History Workshop*, 25 (Spring 1988).

of fathers difficult, especially if they had only vague memories of them. 'The children would not take to me no-how', wrote one father. 'I had looked forward to seeing them, especially young Joey, as he was only ten days old when I left for overseas. I had always fancied them running to me, but they wouldn't come near me, and yelled the place down if I picked them up.'[107] Some men found civilian routines and family life too confining and they missed the comradeship of their unit; some withdrew emotionally, shutting themselves off from their families, or flaring up over petty issues. But the natural problems of coming home were vastly magnified where the trauma of military experience repeatedly resurfaced in night-mares and flashbacks or manifested itself in serious depression, violent rages, or alcoholism. And though countless articles appeared in magazines and advice book-lets proliferated about veterans' needs and how to cope with them, it seems clear that serious nervous disorders often went untreated and that many men, discharged as in good health, were deeply scarred by their experiences.[108]

Two groups of returning veterans—former POWs and disabled servicemen—faced special resettlement difficulties, doubly so for the proportion of men who belonged to both categories. It was anticipated that a high percentage of those in captivity for three years or more would require psychological rehabilitation and courses were prepared to reacquaint ex-prisoners with developments in Britain, and to help them cope with family and social problems. In Europe treatment of POWs was governed by Red Cross–Geneva Convention rules. Officers were usually segregated from 'Other Ranks'; they had special privileges and could not be made to work. Public school-type escapades and daring breakouts may have dominated popular accounts of POW experience, like *The Wooden Horse* and *The Colditz Story*, but for most men the reality had been poor food, spartan conditions, interminable waiting and worrying, and psychological and physical disorders.[109] Those imprisoned by the Japanese were in an especially deplorable state, having been overworked, malnourished, denied medical attention, and in many cases physically abused over long periods. Almost 25 per cent of British POWs in Japanese hands died of malnutrition, disease, or were simply murdered; of the 40,000 who were made to work on the Burma–Siam railway, 16,000 died. There is little hard evidence about the readjustment problems of ex-prisoners; official

[107] B. E. Astbury, 'The effect of long separation on family life', *Social Work*, 3(10) (April 1946), 238; K. Howard (pseud.), *Sex Problems of the Returning Soldier* (Manchester, 1945); Ben Wicks, *Welcome Home: True stories of soldiers returning from World War II* (London, 1991); A. Allport, *Demobbed: Coming home after the Second World War* (New Haven, 2009).

[108] There was a strong collective desire to return to 'normality' and few follow-up studies were made of British ex-servicemen to evaluate the social and psychological impact of their war service. Decades later psychiatrists began to come across increasing numbers of troubled elderly veterans. J. Bourke, '"Going Home": The personal adjustment of British and American servicemen after the war' in R. Bessel and D. Schumann (eds.), *Life After Death: Approaches to a cultural and social history of Europe during the 1940s and 1950s* (Cambridge, 2003).

[109] S. P. Mackenzie, *The Colditz Myth: British and Commonwealth prisoners of war in Nazi Germany* (Oxford, 2004); D. Rolf, *Prisoners of the Reich: Germany's captives 1939–45* (London, 1988); *idem*, 'The education of British prisoners of war in German captivity, 1939–45', *History of Education*, 18(3) (1989); E. Jones and S. Wesseley, 'British prisoners-of-war: From resilience to psychological vulnerability: Reality or perception', *TCBH*, 21(2) (2010).

accounts suggest that re-entry turned out to be easier than had been anticipated in part because most men opted to go directly back to civilian life rather than attend the Civilian Resettlement Units set up by the government (only 19,000 attended). It is likely, however, that families mostly shouldered the burden themselves, although veterans' and ex-POW organizations provided important support networks.[110]

Servicemen from this war who received disability pensions numbered around 300,000. Efforts were made to see that employers hired from the disabled register, although both employers and trade unions resisted proposals to designate certain jobs as especially suitable for disabled servicemen. Only a small number of disabled attended job-training sessions and the special factories established for them by the government employed little more than 10,000; most men found themselves jobs, something that a strong labour market made easier than was the case for their predecessors in the 1920s. Often, however, the jobs they could get were poorly paid and government compensation for injuries was low; pensions for full and partial disability were fixed at First World War levels (or in some cases below them) and generally below those offered by other nations. After 1945, when the majority of males were veterans—either from the two world wars or post-war conscription—such parsimonious treatment is perhaps surprising. Budgetary stringency and concern about costs was the main factor, perhaps supplemented by the assumption that a National Health system and the expansion of social welfare constituted adequate protection. The mantra that everyone had sacrificed, civilians and military alike, may also have had the effect of depreciating the special plight of disabled veterans.[111]

But generalities about pension rates disclose little of the tragic circumstances of men who returned disabled and of widows and their families whose lives continued to be scarred by the war long after the fighting ceased. Here the historian is fortunate to have a remarkable archive of war widows' letters assembled in the 1970s as part of an advocacy campaign to improve their lot. Thousands of women wrote poignant, heart-rending letters, recalling in late-middle or old age their struggles in the post-war years. For them, the boom years of the 1950s do not fit the usual stereotypes and the welfare state appeared anything but beneficent.[112]

---

[110] NA: WO 32/11129, 'British ex-prisoners of war. Rehabilitation of those returning to civil life'; WO 32/10950, 'Psychological aspects of the rehabilitation of repatriated prisoners of war'; WO 32/9906, 'Press announcements and publicity about British prisoners of war 1941–46'. IWM: R. K. Ellis, microfilm; A. E. G. Clapson; J. H. Whitte MS. Also, B. Hately-Broad, *War and Welfare: British POW families, 1939–45* (Manchester, 2009). Local committees of POW families provided mutual support, circulated information, and tried to lobby government, aided by the British Legion and the Soldiers', Sailors' and Airmen's Families Association (SSAFA), the leading national charities serving the armed forces.

[111] P. Reese, *Homecoming Heroes: An account of the reassimilation of British military personnel into civilian life* (London, 1992), chs. 11–12. Between September 1939 and June 1944, 118,000 soldiers were discharged from the British army on psychiatric grounds. There were also in 1948 some 48,000 amputees, many of whom faced delays (as was the case after the First World War) in receiving artificial limbs.

[112] War Widows Archive (WWA): The Iris Strange Collection, Staffordshire University Library, Stoke-on-Trent; Janis Lomas, ' "So I married again": Letters from British widows of the First and Second World Wars', *HWJ*, 38 (Autumn 1994).

In 1945 the average age of war widows was twenty-three years old, many of them with young children. A widow under forty of an army private received a basic pension of £1 a week, which was not raised until 1965; it was also the sole class of war pensions to be taxed. Widows of higher ranks got a little more, so did women over forty years.[113] Among those represented in the archive, many did not remarry, at least while their children were young; they relied heavily on parents and relatives for support. Mrs F., whose husband was killed in Italy in March 1945, leaving her with an infant daughter, recalled: 'the first five years were hell, both mentally and financially, but I was lucky to have a Mum and Dad who tried to help'. A flyer's wife left with a baby son, wrote: 'managed as I lived at home with my parents, whether that was a compensation, don't know'. 'The government left us to starve', wrote another young mother, 'and for years the two of us only received £1 14s 6d and out of that I had to pay 7s a week rent; we had heating, food, and clothes to pay out of the rest and believe me I had to go to work night and day to make ends meet'. Developing tuberculosis after her husband's death in 1945, another widow spent seven months separated from her two small children: 'My brother and I returned home', her daughter recalled, 'and my mother's battle began, not only the battle against poverty, but the battle for life . . . I remember well her not having a decent pair of shoes to wear, or a tidy coat, although she always made sure my brother and I had what was necessary . . . My main memory of childhood is my mother being so ill all the time.'[114]

Wives of disabled men were worn down by poverty as well as hardships of caring for husbands who were wounded physically and psychologically. A woman recalled in 1982:

> I did not appreciate as a child what my father went through but I now know, we never had a normal childhood as Dad was constantly in and out of hospital and whilst at home he would have sudden lapses back into the war. Some nights my Mother had to search for him as he constantly went missing. He could not tolerate any noise as his head gave him pure hell. My Mother cared for my Father right until he died, never leaving him alone as he was frightened to be left alone and lights had to be left on as he was afraid of the dark.

In another case, a POW imprisoned by the Japanese from February 1942 to September 1945 and forced to work building the Burma–Siam railway, arrived home with tuberculosis and incapable of working; his wife caught the disease and spent two years in a sanatorium; their young son was placed in foster care. 'My husband's mental state was terrible as you can imagine. He used to think he was in a Japanese POW camp and one day he had a complete mental breakdown and tried

---

[113] Lomas, ' "So I married again" ', pp. 218–19. Their poor treatment fit into a long and consistent pattern: Janis Lomas, ' "Delicate duties": Issues of class and respectability in government policy towards the wives and widows of British soldiers in the era of the Great War', *Women's History Review*, 9(1) (2000).
[114] The letter writers cannot be identified by name; my references are therefore to WWA Box numbers. Mrs F. Box 44 (8 June 1982); Mrs J. Box 26 (12 February 1982); Mrs M. Box 44 (23 February 1983); Mrs J. Box 27 (31 July 1984).

to kill me, he was taken away and put in a mental home and he was there for 6 years because I was too ill to care for him.' Her husband was never employable; she worked and cared for him until his death in 1979: 'Many times I was told to prepare for the worst but he always pulled through . . . the coroner said I was lucky to have had him so long.' At the war's end he had been twenty-five and she twenty years old: 'we had no married life nor did my son have a home life'. Like many other women in her situation, she was denied a war widow's pension on grounds that the war was not directly responsible for her husband's death.[115]

Unlike after the First World War, disabled men did not have to appear before annual tribunals to have their pension status reaffirmed, nor were children born to them *after* their injury denied special allowances; but large numbers of wives who had nursed them for years were refused widows' pensions when they died because the authorities ruled that the cause of death was not war-related. Appeals were successful in only a minority of cases. This is abundantly illustrated by letters in the archive. Having lost an arm and part of a foot on army service, a well-known professional footballer came back to his wife and children 'a completely changed man'; his career was wrecked and after much illness he died of coronary thrombosis in 1955 at age forty-four; his wife did not receive a war pension. In another case, a sergeant in the Irish Guards was severely wounded at Arnhem and returned a paraplegic; his wife took part-time work, raised their son (two years old at the war's end), and nursed her husband without assistance until his death in 1968—'I had 25 years of hell with no help from anywhere.' At his death the war pension stopped. Acting as unpaid nurses to their sick husbands, it was tacitly assumed, was a wife's duty; it is also clear that many women who went to work were misinformed by local employment offices, being advised not to pay a full stamp since they were already entitled to a war pension and could not receive two. Years later they were outraged to find that they were denied a war pension in their own right and had not contributed enough from their earnings to warrant a full civil pension. In old age, after bearing their burden for decades, they found themselves impoverished, dependent on supplementary benefit.[116]

Like wives of disabled veterans, war widows with young children were especially affected by the closure of wartime public nurseries and cheap childcare facilities. Many could only work part-time or were forced into low-paying domestic service and other jobs that could be more easily combined with motherhood. When her husband, an artilleryman, was killed in Belgium in May 1940, Mrs B. was left with two babies and a total of 35s 5d a week pension. 'While they were very small', she wrote, 'I took in washing and did charring where I could take them with me; when they went to school, I worked out in the fields in all winds and weathers. Life was hard in those days.' Mrs S., also widowed in 1940 with an eighteen-month-old son, fostered another baby to supplement her pension and did part-time cleaning at a

[115] WWA: Mrs J. Box 29 (16 November 1982); Mrs D. Box 29 (25 June 1986 etc.).
[116] WWA: Mrs D. Box 29 (n.d.); Mrs B. Box 29 (n.d.). Boxes 29 and 31 contain hundreds of letters from women who nursed disabled men. Box 30 contains almost a hundred letters from widows who had received false pension information.

doctor's office; Mrs O., left with an eight-month-old daughter when her navy husband was killed off the French coast in 1944, 'worked at home doing dressmaking for the next few years. I was one of the lucky ones because my parents lived quite near so they saw to her after school. Money was a big problem though; people expect dresses to be made for nothing. Anyhow, I did eventually get a better job in office work till I retired when I was 61 . . .' 'I worked from 9 am to 9 pm for more years than I care to admit', wrote Mrs F., widowed in 1945, 'but at least my child was not hungry—I was hungry during the 1930s in Durham and said my child would never know that at least.' Since she got home late and worked on weekends, however, she felt deprived of a closeness to her daughter, who was mostly brought up by her grandmother. Upon re-marriage widows lost their pension rights, even if they were then deserted, divorced, or again widowed; and those who cohabited with a man or gave birth to an illegitimate child risked having their pension discontinued.[117]

But many of these women never remarried; they struggled against poverty and in numerous cases had to part with their children for periods. Widowed in 1942 with a baby boy, Mrs I. was eventually forced to send him to an orphanage and to take up domestic work 'to get a roof over my head'. Her son later went to boarding school, paid for by a fund for naval orphans: 'so I missed all my son's childhood, only seeing him at holidays'. Like many other widows she did not earn enough to qualify for council housing. Another woman with two small children found her earnings diminished after being injured in a factory accident in 1948 and was 'reduced to putting my children into a home until I could get back to normal'. Mrs Iris Strange, whose campaign on behalf of war widows caused these widows to write of their experiences, was also forced to send her rebellious eleven-year-old son to an orphanage, finding it impossible to manage him while holding a full-time job: 'He had already lost his beloved father and he then thought he had lost me and his home.' A prisoner of the Japanese, her husband had survived the 'Railway of Death' only to be killed at sea by Allied bombs towards the very end of the war when he was being transferred to another camp.[118]

Over 4 million men were demobilized by early 1947. Many had been in uniform for five or six years, many had served two or three years overseas. Most came back patriotic and proud of their service but with strong conviction that the discredited

[117] WWA: Mrs B. Box 26 (20 November 1982); Mrs S. Box 25 (1 April 1987); Mrs O. Box 27 (undated 1983); Mrs F. Box 44 (8 June 1982); Mrs K. Box 29 (29 December 1982); Mrs C. Box 44 (14 December 1973); Box 44 (letters and press cuttings) relate the story of Mrs H., whose spouse had died in a POW camp in Borneo, and had her pension discontinued in 1950 after forming a short-lived relationship, although she maintained that the man had never supported her financially—'they left me penniless to bring up 2 children'. After a 15 year fight her pension was reinstated, although she was still fighting for compensation for the missing years when dying from lung cancer in 1978.
[118] WWA: Mrs I. Box 44 (8 January 1984); Mrs S. Box 44 (27 January 1982); Iris Strange Box 44 (25 March 1985). From the early 1970s widows of soldiers who served in Northern Ireland received both the original widows' pension and a second pension; this was extended to widows from the Falklands campaign in 1982. The decision not to award this to Second World War widows led to greater militancy, well documented in the Iris Strange archive. The campaign finally achieved significant increases for Second World War widows in 1990 (and parity with widows from the Falklands and Northern Ireland conflicts). Less than 53,000 Second World War widows survived to collect the additional amount.

pre-war social and political order should be replaced by something more democratic and inclusive. When Slater and Woodside interviewed 200 soldiers and their wives from the London area, many denied any interest in politics: 'politics are a pain in the neck', 'politics is nothing to do with me, we're too busy with our families and jobs'. But when asked about housing, education, the Beveridge Report, or employment, the couples expressed very definite views and preferences. Slater and Woodside added:

> Marxian ideas were common currency. Any passive acceptance of the old social order was disappearing so fast that only its vestiges could be seen. There was a strong feeling in favor of redistribution of wealth, and resentment at real or fancied exploitation and injustice, antagonism towards those with money and power, or hereditary privilege. Both sexes were dominated by the distinction that is expressed in 'We' and 'They' and, even in this war in which all were involved together, by the feeling of a cleft between the two nations... The feeling of belonging to the working class was general in the sample, it was felt to be natural and taken for granted. Some social distance in the interview was accepted, but there was no servility or evidence of inferiority feelings.[119]

Slater and Woodside's observations underscore two major points in this chapter. First, that these veterans had a strong sense of social grievance, which by the end of the war had crystallized into a reform agenda that included more social spending, less social inequality, and a more active state role to assure security and employment. Troops might be cynical when asked about politicians' promises of reform, but expectations were high and they felt that a better future was their due. This sense of entitlement underpinned the growing numbers of protests on ships and bases once the war ended; it also determined the overwhelming preference of ordinary servicemen for Labour in 1945. Theirs was not simply a vote against the Tory past, although it was certainly that; it also reflected the belief that Labour was more likely to translate the rhetoric of reform into reality. Secondly, although wartime films might celebrate the union of classes and regions, military experience reinforced class awareness—even if what prevailed was less a *Marxisant* economic idea of class, than a dichotomous language of 'Them' and 'Us', privileged and 'ordinary people'. Drawn from every part of the country, raw recruits may at first have been struck by their regional and ethnic diversity, but years of carrying out orders, fighting or relaxing together, also fostered camaraderie and class solidarity, especially since the gulf between officers and 'other ranks' reproduced in so many ways the class-stratification of society at large.

The conscription of millions of civilians and early battlefield failures were catalysts of change for the institution of the army and its relationship to society. By D-Day the army was more modern, efficient, and in numerous ways more democratic and sensitive to the needs of ordinary recruits. It had been forced to adapt, introducing a whole array of welfare and educational programmes and overhauling procedures for the placement of soldiers and the selection of officers. As was true in other areas where wartime requirements transformed traditional

---

[119] Slater and Woodside, *Patterns of Marriage*, pp. 254–5.

practices (in industrial relations, for example), the reforms encountered stiff opposition from conservatives and entrenched interests, but in the early war years when Britain's very survival was in question reformers like General Adam gained the upper hand. With victory and the return of peace, however, the tide ebbed and senior officers, believing that discipline had become too lax in many units, strove to reassert pre-war values and regimental 'standards', with increased emphasis upon drills and 'spit and polish'. Gradually, wartime innovations like psychological testing and WOSBs for officer selection were watered down or dispensed with altogether, ABCA was disbanded, and the social background of the officer corps moved closer to its pre-war profile. Not that the regular army of the 1930s returned, for Britain continued to have a mass conscript force throughout the 1950s; but to most national servicemen the army seemed completely divorced from the larger culture, a self-contained bastion of hierarchy and tradition. As Jeremy Crang has written: 'The People's War might have brought the army and nation closer together, but in many ways the army remained a nation apart.'[120]

This resurgence of pre-war values and attitudes also had its counterpart in films depicting the war years. The 1950s saw a spectacular boom in popular war fiction and memoirs. The culture seemed obsessed with the topic and many were turned into films, often with cooperation from the military authorities. In almost every year between 1955 and 1960 the first or second top-grossing films were about war; the public's appetite seemed insatiable. But whereas films of the 1940s, like *Desert Victory* or *The Way Ahead* celebrated a 'people's army' in which national solidarity and collectivist values triumphed over class divisions, the dominant ethos was now quite different. Marcus Collins has examined the cultural resuscitation of the 'gentleman' in the 1950s and these films were part of a broader trend. In such movies as *The Cruel Sea* (1953), *The Colditz Story* (1954), *The Dam Busters* (1954), and *Reach for the Sky* (1956), the 'People's War' has visibly receded before epics of personal achievement, populated by middle- or upper-class officers and technicians. Here the collectivist ethic of wartime is redefined as masculine comradeship and self-proving; women were largely ignored or depicted as waiting wives and girl friends; while ordinary working-class servicemen were assigned bit-parts or relegated to the subgenre of low-budget comedies.[121] It was this kind of refocusing and depoliticizing that led E. P. Thompson to lament 'the uncontested takeover of the moral assets' of the war period.[122] This may be true; and yet ironically post-war films, in their handling of class difference at least, may have mirrored the average veterans' memories more closely than the idealized togetherness of earlier films.

---

[120] Crang, *The British Army and the People's War*, p. 142; also, S. Raven, 'Perish by the Sword' in H. Thomas (ed.), *The Establishment* (London, 1959).

[121] N. Rattigan, 'The last gasp of the middle class: British war films of the 1950s' in W. W. Dixon (ed.), *Re-Viewing British Cinema* (Albany, 1994); J. Ramsden, 'Refocusing "The People's War": British war films of the 1950s', *Journal of Contemporary History*, 33(1) (1998).

[122] Thompson, 'A state of blackmail', p. 131.

8

Wartime Radicals Envision
a New Order, 1940–2

The claim that the Second World War radicalized popular political attitudes was until recently a firmly held, if largely unexamined, 'truth' in modern British history texts. Then came a series of revisionist studies that reopened all aspects of the subject and substituted a narrative of continuity for one of transformation. Under-lying these recent accounts are several key questions. Did the war make a difference in popular attitudes; if so, could the change be regarded as 'fundamental' and was it in any sense lasting? What were the main features of the alleged upsurge of popular radicalism and was the potential for sweeping social and political change contained and nullified principally by the caution and moderation of the Labour Party and trade union movement? If the war did not foster radical political attitudes among the masses, why did many of the nation's political and intellectual elites believe that it had done so? And, finally, how should Labour's electoral victory in 1945 be explained? Was it a positive endorsement of socialism, a yardstick of the shift to the left of public opinion, or should it be viewed more negatively as a rejection of the Conservative Party, a less dramatic change of political winds that deposited victory in Clement Attlee's lap 'like a branch of ripe plums'?[1]

Three major organizing narratives, quite different in emphasis but sometimes overlapping in details, have dominated analyses of wartime politics, each of them extending backwards and forwards to the interwar and post-war decades. The first views the war as a crucial stage in the development of social democracy, interpreting Labour's victory as a consequence of the incremental, but ineluctable formation of working-class consciousness and political power. The second depicts the war as the context in which a cross-party 'middle opinion', already beginning to emerge in the course of the 1930s, triumphed. This interpretation gives special prominence to Keynes and Beveridge as the intellectual fathers of a new consensus among politicians and the Whitehall elites for a reformed capitalism, an ideological convergence cutting across party lines on social policy, a mixed economy, and the role of government.[2] Finally, a third narrative argues that the early war years radicalized political opinion, but ultimately stresses continuity, arguing that the

---

[1] The phrase used by Paul Addison, *The Road to 1945: British politics and the Second World War* (London, 1975), p. 14.
[2] *Ibid.*; A. Marwick, 'Middle opinion in the thirties: Planning, progress and political "agreement"', *The English Historical Review*, 79(311) (April, 1964).

war was a missed opportunity, one that opened a space for sweeping social and political change but failed to deliver. This interpretation emphasizes continuity: the resilience of existing social and political structures and particularly the moderation of the Labour Party and the trade union movement contained more radical possibilities.[3] All of these narratives are heavily inflected by contemporary politics in the post-war era. The first was most popular in the years immediately after Labour's victory and into the 1950s when internecine party divisions quickly gave the Attlee era the hue of a 'golden age'. The second culminated in Paul Addison's masterful study, *The Road to 1945*, published in 1974 just as the post-war boom gave way to more unsettled economic times and political consensus seemed more fragile and endangered. And the third, though a constant critique from the left, was powerfully reinforced by the disappointments of the Wilson years and subsequent internal struggles for the soul of the Labour Party.

Since the 1980s all have come under attack. New studies of the Labour Party depict its development as a lot more uneven, and contingent—better seen as a series of discontinuous conjunctures, with different problems and potentials, rather than a continuous evolutionary movement.[4] They also view politics as a more autonomous realm than earlier works, one in which parties have a complex discursive relationship with their public and play an active role in shaping their voting constituencies; these accounts reject earlier assumptions about the automatic correspondence of class and party that underpinned many *Marxisant* studies. Similarly, while some scholars have continued to stress the degree of consensus that shaped the war years and post-war decades until the 1970s, an increasing number of accounts have questioned whether there had ever been a period when the major parties were so ideologically close as to warrant using the term 'political consensus'.[5] Finally, the argument that the war was a radical moment only half-heartedly grasped has also been heavily criticized by scholars who have questioned the radicalism of the British population in the war years[6] and those that have emphasized the structural constraints that narrowed the Labour leadership's range of policy options.[7]

---

[3] R. Miliband, *Parliamentary Socialism* (London, 1961); J. Saville, *The Labour Movement in Britain* (London, 1988); G. Elliott, *Labourism and the English Genius: The strange death of Labour England?* (London, 1993).

[4] G. Stedman Jones, 'Why is the Labour Party in a mess?' in *Languages of Class: Studies in English working-class history 1832–1982* (Cambridge, 1983); J. Lawrence and M. Taylor (eds.), *Party, State and Society: Electoral behaviour in Britain since 1820* (Aldershot, 1997); S. Ball and I. Holliday (eds), *Mass Conservatism: The Conservatives and the public since the 1880s* (London, 2002).

[5] H. Jones and M. Kandiah, *The Myth of Consensus? New views on British history 1945–1964* (London, 1996).

[6] S. Fielding, P. Thompson, and N. Tiratsoo, *England Arise! The Labour Party and popular politics in 1940s Britain* (Manchester, 1995); S. Fielding, 'What did "the people" want? The meaning of the 1945 general election', *Historical Journal*, 35 (1992); T. Mason and P. Thompson, 'Reflections on a revolution: The political mood of wartime Britain' in N. Tiratsoo (ed.), *The Attlee Years* (London, 1991).

[7] J. Tomlinson, *Democratic Socialism and Economic Policy: The Attlee years, 1945–1951* (Cambridge, 1997); *idem*, 'The iron quadrilateral: Political obstacles to economic reform under the Attlee government', *JBS*, 34 (January 1995).

This chapter and the next seek answers to the questions raised in the first paragraph. The present chapter examines the period up to early 1943, analysing the copious stream of left-wing books and pamphlets critical of government handling of the war; the next focuses chiefly upon the revival of party politics in the final two years and the general election of 1945. Chronology is important here; often when evaluating popular attitudes the war is viewed as an undifferentiated whole, from which evidence can be cited without more precise reference to context. This chapter emphasizes the distinctive character of the early war years: a time of massive destruction of the nation's cities, battlefield defeats, growing anxiety, and dissatisfaction over the conduct of the war. By contrast, from 1943 political attitudes were defined by an expectation of victory, public debates about reconstruction, and by people's aspirations, hopes, and fears as they contemplated the return of peace. In both periods political attitudes were formed in the context of what I have called 'the arena of debate'—which covers not only the media (important though they were in shaping opinion) but suggests the complexly structured space in which ideas and views were communicated, including novel sites of exchange like shelters, hostels, and the altered significance of others like radio or cinema or union meetings and works committees.

ARENA OF PUBLIC DEBATE

By the 1930s Britain had truly become a mass democracy with over 32 million voters compared to 7.7 million in 1910. The fastest growing social strata were white-collar workers, many of them beneficiaries of the threefold increase in secondary education between the wars. Women had been enfranchised by the Acts of 1918 and 1928 and whereas before 1914 only about 27 per cent of the adult population possessed the franchise, the electorate in 1939 included almost all adults of both sexes. These changes redefined the political nation. As Conservative leader Stanley Baldwin put it, democracy had arrived 'at a gallop' and the major political parties faced the problem of integrating these new voters, expanding their party structures and grass-roots organizations, and adjusting their appeals and style of politics to the new environment.[8] As a result they became increasingly proactive—mobilizing their voting constituencies, forging electoral coalitions and reconciling interests, and working to shape the political and social identity of voters. In an age of radio, cinema, mass advertising, and a mass reading public, the interactions of politicians, parties, and voters were changing rapidly. The Conservative Party was especially successful in adapting to the new environment and identifying the party with the public or national interest; but Labour also made great strides in mastering the new techniques and technologies of mass democracy.[9]

---

[8] K. Middlemas and J. Barnes, *Baldwin* (London, 1969), p. 502.
[9] R. McKibbin, 'Class and conventional wisdom: The Conservative Party and the "public" in interwar Britain' in *Ideologies of Class: Social relations in Britain 1880–1950* (Oxford, 1990); L. Beers, *Your Britain: Media and the making of the Labour Party* (Harvard, 2010).

At the same time large numbers of other organizations were engaged in a similar quest to reach and integrate the new mass citizenry. They included co-operative societies and trade unions and also new kinds of non-party civic associations outside the conventional framework of politics. These included the Women's Institutes, Townswomen's Guilds, the YWCA, the Mothers' Union, the National Union of Societies for Equal Citizenship, and other organizations which took up a broad range of social-policy issues on behalf of newly enfranchised women. They also included veterans organizations; rotary clubs; rate-payers and business associations; educational groups, such as the WEA; and others defending civil liberties or promoting peace, like the League of Nations Union. Such organizations generated a vast output of reports, books, lectures, and magazines as well as acting as focal points of social and political debate. A common link between them, Helen McCarthy has argued, was the goal of educating people in democratic participation or active citizenship. For the most part their leaders and membership were middle class and McKibbin has emphasized their pre-war role, typified by an apolitical sociability that was still deeply defined by class, in constructing a broad anti-socialist coalition. McCarthy views them as politically more fluid and diverse, pointing out that in the 1930s at least these civic associations were also were incubators of a new middle-class progressivism and she suggests that they contributed to the relatively easy adjustment of Britain to mass democracy, compared to the Continent, in that political extremes were contained without destabilizing crisis.[10]

Coterminous with the shift to mass democracy was the rapid growth of the mass media. So much of what people already took for granted during the Second World War had entered their lives only recently: radio, movies, mass-market magazines, photojournalism, paperback books, the visual layout of the tabloids, gramophone records; even a national daily paper was relatively new for most of the population. By 1939, 69 per cent of the population read a daily and 82 per cent a Sunday newspaper and the London-based dailies now dominated sales and provincial papers, with a few exceptions, were rapidly losing market share. Magazine circulations increased dramatically, including many aimed exclusively at women readers; so did library loans and sales of paperbacks. Cinema also became a regular part of workers' lives. By the end of the 1930s over 4,000 cinemas entertained an average weekly audience of 20 million, supplying audiences with entertainment and images of fashion, class, celebrities, and places beyond their everyday experience, including a visual commentary on contemporary events through newsreels. Finally, listening to radio became a national pastime. In many working-class homes it was switched on and left on, becoming a constant background to life and a major source of information and news. The BBC's regular listeners tripled in the 1930s and by the end of the decade over 70 per cent of the population had a wireless and almost everyone had access to one. Together these new media technologies produced a democratization of culture, leading some historians to speak of a 'common culture'

---

[10] McKibbin, 'Class and conventional wisdom'; *idem, Classes and Cultures: England 1918–51* (Oxford, 1998). H. McCarthy, 'Parties, voluntary associations and democratic politics in interwar Britain', *Historical Journal*, 50(4) (2007).

in the 1930s which acted as a cohesive force in society.[11] Perhaps 'common culture' suggests more congruity than existed, but there was certainly a growing terrain of shared cultural reference which grew even larger in wartime. New kinds of media stars emerged whose appeal spanned all classes and regions; in addition, the ranks of opinion-makers and cultural commentators became ever larger and more socially and occupationally diverse, less homogeneous than twenty-five years earlier. Different parts of this process have been studied separately and in detail, but what is important to bear in mind here is their cumulative impact.

The outbreak of war and full-scale mobilization brought further changes in the 'arena of public debate'. When Labour entered Churchill's government, party politics were discontinued and a political truce eliminated contests for vacant parliamentary seats. Increasingly, Parliament ceased to matter much in the news, giving way to a system of government committees and agencies. Some civic groups became actively involved in war work and promoted debate about wartime policies; others declined as their membership was conscripted or threw themselves into other, war-related activities. The mass media were subject to varying degrees of official control. The film industry was tightly controlled and was soon engaged in close partnerships with the MoI projecting government-sanctioned images of British values and the nation at war. But film documentaries were also shown on an unprecedented scale in factories, hostels, church and municipal halls, as well as commercial cinemas to convey official messages and raise morale. After a shaky start, the BBC made a conscious effort to respond to working-class listeners more than ever before. Broadcasting was closely monitored and integrated into official publicity policy and programme managers were nervous about giving cause for complaint, fearing, especially with the collapse in France and the threat of invasion, that they might be completely taken over. And yet, well-known social critics like J. B. Priestley, Professor Joad, and Julian Huxley were frequent and popular broadcasters and, as the war continued, more air time was devoted to social and political issues, including a range of programmes about post-war reconstruction.

However, both film and radio were more important in projecting the ethos of patriotic populism and national unity than they were in promoting serious discussion of the war—either conditions on the battlefields or at home. It was the print media, where traditions of free expression were much more firmly rooted, that became the locus of political debate. Radical journalists enjoyed an especially high profile and positions of influence in Fleet Street. Some were determined to expunge the record of press subservience during the Chamberlain Appeasement years. Many felt a strong sense of mission, insisting that their right to debate and criticize was fundamental to what the nation was fighting for—and all the more indispensable under a Coalition government when a political truce suspended normal partisan debate.[12] From the beginning of the war journalists were important catalysts of

---

[11] D. L. LeMahieu, *A Culture for Democracy: Mass communication and the cultivated mind in Britain between the wars* (Oxford, 1988).
[12] R. B. Cockett, 'The government, the press and British politics', PhD Diss., University of London, 1988; *idem, Twilight of Truth: Appeasement and the manipulation of the press* (London, 1989).

public debate—about evacuation, inadequate shelter protection, and inefficiency in production, for example. In more guarded manner, they also analysed the military failures of the early war years. With so many people spending long hours in shelters, barracks, civil-defence posts, and hostels, it is hardly surprising that more news-papers and magazines were read and reached multiple readers. Correspondence columns also flourished; they aired debate, created a rapport between papers and their readers, and enabled journalists to represent themselves as speaking for their readership. Mark Hampton has suggested that the self-perception of the national press shifted between the wars, from an educative ideal to that of a *vox populi*, a representative agency reflecting public opinion and defending popular interests *vis-à-vis* Parliament; this trend reached new heights in the war years.[13] Thus, in early 1941, after its celebrated 'Plan for Britain' issue elicited over 2,000 readers' letters, *Picture Post* even began to experiment with organizing local discussion groups and other direct forms of political pressure. In the following year the *Daily Express* responded to 'a remarkable renaissance of political interest', by organizing commu-nity meetings in large numbers of villages and small towns and the *News of the World* which regularly received a huge postbag of readers' letters invited broadcaster-academic John Hilton to organize an Advice Bureau and hire a team of helpers to reply to them. Soon Hilton and his helpers were dealing with 2–3,000 letters a week.[14]

In political terms the most important change in the war years was the shift to the left of several of the most influential papers. After being taken over by a partnership of the TUC and Odhams Press, sales of the *Daily Herald* surged rapidly and by 1940 circulation was 1.8 million, although it levelled off thereafter. The bolder tabloid style of the *Daily Mirror* produced a still more meteoric rise in circulation during the war: from 1.5 to 2.4 million copies a day. It was especially popular with young workers and the armed forces, especially in the south of England, but its petulant style, lack of deference to those in power, and entertaining articles also allowed it to win over a broad national readership across class barriers. The Liberal *News Chronicle* moved sharply left under the editorial guidance of Gerald Barry; already in the 1930s it developed a close relationship with Labour and during the war embraced both Stafford Cripps and the Second Front campaign in 1942. The position of the Sunday *Observer*, once a staunch supporter of Appeasement, also underwent a dramatic change as the influence of its long-time editor, J. L. Garvin, waned and that of the Astors, its owners, increased. And the winds of change were even blowing in Printing House Square with Geoffrey Dawson's departure; under the prodding of the 'mandarin pink' duo of E. H. Carr and R. M. Barrington Ward, *The Times* became increasingly critical of pre-war politics and an advocate of social and economic reform. As for Lord Beaverbrook's publications, while the *Daily Express* was generally supportive of the government, it was unpredictable like its proprietor and could at times raise Tory hackles. His *Evening*

[13] M. Hampton, *Visions of the Press in Britain, 1850–1950* (Chicago, 2004).
[14] S. K. Smith, '*Picture Post* 1938–45', PhD Diss., Stanford University, 1992; 'Plan for Britain', *Picture Post*, 4 January 1941; 'William Hickey' (Tom Driberg), 'The finger on the pulse of Britain', *Sunday Express*, 9 August 1942. Hilton died suddenly of a cerebral haemorrhage in August 1942. See Edna Nixon, *John Hilton: The story of his life* (London, 1946).

Standard enjoyed greater independence and veered sharply left under the editorial guidance of Frank Owen and Michael Foot. Among magazines, the war enabled Hulton's weekly *Picture Post* (with over 1 million circulation and an estimated 5 million readers) to develop into one of the most important forums for progressive politicians, intellectuals, and planners, while several women's magazines became outspoken on such policy issues as equal compensation for war injuries, childcare, working conditions, and other topics of concern to their readers. The cumulative effect of these changes on wartime debate was large; it also meant that for the first time in the 1945 electoral campaign the balance of press power was fairly evenly divided between Labour and the Conservatives.

Aside from the press, as Conservatives reflected with some bitterness after 1945, radical publishers also played a role in stimulating political debate. Despite a shortage of print and paper large numbers of radical books and pamphlets appeared in the early war years, many of them achieving big sales. It was Orwell who commented: 'the pamphlet ought to be *the* literary form of an age like our own . . . political passions run high, channels of free expression are dwindling, and organized lying exists on a scale never before known. For plugging the holes in history the pamphlet is the ideal form.'[15] Among the most active figures in this area was Victor Gollancz, whose pre-war success with the Left Book Club gave him a very generous paper allotment. Equally important as a voice of radicalism was Penguin Press whose stable of authors included Tom Wintringham, Hugh Dalton, Harold Laski, Sir Richard Acland, and Archbishop Temple. Penguin reached a far broader cross-section of opinion than Gollancz, whose readers were more likely to be already firmly on the left. Other publishers contributed at a more modest level to this flood of writing, among them Secker and Warburg whose radical 'Searchlight Series' by prominent left-wing authors included Orwell's *The Lion and the Unicorn*. These books and tracts, calling for sweeping social and political change, not only sold many copies but their contents were repeatedly recycled in press articles, reviews, editorials, lectures, and broadcasts. While highly evocative, Paul Addison's image of 'Colonel Blimp being pursued through a land of Penguin Specials' scarcely does justice to the numerous band of publishers, large and small, who populated the wartime terrain. The surge of activity among writers and war commentators was a good deal larger and more diverse than his image suggests.[16]

One other characteristic of the 'arena of public debate' in the war years deserves mention—the growth of surveys to measure and evaluate public opinion. Part of the challenge of mass democracy was learning people's views and preferences; it was also clear that the 'public' was diverse, segmented by class, gender, region, education, and age. Advertising, market research, and the related field of public relations developed apace in the 1930s; so did the survey and sampling techniques of

---

[15] *New Statesman and Nation*, 9 January 1943.
[16] R. D. Edwards, *Victor Gollancz* (London, 1987); N. Joicey, 'A paperback guide to progress: Penguin Books, 1935–*c*.1941', *TCBH*, 4(1) (1993); D. R. Costello, 'Searchlight Books and the quest for a "Peoples' War"', *JCH*, 24 (1989); J. Newsinger, 'George Orwell and Searchlight: A radical initiative on the home front', *Socialist History*, 9 (1996); Addison, *The Road to 1945*, p. 188.

academic social-policy researchers. Somewhat more slowly, political parties also began to adopt a more sophisticated understanding of public opinion, although little credence was attached to polling in 1945. The BBC began to engage in systematic listener research in 1936[17] and in the following year both the American Gallup organization (BIPO) and Mass-Observation began surveying British opinion. Recognition of the gulf of understanding between elites and the mass public was one of the strongest themes in Mass-Observation's work and both organizations were propelled by the liberal democratic idea that polls could give voice to those normally unheard; they warned that new communications technologies had given increased power to those who controlled them as well as inflating the claims of organized pressure groups to be representative at the expense of the unorganized.[18] In the war years not only was Mass-Observation recruited by the MoI to investigate public morale, but the government soon sponsored its own Wartime Social Survey. Never before had the nation's views been so closely monitored and so comprehensively documented. Among official surveys, there were, to list only a few: the reports of Home Intelligence and of Regional Information officers (weekly and at times daily surveys of civilian morale), comments collected from the managers of W. H. Smith bookshops and Granada cinemas, War Office morale reports, the Wartime Social Survey, BBC listener research, postal and telegraph censorship, as well as polls commissioned from Gallup and Mass-Observation. In addition, a wide variety of newspapers and non-official organizations, including trade unions, conducted their own surveys to identify public views and sometimes to mobilize support for specific agendas. It is also significant that the results of these polls often found their way into the media, thereby becoming part of public debate.

The print media and civic groups were of central importance to the wartime 'arena of public debate', but the war also created new sites for people to exchange views. Many of these have already been identified in earlier chapters: people spent long periods together in civil-defence posts, workers' hostels, Home Guard units, shelters, barracks, factory canteens, women's voluntary organizations, camps for harvest and forestry work, and so on. There were lectures, clubs, and film shows in factories; London fire stations developed a network of discussion groups; the army established ABCA. Political debate also took place, of course, in trade union branches, workplace committees, and trades councils, while the Communist Party of Great Britain (CP) was active in a range of organizations from the People's Convention to the Women's Parliaments. This is not to say that people were endlessly debating social and political issues, simply that some historians have taken the alleged apathy and disengagement of the mass electorate too far.[19] The public

[17] R. Silvey, *Who's Listening? The story of BBC audience research* (London, 1974).

[18] G. Gallup and S. Forbes Rae, *The Pulse of Democracy: The public opinion poll and how it works* (New York, 1940); on Mass-Observation see the articles in *New Formations*, 44 (Autumn 2001) especially N. Hubble, 'Charles Madge and Mass Observation are at home: From anthropology to war, and after'; Tom Jeffery, *Mass-Observation: A short history* (Birmingham, 1978). BIPO published the aggregate results of its polls in the *News Chronicle* and often the paper's lead editorials took off from the poll results.

[19] See the critique by J. Hinton, '1945 and the apathy school', *HWJ*, 43 (1997).

culture of wartime was often highly political—if we define that as more than party political—and while people might be poorly informed about specific proposals for the reform of education or healthcare or at times alienated and cynical about politics and politicians, none of this necessarily contradicted their having strong political views. Many workers did read radical pamphlets or encountered the same ideas recycled in newspaper columns or trade union papers. It is often difficult to document workers' opinions concretely, but even more dangerous is the assumption that roughly 10 per cent of workers (a curious inverse of 'the submerged tenth'?) can be categorized as a 'thinking minority' while the rest have no opinions worthy of the name.[20] This is especially true of wartime when so much of life was determined by public events and in the broad sense politicized. Contemporary polls offer some insight into the movement of opinion to the left, so do private correspondences. A growing sense that history—especially the history of the Second World War—includes everybody has also produced a rapid increase in the numbers of diaries and letters now being deposited in archives.

WAR RADICALS ENVISION A NEW SOCIETY

The early years of the Second World War enjoy a mythic status in the annals of British patriotism, evoking powerful images of Dunkirk, the Blitz, and a nation united and galvanized into action by the threat to its survival. But while the heightened patriotism of the period is familiar, the sharply radical language in which it was phrased has been masked by subsequent encrustations of myth. Political crisis in Britain in May 1940, followed swiftly by the total collapse of France shook the nation to its core. Responses to the crisis were many: there was a spate of rumours of German landings and fifth-column activity and calls for the internment of aliens. A quarter of a million men volunteered for the newly formed Local Defence Volunteers (soon renamed the Home Guard). Pacifist groups, and the CP, campaigned for a People's Convention and called for a 'people's peace'. In public many affected an insouciance or cheerful fortitude, but as private letters and diaries indicate, people were swept by powerful emotions—of anger, fear, a sense of betrayal, and of desperation. It was, as Orwell wrote, a moment when the nation 'suddenly swings together and does the same thing, like a herd of cattle facing a wolf'.[21] But at the same time some were secretly convinced that Britain had little alternative but to negotiate with Hitler; others suspected that reactionary groups were waiting in the wings to work with Hitler or adopt a British form of Pétainism; and many concluded that Britain's survival depended on a swift and complete break with the policies of the past. Until this point Chamberlainite Conservatism had retained a good deal of popularity; now it was suddenly and totally discredited,

[20] R. Lowe, 'The Second World War, consensus and the foundation of the welfare state', *TCBH*, 1(2) (1990); Addison, *The Road to 1945*, p. 15.
[21] G. Orwell, 'The Lion and the Unicorn' in S. Orwell and I. Angus (eds.), *The Collected Essays, Journalism and Letters of George Orwell* (1940–3), II, p. 66.

replaced by growing recrimination against 'the guilty men' of Appeasement whose
failures had brought the country to the brink of disaster.

The scope and intensity of public disaffection has received less attention than it
deserves, in part because it has been viewed primarily as a personal attack against
Chamberlain, Hoare, Baldwin, and the so-called 'Men of Munich'. The hunt for
individual scapegoats was particularly intense around the time of Dunkirk when
three young Beaverbrook journalists published *Guilty Men* under the pseudonym
'Cato', chosen because he had cleansed the sewers of Rome. This polemic, which
went through twenty-seven printings and sold over 200,000 copies before the
year's end, accused Chamberlain and his political allies of dooming the British
army before it ever took the field and demanded that they be purged from
government.[22] It was the first of many iterations of the 'guilty men' thesis, which
in one sense helped ease the task of building public support for the Coalition by
concentrating responsibility for past failures; but the search for culprits quickly
escalated into a much broader indictment of interwar Conservatism and the pre-
war social and political order. Over a period of two years, sustained by bad news
from the battlefields and dissatisfaction with the speed and efficiency of mobilization on the home front, critics of government policy kept up a continual stream of
radical criticism in books, pamphlets, and press articles. Their ideas were fashioned
in the 1930s, shaped by anti-fascism and public debates about unemployment and
the failure of free-market capitalism. But the dramatic decline of public confidence
in the existing order injected new urgency into left-wing policy discussions and
broadened public receptivity to proposals for sweeping change.[23] Many of these
critics and commentators were well known as writers and broadcasters—like
J. B. Priestley, John Strachey, Julian Huxley, and Cyril Joad, to name only a few;
others, like Orwell at that time, were obscure. Some like Richard Acland, an
MP and the founder of the socialist Common Wealth party, were former Liberals
who had moved sharply left in response to Nazism. Others like Harold Laski and
G. D. H. Cole were prominent in the Labour Party, but were critical of its leaders'
moderation and hoped to radicalize the party from within. Many had been involved
in different pro-planning groups, like PEP, were active in the peace movement in
the 1930s, or advocated European federalism as a way of avoiding war. Others
belonged to the Christian socialist left which had been gaining ground within the
Anglican Church before the war. They were patriotic socialists and though they
may have flirted with communist politics most had rejected Stalinism before the
war; they outlined a specifically British (or, more often, English) brand of socialism
strongly influenced by Ruskin, Tawney, and Cole, which could bring greater
equality and planned efficiency while safeguarding liberal values and freedoms.

---

[22] 'Cato', *Guilty Men* (London, 1940). The authors were Michael Foot, Frank Owen, and Peter
Howard. Also, Geoffrey Mander, *We Were Not All Wrong* (London, 1941). Ex-Tory Capt.
Cunningham-Reid launched several bitter attacks, e.g. *Blame the Old Gang* (London, 1942).
Another pseudonymous book was *Tory MP* (1939) which detailed the family and business
connections of hundreds of Conservative MPs, portraying a close-knit interlocking oligarchy.

[23] P. M. Coupland, 'Voices from nowhere: Utopianism in British political culture 1939–1945',
PhD Diss., Warwick University, 2000.

To Churchill and the political right, of course, their persistent criticism and preoccupation with recasting society in the midst of a war was deeply disloyal—a new *trahison des clercs*, stirring up trouble while the government concentrated on the fighting.[24]

The shock of a second war in the space of twenty years provoked widespread reflection about its larger historical meaning with both conflicts being viewed as stages in the terminal phase of liberal civilization. The events of 1940 constituted, in Laski's eyes, a 'fundamental crisis of capitalism', a historical watershed comparable to the Reformation or the French Revolution.[25] Biologist and popular broadcaster Julian Huxley wrote that 'the old system of capitalist profit-making and individualist competition' was 'falling to bits'; the era of 'economic man' was being overtaken by a new era of 'social man' and this 'reintegration' could either be progressive or reactionary, 'either democratic or else openly or disguisedly fascist'.[26] Others saw the war as a struggle for Christian values against materialism which called for a moral revolution. Malcolm Muggeridge, already in uniform when his book went to press, produced a bitter, despairing chronicle of the thirties, a Spenglerian tale of folly, empty lives, and weak leaders, lacking the moral will to combat fascism and of the masses narcotized by material goods and the mass media.[27] Richard Overy has identified a penchant for doom-laden forecasts, a morbid sense of decay, among intellectuals in the pre-war decades;[28] the war critics echoed many of those themes, but were also utopian with their blueprints for a better society that might yet emerge from the present crisis.

The dominant focus of radical publications, however, was Britain's record of social and political failure since the First World War. Already in 1939, *Tory MP*, published under a pseudonym, had denounced the system of closely interlocking family, business, and political ties that underpinned Conservative power. J. B. Priestley's celebrated radio 'Postscripts' broadcast after the nine o'clock news between early June and late October 1940 sounded many of the same themes, lashing out against the 'idle rich' and officialdom and celebrating the democratic values of ordinary people. Most importantly, Priestley publicized what became the left's master narrative of the interwar years: the broken promises and betrayals of 1918, the dole queues and despair of the 1930s, the increasing gulf between the rich and privileged and the majority of the nation.[29] It was a blunt-spoken critique that was constantly repeated whether in Orwell's indictment of the nation as

[24] Lord Elton, 'Reflections on a new social order', *The Fortnightly Review* (May 1941); *idem*, *Notebook in Wartime* (London, 1941), p. 136.

[25] H. Laski, *Where Do We Go From Here?* (London, 1940); *idem*, *Reflections on the Revolution of Our Time* (London, 1943); J. MacMurray, *The Foundation of Economic Reconstruction*, September 1942, address to the National Peace Council at Oxford (London, 1942).

[26] J. Huxley, 'Economic and social man', *The Fortnightly*, July 1941; *idem*, *Democracy Marches* (London, 1941). Huxley and many others were greatly impressed by a book by the young Austrian refugee and later management studies guru, Peter Drucker, *The End of Economic Man* (London, 1939).

[27] M. Muggeridge, *The Thirties* (London, 1940).

[28] R. Overy, *The Morbid Age: Britain between the wars* (London, 2009).

[29] Simon Haxey (pseud.), *Tory MP* (London, 1939); J. B. Priestley, *All England Listened: The wartime broadcasts of J. B. Priestley* (New York, 1967).

hopelessly 'class-ridden' or the blistering attack by 'Cassandra' on 'the feudal nature of the distribution of property in these islands', or Tosco Fyvel's descriptions of a 'frightened governing class, clinging to its institutions', its confidence extinguished in the mud of the Somme and Passchendaele.[30] Another recurrent topic—surprising at first given all the other problems in 1940, but echoed in contemporary debate about 'the old school tie' and officer selection in the armed forces—was the need to reform or abolish the public schools, seen as the chief structuring agents of the class system which made different social strata unintelligible to each other from infancy. These bastions of privilege, wrote the *New Statesman*'s T. C. Worsley, were responsible for producing conventional, uncreative types, good for the playing fields of Eton but useless for coping with Nazism.[31] Still other attacks focused on unearned capital, arguing that the conscription of labour required an equal conscription of wealth. And growing concern about shortfalls in war production produced increasing accusations that managers and employers were protecting their selfish interests at the expense of the common good. The connecting theme throughout was that British society was too undemocratic, too deeply riven by class and privilege to survive—'fair shares', 'equal sacrifice', and far-reaching social and structural change were necessary if total participation and popular commitment to victory were to be achieved.

But this stream of radical propaganda was not merely an indictment of Conservatism and past failures; it also advanced alternative policies and structures. Some radical writers did little more than make vague appeals for socialism, but others offered detailed and closely argued plans and though, of necessity in this abbreviated description, they are generalized as a group, their ideas were diverse. The dominant themes may be conveniently divided into three: the need for increased state control and central planning; 'common ownership' and sweeping measures of nationalization; and social and economic equality and the creation of an effective democracy. The attack on private capital and 'vested' interests as incapable of efficient organization of the war and basically driven by selfish, sectional priorities rather than common goals underpinned all of this writing. Energetic government direction was needed, it was argued, and too little was being done to control business. Many books and pamphlets called for immediate state control over private investment and overseas trade, while Beveridge's demand for an 'Economic General Staff' to coordinate the economic side of the war became a constant theme in the early war years. Bevin's policy of gradualism was a frequent target: in a pseudonymous publication G. D. H. Cole told Bevin to please 'pull up your socks', 'insist on the power to do the job properly', and make it clear to the Cabinet that workers demanded 'practical assurance that they are not being conscripted for the defence

[30] Orwell, *The Lion and the Unicorn*; T. Fyvel, *The Malady and the Vision* (London, 1940), pp. 153–5; 'Cassandra' (William Connor) of the *Daily Mirror*, *England at War* (London, 1941). Also, J. P. W. Mallalieu, *'Passed to You Please!' Britain's red-tape machine at war* (London, 1942).

[31] F. C. Worsley, *The End of the 'Old School Tie'* (London, 1941); idem, *Barbarians and Philistines* (London, 1940); R. H. Tawney, 'The problem of the public schools', *Political Quarterly*, 14(2) (April–June 1943); H. Dent, 'Education for democracy', *Fortnightly Review* (August 1942). F. Williams, *Ten Angels Swearing or Tomorrow's Politics* (London 1941), pp. 93–102.

of capitalism'.[32] The solution to production bottlenecks and inefficiencies, it was argued, was planning, although many writers did little to define its scope and institutional ramifications; also, few discussed possible conflicts between planning by experts and democratic participation or liberal freedoms, although this issue received much more attention after 1943 amid public debate about post-war reconstruction.[33] Planning was an immediate necessity for national survival but already in January 1941, when *Picture Post* published its 'Plan for Britain', the word became cultural shorthand for a social democratic future conjuring up visions of new planned towns, hygienic schools, healthy families, and an economy without dole queues and poverty. 'Plan we must', wrote town-planner Thomas Sharp in a best-selling Penguin, 'not for the sake of our physical environment only, but to save and fulfil democracy itself.'[34]

Closely linked to this vision was support for 'common ownership' both on moral grounds and as the logical concomitant of wartime planning. Convinced that private capitalism could not resolve the problems of war production, Orwell, Priestley, Cole, Strachey, and Acland, to name only a few, called in 1940–1 for sweeping nationalizations of land, mines, railways, banks, and major industries.[35] Many commentators doubted that large corporations which so recently in the depression had reduced capacity to maintain profits could now achieve the necessary acceleration of output. But they also believed that the changing structure of industry—with cartels, the growing role of banks, and the increasing separation between owners of capital and professional managers—might facilitate the transition to government control.[36] Critics differed over how much nationalization, as opposed to state direction, was possible in the midst of a war. A detailed critique of war production warned that it would 'divide rather than unite the nation . . . rake up old feuds and emphasize differences when the need is to concentrate on our common peril and our common aim'.[37] As a compromise, the wealthy financier and socialist journalist, Nicholas Davenport, proposed a 'common pool' with ownership to be settled later: the state, he suggested, should lease all capital resources for the duration (paying owners a dividend minus a national-defence contribution) and, at the same time, workers should accept a national wage policy. Davenport saw this as a prelude to full nationalization post-war.[38]

---

[32] 'Populus' (G. D. H. Cole), *My Dear Mr Churchill and Other Letters to Persons in Authority* (London, 1941). Quotes from pp. 24 and 38.

[33] G. D. H. Cole *et al.*, *Plan for Britain* (London, 1943); H. Morrison *et al.*, *Can Planning Be Democratic?* (London, 1944)); E. F. M. Durbin, *What We Have to Defend: A brief critical examination of the British social tradition* (London, 1942).

[34] T. Sharp, *Town Planning* (London, 1940), p. 116.

[35] Orwell, *The Lion and the Unicorn*, pp. 95–7; J. B. Priestley, *Out Of the People* (London, 1941); Richard Acland, *What It Will Be Like in the New Britain?* (London, Gollancz, 1942); G. D. H. Cole, 'Private monopoly or public service?' in Cole *et al.*, *Victory or Vested Interest* (London, 1942); John Strachey, *Banks for the People* (London, 1940).

[36] James Burnham's *The Managerial Revolution* (London, 1942) was frequently cited; e.g. D. Routh, 'The twentieth century revolution', *Horizon*, 6(33) (September 1942).

[37] 'Argonaut' (pseud.), *Give Us the Tools: A study of the hindrances to full war production and how to end them* (London, 1942), foreword, dated January 1942.

[38] N. Davenport, *Vested Interest or Common Pool?* (London, 1942); *idem, Memoirs of a City Radical* (London, 1974); M. Edelman, *Production for Victory Not Profit* (London, 1942).

At the heart of radical propaganda was the conviction that survival would compel Britain to become a more socially just and democratic society. The MoI's publicity about 'fair shares' and 'equal sacrifice' and the notion of a 'People's War' seemed to confirm this and commentators saw signs everywhere that ordinary people were becoming active citizens, insistent upon their rights but also aware of their obligations; the phrase 'vital democracy' was used frequently to describe popular participation and the spirit of collectivism: families billeting evacuees, enlistment in the Home Guard, and service in voluntary organizations, shelter committees, and workplace committees were all viewed as examples of a new citizenship of service or contribution. This kind of democracy, it was argued, was a necessary complement to greater planning and state control; socialism in the context of a parliamentary system was viewed as the way to ensure both social justice and liberal freedoms. Moreover, much of this writing was critical of the idea of a class-based politics, arguing that this was outdated; instead, building on the wartime rhetoric of privileged elites versus ordinary citizens, it emphasized the ties of solidarity between productive citizens and, like Orwell, envisioned a progressive politics of both workers and much of the middle class. What is also striking, however, especially in view of the unprecedented wartime mobilization of women, is how little attention was devoted to women's issues and how few of these radical tracts were written by women.

Finally, another salient characteristic of this radical out-pouring, was the moral and Christian tone of much of it. This reinforces the argument of Callum Brown and others that, by focusing upon processes of secularization, historians have underrated the importance of religion in people's lives.[39] During the 1930s the Christian socialist movement expanded rapidly and became increasingly politicized in response to the war in Spain and the growth of fascism. Tawney's exposition of social Christianity was an important influence, while Gollancz's Christian Book Club, which enrolled many Anglican clergy, played a role in encouraging dialogue between Christianity and Marxism. The idea that socialism and Christianity were natural allies gained growing support and played a large role in the popular tide that boosted Stafford Cripps's political career and in building support for the radical Common Wealth Party in 1942. Already in the previous year Archbishop Temple organized a highly publicized conference at Malvern College to consider the new society that was emerging from the war and the Church's role in reconstruction. He also wrote the best-seller, *Christianity and the Social Order*, which sold over 140,000 copies—in part in the hope of containing more left-wing groups within the Church, some of whom, arguing that the Christian faith and capitalism were incompatible, had formed the Council of Clergy and Ministers for Common Ownership.[40]

---

[39] C. G. Brown, *The Death of Christian Britain* (London, 2001); *idem, Religion and Society in Twentieth Century Britain* (Edinburgh, 2006).

[40] D. Ormrod, 'The Christian left and the beginnings of Christian-Marxist dialogue, 1935–45' in J. Obelkevich, L. Roper, and R. Samuel (eds.), *Disciplines of Faith* (London, 1987); K. Robbins, 'Britain, 1940 and "Christian civilization"' in *idem, History, Religion, and Identity in Modern Britain* (London, 1993); R. J. Scrutton, *A People's Runneymede* (1941); T. Sargant, *These Things Shall Be* (London, 1941); Cecil Northcott, *Change Here for Britain: The revolution that is happening* (London, 1942); W. Temple, *Christianity and the Social Order* (London, 1942).

It is difficult to gauge the impact of this barrage of radical commentary. Most historical accounts have focused almost exclusively on negative criticism of 'the old gang' and 'vested interests', while Correlli Barnett's portmanteau term, 'New Jerusalem', used to cover all reformist plans, minimizes the differences between writers like Orwell, Strachey, Cole, and Beveridge. Paul Addison has cautioned that there is a danger of exaggerating the influence of pamphlets and radio talks.[41] But, in recent accounts at least, there is a reverse hazard of minimizing the influence of these radical critics—certainly, conservatives at the time had few illusions about their cumulative effect, nor did they manage much of a response. Many of these books and articles were widely read and, while readers were disproportionately middle class, they reached a wider group in recycled form as press articles and reviews. Arguments that would have been confined to a narrow group before 1914 were listened to, read, or discussed by a much wider public in the war years and similar themes and ideas were circulating in trade union meetings, factory canteens, and Labour Party branches. As Conservatives pointed out angrily, this kind of propaganda was closely aligned to the Labour Party's outlook and agenda—as expressed, for example, in its 1942 programme, *The Old World and the New Society*, which was largely written by Laski. Indeed, the Labour leadership's reluctance to push a socialist agenda—for example, coal and rail transport nationalization—within the Coalition government, produced mounting frustration in radical circles. In a pseudonymous published letter to Attlee, Cole wrote: 'They [the Tories] are in a cleft stick and you—and the nation—ought to be profiting by their dilemma. If you went hard at them now, they would scurry for shelter.'[42] 'We cannot afford to let [social reform] wait', wrote Laski, 'simply because its initiation now is an essential part of the strategy of victory.' In the early war years these critics were convinced that conditions were opportune for a 'revolution by consent', since conservative interests would rather make concessions than face defeat. But they also lacked a means of directly influencing politics until 1942 when public confidence in the government's handling of the war declined sharply.

THE COMMUNIST PARTY

If one indicator of a 'swing to the left' in these early crisis years was this flood of left-wing publications, another was the recruiting activity of radical activists in important sectors of war production and the CP's rapid growth. Remembered fondly as a kind of 'golden age' by communists who were young at the time, the war saw the peak of the party's influence, the one moment when it seemed capable of breaking out of its isolation and acquiring a mass following.

---

[41] Addison, *The Road to 1945*, p. 129.
[42] 'Populus' (G. D. H. Cole), *My Dear Mr Churchill and Other Letters to Persons in Authority*. Quotes from p. 24; H. Laski, 'The need for a European revolution' in *Programmes for Victory* (Fabian Society, London, 1940), pp. 17–18.

Founded in August 1920, the CP made very limited progress in its first decade; its attempts to affiliate with the Labour Party or to work within its structures were blocked, while its efforts to gain influence with the unemployed and within the trade union movement were fiercely contested by the TUC leadership and reached only a small minority of workers. In a few places, it is true, the CP managed to put down strong roots, notably in Stuart MacIntyre's 'Little Moscows': the mining areas of the Rhondda and West Fife; the industrial Vale of Leven, part of the Clydeside conurbation; and among the Jewish working class of East London.[43] But total membership was only 2,500 in 1930, lower than ten years before and significantly below its 10,000 highpoint during the year of the General Strike. Over the next decade the party's fortunes improved and in some industrial sectors—especially engineering, mining, and transport—small cadres of communist trade unionists established rank-and-file movements even penetrating some of the newer industrial centres of the Midlands where unionism was weak. The combination of persistent high levels of unemployment and the growing threat of fascism also won recruits for the party, especially with the Comintern's switch to a popular-front policy and the left's moral crusade against Franco's insurgency in Spain. By the late 1930s the party had gained adherents in youth groups and established a foothold among sections of the middle classes—not simply *la jeunesse dorée* of Oxbridge and the left intellectuals so prominent in studies of the 'Red Decade', but among schoolteachers, technicians, white-collar workers, architects, and suburban professionals, the kind of people who joined the Left Book Club and their local Labour Party branches, many of which quietly ignored official bans.[44] There were also plenty of setbacks, of course; defeat in Spain and Stalin's Moscow purge trials were both demoralizing and divisive but the party's small membership, only 18,000 in 1939, masked its considerably larger cultural and political impact on the eve of war.

The Nazi–Soviet Pact jeopardized these gains, throwing the party into confusion and forcing the ousting of its General-Secretary Harry Pollitt. Revered by the rank and file, his demotion sent shock waves through the party. In the next months many members quit,[45] but others stayed in though confused and angry at the new turn of events or they accepted the explanation that the pact had been forced on the Soviet Union by the Western powers' refusal to agree to an anti-fascist alliance. For some, rejecting a war between capitalist states was what socialists had failed to do in

[43] S. MacIntyre, *Little Moscows: Communism and working-class militancy in inter-war Britain* (London, 1980).

[44] S. R. Parsons, 'Communism in the professions: The organization of the Communist Party among professional workers, 1933–1956', PhD Diss., Warwick University, 1990; K. Morgan, G. Cohen, and A. Flinn, *Communists and British Society, 1920–1991* (London, 2007).

[45] A. Thorpe, 'The membership of the Communist Party of Great Britain, 1920–1945', *HJ*, 43(3) (2000); idem, *The British Communist Party and the Communist International 1919–1943* (Manchester, 2000); K. Layburn, '"About turn": The Communist Party of Great Britain and the Second World War, 1939–41' in K. Layburn and K. Dockray (eds.), *The Representation and Reality of War* (Stroud, 1999); J. Attfield and S. Williams (eds.), *1939: The Communist Party and the war* (London, 1984); W. Thompson and S. Hobbs, 'British Communists on the War, 1939–41', *Oral History*, 16(2) (Autumn 1988).

1914 with catastrophic consequences. Others were motivated by their hatred and distrust of Chamberlain and the Appeasers, whose commitment to the anti-fascist war they continued to doubt. The branches most affected by resignations seem to have been those in areas like Oxford where the popular-front policy was the key to their recent growth and where members were less fully integrated into party culture; the impact of Moscow's abrupt change was also devastating on sympathetic non-members and this turned to outright hostility when Stalin occupied eastern Poland and then opened hostilities against Finland.

In retrospect, however, the most striking aspect of the period before June 1941 is the way the CP bounced back from these blows and began to re-expand its activities and support. In part this reflected the continued existence of earlier anti-war opinion, in the Peace Pledge Union and other groups, and of pressures for a negotiated peace. But the party soon began to distance itself from quasi-Leninist ideas about 'revolutionary defeatism' and 'an imperialist war'. Communist publications might argue that the main struggle of the working class was against its own imperialist government; some even labelled Britain and France as the chief aggressors and made the threat of Nazism secondary to the dangers of incipient fascism at home. But after Dunkirk the anti-war line was applied with greater flexibility; in reality, communists were quietly reverting to the 'war on two fronts' line originally proclaimed by Pollitt which embraced the war against Hitler while attacking governmental failures at home. Activists' responses to the party's official policy varied. Some ignored instructions and volunteered for the armed forces, while many turned their energies to workplace wage struggles and campaigns over civil defence and shelter conditions. It was significant that the party's leadership made no real effort to get district committees and factory cells to push the anti-war position; those that did quickly found it counterproductive among their workmates. In London and other towns communists played an active role on shelter committees and campaigns for deep-shelter protection, while in hard-hit places like Coventry they won public support for their activities during raids—all of which attracted the attentions of police and Home Intelligence. At the same time communist shop stewards in factories focused their efforts upon the defence of trade union rights and craft practices against the encroachments of state and employers.[46] Labour's entry into Coalition with the Conservatives also strengthened the party's position as a vehicle for public discontent over the conduct of the war and the organization of the home front. The clearest evidence of this was the People's Convention held in London in January 1941, attended by over 2,000 delegates who represented a broad array of radical and peace organizations. The Convention's programme was a catch-all of radical causes: anti-fascism, anti-war, plus demands for a popular-front government, improved air-raid protection, nationalization of industry, Indian independence, friendship with the Soviet Union, and so on. However, delegates had no clear plan of action and the movement increasingly saw itself as a forum for voicing left democratic opposition.

[46] K. Morgan, *Against Fascism and War. Ruptures and Continuities in British Communist Politics 1935–41* (Manchester, 1989); *idem, Harry Pollitt* (Manchester, 1993).

There was talk of a second conference to take place in the summer, but Hitler's invasion of Russia brought such plans to an abrupt halt.[47] One result of the Convention, however, was that the government seriously contemplated banning the CP altogether, and it did close down the *Daily Worker* and sharply increased police surveillance of the movement.

It was Hitler's invasion in June 1941 that transformed the CP's situation; its new policy of all-out commitment to the war effort allowed the party to make its influence felt through a wide range of organizations, while the work of its organizers in war factories soon resulted in a rapid surge of membership. 'We almost heaved a sigh of relief, although it was a terrible thing', remembered one activist; 'there was no longer any need to hedge or equivocate', commented another.[48] Pollitt returned to the party's leadership and soon began to emerge as a more important national political figure, speaking tirelessly up and down the country. All references to fascist tendencies within the British government were dropped and the party's prime focus shifted from the vague aims of the Convention to single-issue campaigns such as the demand for Joint Production Committees to maximize output in war factories and an early Second Front in Europe to relieve German pressure on the Red Army. Over the next year the party dramatically expanded its industrial base, although in some factories and industrial sectors hostility remained high, a legacy of earlier conflicts within the labour movement. Some workers were also scornful of the party's sudden switch to all-out commitment to the war or resented its production drives and firm adherence to a no-strike policy. In general, however, the CP's criticism of mismanagement and employer inefficiency struck a responsive chord among the broad public, while in engineering and munitions the expansion of shop-floor organization increased the influence of party militants. As a result in the first six months of 1942 national membership rose from 27,000 to 60,000; gains were especially large in the Midlands where the party quintupled its size in that year while in the London area it more than tripled.[49] In addition, large numbers of other workers drew close to the party, although they never formally joined, electing communist shop stewards, attending dinner-hour lectures, buying party publications, and consulting party organizers on such issues as military exemptions, government allowances, and labour transfers.

An examination of local party files illustrates the prodigious activity of organizers in these years. A fairly complete set of records exists for the Lancashire and Cheshire region. At the end of 1943 membership in the region was 6,704 (in 1940 it had been less than 2,000), divided between 179 factory groups and 77 local branches.

---

[47] J. T. Murphy, *Victory Production* (London, 1942), pp. 43–4; J. Hinton, 'Killing the People's Convention: A letter from Palme Dutt to Harry Pollitt', *Bulletin of the Society for Labour History*, 39 (Autumn 1979).

[48] The first quotation, by Dora Cox: C. Williams, *Democratic Rhondda, Politics and Society 1885–1951* (Cardiff, 1996), p. 162; the second is from Malcolm MacEwen, *The Greening of a Red* (London, 1991). Cox was an organizer in S. Wales; McEwen was on the staff of the *Daily Worker* at the time of the Convention.

[49] N. Fishman, *The British Communist Party and the Trade Unions* (London, 1995), Appendix 1; London Area Reports for 1942 and 1943, CP/LON/DC/00/01, CPGB Archive, Labour History Archive and Study Centre, Manchester.

Aside from work in their unions and on JPCs, communists were active in local trades councils: the Manchester and Liverpool councils, for example, each included a bloc of about forty communists. There were also fifty Anglo-Soviet committees operating throughout the region and the Young Communist League had a little over 300 'real' (as opposed to 700 'on the books') members. In addition, a women's department addressed such issues as childcare, school meals, evacuation, and billeting and the party played a leading role in the Lancashire Women's Parliament. Nor was propaganda work and political education neglected. In 1943 during a three-month period that was not considered exceptional, the Lancashire and Cheshire region sent out over 90,000 leaflets, 9,000 posters, and large numbers of flyers. In addition to regular branch and factory sessions, there were 137 public meetings—an underestimate since, headquarters complained, many branches were negligent in filing reports of their activities. As for party training, a list covering the work of thirty branches during a six-month period in 1943 included: four week-long party schools and four one-day schools at the district level, fifty-three factory courses, sixty-three branch and area courses, another thirty-five one-day schools at branches and sub-districts, forty-seven dinner-hour discussion meetings, and thirty-four courses for new members.[50]

Party records for the London region indicate equally intense activity. By the end of 1942 the London area had 22–26,000 members[51]—well over 40 per cent of the national total. In that year 37 new branches and 379 new factory groups were established, with growth especially in the metal industries, transport, and railways. About 50 Anglo-Soviet committees were functioning in the area and over 800 delegates attended the fourth session of the London Women's Parliament held in late 1943. Statistics for party leaflets distributed and public meetings held were remarkable: over 260,000 copies of party pamphlets were printed in 1942, more than 1.7 million leaflets, and from July to September alone some 1,600 local meetings were held along with hundreds of educational classes for new members.[52] The campaign for a Second Front resulted in some of the biggest rallies of the war with large crowds gathering in London's Trafalgar Square as well as provincial cities to listen to Pollitt and other speakers. The following year, in November 1943, the government's decision to release the fascist leader Oswald Mosley and his wife from gaol produced an explosion of anger and, as a party report put it, 'gave the comrades a feeling of something to grasp and to fight on'. An estimated three-quarters of a million signatures were collected on petitions in the London region alone protesting their release. Mass meetings assembled in the factories and delegates from over 300 factories went to the House of Commons. And in one week attendance at

[50] CP/CENT/ORG/6/4 Lancashire and Cheshire District Files 1943–1960, CPGB Archive. Reports of August to December 1943.
[51] The figures are confusing. Party documents for the London area give 22,000 for October 1942 and 26,087 for the end of November 1942. These totals were compiled from the numbers reported by different branches. CPGB Archive, Manchester, London Report, 30 December 1942.
[52] London Area Reports for 1942 and 1943, CP/LON/DC/00/01, CPGB Archive. NA: HO 45/25572, 'Intelligence reports on Communist Party activities' (1940–1), 25573 (1941–3), 25574 (1941–3) contain police reports on communist public meetings and other activities.

London party meetings surpassed the previous six weeks put together.[53] Memoirs and oral histories about these years record party activists' excitement and confidence. 'These were quite extraordinary times', Malcolm MacEwen, a full-time District Secretary in the North East recalled: 'one really had the feeling . . . that the Party was going places and that it was going to be quite a major force in British politics at the end of the war'.[54]

One result of the mass recruitment of women into war factories was that they became more conspicuous as shop stewards and branch officers,[55] although the trend should not be exaggerated. In the 1930s the percentage of women in the party, many of them wives of male communists, was around 20 per cent (compared to over 40 per cent for the Labour Party) and possibly 25 per cent in the Lancashire textile region. By the end of 1942, women accounted for 27 per cent of the London area membership while at the war's end they were 26 per cent of the national party.[56] In addition to conventional workplace issues, female communists also campaigned on matters of special concern to women and played a large role in the Women's Parliaments. These bodies began as an offshoot of the People's Convention but soon developed a separate momentum of their own; press reporters attended the sessions and their deliberations were quoted in the national press. The first in London in July 1941 was attended by 350 delegates and by its third session in 1942 had 983. Other parliaments followed in Bradford, Manchester, Newcastle, Glasgow, and South Wales. Delegates represented factories, tenants' organizations, trade unions, housewives' committees, and other groups. They debated such issues as working conditions, women's health, public childcare, shopping, rationing, and housing and sent deputations to lobby MPs and local authorities. The TUC put the parliaments on its list of proscribed organizations, much to the anger of many union members, but they were not simply extensions of the Communist Party. By 1945 the London Parliament was working closely with the National Society of Children's Nurseries in a campaign to preserve and even expand public nurseries. Meetings of these bodies might begin with sisterly greetings from such prominent well-wishers as Nancy Astor, Margery Spring-Rice, Megan Lloyd George, and Mrs Pethick-Lawrence. Eleonor Rathbone gave a speech to the Newcastle Parliament; Caroline Haslett, President of the Women's Engineering Association, addressed the London one; and Lady Rhys Williams participated in the one in South Wales.[57]

[53] London Area Report for 1943 (January 1944), CPGB Archive, p. 10 (quote), 2. The notebook of a Brent CP member commented in a review of the party's work in 1943: 'Only on Mosley did we get all-out action.' CP/LON/DC/00/02, CPGB Archive, Manchester.

[54] MacEwen interview quoted in Parsons, 'Communism in the professions', p. 226.

[55] e.g. women were appointed as district organizers for West Yorkshire and the South East Midlands area: Morgan *et al.*, *Communists and British Society*, pp. 161–2, 166; T. Davis, '"What kind of woman is she?' Women and Communist Party politics 1941–1955' in R. Brunt and C. Rowan (eds.), *Feminism, Culture and Politics* (London, 1982). Also, S. Bruley, 'Women against war and fascism: Communism, feminism, and the People's Front' in J. Fyrth (ed.), *Britain, Fascism and the Popular Front* (London, 1985).

[56] Thorpe, 'The membership of the Communist Party of Great Britain, 1920–1945'.

[57] Little has been written about the Women's Parliaments. Some information can be found in: 'Women's Parliaments 1941–44', CP/Org/Misc/1/3 Communist Party Archive, Manchester, which among other things contains some printed summaries of the sessions; 'Women's Parliaments

While large crowds at demonstrations and the influx of new members generated considerable optimism among party organizers, it also raised new concerns. For the first time the party seemed capable of mobilizing a significant portion of the population, but officials worried about a dilution of communist politics and a loss of momentum. As a group the newcomers were quite different from the typical militants of earlier times—for whom the party was a total commitment, a way of life, often bolstered by tight family connections.[58] Many new recruits were reluctant to attend branch meetings or education classes, merely holding a party card and paying their weekly dues. It was difficult to integrate them into party culture and activities or even to maintain contact with them and work previously performed by ordinary members was now done by committees and officials. In consequence, although ambitious recruitment drives were launched and Pollitt spoke of expanding to 100,000 members in 1943, there was a steady exit of members who lost interest. In fact, the party had reached its highpoint in 1942; over the next year it lost about a quarter of its membership declining to about 45,000 where it remained for the rest of the war. Inevitably, tensions arose between the old cadres, who took on increasing burdens, and those they referred to as 'the Red Army volunteers'. By mid-1943 Pollitt himself and regional party reports expressed growing concern about the slackness they found in the party's organization.[59] Officials complained that meetings were poorly attended; branches failed to report regularly on their activities; dues collection was dilatory, causing financial problems; political training was often slighted or of low calibre; and committee members and branch secretaries were constantly turning over.[60] Their disquiet is hard to evaluate since, as the Lancashire and London regional records show, the level of activity seems impressive and perhaps the targets set by King Street and full-time officials were simply unrealistic in the circumstances. Most new recruits, it should also be remembered, were working full-tilt and often had complicated family situations to cope with in wartime.

For every person who joined the CP, there were many who became more sympathetic towards communist views because of the Red Army's courageous resistance to Hitler's invasion. Public hostility towards the Soviet Union, intense after the Nazi–Soviet pact and Stalin's subjugation of eastern Poland and Finland,

1941–44', MSS 292/778.29/2, Modern Records Centre, Warwick University. The ties of the London Parliament to the nursery campaign can be found in the minute books of the National Society of Children's Nurseries (London School of Economics). M-OA Topic collection 32/F, Diary 5390 also includes some information about meetings in 1942. Also, N. Branson, *History of the Communist Party of Great Britain*, III: *1927–1941*, IV: *1941–1951*, pp. 45–7.

[58] T. Linehan, *Communism in Britain 1920–1939: From the cradle to the grave* (Manchester, 2007); R. Samuel, *The Lost World of British Communism* (London, 2006).

[59] Pollitt's concerns in August 1943 ('no use shirking the issue, the mass activity of the party is far from what it ought to be') quoted by N. Redfern, 'The Communist Party of Great Britain, imperialism and war 1935–45', PhD Diss., Manchester Metropolitan University, 1997, p. 104. In individual branches, of course, the mood could also be one of excitement and hope; see e.g. the anonymous diary-notebook of a London party member for 1943–4 in CP/LON/DC/00/02 (1943–4), CPGB Archive.

[60] CP/CENT/ORG/6/4, Lancashire and Cheshire District Files 1943, CPGB Archive.

quickly gave way to admiration once the vast struggle unfolded in the east. The BBC steadily increased its coverage of the Soviet war effort and was soon responding to listener demands for more programmes on Russian culture and Soviet society. There were concerts of Russian music and public salutes to the Red Army, while the BBC's regular 'Russian Commentary' written by Alexander Werth in Moscow was both brilliant and highly sympathetic to the communist system.[61] Cinemas began showing Russian films and newsreels used Russian footage with vivid shots of bitter fighting. Large numbers of local Anglo-Soviet societies also sprang up with representation from all parts of society. Delegations of Russian workers and officials toured factories; shop stewards helped organize aid-to-Russia weeks in war factories; and Beaverbrook capitalized upon popular sentiments by introducing 'Tanks for Russia' campaigns in munitions factories to inspire increased production. The peak of 'Russomania' came with the German surrender at Stalingrad in February 1943. The Red Flag was flown on many public buildings, celebrations and parades took place across the land, and huge crowds flocked to see the jewelled Stalingrad sword as it travelled across the country before being presented to Stalin at the Teheran conference. To some extent the wave of enthusiasm reflected popular radicalism in 1942 and contributed to it, but a good deal was officially orchestrated and conveyed public gratitude towards an ally who was bearing the brunt of the German assault.

In official circles the response to popular enthusiasm was decidedly mixed. While government officials' praise for their Russian ally was effusive, they were concerned that public exuberance might translate into support for the communist political system and the domestic CP. The solution adopted combined encouragement and containment: the activities of the Soviet embassy received strong endorsement while anything associated with the CP met with unfriendly silence. Regional information officers were also quietly encouraged to take charge of local aid-to-Russia campaigns and other expressions of friendship between the two nations, so as to limit the role of local activists. In this they were often aided by Citrine and the TUC which continued to monitor closely communist activities within the labour movement. In practice, however, it was impossible to either control the flow of pro-Soviet propaganda or to completely depoliticize it. Inevitably the picture presented was 'not simply one of Russian strength and fighting spirit, but also that of a resilient, efficient, and popular regime, often held up as an example for the British people to follow'.[62]

In February 1942 Home Intelligence reported: 'Thank God for Russia is a frequent expression of the very deep and fervent feeling for that country which permeates wide sections of the public.'[63] The response was also a measure of public

[61] For BBC coverage of the Soviet Union, S. H. Nicholas, *The Echo of War* (Manchester 1996); I. McLaine, *Ministry of Morale* (London, 1979). NA: INF 1/292, 23–30 March 1943 notes that Werth's radio commentaries were 'widely quoted in factories'.

[62] P. M. H. Bell, *John Bull and the Bear* (London, 1991), pp. 48–9.

[63] NA: INF 1/292, H. I. Weekly Report, 26 January–2 February 1942. A BIPO poll of October 1942 asked whether Britain had taken full advantage of the opportunities offered by the German attack on Russia: 49% answered 'No'; 29%, 'Yes'; and 22%, 'Don't know'.

frustration and anxiety about Britain's military performance and at that specific moment shock over surrender of British forces in Singapore. Intelligence summaries warned that Soviet resilience helped to give socialism a more favourable public image and opinion polls registered 'increased interest in the Russian system of discipline and government' and a growing belief in the superiority of planning and centralized economic direction. Popular admiration, one intelligence report ran, was coupled with 'an almost equally unanimous belief that the success of the Russian armies is due to the political system in that country'. The same document noted that people repeatedly declared that Britain could not return to the way things were pre-war. Pro-Soviet sentiment and the sense of labour's enhanced status within British society complemented each other. In the Soviet Union, it was argued, there were no class divisions to thwart the nation's effort. Russia was described as a workers' republic, a state 'they've created themselves', a 'true country of the ordinary people'.[64] In July 1942 when Gallup asked whether Russia or the United States was more popular with the British people, 62 per cent answered Russia and only 24 per cent the United States.[65] Five months later in December of that year—by which time the tide of battle was moving in a much more favourable direction for the Allies—Gallup asked its sample group to choose between an alliance with Russia or America after the war. The aggregate results which were published showed 45 per cent favoured America, 31 per cent Russia, and 22 per cent answered 'Don't know'. Yet a detailed occupational break-down reveals a more complicated picture with wealthier groups far more favourable towards the US; indeed, industrial wage earners still preferred Russia by more than 39 per cent to 36 per cent.[66]

Much of this enthusiasm was naive and utopian. There was a tendency to see the Soviet regime in the best light. Stalin's face on newsreels elicited spontaneous clapping in cinemas; Russian peasants were depicted in romantic terms, as were the country's women—heroically defending Leningrad and serving in the Soviet armies. Journalists and commentators writing about the Soviet Union were mostly on the left and favourably disposed, while many of the films, posters, photographs, and other materials available for distribution in Britain came from Soviet sources. Soviet planning was also represented as allowing room for grass-roots democracy and liberal freedoms. And while some commentators had deep reservations about Stalinism, these were mostly shelved as people projected onto Russia some of their own democratic socialist aspirations. In immediate political terms, aside from a general reinforcement of left-wing attitudes, this tide of pro-Soviet feeling, contributed—as the next section shows—to the meteoric rise of Sir Stafford Cripps after he returned to London from Moscow. Similarly, it helped to rally public support for opening a 'Second Front Now'—a campaign in which Lord

[64] Bell, *John Bull and the Bear*, pp. 48–9, 90–1.
[65] *Gallup International Polls*, July 1942.
[66] BIPO (Gallup Polls) UK Data Archive Essex, December 1942. There were many factors involved, of course. For one thing Russians and the Soviet army were more remote. The American presence in Britain was growing by the end of 1942 and by December 1943 had reached 760,000.

Beaverbrook, now out of the government, joined forces with the CP and used the power of his *Daily Express* to promote. Large demonstrations in London's Trafalgar Square and other cities were organized to mark the anniversary of Stalin's entry into the war and at the highpoint of the campaign in July–August 1942 polls suggested that some 58–62 per cent of the population supported immediate action to relieve Russia.[67] This figure reflected popular anxiety that further delay might produce a Soviet collapse and growing embarrassment at Britain's battlefield defeats; it was also a way of attacking reactionaries at home.[68] How accurately the campaign reflected popular sentiment for an early Second Front is less clear. The TUC and many trade unionists were strongly opposed to immediate intervention, while the government's industrial relations officer for Glasgow noted that many of the older workers who had fought in France in the previous war urged caution. Those with sons in the forces were also apprehensive and (in Scotland at least) expressed irritation at young engineers who called for a Second Front but were equally insistent about 'the reservation [i.e. call-up exemption] of male workers on munitions'.[69] By October 1942 support for an immediate Second Front had declined and the issue continued to lose steam after the British victory at El Alamein and Soviet success at Stalingrad.[70]

Popular enthusiasm for the Soviet Union, like the growth of the CP, reached its limits in 1942. Both contributed to the radicalization of public opinion and helped broaden acceptance for increase state power and socialist ideas, ironically aiding a Labour Party that remained deeply opposed to working with communists. As the prospect of victory increased from 1943 and the nation began to focus on post-war reconstruction and the return of normal party politics, the choices made by the CP also helped deplete its support. Aside from seeking affiliation with Labour, it had no strategy for the next election and its decision to reorganize, moving away from factory to residential branches, reduced membership. In addition, its continued insistence upon maximum war production and opposition to strikes provoked criticism among workers who were now more worried about redundancies and preserving the gains they had made. Finally, the party's decision to abide by the political truce (which it had never signed) tied its hands; it was unable to benefit from the growing wave of anti-Tory opinion in the last two years of the war. Indeed, until early 1944 communists were still instructed in by-elections to support Tory candidates against left-wing challengers whose platforms echoed their own publicity leaflets.

---

[67] BIPO (Gallup Polls) UK Data Archive, Essex, July–August 1942 (polls 89, 89A, 90). Also Bell, *John Bull and the Bear*, p. 83.

[68] When in May 1941 Minister of Aircraft Production, Moore-Brabazon, said in earshot of some trade unionists that it might be better for Britain if Russia and Germany destroyed one another, his unguarded remark caused an uproar and his dismissal in the Cabinet reshuffle of February 1942. The issue gave rise to stormy debate in the Commons and the TUC annual conference, and angry criticism in the press, including Labour's *Daily Herald*, about anti-Soviet reactionaries in the government.

[69] NA: LAB 10/363, 1 August 1942.

[70] BIPO (Gallup Polls) UK Data Archive Essex, October 1942. Shows public disapproval of public discussion of a Second Front by 46% to 37% (among industrial workers by 44% to 41%).

WHERE DO WE GO FROM HERE? FROM CRIPPS TO COMMON WEALTH

In February 1942 social reformer Violet Markham (no radical) admitted to Kingsley Martin: 'I am getting terribly het up about things in general and am wondering whether anything short of revolution will rouse this country and get rid of our inefficients!' She continued that while 'there must be a whole volume of energy and intelligence running to waste somewhere in this country, we do not seem able to get hold of it and harness it'.[71] In 1941 British forces had been driven out of Greece and Crete; in the Atlantic, German U-boats continued to take a heavy toll; and Japan's entry into the war jeopardized the whole of Britain's empire in South-east Asia and resulted immediately in the sinking of two of the Royal Navy's best ships, *Prince of Wales* and *Repulse*, off Malaya. Bad news was unremitting. The surrender of Singapore with its garrison of 62,000 men came in February 1942, followed by the fall of Rangoon and the loss of Burma. And several months later, in June, Rommel's capture of the fortress of Tobruk was another devastating blow to national confidence. On the domestic front as well, public dissatisfaction over war production reached new heights. Polls evaluating the government's conduct of the war which had been about 60 per cent favourable as late as June 1941, sank to a low of 35 per cent in March 1942 with discontent pervasive in all social groups.[72]

The prime minister himself became more embattled with critics urging him to delegate more and establish some kind of directorate to oversee the war effort. Even within his own party Churchill came under pressure, leading to a motion of censure in the Commons in July which could have been a good deal more damaging but for the incompetence of some of his critics. Asked later what was his most difficult time, Churchill answered without hesitation: 1942. In response to criticism the government tried to rein in the press and even threatened to close down the *Daily Mirror* and *Sunday Pictorial*. Such a move would have been very unwise—that it was even contemplated attests the feeling of beleaguerment in official circles. 'Now I am fairly certain', wrote Orwell early in that year, 'we are on the edge of the political crisis I have been expecting for the better part of two years.'[73]

Troubled by reports that a kind of 'home-made socialism' was spreading fast, the MoI decided in early 1942 to canvas its Regional Information Officers for details. Their responses seemed to validate official concern about a shift in the nation's political mood. The North region reported 'a strong tendency towards the ideal of socialism in all classes' as evidenced by demands for greater equality and resentment of employers 'suspected of resisting changes that might affect their post-war profits'. The North-west Officer wrote: 'We are now on the threshold of an entirely new

[71] Violet Markham to Kingsley Martin, 11 February 1942 (Markham Papers, BLPES London School of Economics).
[72] *Gallup International Polls*, BIPO (Gallup Polls) UK Data Archive Essex.
[73] Orwell, 'Letter to the *Partisan Review*, 8 May 1942' in Orwell and Angus (eds.), *Collected Essays, Journalism*, II, p. 207.

conception of economic and human relationships . . . in which very large incomes will no longer be tolerated, and the motto "Service before Self" must come into its own.' The South-west detected 'a distinct but largely negative swing to what is vaguely called the "Left", directed against the Conservative party insofar as this represents the so-called "Men of Munich", the "old gang!", "Colonel Blimp" and similar diehard types'. Socialist opinion was said to be 'growing like a jungle plant' in the London region: even 'the "employer class" as well as those who formerly voted Conservative' were 'turning to this idea', but 'it appears to have increased considerably among black-coated workers who are said to be reading and discussing a great deal'. Officers in Scotland also described increasing political consciousness and heightened interest in the CP, while the South-east report noted that 'an "inclination to think socially" is said to exist among people who have hitherto never "embraced political socialism"'. Complaints against 'string-pulling behind the scenes' were widespread and blamed for inefficiencies in the war effort. Allegations about 'vested interests' and 'the old gang' were common everywhere and several regions underscored the Soviet Union's impact on popular attitudes, along with the feeling that 'there must and will be "alterations in the present order of society"'. Only in the Southern region did the officer report 'no similar trends of opinion'. Yet, within a month he had changed his tune, informing headquarters: 'It is difficult to exaggerate the growing force of the demand for guarantees that "privilege" not be allowed to lose the next peace . . . individualistic capitalism must yield place to "controlled capitalism"; we ought to be told what we are fighting for etc. Remarks like these can be heard wherever working men gather together.' The ideas were vague, not linked to specific objectives and it is true that some conservative-minded officials may at times have confused an 'inclination to think socially' with socialism, but overall their unanimity is striking.[74]

Into this situation stepped the enigmatic figure of Sir Stafford Cripps. A wealthy, Christian, ascetic barrister, with teetotal and vegetarian habits, he had joined the Labour Party in 1929 and then moved sharply to the left. Frequently at loggerheads with the party leadership over his support for closer ties with the communists and a popular-front coalition, he was expelled in 1939 and only regained his membership at the war's end. Initially frustrated in his efforts to find suitable war work, he was eventually sent to Moscow because of his pro-Soviet views as a kind of semi-official ambassador, where he was distrusted by Stalin and circumvented by Foreign Office officials. After repeated fruitless efforts to get London to send Russia more aid, he quit and returned home in January 1942. His timing could not have been more propitious. After returning he was quickly enveloped in a blaze of publicity. Untainted by the mistakes and failures of the previous two years, his reputation burnished by public enthusiasm for the Soviet alliance (for which he was not responsible), he suddenly found himself the man of the hour.

---

[74] NA: INF 1/292, 'Home-made socialism', Report by the Home Intelligence Division, 24 March 1942. Also INF 1/292, Report for 28 April 1942 (follow-up comment from the Southern region). These reports were compiled from a range of sources: postal censorship, interviews, radio listener research, and so on.

It was not all serendipitous, however. While working-class activists in this period mostly focused on strengthening union networks or the Second Front campaign, middle-class radicals and war commentators sought ways to influence policy both by their writings and broadcasts and more directly by lobbying those with power. In 1940 journalists Ritchie Calder and Hilde Marchant used the first strategy in publicizing the deplorable conditions in London's mass shelters. Spanish Civil War veteran Tom Wintringham used his social connections to set up a private training college for Home Guard volunteers in hopes that these troops might turn into a democratic guerrilla force or people's militia.[75] Another venture was 'the 1941 Committee', which included a politically very mixed group of mostly journalists, publishers, and academics, chaired by Priestley, who met to discuss how the war effort could be organized more efficiently and how to influence 'individuals in key positions'. The main fruits of its deliberations were a memorandum on production, which advocated an immediate state takeover of much of the economy, and its 'Nine Point Programme'[76] which became the basic platform of radical Independents who began to contest by-elections by spring 1942.[77] While Cripps was in Moscow groups of his press friends had helped keep his name in the news and when he landed, he was met and briefed (he had scarcely spent a month in Britain since the start of the war) by David Astor and Tom Harrisson for the 1941 Committee. He also took advice from his old associates George Strauss and Nye Bevan on the Labour back benches.

The press campaign in support of Cripps was exceptional: the *Daily Mirror* and *News Chronicle* welcomed him as someone who could bring new energy and drive to the war effort; the *Sunday Pictorial* ran a banner headline: 'The Astonishing Story of the Man Who Came Back'. He was in close touch with Barrington Ward, the editor of *The Times*, while *Picture Post* found him 'peculiarly English in his instinct for mixing morals and politics, principles and forces'. The hopes projected onto him were a measure of the anxiety that was already building up. But he also helped himself with a highly effective radio broadcast in early February 1942 which exceeded popular expectations and completed his transformation into a figure of national standing. It was a low-key address: earnest, personal, an appeal to his listener's moral sense; Cripps was critical, detecting 'in this country since my return a lack of urgency', and he closed with a question: 'Can you do more than you're doing now to help the Common Cause? Are your hardships and sacrifices comparable to those of the Soviet citizens who are fighting your battle just as you are fighting theirs?' The public response was enormous; his appeal resonated with all

[75] T. Wintringham, *New Ways of War* (1940), *The Politics of Victory* (1941); also David Fernbach, 'Tom Wintringham and socialist defence strategy', *HWJ*, 14 (Autumn 1982).
[76] The points included: greater equality of sacrifice and opportunity; transfer to common ownership of private companies whose inefficiency was hurting the war effort; reorganization of the supply departments; and preliminary plans for post-war construction to mobilize and unify the nation.
[77] T. Hopkinson, *Of This Our Time: A journalist's story* (London, 1982); S. K. Smith, '*Picture Post* 1938–45', PhD Diss., Stanford University, 1992. Those involved in the group included: Richard Acland, J. B. Priestley, David Astor, Thomas Balogh, Ritchie Calder, Vernon Bartlett, Victor Gollancz, Eva Hubback, François Lafitte, Kingsley Martin, Richard Titmuss, Tom Wintringham, C. E. M. Joad, Professor John MacMurray, John Strachey, and Francis Williams.

social groups but especially the progressive middle classes. A schoolteacher and Mass-Observer wrote: 'he describes our weaknesses, points the way to win ... I have wanted to hear him and that kind of speech for months. Unemotional, closely reasoned, tactful. We need all those qualities.' An architect wrote: 'We listened ... with admiration and thankfulness, and the feeling that Here at last is a Man.'[78]

The meteoric rise of Cripps was a measure of public disquiet; but it also reflected the power of the media—Priestley's celebrated 'Postscripts' in 1940 had shown this, while at the end of 1942 it played a crucial role in promoting Beveridge's plan for social insurance. Cripps came across as a man of integrity who was free of party entanglements, an outsider with new ideas. Rather like the 'home-made socialism' referred to earlier, his emergence pointed to the existence of a broad bloc of progressive opinion. Opinion polls continued to show a high rate of personal approval for Churchill, although somewhat lower than earlier. More instructive, however, are the polls evaluating the government's conduct of the war which in March 1942 showed 50 per cent dissatisfied and only 35 per cent satisfied. Equally important, when pollsters asked who should replace Churchill if for some reason the prime minister had to step down, the favourite until now was Foreign Secretary Anthony Eden. In November 1941 only 1 per cent picked Cripps compared to 38 per cent for Anthony Eden. But by April 1942 Cripps had drawn almost even with 34 per cent to Eden's 37 per cent and a London poll by Mass-Observation in March 1942 even placed him ahead of Eden, 39 per cent to 29 per cent.[79] As a possible successor to Churchill, the two leading Labour figures, Attlee and Bevin, never received more than 7 per cent and mostly polled well below that.

Negotiations were already underway to find space in the government for Cripps. Four days after the fall of Singapore when Churchill reconstructed his Cabinet and within little more than a month of his arrival in the country, Cripps became a member of the War Cabinet, Lord Privy Seal, and Leader of the House of Commons. His rise had been super-meteoric; much—too much—was expected of him. The story of the next months has been told several times, most recently and in greatest detail by Peter Clarke.[80] Various interpretations of Cripps's behaviour have been put forward; the confusion stems from the continuously mixed signals he emitted. One recent biographer, Chris Bryant, depicts him as definitely conspiratorial against Churchill. Certainly, for a good deal of time, Cripps believed that Churchill would be unable to hold on to power—that lack of empathy with ordinary people and lack of understanding of the home front would result in the prime minister eventually being pushed aside. Cripps's aunt, Beatrice Webb, confided to her diary: 'He intimated that there were only two possible Prime Ministers: Anthony Eden and himself. Eden had all the right instincts, but was

---

[78] M-OA: FR 1375; also S. Fielding, 'The Second World War and popular radicalism: The significance of the "movement away from party", *History*, 80(258) (February 1995), 45. Also, M-OA: FR 1118 (February 1942); FR 1166 (March 1942).

[79] M-OA: FR 1359 (30 June 1942); FR 1361–2 (July 1942); FR 1375 (August 1942); FR 1394 (August 1942); FR 1411–13 (September 1942); FR 1442–3 (October 1942); FR 1483–4 (November 1942); FR 1524 (December 1942). Some of these surveys may have been financed by Cripps.

[80] Peter Clarke, *The Cripps Version: The life of Sir Stafford Cripps* (London, 2002).

an aristocratic country squire . . . In short, Stafford expects that *he* would succeed Churchill as Prime Minister.'[81] But, as Clarke has argued, ably catching the contradictory impulses of the man, he was also loath to be disloyal and had doubts about how far divisive issues should be pushed in the midst of war. What made him attractive to many of the public—that he was above and apart from party politics— also weakened him in the Cabinet and the Commons. He lacked a firm base of support in Westminster and as a political tactician he was simply outclassed by the prime minister. He soon found himself frozen out of Churchill's inner circle; his schemes for reorganizing the administration of the home front and for a powerful Minister of Defence were fobbed off and his pressure for a clear statement on domestic war aims got nowhere. Finally, Cripps undertook an unsuccessful mission to resolve the growing crisis in India. Later this was viewed as a bad tactical mistake, but at the time his left-wing supporters like Orwell, who were deeply interested in Indian independence, generally applauded the move and had he been successful it would have further boosted his reputation. Frustrated in his efforts, lacking the political base to force changes upon the government, and unwilling to make a move to topple the leader, by September 1942 Cripps was contemplating resignation which would certainly have affected the government negatively.[82]

Ultimately, then, Cripps disappointed his supporters who had projected too much onto him. To many left-wing opinion-makers, he had for a short time seemed like a 'silver bullet', the answer to their hopes: someone to whom they had access, a media figure (albeit a curious one), someone on the inside of government at the highest levels who could bring change quickly without all the complicated problems of building a political organization, a conduit for the left's ideas—ideas that he was seen as sharing fully. In fact, his position was always weaker than it seemed and, as Clarke indicates, he was himself undergoing change. He was slowly relinquishing his hard-left, class views of the 1930s, and he never accepted the position that revolutionary change was either possible or desirable in the middle of a war. 'Altogether he was not the man—or no longer the man—the Left had taken him for.'[83] By the autumn of 1942 his star was fading, although he continued to enjoy a good deal of residual respect in many circles. A forty-year-old worker reflected in early September: 'At Trade Union meetings they're talking a lot against [Cripps]; they say he's going slightly over to the government. Myself, I think he'd do a lot if he had his own way.'[84] The air was draining from the Cripps balloon, but there were still difficult times ahead for Churchill and his close associate Brendan Bracken wrote that the PM 'must win his battle in the desert or

---

[81] C. Bryant, *Stafford Cripps: The first modern chancellor* (London, 1997), p. 316; from Beatrice Webb, unpublished diary, 26 October 1942, Passfield Papers.

[82] Among those urging Cripps to resign and bring things to a head were Carr, Barrington Ward, and Beveridge. Bryant, *Stafford Cripps*, pp. 312–15.

[83] Clarke, *The Cripps Version*, p. 331; Clarke (p. 334) quotes a letter from Harold Laski to Isobel Cripps, 29 September 1942: 'I won't say—yet—that I feel he is the lost leader. But I will say that, for reasons I can't profess to grasp, he is helping Churchill to fight this war on principles of which the outcome seems to make *certain* the victory of reaction in Britain.'

[84] M-OA: FR 1412, 7 September 1942.

get out'.[85] Once victory came at El Alamein in November 1942, Churchill felt secure enough to drop Cripps from the War Cabinet, moving him over to aircraft production.

The sudden rise of Cripps was a temporary threat to Churchill, but it also reflected left-wing dissatisfaction with the Labour leadership. The left wanted more vigorous criticism of Churchill's running of the war and more progress towards post-war social reconstruction, including guarantees on the nationalization of coal. Labour backbenchers Aneurin Bevan and Emanuel Shinwell harassed the leadership, claiming that they lacked the will to compel either a reorganization of the war effort or significant progress towards socialism. Harold Laski, a leading member of Labour's National Executive Committee, infuriated Attlee and Bevin by his outspoken criticisms and his scheming to replace Attlee. As support coalesced around Cripps, so a mood of rebellion against the Coalition and the party machines developed. Electioneering had been suspended by a truce of the major parties, so that when a seat fell vacant through death or resignation it was agreed that the incumbent party would fill it uncontested. But, since only the major parties participated in the truce, challenges were not that uncommon. By-elections are at best an imperfect yardstick for measuring general trends in political opinion owing to the geographical and social peculiarities of individual constituencies, while in wartime the results were further complicated by the constraining effects of the political truce, changes in voter composition due to conscription and large-scale population movements, and generally low turn-outs. Early in the war incumbent candidates mostly faced challengers from anti-war, ILP, communist, and fascist parties, none of whom were capable of getting much support. But by 1942 an increasing number of Conservatives were challenged in by-elections by Independent candidates. In that year over half the vacant Conservative seats were contested and challengers attracted impressive numbers of votes. The change was testimony both to public dissatisfaction with the course of the war and growing unrest among Labour constituency activists.[86]

The biggest shock came in the spring of 1942 when four 'safe' Conservative seats were lost in quick succession. The victors were outsiders or mavericks. These contests at Grantham, Rugby, the Wallasey district of Merseyside, and Malden have attracted detailed analysis.[87] A popular factory manager won Grantham by emphatically disassociating himself from the routine party political game. At Rugby W. J. Brown successfully contested the seat being vacated by the Tory Chief Whip Margesson—a favourite target of those aligned against 'guilty men' and the 'old

---

[85] K. Jefferys, *The Churchill Coalition and Wartime Politics, 1940–1945* (Manchester, 1995), p. 103. In August 1942 Labour MP Ivor Thomas still expected that Cripps, rather than Eden or Attlee, would succeed Churchill. I. Thomas to Tom Jones, 13 August 1942 (Lord Astor Papers, Reading University Library, MS 1066/833) cited in Addison, *The Road to 1945*, pp. 208–9.

[86] During the war 75 of the 141 vacated seats were contested. P. Addison, 'By-elections of the Second World War' in C. Cook and J. Ramsden (eds.), *By-Elections in British Politics* (London, 1973); also Jefferys, *The Churchill Coalition and Wartime Politics, 1940–1945*, ch. 6 and Appendix 2.

[87] Addison, 'By-elections of the Second World War'; G. L. Reakes, *Man of the Mersey* (1956). Reakes won in Wallasey, the seat vacated by Moore-Brabazon.

gang'. Brown, the founder and leader of the Civil Service Clerical Association, had quit the Labour Party in 1931 and since then had been a trenchant critic of the straitjacket of the party machines. Demanding a complete reorganization of the war effort and a state takeover of the nation's major capital assets, Brown tried with other Independents to launch a progressive 'People's Movement' with local constituency branches, but they lacked the stamina or acumen to carry it through.[88] The fact that Brown was a well-known broadcaster certainly helped his candidacy. At both Malden and Wallasey, 1941 Committee veterans played a prominent role, especially at Malden where the insurgent candidate was another colourful media figure, Beaverbrook journalist Tom Driberg (author of the *Daily Express* William Hickey column). Running on the 1941 Committee's 'Nine Point Manifesto', Driberg managed to reduce the Tory vote by 22 per cent in a largely rural constituency. A bevy of well-known progressives came to Essex to speak and canvass on his behalf including Vernon Bartlett, Hannon Swaffer, Tom Wintringham, J. B. Priestley, and Sir Richard Acland. The vote took place immediately after the loss of Tobruk which had a devastating impact on national opinion. 'The Libyan disaster has bitten into the British consciousness greater than any other disaster of the war', the *Manchester Guardian* editorialized. On Driberg's result, it added 'these are healthy political signs', 'most people will feel that it is time the party machines received a sharp knock'.[89] With swings against them ranging from around 9–35 per cent, it seemed as though no Tory seat was safe,[90] although polls registered no great enthusiasm for the Labour Party.

Stephen Fielding has argued that what was happening in 1942 was a 'movement away from party'.[91] Certainly among the broad mass of the public in that year 'politicians' were in bad odour. In October a Home Office report declared: 'There is little doubt that "politics" are suspect, "politicians" as a class distrusted, and political manoeuvring and party politics, national or international, deeply disliked.'[92] But the significance of this 'anti-party temper' should not be exaggerated nor elided with a turning away from politics altogether. Support for Independents in by-elections was symptomatic of several things. For some, casting a ballot for Brown or Driberg was simply a way of registering deep discontent with the handling of the war. Others were angry at the party machines, but far from being disaffected with politics they were bitter because Coalition government blocked their hopes for political change. Radical critics like Acland and Cripps believed that

---

[88] W. J. Brown, *So Far* (London, 1943). His programme included: state ownership of land and minerals, state control of the export trade, a national planning commission, and a central investment board.

[89] T. Driberg, *Ruling Passions: Autobiography* (London, 1977); *Manchester Guardian*, 27 June 1942.

[90] In spring 1942 M-O surveyed people in three areas about who would win the next election. About half gave no opinion. In the London area about 12% expected a Conservative win and 27% a Labour win; in the Midlands it was 14% Conservative and 33% Labour; in the north it was 17% Conservative and 26% Labour. See Addison, 'By-elections of the Second World War', pp. 177–8; also T. Harrison, 'Who'll win?', *Political Quarterly*, 14 (1943), 246.

[91] Fielding, 'The Second World War and popular radicalism'.

[92] NA: HO 262/16, October 1942, Special report on 'Public interest in reconstruction plans'.

the war crisis had created the opportunity for a progressive coalition on the lines of the popular front, first advanced in the pre-war years by G. D. H. Cole and Hugh Dalton as an alternative to the Conservative-dominated National Government. In the spring of 1942 a good many radical critics were convinced that Churchill's Coalition could not last and would, as in the First World War, be replaced by another. To this extent the mood in 1942 was less anti-political than a demand for a different kind of politics. Finally, for many Labour activists, rallying to the Independents offered a way of mobilizing anti-Conservative sentiment and re-energizing local Labour branches. Opinion was highly volatile and traditional party organizations had deteriorated by the middle years of the war. But while a *Manchester Guardian* editorial declared in May 1942, 'we have no right to assume that the party allegiances of 1939 persist in 1942 or will persist in 1944', the next two years would confirm the enormous resilience of the existing party structures.[93] Indisputably many people in 1942, for different reasons, were unhappy about the continuance of the political truce and its exclusion of voters from selecting their representatives. In April 1942, well before battlefield successes focused public attention upon the return of peace, BIPO found that 48 per cent of people approved of Independents contesting by-elections, while 25 per cent were opposed.[94]

Encouraged by the string of Tory electoral reverses Sir Richard Acland also decided that the time was ripe for a new political alternative; capitalizing upon the mood of disappointment and radical impatience after the loss of Tobruk, he announced the birth of the Common Wealth Party in July 1942. Acland was by any standards a curious figure. A grandee landowner from the south-west, he began political life as a Liberal MP and converted to socialism in the mid-1930s, propelled left by the spread of fascism. Ambitious, oddly charismatic (to some at least), often superficial and naive politically, he gained prominence for a short period because, like Cripps, he was seen as a visionary with the courage to challenge the system. He favoured a popular front in the years before the war and still more clearly abandoned his Liberal ties when he published a very successful Penguin Special, *Unser Kampf* (1940), which advocated Christian socialism as the only way to win the war and renew both Britain and Europe. Acland was the moving force in several small radical groups, including Forward March, which sought to develop local branches. He also joined the 1941 Committee and ran into some opposition from Priestley especially when he tried to steer it towards electoral politics. Believing that a crisis was near and that a new government might be set up by the autumn of 1942, Acland was eager to build bridges and create a new progressive force in politics.

Common Wealth's moment of national fame was brief. The party represented a rather awkward and always-conflicted merger of the 1941 Committee and Forward March; for a brief while Priestley acted as its president, but the dominant

---

[93] *Manchester Guardian*, editorial, 1 May 1942.
[94] *Gallup International Polls*, April 1942: 27% had no opinion. Of those who said 'No', 57% disapproved of contesting any by-elections in wartime.

personalities were Acland and the journalist and former communist, Tom Win-tringham.[95] At its peak the party achieved a membership of about 15,000, organized into around 300 local branches.[96] Its political impact was, however, larger than these numbers might suggest and the party's programme and moral appeals struck a chord with a much wider segment of the population. In the next years it won three striking by-election victories that embarrassed the government and it also came close to causing upsets in several other races. For some voters in the last two years of the war it became the chief means of expressing their support for post-war reform and their rejection of Conservatism. As such its history tells us much about opinion on the left and about the inherent weaknesses of the progressive movement that had developed by the middle of the war.

By 1943, with dramatic improvements in the military situation of the Allies, Common Wealth's politics were chiefly identified with post-war reconstruction. At the party's inception, however, the situation was very different; its leaders believed that Churchill's government might fall in the event of more defeats and that socialist measures were necessary right away if victory was to be achieved. Its political agenda, elaborated in a series of books, pamphlets, and manifestos, called for sweeping nationalization, state takeover of credit and financial institutions, independence for the colonies, and 'vital democracy', although the latter remained very ill-defined. The party gave organized expression to central themes of wartime radicalism; but, more than that, it echoed the ethical, religious tenor of much of that writing, justifying its uncompromising position on 'common ownership' purely on moral grounds. Its language was crusading and utopian. 'The structural changes in the shape of society which we propose' it announced 'will lead to the emergence of a new kind of man, with a new kind of mind, new values, a new outlook on life.' Religion and socialism were fused. In fact, Common Wealth denied claims that it was a Christian party, although its principles were rooted in basic Christian tenets, and its meetings, Angus Calder has written, often had something of a Christian revivalist character.[97] It also denied that it was specifically middle class, although those attracted to the movement were overwhelmingly suburban and professional: schoolteachers, managers, students, technicians, lower civil servants, many young people, and members of the armed forces. Its social profile was not dissimilar to the Left Book Club and a good many Club members became supporters. But Gollancz, though fond of Acland whom he had published, did not view Common Wealth as potentially a mass party and decided

[95] Acland Papers and the Common Wealth Party archive (Sussex University); Tom Wintringham Papers (B. Liddell Hart Military Archives, King's College London University); Angus Calder, 'The Common Wealth Party 1942–45', PhD Diss., Sussex University, 1967. Debates within Common Wealth were covered extensively by *Left News* in 1942. Also, M. Hilson and J. Melling, 'Public gifts and political identities: Sir Richard Acland, Common Wealth, and the moral politics of land ownership in the 1940s', *TCBH*, 11(2) (2000). Acland believed that Churchill's government might collapse by the autumn of 1942 and that there would be an opening for a popular front.

[96] Party activists included: Priestley, Gollancz, R. G. Mackay, R. M. Titmuss, Kingsley Martin, François Lafitte, John MacMurray, Keith Ingram, and many others of the Christian left.

[97] A. Calder, *The People's War: Britain 1939–45* (Panther books edition, London 1971), p. 633; R. Acland, *Question and Answer from Common Wealth Meetings* (London, 1943).

not to align his Club with it.[98] Orwell started out dismissive—calling it middle-class 'Socialism minus the class war'—but in 1943 began to take the movement more seriously speculating 'it might develop into the new Socialist party we have all been hoping for'. In fact, Acland greatly admired *The Lion and the Unicorn* and borrowed from it.[99]

While this is not the place to examine Common Wealth's history in detail, its strengths and weaknesses are revealing about the character of the left both in 1942 and the rest of the war. One problem was its own internal divisions. For all its rhetorical emphasis on fellowship, personal feuds and power struggles soon created havoc so that Priestley and several other prominent supporters quit after a few months; these feuds also spilled over into some of the local branches.[100] Moreover, as the party tried to clarify the general principles of the 'Nine Point Programme' which it had taken over from the 1941 Committee, so its ideological divisions assumed more importance. The Christian socialist elements were quickly at logger-heads with Wintringham and others whose socialism grew out of their reading of political and social theory and Marx. Basically, Acland believed that revolutionaries ought to be Christians and those like Wintringham whose viewpoint was secular found themselves accused of subordinating Christianity to planning and secular humanism. The atmosphere of compromise needed to construct a broad progressive alliance was conspicuously lacking among some of the most vocal people in the party. Added to this, Acland's style of leadership was a major problem not only because he made policy pronouncements without consulting others, but because he focused on speeches and writing, giving too little attention to building up party structures or establishing clear rules and procedures. Above all, he had no deep grasp of socialist theory, making do instead with a ragbag of ideas and slogans, and he was out of touch with both the working class and trade unionism. For all its talk of unity—and in contrast to Cripps—the party was never able to win any support from workers or organized labour.[101]

---

[98] Gollancz saw Common Wealth principally as a way of attracting new recruits to socialism. V. Gollancz to R. Acland, 6 October 1944 (Acland Papers, University of Sussex); G. McCulloch, 'Labour, the left and the British general election of 1945', *JBS*, 24 (October 1985), 484. A conference under the auspices of the Left Book Club argued the issue at the very end of May 1942. *Left News* (July 1942) and Edwards, *Victor Gollancz*, pp. 368–71.
[99] Orwell, *Collected Essays, Journalism*, II, pp. 288–9. Also, Introduction to Acland's *What It Will Be Like in the New Britain* (London, 1942) on Orwell's *Lion and the Unicorn*. By early 1943 Common Wealth's by-election results had, in Acland's view, put the government on the defensive and forced Conservatives to pay attention to domestic reforms. 'Finally, these barstards [*sic*] really are shaken now. Something is happening which they don't understand and don't like. The ripples and repercussions of what we are doing spread out in all directions. Winston would never have made that speech putting post-war issues on the map if CW candidates had all lost their deposits.' He added, 'We are far stronger than we suppose and they are far weaker than they suppose. It's only necessary to hit them, and go on hitting them, and get publicity for hitting them and they're finished': R. Acland to Tom Wintringham, 9 April 1943 (Acland Papers, University of Sussex).
[100] J. B. Priestley to Acland, 10 October 1942, Acland Papers. Priestley blamed the Forward March people for trying to take over Common Wealth and forcing out members of the 1941 Committee who disagreed with them. J. B. Priestley to T. Wintringham, 13 October 1942, Wintringham Papers.
[101] On Common Wealth's internal divisions: Tom Wintringham Papers (B. Liddell Hart Military Archives, King's College London University); Acland Papers and the Common Wealth Party archive

Given all these deficits, it is perhaps surprising that Common Wealth was able to achieve the successes it did. There are perhaps several explanations. First, the very considerable enthusiasm that Common Wealth meetings and by-election campaigns were able to generate attests to the permeation of radical ideas and rhetoric among middle-class strata of the population. In this sense, while the circumstances of 1942 provided the opportunity, Common Wealth was a continuation of trends already underway pre-war: the Left Book Clubs, left-wing student politics, Aid Spain committees, fundraising efforts for Basque children, radical Christian groups, refugee aid, and anti-fascist politics. Ideologically it was rooted in pre-war aspirations for a restructuring of progressive politics: the vision of a left coalition, based on moral principles rather than sectional class interests or institutional labour. Secondly, the combination of a Coalition government and a political truce meant that Common Wealth rapidly became an organized way for critics of government policy to vent their feelings. It was also an outlet for protests against a Labour leadership seen as placing socialism 'into the refrigerator' (in François Lafitte's phrase) for the war's duration.[102] Acland spoke of 'immense new moral forces which have been dammed back for ten years by the great dead bulk of the Labour party lying like a fallen tree across the road to progress'. While the labour movement had a crucial role to play, it was unclear, Common Wealth argued, whether the Labour Party 'intends to make a serious attack on the whole capitalist system' or simply advance 'a more privileged position' for industrial workers. Labour leaders, it was argued, seem to lack the will 'to carry through even their declared official policy'.[103]

As partisan politics began to revive in 1943, Common Wealth also became a convenient way for Labour activists to revitalize local politics at a time when they were still hamstrung by the party truce. Even some of Common Wealth's leaders, like R. W. G. Mackay, increasingly saw the movement as a surrogate for Labour and historians have rightly viewed its by-election successes as a harbinger of Conservatism's defeat in 1945.[104] The by-elections also attest the continuing existence of a desire to

---

(University of Sussex), including the draft synopsis of a book by Acland: 'Revolutionaries should be Christians' (March 1943?). Wintringham was particularly troubled by Tom Sargant and Rev. James Parkes whom he viewed as Christian idealists deeply opposed to the more materialist and economically focused socialists in the movement. Wintringham's American wife Kitty also became embroiled in the disputes, accusing Acland of, among other things, excluding women from positions of importance in the movement (Kitty Wintringham to Acland, 10 and 14 November 1943, Wintringham Papers).

[102] N. Deakin, 'Besieging Jericho: Episodes from the early career of François Lafitte 1931–1945', *Cercles*, Occasional Papers Series (2004).

[103] R. Acland to D. Lloyd George, 17 May 1940 (House of Lords Record Office); McCulloch, 'Labour, the left and the British general election of 1945'; Acland, *Question and Answer from Common Wealth Meetings*, pp. 50–1.

[104] Some, however, warned that Forward March and Common Wealth might split and weaken the left: Julian Huxley to Acland, 4 March 1941; Phyllis Bottome to Acland, 3 March 1941; Olaf Stapledon to Acland, 22 September 1943; V. Gollancz to Acland, 6 October 1944, Acland Papers. The popular Christian socialist writer Sidney Dark argued that 'the most advantageous course for the little groups of Malvern minded people is, together, to join their local Labour parties . . . I am sceptical as to whether there are even 50 seats that can be won for socialism without the support of organised

restructure progressive politics as a broad coalition, a more inclusive popular front—an idea that enjoyed considerable support among Labour's grass-roots supporters, if not its leadership, as was evident in party conferences. But Common Wealth's hopes for a new progressive politics were soon overtaken by two powerful forces. The first was the transformation of the war situation. Montgomery's long-awaited victory at El Alamein, the Anglo-American landings in Morocco and Algeria, and the German defeat at Stalingrad made victory seem merely a matter of time. Churchill's position was significantly strengthened, leaving no doubts that the conflict was winnable without sweeping social and political changes. With the prospect of a general election in the not too distant future, Labour was clearly the largest and most feasible vehicle for the left. Like the CP, Common Wealth's chief hope of influencing the outcome of the election and the design of a New Britain lay in achieving an agreement with Labour. The second factor which had a profound impact on Common Wealth was the publication of the Beveridge Report and the impetus it gave to debate about post-war reconstruction. Ironically, the party's successes in the last two years of the war owed much to the growing public discontent over the Coalition's reluctance to fully endorse the Report. It was a mixed blessing for, as by-elections turned into referenda on social security, Acland's radical platform was increasingly hijacked and the party began to lose its separate identity.

The crisis of 1940 undermined Conservative power and produced what in retrospect most historians would agree was one of the most successful Coalition governments in British history. But at times the government's support was far from secure. Deep frustration with the poor showing of the armed forces, production shortfalls, and continuing grievances about 'vested interests' and class inequity resulted in a pervasive dissatisfaction with the course of the war. It was in this context that radical proposals flourished and popular opinion moved to the left. But this 'wartime radicalism', though it possessed many common themes, was disunited, split between what we might call the battle of books and articles carried on by middle-class intellectuals and war commentators, and the politicization going on among workers through industrial disputes, criticism of employers and managers, and local community campaigns about food prices or shelter improvements. The first sought influence through the media, by-elections, Common Wealth, and various civic action groups; the second found its most organized expression in the spread of trade unionism, the campaign for joint production committees, and increased recruitment into the CP. The ideas advanced for reform and restructuring were similar in many respects and workers' views were shaped by debate in the media, but the two groups remained largely separate. From 1943, however, a progressive coalition that combined the two was forged and, ironically, what precipitated it was not a new realignment of politics, as many had predicted in the crisis of 1942, but a revival of traditional party competition over plans for post-war reconstruction.

labour': Sidney Dark, 'Christianity, socialism and the class war', *Left News* (August 1942), p. 2190. By contrast, Wintringham was much more critical of the Labour Party, viewing it as an obstacle to any real Popular Front and 'an organization for tying up the workers to the bosses': T. Wintringham to J. B. Priestley, 7 June 1942.

9

1945 And All That

Six months is a long time in politics under any conditions; in wartime even more so. The difference between September 1942 and February 1943 is striking. In September 1942, four years after the war began, Churchill was still vulnerable. In the House of Commons Labour backbencher Aneurin Bevan attacked the organization of the war effort and called explicitly for the prime minister to go; Cripps was threatening to create a crisis by resigning from the government; even Brendan Bracken, one of Churchill's inner circle, believed him vulnerable. Six months later the Allies were triumphant in North Africa, Hitler's 6th army was surrounded and hammered into submission at Stalingrad, and Churchill's leadership was unassailable. The unveiling of Sir William Beveridge's plan for comprehensive social insurance which fortuitously coincided with these events also helped transform the mood at home. With victory no longer in doubt or even far off in most people's view, questions of military strategy and war production receded; post-war reconstruction moved to the forefront of national debate and party conflict intensified in anticipation of the next general election. More and more, Home Intelligence reported, people demanded to know the kind of post-war society their rulers envisioned. The successive crises of 1942 had unexpectedly culminated with Beveridge who managed to reap the harvest of pent-up radical and reformist hopes.[1]

BEVERIDGE AND PUBLIC ATTITUDES, 1943–5

At first sight the gaunt, irascible, relentlessly self-promoting Beveridge seemed an unlikely popular hero. A patrician figure like Cripps and Acland, he had occupied senior posts in Whitehall and been director of the London School of Economics and master of an Oxford college, all the while maintaining a prodigious output of books and journalism, appearing frequently on radio, and serving on numerous government committees and voluntary boards. A mandarin who believed that reforms were best planned and imposed from above, he had little faith in ordinary voters. But he had a flair for publicity and was a skilled political operator. Far from passively awaiting its reception, Beveridge quickly emerged as the report's chief political salesman. Its contents were selectively leaked beforehand to stimulate

[1] NA: INF 1/864 (21 April 1942, memo.); M-O, 'Social security and Parliament', *Political Quarterly* (July–September, 1943); M-O, *The Journey Home* (London, 1944).

public expectation that it would be 'far-reaching in scope and radical in tone'.[2] And, once it appeared, he began an exhausting schedule of broadcasts and lectures, reaching out beyond the government to the public at large. In this he was assisted by a wide range of groups, but especially by the press. Media coverage was intense and Beveridge had powerful connections; in some ways the campaign was reminiscent of that which had showered Cripps with praise a year before.[3] Few official publications become bestsellers, but this one sold over 100,000 copies in the first month (and over 630,000 eventually); indeed, the night before its publication, long queues of eager purchasers formed outside the His Majesty's Stationery Office in London's Kingsway.

The story of the interdepartmental Committee on Social Insurance and Allied Services has been told many times and requires no lengthy repetition here. It originated with a TUC request in June 1941 for a review of some technical issues and anomalies in existing social insurance benefits and Beveridge's appointment stemmed in large part from Ernest Bevin's desire to move him as far as possible from manpower policy. At the outset there was no intention that the Committee should produce a far-reaching blueprint for domestic reform, but Beveridge had no wish to confine himself to narrow technical discussion of insurance and he expanded his brief to a vision of 'cradle to grave' social security ensuring all citizens of a basic minimum standard of living. He also insisted that to be successful his proposals had to be buttressed by a wider package of commitments—to full employment, a state system of medical care, and family allowances. Simply put, his aim was 'not merely to abolish physical want, but to give a new sense of purpose to democracy, to promote national solidarity and to define the goals of the war'.[4] In fact, the report's proposals were not particularly original. It largely extended the logic of the existing piecemeal structure of state insurance and the contract it envisioned between state and citizen, with an emphasis on containing costs and preserving voluntary action and work incentives, clearly belonged to the tradition of liberal collectivism. Even the slogan, a 'national minimum', was not new but dated from the Edwardian era when, among others, the young Churchill had taken it up. Today most writers view the report as a somewhat conservative document. But in the public imagination it soon achieved the status of a kind of social 'Magna Carta'. 'If it should be adopted and prove workable', one working-class housewife commented, 'it will change the whole face of life for working people and remove the main fears of their lives. I have only to think back on my life and how different it would have been.'[5]

Beveridge's 'Plan' (as it was popularly called) rapidly became the catalyst for debate about post-war reconstruction. Only a fortnight after its release, according to Gallup, 95 per cent of the population had heard of it, with 86 per cent favouring

---

[2] Jose Harris, *William Beveridge: A biography* (1997 edn.), p. 416.
[3] Beveridge also received help from powerful friends such as R. M. Barrington-Ward, E. H. Carr, Edward Hulton, David Astor, Cecil King, and Gerald Barry.
[4] Harris, *William Beveridge*, p. 414.
[5] M-OA: FR 1783, 'Social security and Parliament' (17 May 1943).

its implementation and only 6 per cent opposed. Immediately after its appearance, BIPO conducted a detailed survey of public's reactions with its interviewers fanning out across 150 parliamentary constituencies. This revealed overwhelming popular support from all social classes regardless of whether people felt that they personally would gain from it. The most common objection—from 60 per cent of the sample—was that the provision for old-age pensions was too meagre. But the survey also showed that a sizeable segment of the public also doubted that the Plan would ever be enacted. Fifty-three per cent said 'Yes' it would; 18 per cent, 'No'; and 29 per cent were undecided with lower-income interviewees significantly more sceptical. Government intelligence reports confirmed this: in eleven of thirteen regions surveyed in December 1942 there was 'very real anxiety that the plan will not materialize' because of 'vested interests' (here big business, the insurance companies, and the British Medical Association were specifically mentioned), government reluctance, party wrangling, or resistance to the costs involved. Inevitably, there were also references to the 'betrayal' of hopes after victory in 1918, and some people dismissed the Plan altogether as a smokescreen 'to keep us at it till the war is over'. Postal censorship picked up a similar mixture of enthusiasm, cynicism, and fears that somehow the proposals would be mutilated or blocked.[6] 'Don't know what's going to happen about it', admitted a middle-aged working-class woman to Mass-Observation, 'but they promise you the moon while the war's on. Soon as it's over, they've no further use for you, they'll have a General Election and apologize that they can't stand by the promise of the war government. It'll happen just as it did last time.'[7]

Beveridge seemed to have turned the public's vaguely formulated desires for reform into a concrete programme. But as the Plan's advocates geared up for battle, so those who believed that the country had already moved too far in the direction of socialism also began to rally, arguing that it was too costly, would smother individual initiative, and encourage excessive dependence on the state. Treasury officials worried about its fiscal implications and sections of the Conservative Party looked for ways to shelve the Plan, while part of the right-wing press labelled it 'an Idler's Charter' and the *Daily Telegraph* ascribed to Beveridge words to the effect that he was taking the country 'halfway to Moscow'—a claim that was later withdrawn. Some (but not all) employer groups like the Confederation of British Industries also hoped that the Plan could be welcomed in principle and then amended in the details or discussion of it postponed until later. However, mounting pressure for a parliamentary debate on the issue proved irresistible and when it

[6] R. Mackay, *Half the Battle: Civilian morale in Britain during the Second World War* (Manchester, 2002), pp. 231–40; BIPO, *The Beveridge Report and the Public* (London, early 1943); NA: INF 1/292, weekly reports 1–8 and 8–15 December 1942. Postal censorship mid-November to mid-December 1942 classified the comments of 947 letters on the report: 473 were entirely positive; 193 expressed fears and doubts as to whether it would be enacted, predicting that it might be killed by Parliament or big business; and 281 criticized the report, mostly arguing that it would remove incentives and raise taxes: NA: INF 1/292, 29 December–5 January 1943. M-OA: FR 1568, 12 January 1943; M-OA: FR 1783, 'Social security and Parliament' (17 May 1943).

[7] M-OA: FR 1783, 'Social security and Parliament' (17 May 1943).

came in February 1943 it provoked a serious anti-government revolt. With Conservative speakers intent on making no commitment to the Plan and the Labour front bench unwilling to shake up the Coalition, Labour's rank-and-file MPs carried out their biggest wartime rebellion—all but two voted against the government. This made Bevin, never a fan of Beveridge, furious. He dared the party to expel him, stormed out of a meeting held to patch things up, and for the next fifteen months remained aloof from party meetings, describing himself as a spokesman of the trade unions in the Cabinet rather than a Labour representative. However, as the Welsh Labour MP James Griffiths argued, the rebellious vote was crucial in associating Labour with the Beveridge Plan—something that the party's publicity machine did everything in its power to encourage over the next year.

Not that the enthusiasm of Labour backbenchers or the party's grass roots was rhapsodic or unqualified. But, fearful that the war might soon end without any significant reform being achieved, many were prepared to bury their objections. Some worried that the Beveridge campaign would completely replace more radical demands. *Labour Organiser*, the organ of Labour Party constituency workers, called it 'half a loaf', a 'temporary palliative' that might become a 'substitute for social-ism'.[8] Equal-rights feminists were highly critical of the fact that married women's entitlement to benefits was derived from their status as dependants. And some, like the novelist Ethel Mannin, lamented the translation and attenuation of wartime utopianism into Beveridge; but most Labour women endorsed the Plan strongly and welcomed the enhanced security and health improvements it promised for women. Trade unionists also had reservations about the inclusion of workman's compensation in the general insurance scheme, thereby shifting the obligation from employers to the state. But organized labour no longer objected to the idea of guaranteeing subsistence through contributory insurance. In general, the left regarded the Plan as something to be campaigned for, a rallying point and a step on the right path.[9] '[I]n existing circumstances', wrote Aneurin Bevan, 'wise tactics suggest that we should go for the Report in its entirety'; his wife, Jennie Lee, contesting a by-election seat in Bristol, declared that she was for every sentence, word, and comma of the report. Laski, Tawney, and G. D. H. Cole all praised it highly, while Margaret Cole viewed it not as a palliative 'but an essential prelude to revolution'. She added: 'Social security is to the British worker what the land was to the Russian peasant in 1918 . . . This is no time for picking holes.'[10]

Popular enthusiasm for Beveridge's Plan is beyond doubt, although why people welcomed it as a revolutionary document is less clear. In part it was a measure of the strain of a long war and the nation's impatience for peace and some return for its

[8] *Labour Organiser* (December 1942). Also, *Left News* (January 1943), pp. 2345–6, 2349–52.

[9] E. Abbott and K. Bompass, *The Woman Citizen and Social Security* (London, 1943); K. Parker, 'Women MPs, feminism and domestic policy in the Second World War', D.Phil. Diss., Oxford University, 1994, ch. 4; E. Mannin, *Bread and Roses: A utopian survey and blue-print* (London, 1944), p. 9.

[10] J. Campbell, *Nye Bevan and the Mirage of British Socialism* (London, 1987), p. 127. Margaret Cole's remarks were part of a symposium on Beveridge for *Left News* (January 1943), 2348–9.

sacrifices. But the euphoria was also a reflection of the media blitz surrounding the report: *Picture Post*, the *Daily Mirror*, and the *Daily Herald* kept up a constant stream of articles about the Plan, analysing it in simple, clear bullet points with graphs and diagrams, using fictional examples to indicate the cash implications for an average family and—in the case of the *Herald*—publishing its own brief guide to Beveridge. Press correspondence columns also answered readers' queries, while conveying the sense of national support for the proposals. Coverage in other newspapers and magazines was also massive, while across the country labour organizations, civic associations, and women's groups, like the Townswomen's Guilds and Women's Institutes, organized countless lectures and discussions.[11] ABCA's attempt to publicize the Plan among the armed forces backfired, but the government's foolish decision to withhold a summary booklet written by Beveridge for the troops stirred up further debate, creating a storm of protest in the press and angry criticism in Parliament. In a bid to become the public's mouthpiece, the BBC also jettisoned its earlier caution and plunged into the business of publicizing the report and issues of post-war reconstruction. In short, the vibrant 'arena of public debate', which had developed during the war years, was itself an important contributing factor to the Plan's public reception.

Even the vocabulary used by Beveridge stimulated popular expectations. This, he argued, was 'a time for revolutions not for patching' and—almost like a cleric of the Christian left—he depicted the obstacles blocking the path to reform in Bunyan-esque terms as 'Five Giants' who must be slain: Want, Disease, Ignorance, Squalor, and Idleness. His language was both a tactic to capture the public's imagination and a reflection of the report's long incubation. Jose Harris points to two important influences at the inception of the report. The first was Janet or 'Jessy' Mair (whom Beveridge married in December 1942 right after its publication), who had little sway over the details but encouraged him to 'clothe his practical insurance proposals with a grand vision of a new social and moral order for the world after the war'. Her letters to him contained both a 'millenarian tone' and a 'sense of cataclysmic social change', testimony to the traumatic and transforming impact of the early 1940s when everything seemed to be in flux.[12] A second influence was the socialist economist G. D. H. Cole, whose Nuffield survey of working-class attitudes about welfare was carried out for Beveridge and who helped shape his ideas about manpower and employment. After the French collapse in 1940, Beveridge's views moved sharply to the left. He became a fervent advocate of central planning and was convinced that to defeat Hitler a large measure of state socialism was necessary. His opinions and objectives moderated towards the war's end, but the more sweeping assumptions remained as an 'invisible undercarriage of political

[11] C. Beaumont, 'Women and citizenship: A study of non-feminist women's societies and the women's movement in England, 1928–1950', PhD Diss., Warwick University, 1996, ch. 4.

[12] Harris, *William Beveridge*, pp. 36–9, 375. In her letters Mair railed against Churchill's cronyism: 'How I hope you are going to be able to preach against all gangsters who for their mutual gain support one another in upholding all the rest. For that is really what is happening still in England . . . the whole object of the spider web of interlocked big banks and big businessmen [is] a frantic effort to maintain their own caste' (4 June 1942, quoted by Harris, p. 375).

thought' only hinted at in the report.[13] The result was an incongruity between the Plan's moderate proposals, arrived at by skilful bargaining with various political and social interests, and its radical generalizations and language. Of course, it was precisely this combination and the fact that different groups could read in to it what they wished that enabled the Plan to become the rallying point for a broad reformist alliance in the final years of the conflict.

Interpreting responses to Beveridge's Plan also requires a nuanced grasp of popular attitudes in the last two years of the war. Several historians, mostly relying on one thread in Mass-Observation's research, have emphasized the cynicism and scepticism of workers, linking this to a larger argument about political apathy.[14] But cynicism was also a protective device, a way of guarding against disillusionment by those who had been disappointed before. Popular opinion was multi-layered, volatile, and often contradictory; people were cynical and utopian, hopeful and sceptical—a plurality of feelings that Mass-Observation tried to understand in terms of a shifting relationship between hopes and expectations. After the Commons debate on Beveridge in February 1943 pessimism increased sharply. According to Mass-Observation only 37 per cent of people thought the Plan would be carried out in full and a further 24 per cent thought that parts would be implemented. A BIPO poll on the government's handling of the Beveridge debate found 47 per cent dissatisfied, 28 per cent satisfied, and 24 per cent having no opinion—a highly critical response when the nation was buoyed up by recent military successes. Differences between social groups were unmistakable with disillusionment significantly higher among workers and lower-income groups.[15] Even though the government eventually published a White Paper accepting the gist of the report on *Social Insurance and Allied Services*, Churchill's and the Conservatives' reluctance to guarantee that it would be enacted, galvanized the opposition and played a large role in revitalizing partisan politics. Indeed, Kevin Jefferys has argued that it made a Conservative electoral defeat almost a certainty.[16]

As victory approached, so fears of layoffs increased, together with suspicion that the rhetoric of reform would remain just that. After all the nebulous talk, including Common Wealth's appeals for a 'moral revolution', Beveridge's proposals had the virtue of being concrete—they put some flesh on the bones of all those statements about creating a better New Britain and not returning to the 'bad old days' of the

[13] The papers of Cole's Reconstruction Survey are at Nuffield College, Oxford. J. Harris, 'Did British workers want the welfare state? G. D. H. Cole's survey of 1942' in J. M. Winter (ed.), *The Working Class in Modern British History* (Cambridge, 1983). Also, Beveridge, 'Freedom from idleness' in G. D. H. Cole, *Plan for Britain* (London, 1943). 'Undercarriage' quote: J. Harris, 'Beveridge's social and political thought' in J. Hills *et al.* (eds.), *Beveridge and Social Security: An international retrospective* (Oxford, 1994), p. 29.
[14] S. Fielding, P. Thompson, and N. Tiratsoo, *England Arise! The Labour Party and popular politics in 1940s Britain* (Manchester, 1995).
[15] M-OA: FR 1634; BIPO (Gallup Polls) UK Data Archive Essex, March 1943. Above-average income were satisfied 53–32%; below average dissatisfied 47%–24%; industrial workers dissatisfied 56–24%.
[16] K. Jefferys, *The Churchill Coalition and Wartime Politics, 1940–45* (Manchester 1991), pp. 140, 150–1.

1930s. As a result the Plan became a common denominator, but not the entirety of popular expectations for change. By 1943 people seemed to have a fairly clear vision of what they wanted—not a detailed programme but a loosely conceived social democratic reform agenda. Surveys and contemporary analyses elicited four basic themes. The first was support for an expansion of social services. War had done much to erode popular distrust of the state. It had deepened the realization that human life is social capital—birth, nurturing, work, even death became subject to greater regulation and, on balance, the interventions were considered beneficial. Beveridge's proposals offered the prospect of security and their reliance upon universal contributory insurance got rid of the stigma of charity—everyone was eligible and entitled, welfare was no longer 'reserved for the poor'. Secondly, there was a conviction that the state had both the obligation and the capacity to maintain full employment. With the war drawing to a close this became a topic of intense debate in the press and in trade union, civil service, and political circles. When, in January 1944, BIPO asked its poll sample whether they expected to have difficulty finding a job after the war, 58 per cent of people said 'No', but 32 per cent of industrial workers and 31 per cent of miners said 'Yes'.[17] If government could create jobs in wartime, it was argued, why not in peacetime? Surveys also recorded growing support for public ownership—especially in coal, railways, and land—not simply as the ultimate goal and ethical justification of the labour movement, but as the logical extension of wartime planning and as a way of defeating unemployment. Thirdly, the war promoted confidence in social engineering and planning—a new sense of society, in Jose Harris's words, 'as something that could be molded and modified, made and un-made by acts of political will'.[18] In part this was connected to admiration for the Soviet war effort, but it also resulted from public belief that the controlled war economy had achieved things that would have been impossible otherwise. What was meant by 'planning' was often very vague. For some it evoked simple binary oppositions between bleak images of the unplanned market economy of the thirties and wartime when the nation's resources were harnessed for collective goals. For many, it simply conjured up images of new towns; high rises; airy, hygienic schools; and a modern society where employment was regular. The final aspect of this loose agenda—which informed the others—was popular investment in a language of social citizenship, which implied social levelling and the inclusion of those previously marginalized or excluded from full membership of the community. It was a language that conveyed the priorities of community and the collective good and shaped the way people articulated the obligations and entitlements of citizenship and their aspirations for jobs, housing, education, and family welfare.

Many people had by 1943 a general idea of what they wanted from a post-war settlement. What was unclear was how their expectations might be realized. This

---

[17] For clerical workers and professionals the figures for those expecting to have difficulty were 12% and 5% respectively. BIPO survey made in mid-January 1944 and included in the Home Intelligence report for 10 February 1944, NA: INF 1/292.

[18] J. Harris, 'Society and the state in twentieth century Britain' in F. M. L. Thompson, *The Cambridge Social History of Britain, 1750–1950* (Cambridge, 1990), III, p. 96.

was understandable since the political situation remained very fluid. Anti-Tory attitudes were widespread, but much of the public, including many workers, were also critical of the Labour Party—either for what it had done or had failed to do. Labour officials recognized the danger: while popular political opinion had moved to the left and was thus closely attuned to the party's way of thinking, 'the Party seems in fact to be contemptuously disregarded', as one put it.[19] The two most likely ways in which reform might be achieved were a coalition—either Churchill's or more likely one that was more progressive—and a Labour victory at the polls. A significant segment of the population, influenced by the aftermath of 1918, expected some kind of coalition government to continue. Opinion polls taken in 1943 and 1944 illustrate this, although the surveys are somewhat ambiguous about people's preferences. For example, a BIPO poll of January 1943 has been widely cited as indicative of public discontent with politics and a 'movement away from party'. When asked, Stephen Fielding writes, if the country *should* return to the party system after the war 47 per cent said 'Yes', 19 per cent said 'No', and 34 per cent said 'Don't know'. Fielding emphasizes that 53 per cent either 'refrained from a direct response because they did not care to give the question much time; or they had given the matter some thought but were unconvinced as to the positive merits of the party system'. He adds: 'Whichever is the case, it cannot be said that the return of two-party politics was anticipated with much enthusiasm.' But the question actually asked was: 'Do you think that after the war we *shall* go back to the party system we had before the war?'[20] In this case the high percentage of 'Don't knows' was quite reasonable given the confusing political circumstances of the time; similarly the 47 per cent who said 'Yes' were not necessarily advocating party competition, but simply guessing what was likely to happen. Other polls at the war's end did show considerable preference for a coalition. In August 1944 BIPO found that 35 per cent of its sample wanted some form of 'all-party' government, 26 per cent a Labour administration, and 12 per cent a Conservative one. And as late as March 1945 when BIPO asked voters to choose between the Conservatives and a broad progressive coalition (including Liberals, Labour, Common Wealth, ILP, and the CP) they opted for the coalition by 55 per cent to 24 per cent—a full 13–15 per cent higher than Labour got on its own in polls around the same time. But while these surveys may denote a genuine preference for a progressive coalition, they may also reflect a strategic choice by voters who were doubtful Labour could win and anxious that defeat might scuttle prospects for reform.[21]

As party politics began to revive with the major parties all beginning to position themselves for the next election, Labour began working hard to publicize itself as

---

[19] G. R. Shepherd (the party's national agent) to G. Ridley 10 March 1943, quoted by S. Brooke, 'The Labour Party and the 1945 general election', *Contemporary Record*, 9(1) (Summer 1995), 9.

[20] BIPO (Gallup Polls), UK Data Archive Essex, January 1943; S. Fielding, 'The Second World War and popular radicalism: The significance of the "movement away from party"', *History*, 80(258) (February 1995), 54–5.

[21] BIPO, August 1944; March 1945. Similarly when in April 1945 the BIPO survey asked its panel if they would like to see a Conservative–Labour–Liberal coalition after the General Election, 43% said 'Yes', 43% said 'No', and 14% expressed 'No opinion'. *Gallup International Polls*.

the party of reform. There was no shortage of criticism of Labour in the last two years of the war, but the party redoubled its efforts to seize the opportunity presented by the revolution in popular expectations. At the same time the electorate was beginning to accommodate to the realities of the British voting system; the 'movement away from party' of 1942 was replaced by a quickening interest in politics and a return to party. Evidence for this in the opinion polls is sketchy since between January 1940 and June 1943 BIPO did not ask its survey participants how they would vote 'if a General Election were held tomorrow'. However, a survey of June 1943 and six more prior to the election showed Labour consistently ahead by 12–18 per cent.[22] Labour was not simply the passive beneficiary of public hostility towards Conservatism; the party played a major role in determining its own success.

LABOUR'S ROAD TO RENEWAL

In the years immediately after the Second World War the Labour Party's rise was often depicted as an ineluctable 'forward march' inscribed in the logic of history and the advance of working-class power. This 'whiggish' view owed more to the party faithful's confidence at that particular moment than to close study of the party's history, for Labour's trajectory had been anything but an orderly evolution—more accurately, a story of rapid advances and dramatic retreats in which the two world wars had played a vital role in boosting the party's fortunes.

Labour's early growth certainly seemed rapid to contemporaries; only twenty-four years separated the founding of the Labour Representation Committee in 1900, committed to achieving more independent labour representation in Parliament, and Ramsay MacDonald's taking the seals of office for Labour's first government. The party had originated as an alliance of trade unionists seeking to safeguard their legal rights and small struggling socialist parties. It lacked a clear programme and was not committed to socialism and yet by 1914, thanks to a political strategy of electoral alliance with the Liberals, Labour had managed to win almost forty seats in the Commons and was established as a presence in national politics. It did not have the organizational base or financial resources, however, to launch a real national campaign and was in no position to rival the Liberals, even with working-class voters. The First World War and its strike-torn aftermath transformed this situation. Labour emerged from the war backed by a much stronger trade union movement while the franchise extension of 1918 offered the party prospects for growth. Most importantly, the continuation of Lloyd George's coalition and deep internal rifts within the Liberal Party meant that Labour suddenly found itself occupying the Opposition front bench. By 1918 the party had also adopted an explicitly socialist programme and four years later, although

[22] R. Sibley, 'The swing to Labour during the Second World War: When and why?', *Labour History Review*, 55(1) (1995); BIPO (Gallup Polls) UK Data Archive Essex, June–July 1943.

breaking out of its old bridgeheads of support was hard, it managed to poll 4 million votes or roughly a third of the national total.

Even after the defeat of the 1926 General Strike when union membership contracted and the Trade Disputes Act reduced union contributions to Labour's funds, the party was still able to grow, consolidating its hold on its 'core' regions in the north and making advances in London and other areas where unionism was fairly weak. Continued Liberal decline had opened up a wide space on the left of the political spectrum and Ramsay MacDonald's moderate leadership produced impressive gains, especially in municipal government. By focusing on a range of issues, especially the provision of social welfare, healthcare, and local services, and by its alliance with the Co-operative movement, the party was also successful in recruiting women so that by the mid-1920s its women's sections had expanded to over 200,000 members.[23] And though the accomplishments of Labour's brief minority government in 1924 were modest, it did further undermine the Liberal Party and underscored the fact that politics now offered a choice between Labour and a Conservatism which, as McKibbin has argued, cohered around the theme of anti-socialism. And yet the Liberals were still strong enough to siphon off votes from the Conservative Party in 1929, thereby enabling Labour to become the largest party in the Commons with 287 seats, even if it lacked an overall majority.

This was by far Labour's biggest electoral advance to date: it polled 37 per cent of the national vote and won nearly two-thirds of the large urban seats. But triumph and high expectations rapidly gave way to drift and defeat. Labour had no strategy for coping with mass unemployment and the movement began to fracture over proposed budget cuts and reduced unemployment benefits. And while the party blamed MacDonald's 'betrayal'—his decision to lead an all-party National government dominated by the Conservatives—for the disastrous election result of 1931 when it was reduced to a mere 52 seats, the dramatic loss of popular support was equally a verdict on the government's poor performance in the preceding two years. By 1932 most of Labour's leading politicians had lost their parliamentary seats and the party was again largely confined to its old industrial heartlands of the north and South Wales. Again the trade union movement filled the breach, reasserting its power over policy even though its own membership remained stagnant until the mid-1930s. Labour's failure and disintegration consolidated Conservative hegemony for the rest of the decade.[24]

For the rest of the 1930s Labour was engaged in the tasks of rebuilding. One result was a systematic rethinking of its programme. At first in reaction to its 1931

[23] P. Graves, *Labour Women: Women in British working-class politics 1918–1939* (Cambridge, 1994); M. Worley, *Labour Inside the Gate: A history of the British Labour Party between the wars* (London, 2005).

[24] R. McKibbin, *Parties and People: England 1914–51* (Oxford, 2010), pp. 77–87. The consequences of geography and Britain's 'first past the post' system need always to be taken into account. In 1929, for example, Liberals polled 23.5% of the national vote and got 59 MPs while the Labour Party received 37.8% and 287 seats. In 1931 with 31% of the vote, Labour returned a mere 52 MPs, while the National Liberal Party and breakaway National Labour Party, with only 5.2% of the vote, returned 48 MPs. And in 1935 the Conservative Party received almost 54% of the vote and 432 seats, while Labour's 38% of the vote translated into only 154 MPs.

defeat the party moved to the left, but very soon, pragmatic centrists like Dalton, Morrison, and Attlee came to dominate the reformulation of policy. Large numbers of young economists and planning groups as well as the trade unions were drawn into the process and by 1937 they had hammered out an *Immediate Programme* which designated specific industries for nationalization (coal, gas, electricity, transport, and the Bank of England), a public corporation model for organizing those sectors taken over, a National Investment Board to regulate credit and industrial investment, and a broad social policy agenda. Agreement on immediate objectives also helped to mask continuing ideological differences within the party's ranks. By the outbreak of the Second World War the Labour Party had gone far towards developing the ideas for economic management and blueprints for social legislation that formed the basis of the programme it put forward after 1945.[25] Until now Labour had oscillated between two visions: seeing itself as either a party of the working class or as a movement committed to forging a national constituency of progressive voters. In the 1930s, however, the party's media campaigns consistently addressed this national constituency: courting press editors, revamping the *Daily Herald*, paying more attention to broadcasting, and producing a flood of new print publicity and advertising designed to broaden its support.[26]

Labour also set about rebuilding its local constituency structures, recruiting new members, and making further inroads into local government. Some of the most impressive gains were made in the south-east, including the capital where the electoral machine built by Herbert Morrison gained control of the London County Council in 1934.[27] These gains reflected both the recovery of trade union membership from the mid-1930s and also the growing influence of socialist ideas transmitted by the popular writings of Harold Laski, G. D. H. Cole, John Strachey, and others or through the Left Book Club, the Peace Pledge Union, student organizations, and the columns of *Tribune* and the *New Statesman*. Among middle-class suburbanites especially, socialist intellectuals played a large role in attracting and invigorating new recruits. However, despite all these signs that the party was recovering some of its lost ground, the General Election of 1935 was a disappointment. Labour only managed to recapture seventeen of the seventy-three seats it had won for the first time in 1929; large segments of the working class continued to vote Liberal or Tory; and middle-class socialists remained a fairly small minority. Indeed, Labour seemed to have reached a plateau and looked like settling into permanent opposition. The party was firmly established as *the* political alternative to Conservatism but its supporters were still heavily concentrated in northern and Celtic-fringe industrial areas and there was no sign that it would win the next election in 1940 or challenge Conservative hegemony in the near future. Party intellectual and political scientist Harold Laski for one, grew increasingly

[25] S. Brooke, *Labour's War* (Oxford, 1992), ch. 1; D. Ritschel, *The Politics of Planning: The debate on economic planning in Britain in the 1930s* (Oxford, 1997), ch. 3.

[26] L. Beers, *Your Britain: Media and the making of the Labour Party* (Harvard, 2010), ch. 8.

[27] M. Worley (ed.), *Labour's Grass Roots: Essays on the activities of local Labour parties and members, 1918–1945* (Aldershot, 2005).

pessimistic in the late 1930s that radical change could ever be achieved given public opposition or indifference and the structural obstacles to Labour winning a resounding electoral victory.

Labour's weakness in Parliament gave impetus to groups inside and outside the party who were pushing for some kind of united front to galvanize the left and mobilize public opposition to the National Government. With Hitler's takeover in Germany and the growing threat of fascism, the CP also reversed its policy of attacking socialists or 'social fascists' and advocated a common front along the lines of those that emerged victorious in the French and Spanish elections of 1936. The goal of these efforts—on the part of the ILP, Socialist League, and the CP—was to construct a more unified left; in reality they produced more division and fragmentation. Most of the Labour leadership remained deeply mistrustful of these efforts, in which Stafford Cripps played a major part; their response was to intensify efforts to monitor the party's ideological boundaries, including expelling 'disruptive elements' and those like Cripps who refused to toe the line. Yet another aspect of these pressures for a popular front, often down-played, was closer cooperation with the Liberals—promoted, for example, by the Liberal *News Chronicle* and the Left Book Club. In 1935 the opposition parties had won 46 per cent of the votes, but only 30 per cent of the seats because they split the anti-Conservative vote. However, Labour leaders rebuffed such ideas, fearful that cooperation might revive Liberalism at a time when it seemed fated to disappear. At the local level both before and after 1939 there was unofficial cooperation and interaction among progressives which sometimes resulted in disciplinary action, although Labour officials often turned a blind eye, recognizing that increased restrictions would only drive out more members.[28]

This political landscape was completely reshaped by the outbreak of war, although the conflict's first phase posed a challenge for Labour's leaders, who detested Neville Chamberlain, were unwilling to enter a government led by him, and yet did not want to appear disloyal or unpatriotic. Convinced that Chamberlain could not deliver victory, they were forced to play a waiting game: outright opposition in the midst of the conflict was impossible, but so was close cooperation. Instead they agreed to a party-political truce and sought to offer 'constructive criticism' of official policy, while at the same time trying to contain growing dissatisfaction with the government's uninspiring leadership among the party's rank and file.[29] Labour's leaders were convinced that the war would move Britain closer to socialism and that a much larger measure of central planning and state economic intervention was indispensable to victory. Their collectivist politics had become part of the logic of survival and would now achieve a broader resonance among non-socialists. At the same time the party's leaders repeatedly asserted that

---

[28] M. Pugh, *Speak for Britain: A new history of the Labour Party* (London, 2010); D. Blaazer *The Popular Front and the Progressive Tradition: Socialists, Liberals and the quest for unity 1884–1939* (Cambridge, 2002).

[29] J. Swift, *Labour in Crisis: Clement Attlee and the Labour Party in opposition 1931–1940* (Oxford, 2001).

planning for war could not be divorced from planning for peace; the conflict could and must serve as a vehicle of social transformation, an opportunity to build a better society. 'We remember what happened at the end of the last war', Attlee warned: 'derelict areas, derelict industries, derelict human beings'.[30] Thus, when the failure of British operations in Norway finally brought down Chamberlain's government in May 1940 and Labour entered Churchill's Coalition, its position was that peace aims and reconstruction could not be put off until the conflict was over.

Over the next four years Labour's leaders became national figures, familiar to everyone from the press, newsreels, and broadcasts. Between them the 'big five'— Attlee, Bevin, Morrison, Dalton, and Cripps—already had a great deal of experience of industrial affairs and party policy-making, but their ministerial experience was fairly meagre and only Morrison had previously been (briefly) in a Cabinet.[31] As personalities they could not have been more different. Attlee's lack of personal charisma and the constant tendency of opponents throughout his career to underestimate his intelligence and quiet toughness meant that whenever the going got rough, there were intrigues to unseat him as leader. But a powerful alliance between him and Bevin foiled such plots and his determined, non-confrontational style was essential to holding together the party's leading personalities, both during the war and later. In general, opinion polls showed that Labour's ministers were popular and gained strong approval rates for their performance in office. They shouldered enormous administrative burdens and played vital roles in running the home front war, but only Cripps—in extraordinary circumstances, as shown in chapter 8—was ever viewed as having the charisma to replace Churchill should he have to step down. In 1945, however, their individual and collective achievements were central to Labour's claim to power. As a team they were formidable and what united them—easily forgotten amid the bickerings and personal rivalries—was common adherence to Labour's socialist programme and their sense that the war provided the structural means to implement it. The wartime framework of state controls achieved many of the things Labour had identified as necessary if a socialist administration were to be effective.

But while participation in the Coalition extinguished doubts about the capacity of Labour's leaders to govern, it also placed considerable strains upon party unity and created serious rifts within the left. As we have seen, during the first two years of the Coalition a growing tide of criticism called for sweeping changes in the conduct of the war. Critics demanded swifter and more radical steps to eliminate waste and inefficiency in war production, reform the armed forces, and mobilize the population more effectively behind the war effort. The blaming of Attlee and the other leaders for making too many compromises began on the left in 1940 and never let up. In November 1940 Priestley accused them of 'tamely agreeing' to a 'policy of drift' and buttressing the old order.[32] At the Labour Conference in

[30] Attlee quoted by Brooke, *Labour's War*, p. 42.
[31] Morrison was Minister of Transport 1929–31; Attlee held minor posts: Undersecretary of War in 1924; Postmaster-General and then Chancellor of the Duchy of Lancaster 1929–31.
[32] Priestley to Acland, 9 November 1940, Acland Papers, University of Sussex.

May 1942 TGWU boss Arthur Deakin also jumped into the fray, putting up a resolution for bringing railways, coal, and war production into public ownership during the war.[33] In the House of Commons debate on the Manpower Bill in December 1941 thirty-five Labour backbenchers voted for an amendment which called for the nationalization of transport, coal, and munitions. Further revolts followed, culminating in the mass revolt against the government over Beveridge. Why, critics demanded, had Labour ministers gone along with Tory efforts to gag the press, with inaction over Beveridge, and the decision to release fascist leader Oswald Mosley from prison? Why had they made so little progress towards abolishing the hated Means Test and why did they acquiesce to the use of British troops to suppress the communist resistance in Athens in 1944? The sharpest attacks on the leadership came from Aneurin Bevan and Emanuel Shinwell,[34] but even Citrine, always a team player and no friend of left activists, was increasingly indignant at the failure to amend the Trades Disputes Act which, among other things, blocked the application of the civil service unions for TUC affiliation. Attlee's efforts to obfuscate and dodge the issue, Citrine warned in 1943, were creating a rift between the industrial and political wings of the labour movement.[35]

Frustration over Labour's failure to seize the opportunity and capitalize on its indispensability also underlay the prodigious range of activities undertaken by Harold Laski.[36] By the late 1930s he had become deeply pessimistic, seeing no possible way that socialism was likely to be achieved. But the war offered a solution to his dilemma: the possibility of a 'revolution by consent', of achieving fundamental change without violence and in accordance with the Labour Party's commitment to constitutional legality.[37] The crisis of war, he argued, both enhanced the power and status of labour and made peaceful concessions by the elites more likely. It was therefore imperative that Labour press its claims for a significant advance instalment of socialism immediately. Throughout the war Laski shouldered a huge burden: publishing a continuous stream of books and articles, lecturing all over the country, broadcasting frequently, and taking on an increasing amount of party administrative work. Highly popular with constituency activists, he topped the poll for the party's National Executive Committee (NEC) every year of the war. Within the NEC he lobbied hard and tried to use party conferences to pressure the leadership; he was also the principal author of the party's interim programme on reconstruction, *The Old World and the New Society* (February 1942), which, though vague provided, as Stephen Brooke has noted, a rhetorical framework for more specific policy proposals.[38]

---

[33] Brooke, *Labour's War*, p. 82.

[34] J. Campbell, *Nye Bevan and the Mirage of British Socialism* (London, 1987), chs. 7–10. Also, E. Shinwell, *The Britain I Want* (London, 1943).

[35] W. M. Citrine Papers, BLPES London School of Economics.

[36] Isaac Kramnick and Barry Sheerman, *Harold Laski: A life on the left* (London, 1993).

[37] Jose Harris, 'Labour's social and political thought' in D. Tanner, P. Thane, and N. Tiratsoo (eds.), *Labour's First Century* (Cambridge, 2000), pp. 26–7.

[38] Brooke, *Labour's War*, pp. 107–9.

Laski's interventions were often maladroit and ill-timed and his demands that Labour ministers should carry out the views of the party executive and Conference got nowhere. When Labour leaders failed to secure any tangible gains from Churchill's government reshuffle early in 1942, he even took an extraordinary step of approaching Churchill, whom he admired, and urged him to preside over a sweeping New Deal for Britain. The programme, he argued, must tackle social inequalities, prevent the return of mass unemployment, introduce state control of credit, and create a substantial socialized sector of industry. Regarding Churchill as a Tory rebel who might accept these ideas, Laski suggested quite unrealistically that he could carry the Labour Party executive 'if you would lead the nation on that basis'. Churchill who must have been astonished to get such a letter with its misreading of his own views as well as Laski's own authority within Labour, promised to study its contents.[39] Critical of the CP and convinced that new political organizations like Common Wealth would merely splinter and atomize the left, Laski saw no alternative to the Labour Party which should, he argued, be 'the spinal column of the immense, if unorganized progressive forces of the country'.[40] Viewing Attlee as the major obstacle to progress, he made overtures to Bevin, Dalton, and Morrison to replace the leader. And when no support was forthcoming, he sent a letter to the NEC protesting that the party was being dragged along 'at the tail of the Conservative party' and that in return for a few small reforms 'we are assisting the vested interests of this country to strengthen their hold on state power and . . . to preserve their privileges at the expense of the workers'. '[O]n all fundamental matters', he added, 'we do the giving and the Tories do the taking.' Fearful that a supreme opportunity was being sacrificed Laski favoured pressing Churchill on a minimum programme to the point of breaking up the Coalition—at least, then, he wrote, Churchill would have to call an election which the Conservatives would almost certainly lose.[41] Not surprisingly there were demands for Laski's expulsion from the party, voiced especially among conservative trade unionists. Formally reprimanded by the NEC, in the following year he suffered a serious breakdown, exhausted by his enormous burden of work. When he returned to the public spotlight two years later during the general election campaign it was again as a thorn in Attlee side.

Distrust of leaders, the spectre of MacDonaldism, one historian has written, was 'etched' into the party's psyche;[42] but in the war years as a whole its importance should not be exaggerated. While the belief that Labour ministers were not doing enough to fight for socialist policies within the Coalition was strong among left-wing intellectuals and party members, most of Labour's rank-and-file supporters and trade unionists were supportive of the party leadership. Trade unionism was advancing on all fronts and large sectors of the workforce, including agricultural

[39] For Laski's overtures to Churchill (in February 1941 and again in March 1942): Newman, *Harold Laski: A political biography* (London, 1993), pp. 215–16, 231.

[40] H. Laski, 'Where is the Labour Party going?', *New Statesman*, 10 July 1943.

[41] *NEC minutes*, 9 April 1942.

[42] J. Lawrence, 'Labour: The myths it has lived by' in Tanner, Thane, and Tiratsoo (eds.), *Labour's First Century*, p. 351.

and catering workers who had been largely ignored before, achieved significant gains in pay and conditions. As Stephen Brooke has shown, Labour ministers were far from being hostages to Conservative policies: they contributed to Butler's education reform[43] and got Conservative agreement for Dalton's regional policy designed to steer resources and relocate industrial jobs to formerly 'distressed areas'. Behind the scenes Attlee, Dalton, and Bevin tried to obtain assurances on coal and railway nationalization, but here they encountered firm resistance and by October 1943—with his position much strengthened by victory in North Africa—Churchill made it clear that insistence on coal nationalization would break up the government.[44] For his part Attlee was not disposed to engage in threats or brinkmanship, believing that they endangered the nation and might encourage voters to see the party as unpatriotic, thereby undermining its future electoral chances. Moreover, as early as 1941 the party began serious work on reconstruction planning. Many interlocking centres of the labour movement played a role: policy committees set up by the party itself, groups established by the trade unions and TUC, 'think tanks' like the Fabian Society, occupational bodies such as the Socialist Medical Association and the National Association of Labour Teachers, and many others. They worked on education, family allowances, social insurance, housing, a national health service, employment, the nationalization of industry, regional economic policy, and control of investment and credit. Churchill remained reluctant to give firm pledges about reconstruction before the war's end, although he found himself under increasing pressure to address the issue. It was Labour which forced the pace, moving towards a coherent policy agenda that progressive opinion could unite behind.[45]

In addition, notwithstanding the wartime truce, the Labour leadership took important steps to prepare the party for the resumption of normal politics and the next general election. After Labour's victory in 1945, it became part of Conservative lore that while the Tory party machine had been allowed to atrophy, Labour's organizational structure had been kept in good repair. The implication was that Conservatives had spent more time and energy actually fighting the war. Between the wars it was generally reckoned that better organization gave the Conservatives an edge in every election, contributing to the party's dominance. But in wartime the Conservative Research Department closed down; the position of party chairman lost much of its status; the numbers of Tory salaried agents dwindled rapidly through conscription; and many local associations either met infrequently or suspended operations altogether. In 1943 Conservatives held their first party Conference in six years and then another gap followed until March 1945, whereas Labour's annual Conferences continued and Labour women held their own

---

[43]   Labour MP James Chuter-Ede, Parliamentary Secretary to the Board of Education, played a large role. Bill Bailey, 'James Chuter-Ede and the 1944 Education Act', *History of Education*, 24(3) (1995); Kevin Jefferys (ed.), *Labour and the Wartime Coalition: From the diary of James Chuter-Ede* (London, 1987).

[44]   Brooke, *Labour's War*, p. 88.

[45]   In addition to Brooke and Jefferys, see Abigail L. Beech, 'The Labour Party and the idea of citizenship, *c.*1931–1951', PhD Diss., London University, 1996.

gatherings in several of the war years.[46] Never much of a party man, Churchill had little time or inclination to devote himself to party management. In contrast, Attlee, Morrison, and Dalton paid close attention to their party's machinery. To be sure, Labour enjoyed some basic advantages. Many trade union and party activists were in skilled jobs and, being exempt from the forces, were available for political work. War also reinforced the social importance of trades councils, unions, and the Co-operative movement—all of them integral elements of the Labour movement— while full employment and expanded union membership produced a dramatic improvement in party finances. Thus, there is some truth to the claim that Labour was better prepared than ever before, although the significance of this was often exaggerated. Long working hours, queuing for food, and fire-watching duties left many Labour supporters with little time for party work; evacuation and the increased mobility of people in wartime disrupted party networks; and German raids also brought activity to a virtual standstill in some areas. In addition, while Labour had never enjoyed as many paid agents and full-time organizers as the Conservatives, the ranks of those it had were considerably thinned by conscription and the electoral truce.

At the beginning of the war the party's London headquarters made clear its intention of having local organizations continue their political and social activities as close to normal levels as possible. Conservatives argued that the truce should be defined in a broad sense as covering all political activity and not simply electoral competition, but Labour's leaders never accepted these terms. Local party struc-tures were encouraged to hold public meetings, put out news reports, publish pamphlets and newspapers, and to involve themselves in local affairs. The war was viewed as an opportunity to demonstrate socialist values in action and to strengthen party ties to the community at large. Transport House encouraged Labour suppor-ters to undertake voluntary work (under the party's aegis wherever possible) and to cooperate with civil defence and other public agencies. Local branches soon began lobbying municipal authorities on such issues as evacuation, shelter conditions, emergency housing, and the shopping and childcare difficulties faced by working women. They also established advice bureaux for raid victims, providing information about government compensation, old-age pensions, and dependants' allowances and they were active on local Vigilance Committees, set up to monitor inflation and local food and fuel supplies.

The hub of these activities was the divisional Labour parties, with links to trades councils, union branches, Co-operative societies, the WEA, and other community groups. But while the party's headquarters were more continuously active in keeping local structures alive than the Conservative's Central Office, this also had its price in the form of criticism of the parliamentary leadership, cacophonous annual conferences, and at times open defiance of the guidelines laid down for politics under the truce. Constituency records provide insight into the experiences

---

[46] Conservative women held no annual conference between 1939 and 1946; there were Labour women's conferences in 1940, 1942–3, and 1945. The annual TUC conferences were also widely reported in the press.

of activists at the grass roots and their range of activities.[47] Of course, the party's size, vitality, and its role in municipal government made for varying levels of activity and success. Where a borough council was deeply divided politically or where Labour's own ranks were split, party activists might have little to show for their efforts. This was the case in Liverpool, for example, where pre-war feuding between Catholics and moderates on one side and a more militant left group on the other, continued into the war years.[48] In Gloucester, a prosperous town which had grown rapidly with the rearmament boom of the late 1930s, the major problem was the local party's long history of internecine squabbling between moderates and militants and the division between its political and industrial wings. A rent strike of local council housing tenants which began prior to the war continued to poison the relationship of the different factions. It precipitated a move by local radicals to unseat the party chair, whom they viewed as entirely too cosy with Tories on the local council. He in turn engineered a formal inquiry by the NEC and attempted to expel his opponents. Membership in the constituency declined sharply and the branch was eventually disbanded and then reconstituted. This dispute consumed local energies in Gloucester for over two years.[49] By contrast, in Birmingham where Conservatism and the Chamberlain family had long dominated local politics, a 1939 strike over council rents had done much to increase Labour unity. Here local Labour people, including a highly vocal group on the City Council, successfully pressured Tory councillors and played a leading part in debates over housing, shelters, childcare, and other social issues. The rapid growth of activity in several of the Birmingham branches also reflected the growth of radicalism in middle-class suburbs in the last two years of the war. From surviving records at least it would seem that some of the liveliest debates on policy and strategy often occurred in constituencies where the party had previously faced a difficult time.[50]

One conspicuous wartime trend was the increasing range of constituency business undertaken by women. In March 1943 in the Portsmouth area, for example, seven of the eight local party chairmen and secretaries were women.[51] The Standing Joint Committee of Working Women's Organizations was active in every facet of

---

[47] These comments are based on local Labour Party minutes, including Birmingham, Gloucester, Tottenham (London), Newport, Liverpool, South Shields, Pontypridd, etc. These and local trades council records are now accessible in microform: *The Origins and Development of the Labour Party in Britain at Local Level, Series I and II* (Microform Academic Publishers), gen. ed. Stephen Bird, National Museum of Labour History, Manchester. A detailed analysis of local party activity (including the Conservative Party) now exists: Andrew Thorpe, *Parties at War: Political organization in Second World War Britain* (Oxford, 2009).

[48] *Liverpool Trades Council and Labour Party, 1862–1986* (microfilm), minutes 1939–43.

[49] *Gloucester Labour Party 1899–1951* (microfilm), minutes 1939–45. Prior to the war, the Gloucester party had been split over whether the party should work for a popular front.

[50] Birmingham Borough Labour Party, Executive Minutes 1943–5; Labour Party, Aston Ward Minutes 1942–6; Aston Divisional Labour Party, Minutes and Correspondence 1943–51; Birmingham City Council Labour Group, Minutes 1943–7, Birmingham Central Library. Also, R. P. Hastings, 'The Birmingham Labour Movement, 1918–45', *Midland History* 5 (1979–80); A. Sutcliffe, 'Birmingham and the Second World War' (Typescript. History of Birmingham Seminar no. 3, n.d.), Birmingham Central Library. In contrast South Shields constituency minutes (a seat long occupied by Chuter-Ede) reveal little controversy or vigorous debate.

[51] Fielding, Thompson, and Tiratsoo, *England Arise!*, p. 50.

the war effort, giving advice on evacuation, food rationing, housing, nurseries, women's industrial work, and post-war reconstruction. It also pressed the party to train and adopt more women candidates for the next general election. At the Labour Women's Conference, however, a motion urging committees to select women was defeated; 'feminism' remained a contentious topic for party women who often saw gender as secondary to the party's class priorities and more of a concern to middle-class careerists.[52] Already before 1939 women played an important role in Labour's expanding presence in many areas; around 180,000 belonged to the women's sections and many others, finding sex-segregation somewhat 'old fashioned', became active instead in the party's mixed ward and constituency groups.[53] A growing number of women also entered local government and the pressure of female recruits prompted Labour constituency groups to focus more on 'practical' political issues like the provision of such local services as housing, education, health, and childcare. Wartime conditions further reinforced the centrality of these issues, while the mass recruitment of women into war work focused attention upon 'equal pay for equal work' and the campaign for equal compensation for war injuries. Initially air raids, evacuation, and recruitment into industry or the forces brought a decline in many women's sections, but branch reports indicate that this was often temporary. Party women took up a wide range of volunteer work: 'As socialists', one wrote in *Labour Woman*, 'we practised what we preached: that we were the people to be relied upon for help and comfort and good neighbourliness in difficult times, that we were efficient and resourceful and determined in "getting things done".' In the 1930s they had often been suspicious of 'voluntary work' as primarily the sphere of upper-class Conservative women; now they encouraged such activity as a form of active citizenship, often in partnership with state agencies.[54]

However, as the war dragged on, Labour's organizational base showed clear signs of decay. The level of local activity, of course, varied greatly from one area to another and fluctuated during the course of the war, but it is clear that by the middle war years many party branches had suffered sharp declines and were finding it hard to sustain their operations. Membership statistics are notoriously inaccurate but national figures for individual party membership (affiliated membership remained fairly steady) declined from almost 409,000 in 1939 to a low point of under 219,000 in 1942. The decline was especially large in the London region, so heavily disrupted by bombing and evacuation,[55] while in Scotland, where Labour was

---

[52] The Standing Joint Committee of Working Women's Organizations (SJCWWO) coordinated the work of Labour women and lobbied for them within the party structure. SJCWWO Papers, National Museum of Labour History, Manchester. In February 1943, SJCWWO produced a report arguing that a candidate list of suitable housewives, trade unionists, and professional women should be compiled. SJCWWO February 1943 Exec. Committee minutes, Manchester Labour Archives.

[53] Graves, *Labour Women*. Also C. Collette, 'Questions of gender: Labour and women' in B. Brivati (ed.), *The Labour Party: A centenary history* (London, 2000).

[54] J. Bourne, 'For the community', *Labour Woman* (February 1948). Also, J. Hinton, 'Voluntarism versus Jacobinism: Labour, nation, and citizenship in Britain, 1850–1950', *ILWCH* 48 (Autumn 1995), 82.

[55] 1942 also saw dramatic membership expansion for the CP, especially in the London area.

already weakened by the split with the ILP before the war, individual membership was halved to a paltry 16,000.[56] Thus, while Labour could point to trade union networks that were stronger than ever, it needed to breathe new life into many of its constituency associations where the absence of municipal and parliamentary elections both discouraged new members from joining and made it harder to energize loyal volunteers. 'Our lapse rate has been a tragedy', complained the *Labour Organiser*, which called for renewed recruitment efforts in union branches and more work to enrol the wives of soldiers and industrial workers.[57]

The combination of declining membership, growing evidence of electoral support for Common Wealth and Independents in by-elections, and finally clear signs that national attention was beginning to fasten on the next election, all prompted party managers to take action. Already in mid-1942, Transport House launched a national campaign to revitalize the party machinery and re-engage the membership. Recruitment drives were announced, subsidies for speakers and publicity were increased, and more funds were released to hire full-time organizers. By the year's end six Regional Councils were in operation helping to coordinate recruitment, although they exercised little influence over policy-making. Regional party conferences were also organized to discuss the work of Labour's reconstruction committees. Local associations also began re-hiring paid agents and discussing the selection of candidates for the next general election. Common Wealth's success with middle-class voters also suggested that a large potential reservoir of support existed for Labour in the suburbs. In the last half of 1943, in a series of articles, titled 'Whom do we want in the party?', *Labour Organiser* urged party agents to recruit more actively among black-coated workers, technicians, shopkeepers, managers, clergy, and professionals. Long an advocate of winning over the burgeoning strata of white-collar workers and professionals, Herbert Morrison decided to contest suburban east Lewisham in the next election. 'We have a message for "black-coats" as the well as the millions at the factory bench', he wrote in *Labour Organiser*. 'Our appeal is to the community as a whole . . . for there is no cleavage of interest between hand workers and brain workers, factory workers and office workers . . . The rights of the privileged few must be secondary to the national interest.'[58] Winning cross-class support had long been Labour's stated goal, but the war provided a real opportunity to create a national party and to transcend its trade union and working-class identity. As part of this strategy, the party also worked hard to improve its publicity and capitalize upon its relations with the press, orchestrating a great deal of coverage for Beveridge's Plan and in effect appropriating it. The films circulated by the party

[56] C. Harvie, 'Labour in Scotland during the Second World War', *HJ*, 26(4) (1983); *idem*, 'The recovery of Scottish Labour, 1939–51' in I. Donnachie, C. Harvie, and I. S. Wood (eds.), *Forward! Labour Politics in Scotland, 1888–1988* (Edinburgh, 1989).
[57] *Labour Organiser* (January 1942), 1.
[58] *Labour Organiser* (July–November 1943); H. Morrison, 'We must capture the East Lewishams', *Labour Organiser* (March 1945). Also, K. D. Wald, 'Advance or retreat? The formation of British Labour's electoral strategy', *JBS*, 73(3) (July 1988). The *Daily Herald*, 31 July 1944, distinguished between the 'Blimps of the directors parlours and the Stock Exchange bars' and 'practical men who do the job of management'; 'Licinius', *Vote Labour? Why?* (London 1945) represented socialism as 'the culmination of the managerial revolution'.

and its publications like *Your Home* and *Your Future* repeatedly affirmed its commitment to building homes, providing jobs, and improving healthcare—issues that were increasingly on the minds of voters.[59]

But the revival of activity in many constituencies during 1943 was not simply in response to the prodding of headquarters. Growing anticipation of victory, coupled with an increasing number of by-elections in which Conservatives faced Common Wealth nominees or other challengers, greatly intensified grass-roots Labour hostility to the truce. 'The plain fact', commented the *Labour Organiser*, 'is that the great mass of Labour people . . . do not want to be tied up with the Tories, nor do they want to be asked to use their energies to procure the return of Tory candidates.'[60] Already at the annual Conference in May 1942 thirty-eight resolutions were put forward opposing the truce and a motion for its extension only passed by a narrow majority. A growing number of Labour branches began to break ranks, risking disciplinary action or disaffiliation by refusing to back a Conservative candidate or by actively working for an Independent (or sometimes a Labourite who had temporarily resigned from the party in order to contest the seat).[61] And while some local organizers aided Common Wealth as a useful substitute for powering up local networks, others worried that the fruits of their labours were being harvested by people who 'come along, steal our thunder, and poll our votes'.[62] A new sense of urgency, then, began to permeate Labour's grass roots from mid-1943, aided especially by what was perceived as growing determination among Conservatives to stall over Beveridge and generally proscribe reform proposals. Complaints of apathy and inactivity did not disappear: at Pontypridd in Wales, to take one example, the District Organizer worried about a dangerous tendency to ignore political training and to sit back 'when things are going alright'. Yet, despite his criticism, the Pontypridd minutes show a fair amount of engagement, including debates and lectures about international politics, education, and housing policy; efforts to recruit women workers on the new Bridgend Trading Estate; and strong rank-and-file dissatisfaction over the political truce.[63]

---

[59] Beers, *Your Britain*, pp. 174–7.   [60] *Labour Organiser* (June 1942).

[61] Jefferys writes that Labour activists breached the truce in nearly half the 13 by-elections held in 1942. Jefferys, *The Churchill Coalition*, p. 147. Former Labour people who resigned and stood as Independents included: R. G. Mackay (lost narrowly for Llandaff and Barry, June 1943) and Jennie Lee, the wife of Aneurin Bevan (narrowly defeated for Bristol Central, February 1943). Former Labour members also stood for King's Lynn and Peterborough later in 1943; and in February 1944 Charlie White resigned from Labour to resoundingly defeat the Marquess of Hartington in West Derbyshire. H. Bennett, 'The wartime political truce and hopes for post war coalition: The West Derbyshire by-election, 1944', *Midland History*, 17 (1992).

[62] 'The truce is sick', *Labour Organiser* (March 1943). The need to postpone the party Conference in June 1944 (because of D-Day preparations) may have been a blessing in disguise for the leadership under increasing pressure on this issue.

[63] Pontypridd Labour Party and Trades Council minutes, 4 May 1944. In 1941 the Pontypridd party was at a low ebb, but it revived considerably in the course of 1942–3 with a series of debates on Beveridge, educational reform, and the shape of a post-war world. The membership of many local Labour parties began to increase in 1943 as did membership of local women's sections. F. Bealey, J. Blondel, and W. P. McCann, *Constituency Politics: A study of Newcastle under Lyme* (London, 1965).

By the time the war ended in Europe in May 1945 Labour constituency organizations were in far better shape than two years before. The general revival of party
politics and the initiatives both at the top and at the grass roots produced strong
growth and more efficiency in many local branches as an election drew nearer and
prospective candidates began to be chosen. Even some of the issues in these two years
that tested the relationship between rank-and-file and leadership—for example,
Mosley's release or Bevin's draconian Defence Regulation 1AA (April 1944) which
threatened to imprison strikers, or Labour's endorsement of Churchill's use of British
troops against the communists in Athens—also served to heighten political debate
and engagement. In short, while Labour gained from the movement to the left
of public opinion, its electoral victory was far from being a historic windfall—'falling
like a branch of ripe plums into the lap of Mr Attlee', in Paul Addison evocative
image. Rather it represented a great deal of work and preparation at all levels of
the party.

Finally, another important aspect of Labour's strategy was the leadership's
unshakeable opposition to a popular front or electoral cooperation; the upcoming
election was always represented as a contest between Labour and Conservatives.
This position was nothing new, of course, but it is significant given the fact that
many of the party's leaders were very doubtful that Churchill could be beaten—at
least until the campaign was well underway. Polls published by the *News Chronicle*
might show Labour ahead, but few believed their accuracy and press articles estimated
that three- or four-cornered contests might split the anti-Tory vote and cost Labour up
to fifty seats.[64] The party's leadership had always been on guard against infiltration by
communists and rebuffed successive efforts at affiliation over the years. It also believed
that an agreement with Common Wealth would achieve little. The Liberals, though
badly led and divided, were potentially a more serious problem, especially if they
could capitalize on the huge popularity of Beveridge. In 1935 Liberals had contested
159 seats and siphoned off votes from Labour; in 1945 they put up 306 candidates,
and nobody could be sure that it would be different this time. Labour's mood in the
last year of the war was a mixture of hope and anxiety. The party was probably better
prepared for an election than ever before and many local organizers sensed a strong tide
in their areas in Labour's favour. And yet it was feared that an election might turn
on Churchill's personal stature and his approval rate never went below 80 per cent
after El Alamein. Voters clearly had difficulty seeing any of the Labour leaders, and
Attlee in particular, as the nation's leader. Asked to rate a particular Labour minister's
performance, the public response was mostly favourable, but asked who should replace
the prime minister if he had to step down, they repeatedly opted for Eden (roughly
30 per cent) while none of Labour's ministers reached double figures except for Cripps
and his support plummeted after 1943.[65]

---

[64] *The Economist*, 16 June 1945.

[65] And yet there were signs—ignored at the time—of public uncertainty about Churchill as a
peacetime leader. Asked in September 1944 and again in January 1945 who was most suited to form a
peacetime government, Churchill led Eden by only 3% in the first poll, but in the second it was Eden
by 11% (perhaps this reflected a response to his actions in Greece). F. V. Cantwell, 'The meaning of
the British election', *Political Quarterly*, 9(2) (Summer 1945), 150.

In contrast to Labour, Common Wealth, and the CP were floundering as peace drew nearer. By 1943 Common Wealth was already fragmenting into warring factions and, though it continued to do well against Tories in by-elections, the party remained small and underfinanced, relying heavily for funds upon Acland himself and businessman Alan Good. At the end of 1944 Acland made several approaches to Labour, hoping to arrange some 'organised unity of the left' but his efforts got nowhere and CW quickly began to lose momentum as some of its key figures peeled off[66]—including Acland himself after the election. In 1945 Common Wealth contested only twenty-three strongly Tory seats; in another thirty-three it withdrew in Labour's favour. The only hope for such an independent left party would have been if the Churchill Coalition had remained in being and had fought an election on that basis—a very remote possibility.

As for the CP, it was engaged in a major shift of direction, preparing to embrace a parliamentary strategy in hopes of becoming a more central force in the nation's politics. Pollitt's speeches contained less and less of the old rhetoric of inevitable class antagonism and revolutionary change; now his emphasis was on planning, nationalization, and the possibilities for a piecemeal and peaceful parliamentary transition to socialism. A series of organizational changes shifted the party's emphasis away from factory groups (and factory-based politics) towards residential branches. In place of its large area groups, the CP also developed a structure based on smaller wards replicating the organization of other political parties. Local branches, organized around where members lived would, it was believed, facilitate electoral activity. In fact, the results were overwhelmingly negative. Factory networks that had been patiently built up over the course of a decade were precipitously dismantled and many members were lost for good with little compensatory growth in the residential branches.[67] At the same time the party hoped to forge an electoral pact with Labour. But in December 1942 its application for affiliation was firmly blocked by the NEC and when six months later in May 1943 friendly unions, especially the miners and the AEU, put forward a motion for affiliation or electoral cooperation at the Labour Conference, it was again voted down.

Finally, and most importantly, a shift in Moscow's policy after the Yalta Conference of February 1945 threw the party into confusion. The new line, determined by Stalin's international goals, supported a post-war continuation of the wartime Coalition government, albeit reconstructed with a Labour and progressive majority. Such a coalition, it was argued, should also include 'progressive' Tories who had supported Yalta.[68] As the party's headquarters explained to local branches: 'We need above all to see that the Crimean conference ... calls for such a

---

[66] R. G. Mackay to R. Acland, 30 December 1944, Wintringham Papers, Liddell-Hart Centre for Military Archives, King's College London University.

[67] By the end of 1943 wards covered over half of London, but they varied greatly in activity and quality. London Annual Report 1943, CP Archive; London District Reports 1942, 1943: CP/LON/DC/00/01, CPGB Archive. At the peak during the war there were about 1,200 factory branches in the nation.

[68] N. Redfern, 'Winning the peace: British communists, the Soviet Union and the general election of 1945', *Contemporary British History*, 16(1) (Spring 2002).

change as we are making in respect to the kind of government that should be formed after a General Election...'[69] This abrupt switch threw party branches into turmoil. Members were astonished, some wondering if the new line of 'continued national unity' was predicated upon a conviction that Churchill was unbeatable. Those who had been working hard, preparing for the CP to contest as many seats as possible while also working to ensure a Labour victory, felt that the rug had been pulled out from under them. Rank-and-file communists were minimally consulted—after the fact—about the rulings and many complained of the 'sledge hammer' tactics and 'undemocratic manner in which branches were stampeded into hasty acceptance of this policy'.[70] As so often in the past, the party's rhetoric of democracy and participation belied its practice. By May 1945 when Labour left Churchill's Coalition, the CP had sharply reduced the number of candidates it intended to run so that rank-and-file communists had a choice of working to elect Labour candidates or sitting on the sidelines.

THE GENERAL ELECTION CAMPAIGN OF 1945

By October 1944 Labour's National Executive issued a statement that it would fight the next election as an independent party and two months later the party Conference enthusiastically endorsed this position. An 'odour of dissolution', Churchill remarked, had begun to permeate Westminster. In both major parties the willingness to compromise declined rapidly. Debate about such issues as healthcare and land-use planning[71] became polarized, while the government's decision to send troops against the communists in Greece provoked an outcry, including angry criticism of Labour's ministers from their own back benches.[72] Churchill used the platform of the Conservative Party Conference in March 1945 to denounce Labour's nationalization agenda and what he called their efforts to introduce socialism by stealth.[73] The following month Bevin delivered a counterblast. In a speech at Leeds he condemned Tory misrule between the wars. Aware of rumours that he wanted to preserve the Coalition and might even stick with Churchill if Labour decided to leave, he made it clear that this time there would be no 'coupon'

[69] CP/CENT/EC/01/03 Executive Committee Minutes, 13 March 1945, CPGB Archive.

[70] CP/CENT/EC/01/03 Executive Committee Minutes, 15 March 1945 (report re: Hornsey branch—'sledge hammer'). The second quotation (from a branch resolution at the 1945 Congress) is from Morgan, *Harry Pollitt*, p. 144. For King's Street's effort to contain the anger and guide local leaders in how to respond to it: Executive Committee Minutes, March 1944, 'Draft of political letter on party discussion', CP/CENT/EC/01/03, CPGB Archive.

[71] Jefferys, *The Churchill Coalition*, ch. 7. Conservatives went along with the 1944 White Paper on Full Employment but this was high-water mark of cooperation. In the summer of 1944 the Town and Country Planning Bill—seen as confiscatory by many—was bitterly contested by Conservative backbenchers. Another symptom was a 6-page letter that Attlee sent to Churchill in January 1945 sharply rebuking him for the way he dealt with committee reports in Cabinet. Attlee Papers 2/2 ('Correspondence with Winston Churchill during World War II'), Bodleian Library, Oxford University.

[72] A. Thorpe, 'In a fragile emotional state? The Labour Party and British intervention in Greece, 1944–45', *EHR*, 121 (September 2006).

[73] *The Times*, 16 March 1945.

election to prolong the coalition. 'The coalition', the *Economist* commented, 'is getting more and more threadbare.'[74]

With the precedent of the First World War in mind, Conservatives began to contemplate an early election soon after hostilities ceased, when Churchill's prestige would be higher than ever. Labour's NEC favoured leaving the Coalition once the war in Europe ended, but it wanted the vote to take place in the autumn, allowing time for gratitude towards Churchill to subside. Also, by that time new voting registers could be compiled and many voters now serving overseas in the armed forces would have returned home. However, once Germany surrendered, events moved swiftly. Ten days later on 18 May, Churchill offered Labour a choice between continuing the Coalition until the finish of the Pacific war (expected to last at least another year) and dissolving it at once, with an early election to follow. The prime minister was genuinely unhappy about breaking up the government, but he was also loath to pass up a potential advantage if it was going to end anyway. Fearful of the effect on public opinion and uncertain that Labour could win an election, Attlee, Bevin, and Dalton were highly ambivalent about suddenly quitting the government at this juncture. But Morrison, Bevan, and Laski firmly rejected Churchill's offer and both the NEC and the party Conference were dead set against continued participation. When Attlee communicated this to Chequers, the prime minister's weekend residence, Churchill submitted his resignation and the wartime Coalition ended on 23 May. A Conservative 'caretaker' administration took over but Labour's requests that an election be postponed for some months were ignored, and polling day was set for 5 July.

And so the nation embarked upon its first national election campaign in a decade. What now seems so surprising is the unexpectedness of Labour's victory. Most observers forecast a Conservative win, albeit with a reduced majority. Few paid much attention to poll results which had Labour consistently ahead; rather, most press commentators expected the prime minister's prestige to trump other considerations. In view of this, the two major parties' strategies offered striking contrasts. The Tory campaign was largely built around the totemic figure of Churchill. It downplayed specific programmes and focused more on broad themes and vague statements about a 'four-year plan'. Churchill sought to take credit for the reform proposals that emanated from the Coalition, but the real thrust of the campaign was that he should be given an opportunity 'to finish the job'. Making a triumphant peregrination around the nation, he was greeted by large and enthusiastic crowds wherever he went. But his popularity did not give Conservatives the expected big lift. Often he seemed remote from the everyday worries of people, an old privileged warhorse splendid in the heat of conflict but unsuited for the practical challenges of domestic reconstruction. Even before the Coalition ended Churchill showed signs of exhaustion after five years of constant work and strain and was more apt to ramble in meetings. His high approval ratings were deceptive since many of those who admired him as the architect of victory had doubts that he would make a good peacetime leader. Also, he had never directed a campaign and

[74] Jefferys, *The Churchill Coalition*, p. 182.

his relationship with his party had always been fraught and complicated. Even the attempt to turn the election into a verdict on his leadership made Conservatism look like a one-man band and enabled Labour to highlight the many times he had been at odds with his party.

Labour had few illusions about focusing their campaign around the reticent, enigmatic, understated figure of Clement Attlee; rather the aim was to emphasize the party's reform programme and to present its leadership as a governing team, seasoned by long experience and solidly united in their aims. One can hardly imagine a starker contrast to the triumphal procession across the nation of Churchill and his entourage than Clement Attlee, driven from speech to speech by his wife Vi in their modest Standard Ten car, he quietly absorbed in a crossword and periodically passing her a peppermint. Labour's campaign was intelligent and well-executed with a clear and consistent message. It painted the pre-war period as one of unrelieved disaster for which the Tories were fully responsible. Conservatism, it was argued, had not changed; it still represented 'the forces of property and privilege' and, if elected, would scuttle plans for a New Britain and hand over control to the monopolists and profiteers. Whereas the Conservative manifesto, quaintly titled *Mr Churchill's Declaration of Policy to the Electors*, was a rushed job, vague on details, Labour's election programme, *Let Us Face the Future*, was carefully crafted. Largely drafted by Herbert Morrison, it was an astute combination of socialism and moderate pragmatism, designed to fulfil the expectations of the labour movement and also win over those of the middle classes who had moved left during the war.[75] It opened with a bold declaration of faith—'The Labour Party is a Socialist Party and proud of it'—and went on to lay out a comprehensive programme including social security, housing, full employment, and healthcare. The document championed Beveridge, economic planning, and committed Labour to public ownership of specific industries and services (coal, gas, electricity, inland transport, the Bank of England, iron and steel), defended mostly on grounds of economic efficiency. It was radical but moderate in tone 'striking a balance between a distinctive socialist alternative and a reasonable appeal to the middle ground in public opinion'.[76]

The Conservative vision for post-war Britain was far less coherent. The party had not developed an adequate response to Beveridge and while a group of young Tory reformers were pulling one way, embracing the need for significant reforms, others—including party chairman Ralph Assheton—were moving in the opposite direction and having second thoughts about concessions already made.[77] The

[75] Brooke, 'The Labour Party and the 1945 general election'. The one substantive change to Morrison's draft resulted from an amendment proposed by Ian Mikardo and passed at the 1944 party Conference despite the opposition of the NEC and Morrison. For the vague phrases of the original it substituted more concrete language about nationalizing land, large-scale building, heavy industry, banking, transport, fuel, and power.

[76] Brooke, 'The Labour Party and the 1945 general election', p. 13.

[77] On the Conservative campaign: M. D. Kandiah, 'The Conservative Party and the 1945 general election', *Contemporary Record*, 9(1) (Summer 1945). M. Francis argues that the Conservatives were less collectivist in the late 1940s than in the 1930s: '"Set the People Free"? Conservatives and the state, 1920–1960' in M. Francis and I. Zweiniger-Bargielowska (eds.), *The Conservatives and British Society, 1880–1990* (Cardiff, 1996).

hard-liners, who grew increasingly vocal, wanted to run an ideological campaign that conveyed their view that social reform must be predicated upon prosperity and that this required lower taxes, a dismantling of wartime controls, and speedy return to a competitive, market economy. They saw central planning and collectivist policies as serious constraints upon freedom and, since they lacked a unified message of their own, it is hardly surprising that the Conservative campaign quickly turned into a denunciation of Labour's statist solutions as un-British, at odds with the core values of the nation. Tory candidates found themselves both deploring the growth of the state and an all-powerful bureaucracy, while also claiming credit for the Coalition's White Papers on social welfare reform and employment policy. As a result the party's credibility as a vehicle for social reform continued to suffer, especially since it was the hard-line positions associated with Lord Beaverbrook—reported extensively in his newspapers—that attracted most public attention. Moreover, as the party in power Conservatives also bore the brunt of public frustration with immediate problems. During the campaign, for example, the first squatters or 'housing vigilantes', as they were then called, seized homes in Brighton and Southend, while the British Housewives League began its war on queuing. Labour blamed the Tories for their failure to tackle food and housing shortages—issues on which public patience seemed exhausted[78]—and when ministers replied quite honestly that there were no quick fixes, they met an indignant response from a nation sick of being told to put up with hardship and make do.

Two claims have dominated recent analyses of the 1945 election. First, it has been argued that relatively few substantive policy differences separated Conservatives and Labour, that the election turned primarily upon negative images of pre-war Toryism or who could be trusted to implement an agreed formula for post-war reconstruction; secondly, that the campaign was quiet, dull, and 'low key' with the public uninspired, 'dispirited', 'rather unfocused', and 'considering its opinions under a "cloak of apathy"'.[79] However, both of these claims, which fit into larger arguments about political consensus and voter passivity or disengagement in the post-war decades, are contradicted by much of what happened in the campaign. On the hustings there was little sign of a policy consensus and, if anything, in the course of the struggle party differences became magnified. Conservative reformers were far from controlling their party; it was the election defeat which altered the internal balance of power. The party largely fought the election on a platform of reduced taxes, a return to free enterprise, and an extension of social services, contingent on financial conditions. In addition, while electoral enthusiasm varied from place to place, there was little sign of voter apathy. Meetings in some formerly Conservative

[78] J. Ramsden, *Age of Churchill and Eden 1940–57* (London, 1995), p. 80, points out that '94 per cent of Tory candidates mentioned housing in their electoral addresses, but could not point to actual plans to prepare for a housing drive'. For public criticism of Churchill's caretaker administration: 'Apathy in Whitehall to the public needs', *The People*, 15 July 1945; 'Shop queues grow longer every day', *The People*, 24 June 1945, p. 8; on housing 'vigilantes': *Daily Mirror*, 7 July 1945, pp. 4–5.

[79] S. Fielding, 'What did "the people" want?: The meaning of the 1945 general election', *HJ*, 35(3) (1992), e.g. p. 632; J. Gardiner, *Wartime: Britain 1939–45* (London, 2004), p. 580: 'in the country the prevailing mood seemed to be one of apathy, scepticism and uncertainty'.

strongholds were notably subdued and poorly attended; but memoirs and contemporary accounts also reveal a tough, lively campaign with plenty of signs of public interest. Not only did Churchill, Attlee, Bevin, Eden, Cripps, and other leaders draw huge crowds, but relatively unknown candidates, some of them still in uniform, also found themselves speaking to packed halls. Barbara Betts (later Barbara Castle), running for the first time in Blackburn where the local women's section of the party had insisted on a female candidate, remembered, for example, the eve-of-poll gathering in St George's Hall: 'There were three thousand people there. Every seat occupied, they were lining the walls, they were hanging over the balconies, and there was a sort of unbelievable buoyancy in the atmosphere.' Similarly in rural Huntingdonshire, a National Liberal candidate recalled 'large halls packed with people out of sheer curiosity'. On troopships coming home or going out to the Far East, there were mock elections and in army bases overseas, officers and Other Ranks followed the contest with close interest.[80] Election broadcasts (more than twenty in all) got an average audience of 45 per cent and Churchill reached almost 60 per cent. In addition, there were factory-gate meetings, bomb-site meetings, and doorstep canvassing on a huge scale. As Jon Lawrence notes, in this election voters 'remained keen to meet candidates in the flesh as well as to catch party leaders on the radio or cinema newsreels . . . Direct personal contact remained central to electioneering.'[81]

The campaign was hard fought and nasty for that era: 'the bitterest general election . . . in many years' and 'one of the grubbiest in a dirty sequence' was how *The People* described it.[82] The fact that the two major parties had worked together in government for five years and had separated only five weeks before did not make their divorce any less acrimonious or the campaign any the less ideological. Conservatives blamed Labour for wrecking the Coalition; Labourites accused Churchill of calling a 'snap' election while servicemen were still overseas and before new voting registers were available, potentially excluding many who had relocated during the war. They also argued than an early July election effectively disfranchised over a million people, especially in Lancashire and Scotland, who traditionally took their holiday at that time, although eventually voting was rescheduled in nineteen constituencies. Public debate quickly focused on stark contrasts: private or public enterprise, freedom or centralized control and planning. On 4 June, in his first of four radio broadcasts, Churchill underscored party ideological differences warning that socialism was 'inseparably interwoven with totalitarianism and abject worship of the state' and that if Labour assumed power, it would have to fall back

[80] A. Mitchell, *Election '45: Reflections on the revolution in Britain* (London, 1995), pp. 44, 62; Elwyn Jones, *In My Time* (London, 1983), p. 84. During the 1951 election Charles Wintour of the *Evening Standard* (24 October 1951) reflected: 'The fire of 1945 has been lacking. Six years ago real venom and hatred were abroad.'

[81] J. Lawrence, *Electing Our Masters: The hustings in British politics from Hogarth to Blair* (Oxford, 2009), p. 136.

[82] *The People*, 24 June and 1 July 1945. My conclusions about press coverage are drawn from reading: *The Times, Daily Herald, The People, The Daily Express, Sunday Express, Daily Mirror,* and the *News of the World.* The last 5 of these are now available for the war years in microfilm: 'Popular newspapers during World War II', Adam Matthew Publications, 1993.

on 'some form of Gestapo...no doubt humanely administered in the first instance'. To a public that had recently seen pictures of Belsen and Buchenwald, his rhetoric aimed at familiar and well-regarded figures like Attlee, Bevin, and Morrison, seemed irresponsible and boomeranged. Attlee's riposte the following night was devastating: 'When I listened to the Prime Minister's speech...I realized at once what was his object. He wanted the electors to understand how great was the difference between Winston Churchill the great leader in war and Mr Churchill the Party leader of the Conservatives...I thank him for having disillusioned them so thoroughly. The voice we heard last night was that of Mr Churchill but the mind was that of Lord Beaverbrook.'[83]

In the nation's press the war of words was especially incendiary. A banner headline in Beaverbrook's *Daily Express* predicted a 'Gestapo in Britain if socialists win' (5 June); others regularly referred to 'The National Socialists'. Soon the claim that socialism was a foreign, Marxist imposition was linked to Labour's party chairman Harold Laski—or 'Gauleiter Laski' as he was more often called. With his Jewish, foreign-sounding name Laski was an easier target than Bevin, Dalton, or Attlee, especially when he foolishly questioned whether Attlee should accompany Churchill to the Potsdam peace talks, thereby linking Labour with Tory foreign-policy goals. This quickly escalated into claims that an unelected secret party caucus would hold real power if unthreatening Attlee were to win: 'They would dictate what to say and do, even where to queue', commented the *Daily Express*.[84] Scaremongering headlines abounded: 'Socialists split: Attlee repudiates Laski order' (16 June), 'Socialism even if it means violence' (20 June), 'Shall the Laski "25" rule Great Britain' (21 June), 'What Laski-ism would mean' (1 July), 'Dictators in session' (22 June).[85] Labour compared this barrage to the Zinoviev letter of 1924, a red herring to distract voters from real issues like healthcare, social insurance, housing, and jobs. Eventually Laski sued for libel, but Attlee and other Labour leaders were furious that their own chairman had handed the Tories this non-issue at a crucial moment in the campaign.

For the first time, however, political support in the press was fairly evenly divided and Labour papers retaliated in kind with headlines that screamed: 'Frauds, cheats, wrigglers seeking power', 'More babies die under Tory rule', 'A vote for Churchill is a vote for Franco'. Voters were warned 'Remember the unemployed between the wars' and election leaflets condemned 'The Gestapo methods of

---

[83] Though many believed that Beaverbrook and Bracken were behind these words, Churchill appears to have formulated the phrase himself. Groups of Conservatives, including party chairman Ralph Assheton, were much taken with Friedrich von Hayek's indictment of socialism, *The Road to Serfdom*, and had for some time been urging Churchill to adopt its anti-totalitarian stance as the central theme of the campaign. Richard Cockett describes the Gestapo comment as a clumsy echo of an Assheton speech: R. Cockett, *Thinking the Unthinkable: Think tanks and the economic counter-revolution, 1931–1983* (London, 1995), p. 94.

[84] *Daily Express*, 5 June 1945.

[85] All appeared in the *Daily Express*, except for the last which was the *Evening Standard* headline and referred to Labour's National Executive Committee. J. Thomas, '"Vote for them": The popular press and the 1945 election' in *idem, Popular Newspapers, the Labour Party and British Politics* (London, 2005).

the means test'.[86] Labour propaganda recycled radical critiques from the early war years: the betrayal of 1918 and 'starving Jarrow', guilty Appeasers and the stranglehold of the 'old gang' and 'vested interests'. The issue for Conservatives, argued Aneurin Bevan, was 'how to lie, deceive, cajole, and buy time so as once more to snatch a reprieve for wealth and privilege'. 'Make no mistake', Attlee told a crowd at West Bromwich, 'this is a conspiracy of greedy men who want the opportunity to do what their predecessors did in 1919.'[87] Reports of redundancies and queues at labour exchanges were given prominence. The *Daily Mirror* ran articles on the Tories' closure of tin mines in Cornwall and iron mines in Cumberland. A banner headline announced: 'Bevin answers steel ring: "New scheme to fix prices"'. Since Churchill's popularity was hard to puncture, Beaverbrook became the left's favourite target; he was, declared Bevin, 'the Minister of Chaos' and 'the most dangerous man in British public life'.[88] So recently the object of general adulation, by the campaign's end Churchill suddenly found himself facing hostile crowds and noisy hecklers in Walthamstow and other places in the London area.[89]

It is difficult to gauge the impact of this negative campaigning. Churchill's Gestapo broadcast was almost certainly damaging, while after their defeat many Conservatives blamed Beaverbrook for having injured their cause. Tory attacks also helped unify Labour and erase earlier friction that had developed between the party's leadership and rank and file. Labour's propaganda was more effective since it reiterated themes that had been central to wartime political discourse since Priestley's 'Postscripts' in the summer of 1940. This was especially the case with the campaign waged by the *Daily Mirror*. Throughout the war the *Mirror*'s influence as an independent progressive paper had grown steadily. It was deeply anti-Tory and while not uncritical of Labour's role in the Coalition, gave extensive coverage to leading Labour figures and aligned itself clearly with Beveridge's Plan and a social democratic reform agenda. Its tone was class-conscious, championing ordinary 'people' against 'vested interests' who were eager to return to the good old days of slums and unemployment. With a circulation of almost 2 million, it was influential both in reaching across the usual class boundaries and in attracting many youthful readers who were not normally engaged Labour's supporters. The *Mirror* never explicitly endorsed Labour, but it left no doubt where its preferences lay and its very successful 'Vote for him!' slogan, which quickly found its way into Labour speeches and publicity, was important in pressuring women to vote. Almost daily the paper appealed to wives, and indeed all civilians, to cast their vote for men in the forces, who—it was implied—had been excluded by slow and inefficient

---

[86] J. Thomas, 'Vote for them'; Headlines from *Daily Herald*, 26, 19, and 5 June 1945; the collection of campaign posters, leaflets, and election notices in the Labour History Archive and Study Centre, Manchester.

[87] A. Bevan ('Celticus'), *Why Not Trust the Tories* (London, 1944), p. 13; Attlee: *Daily Herald*, 20 June 1945. Also, *Daily Herald*, 11 June 1945, p.1, headline: 'Attlee: Back to poverty if Tories win'.

[88] *Daily Mirror*, 23 and 30 May 1945; *Daily Mirror*, 12 June 1945, p. 1; also *Daily Herald*, 12 June 1945, p. 1 (Bevin on price rings); *Daily Herald*, 11 June 1945, p. 1 ('Minister of Chaos').

[89] *Daily Express*, 4 July 1945 (Walthamstow); *Daily Express*, 26–7 June 1945 on large turn-outs for Churchill in the north.

registration procedures: 'Your man has fought for you. He is more entitled to have a say than anybody else.'[90] What *he* most wanted, the *Mirror* insisted, was a decent home, a job, security, and the assurance that pre-war inequality and unemployment would not be the reward for his sacrifices.[91]

When the European war ended, the *Mirror* published a legendary cartoon by Philip Zec: 'Here you are don't lose it again!' These words, encompassing promises of peace and social reform, are spoken by a wounded soldier, holding out a laurel wreath and climbing out of a war-torn landscape. The paper used the same image on its front page on polling day, along with its admonition 'Vote for them!' In terms of its visual representation, too, Labour enjoyed an advantage. The war was a 'golden age' of British cartoonists and many of the best—David Low, 'Vicky', and George Whitelaw, as well as Zec—exercised their talents for Labour, providing a political commentary in sharp-edged shorthand that became indelibly imprinted on readers' minds. One thinks of Zec's 'Tory Home Stores' where the 'fruits of victory' are concealed behind the counter, reserved for the rich and privileged. The party's illustrated leaflets and posters, produced in unprecedented quantities, were also clever and memorable. Among the most successful was 'And Now—Win the *Peace*' designed by the painter John Armstrong with its giant V for vote and victory set against a scene of neat houses, emblematic of post-war reconstruction. Equally important were the nine posters designed by Zec, including 'This is our chance to Labour for him' (featuring the smiling British Tommy) and 'Let's build the houses—quick!', which underscored voters' highest priority with its builder's trowel signifying vote and victory. In general, the social democratic visual culture of wartime benefited Labour—whether it was *Picture Post*, official posters, or films, the iconography of a 'People's War' served to reinforce Labour's message of change and a new democratic Britain.[92]

Between the wars Conservatives had successfully branded Labour as a sectional, trade union party—even on the left some had doubts it could ever surmount this and become a national voice of progressive opinion. But, as Paul Ward and Laura Beers have shown, in the 1930s Labour strategists worked hard to overcome this image and in 1945 they succeeded in their dual strategy of presenting the party as both national—the natural home of all progressives whatever their class—and as

---

[90] *Daily Mirror*, 29 June 1945.

[91] A. C. H. Smith, E. Immirzi, and T. Blackwell, *Paper Voices: The popular press and social change 1935–65* (New Jersey, 1975), ch. 3. The appeal also underscored Labour's charge that serving men were being disfranchised by a 'snap' election. What rings loudest today, however, is the slogan's subordination of women through loyalty (a 'sacred trust') and its discordance with wartime rhetoric about women's citizenship rights and obligations. *Daily Mirror* headlines included: 'I'll vote for him' (27 June), 'A sacred trust for women in Britain' (28 June). Some historians have downplayed the *Mirror*'s support for Labour: Fielding, 'What did "the people" want?', p. 64; J. Thomas, 'A "cloak of apathy": Political disengagement, popular politics and the *Daily Mirror* 1940–1945', *Journalism Studies*, 5(4) (2004). But while Cecil King and other important figures on the *Mirror* favoured some kind of left coalition earlier in the war, by 1945 they were committed to Labour.

[92] Donald Zec, *Don't Lose It Again! The life and wartime cartoons of Philip Zec* (London, 2005); J. Gorman, 'The Labour Party's election posters in 1945', *Labour History Review*, 61(3) (Winter 1996); P. Rennie, 'Socialvision: Visual culture and social democracy in Britain during World War II', *Journal of War and Culture Studies*, 1(3) (2008).

the political vehicle of the working class.[93] At times these two identities conflicted, but in the campaign at least such tensions were masked by the unifying language of patriotic populism. Now it was Labour that successfully branded Conservatism as the party of special privilege and narrow class interests. But the fact that Labour was vying for moderate voters did not mean that its rhetoric was moderate; here one needs to distinguish between the campaign at the national and local levels. Compared to later elections, very little central control was exercised over candidates. They endorsed the party's programme, of course, but also retained a good deal of latitude over the tone of their campaign and had little fear of being covered by the national media. As a result, many local candidates went far beyond the party manifesto in their radicalism, calling for a direct challenge to capitalist society. As one London candidate put it: 'It's not a simple question of Box replacing Cox. We have to settle by our votes who is to control the wealth and resources of Britain and in whose interests.'[94] Another result of the latitude permitted to local campaigns was that many Labour candidates accepted help from CP activists. The groundwork had been laid in war years by the growth of support for a popular front and since the CP fielded only twenty-two candidates, many of its organizers felt free to work for Labour. In one constituency, for example, no less than six sub-agents were party members; in another a CP member handled about 15 per cent of the division. In Lancaster, previously a safe Tory seat, where earlier relations with Labour had been very bad, the party was given full responsibility for one ward and at a big eve-of-poll gathering three CP representatives were on the platform. In North Staffordshire about half of party members were estimated to be active in Labour campaigns; in Bristol, CP members canvassed and raised money in the factories for Labour. At Maldon, where journalist Tom Driberg as an Independent had upset the Tory candidate in 1942, the CP's district press officer was in charge of press affairs for Driberg's re-election. Where the races were tight and especially in rural and previously Tory areas, CP assistance was especially welcomed. In Chelmsford the Labour election committee included representatives from the CP, Common Wealth, and the Co-operative Party. In Colchester it was reported that the cooperation had 'become a reality in the election'. In the South Midlands, CP members sat on election committees, spoke at public meetings, and canvassed. In other places, of course, offers of assistance were rejected.[95] But, after their victory,

---

[93] P. Ward, 'Preparing for the People's War: Labour and patriotism in the 1930s', *Labour History Review*, 67(2) (August 2002); Beers, *Your Britain*.

[94] J. Schneer, 'The Labour left and the general election of 1945' in J. M. W. Bean, *The Political Culture of Modern Britain* (London, 1987), p. 269. James Callaghan, then a young naval lieutenant and candidate for Cardiff South, recalled: 'We fought on our own . . . There weren't those quantities of leaflets or instructions or things you ought to concentrate on . . . I'm quite sure I would promise the earth. I had no reason not to. So I wouldn't care for all my speeches made in that election to be known about now': A. Mitchell, 'July days: Memories of Britain's "Modern Revolution"', *History Today*, 45 (July 1995).

[95] CPGB 1945: 'General election campaign' details these local CP activities; the reports are from district officers to Peter Kerrigan at CP/CENT/ORG, Labour History Archive and Study Centre, Manchester. The file did not have a specific location label at the time I read it. In North Aberdeen it was Labour's Election Agent ('a very inefficient and obstinate fellow') who was the major obstacle to

numerous Labour branches wrote letters of appreciation for the help they received. The MP for Portsmouth, for example, thanked the local CP branch profusely for its efforts and, while acknowledging the constraints of Labour's ban on working together, voiced the hope that the next party Conference might usher in 'a new era of unity' by supporting both the affiliation of the CP and Common Wealth. The Labour agent for Barrow-in-Furness wrote: 'Whilst we may disagree on the small details, let us remain united in spirit and in our determination to bring into being the Better World that we have desired for so long.' Also striking was the number of Labour Party post-election parties to which CP members were invited. One East Anglian organizer enquired: 'I don't know whether you have any other cases reported of the Labour party hiring a bus to bring the Communists to a Labour party social?' A number of reports also cited Labour ward committees passing resolutions in favour of further cooperation, especially for the forthcoming municipal elections.[96]

While most of the nation voted on 5 July, the results were not declared until the 26th, permitting additional voting in Scotland and Lancashire and the transportation of the armed forces' ballots from overseas. Even after the campaign, few expected a Labour landslide, although there was a lot of nervous optimism among party supporters. But once the results started coming in, the scale of Labour's victory soon became clear. Harold Macmillan's loss at Stockton was among the first, then came other defeats of front-bench Tories, including Leo Amery, Brendan Bracken, Hore-Belisha, Duncan Sandys, and the party chairman, Ralph Assheton. Labour not only swept its traditional industrial strongholds, but captured numerous seats for the first time. Provincial cities like Plymouth, Taunton, Winchester, York, and Lincoln went Labour, so did suburban seats like Wimbledon, Hendon, and Dulwich, while in Birmingham, which the Chamberlain family had long dominated, Labour took ten of thirteen seats.[97] In English boroughs outside London it won 173 seats, compared to 53 in 1935; the party also carried much of the belt of middle-class suburbs around London where Morrison's victory in East Lewisham was symptomatic, turning a 6,000 vote Conservative majority into a Labour one with a 15,000 vote margin.[98] Even in rural county seats Labour made large gains, dominating those in Wales, drawing almost even with the Conservatives in Scotland, and doing especially well in Norfolk. This, as Clare Griffiths has shown, was the result of a determined effort between the wars to build up Labour organization in the countryside, but the sudden surge of support

cooperation; in Aylesbury the Labour candidate Reg Groves vetoed any help from the CP which included canvassing, although this was reversed under pressure from the local AEU branch.

[96] G. Donald Bruce to local CP (Portsmouth), 22 July 1945; G. Linton (Sec. of Barrow-in-Furness CP branch) to Central Organization Department, CP, 25 July 1945 (reproducing in full a letter of 17 July from the Labour agent, J. Hexham); M. Cornforth, 17 July 1945 (East Anglian weekly report, 9–16 July 1945) on the 'Labour social'; CPGB 1945: 'General election campaign'.

[97] R. P. Hastings, 'The Birmingham Labour movement, 1918–45', *Midland History*, 5 (1979–80), 88; S. Bussey, 'The Labour victory in Winchester in 1945', *Southern History*, 8 (1986).

[98] Arguably the war years created closer community between London and its surrounding suburban belt. The suburbs and the inner city shared the alarms, raids, and destruction and those journeying into jobs by commuter trains and buses experienced daily the devastation of the central districts.

in 1945 showed that agricultural districts had experienced their own wartime shift to the left.[99] The swing towards Labour varied a good deal, the average being 12 per cent, but in Birmingham and the London area it was 23 and 18 per cent respectively.

In all Labour won 393 seats to 213 for the Conservatives and their allies; the Liberals gained only twelve seats and the Communists two. Labour's lead in votes— almost 12 million (48 per cent) to just under 10 million (40 per cent) for the Conservatives—was less dramatic but still large: an increase of 3.5 million for Labour over its 1935 result.[100] For the smaller parties the election was particularly disappointing. Having fielded 306 candidates, the Liberals got only 9 per cent of the total votes, but many of the votes they got came from former Conservatives unwilling to opt for Labour. Even Liberal leader Sir Archibald Sinclair and Beveridge were defeated. As for Common Wealth, the focus of such exaggerated hopes in the last war years, it achieved victory in only one of its twenty-three races.[101] Finally, the CP polled a mere 102,000 votes (0.4 per cent of the total), winning only in West Fife, a party stronghold for many years, and Mile End, Stepney, where the party had developed a loyal following among East End Jews since its pre-war campaigns against Mosley's fascists. Harry Pollitt, who had cultivated the South Wales mining constituency of Rhondda East throughout the war years, lost narrowly to Labour but received 45 per cent of the vote. Given the party's high hopes just two years before, it was a bitter but not unexpected blow. The Labour leadership's gamble that their party constituted the only rational choice for the left and that they could successfully absorb the large bloc of progressive voters had paid off.

In the wake of this defeat some Conservatives blamed the decline of their party machinery, arguing that while Labour spent the previous five years opportunistically promoting its brand of politics and maintaining its party organization, they had focused far more on actually winning the war. It is true that Labour was better prepared and far better financed for this election than previous ones, but a comparison of the two major parties shows that Labour's advantages were often exaggerated. At the national level Transport House was well-organized and it had the backing of an expanded and well-financed trade union movement, but constituency parties varied a good deal in efficiency and leadership quality. In general, recent accounts suggest that the difference this time was that Conservatives failed to gain the electoral 'bonus' that derived from their normally superior organization. Certainly, Labour ran a more effective campaign and not simply because their

---

[99] Clare V. J. Griffiths, *Labour and the Countryside: The politics of rural Britain 1918–39* (Oxford, 2007); J. Stevenson, 'The countryside, planning, and civil society in Britain, 1926–1947' in J. Harris (ed.), *Civil Society in British History: Ideas, identities, institutions* (Oxford, 2004).

[100] The 8% advantage in voting translated into Labour getting 61% of the parliamentary seats.

[101] Liberals increased their total vote over 1935 by 858,000 votes, but they were not decisive in tipping particular seats from Tory to Labour; most voters having decided that they were no longer a viable governing party. The minutes of the King's Norton branch, Birmingham, illustrate Common Wealth's decline, revealing a rapid drop in attendance and activity (Birmingham Central Library). Shortly after the 1945 election the branch disbanded altogether; most of its members joined the Labour Party and the reconstructed Birmingham branch of the Fabian Society.

message was more attuned to voters' aspirations; as a party leader Churchill made serious tactical mistakes and the decision to focus the campaign so heavily upon his personal leadership was dangerous at a time when voters were issue-oriented and polls showed lingering doubts about his capacity as a peacetime leader. But, despite all the problems, the margin between the two parties actually narrowed during the course of the campaign.

Most historical analyses have explained the upset as a consequence of the social, economic, and ideological changes produced by the war. Richard Titmuss, for example, argued that it generated greater social solidarity and a national willingness to accept a large increase in egalitarian policies and state intervention. Arthur Marwick viewed the election as a victory for 'middle opinion'—referring to the numerous cross-party planning and reform groups that emerged in the 1930s— whose 'middle-of-the-road collectivism' was well-suited to the exigencies of war-time society.[102] Most importantly, in *The Road to 1945* Paul Addison traced the development of a broad cross-party consensus about basic principles and policies for post-war reconstruction among the political and civil service elites. In his view, little separated the Labour and Conservative programmes put forward in 1945; rather the election was a rejection of the Tories more than an endorsement of Labour. Many other historians have subscribed to this view that the election focused largely on grudges about the past, rather than hopes for a better future. But while there is obviously truth in this, there is also a danger of exaggeration. Recent studies—by Kevin Jefferys, Stephen Brooke, and Harriet Jones, to list only three—have underscored the ideological and policy differences within the Coali-tion, both the consistency of Conservatism pre- and post-war and the independent evolution of Labour's programme after the political crisis of 1931.[103] Voters did have a choice in 1945 and many were well aware of that. Moreover, interpreting the outcome as primarily a renunciation of Conservatism often has the effect of portraying Labour as the passive beneficiary of a windfall when, in fact, the party played an active role in laying the groundwork for its victory. This emphasis on the negativism of the vote also minimizes popular hopes and expectations at the war's end and the degree to which Labour's message captured the public mood. Stephen Fielding, for example, has argued that many anti-Conservative votes went to Labour because the Liberals were divided and failed to contest half of the seats. But BIPO polls showed that voters overwhelmingly declared they would not have supported a Liberal candidate had one been running in their district.[104] Another claim is that in 1945 'political considerations came a poor second to bread and

---

[102] R. M. Titmuss, *Problems of Social Policy* (London, 1950); A. Marwick, 'Middle opinion in the thirties: Planning, progress and political "agreement"', *EHR*, 79(311) (April 1964); Addison, *The Road to 1945*; D. Ritschel, *The Politics of Planning* (Oxford, 1997).

[103] K. Jefferys, 'British politics and social policy during the Second World War', *HJ*, 30(1) (1987); Brooke, *Labour's War*; H. Jones, '"New Conservatism?": The industrial charter, modernity and the reconstruction of British Conservatism after the war' in B. Conekin, F. Mort, and C. Waters (eds.), *Moments of Modernity: Reconstructing Britain 1945–1964* (London, 1999).

[104] Fielding, 'What did "the people" want?'; G. H. Gallup, *The Gallup International Public Opinion Polls of Great Britain 1937–1975* (New York, 1976), p. 114 (July 1945), p. 116 (August 1945).

butter issues'; soldiers and workers, it is argued, were primarily interested in demobilization, housing, and preserving wartime wage gains, not politics.[105] But this sharp separation of private and political spheres is unconvincing; such issues were intrinsically political and they were central in the campaign. Workers recognized that solutions to these issues were not simply private or personal; their leverage, as producers and citizens, was collective and their political goals embraced general entitlements like healthcare, housing, education, and economic security.[106]

While recent analyses have downplayed the dramatic shift that had taken place in British politics, it certainly seemed sensational at the time—all the more so because unexpected. Conservatism had sustained its largest defeat since the Liberal triumph of 1906. Some punditry was predictably overblown, talking about a Tory Waterloo: 'Without much fuss and without any shooting', *The People* announced, 'we *have* brought about a political revolution.'[107] But, hyperbole aside, many commentators accurately understood that the election had changed the social fault lines of interwar politics and broken the logjam of Conservative dominance.[108] There were large defections to Labour among suburban middle-class voters—not those defined as solidly middle class or upper-middle, but among clerical and service employees, technicians, teachers, lower-paid professionals, and managers. According to sociologist David Lockwood, 47 per cent of clerical workers voted for Labour while John Bonham's analysis of Gallup polls put the figures at 31 per cent of middle-class voters and 44 per cent of the lower-middle-class.[109] *The Economist* announced: 'The greatest paradox of British politics in the past quarter century—the faithfulness to the Tories of the propertyless lower-middle class—is at an end.'[110] The Baldwinite anti-socialist coalition of the pre-war years had been replaced by a concept of the national 'public' which drew a sharp distinction between the interests of 'ordinary people'—industrial workers and lower-middle-class strata—and those of wealthier and privileged groups. Labour also captured the overwhelming support of young people (including those in the armed forces) who had reached voting age since 1935. They had grown up in the 1930s and wartime mobilization had a huge impact on their lives and outlook; in 1945 they constituted by some estimates 20 per cent of the electorate and 67 per cent went for Labour.[111] At the same time the Conservatives lost their traditional advantage with women voters. Already by June 1943, although few contemporaries were aware of it, the 'gender gap' had been eliminated and two years later Labour retained a small lead.

[105] Fielding, Thompson, and Tiratsoo, *England Arise!*, p. 33.

[106] A. Offer, 'British manual workers: From producers to consumers, *c.*1950–2000', *Contemporary British History*, 22(4) (December 2008), 540–1.

[107] *The People*, 29 July 1945, p. 2.

[108] R. McKibbin, 'Class and conventional wisdom: The Conservative Party and the "public" in inter-war Britain' in *idem, The Ideologies of Class* (Oxford, 1990).

[109] D. Lockwood, *The Black-Coated Worker* (London, 1958); J. Bonham, *The Middle-Class Vote* (London, 1954).

[110] *The Economist*, 28 July 1945.

[111] M. Franklin and M. Ladner, 'The undoing of Winston Churchill: Mobilization and conversion in the 1945 realignment of British voters', *British Journal of Political Science*, 25 (1995), 444–5. The authors offer a demographic cohort explanation of the 1945 result which I find only partly convincing.

Working-class women were especially drawn to Labour for both reasons of class solidarity and practical politics. They believed Labour was more likely to enact reforms and they feared that Conservatives might exacerbate shortages by eliminating rationing and controls.[112] Above all 1945 marked a dramatic (and enduring) shift of working-class voters away from Conservatism. In 1935 workers accounted for some 50 per cent of Tory votes; that proportion fell dramatically to 30 per cent in 1945. By most estimates Labour managed to poll about 70 per cent of the working-class vote in 1945 and for the first time the party could convincingly claim to be *the* party of workers. On class, gender, and generational grounds the election had reshaped the earlier social configuration of politics; the big question was whether this new electoral coalition was ephemeral—the product of a distinctive conjuncture—or if it could prove a stable basis for a politics of the left.

The most compelling explanation for this realignment is that the war had moved political opinion to the left and that Labour's programme and rhetoric best accorded with popular hopes for reform and a fresh beginning. Ross McKibbin has suggested that the collapse of confidence in the Conservatives was 'extraordinarily sudden' and they could not have won an election after July 1940.[113] Certainly, public shock over the defeat of France and fears of air raids and an invasion fostered almost an apocalyptic mood in some circles. But the crisis of 1940 was political, focused on Chamberlain and the Appeasers; it took longer to escalate into a broader indictment of the social and political order. In January 1941 postal censorship summarized popular expectations: 'They are looking forward confidently to a post-war levelling of class distinction and a redistribution of wealth.' A Home Office survey in 1942 found that while only a small minority of people were knowledgeable about the details of post-war planning and some felt it almost indecent to talk about reconstruction while Stalingrad was being turned into rubble, when pressed most had definite opinions. They included the usual catch phrases: no return to the pre-war order, a continuation of controls and equal sacrifice after the war, checks on profiteering and property speculation, and an end to the tradition of 'privileged' and 'leisured' classes. By 1943 people expressed definite ideas about what they wanted from a post-war settlement, but were uncertain about whether it would materialize; they emphasized job security, an end to poverty, better housing, educational opportunity, and a more equal society.[114] Disappointment over the government's reception of the Beveridge Report greatly heightened cynicism—and Mass-Observation began trying to measure the

[112] I. Zweiniger-Bargielowska, 'Explaining the gender gap: The Conservative Party and the women's vote, 1945–1964' in M. Francis and I. Zweiniger-Bargielowska (eds.), *The Conservatives and British Society, 1880–1990* (Cardiff, 1996); R. J. Hinton, 'Women and the Labour vote, 1945–50', *Labour History Review*, 57(3) (1992); A. Black and S. Brooke, 'The Labour Party, women, and the problem of gender, 1951–1966', *JBS*, 36(4) (October 1997). In 1945 women voters split 45–43% in Labour's favour, but the BIPO poll of June 1943 showed Labour with almost a 6% margin.
[113] McKibbin, *Parties and People: England 1914–1951*, ch. 4. The poll data are unclear but it does appear that criticism of Chamberlain's government had already grown substantially prior to the war, although that does not mean that Labour could have won an election in 1940.
[114] NA: INF 1/292, 8–15 January 1941; NA: HO 262/16, 'Special investigations by Home Intelligence' (1942–6): October 1942 special report on 'Public interest in reconstruction plans'. On education: M-OA: FR 1269, 'Opinion about post-war education', 21 May 1942.

gap between popular hopes and expectations. Was the defeat of Conservatives inevitable? Quite probably, although dissatisfaction with the Tories did not translate automatically into support for Labour. Had Conservatives been quicker to give guarantees about post-war reform and the Beveridge Report in 1943 they might have been able to capitalize more on Churchill's undeniable popularity. We can agree with Harriet Jones that 'the Beveridge Report was one of those episodes which seemed to bring out the worst judgment in many Conservative politicians'.[115]

Was 1945 a vote for socialism? A BIPO poll of August 1945 is interesting here: when those who had voted for Labour were asked to give their main reason, 51 per cent answered 'best for the working class' or that the party stood for socialism or what they wanted; 9 per cent said they always voted Labour; 11 per cent cited their hatred for the Tories; 19 per cent 'wanted to see a change'.[116] Certainly, the Labour Party made it clear that it was a socialist party and considered its agenda to be a first instalment. Some voters, especially among trade union activists, wanted socialism and had a reasonably clear idea of what they meant by it. Others voted for Beveridge and better housing and believed that they were more likely to get them from Labour. For miners nationalization was a key issue, for other groups it was minor.[117] Some had radical expectations; others were a good deal more modest, having been disappointed before. Electoral victories come from forging diverse coalitions. The tone in 1945 was less strident and the objectives more limited than in the early war years when there was an almost apocalyptic mood, fanned by fears of defeat. But a majority of people voted for significant change, believing that the pre-war order was unfair and unacceptable. Bitter memories of Lloyd George's empty promise of 'homes for heroes' and growing anxiety about housing and unemployment might focus people upon more limited objectives but the rhetoric of radical change was everywhere. And when measured against the bleak images of pre-war unemployment, the rhetoric of planning, social welfare, equal opportunity, and democratic control—the very idea of a 'People's Peace'—seemed to presage a new beginning.

---

[115] H. Jones, 'The Conservative Party and the welfare state', PhD Diss., London University, 1992, p. 69.

[116] Gallup, *The Gallup International Public Opinion Polls*, p. 116 (August 1945). Asked in July 1945 if they expected the government to introduce sweeping changes or govern along existing lines only more efficiently 56% answered 'sweeping changes' to 30% 'existing lines': *ibid.*, p. 114.

[117] Between March 1944 and May 1945 BIPO polls showed the public favouring nationalization of coal (60% to 16%), railways (54% to 26%), land (51% to 31%), and the Bank of England (39% to 20%). *The Gallup International Public Opinion Polls*, pp. 88, 103, 108.

Conclusion

What difference did the war make? This question has been asked many times. It lay behind Richard Titmuss's hugely influential *Problems of Social Policy* (1950) and just about every major study to appear since then. In the mid-1950s Stanislaw Andrzejewski tried to give the question a theoretical framework with his 'military participation ratio'. Simply put, he argued that because modern warfare calls for full participation and sacrifices by all social groups, it has a levelling effect—that marginal groups, especially workers, women, and poorer groups in society, reap the benefit of their efforts in the form of increased social power and new citizenship rights. Arthur Marwick's several studies, originally developed for a course on war and social change at the Open University, adopted a similar perspective, although he placed more emphasis upon social consciousness and war's influence as a catalyst, accelerating social trends already underway. More recent work, however, has often dismissed or seriously qualified claims that the Second World War constituted a 'turning-point' in British history. Studies of the welfare state point to the roots of Labour's legislation in Edwardian and interwar concepts of welfare; research on women has seriously weakened older claims that the war was a liberating experience or had a lasting impact on gender roles; and recent accounts have toned down Titmuss's view that heightened social and national unity generated a 'war-warmed impulse of people for a more generous society'.[1] Labour's electoral victory in 1945, some historians have argued, was chiefly a rejection of Conservatism in a situation where there was not a lot of difference separating the programmes of the two major parties. Others on the left contend that while there was an opportunity for sweeping change, the result was less than it could have been owing to Labour's moderation or the limited horizons of the population at large. Finally, recent accounts of nationalism, emphasizing the divisions produced by gender, class, and ethnicity, have raised doubts about the extent of the much mythicized wartime solidarity.

These works have complicated our view of the war period and, in many cases, have greatly advanced our understanding. But taken together they are conducive to a flattening of the historical landscape, prioritizing continuity over change. There is evidence, however, of a steady counter-flow, a movement to re-emphasize the war

---

[1] R. Titmuss, *Problems of Social Policy* (London, 1950), p. 508. Also, S. Andrzejewski, *Military Organisation and Society* (London, 1954); A Marwick, *Britain in the Century of Total War* (London, 1968); *idem, War and Social Change in the Twentieth Century* (London, 1974); *idem* (ed.), *Total War and Social Change* (London, 1988).

as a historical 'watershed'. Recent studies, including those of John Welshman, have restated the war's importance in shaping the modern 'social service' state; Jose Harris has argued that total war legitimated state power 'in ways that would have been inconceivable in the 1930s, other than in the realm of revolutionary speculation'. Correlli Barnett's provocative studies attack the wartime flowering of 'New Jerusalem' ideals among the elites as a powerful corrosive force, accelerating Britain's decline. David Edgerton has underscored its significance in Britain's development as a 'warfare state' and the creation of a military-scientific elite, while others have argued that 'the importance of the 1940s and 1950s as a social and psychological turning-point is only beginning to be considered seriously'.[2] The argument advanced in *Blood, Sweat, and Toil* also reaffirms the war's major role in shaping Britain's social and political development. In this conclusion, it is helpful to recapitulate some of the social, political, and cultural reasons for such a conclusion.

The war transformed the power and status of the working classes within society. As Bevin understood immediately, the nation's survival in 1940 rested upon the full participation of industrial workers, upon fighting a people's war which carried the promise of a more just and less class-bound society. The war marked the beginning of a long, sustained period of full employment, rising wages, and improving conditions for workers; and while its continuation was not a function of the war, this simple fact, which brought a new level of stability and possibility to the lives of the working class, sharply distinguishes the period from 1940 to the end of the 1960s from earlier decades. Full employment removed the single most important division among workers: between the employed and those on the dole. Industries like coal, shipbuilding, and heavy engineering became vital to the war economy and the communities that depended on them—traditional heartlands of the labour movement in the north, Scotland, and Wales which had languished between the wars—recovered rapidly. Government siting of new war-production facilities in those areas further expanded job opportunities, especially for women, while post-war conversion into trading estates and further government relocation policies bolstered the gains made before 1945.

Among the biggest beneficiaries was the trade union movement. The war years not only revived the old centres of union strength but extended organization to many areas where it had previously been weak. With 9 million members at the war's end (3 million more than at its beginning), trade unionism had become, as Citrine boasted, 'a governing estate of the realm' whose influence extended to all areas of policy. Joint consultation structures stretched from peak policy-making levels all the way down to shop-floor networks and plant-level committees and by the end of 1946 statutory wage agreements covered some 88 per cent of the nation's

---

[2] J. Welshman, 'Evacuation and social policy during the Second World War: Myth and reality', *TCBH*, 9(1) (1998); J. Harris, 'Beveridge's social and political thought' in J. Hills *et al.* (eds.), *Beveridge and Social Security: An international retrospective* (Oxford, 1994), p. 27; D. Edgerton, *Warfare State: Britain 1920–1970* (Cambridge, 2006); C. Barnett, *The Audit of War* (London, 1986); R. Bessel and D. Schumann (eds.), *Life after Death: Approaches to a cultural and social history of Europe during the 1940s and 1950s* (Cambridge, 2003), p. 7. Also, B. Brivati and H. Jones (eds.), *What Difference Did the War Make?* (Leicester, 1993).

labour force. The balance of power between labour and capital had shifted significantly since the 1930s and workers emerged from the war with a stronger collective sense of being a powerful national interest group. When Ferdynand Zweig interviewed manual workers in the late 1940s they repeatedly expressed the view that they were 'the backbone' of the nation.[3]

But the strength and prestige of unions also encouraged complacency. Advocates of trade union reorganization which might eliminate overlaps, encourage amalgamations, or move towards a system of industrial unions covering whole industries, could make no headway at all. The creation of thousands of workplace JPCs which many union organizers at the time and historian James Hinton have characterized as an important initiative towards shared decision-making and industrial citizenship also came to nothing. Many workers had little interest in helping to run things, preferring a clear differentiation of managerial and worker functions, while employers were equally reluctant and uncooperative, viewing them at best as an experiment in improving dialogue and progressive management, rather than a step towards joint decision-making. And while the TUC became an increasingly important pillar of post-war corporatist arrangements and was absorbed into the business of running the country, its ability to exercise authority over affiliated unions was always limited. It relied heavily on persuasion and compromise and the bloc votes of the large unions. Often a target of criticism during periods of industrial conflict, it had little real power over a fragmented union movement.

Arguably, the war strengthened the more conservative sections of trade unionism, making modernization more difficult. It also greatly reinforced public faith in traditional structures of voluntary wage bargaining. If voluntarism had survived the exigencies of total war (and was even deemed crucial in the defeat of Nazism) there was little chance it would be swept aside in peacetime. Both sides of industry believed in a self-regulating system that preserved their autonomy and freedom. Thus while the TUC supported state activism in many areas post-war, it fiercely resisted government regulation of the labour market or a national wage policy. This was one reason (but only one) for the limited nature of post-war economic and industrial planning; once in office the different meanings attached to the wartime mantra of planning became increasingly intractable. Labour retreated from a socialist planned economy to Keynesian demand management techniques similar to those seen by many capitalists as a reasonable alternative to a free market economy.

The war's impact on the lives of working-class women, most historians have concluded, was huge at the time but of limited duration when measured in terms of conventional gender roles, sex-segregated jobs, pay, and employment rates. Post-war decades saw dramatic transformations in the lives of working-class women, but these derived not from the war but the long economic boom and expanding employment opportunities. In general, wartime separations, anxiety about marital breakdown, eugenic worries about low birth rates, and rising alarm about juvenile delinquency all helped strengthen society's focus upon the recreation of family life

---

[3] F. Zweig, *The British Worker* (London, 1952), p. 208.

and with it an emphasis upon a woman's priority as mother, home-maker, and the pivotal figure in the well-being of the family as conceived as a psychological unit. During the war working-class women were disproportionately the target of negative criticism about neglectful parents, and lower sexual standards or 'good time girls'; now they became the focus of discussions about social welfare and domestic science in school curricula. The implementation of Beveridge meant that women gained benefits as dependants of men, while the post-war continuation of austerity and rationing also placed a premium on women's capacities as domestic managers. In all these ways the outcome of the war was to reinforce traditional roles. And yet, as Summerfield has argued, many women believed that their lives and self-esteem were profoundly shaped by their war experiences.[4] I have also suggested that young women conscripted for war work emerged from their experiences conscious of their contribution to the national effort and with a heightened sense of entitlement. They might see their future in conventional terms as wives and mothers, but they wanted more security, better housing, opportunities for their children—in short, a better life than had been the fate of the older generation. When they voted for the first time in 1945 they went heavily for Labour because its programme seemed closely aligned with their goals and most remained loyal to that choice for years thereafter.

In a path-breaking study, *Which People's War?*, Sonya Rose has examined national identity and citizenship in the war years. Her analysis focuses on the efforts of the media and official propaganda to construct and project a unitary concept of the nation. Rose stresses the contradictions between the unity conveyed by the idea of a 'people's war' and the reality of a nation fractured by class, gender, ethnicity, region, and other forms of identity. 'There was', she writes, 'no one-size-fits-all Britishness even when the people of Britain were at war.'[5] The approach produces valuable insights, showing, for example, how women, men, Caribbean contract workers, and social classes experienced citizenship differently and the multiple and contradictory demands upon women. But Rose's image of a tightly formed 'unitary concept' of the nation which acted as a 'master social category' is overdrawn. There were multiple, overlapping versions of the nation and national character in play during the war years even in official and media publicity. Patriotism was open to challenge and redefinition: certainly workers did not accept that loyal citizenship required passivity at home and many in the most troubled industries felt that patriotism had become a convenient tool for limiting workplace demands and eroding traditional practices. But in describing the gap between 'people's war' rhetoric and the reality of social differentiation, Rose also deploys language that overstates the tensions as 'potentially destabilizing' and the nation as 'fragile', 'threatened', and 'riddled with contradictions', where 'the pull to unity was haunted by the spectre of division and difference'.[6] Here it is important to

---

[4] For example, P. Summerfield, 'Approaches to women and social change in the Second World War' in Brivati and Jones (eds.), *What Difference Did the War Make?*

[5] S. Rose, *Which People's War? National identity and citizenship in wartime Britain 1939–1945* (Oxford, 2003), p. 286.

[6] *Ibid.*, pp. 108, 135, 149, 287, and 286.

distinguish between frames of reference—between differences that were perceived as separating Britons and what really defined their common ties, namely the larger external divide between themselves and foreigners (Germans, Italians, Americans, and Russians being especially important for purposes of wartime comparison). Like all such slogans, the 'people's war' was effective because it was vague. People lived with the contradictions; they welcomed, invested in, and were energized by wartime national myths—in, for example, Churchill's speeches to the nation— even as they understood that the prevailing rhetoric of unity, fair shares, and equality was often contradicted by social reality. As *Blood, Sweat, and Toil* argues, wartime debates about evacuation, women's work, leisure, social policy, and the failings of the pre-war political order were all heavily inflected by class. And yet, paradoxically, the sense of national identity and belonging also remained strong throughout the conflict.

What was new and most important for the working class about the dominant national iconography was its inclusivity. The implicit definition and symbolism of the nation underwent a change. For the first time workers were represented as synonymous with the nation: as producers, members of the armed forces, firemen, and raid victims—as good as anyone else. Often class and nation seem to place contradictory claims upon the individual, but discourses about class imply claims about its place in the nation; both are in Benedict Anderson's sense 'imagined communities', interdependent and reciprocally constructed. Wartime multiplied the connections between people's lives and the state; they were constantly addressed as a vital part of the nation and they found ways to assert their own needs. This kind of patriotism underscored the ties that bound different social strata together, but it also generated popular expectations and the idea, however ill-defined, that Britain was moving towards a more democratic and less unequal future. Workers emerged from the war more conscious of their power as producers and citizens; this power was collective, not individual, and its political objectives were universal entitlements, claimed as a right, in the form of jobs, better housing, healthcare, and more opportunity.

This inclusive conception of the nation was a factor in 1945 when Labour succeeded in marketing itself as both the party that best represented the whole nation and as the political vehicle of the working class. Unlike in pre-war elections when Labour was routinely labelled anti-patriotic, in this one it was the Conserva- tives who were branded as the party of narrow, sectional interests. There was no shortage of criticism of Labour earlier in the war, especially in the turbulent year 1942, but as peace drew near it became the most convincing voice of reform and overturned the electoral sociology that sustained pre-war Conservative dominance. Using wartime populist language that contrasted productive citizens and privileged elites, it redefined its natural constituency, winning over a significant segment of middle and especially lower-middle-class voters. Aided by Beveridge, Labour managed to channel the somewhat unfocused radicalism of the early war years, but whether it could hold together its winning coalition of socialists and moderates, trade unionists and suburban middle class, was unclear. The new government pressed forward with its programme of nationalizations and social welfare reform, repeatedly invoking the spirit of wartime egalitarianism and social citizenship; it achieved a great deal in its first three years, which guaranteed the loyalty of its working-class base, but the combination of continuing austerity and controls, high taxes, and socialism in power precipitated a growing middle-class backlash which frayed the sense of national community.

There was no consensus for protracted peacetime austerity and discontent mounted swiftly. The extension of public control and the favour shown to the working class produced an outcry, initially centred in the solidly middle professional classes, against Labour's 'brand new revolting world'.[7] Similar in some respects to the reaction which followed the First World War, it portrayed the middle class who had sacrificed heavily as the chief victims of the peace, crushed by ruinous taxation, and held hostage by big business and big labour. 'It is very noticeable', a London schoolteacher wrote in her diary, 'that nowadays the well-fed, well-clad, sweetly smiling bourgeoisie have disappeared from poster and advertisement. It is the broadly grinning and obviously unwashed "worker" who appears more than life-size on our hoardings and Tube stations.' 'I feel the present government', wrote a woman doctor, 'to be actively and dangerously hostile to me personally and to my standards of life and thought, which I have always considered to be superior to those of the masses.'[8] Press articles abounded about the 'new poor' and 'middle-class plight': there were stories of City gents lunching furtively on jam sandwiches or frequenting pawn-brokers and a stream of 'Letters to the Editor' contrasting pre-war days and the dismal present.[9] If the interwar decades conjured up images of poverty and dole queues for workers, for the middle classes they became a lost Arcadia of low taxes and cheap servants. 'To whittle down the middle class to the wage earner's level', argued economist and broadcaster, Honor Croome, 'is to whittle away not merely economic efficiency, but civilization itself.'[10] For the middle classes it was the early post-war years that reignited their sense of a common identity and solidarity. More broadly, as a reaction to wartime democratization, there was a reassertion of hierarchy and elite social culture which extended from the cult of monarchy and a revival of the debutantes' season to a new conservatism among intellectuals, which American sociologist Edward Shils in a particularly acute essay discerned as nostalgia for gentry values.[11]

---

[7] A. Thirkell, *Peace Breaks Out* (London, 1966). Also N. Humble, *The Feminine Middlebrow Novel, 1920s to 1950s* (Oxford, 2001).

[8] Gladys Langford (teacher) Diary MSS, entry for 2 May 1947, Local History Centre, Finsbury Library, Borough of Islington (London); for the doctor: M-OA: DR (1371) January 1949 on social class ('Middle class, why?').

[9] R. Lewis and A. Maude, *The English Middle Classes* (London, 1949). Press stories about the 'new poor' continued in the *Daily Express* and other papers as late as 1956.

[10] *The Listener*, 11 March 1948; A. J. Cummings, 'Has the class war returned?', *News Chronicle*, 6 May 1947.

[11] E. Shils, 'The intellectuals: Great Britain', *Encounter*, 4(4) (April 1955). Also, M. Collins, 'The fall of the English gentleman: The national character in decline, *c.*1918–1970', *Historical Research*, 75 (2002); F. Mort, *Capital Affairs: London and the making of the permissive society* (New Haven, 2010), chs. 1–2. Comparing two sets of replies from 1939 and 1948 by the Mass-Observation panel to questions about class, Mike Savage argues that overt hostility towards workers became more common and that a new, more meritocratic, middle-class identity was being asserted in the later set, as a more

Conservative efforts to rebuild support for their party capitalized upon this mounting discontent. Continuing scarcities and the hardships of life, which if anything had increased since the war, were blamed upon socialist incompetence, over-regulation, and red tape. Echoing the militant British Housewives League whose demonstrations publicized the low morale of suburban women, Brendan Bracken commented: 'Angry housewives are the most formidable enemy of the socialists, so we must do everything in our power to increase their fury.'[12] The responses of some prominent Labour spokesmen, declaring they did not give a 'tinker's cuss' for the middle class or chastising the 'bleatings' of those 'who believe they have a natural right to live better than the skilled worker because they wear a white collar', added fuel on the fire.[13] Initially, as we have said, debate about the 'new poor' focused on the professions,[14] but this was too narrow an appeal to re-coalesce a broad middle-class alliance, especially since many lower-middle-class voters were well pleased with the national health and other social services. More successful was a well-funded campaign to halt further nationalization and the strategy of defining Labour as the party of trade unionism, bloated bureaucracy, and the infringement of individual liberties. In later years Conservative recovery was often portrayed as a fairly seamless and inevitable process—the fruit of a rigorous party restructuring and the growing influence of Tory reformers like Butler and Macmillan who allowed it to reclaim the political middle ground. In fact, its revival was slow and modest; the degree of continuity with pre-war Conservative thinking was considerable, and ideologically the two parties remained far apart despite later talk of consensus.[15] The new Conservatism, calling for a property-owning democracy, was more of a discursive style than substance in the early post-war years. It was the narrow margin of the Conservative victory in 1951, with Labour polling a larger share of the popular vote, that strengthened the hand of Tory centrists. When he returned to power Churchill recognized the impossibility of dismantling Labour's legislation and was eager to avoid a power struggle with the unions.

---

palatable way of defending class distinctions. M. Savage, 'Affluence and social change in the making of technocratic middle-class identities: Britain 1939–1955', *Contemporary British History*, 22(4) (December 2008). Also, J. Hinton, 'The class complex: Mass Observation and cultural distinction in pre-war Britain', *Past and Present*, 199 (May 2008).

[12] J. Ramsden, *The Age of Churchill and Eden 1940–57* (London, 1995), p. 169.

[13] The first comment was made by Emanuel Shinwell at a meeting of the Electrical Trades Union; the second is from a broadcast by Richard Crossman, 'The Labour Party and the middle classes', *The Listener*, 11 March 1948. Also, in Manchester in July 1948, Aneurin Bevan, Minister of Health, called the Tory Party 'lower than vermin'. P. Martin, 'The Vermin Club 1948–51', *History Today*, 47(6) (June 1997).

[14] *The Economist*, 24 January ('The plight of the professions'); 31 January ('Two million without a party'); 14 February ('Experts without power'); 21 February ('Third party or no party') 1948.

[15] H. Jones, '"New Conservatism?": The industrial charter, modernity and the reconstruction of British Conservatism after the war' in B. Conekin, F. Mort, and C. Waters (eds.), *Moments of Modernity: Reconstructing Britain 1945–1964* (London, 1999); M. Francis, '"Set the people free"? Conservatives and the state, 1920–1960' and H. Jones, 'The cold war and the Santa Claus syndrome: Dilemmas in Conservative social policy-making, 1945–1957' both in M. Francis and I. Zweiniger-Bargielowska (eds.), *The Conservatives and British Society, 1880–1990* (Cardiff, 1996).

The political outcome of the war, then, was first that Labour, which had no say in the post-war settlement of 1918, presided over this one. Had they been victorious in 1945 the Conservatives would have introduced reforms, but their domestic policy in such areas as health, universal eligibility for social services, the position of trade unions, and nationalization would have been different. The second result was a contentious, ideological political climate in the late 1940s[16] and a politics which closely reflected class divisions. In structural terms too the new era was distinctive with the nation divided between two evenly matched parties who between them got 96–98 per cent of the votes cast. Conservatives recaptured their middle-class base and Labour managed to hold on to the bulk of working-class votes.[17] Whereas in the 1930s class had been a weak determinant of voting preferences (with Labour gaining only a minority of workers' votes), the legacy of the war and the Attlee governments combined was a very different political demography where for a very high proportion of the electorate, voting became almost an automatic badge of class identity.[18] If great attention was paid to a minority of so-called 'floating' voters, it was because their 'dealignment' won elections. Paradoxically, while voting statistics might suggest a polarized and partisan society, the general direction of politics in the 1950s was one of convergence in terms of immediate policy agendas. Since each party could rely on a large bloc of class-based support, both needed to cleave to the centre to pick up votes. They were, as David Marquand once put it, like two trains running on parallel lines for a time but headed for different destinations. In the end the Conservatives found this easier and less divisive; Labour's efforts to rethink its objectives unleashed a bitter feud between 'fundamentalists' and 'revisionists' that consumed the party's energies and further eroded its electoral chances.

Assessments of the Attlee governments differ. While it is probably still true to say that a majority of historians view Labour's achievements positively, some on the left criticize their narrow conception of socialism and argue that the electorate, radicalized by the war, was open to a more sweeping reform programme than was introduced. By contrast, in *England Arise!*, Tiratsoo, Fielding, and Thompson argued that it was popular indifference to politics and the paucity of active and informed citizens that was at fault, not Labour's timidity or moderation.[19] As I have tried to show in *Blood, Sweat, and Toil* the projection back into the war years of later popular indifference towards politics seems inaccurate and unconvincing. Even acknowledging popular cynicism—almost a gut reflex to excessive hopes— expectations of reform and a new deal were high at the war's end. In the late 1940s and early 1950s party memberships were at their highest levels; so were election turn-outs; so too was participation in trade unionism and middle-class pressure groups. Voters seemed to feel that they had a political interest to defend and to oppose, and when BIPO asked in September 1948 whether it mattered

---

[16] See e.g. J. Jewkes, *Ordeal by Planning* (London, 1948); I. Thomas, *Socialist Tragedy* (London, 1949).

[17] Labour's share of the votes cast in general elections changed by only a few percentage points: 1945, 47.8%; 1950, 46.1%; 1951, 48.8%; 1955, 46.4%; 1959, 43.8%.

[18] J. Bonham, *The Middle-Class Vote* (London, 1954).

[19] S. Fielding, P. Thompson, and N. Tiratsoo, *England Arise! The Labour Party and Popular Politics in 1940s Britain* (Manchester, 1995).

which political party was in power, 70 per cent of its respondents said 'Yes' and 20 per cent said 'No'.[20] It was in the later 1950s that voters became more passive and disengaged. The convergence of party programmes and the material security provided by economic prosperity, full employment, and the social service state were all influential, making elections seem unimportant or minimally relevant to most people's aspirations and needs. In addition, as Jon Lawrence has shown, TV, the emphasis on national rather than local campaigns, and the market-driven PR quality of the contests all played a part.[21]

Was there an opportunity for a more radical post-war settlement than Labour enacted? In his recent Ford Lectures, Ross McKibbin argues that the war created an unprecedented politicization, disrupted the existing framework of party politics, and created an opening for a more sweeping socialist settlement than Labour was prepared to legislate. Labour's conception of socialism, he argues, was too narrow and compartmentalized, focused on social welfare and nationalization, but unwilling to countenance a broader attack on the social and political institutions that sustained the nation's status hierarchy. The government left alone, he adds, any institution, whether it was the public schools or the sugar industry, that was strongly defended and this fatally undercut its efforts to achieve a 'functioning social democracy'.[22] As a result, what Britain achieved was a remarkable political transformation while retaining its traditional civil institutions so that social democracy never became fully entrenched. This McKibbin largely ascribes to the caution of Labour leaders who believed that institutional reform was 'incidental or of little interest to its electorate' and who were too attached to the status quo themselves.[23] Certainly, by 1945 (in contrast to 1931) Labour leaders were comfortable working within the wartime state; indeed, their attitude was that by creating a much-expanded state machinery the war had provided the structural means for implementing their programme. What is unclear, however, is whether broad support could have been mobilized had Labour tried a bolder attack on established institutions. Here McKibbin focuses heavily on the radicalization that took place in 1940 when the nation's situation was most desperate and many people advanced drastic proposals for social and structural change. By the last war years, however, the mood had shifted and workers' immediate aspirations focused upon the politics of jobs, housing, and social welfare. It is doubtful whether after six years of war the public or the unions (who supplied two-thirds of party funds) would have been receptive to a

---

[20] G. H. Gallup, *The Gallup International Public Opinion Polls of Great Britain 1937–1975* (New York, 1976), p. 197. In October 1949 BIPO asked: 'Are you interested in politics or are there other things that you regard as more important?'—47% replied 'Interested'; 37%, 'Other things'; and 16% 'Don't know'.

[21] J. Lawrence, *Electing Our Masters* (Oxford, 2009); also, D. Marquand, *The Decline of the Public* (Cambridge, 2004); L. Black, *The Political Culture of the Left in Affluent Britain 1951–64* (London, 2003); *idem, Redefining British Politics, Culture, Consumerism and Participation, 1954–70* (London, 2010). Black shows the danger of eliding disengagement from formal party politics and indifference or the decline of politics. Broadening the boundaries of 'politics' he reveals how new kinds of political formations developed in the era of affluence, many of them concerned with quality of life.

[22] R. McKibbin, *Parties and People: England 1914–51* (Oxford, 2010), pp. 162–3, 201.

[23] *Ibid.*, p. 200.

broader *Kulturkampf.* At the same time that the war generated support for reform, it also encouraged a profound institutional conservatism and complacency. The prestige of the monarchy and Parliament was never higher; the same was true of the armed forces; wartime talk of reforming the Lords quickly evaporated. Had Labour pushed for it, they might have successfully carried through reforms of the civil service and challenged the privileged position of the public schools. But these were not things that ordinary people were much concerned about or likely to campaign for. Labour's social and economic legislation did significantly change British society, but it is by no means clear that in the years after 1945 the party could have democratized social and political institutions in the way that McKibbin advocates, even if this had been its priority.

So far, these comments have focused on the social and political results of the war, but the conflict was also a defining moment culturally, played out in the ways that the British perceived themselves and national identity. Much has been written about rituals of commemoration, collective memory, and the war's representation in films, popular fiction, and TV series; but we still lack a comprehensive study of its centrality in the nation's culture over the last sixty-five years.[24] For the vast majority of the population today the war is part of the nation's heritage or belongs to the school curriculum, almost as remote as the Crimean War. Even the generation that grew up in its wake and heard lots of stories about those years has now retired or is about to. Yet fascination with the war seems undimmed, continually retold but selectively to suit changing times and political moods. For some it stands as a touchstone of Britain's declining power post-Suez; for others, like Enoch Powell, it became a commentary on Commonwealth immigration, a period before the 'dark strangers' arrived. Already by the mid-1950s in films like *The Dam Busters* and *The Cruel Sea* the 'People's War' had receded before epics of personal valour, populated mostly by middle-class officers and technicians. By the 1960s, with the illusion of British global presence fading fast, the martial values of wartime were seldom invoked, although they did enjoy a brief and unexpected revival during the Falklands conflict.

What we might call the characterological narrative of the war—the images of popular courage and endurance—has essentially remained the same. It stands unrivalled as a positive marker of stereotypical British qualities: endurance, modesty, individualism, team spirit, and muddling through. Yet in other respects the social symbolism has gone through changes. Portraying the war years as a time of community and social cohesion easily conjures up images of later social fragmentation, welfare dependence, dysfunctional families, and multi-ethnicity. In popular fiction, Roger Bromley has argued, the older social democratic war with its emphasis on the inner city and industrial workers has yielded ground to an

[24] L. Noakes, *War and the British: Gender and national identity 1939–1991* (London, 1998); M. Smith, *Britain and 1940* (London, 2000); M. Connelly, *We Can Take It! Britain and the memory of the Second World War* (Harlow, 2004); C. Waters, '"Dark strangers in our midst": Discourses of race and nation in Britain 1947–1963', *JBS*, 36(2) (April 1997) argues that, once wartime discourses of patriotism and social citizenship had woven the working class 'into the fabric of the national imagery', race replaced class as the chief theme in debate about national cohesion.

emphasis on middle-class experience and suburban streets as emblematic of the nation. Similarly, Geoff Eley has shown the war's centrality in the cultural conflict of the 1970s and '80s as the political right and left asserted their version of the post-war domestic settlement and sought to renegotiate national identity.[25]

Most often in the popular media the war has turned into a sanitized marker of 'the way we were'—at times accenting the more clearly socially stratified society of the 1930s and '40s, at others providing a reservoir of nostalgia for a traditional working-class way of life now bulldozed for slum clearance. Indeed, as Eley perceptively notes, recent versions end up reviving earlier post-war cultural representations 'creating a dense palimpsest of referentiality'.[26] There are, of course, exceptions, including autobiographical films that have used the war to take a hard look at family relationships or others that see it as a terrain for examining sexual and racial themes with more frankness than would have been possible in the 1940s.[27] But most media references remain sentimental and celebratory; exposure to these years has become a trip into a past when things were done differently and seldom are these trips unsettling. If, as in the TV series *Foyle's War*, the nostalgic patriotic narrative is questioned, revisionism is tempered by heritage trappings—the authentic clothes, cars, steam trains, rural and small-town settings, and Foyle himself, an icon of decency and quiet fortitude.[28] As for workers, if they appear it is in quaint forms as fishermen, bobbies, or stereotypical cockney shelterers. Like a silent commentary on the fate of British social democracy and the disappearance of the nation's industrial working class, the huge formations of miners, engineers, and munitions women, the trade unions, and class politics of the 1940s, which are the subject of this book, have somehow disappeared from view.

[25] R. Bromley, *Lost Narratives: Popular fictions, politics, and recent history* (London, 1988). Also, the hugely successful TV series, *A Family At War* (1970–2), shown at a time of high inflation and labour militancy when the country seemed to many to be fragmenting; it depicted the lives and relationships of the middle-class Ashton family. Geoff Eley, 'Finding the People's War: Film, British collective memory, and World War II', *AHR*, 106(3) (June 2001).

[26] *Ibid.*, p. 819.

[27] I am thinking especially of such films as *Hope and Glory* (dir. John Boorman, 1987); *Distant Voices, Still Lives* (dir. Terence Davies, 1983); *Another Time, Another Place* (dir. Michael Radford, 1983); *Land Girls* (dir. David Leland, 1998). See the excellent analyses by Geoff Eley: 'Finding the People's War' and '"*Distant Voices, Still Lives*": The family is a dangerous place: Memory, gender, and the image of the working class' in R. A. Rosenstone (ed.), *Revisioning History: Film and the construction of a new past* (Princeton, 1995).

[28] J. Chapman, 'Policing the people's war: *Foyle's War* and television drama' in M. Paris (ed.), *Repicturing the Second World War* (Basingstoke, 2007).

Index

(pages in *italics* refer to a photograph)

388

Index

child allowances 12, 33
child development 35, 184, 185, 194, 215
child-guidance movement 185, 196, 197
childcare 14, 170, 193, 351
  evacuation billets and 29
  nurseries 137–8, 173, 179, 186–90, 294, 318
  war factory workers 142
children:
  adjustment to returning fathers 290–1
  deprived 190–3, 211
  evacuation of 10–12, 185, *187*
  evacuation's impact on health of 28 n.64, 43
  free school meals and milk 19, 27, 35,
    132, 133
  lack of parental control 195–6, 198
  leisure time 218–19
  London Blitz 43
  neglect and abuse of 18, 31, 32, 190, 192
  psychological damage to 186, 188, 190
  as social capital 184
  summer activities for 223
  welfare of 184–94
Children Act (1948) 193
Children and Young Person's Act (1933)
  194, 197
Children's Minimum Council 19
choral groups 223
Chorley Royal Ordnance Factory 140, 149–50
Christ Church, Spitalfields 48, *61*, 65, *66*
Christian socialism 308, 312, 330, 332
Christianity 224, 312, 331–2, 339
Christie, Agatha 192 n.29
Church-Bliss, Kathleen 158–60
Church of England Temperance Society 48
Churchill, Mary 164
Churchill, Somerset 54
Churchill, Winston 1, 37, 81, 85, 91, 115, 117,
  336, 379
  on air attacks on London 10
  approval ratings 326, 356, 359
  on army education 277
  compulsory cadet training proposal 219
  critics of 323
  on *Daily Mirror* journalists 280
  demobilization plan 286
  election broadcasts 362
  general election (1945) 359–72
  Laski and 349
  Life and Death of Colonel Blimp
    concerns 267
  on nationalization 350, 358
  and officer selection 265
  radio addresses by 36, 227, 377
  on safety of children 30
  and Stafford Cripps 326, 327, 328, 347
  strengthened position after El Alamein 334,
    335, 356
  on surrender regulations 269
  warning on socialism 362–3, 364

cinema 220, 232–7, 249, 302, 306
  newsreels 12, 53, 57, 77, 143, 162, 287, 302,
    320, 321, 347, 362
The Citadel (1938) 111, 235
citizenship 8, 62, 78, 128, 163, 169, 215, 216,
  217, 219, 233, 247, 250, 251, 276–7, 341,
  353, 373, 375, 376, 378
Citrine, Walter 81–2, 91, 123, 125, 131 n.7,
  348, 374
City of Canterbury mutiny (1942) 273–4
civic associations 302, 303, 306, 339
civil defence 40 n.7, 84, 229
Civil Service Clerical Association 39
civil service unions 39, 329, 348
Clark, Sir Kenneth 66, 67, 238–9, 240,
  242, 246
Clarke, Mark 272
Clarke, Peter 326, 327
class 321, 377
  Blitz 55–6, 77–8
  child welfare 184
  cinema and 235–6
  communal shelters and 50
  evacuees 22
  family and 215
  fertility and 213
  handling of Beveridge Report 340
  POWs 291
  radio audience 228, 231–2
  servicemen and 261–8, 296
  voting 380
  war production 127–8, 130–1
  women's auxiliaries 165, 169, 172
  Women's Land Army 169, 172
class consciousness 3, 4, 7, 126–8, 180–1, 183
class identity 4, 5, 6, 126, 282, 354, 380
Clayton, Rifleman William 270–1
clerical workers 39, 130
clothing 15–16, 130, 133, 136, 150
Clydeside 59, 88
  Blitz 71, 72
  CEMA concerts in 243
  Communist Party 314
  evacuees from 11, 15, 20, 21
  industrial action 105, 153
  Irish workers in shipyards 96
  shipyard strikes 87, 107, 110, 114
  shop-floor networks 99
Co-operative movement 5, 50, 163, 344, 351
coal industry, *see* mining industry
Cockett, Richard 363 n.83
Colchester, Essex 366
The Colditz Story (1954) 297
Cole, G. D. H. 308, 310, 311, 313, 330, 338,
  339, 345
Cole, Margaret 13, 338
Cole, Virginia 163, 165
collective bargaining 93, 95, 98, 124, 180
collective memory 1, 382